Rainbows Amidst the Clouds

A Devotional Journey through the Bible

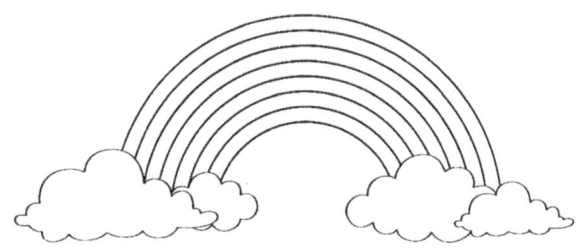

Judy Strand Barcelo

TEACH Services, Inc.
PUBLISHING
www.TEACHServices.com • (800) 367-1844

Copyright © 2024 Judy Strand Barcelo
Copyright © 2024 TEACH Services, Inc.
ISBN-13: 978-1-4796-1688-6 (Paperback)
ISBN-13: 978-1-4796-1690-9 (ePub)
Library of Congress Control Number: 2023920107

Dedication

This book is dedicated to my late father, Fobian Strand, Jr., who first taught me to embrace the rainbows of promise and hope in God's Word, and then set a loving example of how to integrate them into the fabric of everyday life.

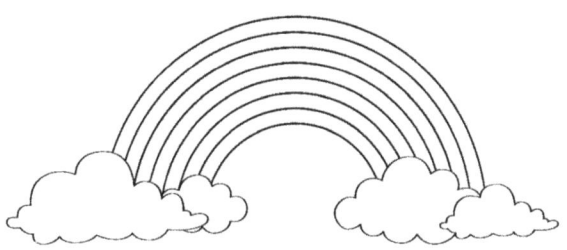

"The memory of the righteous is blessed."
Proverbs 10:7

Table of Contents

Old Testament

January 1	The Gift of Creativity	Genesis 1:27
January 2	The First Sabbath	Genesis 2:3
January 3	Brotherly Love	Genesis 4:9
January 4	God Sees Us	Genesis 16:13
January 5	God Will Provide	Genesis 22:14
January 6	The Mizpah	Genesis 31:49
January 7	The Long View	Genesis 45:5, 8
January 8	Surrender to God's Will	Exodus 4:12
January 9	Stepping Forward in Faith	Exodus 14:13
January 10	Teamwork Prevails	Exodus 17:12
January 11	Strangers among Us	Exodus 22:21
January 12	Workmanship	Exodus 31:2, 3
January 13	The Finger of God	Exodus 32:16
January 14	Restitution	Leviticus 6:4, 5
January 15	Eating and Drinking to God's Glory	Leviticus 10:9, 10
January 16	Tattoos	Leviticus 19:26–28
January 17	Sabbath Services	Leviticus 23:3
January 18	Tithes and Offerings	Leviticus 27:30, 32
January 19	The Priestly Blessing	Numbers 6:24–26
January 20	Retirement	Numbers 8:24–26
January 21	Lapses in Faith	Numbers 11:23
January 22	Equal Rights	Numbers 27:6–8
January 23	Old Testament Ordination	Numbers 27:22, 23
January 24	Cities of Refuge	Numbers 35:11, 15
January 25	Take Courage!	Deuteronomy 1:29–31
January 26	Idol Worship	Deuteronomy 4:39, 40
January 27	Teaching Our Children Diligently	Deuteronomy 6:6, 7
January 28	Empty Handed?	Deuteronomy 16:16, 17
January 29	Unanswered Questions	Deuteronomy 29:29
January 30	Choices	Deuteronomy 30:19, 20
January 31	Strength for the Day	Deuteronomy 33:25, 27
February 1	Promises to a Leader	Joshua 1:8, 9
February 2	The Scarlet Cord	Joshua 2:21
February 3	Dry Ground	Joshua 3:13, 17
February 4	Memorial Stones	Joshua 4:3, 6
February 5	The Sun Stood Still	Joshua 10:13, 14
February 6	Led by a Woman	Judges 4:4, 5
February 7	The Hesitant Warrior	Judges 6:14–16
February 8	A Humble Leader	Judges 8:22, 23
February 9	Physical vs. Moral Strength	Judges 13:4, 5
February 10	Home-Grown Idolatry	Judges 17:5, 6
February 11	Love Pledge	Ruth 1:16
February 12	Wings of Refuge	Ruth 2:11, 12
February 13	The Family Redeemer	Ruth 3:10, 11

February 14	A Happy Ending	Ruth 4:13, 14
February 15	Hannah's Prayer	1 Samuel 2:2, 3
February 16	Not Knowing the Lord	1 Samuel 2:12
February 17	My Ebenezer	1 Samuel 7:12
February 18	Obedience	1 Samuel 15:22
February 19	"Good Looks"	1 Samuel 16:7
February 20	That All the Earth May Know	1 Samuel 17:45–47
February 21	Share and Share Alike	1 Samuel 30:24
February 22	Grace Shown through Kindness	2 Samuel 9:3, 6, 7
February 23	"You Are the Man!"	2 Samuel 12:7–9
February 24	Confronted by Death	2 Samuel 22:5–7
February 25	Your Gentleness	2 Samuel 22:36
February 26	Request Wisdom	1 Kings 4:29
February 27	Taking Advice	1 Kings 12:6–8
February 28	Faith in Action	1 Kings 17:12–14
February 29	Not the Only One	1 Kings 19:18
March 1	What Do You Have?	2 Kings 4:2
March 2	Hospitality	2 Kings 4:10
March 3	Faith Heals	2 Kings 5:3
March 4	Open Our Eyes	2 Kings 6:16, 17
March 5	An Extended Life	2 Kings 20:5, 6
March 6	Led by a Child	2 Kings 22:1, 2
March 7	Ministers of Music	1 Chronicles 6:31, 32
March 8	A Trusted Office	1 Chronicles 9:29, 31
March 9	An Inheritance	1 Chronicles 28:20
March 10	Willingly	1 Chronicles 29:7–9
March 11	Humble Me	2 Chronicles 7:14
March 12	Royal Animals	2 Chronicles 9:21, 22
March 13	God's Victory	2 Chronicles 20:15
March 14	His Prophets	2 Chronicles 20:20
March 15	A King's Letter	Ezra 7:27, 28
March 16	Fasting	Ezra 8:21–23
March 17	The Request	Nehemiah 2:4, 5
March 18	Set Hands	Nehemiah 2:17, 18
March 19	The Plot	Nehemiah 6:2, 3
March 20	Strengthening Joy	Nehemiah 8:10
March 21	Beauty Well Spent	Esther 4:14
March 22	Poetic Justice	Esther 6:6, 11
March 23	Purim	Esther 9:27, 28
March 24	Reactions to Adversity	Job 2:9, 10
March 25	A Friend in Affliction	Job 6:14
March 26	Silence Is Wisdom	Job 13:5
March 27	Words That Break	Job 19:1, 2
March 28	The Hope of Resurrection	Job 19:25, 26
March 29	Hanging Earth	Job 26:7
March 30	Restoration	Job 42:10
March 31	Gender Equality	Job 42:15

April 1	Look Up	Psalms 5:3
April 2	A Refuge in Troubled Times	Psalms 9:9, 10
April 3	Wait	Psalms 27:14
April 4	Morning Joy	Psalms 30:5b
April 5	My Times	Psalms 31:14, 15
April 6	A Broken Heart	Psalms 34:18, 19
April 7	Delightful	Psalms 37:3, 4
April 8	Fretting	Psalms 37:8
April 9	"Though He Fall…"	Psalms 37:23, 24
April 10	Old Age	Psalms 71:9, 18
April 11	Numbering Our Days	Psalms 90:10, 12
April 12	Shout Joyfully!	Psalms 95:1, 2
April 13	Tender Mercies	Psalms 103:1–4
April 14	Say Something!	Psalms 107:2, 8
April 15	Turn Away	Psalms 119:37
April 16	When I Awake	Psalms 139:17, 18
April 17	Happy People	Psalms 144:15b
April 18	Near Us	Psalms 145:18, 19
April 19	Freedom	Psalms 146:5–7
April 20	The Outcasts	Psalms 147:2, 3
April 21	Greedy	Proverbs 1:19
April 22	Do Good!	Proverbs 3:27
April 23	Foolishness	Proverbs 12:15
April 24	Friends	Proverbs 12:26
April 25	Discipline	Proverbs 13:24
April 26	Keeping Watch	Proverbs 15:3
April 27	What's Better?	Proverbs 15:16, 17
April 28	Discretion	Proverbs 19:11
April 29	A Good Reputation	Proverbs 22:1, 2
April 30	Overworked	Proverbs 23:4, 5
May 1	A Wise Child	Proverbs 23:22, 24, 25
May 2	Boasting	Proverbs 27:1, 2
May 3	In Authority	Proverbs 29:2
May 4	An Angry Man	Proverbs 29:20, 22
May 5	The Law of Kindness	Proverbs 31:26
May 6	A Season	Ecclesiastes 3:1, 2
May 7	Walk Prudently	Ecclesiastes 5:1, 2
May 8	Grasping for the Wind	Ecclesiastes 5:15
May 9	Your Might	Ecclesiastes 9:10
May 10	Casting Bread	Ecclesiastes 11:1
May 11	The Conclusion	Ecclesiastes 12:13, 14
May 12	His Banner	Song of Solomon 2:4
May 13	A Hymn of Praise	Isaiah 12:2–6
May 14	Punishment	Isaiah 13:11
May 15	Declaration of Triumph	Isaiah 25:9
May 16	Perfect Peace	Isaiah 26:3

May 17	Talking Clay	Isaiah 29:15, 16
May 18	The Voice	Isaiah 30:21
May 19	Beside All Waters	Isaiah 32:17, 20
May 20	Everlasting Joy	Isaiah 35:10
May 21	Renewed Strength	Isaiah 40:29–31
May 22	Fear Not	Isaiah 41:10
May 23	Return to Me	Isaiah 44:22
May 24	Gray Hairs	Isaiah 46:4
May 25	Beautiful Feet	Isaiah 52:7
May 26	Seek the Lord	Isaiah 55:6, 7
May 27	The Robe of Righteousness	Isaiah 61:10, 11
May 28	Broken Cisterns	Jeremiah 2:13
May 29	True Glory	Jeremiah 9:23, 24
May 30	The Footmen	Jeremiah 12:5
May 31	Our Future	Jeremiah 29:11–13
June 1	His Treasuries	Jeremiah 51:15, 16
June 2	His Faithfulness	Lamentations 3:22, 23
June 3	Self-Examination	Lamentations 3:40, 41
June 4	The Lowest Pit	Lamentations 3:55–57
June 5	Unsuspected Idols	Ezekiel 7:19
June 6	A Heart of Flesh	Ezekiel 11:19, 20
June 7	My Sabbaths	Ezekiel 20:19, 20
June 8	Death of the Wicked	Ezekiel 33:11
June 9	As Native-Born	Ezekiel 47:21–23
June 10	The Cream of the Crop	Daniel 1:19, 20
June 11	Holy Determination	Daniel 3:16–18
June 12	Pride before a Fall	Daniel 4:30, 31, 37
June 13	A Pagan's Faith	Daniel 6:16
June 14	Like the Stars	Daniel 12:3
June 15	Betrothed	Hosea 2:19, 20
June 16	Righteous Rain	Hosea 10:12
June 17	Prudent	Hosea 14:9
June 18	The Outpouring	Joel 2:28, 29
June 19	The Valley of Decision	Joel 3:14–16
June 20	A Mighty Stream	Amos 5:14, 24
June 21	An Unlikely Prophet	Amos 7:14–16
June 22	Deceitful Pride	Obadiah 1:3, 4
June 23	The Belly of Sheol	Jonah 2:1, 2
June 24	Messianic Prophecy	Micah 5:2
June 25	In a Nutshell	Micah 6:8
June 26	The Depths of the Sea	Micah 7:18, 19
June 27	Dust Clouds	Nahum 1:3
June 28	Keep Silence	Habakkuk 2:20
June 29	A Hymn of Faith	Habakkuk 3:17, 18
June 30	Like Deer's Feet	Habakkuk 3:19
July 1	Settled in Complacency	Zephaniah 1:12

July 2	A Singing Lord	Zephaniah 3:17
July 3	Be Strong	Haggai 2:4
July 4	The Apple of His Eye	Zechariah 2:8
July 5	Plucked from the Fire	Zechariah 3:1, 2
July 6	By My Spirit	Zechariah 4:6
July 7	Don't Plan Evil	Zechariah 7:9, 10
July 8	Crown Jewels	Zechariah 9:16
July 9	A Priest's Job Description	Malachi 2:5–7
July 10	Dealing Treacherously	Malachi 2:14–16
July 11	Overflowing Blessings	Malachi 3:10
July 12	A Book of Remembrance	Malachi 3:16, 17
July 13	Turning Hearts	Malachi 4:5, 6

New Testament

July 14	Prophetic Generations	Matthew 1:17
July 15	Divine Affirmation	Matthew 3:16, 17
July 16	Heavenly Sustenance	Matthew 4:4
July 17	The Call	Matthew 4:19
July 18	Be Reconciled	Matthew 5:23, 24
July 19	Don't Worry	Matthew 6:31–33
July 20	Distance Healing	Matthew 8:10, 11, 13
July 21	Words!	Matthew 12:35–37
July 22	Mass Healings	Matthew 15:30, 31
July 23	Dead Last	Matthew 19:29, 30
July 24	Caesar's	Matthew 22:19–21
July 25	Gnats and Camels	Matthew 23:23, 24
July 26	Well Done!	Matthew 25:23
July 27	The Least	Matthew 25:40, 45, 46
July 28	Our Commission	Matthew 28:19, 20
July 29	His Purpose	Mark 1:38
July 30	Called to Repentance	Mark 2:17
July 31	We're Family!	Mark 3:34, 35
August 1	The Seed	Mark 4:26–28
August 2	A Great Calm	Mark 4:39
August 3	Come and Rest	Mark 6:31
August 4	Abundance	Mark 8:19, 20
August 5	Ashamed	Mark 8:38
August 6	Believe	Mark 9:23, 24
August 7	A Little Child	Mark 10:14–16
August 8	Signs of His Coming	Mark 13:26, 27
August 9	Women Disciples	Mark 15:40, 41
August 10	In Favor	Luke 2:52
August 11	His Customs	Luke 4:16
August 12	Covetousness	Luke 12:15
August 13	Angelic Joy	Luke 15:10
August 14	A Great Way Off	Luke 15:20
August 15	Our Faithfulness	Luke 16:10

August 16	Infinite Possibilities	Luke 18:27
August 17	Servant Leadership	Luke 22:25–27
August 18	He Is Risen!	Luke 24:6–8
August 19	Spiritual Comprehension	Luke 24:44, 45
August 20	The Light	John 1:3, 4
August 21	Saved!	John 3:16, 17
August 22	Words of Eternal Life	John 6:66–68
August 23	Doctrine	John 7:16, 17
August 24	Abundant Life	John 10:10
August 25	Other Sheep	John 10:16
August 26	He Shall Live	John 11:25
August 27	Living Peaceably	John 14:27
August 28	The Spirit of Truth	John 16:13
August 29	Future Believers	John 17:20
August 30	Promised Return	Acts 1:9–11
August 31	Such as I Have	Acts 3:6, 8
September 1	Holy Boldness	Acts 4:13
September 2	All Things in Common	Acts 4:32
September 3	Divine Vision	Acts 7:55
September 4	Poisoned and Bound	Acts 8:22, 23
September 5	An About-Face	Acts 9:4–6
September 6	An Epiphany	Acts 10:28
September 7	Holy Joy	Acts 13:51, 52
September 8	Unusual Prisoner	Acts 27:22–24
September 9	Without Excuse	Romans 1:20–22
September 10	Common Ground	Romans 3:23, 24
September 11	Newness of Life	Romans 6:4–7
September 12	It's All Good	Romans 8:28
September 13	Living Sacrifices	Romans 12:1, 2
September 14	A Stumbling Block	Romans 14:12, 13
September 15	Just Imagine	1 Corinthians 2:9
September 16	Such Were Some of You	1 Corinthians 6:9–11
September 17	For Our Admonition	1 Corinthians 10:11–13
September 18	Unity in Diversity	1 Corinthians 12:4–6
September 19	Clanging Symbols	1 Corinthians 13:1, 2
September 20	Incorruptible	1 Corinthians 15:51–53
September 21	Not in Vain	1 Corinthians 15:57, 58
September 22	Sharing Comfort	2 Corinthians 1:3, 4
September 23	Fragrance	2 Corinthians 2:14, 15
September 24	Liberty	2 Corinthians 3:17
September 25	Blinded	2 Corinthians 4:3, 4
September 26	The Inward Man	2 Corinthians 4:16–18
September 27	The Trade	2 Corinthians 8:9
September 28	Strength in Weakness	2 Corinthians 12:8–10
September 29	Sons of God	Galatians 3:26–29
September 30	Works of the Flesh	Galatians 5:19–21

October 1   Fruit of the Spirit .... Galatians 5:22, 23
October 2   Burden Bearing .... Galatians 6:2
October 3   Reaping .... Galatians 6:7
October 4   Hang in There! .... Galatians 6:9, 10
October 5   Heavenly Places .... Ephesians 2:4–6
October 6   The Fullness of God .... Ephesians 3:16–19
October 7   Winds of Doctrine .... Ephesians 4:14, 15
October 8   Grace to the Hearers .... Ephesians 4:29–32
October 9   Bondservants .... Ephesians 6:6, 7
October 10   Knights in Shining Armor .... Ephesians 6:12, 13
October 11   Completed Work .... Philippians 1:6
October 12   Unimaginable Condescension .... Philippians 2:5–8
October 13   Minor Problems? .... Philippians 2:14
October 14   Light Bearers .... Philippians 2:15
October 15   Reaching Forward .... Philippians 3:13, 14
October 16   Citizenship .... Philippians 3:20
October 17   Meditations .... Philippians 4:8
October 18   Promised Provision .... Philippians 4:19
October 19   Spiritual Understanding .... Colossians 1:9–12
October 20   Beware Deceitful Philosophy .... Colossians 2:6–8
October 21   Off with the Old .... Colossians 3:8–10
October 22   The Bond of Perfection .... Colossians 3:12–14
October 23   Singing with Grace .... Colossians 3:16
October 24   "As to the Lord" .... Colossians 3:23, 24
October 25   Mind Your Own Business .... 1 Thessalonians 4:11
October 26   Caught up in the Clouds .... 1 Thessalonians 4:16–18
October 27   Pursue What Is Good .... 1 Thessalonians 5:15
October 28   The Love of the Truth .... 2 Thessalonians 2:9–12
October 29   Everlasting Consolation .... 2 Thessalonians 2:16, 17
October 30   A Place in Ministry .... 1 Timothy 1:12
October 31   Spiritual Exercise .... 1 Timothy 4:7, 8

November 1   Contentment .... 1 Timothy 6:6, 7
November 2   The Love of Money .... 1 Timothy 6:9, 10
November 3   Persuaded .... 2 Timothy 1:12
November 4   Avoid Disputes .... 2 Timothy 2:23–25
November 5   Thoroughly Equipped .... 2 Timothy 3:16, 17
November 6   The Finished Race .... 2 Timothy 4:7, 8
November 7   Good Works .... Titus 3:8
November 8   Thankful Prayers .... Philemon 1:4
November 9   Culture Clashes .... Hebrews 1:1, 2
November 10   Neglect .... Hebrews 2:1–3
November 11   Like His Brethren .... Hebrews 2:17, 18
November 12   The Throne of Grace .... Hebrews 4:15, 16
November 13   Our Anchor .... Hebrews 6:19
November 14   To the Uttermost .... Hebrews 7:25
November 15   The New Covenant .... Hebrews 8:10
November 16   Hold Fast Your Confession .... Hebrews 10:23

November 17	Vengeance	Hebrews 10:29–31
November 18	Saving Faith	Hebrews 11:6
November 19	A Heavenly Country	Hebrews 11:16
November 20	A Cloud of Witnesses	Hebrews 12:1, 2
November 21	Benedictions	Hebrews 13:20–21
November 22	Trials and Tribulations	James 1:2–4
November 23	Good Gifts	James 1:17
November 24	The Implanted Word	James 1:21, 22
November 25	Pure Religion	James 1:27
November 26	The Poor	James 2:1–5
November 27	Dead Faith?	James 2:17, 18
November 28	Fire!	James 3:5
November 29	Sow Peace	James 3:16–18
November 30	Tomorrow?	James 4:13–15
December 1	Fervent Prayer	James 5:16–18
December 2	Wanderers	James 5:19, 20
December 3	Reserved!	1 Peter 1:3, 4
December 4	Living Stones	1 Peter 2:4, 5
December 5	Called to Blessing	1 Peter 3:8, 9
December 6	He Cares	1 Peter 5:7
December 7	The Lion Roars	1 Peter 5:8
December 8	Precious Promises	2 Peter 1:2, 4
December 9	Fruitful Growth	2 Peter 1:5–8
December 10	Eyewitnesses	2 Peter 1:16
December 11	The Sure Word	2 Peter 1:19–21
December 12	Slackness?	2 Peter 3:9
December 13	The Day of the Lord	2 Peter 3:10, 11
December 14	Fellowship	1 John 1:7
December 15	Forgiveness	1 John 1:9
December 16	The Test	1 John 2:3–6
December 17	God's Children	1 John 3:1, 2
December 18	Victory!	1 John 5:4, 5
December 19	The Doctrine of Christ	2 John 1:9
December 20	Health	3 John 1:2
December 21	Glory to God!	Jude 1:24, 25
December 22	The Loveless Church	Revelation 2:7
December 23	The Persecuted Church	Revelation 2:10b-11
December 24	The Compromising Church	Revelation 2:17
December 25	The Corrupt Church	Revelation 2:26, 28
December 26	The Dead Church	Revelation 3:5
December 27	The Faithful Church	Revelation 3:12
December 28	The Lukewarm Church	Revelation 3:21
December 29	All Things Made New	Revelation 21:1–4
December 30	Forever and Ever	Revelation 22:1–5
December 31	The Beginning and the End	Revelation 22:12, 13

Introduction

*A*t the beginning of a recent calendar year, I decided to re-read the Old Testament. I had just finished reading the New Testament over again and made it a practice to focus on one verse that spoke to me personally in each chapter. I found this gave a boost to my spiritual life, making the Bible more relevant to what I was experiencing day by day. Thus, as the new year dawned, I began using this same method, reading one chapter each day as a part of my devotional time and marking the Old Testament verses that I wanted to think about more deeply.

Out of this experience grew a desire to write something about these verses that impacted me the most. This exercise was so helpful that I decided to go back and write about the New Testament verses I had selected the year before. Writing always helps me better dissect and analyze what I read and increases my understanding. As a result, I eventually decided to turn my musings into a devotional book, in the hope that they might be beneficial to other people as well. To accomplish this, I chose some of the special verses I had selected from each book of the Bible until I reached 365 (plus one for February 29, just in case it was needed). Some of these verses were old friends I wanted to linger over, while others I hadn't really noticed or thought about much before and wanted to study them in more detail. I reflected upon, researched, and wrote about these passages, contemplating one per day, until their meaning for my own life became clearer. Sometimes I focused mainly on their significance for me personally, while on other occasions I considered their application to the Christian church at large. Some of the bigger books of the Bible warranted the inclusion of more verses, while the smaller books rendered fewer verses. No book was left out, however, and all verses were arranged in chronological order, just as found in the Bible, from Genesis to Revelation. I used, almost exclusively, the New King James Version (NKJV) for this project.

As a quick disclaimer here at the beginning, I am not a trained theologian and don't presume to "have all the answers," but I believe that Christians throughout the ages have been called to take, eat, and digest the Word of God for themselves so that, with the help of the Holy Spirit, they could understand the deep spiritual truths of the Scriptures and how to apply them to their own daily lives. This effort has helped me do that, and if it can help anyone else, I will be most grateful, knowing that my labors in this regard have not been in vain. With the prophet Jeremiah we want to be able to exclaim, "Your words were found, and I ate them, and Your word was to me the joy and rejoicing of my heart" (Jer. 15:16).

The title of this volume comes from Genesis 9:13, where God declared, "I will put my rainbow in the clouds to be a sign of my promise to the earth" (GW). In this passage, where God is specifically telling Noah that He will never destroy the whole earth again with a flood, I believe we can draw a spiritual parallel. Even though our lives may sometimes be enshrouded in dark clouds, God's promises provide beautiful rainbows of hope. Thus, He covenants to bring us through the storms of life and deliver us safely to the other side of them. Praise God, the Almighty Creator of heaven and earth, for the rainbows!

Dr. Judy Strand Barcelo, Ed.D.

Old Testament

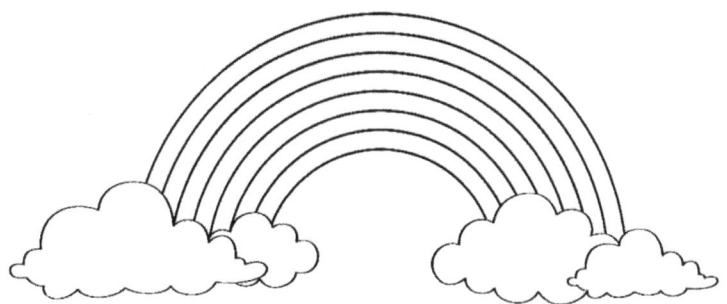

The Gift of Creativity

"So God created man in His own image; in the image of God He created him; male and female He created them" (Genesis 1:27).

How wonderful that God not only made us in His image but that He also shared the gift of creativity with us!

Think what it means to be made in God's image. Although our faculties have been very much diminished by sin, we can still see traces of the characteristics of God in humankind today. Mentally, we can think, imagine, plan, and make decisions. Physically, even though our bodies are mortal, and in that way have a different form than our Maker's, it is nothing short of miraculous what a human body can accomplish with practice and determination. Witness gymnasts or ice skaters in an Olympic competition. A concert pianist playing a classical masterpiece by memory, or a perfectly-matched couple waltzing across the floor in flawless harmony, like poetry in motion.

Socially, we are made in God's image in that we experience feelings of love and feel whole when we share a sense of belonging in families, groups of various kinds, and when we share interests with other people in a collegial manner. Like God, we can also feel joyful, sad, and be filled with compassion for others. And finally, spiritually, we long for a relationship with Him who made us, and we have a God-shaped hole in our hearts until we accept Him as not only our Creator but also as our Redeemer.

God could have just given us the gift of life and stopped there, but He wanted us to feel the wonder and satisfaction of being able to create things as He does. Thus, the world is awash in humanity's creations: inventions (everything from cars and microwaves, to airplanes and computers), not to mention artwork, music, poetry, and prose.

But for me, the greatest gift of creativity is the ability to have our own children. Little people who share our traits and our looks, who copy our gestures and repeat words they have heard us say. It is amazing to watch them grow and develop, still bearing some of our characteristics even into adulthood. What a tremendous opportunity to help mold and guide them into the best people they can be, helping them reach their full potential in this life, while also preparing them for eternal life. It is, at the same time, a wonderful experience and a fearful responsibility! Upon becoming parents, suddenly we understand God's sacrificial love in a whole new way! Like God, we want to protect our children from harm, shield them from evil, spend time with them, give them every advantage, help them make good decisions, and even die in their place, if necessary. God knew that in experiencing this kind of love, we would better comprehend His love for us. And so, He not only created us in His image but also gave us the marvelous capacity to create in our image as well!

The First Sabbath

"Then God blessed the seventh day and sanctified it, because in it He rested from all His work which God had created and made" (Genesis 2:3).

I believe this verse is important to us in several ways. First, it re-affirms the creation narrative that God created everything in six literal days, and then took the seventh day off, not because of exhaustion, but because He wanted time with Adam and Eve to enjoy all the things that He had made for their pleasure and the fulfillment of their needs. As a mother, I liken this to the rush of busyness most parents go through to prepare a wonderful Christmas celebration for their children, and then, when the big day comes, sitting down with their youngsters to share in the delight of the occasion. Together they can enjoy the decorations, the music, the food, the gifts, and most of all, the quality time with each other as a family.

Imagine God, on that first Sabbath, introducing Adam and Eve to the lovely home He had made especially for their enjoyment. The leafy trees from which they could eat delicious fruit, the fragrant and colorful flowers, and the unique birds and animals with whom they shared their garden home. I can see Him talking and laughing with them as He gave them a walking tour of all the beautiful places in their specially-prepared habitat, and sharing the excitement and wonder of their first sunset, with the sky turning into a blazing panoply of color. What a glorious twenty-four hours that first Sabbath must have been!

Another reason this verse stood out to me is that it establishes that the seventh day was not only blessed but also sanctified by God. He set it up as a memorial of creation.

A special time each week when we can remember how God demonstrated His love to us through His awesome and praiseworthy power. Some people think any day will do, but God specifically sanctified the seventh day for this purpose. Finally, I believe God set aside this special time as an example to us so that in our rush to do our daily work and reach our earthly goals, we will take time to stop for a period of time each week to rest from the demands of life and refocus on our need to maintain a healthy relationship with God, as well as those around us.

When working on my dissertation, I had set a goal to complete it in one year, while the demographic data I was presenting was still up-to-date. Although I worked full-time and was a busy wife and mother, I stuck to the challenging schedule I had laid out for myself, and by the time the year ended, I was able to submit my completed document in time to graduate that June. When asked how I accomplished this feat, I explained that I paced myself and made sure to keep the Sabbath every week. I had designated Friday night as a time to rest, Sabbath morning as a time to worship, and Sabbath afternoon and evening to spend with my family. I believe this weekly time of rest recharged my batteries, so to speak, and gave me the stamina to work more effectively the rest of the week so that I could achieve my academic goal. Since then, I have always emphasized to my graduate students the blessings of keeping the Sabbath weekly, not only for their mental and physical health but also to gain the wisdom and strength to accomplish whatever other goals they may have in life. Thank God for the Sabbath that helps keep our lives in balance!

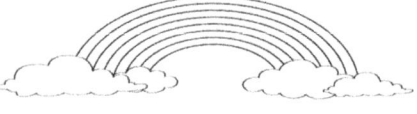

January 3

Brotherly Love

"Then the LORD said to Cain, 'Where is Abel your brother?' He said, 'I do not know. Am I my brother's keeper?'" (Genesis 4:9).

This question the Lord asked Cain so long ago, right after killing his brother, is so poignant that it still haunts us today. Obviously, the Lord knew what had happened to Abel, but by questioning Cain, He gave him the opportunity to reflect on his disastrous deed, as well as a chance to repent and confess his sin, with the possibility of gaining forgiveness and setting out on a better path. Unfortunately, Cain remained intransigent. He "doubled down," as we would say today, not only lying to the Lord about not knowing where Abel was but also giving a petulant answer. "Am I my brother's keeper?" According to the way many people live nowadays, this rebellious question is still being asked, and given a resounding "No!" in response by people who, like Cain, are seeking to defend their evil acts.

As Christians, however, who profess to be representing God in this world, our answer to this age-old question should be a definite "Yes!" When asked about His family on one occasion, Jesus said He considered anyone who believed in Him to be a brother or a sister. Beyond that, in the parable of the good Samaritan, Jesus expanded on that definition by indicating that anyone in need was our "neighbor," thus someone whose welfare we should be concerned about. Of course, the New Testament is replete with verses admonishing Christians to be kind and loving to others. (We'll spend some time on them in the future.)

So, what might that look like in real time in a Christian's everyday life in our modern society? Well, though the answer may seem obvious, the issue of "brotherly love" is so fundamental to Christianity that it bears repeating. I think it's helpful to review our behavior from time to time to make sure we are still on track—that our practice is still in line with our profession.

First, we should probably start close to home by making sure we're treating people in our families with love and respect. Then, of course, we would widen our circle of caring to include our friends and actual neighbors. After that, we would need to be kind and helpful to fellow church members, people with whom we work, and folks we meet in the community.

But it wouldn't stop there. We would even reach out to people very different from us, as the Samaritan did, without regard to their age, gender, language, skin color, social status, belief system, culture, or country of origin.

"How can we be so universally magnanimous?" you might ask. "Especially in a world so filled with hate, jealousy, greed, anger, despair, and crime?" Well, it's not easy. In fact, we can only live like Jesus would in our same circumstances if we ask Him to live in and through us to bless those around us on a daily basis. Thus, we have a need for a daily devotional time, where, unlike Cain, we can surrender our will and ways to the Lord, receive forgiveness for our past mistakes, gain the ability to live in a loving way with our earthly brothers and sisters, and be restored by God's grace to living harmoniously in the wide and inclusive family of God.

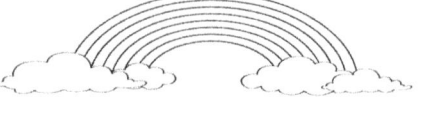

January 4

God Sees Us

"Then she called the name of the LORD who spoke to her, You-Are-the-God-Who-Sees; for she said, 'Have I also here seen Him who sees me?'" (Genesis 16:13).

In this passage we watch a lonely, mistreated, and despairing woman suddenly having an encounter with the just God, who "sees" us at all times, in every circumstance of our lives, even when we think we are totally alone in a cruel and unjust world. In this case, Hagar, the maid of Abraham's wife, Sarah, had run away into the wilderness when Sarah became jealous and angry with her for becoming pregnant when she herself couldn't. Even though it was Sarah's misguided suggestion that her maid become a second wife of Abraham in order to try and bring about God's promise that she and Abraham would have a child in their old age, now she dealt with Hagar harshly. Finally, Hagar couldn't take the injustice of her situation any longer and tried to escape. But in those days, a woman with no social status, money, or transportation didn't have many options.

It was here in the wilderness, "barefoot and pregnant," so to speak, at the lowest and most hopeless time of her life, that the Angel of the Lord comes down, much to her surprise, to speak personally and specifically to Hagar. The Angel began His unexpected visit by gently conversing with her about where she came from and where she was going. When it becomes evident that she really doesn't know where she is going, just that she is fleeing, the Lord rolls out His plans for her life. He tells her that she is going to have a son, and even gives him the name of Ishmael, because "the LORD has heard your affliction" (Gen. 16:11). Then He promises her that He will "multiply her descendants exceedingly, so that they shall not be counted for multitude" (Gen. 16:10). For women in her day and age, having a lot of children was a great honor. It was considered a signal blessing from God, raising one's level of respect in her community. As a result of this surprising conversation, Hagar's perspective on life has quite unexpectedly, and somewhat rapidly, changed. Even though she is told to return to Abraham and Sarah's household, she now has hope and a sense of purpose. She also feels loved because the "God-Who-Sees" actually saw her, actually heard her, and actually had an important role for her to play in the larger scheme of things.

It's amazing how an encounter with God can change our attitudes to the point where we can successfully deal with circumstances that previously seemed untenable to us.

When we come to the end of our rope and see only a black hole in our future, that's the time to cry out to "the-God-Who-Sees." Because of His life and death on this earth, and in order to open the door of salvation to us, our Savior has experienced injustice. He knows what it's like to be mistreated through no fault of His own. He has tasted the bitterness of rejection and abandonment. That's precisely how He understands our plight. He can relate to our suffering. In fact, He longs to bear it for us. Isaiah 61:3 gives us this beautiful picture of what the Lord wants to do for us. He came to provide comfort, "To console those who mourn… to give them beauty for ashes, the oil of joy for mourning, the garment of praise for the spirit of heaviness." Like Hagar, if we turn to the Lord, accepting His guidance, we will be able to gain the comfort, hope, and strength we need to fulfill His benevolent plans for our lives.

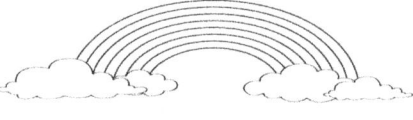

January 5

God Will Provide

"And Abraham called the name of the place, The-LORD-Will-Provide; as it is said to this day, 'In the Mount of the LORD it shall be provided'" (Genesis 22:14).

In my Bible the heading for chapter 22 of Genesis is "Abraham's Faith Confirmed." I think that is a fitting title because if you read the chapter carefully, you find that Abraham had confessed his faith in God before he even arrived at the designated place

of sacrifice. More importantly, he expressed his faith in the presence of his son.

We find the interchange in verses 7 and 8 of this chapter, where, when Isaac asked his father where the sacrifice was, Abraham responded, "My son, God will provide for

Himself the lamb for a burnt offering." Then the Bible says, "So the two of them went together." It paints a picture of a close relationship between Abraham and his beloved son.

Obviously, Isaac had learned to trust his father, just as Abraham had learned to trust God, even when, at least in this case, there was no physical evidence to support their faith. Talk about walking by faith, not by sight!

Too often we focus on the torturous journey from home to the mountain, and I'm sure it was horrible. But in reading the chapter through this time, I was impressed by Abraham's expression of hope and faith, even in the midst of his mental torment, that God would provide what was needed. I believe that faith gave him the strength to push through the pain, and his hope sustained him so that he could move forward through the ordeal. When God did provide

the lamb, it not only confirmed Abraham's faith, but also Isaac's. As well as our own.

I believe that it also unveiled a new vision of the plan of salvation, where God would again provide a lamb for a sacrifice, in the form of Jesus, so that the whole world could be saved. It gave them an indelible, deep, and personal understanding of the mission of the Messiah to come. And today, by reading of their experience, we also gain a better understanding of the plan of salvation and how precious the cost for us to be saved!

Additionally, this story teaches us about the importance of expressing our faith out loud, not only for our own benefit but also for the benefit of those around us. Especially when we can't currently find a solution for our problem. Trusting God through the darkness makes the light, when it appears and God miraculously provides for our needs, even more glorious!

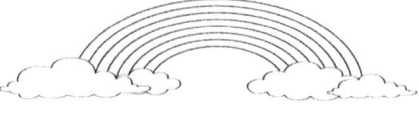

January 6

The Mizpah

"May the LORD watch between you and me when we are absent one from another" (Genesis 31:49).

This benediction, known as "The Mizpah" since it was first pronounced by Laban to Jacob, was a statement of farewell to his family members who were moving away from him. It was not only a type of blessing but a covenant of respect between the two men that they, along with their burgeoning families, would stay on their own

lands, with their large flocks and herds, get over their past differences, and do no harm to one another in the future.

Oh, that all "parting of the ways" might end so amicably. If we are walking close to the Lord and asking for His grace and guidance, we should strive to develop the skill, even in interactions with people we find difficult, to "agree to disagree" when necessary, and move forward, putting them in God's hands, and ultimately wishing them the best.

In the modern era, I have heard variations of this verse, which was originally coined as a peace accord, used as an affectionate way to say goodbye to family and friends, as well as to express hope that we may meet them again. In the meantime, we are committing them to God's watchful care. In Christian circles, it has become part of our blessed hope, that we will see each other again in heaven, if not before.

In my own experience, this simple blessing has brought me comfort, not only at funerals for loved ones but in many other situations where parting with people would otherwise be close to unbearable. It has consoled me when my family and I said goodbye to all of our loved ones prior to moving to the mission field. Then again, when we left the friends we had made in the mission field to return to the United States. We have expressed the phrase out loud to others, as well as breathing it silently in prayer, when saying farewell at graduations at the end of a school year, leaving co-workers at a job we loved, or moving away from dear friends in a church we were attending in order to serve in another community.

Besides hope and comfort, this concise saying has given me peace. This peace comes from knowing that the all-powerful and loving God is taking care of my friends and loved ones while I am separated from them by circumstances, distance, or even death. He can guide them and take care of their needs better than I ever could, so I am satisfied to leave them in His competent and caring hands. Praise God that we don't have to worry about our friends and loved ones as those who have no hope (see 1 Thess. 4:13)! Praise Him that we can anticipate the joy of meeting each other again soon in our wonderful new home in heaven!

January 7

The Long View

"But now, do not therefore be grieved or angry with yourselves because you sold me here; for God sent me before you to preserve life…. So now it was not you who sent me here, but God; and He has made me a father to Pharaoh, and lord of all his house, and a ruler throughout all the land of Egypt" (Genesis 45:5, 8).

Talk about magnanimous! How could Joseph find it in his heart to be so kind and forgiving of his wicked brothers who had sold him into slavery in his youth? They had separated him at a tender age from his home, his beloved father, his country, his culture, and his religion. However, because of Joseph's decision, when stripped of everything else, to cling to his Heavenly Father, they were not able to divest him from his

God. And that decision had made all the difference in Joseph's life.

As we trace Joseph's experience in the previous chapters of Genesis, we see that God honored Joseph's decision to be faithful to Him. In Genesis 39:3, we're told that the master in Egypt who bought him as a slave "...saw that the LORD *was* with him and that the LORD made all he did to prosper in his hand." Would that all of our bosses could say such things about us! Not only that we are trustworthy and competent at our work but also that they can see God is with us and at work in our lives!

Satan, of course, was not happy with this outcome, and due to the lies of Joseph's master's wife, he was thrown into prison. At this point, Joseph might have become so angry or depressed about being treated unfairly again, he might have argued that it wasn't worth it to believe in his God. Instead, he chose to hang on. It wasn't long before his sterling character traits rose to the surface again, and the keeper of the prison put Joseph in charge there. He also saw that the Lord was with Joseph, "and whatever he did, the LORD made *it* prosper" (Gen. 39:23).

We don't know exactly how long Joseph was in the prison before he met Pharaoh's butler and baker there and interpreted their dreams. But we do know that after the butler was restored to his position, it took him two more years before he spoke to Pharaoh about Joseph's ability to decipher the meaning of dreams. As the days drug on, I'm sure that Joseph's faith was tested. He might have given up hope that he would ever be released from prison, becoming bitter against both God and the other people who he had tried to help along the way.

Finally, as He does with us, God revealed that He had a better plan for Joseph's life. Joseph was summoned to interpret Pharaoh's strange dream. Pharaoh was so impressed with Joseph's God-given ability to tell him the meaning of the dream that he decided to put the young Hebrew foreigner in charge of the plan to help Egypt prepare for the coming famine, which had been foretold by his dream. In making that appointment, he said to his servants, "Can we find *such a one* as this, a man in whom *is* the Spirit of God?" (Gen. 41:38). Even Pharaoh saw the reflection of God in Joseph's words and actions. He declared that there was no one as discerning and wise as this person who had so recently been a seemingly forgotten prisoner in a land not his own. And then the amazed young man heard Pharaoh pronounce these words, "See, I have set you over all the land of Egypt" (Gen. 41:41). Suddenly, he became second in command only to Pharaoh himself. In an instant he went from rags to riches, from powerless to powerful, from unknown to famous, not only in Egypt but eventually to the people in surrounding nations who came to buy food from Joseph during the years of famine that followed.

Thus, Joseph found himself in front of his brothers once again. And once again, his character was tested. Would he treat them harshly, sending them away empty-handed to die, similar to what they had done to him? But Joseph took the long view. Upon reflection, he recognized the providence and guidance of God in all of his life's experiences, and so he sought to relieve his brothers' anxieties and guilt by showering them with God's grace. It was a crowning achievement, further demonstrating his God-matured character and illustrating why God could trust him to become a leader in all the circumstances of his life. May God help us to glorify Him wherever we go and whatever we do, just as He helped the faithful Joseph!

January 8

Surrender to God's Will

"Now therefore, go, and I will be with your mouth and teach you what you shall say" (Exodus 4:12).

Have you, like Moses, ever told God that you didn't think you were the right person to do whatever He was asking you to do? In the beginning of the book of Exodus, Moses makes several excuses for why he doesn't think he's up for the job. Certainly, God had chosen the wrong man. At his age, with his "slow tongue" (as he put it), and knowing the god-like power of the Pharaoh, how could he possibly lead the many thousands of people out of their slavery in Egypt? And even if, by some divine miracle, he could convince Pharaoh to let them go, where would he take them? What would they eat and drink, and how could they survive in the desert? Just the sheer number of them was overwhelming! How could one person organize their march through the wilderness, or communicate with them all at the same time to give them instructions, or keep them, including the women, children, and animals, safe from the perils they would experience along their trek to the middle of nowhere?

God, however, wouldn't take no for an answer. He saw the leadership qualities that Moses didn't realize he had. God had hand-picked Moses for this important assignment. Indeed, He had been preparing him for it all of his life. One of the reasons God wanted Moses to lead the people is because God knew that he was humble (meek, the Bible

calls it). He would lean on God and follow His instructions. To bolster the faith of Moses and give him the courage to take on such a fearful responsibility, the Lord promised him three things.

First, He promised to be with Moses. He also supplied some tangible physical support in the person of his brother, Aaron, who had somehow escaped from Egypt and been led to find his brother in the wilderness. He would serve as Moses' right-hand man and help share some of the load. He was still fluent in the Egyptian language and could be a mouthpiece for Moses in Pharaoh's court. God also reminded Moses that He was the Creator of mouths and would help both Moses and Aaron to know what to say. That was His second promise. Third, in Exodus 4:15, God says, "I will teach you what you shall do." At that point, He also supplied Moses with a rod, a simple tool through which God would perform miraculous signs.

Finally, with the assurances Moses had received from God, he moved forward in faith, accepting the challenge. And the rest is history, as they say. We know, from the narrative in Exodus, that there were definite setbacks along the way, such as Pharaoh becoming angry and demanding that the slaves make as many bricks as before, even when he withheld straw from them. But

Moses pressed forward, faithfully delivering the announcement of each successive plague, until the stubborn and rebellious Pharaoh finally agreed to free the Israelites.

Once they had exited Egypt, there were a host of other problems for which to find solutions, just as Moses had feared. True to His promise, however, the Lord was with them and provided everything they needed: food, water, protection from the Egyptians when they came after them, shade by day in a pillar of cloud, and light and warmth by night by a pillar of fire. Through all of this, Moses experienced a rich and rewarding relationship with God, which never would have been his had he declined the Lord's invitation to use his limited talents to accomplish the mighty works of God. Through his surrender, he fulfilled the greatest mission and purpose of his life. What a lesson for us today!

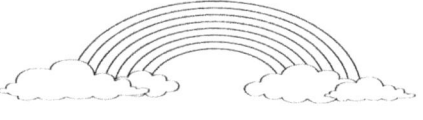

January 9

Stepping Forward in Faith

"Do not be afraid. Stand still, and see the salvation of the LORD, which He will accomplish for you today" (Exodus 14:13).

These are the marvelous, faith-filled words that Moses told the children of Israel when they were camped in the wilderness, and the Egyptians, who had changed their minds about letting their Israeli workforce go, were in hot pursuit of them. Although God had performed amazing miracles for His people in order to lead them out of slavery in the heathen land, they now only saw the Red Sea before them and Pharaoh's powerful war chariots behind them. Their way forward looked impassable, and their chances of surviving looked impossible!

Despite the improbabilities of the situation, Moses continued with his assurances, saying, "For the Egyptians whom you see today, you shall see again no more forever. The LORD will fight for you, and you shall hold your peace" (Exod. 14:13, 14). I can just hear the doubters saying (like in the old classic movie, *The Ten Commandments*), "Of course we won't see them again! We'll be dead!" I'm sure many of them were shaking in their boots, so to speak. Only those with an unshakable faith in God believed the words of Moses, knowing that faith does not depend on actual evidence but trusts God beyond the limits of human understanding. They had seen God work in their lives in the past, and knew that, as the religious writer, Ellen White, says, "Our heavenly Father has a thousand ways to provide for us, of which we know nothing" (*Desire of Ages*, p. 330).

So, when Moses stretched out his rod and the waters of the sea divided, they immediately obeyed his command to march forward. Even though there were high walls of water on either side of them, and the Egyptians were still coming after them, they acted on their faith in God and stepped out onto the path He had provided, despite their unresolved fears. To their amazement and relief, as they focused on obedience, instead of worrying about what negative things could still happen, God, in His time and providence, took care of everything else.

Once they were safely across the Red Sea, they looked back and saw how God had saved them, and true to His promise, destroyed all their enemies. Suddenly, they couldn't help but burst into a song of praise and thanksgiving! Most of Exodus 15 is comprised of this spontaneous hymn of gratitude.

Who of us has not had a problem which looked absolutely unsolvable, yet when we placed it before God in prayer, putting one foot in front of the other in faith, we come to find that God miraculously worked it out on our behalf? Perhaps our whole problem is not solved at once, but if we exercise faith and patience, God eventually works everything out for our good. When He wins these victories for us, we, like the Israelites, should sing out our praise and thanksgiving! This not only brings glory to God but it also deepens our own faith, as well as encourages the faith of those around us.

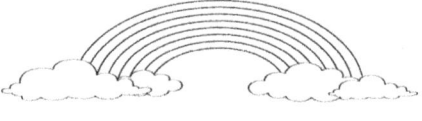

January 10

Teamwork Prevails

"But Moses' hands became heavy; so they took a stone and put it under him, and he sat on it. And Aaron and Hur supported his hands, one on one side, and the other on the other side; and his hands were steady until the going down of the sun" (Exodus 17:12).

Sometime during the Hebrews' wanderings in the desert, the armies of Amalek came out to fight against them. Joshua was asked to choose some men and go to battle against these enemies, while Moses would support the battle by standing on the top of a nearby hill with the rod of God in his hand. Whenever Moses lifted up his hands, the Israelites prevailed, and when he got tired and let down his hands, the Amalekites prevailed.

Then something happened which caught my attention when reading this passage. Two other leaders, Aaron and Hur, went up the hill with Moses. While they were there, looking down at the fighting below, they saw what was happening and immediately went into action to assist their leader. First, they found a large stone to put under him so that he could sit down. Then they took up positions on either side of him, in order to keep his weary hands up until the battle was over, and Israel was victorious.

I would say that these two men had the spiritual gift of helps. They saw what needed to be done, and they did it. Not only did they jump into immediate action but they continued doing the right thing until "the going down of the sun." They stayed at their posts until the job was completed. They didn't look around for someone else to take on their responsibilities or quit when they got tired. I believe they also exhibited the power of teamwork in reaching a goal.

Through the years I have had many people work for me, including teacher's aides, clerks, and secretaries. Somehow, I was never impressed with the "clock watchers," who only stayed on the job until the minimum was done and ran out the door the minute the clock struck 5:00 p.m., or whenever their shift was over. Of course, sometimes people have emergencies, or very tight schedules, where they have to go to an appointment or pick up their children. But the consistent attitude of being engaged with the work at hand, doing it to the best of their ability, and striving to assist their supervisors to reach the organization's goals, are the traits I look for in employees. When they also work well with other members of the team, they distinguish themselves as workers to be treasured!

Two other biblical admonitions about work come to mind (which we'll discuss in more detail later). The first one talks about "whatever your hand finds to do, do *it* with your might" (Eccles. 9:10), and the other says to do our work "as to the Lord, and not to men" (Eph. 6:7). With everyone working together, and each one fulfilling his responsibilities to the best of his ability, the Israelites, with God's help, won the day. I believe that by doing the same today, we can also experience victory in our lives.

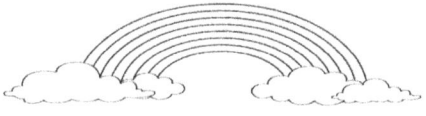

January 11

Strangers among us

"You shall neither mistreat a stranger nor oppress him, for you were strangers in the land of Egypt" (Exodus 22:21).

This verse is found in a section of Exodus titled "Moral and Ceremonial Principles." It strikes a chord with me because, through the years, I have had the privilege of laboring in a foreign country myself, as well as working here in the USA with many foreign students, including a host of immigrants and refugees.

I use the term "laboring" because living and teaching in another country, where the culture and language are not your own, is a hard job. It requires many adjustments, not only of daily culturally-engrained habits but also of general assumptions about the world. Becoming truly competent in a second language means spending many hours listening to and trying to speak that language, which inevitably includes making many, sometimes humorous, and often embarrassing, errors along the way! One time, while working at a college in Mexico, I entered the busy accounting office and inadvertently blurted out that I was pregnant. The shocked workers looked up from their desks, and I realized from their faces that, once again, I had used the wrong word to communicate my thoughts! Another time, while teaching in Puerto Rico, I was asked to give a greeting at the university graduation ceremony in an auditorium filled with hundreds of students, friends, and parents. At the platform microphone, which was also airing the ceremony on a local radio station, I proudly welcomed the listeners on this "hermosa hermana" (beautiful sister), instead of on this "hermosa manana" (beautiful morning)!! Although I quickly corrected myself, I still cringe every time that episode comes to mind!

I share these experiences because, further on, in Exodus 23:9, there is a similar admonition to the verse above, but it gives the Israelites even more motivation to treat strangers kindly, when it says, "Also you shall not oppress a stranger, for you know the heart of a stranger, because you were strangers in the land of Egypt." Having been a stranger in a foreign land, I also "know the heart" of people who have come here from other countries. It can be overwhelming to experience the mismatch of cultural norms, the linguistic mishaps, the identity crises,

feelings of insecurity and inadequacy, as well as the frustration, especially in the early months of the transition, of often feeling out of place. Add homesickness, and for refugees, past memories of poverty, war, or other troublesome experiences to overcome, and it rapidly becomes apparent that these people need our help and support. This is even more true for children and youth, who generally have had no choice in suddenly being thrust into a new and strange environment.

As an American adult, I had great advantages over these "strangers," in a number of ways. I chose to go to another country for a limited amount of time. I knew that if I didn't like it, I could return to the States, and that I would most certainly be able to see my friends and family again. I was healthy and well-educated and had even studied some basic Spanish in school, which at least gave me a little understanding of the language in which I would suddenly be immersed. Fortunately, I didn't come from a background of war or abject poverty, and I was a professional working in a career field I knew well. Despite all these advantages, I still experienced culture shock, so I can only imagine what people from other countries go through when they first come to our competitive, fast-paced, modern life in America.

Fortunately, I have had the opportunity to teach English as a Second Language (ESL) to children, high schoolers, college students, and adults. Some of them were immigrants, others refugees, and still others, the more fortunate, were sent here as foreign exchange students. Over the years I have been inspired by their stories, motivated by their determination, and touched by their courage, as they strive to learn a new language and carve out a new life for themselves and their families.

I guess that's why I get so upset when I see Americans treating foreigners so unfairly or hear hate-filled speech about people who are already battling against such great odds. This is why I believe everyone should have the experience of living in another country for a period of time. They should also try to learn at least one other language. Then, as these verses suggest, because of having "walked in another's shoes," they would demonstrate more understanding and compassion for the "strangers" who live among us.

January 12

Workmanship

"See, I have called by name Bezalel.... And I have filled him with the Spirit of God, in wisdom, in understanding, in knowledge, and in all manner of workmanship" (Exodus 31:2, 3).

This declaration on the part of God occurred six chapters after He had told Moses that He wanted him to build a portable tabernacle that could be carried with the children of Israel as they traveled through the wilderness. He also explained the reason: so that He could dwell among them! Talk about reaching out to develop a relationship! And this was after all He had already done for them in delivering them from Egypt, as well as providing for all their needs since then! What a gracious and loving Heavenly Father, always planning ways to care for His earthly children.

The Lord then spends several chapters talking about the various symbolic parts of the tabernacle with great care, since each part will help to teach them (as well as us, who read the Old Testament hundreds of years later) something about the plan of salvation.

He even goes into detail about things such as what the priests should wear as they go about their ministerial duties!

Finally, and this is what really impressed me, God chose the exact people who would build His tabernacle according to His specifications. He not only knew their names but the names of their fathers and the tribe they were from. In fact, He says He has filled these artisans with all kinds of wisdom and all manner of workmanship, gifting them with the ability to work, not only in gold, silver, and bronze but also in wood and jewels. We're told later that God had given them the skills to engrave and design all manner of artistic works. Besides the tabernacle itself, and all of its furnishings, some of these chosen craftsmen were appointed to make the priestly garments and even the anointing oil and sweet incense that would be used in the sacred services inside the Holy Place of the tabernacle.

Imagine how you would feel if you knew that God called you by name to do a special work for Him! Add to that the confidence it would give you to hear that He had gifted you with just the right talents and skills to exercise your vocation in a masterful way! And what's more, we learn in Exodus 35:34 that Bezalel was also called to help others learn to use their God-given talents. There it says, "And He has put in his heart the ability to teach...." What a blessing it would be, after fulfilling God's purpose for your life, to know that you could leave a legacy of other well-trained people to carry on your good work after you were gone.

So many young people today waste years trying to "find themselves," to figure out what their talents are, and what is their purpose in life. Unfortunately, some older folks also wander aimlessly through life searching for the answer to the question. *Why am I here?* I believe we need to help these people identify the skills and talents they've been given and then to get busy doing the work that is close at hand to the best of their abilities. Asking God to guide them, they should move forward, always in an effort to live a life that will be a blessing to others and will bring glory to God.

Another point to highlight here is that if God has truly called you to do a certain work,

He will supply the abilities and strength you need to accomplish it! (Just as He did for the craftsmen mentioned in Exodus, as well as Moses, Joseph, Mary, Esther, Daniel, Paul, and many others throughout the Bible.) Our assignment may not be easy, but we will have the assurance that we are co-workers with God and doing the work we were born to do!

I think it is noteworthy to mention that this passage teaches us that God values not only mental or strictly religious workers but also those who work with their hands, building, repairing, creating, and designing things for the benefit of those around them. All of us can take encouragement from the Ellen White quotation that says, "Not more surely is the place prepared for us in the heavenly mansions than is the special place designated on earth where we are to work for God" (*Christ's Object Lessons*, p. 326). It is our duty to earnestly ask Him what that work is and then step forward in faith. His providence, our natural skills and talents, and the circumstances of our lives will all help us to find just the right niche for us to work for God, and then I believe that we, too, whether our abilities are great or small, can find purpose in life and fulfillment in our work, similar to what Bezalel was blessed to experience when carrying out his calling.

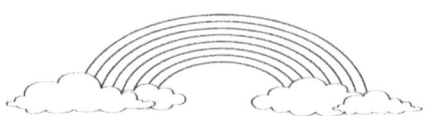

The Finger of God

"Now the tablets were *the work of God, and the writing* was *the writing of God engraved on the tablets" (Exodus 32:16).*

One day when I was working at a Christian college, I had the misfortune to attend a Bible class taught by a well-known and popular professor of religion. The topic under discussion was whether or not we can take the Bible literally. Unfortunately, about ten minutes into the lesson, I realized that he was arguing that we shouldn't and giving several examples of things in the Bible that he couldn't believe actually happened. One of them was the premise of the above verse. "How could God write the commandments with His own finger?" he scoffed. "And why would He use such an antiquated method, when He had the power to just think the words, making them appear instantly on the stone tablets?" I was appalled, realizing the power of his influence on the minds of the younger searchers of truth who sat before him. To their credit, however, several of the young Bible scholars spoke up, using today's text, as well as others, such as Exodus 31:18, which specifically says that the tablets on which the Lord wrote His commandments were "written with the finger of God."

In my recent reading of the book of Exodus, I have found this assertion made in the Scriptures on a number of occasions. Why did God make this point so clear over and over again if it was not important for us to understand His personal involvement in giving us His law? Of course, He could have just spoken the commandments, which according to Exodus 20, He did. But He also put them into writing, which would give His people something tangible, and in a more permanent form, to look at frequently as they thought about how God wanted them to live. Not only did God write on the first tablets, but after they got broken, He did the same thing again for the second set of tablets. In Exodus 34:1, God tells Moses, "...I will write on *these* tablets the words that were on the first tablets which you broke." Then He told Moses exactly where to store these tablets with His law engraved upon them. They would go into the ark of the covenant, under the covering cherubs in the Most Holy Place of the tabernacle.

Obviously, God placed the utmost importance on the Ten Commandments, or He wouldn't have written them out personally... twice! It reminds me of another time, at creation, when God spoke everything into existence. But when it came to creating man, God paused and took more time and care in forming both Adam and Eve into the image of Himself with His own hands! He could have just spoken them into existence, like everything else, or sent an angel down to give them the breath of life. But God gives us a demonstration of how much He values things by actually reaching down and touching them with His own hands!

I suppose some people who chafe at the notion of having to keep the Ten Commandments might seek to diminish their importance by questioning how we received them, or how important they really are to

God. Others may feel that they were given only to the Israelites of the Old Testament, and they do not apply to us now. But even in the New Testament we find many references supporting the keeping of the law. In fact, in John 14:15, Jesus Himself says, "If you love Me, keep My commandments."

Thus, after a thorough reading of it, I believe that those who still have faith that the Bible is the Word of God will be convinced that the Ten Commandments, which He wrote with His own finger, are still important to Him, as well as still binding on us who are trying to live according to His will today.

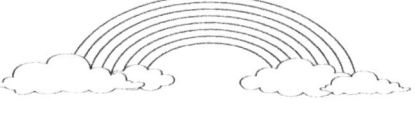

January 14

Restitution

"...Then it shall be, because he has sinned and is guilty, that he shall restore what he has stolen, or the thing which he has extorted, or what was delivered to him for safekeeping, or the lost thing which he found, or all that about which he has sworn falsely. He shall restore its full value, add one-fifth more to it, and give it to whomever it belongs, on the day of his trespass offering" (Leviticus 6:4, 5).

These verses caught my attention because the word "restitution," which appears in the subject heading for parts of chapters 5 and 6 of Leviticus, is one I don't hear people talking about very often these days.

Some of us, especially those in Christian circles, discuss the topic of forgiveness, and occasionally, repentance and even confession, on rare occasions. In modern times, it seems, we feel a bit uncomfortable admitting our errors to others, let alone asking them to forgive us for offending or mistreating them in some way. It's too humiliating and would make us look weak, or at least less than the

perfect-person image we often try to portray. We let ourselves off the hook by thinking that if we have asked God for forgiveness, we really don't have to deal with the down and dirty consequences of our actions on those around us. In fact, we often don't even mention specific sins to God for which we need forgiveness, getting by with just a perfunctory one-size-fits-all prayer of "forgive us all our sins and trespasses," hoping that this general phrase will give us a clean slate before both God and humankind.

Unfortunately, the sins we don't specifically identify, confess to God, and repent of are generally the sins that we will continue to commit. We've never confronted them head on, and actually surrendered them to God, asking for His help to overcome them.

Let's suppose we do get as far as this second paragraph, are we done? No, according to Leviticus, we also need to make restitution for our sins and mistakes. And, it gives us some specific information about how we should do it. First, it says on the very day when the penitent person brings his or her "trespass offering" to God to ask for His forgiveness, that person should also seek to make things right with "whomever" was negatively affected by his or her actions. This means we need try to make things right quickly. Also, and this is the part I've never heard a sermon on, these texts say that the offender should not only "restore the full value of" something but also "add one-fifth more to it." What might that look like in modern-day society?

For things stolen or damaged, finding the full value and paying one-fifth extra could be done fairly easily, although it would certainly be costly. But for less tangible things, such as damaging actions or hurtful words, what might "one-fifth extra" mean? It boggles my imagination. Maybe after a day in which we had said hurtful things to a loved one, we would decide to dedicate at least a day, and a fifth of another one, to using only kind words with that spouse or child? Not only would our family member be pleasantly surprised, but who knows, maybe it would remind us to always speak kindly to each other, helping us develop the much-needed habit of kind and caring speech in our homes?

Obviously, sometimes making restitution may not be possible, as in the case when the person you injured is no longer alive. Or it may not be practical, as in giving someone back a car and one-fifth after it has been stolen. But the principle is clear. The idea is to go above and beyond, the "second mile" if you will, to make things right again.

In any event, if we paid more attention to this counsel on restitution, I'm sure we would think two or three times before committing the same sins and mistakes again. Of course, true repentance and sorrow for the damage we've caused is the goal. But could it be that between the embarrassment and the cost of making restitution, we would find ourselves sinning less? I think that's the point. Making restitution would hold us accountable in a way that could help us improve our behavior and help us heal the wounds our sins and mistakes have inflicted on both God and others. I believe it's a practice that could improve all of our relationships.

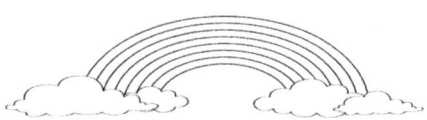

Eating and Drinking to God's Glory

"Do not drink wine or intoxicating drink, you, nor your sons with you, when you go into the tabernacle of meeting, lest you die. …that you may distinguish between holy and unholy, and between unclean and clean"
(Leviticus 10:9, 10).

This passage comes right before God lays out all the animals that are clean and unclean in the famous chapter of Leviticus 11, where the clean animals are the focus of the first half of the chapter and the unclean animals are the focus of the second half. Then God admonishes His people in the last three verses:

> You shall therefore be holy, for I *am* holy. This *is* the law of the animals and the birds and every living creature that moves in the waters, and of every creature that creeps on the earth, to distinguish between the unclean and the clean, and between the animal that may be eaten and the animal that may not be eaten. (Lev. 11:45–47)

Taken together, Leviticus 10 and 11 express not only God's concern for our physical health but also His concern for our spiritual health. Anything, food or drink, that lessens our ability to distinguish between holy and unholy, right or wrong, should be avoided by those who are seeking to become more God-like or "holy," as He is holy.

God was serious enough about His injunction not to imbibe when going into the tabernacle that He told Aaron and his sons they would die if they disobeyed Him on this point. All of Israel needed to understand by this that reverence to God and His sanctuary were not frivolous or joking matters. Sacred duties and holy actions were required by those designated to carry out the priestly ministry, and intoxicating drinks would deaden their sensibilities, causing them to dishonor the God they were enjoined to represent before the Israelites. As modern-day representatives of God to the world, would He require anything less of us?

So, let's discuss this matter of food. Something we might doubt God to even be concerned with, unless we note the care with which He specifically named not only the mammals that were clean and unclean but also the birds, the fish, and even the insects that could be eaten by those who are trying to become holy as He is holy.

This leads me to several questions. Why would God take the time to bother to do this if it wasn't for the good of His followers? And as God, who created everything, wouldn't He be the best source of information on what would be healthy and unhealthy for humans to eat? Finally, who can imagine that after centuries of sin and pollution, the animals that God declared unclean back then could be good for us to eat today?

The fact is that many people nowadays have decided to eliminate meat from their diet altogether, especially where they have a wide variety of nutritious food that is readily available in their part of the world, from which they can obtain enough protein and nutrients to live a healthy life. Vegetarians, who don't eat meat but still use dairy products, are more prevalent than vegans, who limit their diet to solely plant-based foods. But both lifestyles are becoming more popular today as people seek to avoid disease and alleviate concerns of animal cruelty and environmental issues. At the very least, I think we would do well to listen to our Creator's instructions about what things to avoid in order to be happy, healthy, and even, as He suggests, holy!

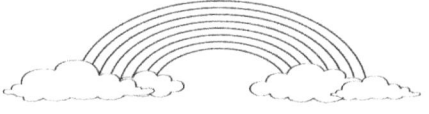

January 16

Tattoos

"You shall not eat anything with the blood, nor shall you practice divination or soothsaying. You shall not shave around the sides of your head, nor shall you disfigure the edges of your beard. You shall not make any cuttings in your flesh for the dead, nor tattoo any marks on you: I am the Lord"
(Leviticus 19:26–28).

Leviticus 19 enumerates a whole host of moral and ceremonial laws. Among them are the ones stated in the three verses cited above. These caught my eye for three reasons.

First, I would not readily equate eating something with blood in it to practicing something as generally considered to be heathen as "soothsaying." However, the Lord has just delineated what was clean and unclean for food earlier in this book of injunctions, and He apparently took it seriously enough to expect obedience in eating habits, right along with His other requirements. As far as soothsaying is concerned, in chapter 20 God reiterates His displeasure with these types of activities when He says He will set His face against that person who turns to mediums and familiar spirits.

Second, I found the prohibition to shave one's head or cut one's beard interesting. As I continued my reading, it was curious to note that priests, specifically, were not allowed to make "any bald *place* on their heads" (Lev. 21:5). While I don't fully understand the rationale behind these regulations, I'm sure God had His reasons for establishing them. Some people have suggested that these were practices of the heathens who lived around them, and God wanted His people to be set apart so that even in their appearance they represented the one and only true God, as opposed to adopting customs that might affiliate them with any false gods.

Third, I was surprised to actually find the word "tattoo" in Scripture. In the past, I have heard Christians make vague references to the fact that people should not use tattoos, but this was the first time I had seen this injunction in the Bible myself, clearly stated in black and white. This, along with the admonition not to cut oneself, is much easier to understand, given that these kinds of activities were practiced for many years by those who served other gods and worshipped idols.

Amazingly, tattooing oneself has become very popular in our modern culture today. Not just by cult worshippers and people involved in satanic rituals but by people who want to define themselves as gang members, rock stars, movie stars, and other famous people in our society. Unfortunately, many young people are following their example, understanding neither the symbolism of their actions nor the pain and difficulty they will experience if they later decide to try to remove the deep stains from their skin. God, who made our bodies, claims them as His. We don't need any etchings in our flesh to identify ourselves as part of His family. In fact, His emphasis is what our characters look like on the inside rather than any bodily marks on the outside.

While the instructions found in Leviticus were given to the Israelites, I believe they illustrate principles that should still be followed in our time by people who are trying to serve and represent God in our present context. My conclusion here is that even when we don't understand all of His biddings, we should try our best to follow them, trusting that our loving heavenly Father knows what's best for us, as well as for those we are seeking to influence for good in the world around us.

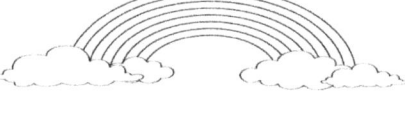

January 17

Sabbath Services

"Six days shall work be done, but the seventh day is a Sabbath of solemn rest, a holy convocation. You shall do no work on it; it is the Sabbath of the LORD in all your dwellings" (Leviticus 23:3).

Interestingly enough, when the Lord is describing the various religious feasts (what we would call holidays—derived, of course, from the term "holy days") that He wants His people to celebrate each year, He pauses for a moment to reiterate how the weekly seventh-day Sabbath should be kept. In this chapter, the seventh-day Sabbath is distinguished from any other days of sabbath rest experienced on a holiday by a capital letter. Although I've read my Bible for years, this was the first time I had noticed this fact.

Here the Lord reminds us that we should not work on Sabbath and that it is a time of solemn (I take this as meaning "reflective" in a spiritual sense) rest. But He also adds that it should be a time of "holy convocation." This is the first time I have registered seeing this term in conjunction with appropriate Sabbath activities. A convocation is a coming together of many people, and if it is for a holy purpose, I read that as meaning a time for a lot of people to get together and worship God, which would provide a premise for why we conduct church services on the Sabbath today. It's biblical.

Unfortunately, some modern Christians see Sabbath church services as unnecessary. They would rather sleep in, watch something religious on television, or plan activities in the great outdoors. While sleeping, watching a sermon on tv, or going on a hike in nature are all activities that might be considered to be appropriate on Sabbath, they do not take the place of meeting together with like believers to praise and worship the Lord. There is something about coming together on Sabbath to sing, pray, worship together, and fellowship with others that helps keep our spiritual lives thriving. (*See note below.)

Some people make excuses for not attending Sabbath services, saying that they don't like the sermons, or the music, or the style of worship in their local congregation. I have two recommendations for these folks. First, ask the Lord to help you use your gifts to make the services more uplifting for you and your fellow parishioners. Or, if you live in an area where there are several churches within a reasonable driving distance, vote with your feet, and start attending a church that better fits your spiritual needs and worship-style preferences.

Many have found that skipping church over time has weakened their Christian experience. The longer you don't attend church, the harder it is to go back because you feel more like a stranger than a member of the congregational family. Also, you get out of the habit of going, and Satan is quick to get you involved in other activities to usurp that time, making you feel that you are too busy or have other more interesting things to do than go to church. Slowly, step by step, he is able to use this tactic to lead you away from the things of God and into the things of the world.

One other interesting point about Leviticus 23 is that in verse 32 is where we find the rationale for keeping Sabbath from evening to evening. Apparently, this marked the beginning and ending of each "holy day" and is why modern-day Jews still celebrate not only Sabbath but all of their holidays from sundown to sundown. This can sometimes be challenging when living in a place "where the sun never sets," like parts of Alaska, but the general principle is still followed, and many Christians solve this dilemma by keeping the Sabbath from 6:00 p.m. Friday to 6:00 p.m. Saturday throughout the year.

In any event, Leviticus 23 reminds us of how important the seventh-day Sabbath is to the Lord, and that on it we should participate, whenever possible, in a "holy convocation."

(*Note: This was written prior to the coronavirus pandemic. Naturally, there are times when we can't attend regular church services because of sickness, or for public health reasons, such as when a church is shut down for a period of time. Under normal circumstances, however, it should be our privilege and our goal to attend Sabbath services whenever we can.)

Tithes and Offerings

"And all the tithe of the Lord, whether of the seed of the land or of the fruit of the tree, is the LORD's. It is holy to the LORD. And concerning the tithe of the herd or the flock, of whatever passes under the rod, the tenth one shall be holy to the LORD" (Leviticus 27:30, 32).

Here, in the last chapter of Leviticus, where the Lord is wrapping up His instructions to Moses for the children of Israel, He reminds them of their duty to continue paying tithe, not only in a monetary sense but out of all their increase. Once they took possession of Canaan, besides their flocks and herds of animals, they would now own land on which they would generate crops from fields and orchards. By paying tithe regularly they would remember that everything they did was done in the strength that the Lord had given them, and everything they possessed was a gift from the Lord. Undoubtedly, the purpose was to keep them loyal and grateful to the true God of heaven, instead of being influenced by the people around them to serve and worship false gods.

It surprised me when my mother-in-law counted all the fruit borne by each of her fruit trees each year. Then I realized that she took this injunction of paying tithe on her increase quite literally, having grown up in a largely agricultural community in Mexico. Upon moving to the United States, she simply brought this practice with her, thereby continuing to demonstrate her gratitude and commitment to God for all His blessings to her and her family.

Many modern Christians, most of whom are not involved in an agrarian lifestyle, chafe over the idea of paying tithe even on just their monetary income. Some say that paying one-tenth of their increase is too much, and that it is an arbitrary and unreasonable demand on them from church administrators who are trying to make money for the church at their expense. These people show their lack of acquaintance with the Old Testament Scriptures, which make a number of references to the requirement to pay tithe, defining it clearly as one-tenth of our increase. Today's verses, found near the end of Leviticus, are simply one last reminder to God's people of His command in this regard.

Other folks claim that they don't believe in paying tithe, either because they don't know exactly where it is going, or they choose to think that their funds are being misappropriated in some way. While the misuse of money may happen on a rare occasion, God holds us responsible for our actions, not the actions of others. Where do our motivations lie? Are we, personally, doing our duty to show our love and gratitude to God by returning a faithful tithe?

We all know that "God loves a cheerful giver" (2 Cor. 9:7). This, of course, includes not only tithe but also offerings. In fact, when the Israelites came to celebrate feasts and holy convocations, they were instructed that no one should come with empty hands before the Lord. All were expected to bring offerings and gifts to the Lord as part of their regular worship activities. So, if we are falling short in this spiritual dimension of our life, what should we do about it?

Two things that have helped me come to mind. First, I must determine that I am going to pay my tithe faithfully, making it the first check I write after receiving my paycheck, knowing that God will bless me if I am obedient to Him. After all, that is what He promises in Malachi 3:10. In fact, He says there that He will pour out so many blessings that we will not have room to receive them! Second, I must ask Him to guide and improve my motivations for paying both tithe and offerings, making me a truly willing and cheerful giver.

January 19

The Priestly Blessing

"The LORD bless you and keep you; The LORD make His face shine upon you, and be gracious to you; The LORD lift up His countenance upon you, and give you peace" (Numbers 6:24–26).

Several chapters into the book of Numbers, the Lord instructs Moses to give this beautiful priestly blessing to Aaron so that he, and the other priests, can pronounce it upon the children of Israel. Then, in verse 27, He says, "So they shall put My name on the children of Israel, and I will bless them."

I believe this blessing demonstrates the love and care the Lord longs to shower upon His people, even today. It is an expression of His longing to be close to us and His desire to guide us into safe and blessed paths throughout our lives.

Embedded in this ancient, yet ever relevant, pronouncement are several promises the Lord makes to those who follow Him. First, their lives will be filled with blessings. Second, that He will "keep" us, or watch over us, keeping us in His care. Next, that He will be gracious (including merciful) to us. And finally, that He will grant us peace. To me, the phrases, "make His face shine upon you," and "lift up His countenance upon you," paint a picture of a tender, loving Father, who is always attentive to His children's needs and whose face shines with love and pride as He looks upon His family.

Perhaps this image is reinforced by the fact that, from the time our daughter was a tiny baby, my husband used to hold her up above his head and repeat this blessing, usually in his native Spanish language, dedicating her to the Lord. Although she participated in two formal baby dedications, one in our church, and one in his family's church, he never tired of punctuating the days, both before and after, with this impromptu prayer of blessing. It didn't matter where we were or who else was within earshot. Whenever he was overcome with love, joy, and thankfulness for our daughter, he would burst into this sacred ritual up until she was school age and could no longer be easily lifted over his head. Then, instead, he would repeat the now familiar blessing to her, at least once a week, before putting her to bed. Eventually, of course, after hearing them so often, she memorized the meaningful words, and we have no doubt she will also repeat them to her children. Talk about a legacy of blessing!

Today, in looking back, we can only stand amazed and praise the Lord for the way He has blessed and cared for our daughter throughout all the days of her life. We have seen many evidences that the Lord has taken our recitation of the priestly blessing seriously, and we are so thankful that our many prayers and petitions to the Lord on her behalf have not been in vain. The Lord keeps His promises, and for that we praise His holy name! It makes me want to burst into song! This is the first verse of the first hymn in the *Seventh-day Adventist Hymnal*. Join me if you would like:

> "Praise to the Lord, the Almighty, the King of creation,
> O my soul, praise Him, for He is thy health and salvation!
> All ye who hear, now to His temple draw near; join ye in glad adoration!"

January 20

Retirement

"This is what pertains to the Levites: From twenty-five years old and above one may enter to perform service in the work of the tabernacle of meeting; and at the age of fifty years they must cease performing this work, and shall work no more. They may minister with their brethren in the tabernacle of meeting, to attend to needs, but they themselves shall do no work. Thus you shall do to the Levites regarding their duties" (Numbers 8:24–26).

When I first read these verses, I was amazed. "See," I said to my spouse, "Even God believes there is a time for retirement." I had been lobbying for us to quit working, buy an RV, and travel around exploring parts of the country we had not yet seen. Through the years we had made it a goal to visit all fifty states on our various vacations, but I was sure there were still many adventures out there just waiting for us to enjoy in our golden years!

My husband, however, had tried being retired for a few months and decided he didn't like it. "As long as I have my health, I want to keep working," he told me. "Besides, if I stop working now, we won't be able to afford to travel anywhere."

As a result, I have had to content myself with weekend and vacation getaways, but I'm still in the market for a nice, used RV so that once we are both fully retired, we can go exploring!

Looking at these texts again, it is interesting that the Lord prescribed both a beginning and an ending age for priests to work in the tabernacle. At the age of twenty-five, young people were considered totally eligible to take on all the regular duties of the priesthood. After twenty-five years, however, at the age of fifty, they were officially retired. Reflecting on this, I think there comes a time when those of us who are older should move aside, passing the torch over to the younger folks, giving them a chance to exercise their God-given talents and abilities in the cause of God.

I'm comforted by the fact that the Lord doesn't push those of us who are older completely aside. Here He tells Moses that priests over fifty years old may still do some light work with their brethren in the tabernacle "to attend to needs," as long as they leave the heavier priestly duties to those younger than themselves. So, although it is time for us, as retired members of God's family, to slow down, there are still some things we can do to assist in the work of attending to the needs of others.

Some may argue that the age of fifty seems too young to retire, but apparently the Lord thought it was appropriate for the kind of work the priests were doing in that time and place. Today, in modern American society, people are always arguing over whether retirement age should be set at fifty-five, sixty-two, sixty-five, or later. It seems as soon as one reaches the magic number, the goal posts are changed again, putting "senior discounts and benefits" just out of reach! If we live long enough, based on our individual circumstances, our health, our financial situation, and the type of work we do, we will each need to make the decision about when to retire for ourselves, to the best of our ability, and in consultation with God and our families.

Regardless of when we retire, as our health and energy allow, I believe we each need to seek the Lord's wisdom for how, using the gifts and resources He has given us, we can still make ourselves useful in some way, perhaps through our prayers, our sage counsel, or offerings dedicated to specific projects in advancing His kingdom. At the same time, I rejoice in the fact that the Lord "remembers that we *are* dust" (Ps. 103:14). After all, Ecclesiastes 3 admonishes us that "to everything *there is* a season." Knowing this, there is actually a time when He calls us to relax, enjoy the fruits of our life of labor, spend time with loved ones, and give thanks for God's continued blessings during our retirement years.

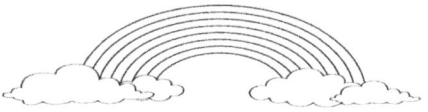

Lapses in Faith

"And the LORD said to Moses, 'Has the LORD's arm been shortened? Now you shall see whether what I say will happen to you or not'" (Numbers 11:23).

Amazingly, this verse shows us that even Moses, that great man of God, through whom God performed so many powerful and incredible miracles, had occasional lapses in his faith. This was one of those times. The Lord heard the people's complaints of being tired of just eating manna all the time, and remembering the flesh pots of Egypt, they begged Moses to provide them with meat. At this request, Moses was overwhelmed, for the multitude of people he now led numbered 600,000 men alone, not counting the women and children. He was also angry that the people were so ungrateful for all that the Lord had done for them throughout their journey, starting with the miracles that finally convinced their masters in Egypt to let them go free.

Yet, hearing their cries to Moses that they never should have left Egypt, God had promised that He would give the Israelites meat, not only for one meal but enough for a whole month! (This was one of those situations in which the phrase, "Be careful what you ask for because you might get it," would be appropriate.) In fact, they would have so much meat that they would come to loathe it!

It was at this point that Moses became incredulous. Focusing on the impossibilities, instead of the fact that with God "all things are possible," he argued with God, as we often do. "Shall flocks and herds be slaughtered for them, to provide enough for them? Or shall all the fish of the sea be gathered together for them?" (Num. 11:22).

Momentarily forgetting that he was talking to the Creator of the whole universe, the One who caused the plagues to fall upon Egypt, who miraculously parted the Red Sea for them, brought water from a rock, shielded them with a pillar of fire by night, guided them with a shade-producing cloud by day, and made manna fall from heaven to feed them year after year, he petulantly expressed his doubt.

In today's text, the Lord simply responds to Moses by asking the question, "Has the Lord's arm been shortened?" In other words, was God less powerful now than He had been in Egypt, or when performing miracles for them throughout their wilderness sojourn so far? Then he admonishes Moses to observe what happens next, saying, "Now you shall see whether what I say will happen to you or not." Suddenly, a strong wind begins to blow, and with it come more quail than the people could count. They spent the next several days, and even one night, collecting enough quail for all of them for a month, just as the Lord had said would happen.

Unfortunately, modern Christians often have the same problem believing God when a huge problem looms up before them. We forget that the God we serve is still all-knowing and all-powerful. A famous quote from Ellen White tells us that, "We have nothing to fear for the future, except as we shall forget the way the Lord has led us, and His teaching in our past history" (*Life Sketches of Ellen G. White*, p. 196). As we recount what the

Lord has done for us, the circumstances He has arranged in our lives, and the blessings He's poured out upon us, our faith should be strengthened, and when the doubt-filled question, "Has the Lord's arm been shortened?" comes to mind, we should be ready to shout out a resounding, "No!" Our God is the same mighty, heavenly Father that He was at the time of Creation, in the time of the Israelites, and in the time when Jesus walked on earth performing miracles of healing and salvation. Indeed, our strong and ever-vigilant God is the same yesterday, today, and forever!

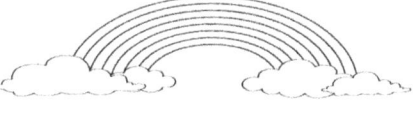

January 22

Equal Rights

"And the LORD spoke to Moses, saying: 'The daughters of Zelophehad speak what is right; you shall surely give them a possession of inheritance among their father's brothers, and cause the inheritance of their father to pass to them. And you shall speak to the children of Israel, saying: 'If a man dies and has no son, then you shall cause his inheritance to pass to his daughter'" (Numbers 27:6–8).

These verses appear in the middle of a discussion about inheritance laws for the children of Israel. They had just undergone a census to see how many men there were in each tribe. These numbers helped Moses decide how much land in Canaan each tribe should be given as an inheritance. Larger tribes would receive more land, and smaller tribes would receive less land. But there was a problem. In the tribe of Manasseh, of the descendants of Joseph, there were no sons in this generation to receive an inheritance in the land flowing with milk and honey.

It was brave of five women, the daughters of Zelophehad, to step forward and request that Moses consider their case and grant them the land that normally would have gone to a male in their family, if they had had a brother. They spoke up in front of not only Moses but also Eleazar, the priest, as well as the leaders and all the congregation of Israel. Boldly they asked for a possession among their father's brothers.

Since this situation was unprecedented, Moses brought their case before the Lord. And today's text records the Lord's answer. Not only did He resolve the case of the four daughters of Zelophehad but He commanded Moses to deal fairly with other families that had daughters and no sons, in this same manner. Thus, this incident guided the

Israelites' decisions as they divided inheritances into the future.

I have several observations here. First, how important it was that these five women, Mahlah, Noah, Hoglah, Milcah, and Tirzah, spoke up. They did so at an appropriate time and place, and in front of the whole congregation so that everyone would know the outcome of their petition. Ultimately, they benefitted by doing so, but they also helped other women who came behind them by their judicious presentation.

Second, I am impressed by the fact that, although women were not generally granted land in the time of Moses, he was open-minded enough to listen to their plea and wise enough to seek the Lord for counsel before making a decision. Two valuable traits for a good leader even today.

Third, I'm thankful that the Lord made His position clear on this matter, showing again that He is a God who is fair and treats us all equally. It's comforting to know that He is ever mindful of our needs, regardless of our gender, or any other distinctions that societies artificially set up to make us think that one class of people is better than another. May the Lord help us to be as accepting and magnanimous as He is!

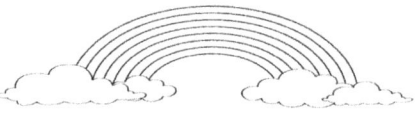

January 23

Old Testament Ordination

"So Moses did as the LORD commanded him. He took Joshua and set him before Eleazar the priest and before all the congregation. And he laid his hands on him and inaugurated him, just as the LORD commanded by the hand of Moses" (Numbers 27:22, 23).

The last half of Numbers 27 tells us how a new leader of Israel was chosen shortly before the death of Moses. Always a humble and thoughtful leader, when he knew he would pass away before the children of Israel would cross over the Jordan into the promised land, he asked the Lord to name a successor to take his place so that the people would "not be like sheep who have no shepherd" (Num. 27:17).

Helping to choose and train a person to take your place is one of the marks of a dedicated and faithful leader. Also, Moses knew that if he put his blessing on the new man in charge, that person would be more well-accepted by the congregation. Change is always hard, and a formal gesture of approval by Moses would make the transition go more smoothly.

Of course, the Lord was way ahead of Moses. He had already picked a new young leader, a man filled with the Spirit, and had already planned for how he would be introduced. He told Moses to take Joshua before Eleazar, the high priest who had succeeded Aaron, as well as before the whole congregation of Israelites. Then Moses was to place his hands on Joshua and inaugurate him publicly and formally as the new leader of the people.

So the custom of "inaugurating" leaders by laying hands on them and pronouncing a public blessing on them as they take up the proverbial "torch" that has been passed down to them began. Synonyms of the word inauguration include dedication, commission, ordination, and installation. Sometimes we argue over which terms to use, but the activity is the same. It's the acknowledgment that a person has been set aside for a special work, in the presence of God and the community which they will serve.

Another detail here is worth mentioning. In verse 20 of this chapter, the Lord tells Moses to start by giving Joshua some of his authority, which implies that Moses was to take a mentorship-type role while the young leader was learning the ropes of his new position. No matter how competent a person is, the quality of the orientation to their new role and setting can make or break their success in their new assignment. Thus, for a period of time, we don't know how long, Joshua was able to enjoy a type of apprenticeship program until Moses felt he could fully surrender the reins of leadership and rest in peace.

This narrative presents a great model for how to successfully transfer leadership, not only from one person to another but from one generation to another.

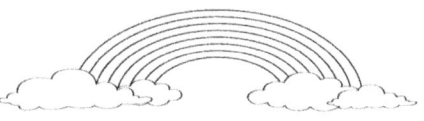

January 24

Cities of Refuge

"Then you shall appoint cities to be cities of refuge for you, that the manslayer who kills any person accidentally may flee there. These six cities shall be for refuge for the children of Israel, for the stranger, and for the sojourner among them, that anyone who kills a person accidentally may flee there" (Numbers 35:11, 15).

When the time came to divide the inheritance among the children of Israel in the land of Canaan, the Lord individually named a leader from each tribe to do this work. In order to be fair, larger tribes were granted more land, and smaller tribes were given less land. But the Levites, who were the priests for the

Israelites, were not assigned their own land. Instead, each tribe was directed to give some of its cities, in proportion to the amount of land that they received, to the Levites. These cities, as well as the common land around them for two thousand cubits on each side for their cattle, herds, and other animals, were to be reserved especially for the Levites. In total, forty-eight cities, spread throughout the land of Canaan, were dedicated to this purpose. Among them, six cities were to be appointed as special "cities of refuge," at the Lord's direction.

Then the Lord explained the reason for these cities. They would be a haven for people who accidentally killed someone, until they had the chance to stand before the congregation for judgment. In those days of "an eye for an eye, and a tooth for a tooth," if the manslayer was found outside a city of refuge, an avenger, someone from the dead person's family, could kill the person who had accidently killed their loved one.

To clarify, a murderer has intent to kill (the death is premeditated), while a person who accidentally kills someone else is called a manslayer, from which we derive the current legal charge of manslaughter. This chapter goes on to say that, after judgment by the congregation, if the one who has fled to the city of refuge is found guilty of murder, he shall be put to death. Whereas, if he is found to have killed a person accidentally, he shall be acquitted. Nevertheless, he must remain in the city of refuge until the death of

the current high priest, perhaps to wait until the emotions of any would-be avengers had settled down. Only then can the manslayer return to the land of his possession.

This chapter also cites several specific examples of scenarios where a person would be charged with either murder or manslaughter. It also states that the murderer would be put to death on the testimony of witnesses, but that only one witness is not enough to give someone the death penalty. I'm surprised at the level of detail the Lord gives the children of Israel here in order to guide them in judging each other fairly in their new, developing society.

The creation of these cities speaks not only to God's justice but also to His grace. Notice that in verse 15, the Lord says these special places will provide a refuge, not only to the children of Israel but also for the stranger and for the sojourner. Anyone who accidentally took a life might flee there.

I can only surmise that this practice provided inspiration for our modern-day "sanctuary cities." Although the crimes and legal proceedings may be different, the idea of giving people grace until a just settlement of their case can be reached seems fair in the light of the instructions given to the Israelites in the Old Testament. To me, this open-armed acceptance, this opportunity for a second chance in life for people who have made terrible mistakes, is a demonstration of the wideness of God's mercy and should be an encouragement to us all.

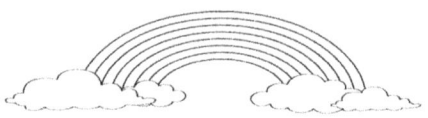

Take Courage!

"Then I said to you, 'Do not be terrified, or afraid of them. The LORD your God, who goes before you, He will fight for you, according to all He did for you in Egypt before your eyes, and in the wilderness where you saw how the LORD your God carried you, as a man carries his son, in all the way that you went until you came to this place'" (Deuteronomy 1:29–31).

It was time to pass over the Jordan River into the Promised Land. There was great anticipation in the ranks of the desert-weary people, but a problem arose. The leaders, one from each tribe, had just come back with a negative report, not about the land itself, which was beautiful, and truly a land flowing with milk and honey as the Lord had promised. The concern was about the people they would have to fight to gain possession of the land of Canaan. According to the returned spies, the people were giants! They were both taller and stronger than the Israelites, and the huge and numerous cities were "fortified up to heaven" (Deut. 1:28).

All but two of the leaders who had scoped out the land focused on the negative aspects of the situation, spreading doubt and discouragement throughout the whole camp. What a lesson to leaders of how important their words are, fostering either hope or despair in those who follow them! This principle holds true in all the areas of life; at home, at work, at school, and at church. A small expression of doubt can go a long way in squelching new ideas and destroying innovative initiatives.

It's not that we should abandon reality in our goals and aspirations. We need to keep our feet on the ground, so to speak. Nor should we adopt a Pollyanna naivete or stick our heads in the ground, hoping that the difficult decisions will disappear before we come up for air. In this life we will all have unplanned and unpleasant circumstances to maneuver through and crucial decisions to make, which will change the direction of our lives and the lives of those around us, sometimes for many years to come. Thus, the importance of seeking counsel of God, as well as remembering all the ways He has led us in the past. When our faith is tested, focusing on at least these two things can be helpful. First, that God is all-powerful. Things that are impossible for us, are, of course, possible with God. Second, our faith will be bolstered when we remember all the ways that God has led us in our past experiences.

In the verses above, Moses, being the faithful leader that he was even into his old age, sought to turn the thoughts of the children of Israel to a remembrance of all the recent miracles the Lord had done to bring them out of bondage in Egypt. How could they forget so soon His power, and the tenderness of His watchful care as they had traveled through the hostile desert? As humans, we have so many fears about all the terrible things that could go wrong in our lives that we often forget to reflect on the good experiences of the past, on the answered prayers, and the blessings God has poured out upon us. As a result, our faith sometimes falters, just as it did for God's people as they were poised to take possession of the land of Canaan. We need to take courage, knowing that the Lord is on our side!

May God help us, as we are waiting on the verge of entering the heavenly Canaan, to talk with faith, to know that God has promised to calm our fears and to fight for us, and even to carry us "as a man carries his son" when the way gets too difficult for us to manage. Let us encourage one another with uplifting and positive words so that together we can accomplish all the victories that the Lord has in mind for us. If we follow His leading, He will make us more than conquerors.

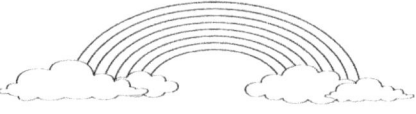

January 26

Idol Worship

"Therefore know this day, and consider it in your heart, that the LORD Himself is God in heaven above and on the earth beneath: there is no other. You shall therefore keep His statutes and His commandments which I command you today, that it may go well with you and with your children after you..." (Deuteronomy 4:39, 40).

What a powerful declaration against idolatry! In this chapter, Moses is about to part ways with the children of Israel. The Lord has informed him that his time as the leader of his people has almost come to an end. He will not be passing over the Jordan with them into the Promised Land, for God has other, ultimately more exciting, plans for him. Although he will die, we know from the New Testament that God will later resurrect him, and he will actually be one of the people sent from heaven to comfort and strengthen Jesus in the hour of His transfiguration prior to His death on the cross.

Here then, Moses uses his last bit of time with the Israelites giving them admonitions to keep in mind after he is no longer with them. In Deuteronomy 4, he pleads with them to remember all the Lord has done for them, to obey His commandments, and to teach not only their children but also their grandchildren about the Lord and His statutes. We see Moses doing everything possible to help his people remember to observe God's righteous requirements as they move into the land of Canaan. He also gives them a stern warning about falling into idolatry by worshiping the "gods" created of wood and stone by the Canaanites, who will be living all around them. Knowing the power of peer pressure, and how, as humans, we are so prone to be influenced by those around us,

Moses recites the negative consequences of turning away from their true God, the One who made all of heaven and earth. He also reinforces their faith by telling them that even though their all-powerful Creator cannot be seen, if they seek Him with all their hearts, they will find Him (verse 29).

Some of the Israelites would probably be tempted, like us today, to keep serving God, while also giving homage to other gods and idols, just to be sure we've covered all our bases, or to fit in better with the people around us. But Moses asserts that "there is no other" God like Jehovah. Only He is all-powerful, all-knowing, all-loving, and only He can satisfy our built-in need to worship Someone greater than ourselves. Bowing down or praying before a statue or other object made by human hands is degrading for a child of God, who is made in His image. It is a waste of time, energy, and resources, and it will leave us spiritually empty. On the other hand, we are told that it will "go well with us" if we worship and obey the Lord

Being convinced that worshiping idols is condemned by the Bible, many Christians today, who would judge this practice as wrong and a sign of ignorance, are unwittingly worshiping other things, such as clothes, cars, riches, politics, sports, music, and even other people. May God help us to recognize and set aside our modern idols so that nothing will interfere with our relationship with the one true, eternal God, who alone is worthy of our time, money, energy, praise, and everlasting worship!

January 27

Teaching Our Children Diligently

"And these words which I command you today shall be in your heart. You shall teach them diligently to your children, and shall talk of them when you sit in your house, when you walk by the way, when you lie down, and when you rise up" (Deuteronomy 6:6, 7).

Whenever I read these words, I think of my father. He memorized more Scripture than anyone I have ever known. And he shared it, often repeating long passages. But he would also punctuate his conversations with a short one-verse zinger ("a word in season") at just the time someone with whom he was talking needed it. His children were no exception. He would apply God's promises like band-aids whenever we needed wisdom, warnings, or comfort. Whatever the situation warranted, he had a verse or two at the ready to share with us.

Our location made no difference, for he took verse 6 literally when it said we should put these words in our hearts. Thus, he was constantly working on memorizing verses: while shaving, while waiting in line for something, while washing dishes, or during his hour-long daily devotions. He followed the admonition to teach them "diligently to your children" in that he also required us to memorize verses, sometimes during family worships, or before we went out to play in the mornings. Recitation of Bible verses was a common occurrence in our house, whether we were sitting down, lying down, or walking around, as suggested by verse 7 of today's passage.

As a result, people often sought my father out as a spiritual counselor, of sorts. They asked for his advice or requested him to pray for them. He would listen patiently to long tales of woe from folks who were considered outcasts by others, comforting and encouraging them with texts and promises from the Bible. Whenever Christians from other faiths appeared at our door to witness, they soon learned that they had "bitten off more than they could chew," as my father peppered them with verse after verse from both testaments, in support of his doctrinal beliefs. In his younger days, when he was asked to share his testimony about how he had survived as a Christian through more than a decade of military service during the end of World War II and the Korean conflict, he was always happy to share the promises from God's Word that had bolstered his faith and sustained him through those difficult times.

While I can't speak for my siblings, I know what affect my father's unshakable faith in the sacredness and power of God's Word had on me. First, I grew up with a respect for the Bible and an appreciation for its promises. Second, the importance of obeying God's commands was impressed upon me at an early age. Third, I enjoyed a confidence in the doctrines I'd been taught, knowing they were based on God's Word. Fourth, I also felt a sense of direction and self-worth as I began to comprehend, from information garnered from the Bible, where I came from, why I was on this earth, and where I was going after death. Understanding where I stood in the big picture of the universal conflict between good and evil helped me live a much more purpose-driven life as well as a more fulfilling one.

As I contemplate these texts anew, I wonder if I followed them close enough in the raising of my own daughter. I hope so. I wanted her to experience the same blessings I gleaned from a father who took them very seriously and did his best to inculcate in his children an enduring trust in God and an unshakable belief in His Word from an early age. May we all, as parents, grandparents, and anyone having influence over the young people all around us, seek to do the same, so the spiritual blessings of knowing God will continue to be poured out on generation after generation as long as we remain on this earth.

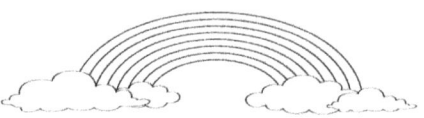

January 28

Empty Handed?

"Three times a year all your males shall appear before the LORD your God in the place which He chooses: at the Feast of Unleavened Bread, at the Feast of Weeks, and at the Feast of Tabernacles; and they shall not appear before the LORD empty-handed. Every man shall give as he is able, according to the blessing of the LORD your God which He has given you" (Deuteronomy 16:16, 17).

Two things struck me about this passage. First, that the Lord recognized humanity's need to *come apart and rest awhile* from their usual day-to-day labors to celebrate various feasts, or holidays, as we would think of them today. These special times provided not only for rest but also for socialization and spiritual edification. The closest thing we have to this now is probably our summer camp meetings across the United States. These feasts were designed to help the people reflect, give thanks to God for the blessings He had poured out upon them, and reorder their priorities. Instead of earthly concerns, they were enabled to stop their usual work to focus on heavenly themes. It was for recentering, if you will.

Naturally, feasting and fellowshipping were important aspects of these meetings, as they are in our current celebration of holidays. Unfortunately, society has downplayed, and continues to do so more and more, the religious elements of our most treasured holidays, such as Thanksgiving, Christmas, and even Easter. It seems to me that, as Christians, re-emphasizing the spiritual implications of the days we celebrate, would go a long way toward helping us to return to our daily work refreshed and revitalized, as well as with a renewed sense of gratitude to God for our many blessings,

just as the Lord intended "holy days" to do when He gave them to the children of Israel so many years ago.

Second, this passage reminds us of our stewardship when the text says, "...they shall not appear before the LORD empty-handed." I thought about this verse for a while. What if every time we came before the Lord we brought an offering, as the Israelites were required to do? What if, besides our regular offerings, we brought special gifts of gratitude to the Lord on holidays, instead of only thinking about gifting ourselves and other people? Imagine how much money the church would receive to accomplish its work in the world! And remember, these offerings were all in addition to the regular tithe, the ten percent of all their increase, that the congregants were expected to bring before the Lord. Recent statistics tell us that currently, only about 36 percent of church members pay an honest tithe, never mind offerings!

Reflecting on these verses, it seems the Lord was trying to teach His people, both then and now, to take time in our busy lives to stop and thank Him for His blessings in order to strengthen our relationship with Him at regular intervals. He also wants us to practice generosity by being faithful in our offerings. This habit would stifle our selfishness, as well as make us better stewards of the means that flow through our hands to the benefit of others. Since reading these texts, I have become more mindful of my offerings, planning ahead for what I will give, and trying to bring offerings of praise, in addition to money, whenever I arrive at the church to worship the Lord.

January 29

Unanswered Questions

"The secret things belong to the LORD our God, but those things which are revealed belong to us and to our children forever, that we may do all the words of this law" (Deuteronomy 29:29).

Working as a college professor, I was confronted at times by students who had serious existential questions, often about God but also about life, in general. These were questions that were not easy to answer. On occasion, through research or my own life experiences, I was able to provide a satisfactory response, but I frequently had to admit that I didn't know, and we would probably have to wait until we got to heaven, where the Lord Himself would be able to explain why things happened the way they did on earth. Of course, He will also reveal more about Himself, as well as spiritual insights that either we would not be able to understand or weren't yet ready for during our time here.

This verse reminds us that God is omniscient, and we are not. We were created by Him, thus He understands our curiosity and quest for knowledge. But suggesting that a finite human brain, which has been deteriorated by thousands of years of sin, can understand the all-knowing, all-wise, infinite mind of God, is somewhat akin to saying that an ordinary ant crawling on the ground can look up and understand the mind of a person standing above him! Does this mean the college student, or anyone else, should be told not to ask questions? No, it only means that as humans we need to recognize that our earthly brains have certain limitations.

In the spiritual realm this means that once we have studied everything God has revealed to us on a given topic, we need to leave the rest to Him, knowing that in the eternal sinless world where we are going, He will show us all we need to know when we need to know it. And we will be satisfied. This assumes two things from the searcher. First, that he or she has spent time studying what God has already revealed upon a subject. Second, that he or she has decided to trust God to provide the other pieces of the puzzle on God's own perfect time schedule, instead of insisting all the answers must be known NOW in order to believe in and surrender his or her life to the Lord.

As parents, we follow a similar pattern in dealing with our own children. When they are infants, we don't try to explain everything we know about math, science, world history, etc., because we realize that they are not yet developmentally ready to receive this outpouring of knowledge. Even when they are a little older, we sometimes choose not to share things with them that might hurt them or cause them to be afraid of the future. We want to wait until we feel they are ready to receive what we are sharing with them and deal with the facts in a mature and effective manner. We tell them things when we believe they can either benefit from the information at this stage of their lives or when it will prepare them emotionally, intellectually, or psychologically for what lies ahead.

Even Jesus, when He walked here on earth with His disciples, told them, "I still have many things to share with you, but you cannot bear *them* now" (John 16:12). This did not preclude them, however, from acting on the information they had received from Him up to that time. We, like them, have plenty to keep us busy just acting on the information the Lord has already so mercifully seen fit to give us. When we have lived up to all the light we have, then we may be in a position to ask for more light, always realizing that the Lord, in His infinite wisdom, knows what's best for us.

Although there will always be room to doubt God, because of the all-important gift of free will He has granted us, if we choose to walk that dark path, we will reap the sad consequences both now and in eternity. On the other hand, we will be much better served by choosing to trust Him as our kind, loving, and thoughtful heavenly Parent. One who we see, not as someone who is trying to keep secrets from us, but as One who, through the Bible, prophets, the life of Jesus on this earth, and the Holy Spirit has provided all the information we need now in order to be saved.

During our earthly journey, "we see through a glass, darkly" (1 Cor. 13:12, KJV), but when we reach heaven, God has promised to open His storehouses of knowledge to our understanding, and we will know why things happened the way they did during our lifetimes. Not only will we be given answers to all our questions but our curiosity will be continually satisfied. Our new, immortal, and revitalized minds will delight in learning great and wonderful things, both about God and His marvelous creations across the limitless universe throughout the ceaseless ages!

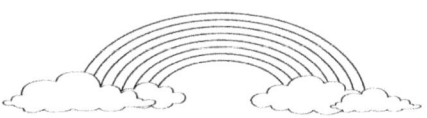

January 30

Choices

"I call heaven and earth as witnesses today against you, that *I have set before you life and death, blessing and cursing; therefore choose life, that both you and your descendants may live; that you may love the LORD your God, that you may obey His voice, and that you may cling to Him, for He is your life and the length of your days..." (Deuteronomy 30:19, 20).*

Knowing his time is short, Moses here makes one more passionate appeal to the children of Israel to obey and follow the Lord as they are about to move into their new phase of life in the land of Canaan. He outlines again the consequences of choosing to obey, as opposed to choosing to go their own way, once they are surrounded by people who worship other gods. This choice cannot be avoided. It must be made one way or the other. He makes clear that this is a decision of the utmost importance, one that will be witnessed not only on earth but also in heaven. What's more, the ramifications of their choice will affect both them and their descendants, for good or evil, for years to come.

This week, some friends of mine just dropped their son off at college. He is going to live in the dorm, away from his family and far from home for the first time. I can just hear them, like Moses, but perhaps in more modern terms, trying to give him their best advice about his choices and what the consequences might be, as he moves into his new phase of life. Suddenly, he will be surrounded by a host of new influences, some good and some bad. He will now be free to make his own decisions. His parents have tried to teach and guide him for eighteen years. Now, it's up to him whether to heed their counsel.

He will decide for himself how he wants to conduct himself in his new environment. Will he study diligently or party every week? Will he choose good friends or those who will lead him astray? Will he keep a neat room, clean clothes and eat healthy food or will he live a messy, careless, and slovenly existence? Will he avoid the numerous addiction traps that so many young people fall into or will he remember the advice of his praying parents and choose to continue to serve the God of his fathers? Not unlike the children of Israel, the choices he makes now (in his case, especially about his lifestyle, his career, and his life partner) will impact both his future and the future of his offspring. I'm praying with his parents that he will choose to serve God, following a path of fulfillment and blessing as a result.

In life we all pass through a number of phases. Once we complete our academic training, there are many other challenges to which we must adjust. Married life, a new job, moving to a new town, parenthood. And that's not all. There's the phase of grandparenthood and retirement. Sometimes we have to adjust to sickness, disability, becoming caretakers, or requiring care ourselves. Other times we are confronted with major changes in our lives, such as divorce, widowhood, remarriage, becoming a stepparent, or living in a foreign country. Whenever we pass into any of these new stages of life, among all the other decisions we'll need to make is that all-important spiritual choice again. Will we continue to serve God or let our new circumstances and surroundings separate us from Him? May the Lord help us, in whatever stage we find ourselves, to cling tightly to Him throughout our whole life's journey.

January 31

Strength for the Day

"...As your days, so shall your strength be…. The eternal God is your refuge, and underneath are the everlasting arms"
(Deuteronomy 33:25, 27).

As I came to the end of the Pentateuch, the five books of the Bible that Moses left to the Israelites, I was blessed anew by the promises found in chapter 33, especially the ones found in verses 25 and 27.

"As your days, so shall your strength be," has been my mantra when going through physically or even emotionally difficult times. One year ago, when we moved to a new home in another state, I remember leaning heavily on this promise. There was so much to do! All the packing, deciding what to sell, give away, or throw away, the planning of who would help move us and when, disconnecting utilities in one city and scheduling them to be connected in another, reviewing and signing final documents on the house we had purchased, the list went on and on. Finally, on the last day, when everything had been moved out of the old house, it was time to do some serious cleaning. We were already exhausted from moving furniture, lifting boxes, and making what felt like a hundred trips carrying smaller items to our cars. After a long drive, we would still need to unload enough things to be able to spend the first night in our new home.

We decided we would need to make another trip all the way back to the old house to clean it on the following day. After that, I needed to spend a day cleaning shelves and cupboards in the new house before unpacking our belongings there. Although the Lord sent us some wonderful movers, who placed our large pieces of furniture where we wanted them, it still took us about a month to unpack the sea of boxes surrounding us in almost every room! I had experienced some heart issues the year before and didn't feel up to the task, but I worked methodically from dawn to dusk every day, before, during, and after our move, earnestly claiming God's promise for strength to get through each twenty-four-hour period.

When we were finally settled, we knew we had been working hard, not only from our sore muscles but because of the fact that my husband and I had both lost about five pounds in the process! I am still praising the Lord every time I think about this experience. He made what I thought was an impossible task possible through the strength He provided us, based on this precious promise!

Meanwhile, the sister promise for today, found in verse 27, is a powerful expression of God's omnipotent love and care and has brought comfort and calm to me, especially after surgeries, when I felt totally helpless on my own and knew that I could just rest in God's "everlasting arms" until I felt better. Knowing during times of searing emotional pain that God is our refuge, "our hiding place," as Corrie Ten Boom put it when writing about her experience during the Holocaust, can provide a spiritual strength and patient trust that helps shield us from Satan's worst attacks on our faith and hope. Finding God as our refuge during life's most difficult moments sustains us until we can see the light at the end of our dark tunnel. We come to realize that, through God's protection and providence, we have not only survived but now have a testimony to share with others about God's gracious power to bring us through life's roughest storms. Surely, the eternal God is our refuge, and underneath are His everlasting arms!

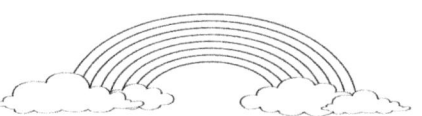

Promises to a Leader

"This Book of the Law shall not depart from your mouth, but you shall meditate in it day and night, that you may observe to do according to all that is written in it. For then you will make your way prosperous, and then you will have good success. Have I not commanded you? Be strong and of good courage; do not be afraid, nor be dismayed, for the LORD your God is with you wherever you go" (Joshua 1:8, 9).

It's a new day for the Israelites, but especially for Joshua, as he now takes up his new leadership position among them. He can no longer lean on Moses. The responsibility to lead and guide this multitude of people now falls squarely and heavily on his shoulders alone. He has just received marching orders from God to "arise, go over this Jordan, you and all this people…" (Josh. 1:2). Naturally, he would feel some trepidation as they entered the land of Canaan for the first time and confronted the people who were living there.

How gracious, then, for the Lord to give him a number of wonderful and reassuring promises at the outset of his administration. The first chapter of Joshua is replete with these encouraging utterances. After reminding Joshua to meditate on the Book of the Law, which had been handed down by Moses, he also admonished him to observe what was written in it. Then a cascade of promises followed: Joshua's way would be prosperous; he would be blessed with success; the Lord would strengthen and encourage him; he would not have to be afraid nor even dismayed. Finally, God told Joshua that He would be with him wherever he went!

What president, military commander, or CEO of an organization could ask for more! In fact, I think it would be advisable for anyone starting in a new leadership position, whether a pastor, teacher, school principal, college president, or owner of a new business endeavor, to claim these promises as well. Even parents, especially those who are moving into this role for the first time, could benefit from the blessings poured out in these verses.

Imagine not being fearful, or even dismayed, about things that could happen in the future. Meditate on the fact that the Lord has said He would strengthen and be present with us wherever we go. As long as we are following God's leading, it doesn't matter which job we've been assigned, or in which house, neighborhood, city, or country we've been called to work. We can be confident that the Lord will be there with us, and our labors will not be in vain.

Who wouldn't covet the assurance that you could be prosperous and successful in reaching both your personal goals and your business potential? Not just in a monetary or military way but in a way that brings purpose and fulfillment into your life.

Our part to play is simply two-fold. Observe God's law and claim these promises for our own. He even pledges to give us the strength and courage we'll need to accomplish these things, as we move forward in faith. What a small price to pay for such a good deal with God!

February 2

The Scarlet Cord

"Then she said, 'According to your words, so be it.' And she sent them away, and they departed. And she bound the scarlet cord in the window"
(Joshua 2:21).

Has anyone, who you initially thought was "below you" for some reason, ever saved your life? The story of Desmond Doss comes to mind. You may have seen the movie Hacksaw Ridge, where the young Christian soldier signs up to be a medic in World War II. Because he was a conscientious objector, he was persecuted, rejected, and maligned by his fellow soldiers. They ridiculed him and called him a coward. But once they went to war, and he was the one who bravely saved the lives of many of them, their opinion of him changed rapidly, and their low estimation of him turned to gratitude and respect.

Sometimes it's easy for us to think ourselves better than people who are poorer, who work at low status jobs, or who don't speak English well. Working with foreign students for many years has taught me not to underestimate people at first glance. Getting to know them over a semester or so, I am continually impressed with their intelligence, their kindness, their determination to keep pressing forward despite the hardships they may have suffered in life. It's inspiring as well as humbling. Their humanity, friendship, and generosity throughout the years have taught me to be less task-oriented and more people-oriented.

In the story told in Joshua 2, God uses a woman to help the Israeli spies who Joshua has sent to check out the cities and the people in the land of Canaan, where they will

soon be dwelling. Besides being a woman, she was a foreign person. In fact, someone who they would usually consider an enemy. Not only that but she was also a prostitute by profession. What an unlikely rescuer! Providentially, however, the spies lodge in her house. In the process they learn that she is a believer in the God of heaven, the true and powerful God of the children of Israel. When word gets out that Israeli spies are in her house, she courageously hides the two men on her housetop, protects them from discovery, and helps them escape safely. Before they leave, however, she asks that they will remember her kindness and spare her and her family when Jericho is destroyed. The men agree on the condition that she tie a scarlet ribbon in her window to let the Hebrew soldiers know which house not to attack. They promised that she, and whoever of her family were found in the house with her, would be saved. Thus, her bravery and faith in God saved not only her life but the lives of those in her family. If only all of us could be similarly blessed.

I have read that the scarlet ribbon symbolized the red blood of our Savior, which was poured out for our redemption, and that by hanging it out her window, Rahab was demonstrating her faith in the one true God, whom she believed could save both herself and her family. For this act of faith, she is mentioned, along with patriarchs, prophets, and kings in the famous faith chapter

58

of Hebrews 11 many years later. This story teaches us more about God's mercy, His grace, and His impartiality. He is willing to choose anyone who has faith in Him to do great and wonderful things!

February 3

Dry Ground

"And it shall come to pass, as soon as the soles of the feet of the priests who bear the ark of the LORD, the Lord of all the earth, shall rest in the waters of the Jordan, that the waters of the Jordan shall be cut off, the waters that come down from upstream, and they shall stand as a heap... Then the priests who bore the ark of the covenant of the LORD stood firm on dry ground in the midst of the Jordan; and all Israel crossed over on dry ground, until all the people had crossed completely over the Jordan" (Joshua 3:13, 17).

Today's devotional warrants two verses because the second is the fulfillment of the promise found in the first. In verse 13, Joshua is encouraging the children of Israel to trust in the Lord, saying that this miracle of the stoppage of the Jordan River would be a sign unto them that the living God was among them and that He would make them victorious in their battles once they had entered Canaan. First, however, they would have to walk by faith, with the priests actually stepping into the flowing water, even though, from all indications, it was still rushing downstream at full force. What a lesson for us. We can't wait until the path before us is totally clear of obstructions before we step forward in the direction God has marked out for us to follow. Sometimes the way ahead looks impossible to us, but if

we continue to walk forward in faith, we will be amazed at the miracles the Lord will perform on our behalf and to His glory.

In verse 17 we have the historical account of what happened when the Israelites obeyed the Lord's command. Not only did the waters of the Jordan stop but the bottom of the river became "dry ground," making it possible for all the Israelites to cross safely over to the other side. As Christians, we need to be cognizant of the fact that our influence is a powerful gift from God. When we take a firm stand of faith, despite whatever difficulties may present themselves, only heaven will reveal how many others will be influenced by our example to be faithful to God's call in their lives as well. If we want our children, our friends, and our neighbors to be saved, we need to set the example of walking by faith. Then we should share our testimonies of how God has opened doors and created new and amazing interventions in our lives that previously couldn't have been imagined when we were waiting to have all our questions answered before following His leading.

I have been blessed with a number of experiences related to "walking by faith, not by sight," but the one that stands out most clearly in my mind was when I was asked to create a master's in education program while I was a missionary at a university in Puerto Rico. The task seemed overwhelming

at first, but little by little, with a lot of prayer and effort, the program began to take shape. Students were recruited, professors were hired, study materials were purchased, and at the end of three arduous years, our first fourteen graduates earned their master's degrees! The program was also accredited by two different accreditation agencies in the United States as well as one in Puerto Rico! There had been obstacles at every turn, but by trusting in God's grace and awesome power, the "waters had parted," and the impossible had been accomplished! Praise and gratitude spring from my heart whenever I remember this marvelous experience!

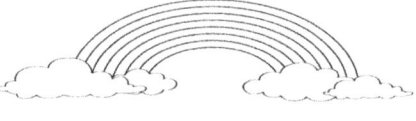

February 4

Memorial Stones

"...'Take for yourselves twelve stones from here, out of the midst of the Jordan, from the place where the priests' feet stood firm. You shall carry them over with you and leave them in the lodging place where you lodge tonight.' ...that this may be a sign among you when your children ask in time to come, saying, 'What do these stones mean to you?'" (Joshua 4:3, 6).

Continuing with the story from yesterday, as the people were crossing over the Jordan, Joshua was instructed by the Lord to appoint twelve men, one from each of the tribes of Israel, to choose one stone to carry up out of the riverbed on their shoulders. With these stones, a memorial was to be set up on the other side of the river to commemorate the miracle the Lord had

performed for them as they were entering the Promised Land. Not only would it help the Israelites remember that their all-powerful God was with them but it would also give them an opportunity to tell the next generation what the Lord had done for them.

When their children and grandchildren asked the meaning of that pile of stones, they would explain how the waters of the Jordan were held back until all of the Israelites crossed over, giving them a sign that God, the same One who dried up the waters of the Red Sea when their ancestors were first delivered from Egypt, would be with them and give them victory in their battles in their new country. What a comfort this miracle must have been, alleviating their doubts and fears, and assuring them anew that the Lord was still with them, even though they were following a new leader into a strange and different land.

As I thought about these memorial stones, I wondered what reminders we have given ourselves of God's providences along our life's journey. What monuments of the Lord's grace and deliverance in our personal lives have we set up in order to bolster the faith of our posterity? Do our children know how the Lord has led us and the miracles He has performed in our lives to alleviate our doubts and fears? What about the blessings we've received, the prayers that have been answered, the forgiveness granted, and the spiritual battles He has helped us win? If we haven't shared these experiences with our children, as well as others in our sphere of influence, are we shirking our duty? By withholding our testimonies of what the Lord has done in our lives, are we robbing God of the praise and glory due Him? I would contend that not sharing what the Lord has done for us makes us forget all the benefits we have received from his hand, thus weakening our faith over time. It also prevents us from helping to build up the faith of the other people that God brings into our lives.

Thus, I've started thinking about practical ways to do this in everyday life. What I've come up with so far is this list of suggestions: marking promises in the Bible that God has fulfilled in my life and sharing them with others, as the Lord provides opportunities; sharing answered prayers in prayer meetings and other church gatherings; reserving some time during family worship where each person is invited to share something the Lord has done for them in the recent past; committing to writing ways the Lord has guided and blessed us through memoirs, short stories, poems, and letters. I'm sure there are many other ways to preserve and share our testimonies, and I'm convinced that if we ask the Lord to set up more "divine appointments," He will bring people across our path who need to hear what we have to share.

After all, the Lord longs for us to tell others what He has done for us, so they can come into a trusting and saving relationship with Him as well. Sermons, Bible studies, distributing Christian literature, all have their place in evangelism, but little is as effective as an individual remembering what God has done in his or her life and sharing it with a searching soul. People can argue with doctrines, denominational beliefs, and even historical facts, but they frequently find it difficult to resist the humble, Spirit-filled testimony of a believer who has experienced the transforming, miracle-working power of God in his or her own life.

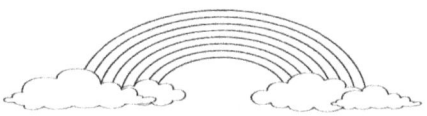

The Sun Stood Still

"So the sun stood still, and the moon stopped, till the people had revenge upon their enemies. ...So the sun stood still in the midst of heaven, and did not hasten to go down for about a whole day. And there has been no day like that, before it or after it, that the LORD heeded the voice of a man; for the LORD fought for Israel" (Joshua 10:13, 14).

As the children of Israel were fighting for possession of the Promised Land, five kings heard of their victories over Ai and Jericho and decided to band together to fight against Joshua and his mighty men of valor. They comprised a vast army. The Israelites had reason to feel intimidated, but the Lord told Joshua not to fear because He would deliver the hosts of the Amorites into his hand. Therefore, in front of all the children of Israel, to give them courage and to ensure that the glory for winning the battle that day would be ascribed to God's intervention, Joshua asked that the sun stand still until they had won the victory over their enemies. It was a bold request. As verse 14 says, "...there has been no day like that, before it or after it...." Yet acting on God's promise, Joshua had the faith to publicly ask God to intervene in a way that He never had before. Honoring the young leader's faith, the Lord "heeded the voice" of Joshua, and the Israelites gained the promised victory.

Have you ever asked God to intervene in your life in a way He's never done before? It's a daring proposition. But look at all the stories in the Bible where God did just that. Seemingly impossible things that had never been heard of before. Reflect on the saving of Noah and his family in a special ark when it had never rained before. Then there was the birth of the promised son to Abraham and Sarah in their old age. Think of Gideon's fleece, Elijah being taken up to heaven in a fiery chariot, Elisha making an iron axe head float, not to mention all the wonders the Lord performed in Egypt to free the Hebrew slaves, and the marvelous, never-seen-before actions that God took to care for them during their journey through the wilderness: the manna that God provided for them to eat for forty years, water from a rock, and a cloud to both protect and guide them on their trek. Just think of all the other instances of God's marvelous power delineated in the Old Testament, some of which we have recently been discussing, like the Jordan River drying up so the Israelites could cross over into Canaan on dry ground. Meanwhile, in the New Testament we have the virgin birth, the raising of Lazarus from death, and the many healing miracles of Jesus, just to name a few of the unexpected and usually thought to be impossible actions of God on behalf of humankind.

So the next question to follow is, if we haven't seen any of these miraculous interactions in our lives today, why not? Should we? Is it our lack of faith that is keeping us from experiencing signs and wonders in our lives similar to what people experienced in Bible times? These questions certainly give us food for thought. Surely, part of the problem is our lack of faith. But I do look forward to the time of the "latter rain," described in God's Word as a period near the end of time when God's Spirit will be poured out on His people, and they, through the Lord's power, will perform many signs and wonders.

In the meantime, I think it behooves us to recognize the smaller, everyday interventions of God in our lives that we often overlook because they have become so commonplace to us. Little things we take for granted that we couldn't do without God's power. That our hearts keep beating day after day, that the food we eat is digested and converted into energy to keep us going, that babies are born, people still recuperate from various diseases, and earnest prayers are still answered in myriad ways! In fact, my experience has been that the more I thank and praise God for the little miracles He does in my life, the more they seem to multiply! So, I am led to believe that if we trust in the Lord and rejoice in the smaller "everyday miracles," He will send the big ones, like the sun standing still, if and when we need them most.

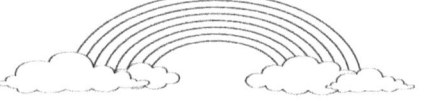

February 6

Led by a Woman

"Now Deborah, a prophetess, the wife of Lapidoth, was judging Israel at that time. And she would sit under the palm tree of Deborah, between Ramah and Bethel in the mountains of Ephraim. And the children of Israel came up to her for judgment" (Judges 4:4, 5).

As we move into the book of Judges, the leadership of Joshua comes to an end with his death. He had been a faithful leader, encouraging the Israelites to follow the Lord, reminding them of all the victories He had helped them win in their new land, and warning them what the consequences would be if they turned their backs on God in the future. For the next several hundred years, the Lord raised up a series of military champions and local judges to lead His people. The Hebrew word for judges can also mean rulers, deliverers, or liberators. Besides helping to free the people from their oppressors, it was their assigned task to maintain justice and settle disputes between the Israelites.

Surprisingly, among these colorful characters whose stories are delineated in the book of Judges, we find Deborah. Most of chapters 4 and 5 are devoted to her. Not only was she a judge but the Bible says that she was also a prophetess—a fearless one at that. When she told a man named Barak that God had called him to fight against their oppressors, he said he would only go to battle if she went with him. Although the Lord had already promised victory, Barak did not have the courage to enter the fight without the prophetess at his side. Gladly she agreed to go, giving him more words of encouragement just as he was about to attack Sisera, his armies, and his nine hundred chariots of iron. As promised, God gave Barak the victory that day. Then, Deborah, who called herself a "mother in Israel," led out in a rousing song of praise! After that incident, Israel enjoyed peace for the next forty years.

I am always amazed when the Lord goes counter to the popular culture of her given context and chooses a woman to do a special job for Him. Fortunately, God is not bound by our cultural social constructs, role limitations, or traditional human mores. Being "no respecter of persons," He uses anyone who makes themselves available to be utilized by Him in a specific time and place. Here, several other female examples come to mind. Mary, the mother of Jesus; Anna, the prophetess in the temple when Jesus was dedicated; the humble widow who helped keep the great prophet Elijah alive during a fearsome famine; the woman at the well in Samaria who evangelized her whole town; and in more modern times, an American woman named Ellen White, who was called by God to be not only a prophet but also a powerful speaker, prolific writer, and wise leader when the Seventh-day Adventist Church was established in the 1800s, continuing her work until the time of her death in 1915 (a mere seven years before my own mother was born).

In fact, the Lord often uses those whom we least expect to do great things for Him. At these times, it's as if He is trying to break down our small, narrow-minded tendencies and stretch our horizons. Think of how God can use those who do not have abundant wealth, education, or status. Sometimes God uses people from other races, cultures, or language groups other than our own. Children, adolescents, and especially some of us seniors in our "golden years" can still be valuable co-workers in the Lord's cause. I think of Namaan's poor little slave girl, torn from her family at a young age, but rich in faith, who saved her master and his household. Then there's the old woman, also poor and disenfranchised, who gave her two mites as she entered the temple. Jesus has used her simple act to encourage other folks to give generously throughout the ages ever since her story was first told. Simon, a person from a different race and country, carried the cross to Calvary for Jesus. And Mary Magdalene, who had been a woman of ill-repute before her conversion, was the first person to announce His resurrection!

Reflecting on God's grace, love for the human family, and His warm acceptance of all those who choose to serve Him makes me remember the words to that old hymn that says, "There's a wideness, in God's mercy, like the wideness of the sea" (*The Seventh-day Adventist Hymnal*, hymn 114). Lord, please make us who claim to be your followers as open-minded and marvelously magnanimous as you are!

The Hesitant Warrior

"Then the LORD turned to him and said, 'Go in this might of yours, and you shall save Israel from the hand of the Midianites. Have I not sent you?' So he said to Him, 'O my Lord, how can I save Israel? Indeed, my clan is the weakest in Manasseh, and I am the least in my father's house.' And the LORD said to him, 'Surely I will be with you, and you shall defeat the Midianites as one man'" (Judges 6:14–16).

In the story of Gideon, we find a follower of God who was hesitant, doubting, and argumentative with the Lord. In the verses just before those written here, when the Lord first talks to him, calling him a "mighty man of valor" (verse 12), Gideon dares to answer back like a sassy teenager. He asks about where God has been while the Israelites are suffering under the cruel hand of their enemies, the Midianites. He also asks about the miracles their fathers had told them about when God had delivered them from Egypt, which they hadn't see performed in their day. Then he asks why God had forsaken them.

Amazingly, the Lord ignores Gideon's impertinence and doesn't argue with him. Instead, He reveals that He is calling him to rectify the very situation that he is complaining about. He gives Gideon a few more words of encouragement, states clearly that He is sending Gideon to deliver his people, and tells him that He will be with him and give him victory over the Midianites. When what the Lord is asking him to do sets in, he, like many of us, begins making excuses for why he can't possibly do what God is asking of him. After all, he's from a weak clan, and he's the youngest in his family. Surely the Lord is asking the wrong person to take on such a daunting task.

Never mind that the Lord, Himself, is speaking to Gideon, the doubting warrior now asks for a sign that this truly is what he is being called to do. So, in order to build up his faith, the Lord starts performing miracles. First, the food Gideon brings out is consumed by fire. Later in this same chapter, we find the famous story of Gideon's fleece. He puts out a piece of fleece and asks that the Lord will make it wet while the surrounding ground is dry in the morning. The Lord condescends to grant the sign he requests. Incredibly, still needing to be convinced further, he asks the Lord to make the fleece dry, while the ground around it is wet the next morning. When this sign is also granted to Gideon, he finally believes enough to get on board with God's plan. What a patient and merciful God we serve!

Finally, Gideon sounds the battle cry, and 22,000 soldiers respond to fight against the vast armies of the Midianites. Knowing that many of the Israelites were afraid and not spiritually ready to trust that God could deliver them, He directed Gideon to tell them that if they were fearful, they could go back home. All but 10,000 left. Then the Lord went even further to separate out the men He wanted by asking them all to drink water while crossing the river. Those who took the time to kneel down and take a leisurely drink were also sent home. Now only 300 men, those who had lapped the water as they were moving forward, demonstrating their eagerness to engage in the battle, were left. Following God's leading, Gideon put the men into three groups of one hundred each on different sides of the enemy army. They used torches and the noise of trumpets and of breaking pitchers to confuse the Midianites, who fled in fear. Israel not only experienced a resounding victory that day but they lived in peace from their enemies for the next forty years. God's way is always best, even though to our human ways of thinking, we sometimes feel He is being illogical. Who would think to fight thousands of professional soldiers with only 300 ragtag volunteers? Who would call a humble, doubting man with weak faith to become a courageous and successful leader of His people?

What a reminder that "with God all things are possible" (Matt. 19:26). And, I dare say, the story of this hesitant warrior can give all of us hope—hope that God can use even the weakest of us to do great things for Him if we will only trust Him, surrendering our will to His all-wise plan for our lives.

February 8

𝓐 Humble Leader

"Then the men of Israel said to Gideon, 'Rule over us, both you and your son, and your grandson also; for you have delivered us from the hand of Midian.' But Gideon said to them, 'I will not rule over you, nor shall my son rule over you; the LORD shall rule over you'" (Judges 8:22, 23).

After Gideon's success against the Midianites, the people of Israel immediately wanted to make him their king. Gideon's response shows that even after the Lord had used him in a mighty way, he didn't let it go to his head. He retained his humility, knowing that it was the Lord who had gained them the victory over their enemies. He gave God the glory, pointing the people to Him as the true Deliverer and rightful Ruler over the Israelites. Perhaps this is the reason God selected Gideon in the first place, even though initially he appeared to be a "doubting Thomas."

The characteristic of humility is in short supply in those who rule over others today. It seems that just about everyone in politics, in business, and even in the church is always trying to get credit for anything good that happens, attempting to clamber to the top so that they can become more famous and powerful. Once they achieve their goals, however, they often are not satisfied, first because they suddenly realize all the responsibility that lies on the shoulders of leaders, and second, because their lust for power has become so great they are driven to continue to look for an even higher position, with even more power, riches, and fame. They boast about their accomplishments; they take advantage of people in lesser positions; and they feel that their ends justify their means, just as long as they can selfishly claim more and more for themselves.

Where did this unquenchable grasping for power come from? Recently, my husband and I have been reading about how sin began in heaven with Lucifer's rebellion against God. Despite his high position, he began to foster a seed of discontent and selfish ambition. He wanted to have the position of Jesus and was jealous of His power. Slowly, he began to murmur and complain about God to the other angels until this seed bore fruit in convincing one-third of his heavenly companions that God was unfair. The war in heaven, a place of utter peace and sheer happiness up to that point in time, was the result. And, ever since, as

residents in a sinful world with naturally carnal natures, we see the same tendency to fight for supremacy and power play itself out in our own lives and in the lives of those around us. Even as small children we see fighting between youngsters over who gets the biggest piece of pie or to be first in line.

Then, as adults, we often complain about our leaders, envying their power. We talk behind their backs, undermining their authority, and besmirching their character and motives. In an effort to build ourselves up, we try to tear others down. Many times we aren't satisfied until we've turned a previously happy home, workplace, community, or church into a toxic environment. This is not to say that leaders are perfect or that it isn't good to reflect on ways to improve a situation. But we all need God to help us examine our motives and guide us into unselfish and appropriate ways to work together with others to solve problems or make improvements in a particular setting. And when there are victories, let's follow Gideon's example in giving God the glory as well as our heartfelt homage and thanks.

Physical vs. Moral Strength

"Now therefore, please be careful not to drink wine or similar drink, and not to eat anything unclean. For behold, you shall conceive and bear a son. And no razor shall come upon his head, for the child shall be a Nazirite to God from the womb; and he shall begin to deliver Israel out of the hand of the Philistines" (Judges 13:4, 5).

In this chapter of Judges, we find the story of Samson's birth. Similar to the amazing experiences of the mothers of John the Baptist and Jesus that are found in the New Testament, an Angel of the Lord appears to Samson's mother and tells her that she has been chosen for a special assignment: to bear a son who will play an important role in God's dealings with His people. In addition to giving the previously barren woman the good news that she will soon be having a son, He gives her some specific instructions regarding how to raise him. These directions are found in the two verses cited above.

First, she was told how to care for her own body while she was carrying the child and then, subsequently, how to care for him. They were not to drink wine or anything else from the vine, and they were advised to avoid any meats that had been declared unclean. In addition to these dietary restrictions, the outward sign that this child was a Nazarite, in other words a person set aside to serve God for a special purpose, was that he was not to cut his hair. Literally, no razor should ever be used on his head.

While Samson's parents complied with these restrictions, Samson himself was not as careful to obey God's claims on him. He gloried in the extraordinary strength with which the Lord had gifted him, using it on several occasions to destroy pockets of Israel's enemies, the much-feared Philistines. But becoming something of a party boy in his youth and young adulthood, he strayed from God's purpose for his life. The infamous story of his cavorting around with Delilah, her betrayal, and his captivity by the cruel Philistines is well known.

Eventually, while still imprisoned and having been blinded by his enemies, he came to his senses, and in one final act of faith and moment of God-given strength, he pulled their temple down on them so that the number of Philistines he killed at his death was greater than the number of them he had killed in his lifetime. Since Samson's name is included in the faith chapter of Hebrews 11, we believe that, ultimately, he will be saved. But just imagine how different his story might have played out and the wonderful things the Lord would have been able to accomplish through him if he had faithfully followed God's will for his life.

Sometimes, when in our youth, we think our unwise choices and capricious activities won't really have much of an impact on our future lives as adults. We move away from the things our godly parents have taught us, thinking there will be plenty of time to mend our ways when we are older. Occasionally, we wake up in time to turn our lives around. More often, however, we become enmeshed in addictions, unsavory relationships, and deceptive ideas that take such a strong hold on us that we never fully recover. Satan has made an art form of deceiving us into thinking that life is all about having what he calls "fun" and living just for the moment, without any regard for the fearsome consequences that will be reaped, not only in this life but in the life to come.

This topic really hits home for me, having worked with young people most of my life. But the brevity and uncertainty of life warrants making this warning even more serious. One youthful indiscretion that haunts me most was when four of my daughter's classmates in high school decided to go out one January afternoon and have some "fun," driving as fast as they could on a narrow and hilly residential road. The car they were in hit a patch of ice and slammed into a tree, killing three of them.

Of course, the brevity and uncertainty of life is something of which even we, as adults, need to be mindful when Satan tempts us to follow his leading, even in small ways or for a short period of time. Our only safety is in asking the Lord to keep us close to Him, surrendering our will to His plan for our lives, at each step of our earthly journey.

February 10

Home-Grown idolatry

"The man Micah had a shrine and made an ephod and household idols; and he consecrated one of his sons, who became his priest. In those days there was no king in Israel; everyone did what was right in his own eyes" (Judges 17:5, 6).

During a time when there were no judges or kings over Israel, their society degenerated into idolatry after the pattern of the Canaanites who lived all around them. Without a leader to guide and admonish them, they forgot the Lord's command to worship only Him. Being accountable to no one, they didn't remember the third commandment, which forbade them from making and bowing down to idols or graven images of anything in heaven or earth. As stated in the above verse, "...everyone did *what was* right in his own eyes."

Interestingly, humankind always seems to be looking for something to worship. There is a hole in human hearts that can only be filled by God. However, once God has been dismissed from people's lives, they replace Him with myriad other things to try to fill the gap in their souls. In Old

Testament times, they conjured up all kinds of false gods...everything from golden calves to statues carved from wood to heavenly bodies, such as the sun, moon, and stars. Today, most of us look down on worshipping those types of idols, substituting more modern things like money, cars, celebrities, sports, or even addictions to drugs, alcohol, unhealthy lifestyles, or technology of various varieties. Nowadays, people's time, money, and energy are too often wasted on social media and video games. Unfortunately, all of these idols, together with any others that tend to turn our attention away from God, are wreaking havoc on our spiritual lives.

In Micah's case, some might laud him for at least trying to worship God. The problem is that he was trying to do it in all the wrong ways—in ways that were "right in his own eyes" but not in God's eyes. Like Cain, he ignored God's instructions on how to worship Him correctly and chose his own way to worship and his own kind of sacrifice, which was not in accordance with what the Lord had requested of him. He also selected one of his own sons to be a priest, instead of sticking with God's requirement that only Levites were to serve as priests. Like all of us, Micah had an influence on his peers, and it wasn't long before others were following his idolatrous example.

Have you ever heard anyone say, "It doesn't matter what you believe, just so you're sincere about it"? Or, "It doesn't matter what god you serve, as long as you believe in a 'higher power'"? Micah's worship, while it might have been well-intended, was considered idolatry by God. By just doing what was right in his own eyes, he was disobeying God's specific instructions regarding who to worship and who or what not to worship. The Lord has given us the opportunity, and even the duty, through His word (and it is more available to us now, in many different formats, than ever) to learn about who He is as well as how to worship Him "in spirit and in truth" (John 4:24). Like Cain and Micah and many other people described in the Bible, if we only choose to do what is right in our own eyes instead of what the Lord has clearly asked us to do, unfortunately, we will be counted among the "idolators" and found wanting on that final day of judgment when He returns to take His faithful followers home.

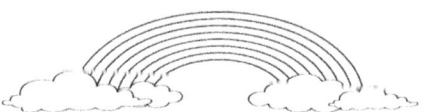

Love Pledge

"...'Entreat me not to leave you, or to turn back from following after you; for wherever you go, I will go; and wherever you lodge, I will lodge; your people shall be my people, and your God, my God'" (Ruth 1:16).

As I began reading the "romance novel" of Ruth, I had to pause to further contemplate this famous pledge of love that Ruth declares to her mother-in-law, Naomi. Her loyalty and devotion amaze me for a number of reasons.

First, we are talking about her mother-in-law, the infamous relationship that often causes the most stress in family interactions. Obviously, this was not the case between Naomi and her two daughters-in-law since she had lived in Moab for at least ten years, and they both chose to stay with her even after the death of their husbands.

Second, Naomi was a foreigner in Moab, bound to have very different cultural perspectives and ways of doing things than Ruth and Orpah. Eventually, when Naomi decided to go back to her country of origin, Orpah was convinced that it would be better for her to stay in Moab and return to her family. Ruth, on the other hand, had grown to love Naomi so much that she couldn't bring herself to part with her, even though it meant leaving her country, her cultural background, and her family.

Third, Naomi was a different religion than Ruth. Apparently, Naomi had lived such an exemplary life, despite the fact that she was going through difficult times after the loss of her husband and sons, that Ruth had come to know the God of Israel and was ready to abandon the worship of other gods and serve only Him.

I'm also impressed by Ruth's ability to express her love and devotion in such tender and affectionate words. Surely, Naomi felt comforted in her older age and loneliness when Ruth pledged to stay by her side. This makes me think about how important it is that we confess our love to those around us, not just at the altar when getting married, which is where this pledge is so often repeated, but throughout our lifetimes. It also points out the fact that people other than our spouses (parents, children, grandchildren, siblings, and even in-laws!) need to know how much we care for them. Think how much happier our homes and relationships would be if everyone around us was assured regularly of how much we loved them. Feeling such comfort, security, and joy when wrapped in a supportive environment of faithful affection, just think how much more successful and fulfilling the lives of our loved ones would be.

Why, then, are we so reticent to shower others with loving words? It doesn't take more than a few minutes, only a little bit of effort, and it costs nothing. It must be our pride and selfishness that gets in the way. But if we are going to be prepared to live in heaven someday soon, we need to break our old habits of criticism, bickering, and complaining, replacing them with the habit of speaking only edifying words of encouragement, kindness, and committed love. How better to get ready to live in heaven than to start speaking its language of love now?

Wings of Refuge

"And Boaz answered and said to her, 'It has been fully reported to me, all that you have done for your mother-in-law since the death of your husband, and how you have left your father and your mother and the land of your birth, and have come to a people whom you did not know before. The LORD repay your work, and a full reward be given you by the LORD God of Israel, under whose wings you have come for refuge'" (Ruth 2:11, 12).

Not only did Ruth express her love in words but she backed them up by her actions. As soon as she and Naomi had settled back in Bethlehem, she began gleaning in a field of barley in order to provide for herself and her mother-in-law. As it turned out, Boaz, a wealthy distant relative, owned the field where she was working. When he came to the field to see how the work was coming along, he saw the new reaper and asked who she was. Upon learning her story, and how she had left her own country to serve and support Naomi in her widowhood, he asked the overseer of the work to leave extra amounts of the barley behind as they were reaping, so she would be able to collect plenty of grain for the sustenance of both her and her mother-in-law.

Surprisingly, the gracious Boaz spoke to her kindly, bringing comfort to the foreigner. Then he went even further, making sure she had water to drink during the day and going the second or third mile by inviting her to come and join him and the other workers to eat something at mealtime. He also encouraged her relationship with the Lord, saying that she had come under His wings for refuge, thereby assuring her that all would be well here in her new land.

By his words and actions, Boaz here illustrates what it means to come under someone's wings for refuge. In this way, he is a representative of the Lord in this story. He demonstrates the Lord's magnanimous character, together with His tender and faithful provision for those who choose to put themselves under His care. We are reminded that if we seek refuge from the Lord, He will accept us, regardless of our lack of status, financial standing, gender, or country of origin.

Finally, in this passage, we find that Boaz pronounces a blessing upon Ruth that the Lord would repay her work and that a full reward be given her by the Lord God of Israel. Imagine how Ruth must have felt at this point. I'm sure that at least some of her apprehension about the future, some of the culture shock of living in a foreign land, and some of the loneliness of missing her family must have drained away, as she took hope and consolation from the encouraging words of this important man in the community. Who of us doesn't appreciate words of affirmation when we have worked hard? As far as a "full reward" is concerned, in the following chapters of Ruth, we see that the Lord uses Boaz himself to help fulfill this part of his blessing.

It wasn't until she arrived home, sharing the barley she had gleaned and her excitement over the wonderful treatment she had received in Boaz's field, that she learned from Naomi how blessed she had truly been in meeting the wealthy distant relative who, in keeping with local customs, might be able to redeem her, turning her whole life upside down! What incredible surprises the Lord has in store for us when we take refuge under His loving wings!

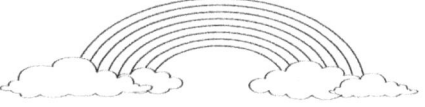

February 13

The Family Redeemer

"Then he said, 'Blessed are you of the LORD, my daughter! For you have shown more kindness at the end than at the beginning, in that you did not go after young men, whether poor or rich. And now, my daughter, do not fear. I will do for you all that you request, for all the people of my town know that you are a virtuous woman'" (Ruth 3:10, 11).

In chapter 3, the saga continues. Ruth was elated once she realized that since Boaz was a relative, according to Jewish custom, the kind and wealthy man could actually marry her, buy back the property that had belonged to her deceased husband, and thereby assure that his name and inheritance would be carried on to future generations. Boaz could buy the land of not just her husband but also her brother-in-law and father-in-law, so Naomi's economic future would be secured as well.

First, however, there were a couple of other matters to be addressed. One was that Ruth and Naomi had to formally ask Boaz if he would be willing to take on the role of the family redeemer. As evidenced in the above verses, Ruth was quite a bit younger than Boaz, which is why he used the affectionate term "daughter" when he addressed her.

Bringing Ruth and Naomi "in from the cold" (so to speak, since women without fathers and sons in that time and place were often destitute) would also be a costly proposition. Fortunately, Boaz decided he was up for the challenge. After all, not only had he noticed her appearance when she started gleaning in his fields but he had also been attracted by her character, her work ethic, and her concern for her aging mother-in-law. It also impressed him that she didn't go chasing around after young men. All this had given her a good name in the community. He was happy to help her, seeing through her words and actions that she was, indeed, a "virtuous woman."

The other hurdle, though, was that there was someone else in the town who was a closer relative, and thus had "first dibs" on the opportunity to redeem Ruth's deceased husband's inheritance. If he chose to buy the land back and marry Ruth, Boaz would not have been able to move forward with his plan. Fortunately, the other gentleman finally decided it wasn't in his best interest to do so, and Boaz was able to seal the deal.

In this story we see a small vignette of what our Redeemer has done for us. We were trapped by our circumstances, living here in this world of sin. Before knowing the Lord, we were foreigners to His grace. But as we came to know Him and asked for His assistance, He took us under His wings. Instead of spiritual poverty, He gave us heavenly riches.

Instead of despair, He gave us faith and hope for a glorious future with Him. Instead of loneliness and isolation, He surrounded us with His loving companionship and put us in good standing as a valuable part of the body of Christ. At great cost to Himself, He gladly took our sadness and turned it into joy. Moreover, if we are faithful to our calling in life, as was Ruth, we have eternal rewards awaiting us in heaven! What a beautiful picture this story paints of how much the Lord loves us and how much He wants to be our personal Redeemer!

February 14

A Happy Ending

"So Boaz took Ruth and she became his wife; …and she bore a son. Then the women said to Naomi, 'Blessed be the LORD, who has not left you this day without a close relative; and may his name be famous in Israel!'" (Ruth 4:13, 14).

How appropriate that we can say that Ruth and Boaz "lived happily ever after" on Valentine's Day! In one fell swoop, all of Ruth's dreams came true. However, other people were also blessed by this union. Naomi was ecstatic to have a grandchild who would carry on the name for her family, and the whole community rejoiced with her! This child was named Obed, who later became the father of Jesse, who was the father of King David. As we know, Jesus was born in the lineage of David. Thus,

unbeknownst to her at the time, Ruth, the young foreigner from Moab, became one of the ancestors of the world's Redeemer! Thus, indirectly, all of us have been blessed by this poignant romance recorded in the small book of Ruth.

Once again, it's hard not to see the spiritual implications of this short story. Jesus has done for us what Boaz did for Ruth. Despite the fact that we were strangers and outsiders, He has accepted us "in the Beloved" (see Eph. 1:6), purchased us, and made us

His bride. Because of His redeeming love, He has changed the whole direction and purpose of our lives. Now, whatever happens to us on this earth, we know that our story, too, will have a happy ending.

In the meantime, He also provides amazing serendipity experiences from time to time to demonstrate His love for us and cheer us along life's pathway. Here, I am reminded of one of these events in my own history.

I had just gone through a very difficult breakup, in the wake of which I started a new job to support myself. I was working as an administrative secretary in a large hospital. Having just moved to the area, I felt friendless and alone. One day, when the Lord knew I needed it, another one of the administrative secretaries who was about my age peeked into my office, and with a sweet smile, she asked if I wanted to go to lunch with her. Her friendship became a ray of sunshine in my previously dark and lonely existence. What a Godsend she was! Soon, she had invited me to attend a weekly worship service at her home, where she and her husband treated me like family.

But wait until you hear the happy ending, which convinced me that all along the Lord had been planning for me in love. As my friend and I got to know each other better, we discovered that our fathers had both been in South Korea during the Korean Conflict in the early 1950s. My father was serving there in the military as a medic. While her father, along with his family, was serving as a missionary pastor in the same region. On weekends my father had actually attended services at her father's church. Not only that but the pastor had invited him, along with other homesick young American soldiers, over to his home for fellowship and a meal on several occasions! Thinking back to that time, amazingly, my father could even remember my friend as a little girl, standing on a step stool, trying to help her mother with the many dishes created by the visitors to their home.

Now, more than two decades later, and on the other side of the world, the Lord arranged for my friend and I to converge at the same place of employment at the same time so that his daughter could bring sunshine into my life, the same way her father had brought sunshine into my father's life so many years before! What a glorious revelation this was! How could I continue to feel depressed when the Lord had been planning for me in love, even before I was born? Our wonderful friendship has made a tremendous impact on my life.

If you've been walking with the Lord, I'm sure you can think back to similar marvelously serendipitous experiences that gave you hope as well as an amazing sense of God's providence in your life. These events not only give us more zest for this life but also help prepare us for all of the wonderful surprises God has in store for us when we reach our heavenly home, our very own "happily ever after!"

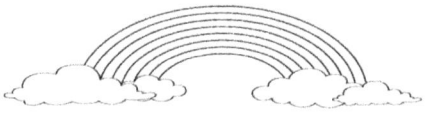

Hannah's Prayer

"No one is holy like the LORD, for there is none besides You, nor is there any rock like our God. Talk no more so very proudly; let no arrogance come from your mouth, for the LORD is the God of knowledge; and by Him actions are weighed" (1 Samuel 2:2, 3).

After years of longing to have a child, the Lord answered Hannah's prayer. When her first son, Samuel, was born, her joy knew no bounds. As she had promised the Lord, she loaned him to the temple in Shiloh where he could learn the duties of the priesthood. Samuel grew in favor with God and humankind, becoming a prophet as well as a wise counselor for the people of Israel.

Happily, after Samuel, the Lord honored Hannah's faith and devotion with three more sons and two daughters. In her day, not bearing children was a shameful thing, and the other wife of her husband, who had borne children first, had made Hannah's life miserable by reminding her frequently that she was barren. For this reason, when Hannah finally did have children, she broke out in a song of praise and thanksgiving, as recorded in the second chapter of 1 Samuel.

Have you ever known someone who didn't seem to be able to have children? Sometimes for physical reasons, other times for sickness, or perhaps the timing wasn't quite right. While some of these people may remain barren for life, others find that after certain significant events, or just waiting until their bodies are ready, children are born to them. I think of a young woman we know who never had children until she adopted a child. Apparently, taking care of this little one awakened her maternal instincts, and before too long, she got pregnant and had two more daughters and a son of her own. She now laughs and says they went from infertile to insanity, with a passel of kids filling all her house with clothes, toys, baby things, and the pitter-patter of little feet. This reminded her of the old adage, "Be careful what you ask for!" Her whole life has been turned upside down, but she wouldn't have it any other way!

I have cited these two verses because here Hannah reminds us that there's no room for arrogance and boasting about who we are, or what we have, since it all comes from the Lord. Having suffered the cruel taunts directed at her in her time of distress, she knew how painful this attitude of superiority can be for those surrounding us. Instead of gloating about the gifts God has seen fit to give us, we should, like Hannah, spend our time thanking and praising Him for His outpouring of goodness, love, and grace in our lives.

Have you ever been in the company of a proud boaster? It soon becomes obvious that this person is only concerned about him or herself, not caring about the feelings of those within hearing distance. Worse yet, they haven't yet come to realize that everything they have is because the Lord has blessed them, whether with health, wealth, talent, position, citizenship in a given place, houses, lands, children, or myriad other material possessions. By speaking in a proud manner and acting as if any of these things makes us better than other people, we both misrepresent God and rob Him of the glory only He deserves.

Not Knowing the Lord

"Now the sons of Eli were corrupt; they did not know the LORD" (1 Samuel 2:12).

This verse "stuck in my craw" because it is so disheartening. How could Eli, the high priest of Israel, have sons who, although going through the motions of being priests themselves, didn't know the Lord? They grew up in the church. They had a godly father as a role model. Even though he was younger, they even had the pious example of Samuel. Their daily work was to receive the offerings of the people who came to the temple to worship.

Unfortunately, none of these things seemed to keep them from turning away from God. Their rebellion, selfishness, and irreverence turned to violence when the people did not give them the meat from their sacrifices in the way they wanted it. Despite God's instructions on how to receive the sacrifices, and their father's occasional warnings regarding the sexual immorality they practiced on the side, they continued in their iniquity. Soon they became infamous for their evil ways, discouraging some of the people of God from even coming to offer their sacrifices anymore.

Eli heard the complaints of the people, yet somehow he either could not, or would not, restrain his sons. The Lord found this situation unacceptable and, through messages given to the young yet faithful Samuel, communicated to Eli His displeasure as well as what He would do about it. Shortly thereafter a battle with the Philistines ensued, and both of Eli's sons were killed. Upon hearing the news, Eli himself passed away. He had been a priest and judge for the people of Israel for forty years. Upon his death, Samuel, who was now recognized as a prophet, also became a judge over the Israelites, serving in that capacity for the rest of his life.

This story brings up a number of difficult questions. Is it the parents' fault when their children decide to stray from the Lord? Why do so many children of righteous and godly parents choose a rebellious and vile lifestyle? Is the child not responsible for his or her own choices regarding whether or not he or she comes to know the Lord personally? Should people who are obviously living in sin be allowed to continue to minister in

God's church? If so, what message does this send to the parishioners?

Obviously, we don't have all the answers. I believe these are questions we need to give more thought to, realizing that every particular situation has grown out of myriad variables and circumstances of life. However, I would dare to make a couple of observations. First, God does expect us to discipline our children as well as teach them to know the Lord to the best of our ability. Second, sometimes, in spite of our instruction and example, our children may choose to follow a different path. After all, even in a place as perfect as heaven, one of God's children, Lucifer, chose to go his own way. So, we can take comfort in the thought that the Lord understands the pain this causes us. We can also take consolation in the knowledge that while there's life, there's hope. At any point through the mazes of life, a soul can exercise its free, voluntary will to choose to come to the Lord. Thus, it's essential that we continue to pray for our prodigal children, knowing that the Lord loves them and wants them to experience His salvation even more than we do. Sometimes our prayers for our children are answered after we have already passed from this earth, which means we will have some happy surprises awaiting us when we get to heaven.

Third, being the child of a priest (or pastor) can be difficult in some ways. Although enjoying living in an atmosphere of spirituality, there are higher expectations for these kids. Sometimes the child of a famous or popular pastor has trouble finding their own identity when standing in the shadow of their father. Also, it seems that Satan works even harder to tempt pastor's children to do wrong, knowing that any scandal will hurt not only the pastor and his family but also the whole congregation, leaving a black mark on the cause of God. For this reason, as a congregation, we need to wrap the pastor and his family in a thick blanket of consistent and loving prayer.

Lastly, just a few comments about allowing people living in open sin to continue in ministry. In recent years, we have seen on the news the dire consequences of this practice in Roman Catholicism. Many young people have been molested and abused by those who were supposed to be their spiritual leaders. Not only are these priests a bad example of Christianity but they also misrepresent God and have actually turned many people into confused and embittered non-believers. Of course, we know that God can forgive these leaders if they repent, but that doesn't mean they should continue to be placed in positions of authority where others may be harmed by them in the future. If they are truly sorry and still want to serve God, they should humbly accept duties where they have little or no influence, being placed where they can use their talents in a totally different capacity. A church or congregation that deals with errant spiritual leaders otherwise will be held morally (by God) and legally (by humanity) responsible for perpetuating the crimes of the past.

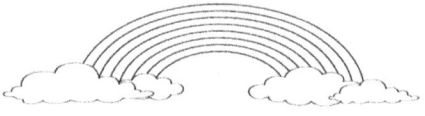

My Ebenezer

"Then Samuel took a stone and set it up between Mizpah and Shen, and called its name Ebenezer, saying, 'Thus far the LORD has helped us'" (1 Samuel 7:12).

From my youth I have loved the old hymn "Come, Thou Fount of Every Blessing," although I have always questioned the meaning of the word 'Ebenezer' which is found in the second stanza of hymn 334 in *The Seventh-day Adventist Hymnal.* The verse goes like this:

Here I raise my Ebenezer, hither by Thy
help I've come,
and I hope by Thy good pleasure safely to
arrive at home.
Jesus sought me when a stranger, wandering from the fold of God;
He to rescue me from danger interposed
His precious blood.

Obviously, the strange word had something to do with God helping one of His servants, but I didn't know who first used that term or anything about the context. After reading 1 Samuel 7, I was finally able to fill in some of the blanks. The Israelites were about to engage in one of their many battles against the Philistines. Due to their fear, they asked Samuel to pray for them and that the Lord would give them success. In response, Samuel asked them to get rid of all their false gods and idols, fast, and pray to the Lord before the fight began. As they gathered together at a place called Mizpah to do this, the Philistines saw their chance to attack them all at once.

When the Israelites heard that the Philistines were already on their way to Mizpah, they cried out again for Samuel to pray for them. Not only did Samuel pray but he also offered up a burnt sacrifice to the Lord on behalf of the fearful soldiers. As he was doing this, the Lord, in answer to their petitions for help, caused a "loud thunder" (verse 10) to fall upon the Philistines, confusing them so that the Israelite forces were able to overcome them and drive them out of their land. They experienced a great victory that day because they had put their trust in the Lord. Not only that but the Bible says that they didn't have any problems with the Philistines for the rest of Samuel's tenure as a judge over Israel.

It was just after this amazing victory that Samuel, wanting to give praise and thanksgiving to the Lord for his miraculous help in defeating their constantly-harassing enemies, set up a stone as a memorial. He called this stone, which must have been fairly large, Ebenezer. Then he explained what he meant. It was to be a reminder that the Lord had helped them up to this point as well as the fact that just as God had given them a wonderful victory in this battle, He would assist them in all their battles to come, if they would just turn to Him with all their hearts. It was something he wanted them never to forget, even after he was no longer their spiritual leader.

So, how do we set up an Ebenezer of our own? I have started a "Thanksgiving and Praise List." I spend a little time each week on it, writing down the prayers the Lord has answered for me recently as well as extra blessings in the last week for which I want to praise Him. It's great because when I get discouraged or think a given problem is impossible to solve, I can just look at my list, remember that "hitherto hath the Lord helped me" in the past, and know that if I turn to Him, He will help me both now and in the future. If I have financial worries, I know He has kept us afloat before, and He "has a thousand ways to provide for us, of which we know nothing" (*The Desire of Ages*, p. 330). If I have physical challenges, I know that He will give me strength for the day. If I have relationship problems, I surrender them to Him, knowing I can cast all my care upon Him, because He cares for me (see 1 Peter 5:7). And if I am experiencing spiritual challenges, I can trust in His promises to see me through. The main problem is in remembering all He has done for us in the past and keeping faith that He will continue to help us in the future. That's why we each need to raise our own "Ebenezer" stone.

February 18

Obedience

"…'Has the LORD as great delight in burnt offerings and sacrifices, as in obeying the voice of the LORD? Behold, to obey is better than sacrifice, and to heed than the fat of rams" (1 Samuel 15:22).

When I came upon this verse in my re-reading of the Old Testament recently, it had a very familiar ring to my ears. As a child, my father used to quote this text to us from time to time to remind us of the importance of obedience, especially when we would try to make excuses for why we hadn't obeyed him. He believed it was his duty to teach us to respect and obey him when we were young so that we would know how to respect and obey the Lord when we were older and making decisions on our own. "As the twig is bent, so grows the tree," was an expression he used often.

In this story about King Saul, God had given him, through Samuel, explicit instructions about how to conduct a battle against the Amalekites. Saul disregarded those instructions, keeping some of the spoils of battle for himself and those who fought with him. In those days, animals such as sheep and oxen were considered part of the spoils. When God sent Samuel to confront Saul about disobeying the commandment of the Lord, Saul made matters worse by lying. First, he claimed that he had obeyed the Lord. Then, when Samuel asked him about the bleating of sheep and the lowing of oxen that he was hearing (see verse 14), Saul made up an excuse. It was the fault of the people who were with him. Finally, he tried to white-wash the whole incident by saying that the reason they had kept all the Amalekites' animals, after all, was so that they could sacrifice them to the Lord. It was at this point that Samuel, seeing through his smokescreen, told Saul that his lies and excuses were not acceptable. Sacrifices meant nothing if offered by a disobedient servant. Now that Saul had been tested and shown to be disobedient to the Lord's commands, the kingdom would be taken from him and given to someone who would "hearken unto the Lord."

Obedience is an unpopular word these days. In modern American society, we value independence and freedom from any kind of restraint to our individual wishes. Now it is commonplace to see children disrespecting and disobeying their parents. Students often lack respect for their teachers, disregarding their instructions, and many people show disrespect for anyone of authority as well as blatantly ignoring the laws of the land. In fact, in the face of rampant political discord and increases in crime and mass shootings, we suffer mistrust of even our own fellow citizens. Only the Lord knows where all this will end. Certainly, we must be racing rapidly to the close of probation.

In the meantime, the Lord still requires obedience from those who have decided to follow Him. That's why He tells us plainly in John 14:15, "If you love Me, keep My commandments." No ifs, ands, or buts about it. No whitewashing our errant ways with excuses that other people made us do it or that our motives were good. We can be very sincere and still end up at the wrong destination if we disregard the map. Of course, we know that the only way we can keep God's commands properly is to study His instructions in His word, which He has given us to guide us, and to pray daily for the help of His Holy Spirit to keep us living within His will.

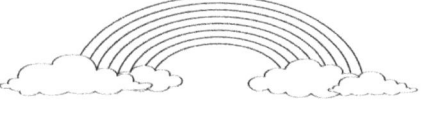

February 19

"Good Looks"

"But the LORD said to Samuel, 'Do not look at his appearance or at his physical stature, because I have refused him. For the LORD does not see as man sees; for man looks at the outward appearance, but the LORD looks at the heart'" (1 Samuel 16:7).

As humans, we seem to be immediately attracted to people with good looks. We admire their smile, their eyes, their hair, their height, etc. People with a pleasant outward appearance are more generally chosen for jobs, leadership positions, movie roles, spouses, and so forth. Thus, when God's prophet, Samuel, was told to go and anoint a person from the sons of Jesse to replace Saul as king, he was naturally drawn to the tall, good-looking, mature ones, who he thought possessed more of a kingly bearing. However, as the handsome young men passed before him, the Lord indicated that none of them were the chosen future king. When Samuel asked if Jesse had any other sons, David, the youngest, was called in from the fields where he was keeping sheep. Not bad looking, but the youngest, smaller, and with the least life experience, he would not naturally have been the prophet's first choice. Yet God, knowing David's heart, selected him to be anointed as the future king of His people.

Have you ever known anyone who was so obsessed with their looks that you soon found other companions, not so shallow, with whom to spend your time? Trying to look one's best is not wrong, but like anything that becomes an idol to us, over time it changes our character for the worse instead of for the better. It can make us self-focused, inhibiting the good use of our talents when we think we don't measure up, or proud, giving us a false sense of superiority when we think we look better than others. Some people spend exorbitant amounts of money on make-up, clothes, hairstyles, diets, and gym fees, which could much better be spent to help those around them in need or dedicated to projects that would advance the cause of God in the world.

This passage teaches us that what God values is our heart, our character, who we are on the inside. Unlike humans, He looks right past the externals and focuses on our thoughts, motives, and actions. What is our relationship with Him? How much do we think of others? Do we strive to become ever-better versions of ourselves in order to use our God-given gifts to serve Him and others to the best of our abilities? Do we live up to our potential and use every opportunity to bring God glory? How do we use our time, money, and influence over those around us? Do we study to show ourselves approved unto God, "rightly dividing the word of truth" (2 Tim. 2:15)? Do our daily actions show that we are children of our gracious heavenly Father? These are the questions we need to ask ourselves when we are looking to define true beauty. These questions of "internal good looks" are also ones to consider when choosing someone for a job, leadership position, friend, and definitely when choosing a spouse! We are reminded in this story that outward appearance should never be our only or strongest criterion.

One other interesting point here that shouldn't be overlooked is that God is not concerned with David's age. How encouraging to know that, regardless of a person's age, God still values a relationship with them, watches the steady growth of their character, and has a special work for them to do if they sincerely dedicate their young lives and talents to Him.

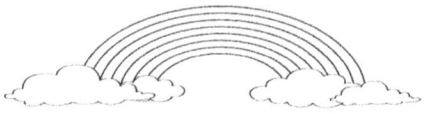

That All the Earth May Know

"Then David said to the Philistine, 'You come to me with a sword, with a spear, and with a javelin. But I come to you in the name of the LORD of hosts, the God of the armies of Israel, whom you have defied. This day the LORD will deliver you into my hand...that all the earth may know that there is a God in Israel. Then all this assembly shall know that the LORD does not save with sword and spear; for the battle is the LORD's, and He will give you into our hands'" (1 Samuel 17:45–47).

No story of the life of David would be complete without mentioning his victorious encounter with Goliath, the infamous giant warrior of the Philistines. Just as the greatest challenges in our lives bring out the hidden characteristics of the heart, so all those positive traits that the Lord had seen in young David when He anointed him as Israel's future king were manifested in this momentous event: his courage, his zeal, his fearlessness, his utter faith in the God he had come to know, and especially his sense of injustice that God's name was being drug through the mud with nobody standing up to defend it.

Albeit still a youth, he was a man of action. When no one else, not the king, the soldiers, or his older brothers, had the courage and faith to step forward against this fearsome foe, David did. Without flinching he boldly declared, "This day the LORD will deliver you into my hand...that all the earth may know that there is a God in Israel." His faith in God, throughout all the experiences of his young life, had taught him that in every emergency that "the battle *is* the LORD's." No matter how dire the circumstances or how impossible the situation seemed, when he had surrendered it to God, he had come off victorious. Thus, even in

this tremendous conflict, when everything was stacked against him, David confidently went forth to war, never doubting that the Lord would bring an overwhelming victory to His people!

Oh, to have such faith when fighting our modern everyday conflicts! The secret was that David had trusted in God consistently, practicing his faith day by day, until it became integrated into his very character. Over and over again, when he asked for God's help, he had watched as the Lord had protected him, saving his life from the lion and from the bear (see 1 Sam. 17:37). As he wrote later, in the beautiful and poetic Psalm 23, the Lord had become his Shepherd, leading and guiding him through the ups and downs of life, even through the valley of the shadow of death. Through it all, his testimony was that the Lord restored his soul, and he triumphantly declared, "Surely goodness and mercy shall follow me all the days of my life; and I will dwell in the house of the LORD forever" (Ps. 23:6).

If we had David's faith, I'm sure we would score many more victories in life. Even so, faith is not only about earthly victories. If it were, some people would serve God only for that reason. True faith grasps the reality that God is with us, even through the difficult times, which, of course, is what makes them bearable. But it is also the far-sighted view of the great controversy between Christ and Satan that helps us know that no matter what temporary setbacks we may experience here, ultimately, our God wins! And He has promised that we who are faithful will also not only win but will also have the blessed privilege of the joy of His presence throughout eternity!

Like David, I want to let the world know that there is a God in heaven and that the battle is His, not ours. Our part is to maintain a strong faith in Him until all the fighting is over, when the winning team can go home to celebrate forever!

February 21

Share and Share Alike

"…But as his part is who goes down to the battle, so shall his part be who stays by the supplies; they shall share alike" (1 Samuel 30:24).

Near the end of the book of 1 Samuel, there is an interesting and often overlooked little verse which I think merits our attention. Let's first provide some context. So, David was pursuing his enemies with 600 soldiers under his command. When they came to a certain brook in that area, 200 of the men were too weary to go on. As a result, they were asked to stay by the supplies. (The King James Version calls it "the stuff" in verse 24.) At any rate, when the battle was over, and David returned victorious, along with the 400 men who had continued with him, some of them suggested that 200 men who had stayed behind with their belongings should not receive any of the spoils of battle since they had not actually engaged in the fighting. This pricked David's sense of justice, and he rebuked the selfish

soldiers who did not want to share anything with their weaker brethren who, while not able to go on, did their part by guarding the supplies. After all, he reminded them, it was the Lord who preserved us and gave us the victory as well as the spoils that fell into our hands. Then he uttered the words recorded above. In fact, he felt so strongly about it that he declared it a statute and an ordinance to be practiced throughout Israel.

Upon reading this verse, I think of the many people who, for whatever reasons, cannot fight on the frontlines of the battle between good and evil but still support God's cause in whatever way they can. Some folks, although willing, have not had the opportunities or natural abilities to become great evangelists or preachers. Others, who may have wished to teach or go into medical fields, have been hindered by life's obligations, lack of finances, or other unanticipated circumstances. Obstacles may have prevented some with lofty plans from serving in mission fields, near or far. Even if able to work in public fields of service during their youth, older folks sometimes find that their age, health, or energy levels now preclude them from active service. We often overlook the fact, however, that there are still effective ways to support God's work. Helping with our means, a listening ear, an encouraging word, and our prayers are all ways to continue to do our part in winning the battle. This verse assures us that if we do what we are able to do to the best of our ability, God values and honors our contributions.

This verse also makes me think of the many faithful wives and mothers who have stayed in the background holding down the fort while their husbands have gone off to do great things for the Lord. Putting your life goals on hold to support a spouse gaining an education, taking care of small children, caring for aged loved ones, sitting at home taking care of business while a spouse is traveling the world, or ministering to others for days on end, can all be huge and sacrificial offerings to the cause of God's work. And it is comforting to know that God sees these humble gifts, understands the faithfulness they require, and has not forgotten us. Now we just need to know that our spouses and others in parts of the battle that garner more recognition appreciate the steady foundation we have provided by "staying by the stuff." If they do, they'll generously show it by freely sharing the blessings and gifts of victory with us when they return home.

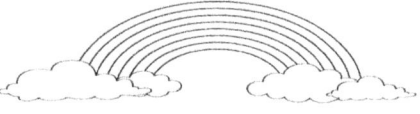

February 22

Grace Shown through Kindness

"Then the king said, 'Is there not still someone of the house of Saul, to whom I may show the kindness of God?' ... Now when Mephibosheth the son of Jonathan, the son of Saul, had come to David, he fell on his face and prostrated himself. ... So David said to him, 'Do not fear, for I will surely show you kindness for Jonathan your father's sake, and will restore to you all the land of Saul your grandfather; and you shall eat bread at my table continually'" (2 Samuel 9:3, 6, 7).

By this time, David had won many conquests with the Lord's help, and he had been installed as king not only of Judah but of all Israel. He had moved to Jerusalem, established his administration, and in gratitude, was looking for additional ways to thank the Lord for His goodness. It's interesting to note that when we recognize that we have been the recipients of God's grace, we naturally want to shower some of it upon others. Thus, David's question to his servant was, "*Is* there not still someone of the house of Saul, to whom I may show the kindness of God?"

Let's stop and remember for a moment who Saul was: the previous king, his rival in the last years of Saul's life, the man who tried to kill him repeatedly, and who chased him into the wilderness where David and his men had to live in caves and struggle to survive. Not only that but most new kings coming into power only sought out relatives of the previous ruler in order to annihilate them and secure their own throne. So why would David want to show kindness to any remnants of the house of Saul? Grace. Just a desire to share God's goodness. True grace, outside of the influence of God in our lives, is always inexplicable.

Nevertheless, when David found out that one of Saul's descendants had survived and, better yet, was the son of his old best friend, Jonathan, he sent for him immediately. The young man, Mephibosheth, had been dropped by his nursemaid when he was only five, as she was fleeing after hearing that both Saul and Jonathan had been defeated in battle. As a result, the Bible tells us that he was lame in both his feet. Needless to say, Mephibosheth was terrified when he was summoned to see King David, falling on his face and prostrating himself before the powerful monarch who now held his life in his hands.

How utterly surprised and relieved he must have been when the first words out of David's mouth were, "Do not fear." And his amazement only grew as David not only pledged to treat him with kindness but to restore the land of his grandfather, Saul, to him, and invited him to actually eat at the king's very own table as if he were part of the royal family! If that weren't enough, David commanded his servants to work the land of Saul and bring in the harvest since the disabled new landowner would not be able to care for the land himself. Talk about going the second and even third mile, and beyond, for someone who could never repay your kindness!

Actually, this story paints a very good picture of God's kindness towards us. It was our fellow humans who rejected and killed Him when He came to save us. We have done nothing to deserve God's grace and are totally unable to help ourselves be saved. Spiritually-speaking, we are poor, weak orphans, coming from a long line of enemies against God. Why would God want to show us grace and mercy? Why would He want to adopt us into His own royal family, to eat at His table of blessings continually? Why would He assign angels to watch over us and prophets to explain things we could never understand on our own? Why would we be chosen to receive God's amazing love in a way that could change our lives for the better forever? Simply grace—the inexplicable grace of God, which overflows from His beautiful character of love, unexpectedly filling our empty lives with overwhelming joy and thanksgiving! Like David, let's pass some of it on to those around us today!

"You Are the Man!"

"Then Nathan said to David, 'You are the man! Thus says the LORD God of Israel: 'I anointed you king over Israel, and I delivered you from the hand of Saul. I gave you your master's house and your master's wives into your keeping, and gave you the house of Israel and Judah. And if that had been too little, I also would have given you much more! Why have you despised the commandment of the LORD, to do evil in His sight? You have killed Uriah...with the sword; you have taken his wife to be your wife, and have killed him with the sword of the people of Ammon'" (2 Sam. 12:7–9).

Generally, in today's culture, when someone says, "You are the man!" they're talking about your strong and admirable qualities. Unfortunately, in this instance, the prophet Nathan had been sent to David to tell him a story that would arouse his pity and incite his indignation against someone who had treated another person unfairly. Upon hearing the tale of woe, David declared that the perpetrator of the described crime should be punished immediately. It was at that moment that Nathan pointed the finger at David, announcing that he was the one who had committed a sinful injustice, not only against his faithful servant, Uriah, but also against God.

Suddenly, the Spirit of God awakened David to the magnitude of his own iniquity in arranging for Uriah to be killed in battle so that he could take Bathsheba, his wife, for himself. He thought he had covered his tracks pretty well, but the Lord knew all about his scheming, his recent selfish and sinful actions, and would not allow David to continue to deceive himself and his nation by living as if nothing so evil had occurred. In a moment of clarity David realized the truth that his sin was not only against Uriah but also against God, who had entrusted him with so many blessings, making him king of the nation and a spiritual leader among his people.

This is a sad chapter in the life of David. He had started out with such a sterling character. He had been God's man, full of courage and faith, and an inspiration to his nation. How could he have sunk so low? I think there are two lessons we can draw from this story. First, none of us on this sinful planet is above being tempted. We all carry around an innate human tendency to sin. It is part of our carnal nature, which means we all need to constantly be on the lookout for ways in which Satan is trying to trip us up, so we can ask the Lord to strengthen us and avoid the pitfalls. Second, sometimes when we get a little too comfortable in our situation, we are at greatest risk of letting go of the hand of God and confidently trying to live life on our own. We think that surely we have the wisdom, intelligence, and strength to navigate our own course through life. Other times, however, we are just wayward and choose to go astray despite any red flags our conscience might be waving to make us think twice!

In any event, the more edifying part of this story can be found at the end, where David fully repents of his sin and sincerely and humbly asks God for forgiveness. Like with all sin, there were consequences to pay, and David's spiritual influence was weakened as a result. But his later psalms reveal the gratitude, relief, and joy David felt when he knew he had secured the forgiveness of the Lord. After this unfortunate stumble, thankfully, by turning back to God with his whole heart, he learned about God's love, mercy, and grace in a new and very personal way.

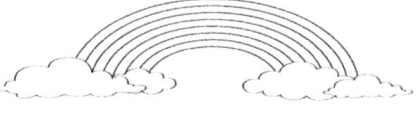

February 24

Confronted by Death

"When the waves of death surrounded me, the flood of ungodliness made me afraid. The sorrows of Sheol surrounded me; the snares of death confronted me. In my distress I called upon the LORD, and cried out to my God; He heard my voice from His temple, and my cry entered His ears" (2 Samuel 22:5–7).

These words are actually part of a song of praise that David sang to the Lord after being delivered from all his enemies, including four Philistine giants who had been harassing the Israelites off and on for a number of years. At one time during a particular battle against these foes, David, who was a little older now, grew faint and looked death squarely in the face. Providentially, one of his mighty men came to his aid, and he survived yet another conflict. But his realization of how close he had come to death inspired the words of this passage as an offering of thanksgiving to God for once again sparing his life.

Have you ever been confronted directly by death? I have on at least two occasions: once when diagnosed with cancer, and again when I was told I had heart issues that would require medications to keep me alive. I'm sure there were other times when I experienced near-death events, some of which I probably didn't even realize...such as just missing a car accident or during a number of earlier surgical procedures where I was under anesthesia. But these were the two incidents, happening about two years apart, where I was most suddenly and directly faced with my own mortality. Perhaps they struck me harder now that I had reached retirement age, knowing that many people in their sixties have died from such ailments.

In any event, they both triggered some serious reflection about life's existential questions. Was I ready to die? Was my house in order? Had I fulfilled the purposes God had for my life? Had I accomplished what I had wanted to achieve during my tenure on earth? At this point, did I have a "bucket list" of things I still wanted to do in whatever time was left to me? The questions, both mundane and momentous, tumbled through my mind, begging for answers.

I have discovered that the best remedy for times like this is to spend time with God. He calms us with His promises and comforts us with His presence. Then we are reminded that, just as He has taken care of our past, He will take care of our future, one step at a time. We just need to keep trusting Him, and things will work out, one way or the other, for the best.

Eventually, surgery took care of my cancer, and medications took care of my heart problems, and life went on. Although I was forced to retire, with time I began to see the upside of my health challenges. In retirement I had more time to spend with family and friends, more time to do things at church, and more time to write and participate in hobbies that I enjoy.

Like David, after coming out the other side of the immediate experience, I, too, felt a surge of both gratitude and praise—gratitude that I was still alive and praise that God is still the Sovereign Lord in control of all that concerns us. What a joy to know that, when confronted with death, He hears our cries all the way from heaven!

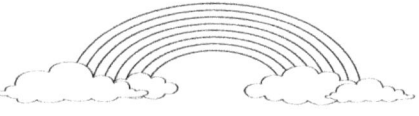

February 25

Your Gentleness

"You have also given me the shield of Your salvation; Your gentleness has made me great" (2 Samuel 22:36).

David is now nearing the end of his long and productive life. His last recorded words contain many praises to God, including his declarations that the Lord has been his shield, his rock, his refuge, and his strength. Amid these, we find an interesting assertion that it is the Lord's gentleness that has made him great.

In our society today, gentleness is a very underrated characteristic. Generally, when we think of greatness, we associate it with someone who exhibits ambition, aggression, strength, and power. So it's ironic to hear someone who was known as a "warrior king" talk about the value of gentleness. Although David had fought in many battles, apparently as he neared the end of his journey, like all of us, he reflected upon what was really important in life.

After his moral downfall and repentance, and after experiencing an overwhelming sense of God's unmerited mercy and grace, it appears he really began to appreciate how much God had nurtured, forgiven, and carefully guided him along with lovingkindness, hearkening back to the time in his youth when he had shepherded his own sheep. He realized the amount of patience and tenderness required of a good Shepherd and recognized how God treated His people in the same way. Without gentleness, neither the sheep nor God's people would be able to survive the vicissitudes of life.

Later, in the New Testament, we find Jesus Himself expounding on virtues related to gentleness during His sermon on the mount. He blesses the meek, the merciful, and the peacemakers. Gentleness is also mentioned, along with other qualities such as longsuffering, kindness, and goodness, in the fruits of the Spirit identified by Paul in Galatians 5:22, 23.

Just think of the times you have experienced gentleness and what a difference it has made in your own life. In my mind I see a mother's loving care for her young children. I see a nurse tenderly dressing a patient's painful wound. I see a teacher patiently working with a slow learner. A father helping his toddler learn how to walk and comforting him when he falls. And I hear the voice of God saying, "Come to Me, all *you* who labor and are heavy laden, and I will give you rest. Take My yoke upon you and learn from Me, for I am gentle and lowly in heart, and you will find rest for your souls" (Matt. 11:28, 29). It's interesting to note that in this passage Jesus describes Himself as "gentle" while at the same time demonstrating gentleness in His kind invitation to us to find rest in Him. It follows then that all of us who wish to be "great" as our Lord is will also need to be gentle as He is.

In today's verse, David is acknowledging that God's gentleness with him personally has been the source of all his material and spiritual blessings. His re-establishment as a man after God's own heart (see 1 Sam. 13:14), his health, strength, influence, crown, and kingdom can all be attributed to God's gentleness toward him, filling his heart with this simple expression of gratitude.

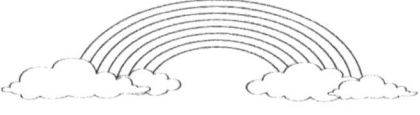

February 26

Request Wisdom

"And God gave Solomon wisdom and exceedingly great understanding, and largeness of heart like the sand on the seashore" (1 Kings 4:29).

After David's death, his son, Solomon, became king. Solomon was young and inexperienced but smart enough to know that he needed to ask for wisdom from the Lord in order to be a good king. So, early in his reign, when the Lord appeared to him in a dream, asking what He could give him, Solomon was prepared to make his request for wisdom and understanding so that he could properly judge the people and rule the nation successfully.

The Lord was so pleased with this petition that he gave Solomon not just wisdom but also long life, honor, and riches. These were all things that Solomon had not specifically requested but that would bless him throughout his reign. Shortly thereafter, he was called upon to settle a dispute between two women. Both had borne a child, but one of the babies had died. When both mothers claimed the baby who survived as her own, the case was brought before the king. Solomon suggested that the remaining baby could be cut in half so that each mother would have at least a part of the baby. Of course, the real mother protested strongly in order to save the life of her child. At that moment, her compassion and love for the child identified her as the real mother, and the baby was given to her. When word got out about how Solomon solved this case, all Israel lauded him for his wisdom and justice.

As Solomon became richer, he acquired all kinds of animals, which he studied, along with birds and fish. His wide-ranging interests motivated him to learn all about trees and plants as well. He became such an expert on these things that men from many nations came to hear him share his remarkable knowledge. What interesting science classes he must have conducted!

Then there was his collection of musical instruments: harps, stringed instruments, and trumpets. The Bible says that Solomon spoke 3,000 proverbs, and his songs numbered 1,005! In addition, he brought peace and prosperity to Israel and raised up a labor force of 30,000 men to help him build a beautiful new temple for the Lord in the city of Jerusalem.

As Solomon's fame spread, the stories of his wealth and wisdom reached as far as Egypt. Soon, even the Queen of Sheba decided to visit Jerusalem herself to see if all the fantastic tales she had heard about Israel's king were really true. She brought her whole retinue along with her as well as her hardest questions. Chapter 10 tells us that "there was nothing so difficult for the king that he could not explain *it* to her" (verse 3). Then she had the privilege of receiving a royal tour of the city, including Solomon's luxurious home, and the magnificent temple for the true God of heaven. When her visit was over, the queen exclaimed that not only were the reports she had heard at home true but that not even half of Solomon's wisdom and prosperity had been told to her, and she only believed it now because she had seen it with her own eyes! 1 Kings 10:23 sums it all up with this statement: "So King Solomon surpassed all the kings of the earth in riches and wisdom."

Why? Simply because he asked God for wisdom. Could it be that we are only experiencing a small number of the blessings God wants to shower upon us because we have never asked for wisdom? We are all invited to ask by the promise found in James 1:5, which says, "If any of you lacks wisdom, let him ask of God, who gives to all liberally and without reproach, and it will be given to him." We are not all called to be the king of a nation, but we still need help in making wise decisions every day at home, school, work, and wherever else our assigned responsibilities take us in life. Let's request wisdom!

Taking Advice

"Then King Rehoboam consulted the elders who stood before his father Solomon while he still lived, and he said, 'How do you advise me to answer these people?' And they spoke to him, saying, 'If you will...speak good words to them, then they will be your servants forever.' But he rejected the advice which the elders had given him, and consulted the young men who had grown up with him, who stood before him" (1 Kings 12:6–8).

When was the last time you asked for advice? When was the last time you took someone's advice? In this vignette, Rehoboam has just been established as king of Israel after Solomon's death, and he was wise enough to ask advice of those who had served in his father's just and prosperous government. These elder statesmen were experienced, and their advice to treat the surrounding tribes of Israel kindly was sound. Unfortunately, Rehoboam was not wise enough to follow the advice he received from these counselors, in favor of the advice given by younger, less experienced advisors with which he had surrounded himself. They suggested that Rehoboam should assert himself as a powerful leader by speaking harshly to the assembly of Israel, telling them that he would make their "yoke" harder and chastising them more strongly than his father ever had!

The consequences of his hasty speech and unwise actions were catastrophic not only to his kingdom but also for the children of Israel as a nation. The Israelites decided to choose a different leader to rule over them and crowned Jeroboam as their king. Only the tribe of Judah continued to acknowledge Rehoboam as their king after this incident. It was here that the Israelites were split into two different nations, which came to be known as the northern kingdom of Israel and the southern kingdom of Judah. This sad state of affairs continued for many years thereafter, all because of a young king taking some bad advice.

There were not only political ramifications of this division in the tribes of Israel but also spiritual ones. Jeroboam was afraid that the people over whom he reigned would want to return to Jerusalem to worship in the house of the Lord there. Subsequently, he feared that many of them would return to pledging their allegiance to Rehoboam over time. As a result, he also took some bad advice and decided to create two golden calves that the people could worship within his territory. He didn't stop there, however. He developed a whole other system of worship for his subjects, building shrines in high places, naming common people as priests (instead of the sons of Levi), and devising a false feast day on which the people were to come together to sacrifice to idols and burn incense. Thus, by retaining some of the trappings of the old religious customs of the people, he gradually led them to abandon the worship of the true God, stay in the northern kingdom to follow these false worship practices, and continue accepting himself as their king. How easily human beings allow themselves to be manipulated and deceived!

How important, then, as emphasized in yesterday's devotional reading, that we continually ask God for His wisdom in making decisions, large or small, and in all the circumstances of life so that the bad advice all around us does not lead us down the path to perdition!

February 28

Faith in Action

"So she said, 'As the LORD your God lives, I do not have bread, only a handful of flour in a bin, and a little oil in a jar; and see, I am gathering a couple of sticks that I may go in and prepare it for myself and my son, that we may eat it, and die.' And Elijah said to her, 'Do not fear; go and do as you have said, but make me a small cake from it first, and bring it to me; and afterward make some for yourself and your son. For thus says the LORD God of Israel: 'The bin of flour shall not be used up, nor shall the jar of oil run dry, until the day the LORD sends rain on the earth'" (1 Kings 17:12–14).

The next verse in this passage is surprising because it says that the widow of Zarephath "went away and did according to the word of Elijah" (verse 15). Would you or I have had such faith? At first glance, this strange request from Elijah seems a bit inappropriate, if not downright selfish. Taking the last bite of food from a poor widow and her child in the midst of a drought? It seems unthinkable.

But here God was testing both the faith of Elijah and the faith of the widow. God would be true to His promise to provide for them. Although this woman was poor in worldly goods, she proved herself to be rich in faith, and the Lord rewarded her, her son, and Elijah by miraculously supplying food for all three of them "for many days" (1 Kings 17:15). If the widow had not been both faithful and generous with the little she had, she never would have experienced the ongoing miraculous faithfulness of God at work in her life in such a special and personal way!

It makes me wonder what special blessings I might be missing out on due to my lack of faith. Perhaps one of the reasons the Lord asks us to pay tithe, even though He owns the "cattle on a thousand hills" (Ps. 50:10), is to test our faith in His ability and willingness to provide for our needs. Even though we might have little, and despite the fact that we cannot see what will happen to us in the future, it's really an exercise in learning to trust the Lord month by month.

But His promise is that if we choose to obey Him, He will pour out so many blessings on us that we won't have room to receive them (see Mal. 3:10)! It also makes our belief in Him not just theoretical but something practical and personal, as we witness Him working things together for good within our very own lives. This, in turn, gives us a testimony of His faithfulness that we can share to help build the faith of those around us, the ripple effect of which we may never know until we reach eternity!

Just think how pleasantly surprised the widow of Zarephath will be when she learns how many people her simple faith has touched and inspired throughout the ensuing years of earth's history!

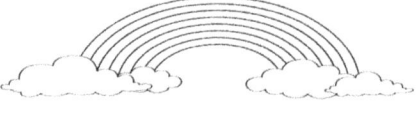

February 29

Not the Only One

"Yet I have reserved seven thousand in Israel, all whose knees have not bowed to Baal, and every mouth that has not kissed him" (1 Kings 19:18).

Have you ever felt like you were the only one in the vast world who cared anything about spiritual matters and was trying to follow the Lord in your life? Elijah, that great prophet who prayed fire down from heaven in a mighty showdown between him and the priests of Baal, did. Shortly after his great victory on Mount Carmel, where he confirmed to the Israelites that only the God of heaven was the true Sovereign God worthy of worship and destroyed the priests of Baal, he received word that the wicked Queen Jezebel had sworn to kill him within twenty-four hours.

At this news, and probably because he was so physically exhausted and emotionally drained after the amazing events of the last day, he fell into a deep depression and even prayed that he might die. He went and hid a day's journey into the wilderness, where he wailed out his woes to the Lord. He cried, "...I have been very zealous for the LORD God of hosts; for the children of Israel have forsaken Your covenant, torn down Your altars, and killed Your prophets with the sword. I alone am left; and they seek to take my life" (1 Kings 19:10).

After sending two angels to bring food and drink to Elijah in his wilderness hideout under a broom tree, the Lord followed him to a cave in Horeb, where He asked him in a still small voice, "What are you doing here, Elijah?" (1 Kings 19:13). Then, after telling Elijah He still had work for him to do, He revealed the encouraging truth presented in today's text. The Lord still had 7,000 faithful followers in

Israel who were not Baal worshipers. Elijah may not have known them, but the Lord did and was continuing to fulfill His purposes through them in the land of Israel. Elijah was not the only one, as he had thought.

Have you ever been in a place, emotionally or physically, where you heard the Lord's small voice in your conscience asking what you were doing there? I have. It is a gentle reminder of our identity as a child of the Sovereign God as well as a call to return to the service of the Lord, where He still has a purpose for our lives. We can never be happy and fulfilled when we try to run away from God, hiding from what we know He is calling us to do.

I think we can take heart from Elijah's story, recognizing that even great men and women are only human and get discouraged from time to time. But it is comforting to know that on those difficult days, when everything looks hopeless, the Lord does not forsake us. He understands that "we *are* dust" (Ps. 103:14) and gently works to restore us to our best selves.

This story also reminds us that it is not up to us to count how many other people we think are serving God in a certain place and time. Our job is to concentrate on what the Lord is asking us to do, personally, and leave the number counting up to God. We can rest assured that there are others who are serving Him. He always preserves a remnant of faithful followers, who, even when in the minority, continue to do God's work in the world.

What Do You Have?

"So Elisha said to her, 'What shall I do for you? Tell me, what do you have in the house?' And she said, 'Your maidservant has nothing in the house but a jar of oil'" (2 Kings 4:2).

How interesting that shortly after taking on the mantel of his mentor, Elijah, the young prophet Elisha also had an encounter with a widow who proved her faith by her obedient actions. In this case, the creditors had come to take this poor woman's sons and sell them as slaves. In this emergency, the widow took her first wise action by crying out to God's prophet for advice on what to do.

Then, her next step, in answer to Elisha's question was to take inventory of what she had and what she didn't have. Her honest and humble assessment was that she had "nothing in the house but a jar of oil." Similarly, when we ask God for help, we should humbly and honestly acknowledge our situation and identify our needs while at the same time recognizing whatever gifts the Lord has given us. The words of the song, "Ordinary People" by Danniebelle Hall, come to mind here. They tell us that our little will become much when we put it in God's hands.

Of course, that's what happened. Once Elisha gave the advice to the woman to use the one thing she had, she immediately obeyed. She and her sons borrowed every empty jar they could find in their neighborhood, filling each one with the oil she had in her house until all the jars were filled to the brim, and there were none left to borrow. Only then did the oil in her one jar stop flowing. It reminds me of how the Lord kept the manna falling to feed the Israelites in the wilderness for forty years until they entered the Promised Land, and it was no longer necessary.

Finally, the widow went to the man of God to report on the miracle the Lord had done for them. There she joyfully heard Elisha declare that she should go and sell the oil, pay her debt, and use the rest of the money they earned to support herself and her sons into the foreseeable future. The threat of being sold into slavery was history!

Some people enjoy a multiplicity of gifts while others have been given just one major or minor talent. Either way, the talents we dedicate to the Lord, following His bidding on how to use them effectively for Him, are the ones that will produce a ripple effect of blessing for time and eternity! Just think of all the miracles wrought by God's rod when Moses, in faith, used it according to the Lord's direction to free His people in the Old Testament. And the widow's mite, when Jesus used her small and singular gift to inspire other people to be generous, not only in the New Testament but all the way down to the present.

This story of the widow with a jar of oil may be short, just a few verses, but it is packed with spiritual lessons for us: ask for God's help, identify what we possess, obey God's instructions, put our talents to work, and then thank God for His work in our lives. Doing this can inspire others to experience the joy and fulfillment of using what God has given them to make a difference in the world while at the same time bringing praise and glory to His name!

Hospitality

"Please, let us make a small upper room on the wall; and let us put a bed for him there, and a table and a chair and a lampstand; so it will be, whenever he comes to us, he can turn in there" (2 Kings 4:10).

Shortly after his experience with the widow with the miracle oil, Elisha was passing by a residence of a notable woman in Shunem, who invited him to eat. It was such a pleasant meal that, from then on, every time he was walking by that household, which was fairly frequently, he would stop in to eat something. Eventually, the hospitable woman talked to her husband about making a guest room right there at their house for the man of God.

The kind husband agreed with the plan. Soon, Elisha had a nice upper room to stay in when he was in Shunem as well as good food to sustain him as he did his work for the Lord in that area. What a blessing! He was so thankful that he began to think about ways to show the generous couple his gratitude.

One day, when Elisha was talking with his servant about this, Gehazi had an idea. The thoughtful woman had no son, and her husband was getting old. Wouldn't it be a great way to show their appreciation if she could bear a son? When Elisha called her and told her about the plan, she was incredulous. But a year later, just as the prophet had predicted, she bore a son!

Everything went well, until one day, when the boy was old enough to go out into the field with his father, he got a terrible headache. By noon, he had died! In great distress, the woman went to find Elisha, encountering him at Mount Carmel. Elisha sent his servant ahead, but the distraught mother would not go home until Elisha, himself, went with her. Upon their arrival, Elisha went straight to where the boy was, immediately praying for him and stretching his warm body over the child's. He repeated this twice until the child sneezed and came to. When the Shunammite woman was called to the room, she fell to the ground in worship before picking up her son and rushing out of the room with him. Imagine her relief and joy!

This couple's hospitality was not shown to Elisha for any earthly gain. They kindly provided a place for him to stay simply out of the goodness of their hearts and before he had done anything for them. They felt satisfied knowing that the man of God had a safe and comfortable place to stay in their home. Receiving a son, although unanticipated, was a wonderful and surprising reward for their efforts. And when Elisha brought him back to life after his illness, that was the "frosting on the cake" of their happiness!

When is the last time you went out of your way to be hospitable to someone? In my experience, although it often takes planning and hard work, the blessings received by both the guests and our family are worth the effort. Friendship, prayer partners, increased faith, new recipes, and even being left with more food than we started with because of dishes brought by our guests at times have all been benefits we have gained from being hospitable. What better way to get to know your neighbors, other church members, and even members of your family!

Faith Heals

"Then she said to her mistress, 'If only my master were with the prophet who is in Samaria! For he would heal him of his leprosy'" (2 Kings 5:3).

I especially like this story because it has a child heroine. Raiding bands of Syrians had gone into Israel and captured some of its inhabitants, making them their slaves. This young girl had been made a servant of Naaman's wife. Naaman was a commander of the army of the king of Syria, and as such, he was an avowed and much-feared enemy of the Israelites. Not only had the child been taken from her home and family but she was being forced to serve, through no choice of her own, in the household of one of the warriors responsible for her own slavery as well as that of many of her people. She was suddenly thrust into a heathen environment and a totally different culture than her own. Imagine what it would be like to be in her shoes.

Under such circumstances, you would think she might have become angry, depressed, and rebellious against those who were causing her suffering and keeping her at a painful distance from her loved ones. Who knew what had happened to her parents or what might happen to her in the future in this strange land? Certainly, there must have been times when she felt very lonely and fearful.

Yet the Bible paints a surprisingly different picture of this young girl. Upon finding out that Naaman had contracted leprosy, she spoke to his wife, her mistress, in a kind and thoughtful way, expressing faith and hope that he could be healed if only he could meet with Israel's prophet. I can almost hear her cheerful voice, suggesting a remedy for Naaman's horrible malady. It's as though she had forgotten completely about her own predicament in her desire to help alleviate someone else's suffering. How amazing that, no matter our age, faith can lift us up to a whole other level of existence above the trials and tribulations of this dark world.

The fact that both Naaman and his wife took the little girl's words seriously speaks volumes about the quality of her work, her positive attitude, and the influence her daily life had made upon them. Her faith inspired faith in them. Even though it would be a humbling experience for the Syrian commander to present himself to Israel's prophet, the little maid's words had sparked an inkling of hope in the couple's hearts. And so arrangements were made between the king of Syria and the king of Israel for Naaman to visit Elisha. Israel's king thought it was just some kind of a set-up to cause more conflict between the two nations, but when Elisha heard about it, he encouraged Naaman to come, knowing that ultimately, through the healing that would take place, God would be glorified.

Thus, Naaman and his entourage arrived at Elisha's doorstep, only to have the prophet send out a messenger telling him to go and wash in the Jordan River seven times. Of course, the commander was incensed and humiliated by such strange instructions. For one thing, Elisha didn't even pay him the courtesy of coming out to talk to him, and then he was told that to "be clean" (2 Kings 5:10) he had to wash in Israel's dirty Jordan River? There were what he considered to be much better rivers in his home territory. Finally, however, since it seemed to be his last hope of getting well, his servants convinced him to at least try what the prophet had suggested. Down into the river he went, noticing nothing different the first several times he went under, but after dipping himself in the water the seventh time, the Bible says "his flesh was restored like the flesh of a little child, and he was clean" (2 Kings 5:14). Faith that he could be healed and

obedience to the instructions given resulted in a miracle!

Best of all, Naaman had become a believer in the same God as his little Israelite maid at home, declaring his faith when he came to thank Elisha by saying, "Indeed, now I know that *there is* no God in all the earth, except in Israel" (2 Kings 5:15). Who knows how many people with whom Naaman shared his faith in the true God after he was healed of leprosy? It's incredible to consider, but it all started with the simple belief of a faithful young maiden in a foreign land. Faith heals.

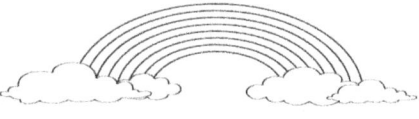

March 4

Open Our Eyes

"So he answered, 'Do not fear, for those who are with us are more than those who are with them.' And Elisha prayed, and said, 'LORD, I pray, open his eyes that he may see.' Then the LORD opened the eyes of the young man, and he saw. And behold, the mountain was full of horses and chariots of fire all around Elisha" (2 Kings 6:16, 17).

This story is amazing for several reasons. First, because Elisha had enough faith to believe that God had the situation under control, and although the troops were invisible, he knew that he and his servant were surrounded by the mighty army of God! And he knew that God's army was more powerful than the amassed forces of the enemy.

Second, that through Elisha's simple prayer of faith, God opened the eyes of his servant to see the spiritual realities all around them. So often, we are like Elisha's servant, totally oblivious to the intense and furious battle between good and evil that is raging all around us. With our limited human eyesight, we usually only see things from an earthly perspective, thus losing our courage when confronted with seemingly insurmountable challenges and giving in to fear and despair, feeling that all is lost before the fight has even begun!

But the story continues. Elisha is about to use two powerful weapons to win not only this battle but the whole war: blindness and kindness. He asks the Lord to strike the approaching Syrian soldiers with blindness, so they are rendered useless to carry on the fight. Then he leads them right into the midst of Samaria, where the king of Israel is waiting breathlessly to kill them.

Elisha, however, has a totally different plan. Asking that their eyes be opened so they could see where they were, he then instructs the king to bring food and drink to the Syrian soldiers before sending them home in peace with the shock of this kindness seared into their collective memory. Surprisingly, to both the Israeli and Syrian armies, they ended up feasting instead of fighting!

So, what was the result? The Bible says that "the bands of Syrian *raiders* came no more into the land of Israel" (2 Kings 6:23). Without one shot being fired, and without one soldier being killed, the war was over. Better yet, the Israelites entered a wonderful period of peace in their land. And the proverbial "frosting on the cake" was the fact that God's people were finally enabled to rightly represent His character of mercy and grace to the heathen nations that surrounded them.

What a reminder that we, when struggling with seemingly impossible situations, need to stop and ask God for spiritual eyesight so that we can see things as God sees them. Through faith in God's promises, claiming His strength, and resting in the fact that He is still the Sovereign Creator of the universe, we can also come off as more than conquerors! Our faith, like Elisha's, has the power to lift us into a whole new realm of existence where we can trust God to ultimately work everything out for our good. After all, "those who *are* with us *are* more than those who *are* with them." We just need to ask the Lord to open our eyes!

An Extended Life

*"Return and tell Hezekiah the leader of My people, 'Thus says the LORD …
"I have heard your prayer, I have seen your tears; surely I will heal you. On
the third day you shall go up to the house of the LORD. And I will add to your
days fifteen years. I will deliver you and this city from the hand of the king of
Assyria…" ' " (2 Kings 20:5, 6).*

Isaiah, God's prophet in those days, had just finished telling King Hezekiah to set his house in order because he was going to die. The despairing ruler turned his face to the wall, weeping, pleading his case, and praying that God would extend his life. Immediately, the Lord heard and answered his prayer! Before the prophet had even left the middle court of the king's property, the Lord told him to turn around. He was instructed to deliver a new message to the ailing monarch. Not only would the Lord heal him but he would be given fifteen more years of life. On top of that, the Lord pledged that the king's city would be delivered from their enemies, the Syrians.

Despite this amazing turn of events, Hezekiah, like many of us when asking a special petition of the Lord, asked for a sign. In an amazing display of grace and forbearance, the Lord condescends to the doubting king's request.

Hezekiah asks that the shadow on the sun dial go backward by ten degrees! Then he would know that the Lord would do as He had promised. As if the Lord could not be trusted to keep His word! How sad that the leader of God's own people showed such a lack of faith! But the Lord's mercy and kindness prevailed, as it so often does in His dealings with His children. The sun dial's shadow went backward, and Hezekiah was healed within three days!

The king received a second chance, a new lease on life. What would he do with his fifteen additional years? What would you do? Unfortunately, many of us make promises when we are bargaining with God for a longer life, which we fail to keep when our wish is granted. Over the years, my husband has worked to provide counseling services to prisoners in an effort to reduce recidivism rates. While some of the inmates actually keep their promises to live a changed life once they are no longer incarcerated, many others forget all about their new intentions, slipping back into a life of crime. As sinners, we have all experienced a similar phenomenon at various times in our lives. We make New Year's resolutions that only last a few weeks; we make appointments with people that we sometimes forget; we swear that we're going to break a bad habit, which pulls us in again at the slightest temptation. We find that even when "the spirit indeed *is* willing… the flesh *is* weak" (Matt. 26:41). Only by staying close to the Lord and trusting in His strength can we break away from old and destructive patterns and truly live the kind of life the Lord planned for us to live from the beginning.

It seems that, although Hezekiah did some good things in his fifteen remaining years, he also made a very grave mistake during his extended life. When envoys came to visit him from Babylon, he showed them all of the treasures in his house and dominion. Instead of just thanking the Lord for His goodness and praising the Lord for his possessions, he proudly showed them off, bragging about all that was his: silver and gold, ointments and spices, weapons, precious items passed down to him from previous generations, as well as his architectural accomplishments! Unfortunately, when the Babylonians raided his city years later, after his eventual death, they knew exactly where to find the kingdom's treasures and carried them all away to Babylon.

So, was it good that Hezekiah lived an additional fifteen years? I suppose we will only learn the answer to that question on Judgment Day. Meanwhile, each of us receives a brand new slate every morning, our own version of a new lease on life! Will we spend the time extended to us in showing off our possessions and boasting about our accomplishments or in telling others about God's loving kindness and praising Him for the miracles He's done in our lives? Regardless of however much time we have left in this life, whether the Lord grants us many more years or just a few, we each get to decide anew to make it a life that is truly worth living!

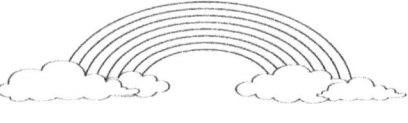

March 6

Led by a Child

"Josiah was eight years old when he became king, and he reigned thirty-one years in Jerusalem. ...And he did what was right in the sight of the LORD, and walked in all the ways of his father David; he did not turn aside to the right hand or to the left" (2 Kings 22:1, 2).

The book of 2 Kings has several inspirational stories about children making a difference in the lives of those around them. This time it was a young boy. At only eight years of age, Josiah became king in Jerusalem. From the beginning, he "did *what was* right in the sight of the LORD," unlike his wicked grandfather, Manasseh, and his wayward father, Amon.

In Josiah's eighteenth year, while making reparations to the house of the Lord, the high priest, Hilkiah, found the Book of the Law there. He gave it to Shaphan, the scribe, to read to the king. What was so remarkable about Josiah is that as soon as he found out about the law of God and what the Israelites were supposed to be doing to maintain their covenant relationship with the Lord, he immediately set out to rectify the errors of his people, destroying their many idols and seeking to re-establish their commitment to the one and only true God.

Josiah was obviously a young man of action. He wasted no time in seeking out Huldah, the prophetess, to inquire of the Lord what to do. He must restore true worship, which he does by gathering all the elders of Judah together with all the inhabitants of Jerusalem to publicly read the Book of the Covenant in their hearing. Then he leads by making a personal commitment to following all the Lord's commandments, testimonies, and statutes "with all *his* heart and with all *his* soul" (2 Kings 23:3). What a great example! The people are so moved by his passion to do what is right that they follow his lead and renew their commitment to obey the words of the covenant.

This prepares the people for the next step, which is to purge the land of all of its many idols: to Baal, the sun, the moon, the constellations, Ashtoreth, Molech, and others. He destroyed their altars, images, pillars, and the shrines on the high places where they practiced their abominations. Then he asked the people to clean out any signs of idolatry from their homes, the temple, and the cities of Judah. Finally, he executes the idolatrous priests and banishes all mediums, spiritualists, and anyone else who had led out in any type of false worship.

Now he is ready to reinstitute worship to the God of their fathers by declaring a huge religious holiday. They will celebrate a Passover such has not been kept in Jerusalem since even before it started having kings! Everything was done according to what had been written in the Book of the Covenant. The Lord promised Josiah that, because his heart was tender and he was humble enough to recognize Israel's sin and obedient enough to re-establish true worship, he would not see the destruction of Jerusalem during his lifetime.

I believe this vignette is a model for those who wish to be leaders in God's cause today. Josiah was a good ruler because he first explained why the people's religious practices needed to be changed. He publicly committed to serving the God of heaven and following all of His commandments. Then he enlisted the people's help in eliminating idolatry from the kingdom. When the task was done, he stopped to celebrate a feast to the Lord with them. This Passover marked the end of false worship and the beginning of true worship for all Josiah's subjects for the remainder of his long, peaceful, and prosperous reign. If only we all had such wise and wonderful leaders, whether young or old!

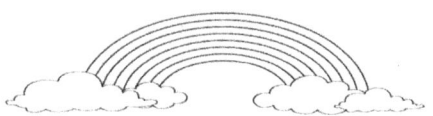

Ministers of Music

"Now these are the men whom David appointed over the service of song in the house of the LORD, after the ark came to rest. They were ministering with music before the dwelling place of the tabernacle of meeting, until Solomon had built the house of the LORD in Jerusalem, and they served in their office according to their order" (1 Chronicles 6:31, 32).

The books of First and Second Chronicles go back and fill in some of the history and details of events that occurred in previous books of the Old Testament. In this chapter of First Chronicles, the various responsibilities of the family of Levi are delineated. The Levites, although usually thought of as the priests, were also appointed to every kind of service of the tabernacle of the house of God, according to verse 48. Some were assigned to be gatekeepers while others had oversight of the tabernacle treasury. Others were in charge of the tabernacle furnishings or made incense or baked the shewbread used in the temple services. And then there were the musicians.

When I first heard the term "minister of music," I didn't really take it seriously because everybody knows it is the pastor who actually ministers to the people in his congregation, right? As I kept reading through the next several chapters of First Chronicles, however, I became aware of what an important role these people played in the worship of God in ancient times, causing me to re-evaluate my attitude toward our modern-day ministers of music. Don't get me wrong. I have always loved and been inspired by great sacred music, but I guess I just didn't think of it as a full-time occupation, per se.

In 1 Chronicles 9:33, I learned that the singers lived in the temple chambers and were "free *from other duties;* for they were employed in *that* work day and night." These were not small groups of singers. They were more on the order of a huge choral group, perhaps akin to the Mormon Tabernacle Choir of our day. In fact, in 1 Chronicles 25:7, it says that in one group, all those who had been "instructed in the songs of the LORD," were 288 singers! They certainly must have sounded like a great choir of angels!

Then, I found that on one occasion "four thousand praised the LORD with *musical instruments*" (1 Chron. 23:5). These instruments, which David had made, included harps, stringed instruments, tambourines, trumpets, and cymbals. With an ensemble like that, imagine how the courts of the temple must have resounded with joyful praise! What an inspiration for the people of God that must have been, helping to turn their hearts and minds to Him anew at each religious gathering.

The closest thing I can compare it to in my own experience is listening to a mass choir, accompanied by a full orchestra, singing the "Hallelujah Chorus" in a church with great acoustics. Being a participant in such a glorious musical rapture is even better, gifting me with an all-encompassing foretaste of the amazing auditory delights awaiting us in heaven! In the meantime, perhaps we should better value and assist those who are charged with the responsibility of planning and conducting our own local church's music ministry.

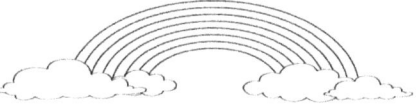

March 8

A Trusted Office

"Some of them were appointed over the furnishings and over all the implements of the sanctuary, and over the fine flour and the wine and the oil and the incense and the spices. Mattithiah of the Levites, the firstborn of Shallum the Korahite, had the trusted office over the things that were baked in the pans" (1 Chronicles 9:29, 31).

Chapter 9 continues to describe the many temple-related assignments given to some of the members of the tribe of the Levites, in addition to the more commonly-acknowledged priestly duties carried out by so many of their brethren. What surprised me was the value and importance given to each one of these responsibilities. Notice that even those who were responsible for baking the temple showbread were considered to hold "a trusted office" by the Lord. And many of these workers—carpenters, cleaners, cooks, incense makers, those who created precious spices, bakers, and gatekeepers—were actually individually named in these passages. Talk about knowing what God's plan is for your life!

So here, again, God's Word confirms the worth of every individual as well as the fact that we all have different talents, yet we all hold what God considers to be a "trusted" place in His master plan. When we all exercise our gifts harmoniously together, truly great, well-organized, and marvelous things can be accomplished! It's reassuring to know that God is not looking for cookie-cutter followers. He just wants people who will follow the injunction that says, "whatever you do, do all to the glory of God" (1 Cor. 10:31).

When I was growing up, my folks did not make enough money to send me to church school, which meant I had to work to help defray my tuition expenses. I did a little babysitting when I could. My freshman year of high school, when I was finally deemed old enough to work part time at the school itself, the only job left by the time I registered was custodial work. My first official job was to clean the large girls' bathroom in the administrative wing of the academy I attended. So, each day after classes, I would head to the janitor's closet to gather my supplies and then go straight to work with the goal of finishing the task before my ride came to pick me up. At that time, I was working only about five hours a week, and if I remember correctly, I made a whopping seventy-five cents per hour! But every little bit helped. My father had ingrained the adage, "Whatever your hand finds to do, do *it* with your might," (Eccles. 9:10), into our heads from the time my brother, sister, and I were in elementary school just doing our simple chores at home. As a result, I found I enjoyed work, making it into a game or a contest whenever I could.

That was good because by my sophomore year, I started attending a boarding academy in another state with board and room costs in addition to the money needed for tuition and books. I was lucky enough to be able to work about twenty hours a week, boasting a pay rate of a little under a dollar per hour! That year I worked in the cafeteria, preparing meals

and washing dishes. My junior year I worked in the bakery, making sixty loaves of bread a day as well as cookies, cakes, and cinnamon rolls (my favorite!). Maybe that's why the verse about a baker holding a "trusted office" snagged my attention. By my senior year, though, I found a job in the school's furniture factory where I could make more money. Between that, and staying at the school to work during holiday periods as well as during summer vacations, my parents and I, working together, were able to wipe out my high school debt, so I was ready to start college free and clear of other financial obligations.

All this to say that, at an early age, I found different kinds of work to be both honorable and enjoyable. Knowing that God valued their work and gave each one of them the wisdom and strength to do their varied occupations to the best of their ability must have been a real source of blessing to the Levites, just as it should be to us today!

March 9

An Inheritance

"And David said to his son Solomon, 'Be strong and of good courage, and do it; do not fear nor be dismayed, for the LORD God—my God—will be with you. He will not leave you nor forsake you, until you have finished all the work for the service of the house of the LORD'" (1 Chronicles 28:20).

At my mother-in-law's funeral, her eldest son talked about the rich inheritance he and his siblings had received from their mother. She was not a rich person, had few material possessions, little formal education, could only speak a few words of English, and was not well-connected socially in the usual sense of the term. How then could she have left so much to her children?

My brother-in-law went on to explain in his eulogy that the priceless legacy of faith, which she had passed down to them, was worth more than any earthly inheritance. Through her example of a living faith, her sacrifices, her training, and her prayers, her family had been blessed to receive spiritual preparation for living this temporary life successfully as well as being equipped to look forward with hope and anticipation to the permanent life to come. No parent is perfect, but she had done all she could to attach their affections to the God who would one day reunite her with her family and friends in a heavenly home where they would never be parted again. What a treasured inheritance!

As parents, we can only hope to leave this kind of legacy for those who follow behind us. In today's text, David is attempting to reach that same goal in his admonition to his son, Solomon. He tells him to be strong, courageous, energetic to accomplish what is good (in this case the building of the temple), and not to be fearful or discouraged because God would never leave him or forsake him. But the phrase that really touched me is when he said, "My God—*will be* with you." David's own experience with God had been a testimony of how to live a life of faith, and

now, before his death, he wanted to make sure that he had passed the contagion of his faith down to the next generation. He wanted Solomon to be connected to the same Source of power, wisdom, and grace that he had depended upon throughout his own lifetime. Of course, as king, David undoubtedly left wealth, property, power, and position to his son, but, most importantly, was leaving his son with a love for and desire to trust his God. He knew that would be the most valuable gift he could leave to his posterity.

So, what about us? Do our children know our God? Have they seen Him in our example and heard our testimony of His goodness? Have we thrown the whole weight of our influence on the side of doing what is good? Do our words and actions convince them that our God is the same One that they will want to have as their friend and guide throughout life? If not, it should give us food for thought. Where are our priorities? Are we so busy with the daily rat race, with focusing on the temporal needs and desires of this life and the distracting worldliness all around us, that we are missing out on the most important things we need to provide for our children? What will our inheritance be, not only for our children but also for our grandchildren, great-grandchildren, and all those who fall within the shadow of our influence? May the Lord help us.

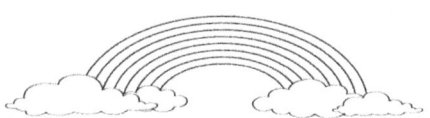

Willingly

"They gave for the work of the house of God five thousand talents and ten thousand darics of gold, ten thousand talents of silver, eighteen thousand talents of bronze, and one hundred thousand talents of iron. And whoever had precious *stones gave* them *to the treasury of the house of the LORD… Then the people rejoiced, for they had offered willingly, because with a loyal heart they had offered willingly to the LORD; and King David also rejoiced greatly" (1 Chronicles 29:7–9).*

Reading this passage, we are reminded of how the Israelites gave so willingly of all they had when Moses asked for donations in order to build the tabernacle in the wilderness. Eventually, he actually had to tell them to stop making offerings for that purpose because they had received enough!

Now, we see David, in one of his final acts, petitioning the people to generously give of their possessions for the building of the great temple his son would be constructing in Jerusalem. As was his custom, he led by example, donating 3,000 talents of gold and 7,000 talents of refined silver from his own treasury. But then, before any of the officers of the tribes had given, he took another critical action. He challenged the leaders to consecrate themselves to the Lord. David had lived long enough to have learned that once people have truly committed to serve the Lord, they give willingly, from their hearts, to God's causes in the world. He didn't have to "pull teeth" or beg repeatedly for the necessary funds to go forward with the sacred project. The Bible says that the people "rejoiced" and gave willingly. These were no meager offerings. As delineated in today's texts, they brought thousands of talents of gold, silver, bronze, and iron as well as precious stones for the upbuilding of the great temple which Solomon would raise in their midst for the glory and honor of their worthy God.

When David saw the abundance of the offerings the people gave so willingly and generously, he was overwhelmed and broke out in joyful praise to the Lord, as recorded in verses 10 to 17 of this same chapter. Here he also takes the opportunity to express his gratitude to the Lord that the people brought their gifts so willingly as well as acknowledge that all they had originally came from the Lord's hand. Now they were simply returning a portion of it.

Finally, David entreated everyone in the assembly to "bless the LORD your God" (1 Chron. 29:20) before dismissing them with his words of praise and thanksgiving to God still ringing in their ears. I can only imagine some of the sentiments they must have felt on their way home that day: personal satisfaction that they had dedicated part of their wealth to God's cause in answer to their beloved leader's request and the moving of the Spirit; a sense of teamwork because they were working together with their brethren for a common and worthwhile goal; and, last but not least, the joy of knowing that they had become co-workers with God to advance His great purposes in the world! I am convinced that the same blessings can be felt today by all those who bring their offerings willingly to the Lord. My gifts may not be as large, but when I give them cheerfully, I always return home fulfilled, knowing that the smile of God rests upon me.

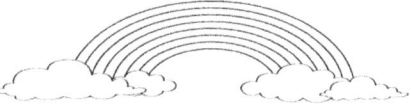

March 11

Humble Me

"If My people who are called by My name will humble themselves, and pray and seek My face, and turn from their wicked ways, then I will hear from heaven, and will forgive their sin and heal their land" (2 Chronicles 7:14).

Here, the Lord personally appears to King Solomon at night and directly communicates His message to the ruler of His people. I find this verse interesting because three actions are specifically requested by God followed by three promises God makes to His people. The three spiritual exercises God enjoins on His people are to humble themselves, seek Him in prayer, and turn away from sin. The three blessings God promises in return are to hear the people's prayers, to forgive their sins, and to heal their land. Talk about knowing the will of God. The Lord could not have been more straightforward in clearly outlining what He expected from those who were to represent Him to the rest of the world. By every indication in the Scriptures, God's requirements for His modern-day people have not changed.

Thinking about how to apply this message to my own life, I first thought about what it means to humble oneself. The old chorus comes to mind: "Humble me, humble me, oh Lord, humble me, humble me so I can do your will." I don't see this as someone groveling or flagellating themselves, trying to punish themselves into heaven, rather as someone who has realized God's omniscience and humankind's intellectual, social, and spiritual limitations. I see it as a human being approaching his or her Maker with an open and teachable spirit. Laying aside pre-conceived beliefs, opinions, and biases, surrendering our lives and plans to Him, and coming into His presence willingly to learn what the great Master Teacher wants to teach us.

Let's look at a few Biblical examples. First, those who were humble enough to be ready for God to do miracles in their lives. I think of Mary, the mother of Jesus; Zacchaeus, the converted tax collector; Joseph, waiting patiently in an Egyptian prison; and Samuel's mother, who earnestly prayed for a child to raise in the fear and admonition of the Lord. Now, some who refused to humble themselves: the rich, young ruler, the loud-praying religious man who thought himself better than the commoner praying beside him, and, of course, the supposed religious leaders of the Israelites. Although they thought they were superior to others, they all "missed the boat." One of the greatest sins of the Pharisees of Jesus' day was their pride. The feeling that they knew it all when it came to religious topics, which was actually the thing that blinded them to the fact that Jesus really was the long-awaited Messiah. It made them impervious to the gospel!

So, first I need to come to the Lord with a teachable spirit. Then, according to the formula delineated above, I need to seek Him in prayer. Next, as the Lord indicates through the still, small voice of His Holy Spirit, I need to turn away from the sins He points out in my life. What happens next? The Bible promises that He hears my prayer, forgives my sins, and begins to heal my environment, starting with my cleansed and renewed influence in the world around me. Suddenly, following God's will in my life doesn't look as complicated as I have sometimes made it.

March 12

Royal Animals

"For the king's ships went to Tarshish with the servants of Hiram. Once every three years the merchant ships came, bringing gold, silver, ivory, apes, and monkeys. So King Solomon surpassed all the kings of the earth in riches and wisdom" (2 Chronicles 9:21, 22).

I was truly surprised when I came upon this passage of Scripture. In all my years of reading the Bible, I don't ever remember coming across this information before. If I did, I must have just scanned over it, not really paying much attention to what it said. But now, reading and studying the Bible more closely, chapter by chapter, this verse jumped out at me. In addition to gold, silver, ivory, and other merchant wares, we see that Solomon brought apes and monkeys into his kingdom. Later in this same chapter it tells us that surrounding rulers also brought horses from Egypt and other countries. Could it be that Solomon started the first zoo for the entertainment of his subjects? We don't know, but it's an interesting idea to ponder.

In verse 22 it says that Solomon's wisdom surpassed that of all the other kings of the earth at that time. It may be that he acquired animals not only for enjoyment but also to study and learn about them, so he could share that knowledge with others. The Queen of Sheba was one of the people who came to him and benefitted from his wisdom on a wide array of topics. Although she asked many difficult questions, there were none that Solomon could not answer. At the end of her visit she exclaimed, "...indeed the half of the greatness of your wisdom was not told me" (2 Chron. 9:6).

Solomon must have known a great deal about horses since he had so many of them, and they had been used in battles for years by the time he took the throne. Camels, such as the ones the Queen of Sheba's retinue used, were common modes of transportation in the more desert-like regions of the Middle East. It's also interesting to note that Solomon must have learned something about lions because he had a dozen of them made to stand on the two sides of the six steps leading up to his throne, as well as placing one beside each royal armrest. Because of his interest in animals, I wonder if he didn't also have a number of exotic birds from different parts of the then-known world.

In any event, just thinking about the value that the richest and wisest man who ever lived placed on his collection of "royal animals" makes me more appreciative of the many kinds of animals the Lord has created for all of us to enjoy. Nowadays, we don't have to be rich or a king to possess a number of animals of our own. Animals have benefitted humanity in so many ways over the years and still continue to do so. They can provide food, clothing, protection, entertainment, transportation, and probably the greatest blessing they bring us today is their faithful companionship. Many a single, sick, or elderly person has been able to stave off loneliness through adoption of a pet. Recent studies have even shown that pet owners live longer than their peers since the need to care for their animals keeps them active and gives them a reason to get up in the morning. The comfort and loyalty of a good pet has proven to enrich the lives of many of us humans. Thank you, Lord, for the often-overlooked blessing of animals!

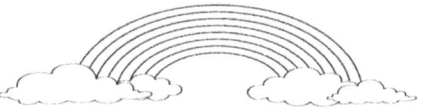

March 13

God's Victory

"...Thus says the LORD to you: 'Do not be afraid nor dismayed because of this great multitude, for the battle is not yours, but God's'" (2 Chronicles 20:15).

What courage this promise has given me through the years! How wonderful it is to trust that, when confronted with an apparently insurmountable problem, God is going to find a way to win our battles for us! In the meantime, He tells us not to be afraid and not even to be dismayed about them!

In this particular instance, King Jehoshaphat was up against the armies of Ammon, Moab, and Mount Seir, who had united to attack the tribe of Judah and Jerusalem. These enemies were called "a great multitude" (verse 2), and Jehoshaphat was immediately filled with fear when he was told of their coming. But, fortunately, the king knew where to go to ask for help. At once, he turned to the Lord. He prayed, proclaimed a fast throughout all of Judah, and brought the people together before the temple, so the whole assembly could seek God's help together.

Then he petitioned the Lord for help in the presence of the men, women, and children of his kingdom with these words, which declared his faith in God's power: "O LORD God of our fathers, *are* You not God in heaven, and do You *not* rule over all the kingdoms of the nations, and in Your hand *is there not* power and might, so that no one is able to withstand You?" (verse 6). He continued to cry out to the Lord and finally ended his public prayer by saying, "O our God, will You not judge them? For we have no power against this great multitude that is coming against us; nor do we know what to do, but our eyes *are* upon You" (verse 12). This prayer is a great model for us when seeking God's help. First, Jehoshaphat declared their helplessness, then he expressed his faith in God's power to do something about the situation, and finally, he committed himself and his people to trusting that the Lord would come to their aid.

In response the Lord filled a prophet in their midst, Jahaziel, with His Spirit, and he pronounced the beautiful promise found in today's text to the king, the inhabitants of Jerusalem, and all the people of the tribe of Judah. And to us, by virtue of the fact that it was recorded in the Old Testament for our edification as well.

Of course, the story ends with a great victory wrought by the God of heaven and earth. In fact, in verse 17, the people were told that they would not even need to fight in this battle. Instead they were told: "Position yourselves, stand still and see the salvation of the LORD, who is with you!" Then, amazingly, while they worshipped and sang to the Lord, He defeated their enemies. Wow! There is so much to gain from this story. We may face all sorts of great battles, be it emotional, spiritual, financial, or any other kind that we typically have to confront in this life. Whenever we find ourselves up against a "great multitude" of evil forces, the winning formula is to turn to the Lord and express our need, our faith in His power, and our trust in His providence. After putting the battle in His hands, our job is simply to give Him our worship and praise while we watch Him win the victory!

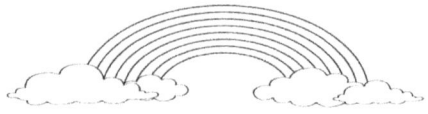

His Prophets

"So they rose early in the morning and went out into the Wilderness of Tekoa; and as they went out, Jehoshaphat stood and said, 'Hear me, O Judah and you inhabitants of Jerusalem: Believe in the LORD your God, and you shall be established; believe His prophets, and you shall prosper'" (2 Chronicles 20:20).

Here the story of yesterday continues. At this point in the chapter, Jehoshaphat is inspired to give his people this significant admonition before the battle had even begun. And his good advice trickles all the way down to our day.

We are also established when we believe in God. What does that mean? To me, the word "established" conjures up pictures of people who are calm, safe, and secure. People who don't need to worry because they are settled in to the idea that their all-wise God is in control.

Then we come upon the phrase, "believe His prophets, and you shall prosper." The word "prosper" here connotes more than just doing well financially. We will do well spiritually. We will do better in life, in general, because the prophets who our omniscient God sends to us are inspired by Him to provide us with wise council and help to guide us into all truth.

Of course, at this point, we need to make sure that we are listening to the voice of a true prophet rather than one of the many false prophets who have arisen at different times in the history of the world. How will we know the difference? The Bible itself gives us a couple of clues. First, it tells us that, "To the law and to the testimony! If they do not speak according to this word, *it is* because *there is* no light in them" (Isa. 8:20). And then, "...By their fruits you will know them" (Matt. 7:20). So, the first test of a true prophet is whether a person who claims to have messages from God is speaking according to biblical principles while the second test is whether that person is living according to biblical principles.

As a young person, Ellen G. White was considered a true modern-day prophet (prophetess, if you will) by my parents, and they frequently read from her writings during our family worship time. But it wasn't until I got to academy and started reading from her books on my own that I really started to appreciate what a gift God had given to the church through the Spirit of Prophecy, as her books are often called. I not only gained deeper spiritual insights into biblical passages but I also felt my own walk with God growing stronger. This is why, whenever I hear people expressing doubt about whether Mrs. White is a true prophet of God, I always encourage them to start reading her writings for themselves and then to measure the results in their own personal spiritual life. After that, I leave the rest to the Holy Spirit.

I only know that in my own experience, believing in both God and the prophet He has provided for our time and place, I have been richly blessed, comforted, convicted, and guided at various critical points in my life's journey. It's good to know that, just like His dealings with the Israelites, the Lord has not left us to fight our battles alone here on this earth. It's our job to simply follow His directions, and it's His job to win the war!

A King's Letter

"Blessed be the LORD God of our fathers, who has put such a thing as this in the king's heart, to beautify the house of the LORD which is in Jerusalem, and has extended mercy to me before the king and his counselors, and before all the king's mighty princes. So I was encouraged as the hand of the LORD my God was upon me; and I gathered leading men of Israel to go up with me" (Ezra 7:27, 28).

When Artaxerxes was the king of Persia and Ezra worked as a priest and scribe in his kingdom, something truly amazing happened. A small contingent of Israelites had already left their captivity in Babylon to return to Jerusalem and rebuild the temple under the decree of Cyrus, the previous king of Persia. Ezra believed it was his mission to now return to Jerusalem to seek "the Law of the LORD" (verse 10) and to teach its statutes and ordinances in Israel.

As surprising as King Cyrus' supportive declaration had been some sixty years earlier for those who chose to return to Jerusalem, King Artaxerxes made a similarly generous proclamation in support of Ezra and those who wanted to travel with him to Jerusalem. This decree was expressed not only verbally but the king also put his mandate in writing in the form of a long letter (see Ezra 7:12–26), which virtually gave Ezra *carte blanche* for anything he would need on his important quest. We are not told what Ezra had done to earn such favor from the king, but it appears that Artaxerxes had become a believer in the God of the Israelites because he not only sends Ezra off with large quantities of silver and gold but also instructs the treasurers all along the journey to provide whatever else Ezra may need for the "house of the God of heaven" (Ezra 7:23).

In this amazing letter from the king, I counted at least seven ways Artaxerxes provided for Ezra's mission to be completed successfully. First, he declared that anyone who wanted to volunteer to go to Jerusalem with Ezra would be allowed to do so. Then, he sent freewill offerings for the project in Jerusalem from the priests and people who would be staying in Babylon. This was in addition to the silver and gold already mentioned above. He also sent articles that would be used in the services of God's house, adding that anything else Ezra needed could be paid for from the king's own treasury! What an unexpected windfall! But the king was not finished. He declared that taxes should not be imposed on Ezra or any of the servants of the house of God, including priests, Levites, singers, gatekeepers, and others. Once Ezra arrived at his destination, he was given the power to choose the magistrates and judges who would assist him in teaching the laws of God to the people as well as determine what punishment would be given to any who would not observe God's laws. Ezra could not have asked or received more if the king himself had been an Israelite!

It was at this point that Ezra broke out in praise to God as found in today's verses. He could not contain himself, for he knew that the "God of our fathers" had put "*such a thing* as this in the king's heart." Energized and encouraged, under the authority of the king, and the approbation of his God, Ezra chose the best Israeli leaders he could find to attend him on his journey, and they set off for Jerusalem to accomplish the sacred mission to which he had been called.

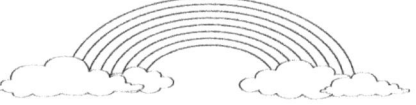

March 16

Fasting

"Then I proclaimed a fast there at the river of Ahava, that we might humble ourselves before our God, to seek from Him the right way for us and our little ones and all our possessions. For I was ashamed to request of the king an escort of soldiers and horsemen to help us against the enemy on the road ... So we fasted and entreated our God for this, and He answered our prayer" (*Ezra 8:21–23*).

Fasting is not something I know a lot about since it doesn't really seem to be "in vogue" in modern-day religious circles. I remember, though, that on occasion, my father, who was a very devout Christian, would fast and pray over matters and for people he was very concerned about, such as when one of his children was in trouble. And I must say that through the years, I was witness to many of his answered prayers, some of which are still being answered even after his death!

Later I learned, when I was teaching English as a second language to college-aged foreign students, that true Muslims fast for the whole day during Ramadan, not eating or even drinking anything, until after sundown in celebration of their religious holiday. As an adult, I have slowly come to the realization that devout believers in a number of different faiths have adopted the custom of fasting as a religious discipline, although it seems to have begun with the Jews and then later to have spread to the Christians. The New Testament asserts that Jesus, as well as His disciples, resorted to fasting from time to time.

In order to gain a little more insight on the topic, I looked these verses up in volume three of *The Seventh-day Adventist Bible Commentary*. There I found this explanation: "Fasting was usually symbolic of repentance, and often accompanied a disaster that had occurred or was expected. In this case, however, it was held in connection with prayer for a safe journey" (*The SDA Bible Commentary*, vol. 3, p. 377). Apparently, the route from Babylon to Jerusalem passed through long stretches of dangerous wilderness, and many of the men selected to accompany Ezra had brought their families, including some little ones, who were not prone to travel quickly nor prepared to engage in war along the way. Given the great quantity of treasure they were carrying, Ezra realized the danger they were in as well as their need for divine protection.

He, of course, could have asked for protection from King Artaxerxes, but the ruler had already been exceedingly generous, and Ezra had so strongly emphasized to the king the power of the true God that now, as they were starting out for Jerusalem, he knew his best course was to entreat that same all-powerful God for a merciful journey rather than any earthly monarch. His first step was to declare a fast among the travelers. This gave them a time to humble themselves before God and search their lives to remove any known sin before moving forward. Ezra wanted to make sure there was nothing between the Lord and his people that might preclude His protection of them.

I especially like verse 23, where Ezra sums up what happened after that with this succinct declaration. "So we fasted and entreated our God for this, and He answered our prayer." It has made me reconsider the practice of fasting.

March 17

The Request

"Then the king said to me, 'What do you request?' So I prayed to the God of heaven. And I said to the king, 'If it pleases the king, and if your servant has found favor in your sight, I ask that you send me to Judah, to the city of my fathers' tombs, that I may rebuild it'" (Nehemiah 2:4, 5).

Thirteen years after Ezra's trip, in the twentieth year of king Artaxerxes' reign, another Israelite felt called to return to Jerusalem. This time it was Nehemiah, who was actually employed in the king's palace as a cup bearer at the time. The king knew him well. So one day, as he was going about his daily work, the king noticed that Nehemiah's usually cheerful countenance seemed troubled about something. When the king asked Nehemiah why he was so sad, at first he was a little surprised that the king was paying so much attention to his mood. But then, realizing this was his chance to ask the king for a favor, he quickly shot a prayer for wisdom up to the "God of heaven."

While Ezra had asked permission to go help rebuild the temple in Jerusalem, Nehemiah's wish was to rebuild the wall, along with some of the buildings that had been destroyed within the ancient sacred city way back when the Babylonians had first taken the Israelites captive. The fact that his ancestral city still lay in ruins was something he had been mourning over for days now, ever since receiving a recent negative report about the continued disastrous condition of Jerusalem. As a devout believer in the true God, he had made it a subject of fasting and prayer. Now, the king had given him an opening to make a special request, and he politely, yet boldly, announced to the king what it was that had become his passion. He needed the king's approval and blessing to go to Jerusalem and help restore the city, starting with the wall, which had previously surrounded and protected it from dangerous intruders and raiders.

It took both faith and courage to make this petition to the Persian monarch because if he became upset or displeased by Nehemiah's plea, he could immediately have him executed or imprisoned. When Nehemiah saw from the king's reaction that the Lord had softened his heart, and he didn't seem to oppose the idea, he took his request a bit further. He ventured to ask that the king give him letters for the governors in the lands through which he would need to travel authorizing his mission. Surprisingly, Artaxerxes not only agreed but this time he also provided captains of his army, along with horsemen, to help protect the caravan on its journey!

Thus, Nehemiah headed to Jerusalem to fulfill his real life's calling. Although he originally thought the task upon which he was about to embark might take him a couple of years, he actually spent the next twelve years supplying leadership and inspiration to the Jews living in and around Jerusalem, as they reconstructed the wall and other wasted parts of that historic city.

Leaders, who are charged by God to carry out a great work, would do well to follow Nehemiah's worthy example. Initially, upon hearing of the desolation in his homeland, he found out all he could about what needed to be done. Subsequently, he spent much time fasting and praying about the situation, as well as thinking about what the solution to the problem could look like. He asked what he himself might do to help. Then, when he saw the providence of God working in his favor, he didn't hesitate to courageously request what was needed for the task at hand. As the Lord opened the way, Nehemiah acted in a timely fashion. He stepped up to the challenge, and God blessed his faith, his work, and his commitment with success.

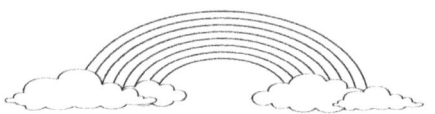

Set Hands

"Then I said to them, 'You see the distress that we are in, how Jerusalem lies waste, and its gates are burned with fire. Come and let us build the wall of Jerusalem, that we may no longer be a reproach.' And I told them of the hand of my God which had been good upon me, and also of the king's words that he had spoken to me. So they said, 'Let us rise up and build.' Then they set their hands to this good work" (Nehemiah 2:17, 18).

Once he arrived safely in Jerusalem, Nehemiah took several days to assess the situation and scope out the work that needed to be done. Only then did he gather the Jews in the area, including the priests, the nobles, and the officials, to speak to them about his intentions and encourage them to join him in the great task before them. Obviously, he was convincing because the people responded in the affirmative. Not only did they say, "Let us rise up and build," but the Bible tells us that they "set their hands to *this* good *work*," showing their level of commitment to rebuilding Jerusalem's wall.

And so the arduous work began! As usual, when a group of people set out to accomplish something worthwhile, there are detractors. In this case, Sanballat and Tobiah, governors of lands in the surrounding regions, were disturbed that Nehemiah had come to assist the Jews in strengthening Jerusalem. But the former cup bearer did not allow their taunting and scorn to dissuade him from his purpose. Boldly he declared, "The God of heaven Himself will prosper us; therefore we His servants will arise and build..." (verse 20).

The genius of the project was that each family unit set about to build a portion of the wall, taking ownership for that section.

Then, when their enemies threatened to stop the work by attacking them, each family also took responsibility for protecting their part of the wall. Several effective strategies were employed by the faithful workers so that their work would not be hindered. For a time, half of the people worked at construction while half carried weapons. Some others actually carried their weapons with them while they were building the wall! Then they worked in shifts so that someone could always be on guard against enemies, even at night, to allow the work to go on uninterrupted. Meanwhile, Nehemiah reminded the people that "Our God will fight for us," (Neh. 4:20) and encouraged them to keep building until the job was completed.

And the Lord did protect and bless this dedicated group of laborers, helping them finish the entire wall in just fifty-two days- less than two months! What a great reminder that perseverance and determination can help us accomplish seemingly impossible tasks when we faithfully "set our hands to the work" and follow God's leading one step at a time.

Recently, I was asked to head up a team of people who were charged with producing a school accreditation document in a time period of about three months. Usually this type of paperwork is started a year or more before an impending accreditation visit from the powers that be. Several folks in the group complained that they didn't even know how to get started, and even if they did, it would be impossible to complete the project on time. A few others suggested that maybe we should just give up before we started. We decided to take home the instructions we had been given, read them over, and meet a week later to decide what to do. As I read through the book that outlined the requirements for a thorough self-study of our overall school program, which would then guide the writing of our school improvement document, I became convinced that the task, though very labor intensive, was doable. As I thought and prayed about the project, an old Chinese proverb came to mind: "A journey of a thousand miles begins with a single step." That was the encouragement I needed to move forward.

When we met again, we divided the work up into sections (like Nehemiah's work crew), made a calendar of activities that would help us finish the project in a timely fashion, and committed to work hard together, one step at a time, for the next three months. We "set our hands" to reach our goal, and the Lord guided and prospered us, helping us produce a beautiful school improvement plan of which we could be proud! Not to mention the added blessing of the full accreditation status that we had been seeking!

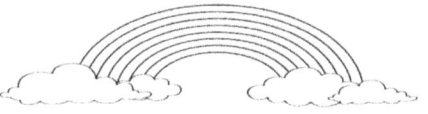

March 19

The Plot

"…Sanballat and Geshem sent to me, saying, 'Come, let us meet together among the villages in the plain of Ono.' But they thought to do me harm. So I sent messengers to them, saying, 'I am doing a great work, so that I cannot come down. Why should the work cease while I leave it and go down to you?'" (Nehemiah 6:2, 3).

Nehemiah's two strongest enemies during the whole time he was trying to accomplish his mission, Sanballat and Geshem, finally realized that they were not going to be successful in bringing the construction project to a halt by their threats of war. Thus, they decided to change their strategy, resulting in a plot to pretend they were friendly and just wanted to meet with him to talk about their concerns. Once he was separated from his Jewish brethren, they could both stop the work on the wall and eliminate the leader who was causing them such consternation.

Fortunately, however, Nehemiah was wise enough to see through their ill-intentioned plan, replying that he was too busy with his important work to set it aside in order to meet with them. But they did not give up easily. Four times they sent a messenger with the same seemingly benign invitation. Finally, they sent a letter accusing Nehemiah of treason, saying that he was trying to stir up a rebellion in Jerusalem and set himself up as a king. They threatened to send these false reports to the king of Babylon if Nehemiah did not come to "consult" with them. Seeing through their deceptive plans again, Nehemiah responded that their accusations were not true and that though they had hoped to scare the Israelites into discontinuing the work, it would go forward. In fact, Nehemiah was even more determined to finish the project, crying out *"O God, strengthen my hands"* (verse 9).

One would think that Nehemiah's enemies would give up trying to dissuade him from his mission, but they had one more trick up their sleeve. This time they hired a secret informer to declare a false prophecy that someone was coming to kill Nehemiah at night, so he should run and hide in the temple, closing the doors behind him. Several other false prophets repeated this prophecy

to Nehemiah in an effort to make him afraid. But the man of God stood firm, confident not only in who he was but also in the work God had called him to do. He exclaimed, "Should such a man as I flee?" (Neh. 6:11). His faith left no room for fear.

As the story ends, it is the enemies in the surrounding nations who become disheartened rather than Nehemiah and his co-workers. In fact, when the wall was completed in such a short period of time, even they had to admit that the work was finished because of the Israelites' God.

Have you ever set out to accomplish a seemingly impossible task, knowing that it could only be completed through God's wisdom and strength? Then as you are working through the details, you are challenged by one obstacle after another. Distractions abound, and it is tempting, on occasion, to become discouraged and just give up. But, finally, through faith and perseverance, the goal is reached! I have seen it over and over again, not only in my life but in the lives of those around me. Nehemiah's experience reminds us again of the glorious things God can do through us when we are wholly committed to His cause.

Strengthening Joy

"Then he said to them, 'Go your way, eat the fat, drink the sweet, and send portions to those for whom nothing is prepared; for this *day is holy to our Lord. Do not sorrow, for the joy of the LORD is your strength'"*
(Nehemiah 8:10).

After the wall of Jerusalem was rebuilt, Nehemiah was named its governor while his contemporary, Ezra, served as the priest and scribe. These two men of God decided it was now time to focus on rebuilding the spirituality of the people. Thus, they brought out the Law of God and read it aloud in the open square. The Levites, meanwhile, made sure the people understood what was being read. This chapter tells us that when the people heard the Law, they began to weep, understanding, some of them for the first time, how far they had strayed from the Lord's instructions.

Nehemiah, however, told the people to rejoice for the blessing of being able to hear God's Law again, quipping the phrase found in today's verse: "The joy of the LORD is your strength." In fact, he suggested that the whole assembly should celebrate the ancient Feast of Tabernacles that they had read about there. So, for a whole week, the people participated in a kind of camp meeting assembly, living in booths made of tree branches, confessing their sins, and seeking to draw close to the Lord again. The Bible tells us that there "was very great gladness" (verse 17) among the people during this time. Now, as then, getting ourselves right with God produces joy. Receiving His mercy and grace gives us a clean slate.

Whenever I hear the phrase "the joy of the LORD is your strength," I can't help remembering past youth retreats and summer camps where we sang out these words in a short chorus that someone had the wisdom to create. I still find myself humming the catchy little tune from time to time. It encourages me.

In any discussion about joy, I always remember my father's cheerful influence. I can still hear his joyful greeting as he woke us up in the morning, saying, "Rise and shine!" Then he would make his way from one window to another to open all the blinds, while singing, "Let the blessed sunlight in!" He was always singing, humming, or whistling a hymn, so we knew that he was coming home when he was still a block away. While shaving, waiting in line, or riding in a car, he invested his extra minutes in memorizing a verse of Scripture, which he would use to encourage someone who crossed his path here and there along the way. He smiled so much that people would actually ask him why he was so happy, to which he would reply, "Because God loves me!"

To what do I attribute his exuberant joy? Was his life easier or did he have fewer trials and tribulations than other people? No. In fact, he served as a medic in both World War II and the Korean War, so I realize now, as an adult, that during the twelve years he served in the military, he must have both seen and been involved in horrific experiences that only war can produce. He never shared any of those dark moments with us, choosing instead to focus on the positive things of life. There were many times through the years when he struggled financially, and later, he wrestled with a number of troubling health issues. But, as my brother, sister, and I were growing up, he made it a point to speak lovingly to us, showing us compassion when we needed it and encouraging us in all of our endeavors as my siblings and I made our way into adulthood.

Reflecting upon it now, I believe the secret to his nearly constant contentment was his hour-long daily devotional life. Being fortunate enough to have been his daughter, I can attest to the fact that, truly, the joy of the Lord was his strength!

March 21

Beauty Well Spent

"For if you remain completely silent at this time, relief and deliverance will arise for the Jews from another place, but you and your father's house will perish. Yet who knows whether you have come to the kingdom for such a time as this?" (Esther 4:14).

The most well-known part of the book of Esther, of course, is the story about her winning the king's beauty pageant. It is a rags-to-riches tale that quickly grabs our attention, as we watch Esther go from a young orphan who lost both of her parents at an early age to the queen of the Medes and the Persians, whose territory extended from Ethiopia in Africa to India in the east.

Fortunately, her older cousin, Mordecai, adopted her and raised her as if she were his own daughter, providing her with opportunities which otherwise she most probably would have missed. Providentially, she was just coming of age at the time that King Ahasuerus decided it was time to change the queen. Being both lovely and beautiful, as the Bible describes her, she immediately gained the favor of the king's servants. She was given extra beauty treatments while waiting to meet the king, as well as seven maidservants from the palace to help her prepare for the big day. When it finally arrived, Esther 2:17 tells us that "The king loved Esther more than all the *other* women, and she obtained grace and favor in his sight ... so he set the royal crown upon her head and made her queen...." If that wasn't enough, he called for a new holiday in all the provinces called the Feast of Esther. Talk about a whirlwind Cinderella story!

Meanwhile, however, Mordecai had learned of a threat against the king's life. Treason was in the air. He told Esther about the plot immediately so that she could warn the king directly. As soon as Ahasuerus found out, the traitors were executed, and the king owed a debt of gratitude to Esther and Mordecai. But we'll talk more about that part of the story in the coming days. Suffice it to say that because of Esther being in the right place with the right attitude at the right time, her people were saved. Of course, as Christians, we can trace God's hand working behind the scenes. It's amazing that when we lend our talents to the Lord, even the advantage of our good looks (if we have them), God can work wonders! It doesn't matter if we're young or old, male or female, good-looking or not (some of us have other gifts!), God has a place for us so that we can fulfill His purposes in the world. Even with the most meager of talents, we can bless those around us and bring glory to God.

I think it's important to note here the difference an attitude of service made. After enjoying the luxuries of the palace for a while, Esther could have decided not to risk losing the favor of the king, to simply relish her new role, and forget about the problems of her people. But in Mordecai's question about her coming to the kingdom "for *such* a time as this," she heard the call of God and knew what she had to do. First, however, she asked the Jews to fast and pray, along with her and her handmaidens, for three days. She realized that she was on God's mission and dared not go forward until she had received the courage and wisdom that only He could supply. As a result, she was successful in accomplishing her important role in God's work. Nothing is a feeling more satisfying than that! What is it that the Lord is calling you to do?

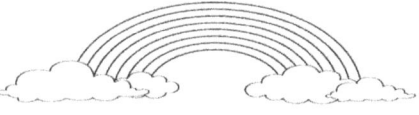

March 22

Poetic Justice

"So Haman came in, and the king asked him, 'What shall be done for the man whom the king delights to honor?' Now Haman thought in his heart, 'Whom would the king delight to honor more than me?' ...So Haman took the robe and the horse, arrayed Mordecai and led him on horseback through the city square, and proclaimed before him, 'Thus shall it be done to the man whom the king delights to honor'" (Esther 6:6, 11).

After Mordecai requested Queen Esther's help in saving the Jews, she developed a plan. First, she would invite the king and Haman, the king's second in command and the one who came up with the heinous plot to kill all the Jews within Ahasuerus' kingdom, to a banquet. They didn't yet know that she was Jewish or that she knew anything about Haman's murderous plans for the Jewish people. After garnering some rapport with the king and his guest, she would invite them for another banquet the next day when she would appeal to the king to save the Jews.

Meanwhile, Haman had been developing a strong hatred for Mordecai, who refused to stand before him to pay homage to his newly-acquired high position in the king's service. When he complained to his friends and family about this, they suggested Haman build a gallows on which to hang Mordecai. All this came to a head the day before the second banquet, so Haman determined to suggest to the king that very morning that Mordecai be hanged on the gallows he had made. The previous night, however, when the king was having trouble sleeping, his servants were summoned to read the book of the records of the chronicles to him, where he was reminded of his life being saved when Mordecai reported the treasonous plans of two of his doorkeepers. When the king asked what had been done to honor Mordecai, the answer was nothing.

It was just at this point that Haman showed up at the court, preparing to make his cruel petition to have Mordecai killed. Instead, the king brought him in and asked the question found in verse 6 above. What should the king do to show honor to someone with whom he was pleased? To this, the self-centered Haman thought the king was wanting to honor him, so he came up with the elaborate plan of dressing the honored one in the king's robe, mounting him on the king's horse, and parading him throughout the city telling everyone how much the king honored the person. The king liked the plan so much that he immediately ordered Haman to carry it out—not for himself but for Mordecai!

The shocked and humiliated Haman could do nothing but carry out the king's orders. His plan to kill Mordecai had been turned totally on its head! As he was still mourning and complaining to his wife about the day's strange events, the king's servants came to quickly remind him of his appointment at the palace for the queen's second banquet. It was here that the king encouraged Esther to make her petition for whatever she wanted, up to half of the kingdom. This was her moment. Not only did she ask that her life and the life of her people be spared but she also revealed Haman as the instigator of the merciless plan. Upon receiving this news, the king became so angry that he arose and went to the garden. When he returned, Haman had fallen across the queen's couch to beg for his life, making the king think that he was attacking the queen right there in the palace. In his fury, when he was trying to decide what to do with Haman, one of his servants pointed to the gallows that Haman had made to hang Mordecai on, and the king commanded that Haman be hanged on it instead! Thus, poetic justice was served.

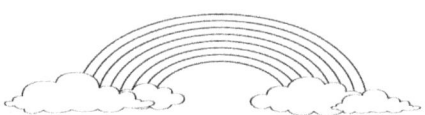

Purim

"The Jews established and imposed it upon themselves and their descendants and all who would join them, that without fail they should celebrate these two days every year, according to the written instructions and according to the prescribed time, that these days should be remembered and kept throughout every generation, every family, every province, and every city, that these days of Purim should not fail to be observed among the Jews, and that the memory of them should not perish among their descendants" (Esther 9:27, 28).

After the death of the wicked Haman, Esther realized her work was not finished if she was going to save her people. The decree to destroy the Jewish people on the thirteenth day of the twelfth month had already gone out to all 127 provinces of the kingdom of Ahasuerus. So, again, she threw herself at the king's feet, seeking his favor and mercy, and imploring him to revoke the letters that had gone out announcing the day of slaughter.

By this time, the king fully understood who Haman had been, who Esther was, and who he wanted Mordecai to be in his administration, despite the fact that both Esther and Mordecai were Jews. But the edict to destroy the Jews throughout his kingdom could not be altered, for whatever was written in the king's name and sealed with the king's signet ring could not be revoked. However, the king could issue another decree that would supersede the first one, essentially making it null and void. It was only the third month of the year, so there was still time to issue a new command and send it to all the people throughout his domain from India to Ethiopia. He assigned this clever task to Esther and Mordecai.

Calling in the scribes, they drafted a letter that allowed the Jewish people to rise up and defend themselves on the indicated day of slaughter. They were encouraged to "avenge themselves" against their enemies and even to plunder the possessions of anyone who tried to attack them (Esther 8:13). Then the mandate was sent under the name of the king and sealed with his signet ring so that it couldn't be changed. To make sure everyone understood that the Jewish people would be ready for war on the thirteenth day of the twelfth month, the edict was sent out in all the languages of the kingdom.

When the dreaded day arrived, the Jewish people were prepared to defend themselves wherever they lived in the kingdom. The other people in the lands where they lived feared them, and some even decided to become Jews themselves! The fighting went on a second day, but by the third day, Mordecai established a two-day holiday for all Jews throughout the kingdom. This holiday would be called Purim, to be celebrated in perpetuity for all the children of Israel. It would be celebrated yearly on the fourteenth and fifteenth days of the month of Adar and would become a time of feasting and joy as well as a time when the Jewish people would send gifts to one another and to the poor. And, as we know, this holiday is still celebrated today.

All of this took place because of the courage and faithfulness of one orphaned young woman, who believed that God had raised her from obscurity to the throne of the kingdom for a special purpose at a specific time in the history of her people. The story of Queen Esther inspires us to believe that despite the difficult circumstances that surround us, God works to bring about good and blessings for His people.

March 24

Reactions to Adversity

"Then his wife said to him, 'Do you still hold fast to your integrity? Curse God and die!' But he said to her, 'You speak as one of the foolish women speaks. Shall we indeed accept good from God, and shall we not accept adversity?' In all this Job did not sin with his lips" (Job 2:9, 10).

How do we react when adversity falls upon us? Some of us read Job's famous story, and knowing that it ends on a positive note, we don't stop to consider the full impact of his suffering. He endured emotional, physical, relational, and spiritual pain in quick succession! In one day his wealth was wiped out: the oxen, donkeys, sheep, and camels, signs of wealth and status in his culture, were all taken from him. Just as he was dealing with these waves of bad news, another servant arrived to sadly announce the tragic death of all ten of his children—seven sons and three daughters—who had been feasting together when a strong wind came and destroyed the house where they were gathered, instantly killing them all!

Nevertheless, Job, although overwhelmed with sorrow and loss, did not curse God but fell to the ground and worshipped Him, saying, "Naked I came from my mother's womb, and naked shall I return there. The LORD gave, and the LORD has taken away; Blessed be the name of the LORD" (Job 1:21). What an incredible reaction to his sudden and inexplicable adversity!

Satan, however, was still not satisfied that Job would remain faithful to God regardless of what happened to him. Thus, Job was struck with terrible boils from head to foot. Then, to make matters even worse, he influenced Job's grieving wife to encourage him, not to maintain his faith in God, but to curse God and just give up and die! I'm sure that was probably how she, who had suffered these horrible tragedies along with Job, was feeling at the time. After all, her wealth and status had also been wiped out in a day, her husband had a loathsome condition and was sitting in an ash heap scraping his painful sores, and she had suffered the loss of all of her children in one fell swoop! I think that perhaps some of us, who are reading the story from a distance today, judge Job's wife too harshly. How would we have felt passing through the same horrible experiences? How do we respond now when even one terrible experience at a time suddenly hits our life? Common modern reactions to such things include anger, depression, and a loss of trust in God. It's a sobering thought that requires some reflection.

Job, though, amazingly enough, hung on to his faith, even when his three friends who showed up to comfort him actually discouraged him with their pompous and judgmental comments. Let's not overlook the point here: sometimes we also misjudge or discourage others with our inappropriate words and advice during their time of adversity. How important that we ask God for wisdom in these delicate circumstances to choose our words carefully, or simply share their burdens in silence, which is often the best comfort of all. I see our reactions to adversity as an indication of the depth of our relationship with God. I also believe that people process their grief in different ways and at different rates of speed, and it is not for me to judge how another deals with tragedy. May the Lord give us each the strength we need to maintain our trust in God, as Job did, even in the face of life's most difficult moments.

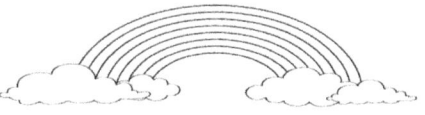

March 25

A Friend in Affliction

"To him who is afflicted, kindness should be shown by his friend, even though he forsakes the fear of the Almighty" (Job 6:14).

Unlike Job, many of us have strayed from God during times of affliction. I know I have. After a particularly painful divorce, I was mad at God. I ceased my daily devotional, which had been my custom since before academy days, and I eventually quit going to church for a couple of years. I kept asking why God would permit such a horrible thing to happen to me. To me, who up to that point had always maintained a trusting relationship with Him and was even planning on going to the mission field someday to serve Him! The age-old question of "Why do bad things happen to good people?" kept rattling around in my mind. I concluded that it was not fair! So why did God, who is all-powerful, allow such difficulties to assail and harass us?

One thing led to another, and eventually I had become a *bona fide* worldling. Fortunately, the Lord didn't give up on me. He gave me patient, caring parents, who prayed for me incessantly, good friends to encourage me, and a nearby church who was accepting of singles and provided activities for people who felt disenfranchised by unexpected life circumstances. Slowly I began to be less angry, as I realized that I still had a future that could be happy, perhaps even more happy, than before divorce had wreaked havoc on my life. As hope grew, I started to heal and even began to attend church again from time to time. After all, I still believed all the church doctrines, even though I initially felt like a misfit there. I was a woman without a country, so to speak. I didn't really belong in the world either. When I turned to it for comfort, I found only shallow answers and broken cisterns that didn't satisfy my spiritual needs or restore an existential purpose to my life.

Finally, I was re-baptized. I decided to start over with God and chose to trust Him, even though I still did not have all the answers about why things happen as they do. It dawned on me that as the universal great controversy plays out, part of living in a dominion of sin is that none of us is exempt from suffering. Even the totally innocent Jesus, who died to rescue us from Satan's grasp and save us eternally, was not treated "fairly" during His time on earth. So who was I to complain? I realized that many people have suffered unjustly in this world, many in worse ways than I, so it was time to quit "licking my wounds" and get on with a life worth living again! In the larger picture, my pain and problems will one day seem brief indeed, and when we finally get to heaven, Jesus Himself has promised to explain to us why things in our earthly life happened the way that they did, and how He was always working in the background to bless us. One of the best blessings I received was the friends the Lord gave me during that time, who accepted and loved me even while I was wandering in the world. So, I can relate to what Job is saying in today's verse. If you have friends or loved ones who have left the Lord and the church, don't criticize and condemn them, as Job's unfaithful friends did to him. Instead, pray for them, invite them to wholesome activities, demonstrate through your words and actions that the Lord still loves them. Then, stand back and observe how the Holy Spirit gently woos them back into the family of God!

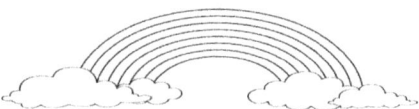

Silence is Wisdom

"Oh, that you would be silent, and it would be your wisdom!" (Job 13:5).

This pithy declaration was directed at Job's "friends," who were serving as his critics instead of encouraging him in his time of tribulation. He was grieved by their attitude, very prevalent in the culture of his day, that he must have done something terribly wrong in order to have lost his wealth, health, and family. Certainly, God must be judging him for some secret sin or blatant disobedience. Although Job knew he was not perfect, he also knew that he had been living a godly life and had not committed any wrongdoing that would have brought this destruction to him and his family. He had served God in prosperity and was determined to continue to serve Him in adversity. In fact, in Job 23:10–12, he asserts,

> But He knows the way that I take; *when* He has tested me, I shall come forth as gold. My foot has held fast to His steps; I have kept His way and not turned aside. I have not departed from the commandment of His lips; I have treasured the words of His mouth more than my necessary *food.*

So, although Job did not understand the cosmic reasons for his difficulties, he made a decision to trust God anyway. Later in this chapter we read the most significant passage in the whole book. Job declares, "Though He slay me, yet will I trust in Him" (Job 13:15). If only we could all exemplify that type of faith! From our own life experiences, however, we know that to say such a thing might be possible, but to live according to

it is extremely difficult. Job has set a very high bar. Of course, the Lord did know what was happening in Job's life, and He did know that Job would "come forth as gold," which is why He chose him to prove not only to Satan but to the whole on-looking universe that a life of faithfulness could be lived on this sinful planet, despite the trials and tribulations that God's people might experience during our tenure here.

Unfortunately, Job's friends, who thought they had all the answers, did not see or understand the larger picture of what was going on behind the scenes in the great controversy between good and evil. They didn't know that Job had actually been singled out to endure his problems because of his faithfulness, not as a result of his iniquity! As they continued to preach to him about his supposed faults, his painful journey was made more bitter, and he referred to them in this same chapter as "worthless physicians" (Job 13:4). Later he told them, "Your platitudes *are* proverbs of ashes" (Job 13:12).

So, what should Job's friends have said? As we discussed yesterday, sometimes just sitting with the person silently and letting him or her know we care for them is the best thing we can do. After all, unless we have walked in their shoes, none of us really understands another person's plight. I can reiterate this based on my own experience. One day when I was totally overwhelmed with grief due to the complications of my divorce, all I could do was lay on my bed and weep. My father, who was visiting at the time, in an effort to show solidarity, just sat silently by the side of my bed quietly praying. He had exhausted his words of comfort, but his mere presence helped me understand that he was sharing my burden of grief just by passing through it with me. It was a powerful experience I will never forget. It also continues to remind me that Jesus, our best friend, does the same, suffering right along beside us, bringing us comfort and strength to bear our difficulties just by token of His healing presence. I believe our goal as a friend to someone in need is to be more like Jesus. We need to do less talking and more listening, less bemoaning the situation and more praying. Less absent when they are suffering and more present, showing by our actions and mere presence that we care.

March 27

Words That Break

"Then Job answered and said: 'How long will you torment my soul, and break me in pieces with words?'" (Job 19:1, 2).

In this chapter, Job acknowledges that the words of his supposed friends have tormented his already suffering soul, and he laments the fact that their words have broken him in pieces. He also expresses his feelings that not only his friends but also his relatives have failed him. In verse 19, his tortured voice and spirit cry out, "All my close friends abhor me, and those whom I love have turned against me." At the time when Job needed them most, those on whom he should have been able to lean for moral support and to turn to for words of encouragement and hope were simply not there for him. In fact, instead of providing comfort and solace, they made matters worse by their harsh expressions of judgment and condemnation.

During my short tenure on earth, I have been the recipient of both words that break and words that heal. From my own experience I can vouch for the fact that words truly do matter, especially when uttered by people we love, respect, or look up to. Words that break are often delivered in a loud and angry manner, but they can also be spoken in a soft and serious tone, hitting their target directly in the core of a sore and aching heart. People my age can remember an old song that described this kind of event as someone "killing me softly" with his words.

Regardless of how they are delivered, words that break are generally not regarded as being as damaging as some catastrophic occurrence, but they have the power of being remembered over and over again, slowly eroding our courage, our perseverance, and any glimmer of hope for the future that we may be trying to cling to. I have seen the light of joy and excitement in the eyes of too many youngsters be extinguished by the harsh and discouraging words of a parent, a teacher, or a supposed mentor. I have witnessed a husband demean and destroy his wife's self-esteem, effectively crushing any tender plant of love that might be trying to grow between them, by his cruel and thoughtless outbursts thrown at her in public. I could go on, but unfortunately, all of us living in today's world have either heard or personally felt the sting of words that break and seen the trail of misery and tears left in their wake.

What Job really needed in his darkest hours were friends who, when they did speak, would share wise and carefully-chosen words of courage and comfort. Think of the times you've heard a mother comfort her baby with soft and loving words. Or a father encouraging his child to try a difficult task, like riding a bike, motivating him to keep trying until he was successful. How about a teacher, assuring a struggling student that she could learn to read or that a high schooler could reach his dream of becoming a doctor one day? Or a suitor whispering sweet nothings to the one he loves? Or a health professional speaking words of hope and healing to an ailing patient? Or a pastor pronouncing words of faith and blessing upon a parishioner?

What a different world it would be if we all determined to use our gift of speech, not to wound, break, and discourage like Job's misguided friends, but to comfort, heal, and encourage our family members, friends, students, employees, colleagues, and whoever else the Lord sees fit to bring across our path from day to day. Lord, please give us wisdom to speak in this way to people we know and love, especially during moments of adversity.

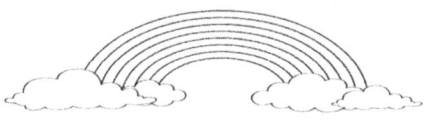

March 28

The Hope of Resurrection

"For I know that my Redeemer lives, and He shall stand at last on the earth; and after my skin is destroyed, this I know, that in my flesh I shall see God" (Job 19:25, 26).

Just after Job laments the fact that all of his friends and family have failed him in his greatest time of need, he bursts forth with this famous expression of faith in God and in the blessed hope he has in the resurrection. It's as if one is struggling to find their way through a dark tunnel, when suddenly, somebody turns the light on, and the way is made clear. In Job's case, the Holy Spirit seems to bring to mind a quick glimpse of a higher and wider perspective, where everything in this world is temporary, and soon, all suffering will come to an eternal end with the resurrection of those who trust in God.

In light of the resurrection, we, along with Job, can find glimmers of hope despite whatever we are going through in the moment. First, the simple acknowledgment that, at that grand event, justice will finally be served. God will make everything right in the universe, and we will finally have all our questions answered. Second, our bodies will be whole again and strengthened with the gift of immortality. Looking back from eternity, the problems we grappled with on earth will seem short-lived and small. Third, we will see our loved ones again. And finally, we shall actually meet our Lord face-to-face and live in the safety and joy of His presence throughout the ages to come.

No wonder, in verse 27, Job exclaims, "*How* my heart yearns within me!" For a few brief moments he is lifted to a higher plain, forgetting his present afflictions, and through the eyes of faith, he contemplates his future blessings!

I believe modern-day Christians can have a similar experience by focusing on God's promises, which are scattered generously throughout His Word. My belief in this is bolstered by the example of my father, who I have written about before. Permit me to give a brief recap to illustrate my point. Although not a man of means and afflicted with many problems throughout his lifetime, he was the happiest man I ever knew. He was frequently smiling or whistling a hymn wherever he went, spreading joy and dropping words of encouragement to those who were discouraged. When people asked him why he was so happy he would reply, "Because God loves me." Then he would quote one of the many promises from the Bible that he was always memorizing. While concentrating on the things of heaven, the things of earth seemed transitory and far less important.

This is a lesson I am still trying to learn. Even though it fosters more misery, it seems so much more natural to recite all the problems in life. Poor health, difficult people, bitter past experiences, financial difficulties, and fears for the future, all seem to command the greater part of our attention when we would be better served by focusing on the more positive aspects of our existence. This includes not only counting our blessings but also utilizing the gift of God's promises, which are designed to give us the courage and strength we need to navigate life's stormy waters. And, like Job, despite the difficulties we are experiencing now, we can and should maintain our faith in the resurrection with all its attendant blessings!

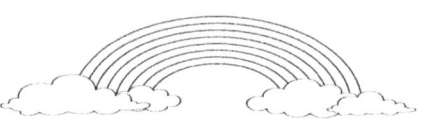

Hanging Earth

"He stretches out the north over empty space; He hangs the earth on nothing"
(Job 26:7).

After listening, without any real benefit, to what his ineffective friends had to say, Job begins to philosophize about humanity's frailty and God's majesty. In this chapter, Job contemplates God's amazing and inexplicable creative power. The very God he serves made the heavens and adorned them; He created the clouds, controls the waves of the sea, and whispers through the thunder! More than this, He created all life forms and "hangs the earth on nothing!" And these, exclaims Job, "*are* the mere edges of His ways" (verse 14)!

His unavoidable conclusion, then, was 'Who is humankind to question God?' (see Job 12). An inadequate yet somewhat useful illustration here would be to picture a flea, trying to question and analyze a person about what they are doing and why they are doing it. How can human beings, with their limited wisdom and understanding, even attempt to comprehend the Ruler of the universe, the Creator and Sustainer of the earth, the all-knowing and all-powerful Sovereign God? Having been privileged to experience a close relationship with this God, Job also knows that He is all-loving. And so, he comes to a turning point. He makes a conscience decision to trust this omnipotent Friend, even though he may never understand God's purposes for the difficulties that have occurred in his life while on this earth. In spite of everything, he steps out in faith, and re-affirms his commitment to the Lord with the declaration, "Though He slay me, yet will I trust Him" (Job 13:15). Wow! What impressive faith!

Of course, God knew all along that Job would prove to the watching universe that a human being could be faithful to Him, despite losing all blessings and possessions. In the great cosmic battle between good and evil, Job demonstrated that it was possible for a human being to love God, for Himself, not solely for the benefits that the person could accrue from such a relationship. It seems that even Job had an inkling, during the ordeal, that he would continue to trust in his God because that was the choice he had decided to make. In Job 23:10 he had predicted, "But He knows the way that I take; *when* He has tested me, I shall come forth as gold." Not only did this prophecy come to pass, but Job's shining influence still challenges and inspires us today.

I found that the experience of parenthood brought many spiritual insights into sharper focus. When my daughter was small, although we made sure to give her a host of positive experiences, there were many negative things that we withheld from her. Sometimes these were things that a number of other children her age were involved with. At times, we could easily explain why we wanted her to avoid certain activities or experiences, but other times we could not. At those times, we would simply say, "As your parents, we are trying to do what's best for you. You may not understand why we are saying 'no' now, but you'll have to trust us, and someday, when you become a parent, you will understand why." In the meantime, she just had to surrender to what we thought was best, loving and trusting us, until she became an adult and understood these things from a parent's perspective. In the meantime, our close relationship with her in the good times helped us to be able to maintain a healthy relationship with her in the more difficult times.

I think our relationship with God is like that. We don't understand everything here, but knowing that our all-wise heavenly Father loves us and ultimately wants what's best for us all, we should be willing to trust Him until, one day soon, we will see everything from God's perspective and be more than satisfied! In fact, in the New Testament, we are told that in the end, every knee will bow to the Lord (Phil. 2:9, 10), and everyone will proclaim, "Just and true *are* Your ways, o King of the saints!" (Rev. 15:3).

March 30

Restoration

"And the LORD restored Job's losses when he prayed for his friends. Indeed, the LORD gave Job twice as much as he had before" (Job 42:10).

After meditating on God's majesty for a while, Job was able to see his friends in a different light. Instead of resenting them for their condemnation and lack of support, he decided to pray for them. With this act, it was obvious to everyone watching in the universe, including God and Satan, that Job had passed the test of his loyalty and faithfulness to God with flying colors!

And so, we're told in today's verse that the Lord not only restored all that Job had lost but He actually gave him twice as much as he had before his ordeal. He regained his health, living an additional 140 years. He had more wealth, more status, more sheep, camels, oxen, and donkeys than before. He even had more children, and the Bible says he saw his grandchildren for four generations before he passed away!

Right about now I can hear somebody asking, "But how was that fair to Job's original children?" Fair. In this world of sin, we all have many experiences that are not fair. May I remind you again that even Jesus Himself, upon coming to earth to save us, was not treated fairly. However, and this comment is not made to make light of the question, we do know that, when Jesus comes again, He will bring justice with Him, and the things we saw only "through a glass, darkly" (1 Cor.

13:12, KJV) will then be clearly seen and understood from a much broader perspective than we can have now. When I grapple with this concept, I am always comforted by the fact that, because of the resurrection, we know Job will see his original children again and be able to live with them in a much more blissful existence throughout eternity!

Where does that leave us, then, at the end of Job's story? Do we just give a Pollyanna-like shrug, pretending his pain wasn't real or doesn't matter? Of course, it matters! It proved to the universe God's point about humanity's ability to continue trusting in Him through thick and thin, as well as convincing all who watched of the cruelty and injustice that sin brings in its wake.

Similarly, we could ask if the pain of Jesus mattered. We can answer with a resounding, "Yes!" Because through it, He provided for our salvation! The Bible even tells us that when He looked at the travail of His soul here on earth, He was satisfied, knowing it would bring "many sons to glory" (Heb. 2:10)! Though hard to believe now, even our current pain will be worth it, if we, like Job, remain faithful until the end. For we are assured that this "light affliction, which is but for a moment, is working for us a far more exceeding *and* eternal weight of glory" (2 Cor. 4:17). At times, this seems impossible, but Jesus has promised to walk with us through all of the phases of our life, including the darkest and most difficult ones. Not only that but He will more than restore all that we have lost in this life when we finally arrive in our heavenly home. Ellen White tells us that, looking back, all of our trials and tribulations on this earth will appear as insignificant, in comparison to the indescribable glories of the earth made new (see *Early Writings*, p. 67)!

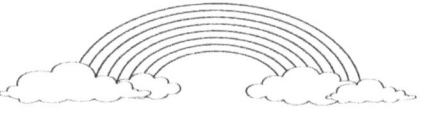

March 31

Gender Equality

"In all the land were found no women so beautiful as the daughters of Job; and their father gave them an inheritance among their brothers" (Job 42:15).

In this last chapter of the book of Job, we find more detailed information about his restoration, including this declaration: "Now the LORD blessed the latter *days* of Job more than his beginning" (verse 12). He had been rich before his adversity struck, but now he was doubly wealthy. He had so much that he wanted to make sure his children would each enjoy an abundant inheritance from him. This was not an unusual gesture on the part of men of means who were living in his day. What was unusual, however, was the fact that he made sure his three daughters, in addition to his seven sons, received their fair share of all that he possessed.

In many of the surrounding heathen cultures of that time, the worth of a woman was similar only to that of a slave. She herself was generally considered a possession to either her father or her husband. Her destiny was often tied to whichever man had authority over her at the time. But as Job passed through his ordeal, he had experienced a deeper conversion. One that taught him more about who God was, and he gained a clearer perspective of how God valued people. All people, including women. So, instead of overlooking his daughters, Job ignored the customs of those pagan societies all around him and made sure to give each of his daughters an equal share of his inheritance.

Whether Job had a vision or just a spiritual epiphany, in this chapter he says, "I have heard of You by the hearing of the ear, but now my eye sees You" (verse 5). Arguably, in "seeing" the Lord, he also saw more of God's character and was changed by the sight. He became more just, more fair, and more generous himself.

I have observed that the same thing often happens with people who have become acquainted with suffering of some kind today. They become more merciful and compassionate with others who are suffering. They develop more empathy for the sorrowing and can become more generous with those in need. At least for Christians, they focus more on what God would do for those in pain or adversity and less on what those around them would do—or fail to do.

Bringing it down to the personal level, after I have walked through several of my own dark valleys, it's as if the scales have fallen from my eyes, and I am suddenly aware of the many other people all around me who are also struggling with pain. It may not be caused by the same circumstances. So many factors make life difficult nowadays: illness, death, divorce, financial losses, broken relationships with friends and family members, job stresses, loneliness, addictions, etc. But having walked a little while in some of their shoes, I find I am more motivated to try to help alleviate their discomfort in some way. I know from my own experience that just seeing someone else who has traveled through a similar long, dark tunnel and come out successfully on the other side gave me courage and hope to keep going forward until I found the proverbial light at the end of it.

Thus, unbelievably perhaps, I have found three possibly good outcomes of suffering, depending on how we respond to it. 1) We can draw closer to God because we better realize our need for His help, and we know that He can understand us because He also suffered when He came to live on this earth. 2) Our characters can improve as our stony hearts become hearts of flesh because of our new understanding of what others are going through, and 3) We can become more compassionate and fairer in our interactions with others, especially those who have generally been marginalized by society, treating them with respect and equality, regardless of their race, religion, language, age, country of origin, or like Job, even their gender.

Look Up

"My voice You shall hear in the morning, O LORD; in the morning I will direct it to You, and I will look up" (Psalm 5:3).

I am so happy to be looking at the book of Psalms this month. It is the favorite of many Bible readers, including me, because of its many songs, poems, praises, and promises. It is a rich treasure house for fostering reflective thought, especially as we consider David's experience, who stumbled like us, yet he was a man after God's own heart because when he made mistakes, he repented and kept seeking a closer relationship with the Lord. Although it will be difficult, I am going to try to limit myself to discussing only twenty of the marvelous texts found in Psalms before continuing my journey through the rest of the Bible this year.

As humans, sometimes we wake up cheerful and excited to begin the activities of a new day, and other times, at first consciousness, we feel grumpy, and all we want to do is pull the covers back over our head and not even think about getting out of bed. Who hasn't heard the term, "He got up on the wrong side of the bed this morning"? It happens to all of us on occasion. Sometimes because we've suffered through a restless night, and other times because after waking up from a bad dream, it takes us a few minutes to shake it off and come back to reality. In any event, I've found that starting the day with some devotional time when I first wake up centers me. It dispels any bad mood and helps me to focus on who I am (God's child) and what I should be doing on a given day (trying to align with God's will). In other words, looking up to God in the morning helps me not to look down at my problems. It carries me to a higher plane where I can look at life's difficulties from heaven's perspective, which brings me peace and joy. But I must make the choice, every day, to dedicate my first few minutes to this purpose.

On those glorious mornings, like what David refers to here, when all seems bright and fair, those of us who are Christians can hardly contain our expressions of thanksgiving and praise to God. In my own experience, however, I've discovered there are several things that have enhanced my morning meeting with God, making it even more meaningful. One is simply scheduling this time and making it a daily priority until it becomes a well-ingrained habit. Then, to me, the location matters, and I try to be where there will be as few distractions as possible. In the place where I generally have my morning worship, there is a large, lovely window, from which I can view the stately mountains, the bright blue sky above them, with a few wispy white clouds, and the trees in my back yard dancing to an occasional breeze. These sights remind me of the omnipotence of my Creator God, assure me that He is still in control, and inspire me to continue to trust Him with all the concerns of my life.

Another thing I've found helpful is to include several different components in my worship time. First, I thank and praise God for His blessings as well as for the day ahead. I then read a morning devotional book after which I study an adult Bible lesson. After that, I read at least a chapter a day from the Bible, and finally tackle my prayer list. This morning routine has been a blessing to me spiritually, and it helps to keep me "looking up" for the rest of the day.

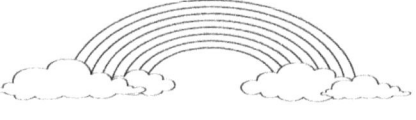

April 2

A Refuge in Troubled Times

"The LORD also will be a refuge for the oppressed, a refuge in times of trouble. And those who know Your name will put their trust in You; for You, LORD, have not forsaken those who seek You" (Psalm 9:9, 10).

Forsaken, abandoned, isolated, forgotten, left alone—feelings we've all had from time to time. Even as Christians, these feelings sometimes get the best of us. The problem is that when we're in the thick of something that is causing us pain, it's our tendency to focus on the situation, rather than to trust in God, who at times, can feel very far away from us. The times we feel least like looking at God's promises are the times we need to bathe ourselves in them the most in order to hang on until things get better.

When reflecting upon people of God who made it through tough times by choosing to find a refuge in the Lord, several names come to mind. In the Old Testament, there are a number of stellar examples. There was Noah, the last head of household who believed God's word, warning the entire antediluvian world about the coming flood, while the people of his day isolated and mocked him. Then, Joseph, my favorite, sitting abandoned in an Egyptian jail for a crime he didn't commit. Daniel, thrown alone into the lion's den because of praying openly to his God. And the minor prophets, often feeling ignored, rejected, and mistreated by the very societies with whom they were trying to share God's messages. David himself knew what it was to be oppressed, when, as a young man, he had to flee to the wilderness in order to escape the insane wrath and jealousy of King Saul. Albeit, this very experience is what taught him that God could be trusted to be a refuge in times of trouble.

In the New Testament, besides Jesus Himself making God His refuge in every fearsome trial and tribulation, there was John the Baptist, languishing in a prison while Jesus had begun His miraculous ministry. Later, Stephen, Peter, and Paul, all who courageously preached the gospel wherever they went had to learn to trust in the Lord, making Him their strength and refuge throughout the difficult and dangerous times of their lives. Sometimes their lives were spared, sometimes not, but they are all guaranteed eternal life.

We even have some modern-era heroes, who made God their refuge when under the pressure of terrible circumstances. I think of Desmond Doss, the World War II medic I've mentioned previously, who asked for God's shelter as he selflessly saved many other soldiers during an exceptionally bloody battle. And Corrie ten Boom, a young Christian girl, who was assigned to a Nazi concentration camp for helping her family shelter Jews during Hitler's reign of terror. She penned the words that the Lord was her "hiding place" throughout her ordeal. I also think of leaders in their widely different fields, like Abraham Lincoln and Ellen G. White, who must have often felt alone when struggling under their great responsibilities and facing the criticism heaped upon them by their detractors. Both had to seek refuge from the Lord in order to carry out their work. And so should we.

Only the Lord knows how much time we have left on this earth to finish the tasks He has assigned us. But we can only do them well by asking Him to be our Refuge, the Source of our strength, fortitude, and peace, trusting Him to shelter and walk beside us, even when we don't feel Him there and rejoicing in His presence when we do, until the purposes of our lives are fulfilled.

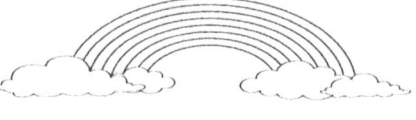

April 3

Wait

"Wait on the LORD; be of good courage, and He shall strengthen your heart; wait, I say, on the LORD!" (Psalm 27:14).

Almost everyone hates waiting for something, whether it's in a grocery store checkout line, at the doctor's office, or "holding" on the telephone. Most of us have a story to tell about something we've had to wait for that really tried our patience. Depending on our life stage, we have to wait for school to be out for the summer, wait to get our driver's license, wait for a college admittance letter, wait to get married, wait for a child to be born, wait to hear if we got the job we interviewed for, wait to receive a medical diagnosis, wait to see if we were granted the mortgage loan for that house we wanted, wait for a special phone call from someone we love, or wait to be eligible for retirement. The list goes on and on. Many of these "wait times" make us anxious or irritated. But some things are easier to wait for because we expect the final result will be pleasant or fulfilling, like, for example, having a baby. Similarly, waiting on the Lord should be one of our most enjoyable and productive times.

As humans, however, even waiting on the Lord can be difficult for us. First, because patience is often not a well-developed fruit of the Spirit since it goes against the grain of our carnal natures, and second, because it implies a surrender to God's will for our lives. Instead of making decisions on our own and rushing into situations we think we can handle with our own wisdom and strength, waiting on the Lord involves laying our plans before the Lord and then watching and listening for His guidance on a given matter.

It's a type of spiritual discipline that David has experienced for himself, and He can attest to the fact that it brings positive results. Thus, in this powerful declaration, David suggests that others develop the life-changing habit of waiting on the Lord. While we're waiting, we often overlook the next suggestion in this verse, which is to "be of good courage." To me, this simple phrase implies that, after we have presented our question or issue to the Lord, we should quit worrying about it, knowing that it is in the Lord's hands and maintain our faith that He will do what is best. Then comes the promise in the center of this verse: "He shall strengthen your heart." If we are truly waiting and depending on Him, He will banish all fear, doubt, weakness, and feelings of inadequacy, empowering us to move forward to accomplish His will in our lives.

So now to the crux of the matter. How do we develop this habit that will give us fewer headaches, less ulcers, reduced stress, and more serenity and surety in our Christian walk? We need to carve time out of our daily schedules to spend with the Lord. Reading His Word, praying about the specific concerns, small or large, and seeking to maintain a connection with Him throughout the day will help us get closer to Him so that we will better discern His voice speaking to our souls and be enabled to more closely follow His guidance. In a day of fast food, instant breakfast, speed dating, and Quik Stop markets, asking people to intentionally dedicate a daily, unhurried period of time to waiting on the Lord is a tall order, but it's one that David assures us will be worth the wait!

April 4

Morning Joy

"Weeping may endure for a night, but joy comes in the morning" (Psalm 30:5b).

There are so many precious promises and glorious passages here in the thick of the book of Psalms that I had trouble choosing which ones to reflect upon. This text, however, jumped out at me. I had already marked it during some previous reading when I had needed the hope and comfort that it provides. Today, though, it demands comment since it serves as a reminder of God's power and grace to save me from dark places in my life where I couldn't see any light at the end of the tunnel. I believe this assertion can be appreciated as a testimony of what the Lord has done for me in the past as well as providing assurance for the present and bright hope for the future.

There were at least two times in the past when I had felt hopeless and as if there was no future for me—no reason to go on. All I could see was hurt, despair, grief, and discouragement. I cried until it seemed there were no tears left to shed. I groaned and moaned and complained to the Lord about what I was going through, even though, at those two specific times, I felt quite distant from Him. I lost my appetite for both food and life, in general. It was difficult to put one foot in front of the other. A Christian counselor helped me through the first dark episode by encouraging me to focus on living just one day at a time. As I've mentioned before in this book, my friends and family encouraged and supported me, helping me pass through the second period of crisis, and finally heal enough to start seeing things in a more positive light again.

Even though life had not gone the way I planned, I began to see another way forward. The little pinhole of light at the tunnel's end began to get brighter and brighter until one day I found myself stepping out into the full and resplendent sunshine! Life was worth living. I could still live a purpose-filled life that would make a difference in the world. In fact, now I had a new bag of tools I could use to turn around and help other people who were going through something similar. Just seeing that someone else had survived having their life torn apart by unexpected circumstances, and was now happy again, often served to reignite their hope that life would eventually get better for them, too.

Applying this verse to my present state of existence gives me a calm assurance that just as the Lord has turned my sorrow into joy in the past, He will be able to do it again as I trust in Him in the future. Also, I have a broader perspective now, realizing that my earthly troubles are fleeting. Like everything else in this world, they are only temporary. Darkness and light, sorrow and joy, come and go throughout the seasons of our seven or eight decades here.

Contemplating this text as it applies to us in the future, it becomes a promise of a joy-filled eternal life once our years of struggle and strife on this sin-dominated planet are over. As Christians, the sorrow of every funeral is mitigated by our blessed hope in the resurrection. We know that one day soon our Redeemer will wipe away all tears from our eyes, and our morning will be the new dawn of a blissful eternity in a place where we will never have to experience disappointment, pain, sorrow, sickness, despair, or death ever again! So, with David we can proclaim, "Weeping may endure for a night, but joy *comes* in the morning." Praise the Lord!

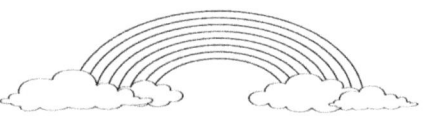

My Times

"But as for me, I trust in You, O Lord; I say, 'You are my God.' My times are in Your hand; deliver me from the hand of my enemies, and from those who persecute me" (Psalm 31:14, 15).

I first marked this passage in my Bible at a time when I was struggling about leaving the job I was at and moving to another more challenging one. As with every decision, there were both pros and cons to consider. Finally, when I was almost driven to distraction with the arguments going on in my head, I came upon this verse which simply assured me, "My times *are* in Your hand." With a sigh of relief, I turned the whole thing over to the Lord, saying, "Lord, You know what is best. Please work through circumstances to indicate to me which way I should go because only You know what the future holds, and You know what's the best road for me to take." With surrender to His will, whatever it was, I found peace.

Since then, I have been blessed to turn to the comfort and assurance brought by these verses on a number of sticky occasions. Not just for career-related decisions but also for personal, relational, and spiritual situations where I needed God's help and guidance throughout the various phases of my life.

We all experience ups and downs, good times and bad times, laughter and tears, times of exuberant faith and rough patches when our faith wears thin. We can also be wearied by stress or fighting illness, which saps our physical and mental strength. Sometimes, our unknown future overwhelms us with doubt and uncertainty. I'm sure that was as true for David, the author of this psalm, as it is for us today. Surely he felt even more desperate when King Saul was persecuting him, through no fault of his own, and chasing him down to destroy his life.

The antidote for his powerful and dark emotions can also be a source of centering and stabilizing us. He decided not only to trust his life into God's almighty hand but also to cry out for deliverance from his enemies and those who would destroy him completely if given the slightest opportunity. Although we don't think of it often, so preoccupied as we are with the daily rat race, and frequent conflicts with others at home, school, and work, we also have someone pursuing us and ready to destroy us wherever and whenever he can. The Bible tells us that "the devil walks about like a roaring lion, seeking whom he may devour" (1 Peter 5:8). And his evil angels are just as intent upon tripping us up and destroying us, as Saul's vicious army was determined to take away David's life and bright future.

How comforting then, to know that our loving heavenly Father, who is much stronger than any of our foes, material or spiritual, has "got our back," as the saying goes, and will provide those who ask Him with shelter, protection, and guidance during all the times of our life. Only He has the game plan, the resources, the tools, the foresight, and the wisdom, as well as the love and grace, to help us win not only the war (between good and evil) but also all the smaller battles along the way. We just need to keep focusing on staying surrendered and placing all of our times within His trustworthy hand.

A Broken Heart

"The LORD is near to those who have a broken heart, and saves such as have a contrite spirit. Many are the afflictions of the righteous, but the LORD delivers him out of them all" (Psalm 34:18, 19).

Have you ever had a broken heart? If so, you know that emotional pain can sometimes be even worse than physical pain. We are told that this was true for Jesus when He died on the cross because of the agony of being separated from His Heavenly Father. I'm sure the pain of rejection by many of those who He came to save was also excruciating.

A broken heart can sometimes come from circumstances such as a lost job, a destroyed dream, suffering from some kind of violence, or the death of a loved one. But generally, the cause is a relationship that has gone awry. The end of a romantic relationship, a divorce, a wayward child, a betrayal by a trusted friend, a forced separation from a soulmate, or even an unfair and unexpected character assassination in the workplace or the community, which can ultimately change the course of a life.

As mentioned by the verses above, we all go through many afflictions in life, but the first time I remember my heart really being broken is when my first husband left me, filed for a divorce, and started dating someone who I had previously considered a trusted friend. Fortunately, by this time, he had moved back to his home state, so at least I didn't have to run into the two of them when doing errands in my new place of residence. But that didn't keep me from wanting to take up the fetal position, roll under my bed where nobody would ever see me again,

and die. I really did think that, for all practical purposes, my life was over.

Even though the relationship had sometimes been rocky, and his harsh and angry words had often made me wince in pain, I hadn't considered divorce as an option since I didn't believe in it. Despite my beliefs, I now found myself a divorcee. I felt ashamed, as if I was wearing a big scarlet "D" on my blouse, making me a misfit in society. Since we had just moved, I didn't know my neighbors, I hadn't yet found a job, and I was embarrassed to go to church, feeling that everyone there would judge me as a bad person when they found out that I was divorced. (This was about forty years ago, when people talked less openly about being divorced than they do today, especially in religious circles.) Everywhere I went I felt incomplete, as if half of my body was missing. I slowly moved through all of the stages of grief. Denial, anger, guilt, sorrow, etc., etc. When I learned that he had been unfaithful to me all along, I also felt foolish. How could I have been so naïve? I found myself living in a reality I didn't want to accept for my life. However, I really didn't believe in suicide, so there was nothing for me to do but to force myself out of the house, keep putting one foot in front of the other, and just live through one painful day at a time.

Fortunately, the Lord led me to a Christian counselor who helped me see that I was not the only one who had ever suffered this kind of pain. He shared many examples of other people who had kept going until the pain subsided enough that they began to have hope again, and even began to live purposeful and fulfilling lives once they got to the end of their personal dark tunnels.

I believe it was about this time that I stumbled upon this verse. "The LORD *is* near to those who have a broken heart." It was like healing oil being poured onto a gaping wound or sparkling water poured over a thirsty soul who had walked many days through a dry and barren desert! It was my introduction to the presence of God in my life through the Holy Spirit—the Comforter. I believed in Him because I had heard of Him and studied Him as the third person of the Godhead all of my life. But now, in my time of need, I was blessed to experience Him. He became my companion, walking with me through my various stages of healing. Like many spiritual realities, it's hard to explain. I only know that since my first broken heart, He has become a comforting Friend and treasured Gift, making God's presence feel near to me whenever I claim this promise as I move through the unexpected and sometimes painful parts of life.

April 7

Delightful

"Trust in the LORD, and do good; dwell in the land, and feed on His faithfulness. Delight yourself also in the LORD, and He shall give you the desires of your heart" (Psalm 37:3, 4).

These verses are among my husband's favorite. He grew up on a poor ranch in the middle of Mexico with little likelihood of ever gaining a Christian education. After all, his parents had very little schooling, and he had three siblings to compete with for his share of the family's resources. They lived in a fairly remote location, and the nearest small primary school scheduled classes only during months of the year when the students weren't needed to help with planting or harvesting chores at home. Thus, his education was off to a rocky and somewhat limited start.

By the time the three older children were ready for secondary school, his parents had been able to move to a place near a Christian school with a more reliable schedule and a more robust curriculum. It was a boarding academy where many students lived in dorms on campus, going home only on long weekends and holidays. The students studied, worked, and worshiped at the school. My husband's father had found a job as manager of the school's farm, however, so they lived close enough that he and his siblings were able to save some money by living at home. It was my mother and father-in-law's dream that all of their children would get a good Christian education, so they prayed and worked hard until their dream came true. Eventually, all four of their children made it not only through secondary school but also through college! Such is the power of faith and parental visions!

Seeing the hard work and dedication of his parents on his behalf, my husband also made it his personal goal to finish his education, waiting to marry or become involved with any other distractions until after he had his master of divinity degree in hand. It took a great deal of discipline, determination, and the deferral of many things that others his age were enjoying. But during those years of sacrifice, the passage above encouraged him that if he continued serving the Lord and delighting in Him, eventually the Lord would grant him the desires of his heart. And so, he

finally started to do all the things that most young adults do sooner. He married, was privileged to have a beautiful and intelligent daughter, became a professional minister and counselor, and enjoyed the blessing of buying several homes over the years. Now, close to retirement, his testimony is that the Lord kept His promise, giving him the desires of his heart.

So what does it mean to delight ourselves in the Lord, which, according to these verses, is our part of the bargain? To me, it means staying close to Him through private and corporate worship, walking within His will to the best of our ability, serving Him and others through the wise use of all that He has given us, and finding joy in His presence, feeling grateful for all of the love and blessings He continually showers upon us. His promises are part of the blessings with which He has gifted us. Just claiming them and seeing how God fulfills them in our everyday lives over the years is one of the best ways I know of for Christians to become delightful—full of delight!

April 8

Fretting

"Cease from anger, and forsake wrath; do not fret—it only causes harm"
(Psalm 37:8).

T he little word "fret," which can be termed a more colloquial expression of the word "worry," is found a couple of times in this psalm. Here we are told not to fret because it only causes harm. Harm to whom? I can only surmise from the context that the harm is being done to the one who is fretting. In trying to identify several negative results fretting could cause to a worrier, I came up with this list: anxiety, insecurity, upset stomach, insomnia, erosion of faith, and loss of thankfulness and joy over current and past blessings. You might be able to come up with several additional negative effects of being a worrywart.

In any event, this general admonition not to worry is matched in this chapter with a more specific one in verse 7 that tells us, "Rest in the LORD, and wait patiently for Him; do not fret because of him who prospers in his way...." After this, a discussion ensues about the future of those who do evil, saying that they shall be "cut off" (verse 9). We are brought to a sense of justice when verse 10 says that in "yet a little while and the wicked *shall be no more.*" So, of all the things we find to worry about, we can cross the one about when justice will be meted out to the wicked off of our list. The Lord, when He sees the time is right, will take care of it. Mirroring that concern, we can also relax, knowing that the righteous will receive their reward from the Lord in due time. He promises, in verse 11, that the "meek shall inherit the earth, and shall delight themselves in the abundance of peace." Of course, this is only one place out of many in the Scriptures where we are told of the end of the wicked as well as the rewards that will be showered upon the just when Jesus comes again. In the meantime, we should do what we can to help maintain justice in the world in which we live today, where there is so much injustice. But we take hope and comfort from our knowledge that one day soon, Jesus, our righteous Judge, is going to make everything right. So, we don't have to lie awake at night worrying about it.

Nor should we worry about all of the other things that steal our peace and joy. There are so many of them: financial pressures, health issues, our work, our relationships, our children, our futures, in general. But thankfully, for the sake of our own health and well-being, the Lord has asked us to turn all of our burdens over to Him rather than waste time worrying about them. This does not imply that we become careless or irresponsible about the issues of life over which we have control. Just that we pray about each one and realize that the Lord will help us solve the problems we can; He will take care of the issues and difficulties that we can't solve ourselves. Sometimes, of course, this will try our faith and require us to be patient since God will take care of our worries on His time schedule rather than ours. But we know that, ultimately, He will take care of them in the best way possible.

In thinking about this topic, I can't help but quote the marvelous passage found in Philippians 4:6, 7: "Be anxious for nothing, but in everything, by prayer and supplication, with thanksgiving, let your requests be made known to God; and the peace of God, which surpasses all understanding, will guard your hearts and minds through Christ Jesus." So, quit worrying!

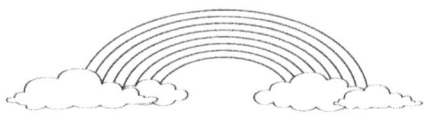

April 9

"Though He Fall..."

"The steps of a good man are ordered by the LORD, and He delights in his way. Though he fall, he shall not be utterly cast down; for the LORD upholds him with His hand" (Psalm 37:23, 24).

Whew! What a relief! Who of us, whether we've followed the Lord for just a short time or all of our life hasn't made a serious blunder here or there along the way? Sometimes, even though our initial intentions may be good, we do or say something that injures those around us. Other times, we become angry or headstrong and actually choose to abandon the Lord and His ways for whatever reason we rationalize as justifying our behavior in that situation. It is also possible, in the hectic world in which we live, to just slowly slide off the track because of business or carelessness.

The problem that I've been wrestling with lately falls into the first category. Being a strong extrovert, I sometimes blurt something out that, had I taken time to stop and reflect before opening my mouth, I would not have uttered. Later, when I think back on certain conversations, I ask myself why I used THAT word or even THAT tone or slipped into gossip gear or judgement mode. Then, I repent, and remembering that the Lord will forgive me, I claim this promise, asking that the Lord will uphold me with His hand and give me the wisdom to speak more judiciously in the future.

Of course, like most people, there have also been instances in the past where I was just plain angry with the injustices in the world, especially ones that collided with my life plan, and unhappy that God, the all-powerful One, didn't iron them all out

quickly in order to immediately reduce my suffering. As a result, there were times when I simply turned my back on Him and walked the other way. Fortunately, God was patient with me, and His Spirit continued to work in my life until, eventually, I found my way back to Him. Ultimately, we learn that the broken cisterns of the world can never satisfy our spiritual thirst like the Living Water of Jesus can, and because of God's grace, we know He will accept us with open arms when we return from our backslidden wanderings.

When it comes to the third way we go astray, I'm reminded of a story I read recently, where a generally decent young man, only about eighteen or nineteen, finished high school in his small town and then looked around for something interesting to do with his life. One day, when he was feeling a little bored, a friend suggested that they rob a bank, just for the fun of it. The excitement of the heist was exhilarating, so they robbed a couple of other banks. Soon, of course, their shenanigans came to an end, when they were caught and both sent to jail. When Jack (we'll call him) got out, he now had a record, making it harder for him to find a good job. Soon, he was hanging out with people who partied and did drugs, sliding into a deep addiction, which he found it almost impossible to shake. After wasting away his young adulthood, in and out of trouble, and strung out on the drugs he both hated and craved, He found the gospel, was helped by a Christian rehabilitation program, and found his purpose in working with other young adults who had made bad choices, simply out of carelessness or a lack of direction in their lives.

How glad we should be that, in whatever way we have fallen into sin or error, this passage encourages us that we do not need to be "utterly cast down," for the Lord has promised that when we turn to Him to help us get back on the right path, He will lift us up again with His own hand. We can come home again. We can get a second (or third or fourth) chance. We can start over. Praise the Lord for His mercy and grace!

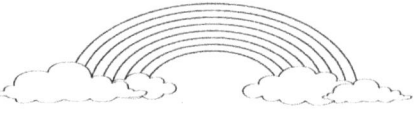

April 10

Old Age

"Do not cast me off in the time of old age; do not forsake me when my strength fails. …Now also when I am old and grayheaded, O God, do not forsake me, until I declare Your strength to this generation, Your power to everyone who is to come" (Psalm 71:9, 18).

These two verses fit together so well that I decided to cover them both at the same time in this devotional reflection. Now that David is aging and his strength waning, he feels his need of God's presence and strength in his life more than ever. It is interesting to note, however, that this is not just a selfish request. He has a critical purpose in mind. He is eager to make sure that he has infused his testimony and faith into not only those of the next generation but also to all his posterity to come. For David, writing songs and poems was one very important method he used in order to ensure his legacy. Here, he entreats the Lord to continue to assist him until his mission is completed.

As I age, I can relate. Our bodies aren't as strong physically as they used to be. (I now have to wear glasses to read, and family members are called upon to help me open jam jars and the like.) The ravages of wear and tear over time begin to take their toll. As our immune systems weaken, we are more prone to experience illness, and some body parts don't work as well as they used to. Our memories are not as sharp. (What was that person's name, again?) Emotionally, we may feel more sensitive or lonely. Or less able to tackle the many issues and stressors of life, as we did when we were young and more resilient.

Spiritually, however, I think that our golden years are a time when our relationship with the Lord can actually grow stronger. Why? Because as we become weaker, we can learn to depend more upon His strength. We have more time to pray for ourselves and others. We have fewer worldly distractions and can concentrate more on spiritual themes. And realizing the shortness of life, we can also now determine, as David did, to use the time we have left to complete our life purposes, making sure that our influence has a meaningful and eternal impact, not only on our children but on all those with whom we come in contact. It's a tall order, but when leaning on the Lord's strength, it is one that we can accomplish.

As a result, now that I'm retired, I find these verses very comforting in a way I didn't really appreciate before. They give me courage, knowing that as I finish out my days, the Lord will not forsake me or cast me off as useless. They tell me that He will still sustain me with His presence and that He still values me as a co-worker with Him.

This line of thought reminds me of two very special ladies my husband and I met several years ago when our church was involved with a nursing home ministry. One was named Beverly, and the other was named Thelma. Although Beverly was bedbound, she always gave us a sweet smile when we came to sing at her bedside. She knew all the old familiar hymns and often sang them along with us. Sharing a text and prayer with her before leaving each week was

as much a blessing for us as it was for her. She's gone now, finally succumbing to the ravages of her sickness, but we are confident that we will worship with her again someday soon in heaven.

Visiting Thelma was another blessing we will always cherish. Though in her nineties when she came to the nursing home, she asked the nurses to call the local church pastor to come and visit her. First, my husband went alone, spending time each Friday night having sundown worship with her. Hearing about her bright and outgoing personality, soon I and several other members of our congregation began to go and worship with her every Sabbath afternoon. My husband played his harmonica and guitar, and after sharing a brief thought, we would pray together. So many patients were attracted to the music that before we knew it, we had a dozen or so attendees at our little gatherings, and we had to meet in the long-term care center's dining room. Even the nurses would stop in to listen or sing a snippet of a song they knew from time to time. We became regular volunteers at the facility and were able to continue our ministry there for several years, all because of Thelma's beautiful witness to all those who came in contact with her, and because of her strong faith in the Lord, even as she approached the century mark. May we all be as faithful as Thelma, as the Lord carries us through our final years!

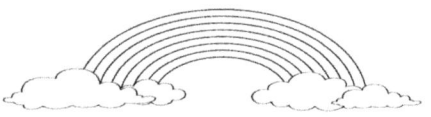

Numbering Our Days

"The days of our lives are seventy years; and if by reason of strength they are eighty years, yet their boast is only labor and sorrow; for it is soon cut off, and we fly away. So teach us to number our days, that we may gain a heart of wisdom" (Psalm 90:10, 12).

Some twenty chapters later than yesterday's comments about age, we see the Psalms returning to a theme related to aging, but in this instance, the clear emphasis is on how we spend the brief time we each have on this earth. My pastor husband likes taking the admonition to "number our days" literally. Whenever someone we know has a birthday, he finds out when that person was born and quickly does the math, so he can announce to them exactly how many days they have lived so far. We laugh, but it serves as both a shocking reminder of how quickly our lives have passed, and it is a wake-up call to use the days we have left more wisely.

Again, I must admit I have read these verses many times, skipping over them rather lightly, since they were obviously addressed to someone else—some elderly person who was on the brink of death. Not me, in the prime of life. However, now that I myself am approaching seventy years of age, they suddenly have more relevance. Seventy years? Perhaps eighty, if I follow a healthy lifestyle and don't develop some type of catastrophic illness. This calls for some serious reflection. What have I accomplished in the years of life? What's more, what do I want to do in whatever time is granted me in the few years to come? What have I left undone that definitely needs to go on my "bucket list?" The problem is, now that we are in our golden years, we sometimes don't have the

energy, health, financial resources, or even motivation to accomplish some of the goals we held as dear in our younger years.

This is why I have recently decided that these verses are also very appropriate for the younger set. Heeding the caution to choose carefully how their time is spent will lead to a far more productive and fulfilling life. When they come to the end of it and look back, despite all the vicissitudes and obstacles, they can enjoy a sense of gratitude and satisfaction that they have lived, as much as possible, within God's will. They will have "finished the course" knowing that they did their best to fulfill God's purposes for their lives in this world.

Unfortunately, those who do not know God often find themselves adrift in a sea of purposelessness, not understanding why they were born, why they are here, and where they are going when their seven or so decades of meaninglessness finally grind to a halt. How important, then, that we need to rescue these folks, giving them back a sense of self-worth, a purpose for living, and hope for the future before it is too late—too late for us to share and too late for them to hear and understand God's gracious invitation to all humanity.

Thus, it is never too early to become a co-worker with God to help others find Him, and as long as we have life and sufficient mental capacity, it is still not too late for us "old-timers" to join the rescue team, even in the last decades of our life. It will be time well spent. I think of my father-in-law, who had very little education and had never mastered English, still giving Bible studies to Spanish speakers in his community here in the USA, even into his seventies. I think of my own father, who though beset with pain and infirmities, continued to witness and be a prayer warrior for others until his death at age seventy-nine. And, of course, I think of the two wonderful Christian ladies I told you about yesterday, each in her own way, bringing light and blessing into the nursing home where they were confined until the last days of their lives.

On our next birthday, I think it would behoove each of us to actually number our days, as the text admonishes, "that we may gain a heart of wisdom."

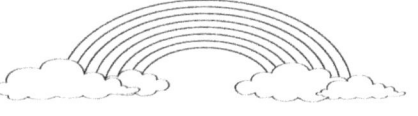

April 12

Shout Joyfully

"Oh come, let us sing to the LORD! Let us shout joyfully to the Rock of our salvation. Let us come before His presence with thanksgiving; let us shout joyfully to Him with psalms" (Psalm 95:1, 2).

The whole first half of Psalm 95 is an exuberant call to worship our Creator and the "Rock of our salvation" with our whole being. A study of the various activities outlined in the first seven verses tell us what that whole-hearted worship might entail. We are to sing, shout joyfully, come before His presence with thanksgiving, use psalms (which infers using His words as found in the Bible), exalt Him as the great King that He is, and worship and bow down, or kneel, "before the LORD our Maker" (verse 6). This would also be a time in which we acknowledge that we "*are* the people of His pasture, and the sheep of His hand" (verse 7). In other words, to recognize that the eternal Rock not only watches over us but tenderly cares for us as a shepherd watches over and cares for his sheep. No wonder we have something to shout joyfully about!

For many people, going to a religious service reminds them of going to a funeral. They imagine everybody being very silent and somber. Unfortunately, the services in some churches today do seem more like places that are dry and boring, with little fellowship or praise, as the stone-faced participants move through old and dusty rituals that don't seem to have much relevance in their everyday lives.

On the other hand, when people are invited to a sports event or a concert, they immediately think about the wonderful time they are going to have as well as the camaraderie with other fans who share their interest in the given activity. Joyful shouting is often something that occurs at these events, especially when a person's favorite team makes a score. I am reminded of the shouts of excitement that my husband makes when someone scores a goal in soccer or that my son-in-law elicits when his preferred baseball team hits a home run! I have often thought how wonderful it would be if worshipping the Lord could generate that same kind of joy and excitement in parishioners.

This begs the question of how to make our worship services more alive and exciting while still maintaining due reverence and appropriate decorum. As a pastor's wife, and a person who has attended various church services for most of my life, this is a topic to which I've given quite a bit of thought. Few discussions get more heated than those that center around preferred worship styles. This is particularly a sticky question when people from different cultural backgrounds, or differing generations, are involved. So many facets of worship come under scrutiny.

Everything from what kind of music should be played to how long the service should be. Then there is the order of service, who should and shouldn't be on the platform, and how should people dress when they come to church? The list goes on.

After living in a number of different cultures and participating in services with diverse worship styles, I have concluded that people don't have to all worship in the same manner. The Lord still loves us whether we pick up the offering at the beginning or the end of the worship service. Obviously, we need to be sensitive and respect others' worship preferences by not forcing them to worship God in the exact same way that we do. God's people should be creative enough to conduct varying types of services at a variety of times, in different places, and for different populations. Church services should facilitate people worshiping in ways that are meaningful to them, culturally, or generationally, just as long as the elements highlighted in Psalm 95 are included, and they are able to do so with their whole hearts with enthusiasm and joy!

April 13

Tender Mercies

"Bless the LORD, O my soul; and all that is within me, bless His holy name! Bless the LORD, O my soul, and forget not all His benefits: who forgives all your iniquities, who heals all your diseases, who redeems your life from destruction, who crowns you with lovingkindness and tender mercies" (Psalm 103:1–4).

This passage is so beautiful I couldn't help but include all four of the first verses of Psalm 103 in today's reflection. It starts us off with a list of some of the ways that the Lord faithfully showers us with lovingkindness and His tender mercies. The term "tender mercies" appears various places in the Scriptures, but I never paid much attention to it until I saw an old movie one evening that was entitled *Tender Mercies.* It was about a worldly man, around retirement age, who had a drinking problem and had finally hit rock bottom with regard to his career, his family, and his future. I don't want to ruin the end of the story for you, but suffice it to say that God's grace and mercy reached down into the depths of this man's despair and tenderly set him on his feet again with a whole new perspective and purpose in life. I thought the movie was aptly titled and was a good demonstration of how God's tender mercies, including His forgiveness, patience, mercy, and grace, can turn our lives around if we will only respond to His lovingkindness.

The phrase "forget not all His benefits" also draws my attention here because it is so easy to do just that. Life is so busy, and we face so many challenges from day to day, that it somehow seems easier to complain about things rather than recount God's blessings in our lives. Why is that the habit of complaining just makes our lives more dark and dismal while the habit of thanking and praising God makes them so much brighter and happier? Not only for ourselves but also for those who have to live with us!

Now that I'm retired and have a little more time for my daily devotions, I have picked one day a week where, instead of asking God for things, I just dedicate my prayer time to thanking and praising Him for all of the blessings He has poured out, and all of the prayers He has answered for me over the last seven days. What a difference it makes on my outlook! I've taken to calling that day "wonderful Wednesday." If I wait longer than a week, I find that it is easier to forget all of the little blessings He has strewn across my path. I also find that writing the good things down helps me to be able to review them from time to time, especially when I am tempted to think that God is not active in my life. This little exercise strengthens my faith and assures me that God is hearing and answering my prayers. It also gives me fresh content to use for praising God or when the Lord sends me to someone who needs a word of encouragement about His goodness.

After all, I believe the words, "Bless the Lord," as used in these verses, could actually be translated "Praise the Lord." It's something of which we do too little. But something the Lord takes pleasure in, whether it is done in private or in public. May the Lord teach us how to edify the church and the world through our praise to God for all of His tender mercies!

Say Something!

"Let the redeemed of the LORD say so, whom He has redeemed from the hand of the enemy... Oh, that men would give thanks to the LORD for His goodness, and for His wonderful works to the children of men!" (Psalm 107:2, 8).

Now we are on a roll. These verses fit right in with yesterday's devotional thought about the need to praise the Lord, only this time there is more emphasis on the aspect of thanksgiving. Think back over your recent conversations, even with Christians, and count how many times they have said, "Thank the Lord," or "Praise the Lord," or even its equivalent, "Hallelujah!" How many times in the last week or so have you yourself uttered them during your conversations with others? If you're like me, not nearly enough.

Here I'd like to quote verse 6 of this same chapter, which says, "Then they cried out to the LORD in their trouble, *and* He delivered them out of their distresses." As Christians, all of us have suffered some kind of pain, problem, or circumstance where we have fallen on our knees and begged earnestly for the Lord to come to our aid. When He does resolve the situation, do we also fall on our knees in gratitude and praise? Or do we forget all about our request that brought the Lord's intervention on our behalf? Or, worse yet, just chalk the resolution of the problem up to circumstance or coincidence, failing to thank Him altogether? Why are we so slow to give God the credit He deserves? If we asked an earthly friend for some huge favor, and he did it, how long would he continue to be our friend if we never showed him any gratitude? Yet our gracious God helps us over and over again throughout the course of our lives, sometimes in ways we won't even realize until they are revealed to us in eternity.

No wonder my father, always an advocate for learning Scripture by heart, required my siblings and I to memorize Psalm 107:2 in our youth. He wanted to make sure that we understood, from an early age, the importance of putting our praise and thanksgiving into words that would bring glory to our kind and faithful heavenly Benefactor. Instead of taking God's grace and goodness for granted, like an ungrateful child who is unmindful of the constant care and sacrifice of his or her parents, we need to say something!

Some of the arguments I've heard against verbally uttering words of praise is that it "might offend some people" or that "I live my praise, so I don't really need to speak it out loud." While both those objections might have some merit, and I agree that we need to use our words judiciously, I can't help but wonder what would have happened the night that Paul and Silas were singing songs of praise to God while they were being held in jail for witnessing about Jesus, if they had not voiced their praise? Would the jailer and his whole family have been baptized? In fact, would the gospel message have gone to the whole then-known world if the disciples had been timid about verbally sharing God's goodness and greatness? Perhaps we are too much influenced by the secular society around us, worrying more about what they will think than what the Lord is asking us to do. As far as living out our praise, that, of course, is an important part of our Christian duty, but I don't think it excuses us from also speaking words of thanksgiving and praise, as we are encouraged to do by today's verses.

I realize that for some people, especially the introverts among us, this might seem like a difficult task, especially if we have never done it before. But I'm sure we will be doing a lot of it in heaven, so there's no time to start practicing like the present. A good place to start is in church. Some churches I know include a "praise and prayer time" as part of their regular weekly worship service. What a great idea! Parishioners have

a chance during this time not only to ask for prayers from their Christian family but also to voice their thanksgiving and praise to the Lord for the blessings they have received from His hand over the last week.

Obviously, whenever we are going to verbally praise the Lord, we need to ask for His guidance and courage, as well as His wisdom, so that we will be able to "speak a word in season" for our listeners (see Isa. 50:4). But wherever we share our testimony of God's goodness through praise and thanksgiving, we can be assured of bringing glory to God as well as deepening our own faith and bolstering the faith of our hearers. So, let's speak up!

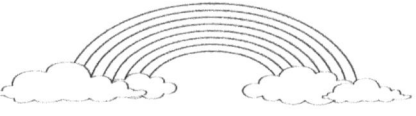

April 15

Turn Away

"Turn away my eyes from looking at worthless things, and revive me in Your way" (Psalm 119:37).

Casually reading along in this part of the Psalms recently, enjoying the verses about the excellencies of God's Word and our need to thank and praise Him, I was surprised when this verse jumped out at me and grabbed my attention. Immediately, I felt convicted about my TV watching. I do try to guard the gates of my mind by not watching anything too violent, sexually explicit, sinister, with a lot of objectionable language, or having to do with the occult, which, in this day and age, can be a challenge. But, as a

retired person, I now watch more TV than I used to, finding it helps to fill in the emotional void I sometimes feel by being at home without all the social interactions I enjoyed when surrounded by co-workers and friends out in the working world. So, now, I am making a more conscious effort to stick by my viewing standards in order to claim the last part of this verse, which states that if we turn away from seeing evil things with our eyes, then He will revive us in His way. And we all need revival, since it will bring us closer to the Lord.

I say this, knowing how difficult it is to only watch uplifting things, surrounded as we are by a very secular society with very low standards of decency for what is acceptable for viewing audiences to watch. Sometimes, even advertisements or newscasts are shocking in what they decide to broadcast. Since there often seem to be few, or woefully ineffective, filters in the entertainment industry, it falls to us to set up our own limits not only for ourselves but especially for any of the highly-impressionable children or youth living within the four walls of our residence.

Of course, this verse also admonishes us to turn away not just from "bad" content but from "worthless things" as well. I believe this significantly expands the circle of things that serious Christians will avoid, including R-rated movies, objectionable video games, and inappropriate internet (and social media) material. Nowadays, even many magazines or books should be excluded from our reading lists, if we are trying to grow in our Christian walk with the Lord.

So, the question arises, must we turn away from any type of visual entertainment? The answer, of course, is no. Fortunately, if we search, we can still find programs, movies, etc., that have a modicum of social value. Historical documentaries, biographies, musical presentations, and children's programs that are educational or that teach values and important life lessons are some that come to mind. And of course, to remain prepared, informed, and relevant, we will need to keep up with the news and weather forecasts. Naturally, each responsible adult has to choose the entertainment that they find acceptable for their own Christian home.

Televisions, like many other things (money, guitars, etc.), are not evil in themselves. It's how they are used that matters. One bright spot I see here is that today a number of Christians have become proactive in this regard, broadcasting Christian content, such as music, sermons, lifestyle tips, mission stories, Bible stories for children, and evangelistic meetings. They have taken visual media hardware, which has too often been used for detrimental purposes, and provided uplifting programming, which edifies the church while also blessing those who choose to tune in to these channels. Computer software has also been produced over the last couple of decades, including livestream and archived sermons, musical programs, and Bible study courses in many languages. It's as if the Lord, foreseeing how difficult it would be for us to turn our sight to good things in the last days, has risen creative people up with special talents, who could benefit us by providing healthy and spiritually-uplifting visual programming, to assist us in our quest to experience a revival of godliness. Now it's up to us, with the Lord's help, to make the right day-to-day choices regarding where to set our sights.

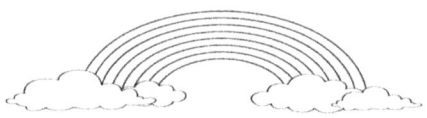

When I Awake

"How precious also are Your thoughts to me, O God! How great is the sum of them! If I should count them, they would be more in number than the sand; when I awake, I am still with You" (Psalm 139:17, 18).

What a precious and reassuring passage this is! Just to think that the Creator God, who made everything throughout the vast, limitless universe, thinks about me is more than I can wrap my head around! I recently saw a picture of our solar system, in which our planet seemed very small. Yet, as astronomers tell us, our solar system is just one among numberless others in a universe so massive that, as humans, we will never be able to discover its lengths, heights, and depths!

Not only does this all-powerful God think about me, this one little human being, among millions of others, but if I were to count the times He thinks of me, it would be "more in number than the sand!" It's incomprehensible! Unbelievable! But it's right there, in writing, in the middle of the Bible. So, as a Christian who believes that the Bible is the inspired Word of God, I have no choice but to believe it.

Growing up near the Pacific Ocean in Southern California, and later, serving as a professor at a college on the island of Puerto Rico, I have spent a great deal of time on beaches. As a result, I have had the opportunity to stroll across vast expanses of sand on many different beaches, and I can tell you that the sand on even one of them is far more than I could ever count! Since my lifespan will probably only be seventy or eighty years, this pretty much means that God is thinking about me all of the time!

The last part of verse 18 states, "when I awake, I am still with You." To me, this assures us that the Lord does not quit His vigilance over us, even when we are asleep. When we awake, as soon as we are conscious, we should realize that we are still under His watch care. He is immediately available to us. We don't have to make an appointment or stand in a long line somewhere in order to gain an audience with Him. No long wait, such as we are used to experiencing when wanting to talk with some earthly executive, is required. No formal attire or uniform is needed. We simply need to open our hearts to Him as our kind and generous heavenly Father. He is always ready to hear our concerns and petitions as well as our thanksgiving and praise! What a glorious God we serve!

There have been times when I have awakened from a dead sleep, after struggling my way through a bad dream, and I was in a foul mood, with negative thoughts still swirling around in my head. It was like my brain was left "with a bad taste in its mouth." But when I remember this text and choose to turn to the Lord, the negative thoughts flee away, like fog melting in the morning sun.

I have found that making it a habit to turn my first thoughts of the day to the Lord has made a real difference in my life. Having talked with Him about my concerns, He, the One who is thinking about me constantly, gives me peace. After sharing my petitions with Him, I start the day out with hope, knowing that He, who loves me so much, will grant what is best for me. Lastly, taking time to thank and praise God for the blessings He has already showered upon me gives me joy and confidence to face each new day, with the assurance that He, who has been my Helper and Sustainer in the past, will continue to guide and bless me all the remaining days of my life. I love waking up in the morning knowing that He is still with me and that I am still with Him!

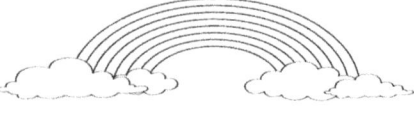

April 17

Happy People

"Happy are the people whose God is the LORD!" (Psalm 144:15b).

What a short and sweet declaration! It set me thinking about what benefits I have received that have brought me happiness as a result of my relationship with God. Upon reflection, I came up with at least four different categories of blessings that have brought me contentment as a Christian.

First, physical blessings. As a creationist, I believe one of the most wonderful gifts God gave us is our bodies. When I studied something in college about anatomy and physiology, I was truly in awe and amazement about how wonderfully the various miraculous systems of our body work and interact with each other so that we can function day by day. Realizing that God loved and designed us so that we could do all the things humans have accomplished in this world is truly awe-inspiring! Every Olympic season, people are able to push their bodies to break new physical records we previously thought were impossible, demonstrating how efficient and powerful a well-trained human body can be. Women (with the help of men) can also procreate and lactate, helping to bring precious children into existence. Every new baby, including my daughter, is an unfathomable miracle of life. I personally am happy that I can walk, talk, see, hear, touch, and feel things around me as well as smell and taste such a wide array of delicious foods that the Lord has provided. I'm thankful that I can think, plan, and achieve life goals, read, write, sing, create music, and utilize my free voluntary will as an individual. My body can heal and rejuvenate itself if I treat it with care. Understanding that all of these gifts are from the hand of our loving Lord makes me happy.

Emotional blessings that I appreciate include being able to feel the joy of belonging to the family of God. Sharing love, compassion, and even sorrow at someone else's loss. Feeling the sympathy and support of others when I suffer loss. Experiencing a kind of holy pride when my children or students accomplish something great. And the unbridled movement of my soul when I see a sudden rainbow, a magnificent snow-capped mountain range, a beautiful flower, or an incredibly colorful sunset! I feel happy that the Lord made me, not as an unfeeling robot or piece of machinery, like a cog in a wheel, but as a living, feeling human being made in His own image!

Social interactions from which I gain contentment are, of course, closely related to the fact that I am blessed with the emotions mentioned above. In this category, I find a kind of contented fulfillment in social engagement with my family, with old and new friends, with mentors and children, and with my brothers and sisters in the church. Even with random, interesting people I meet when I travel, take a class, or join some type of special-interest club in the community. Of course, those who are not Christians can also experience happiness from their social interactions, but believing that God is active in your life and that He guides your steps gives all of your relationships more meaning. It makes your life richer, giving you more joy and satisfaction, thus providing additional reasons to thank and praise the Lord, who is the Giver of every good gift we receive.

Finally, because of choosing to be one of God's people, I experience numerous spiritual blessings. Among them I count knowing I am forgiven for any mistakes I have made in the past and that the Lord has given me a clean slate and accepts me as His child. I also appreciate the ability to claim all the promises in the Bible as my own, giving me the strength and courage to face life's challenges as they come. The enjoyment of God's second book of nature, giving Him the glory for creating it all—including the autumn trees, the changing seasons, the forest waterfalls, and waves of the sea, as well as all the amazing animals the Lord has given to entertain us, for us to study and care for, and even to domesticate into loving pets. Every week, when I take a Sabbath rest, I thank the Lord for providing this time for worship, for communion with Him, for fellowship with other believers, and for rest and relaxation. It is a spiritual blessing that reduces anxiety and pressure, leaving me recharged for whatever lies ahead. My relationship with God makes me happy not only in all these ways but because He gives my life purpose in the present as well as a glorious hope for the future!

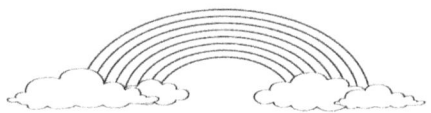

April 18

Near Us

"The LORD is near to all who call upon Him, to all who call upon Him in truth. He will fulfill the desire of those who fear Him; He also will hear their cry and save them" (Psalm 145:18, 19).

Recently I have been looking at our town's newspaper ads in order to get estimates on several home improvement projects. Whenever I see the words "Near You," I read the ad more carefully since I want to hire someone local. I want someone who knows our community and who our community knows and can vouch for in case I want to get a recommendation. Local businesspeople can usually get the job done sooner and often for a better price. Also, if the business is nearby, I feel like it's easier to call them back to check on something or to do another project for me in the future now that I've built up a relationship of trust with the individual.

In prayer, it's also important to build up a relationship of trust. The more we pray and the more we see God actively working in our lives, the more confidence we'll have to turn to Him again and again. Sometimes when we pray, we feel like God is far away and that our prayers aren't going any higher than the ceiling. When we feel that way, it's time to dust off this promise and realize that God is near to us when we pray and that He hears us and is working in the background on our behalf, even if we do not immediately see the answer to our prayers.

We need to exercise our faith, not depending on our feelings. It is human nature not to trust in things we cannot see or feel, and in the midst of difficult circumstances, we sometimes become overwhelmed with doubt. Here is where we need to claim today's promise for ourselves and ask God to increase our faith.

I remember being by my father's side shortly before he passed away. He had been placed in a hospice ward in a gray-walled veteran's facility, and he was in a pain-killer-induced state of semi-consciousness most of the time. I had traveled from another state on the other side of the country to spend a few days with him at the impending end of his life and to provide what moral support I could to the rest of the family. On what turned out to be his last night, as it got late, all the other visitors seemed to have left the vacuous building. I stayed on, feeling the sense of death in the austere room. Knowing that he had always been a man of prayer, and that these might be our last moments together, I was compelled to pray with him before I left, even though I found it hard to find the right words, and my prayer seemed very weak and inadequate in the face of such a dark and malicious enemy as death. It was as if evil forces were crowding in around us, making it difficult for me to form the simple words I finally uttered, leaning strongly on the faith my father had always taught me. Although I'm sure he would have been comforted by my last halting petition for God's peace and presence to surround him, I'm still not sure if he heard me, but because of the passage above, I know God did. In the middle of the night, several hours after I had left the hospital, the hospice nurse called to inform us that my father had passed away in his sleep. The pain and struggles of life were behind him. He was at peace. Looking back, I don't think I ever prayed such an ineloquent prayer in my life, but I believe that the Lord heard my cry and came near to us in our time of need, pushing away the shadows, filling the room with His comforting presence, and staying right by my father's bedside until the end.

April 19

Freedom

"Happy is he *who has the God of Jacob for his help, whose hope* is *in the LORD his God, who made heaven and earth, the sea, and all that* is *in them, who keeps truth forever, who executes justice for the oppressed, who gives food to the hungry. The LORD gives freedom to the prisoners"* (Psalm 146:5–7).

When I decided to retire a few years ago due to health issues, my husband, who is the same age, decided he was not ready to retire and searched for other ways to engage himself. He tried house painting and Uber driving for a while, but decided that neither of those jobs was really his calling. Eventually, he found work at a state prison as a substance abuse counselor, which he felt was right up his alley. He had done this kind of counseling before and enjoys interacting with the prisoners, trying to give them some perspective about the benefits of a substance-free life and encouraging them that there is still hope for them to live a better life in the future. Some people in prison give up on trying to change their lives, feeling that all hope is gone. They have reached the end of a purposeful existence, rejected by both God and humanity. Others resist any effort to change, choosing to go on in their rebellion, making themselves and everyone around them as miserable as possible. Thankfully, there is a third group. These are inmates who have hit rock bottom, so to speak, and know that it is time for them to begin making wiser decisions in order to salvage any time they have left on this earth. They choose to do whatever they can to turn their lives around and determine to become good, productive citizens upon their reentry into society. Whatever group they fall into, fortunately, we serve a God of forgiveness, second chances, power, and redemption!

The old adage, "Where there's life, there's hope," applies here. We have personally known a number of cases where ex-cons have totally changed the course of their lives after completing their sentences, some of whom have decided to dedicate their remaining days to helping other people who are struggling not to fall into the same pitfalls along the road that they themselves did. Those who become Christians, whether serving sentences short or long, or even for life, suddenly know the wonderful freedom that Jesus brings into their lives. Not only does He give them victory over drugs, alcohol, and other addictions but He also provides freedom from their guilt, anger, and fear of what the future will bring. What powerful testimonies they have to share about the power of God to break their chains of sin and captivity to evil thoughts and habits!

My own brother-in-law is an example of a person who has experienced this marvelous freedom that only God can give. We had been praying for him for years, but when he was finally arrested and sent to prison, we basically gave up on him. The Spirit of God, however, is not detained by prison walls, gates, and locks. It can permeate hearts wherever a soul chooses to reach out to Him. Sitting in jail, my brother-in-law did just that. He started attending Bible study class once a week, and it wasn't long before he gave his life to the Lord! Our feeble prayers had been answered, not immediately, but at the time that was best for him. He experienced God's mighty power and walked out of his cell a different man than the one who walked in. Praise God for the amazing freedom that only Christ can give!

April 20

The Outcasts

"The LORD builds up Jerusalem; He gathers together the outcasts of Israel. He heals the brokenhearted and binds up their wounds" (Psalm 147:2, 3).

Who are the outcasts today? The poor, the sick, the old, disabled people, the homeless, orphans, foreigners, anyone who looks or acts differently than the mainstream? Those of us who have never been marginalized find it hard to have compassion or understand the feelings of people who live on the periphery of society. This is why it is beneficial for us to step out of our comfort zones once in a while. Walking in someone else's shoes, so to speak, can give us insights we would never gain in any other way.

Growing up in the United States, in a white, protestant, lower middle-class family, I enjoyed all the rights and privileges that come from being a citizen of the strongest nation in the world. Although we often struggled financially to make ends meet, I only discovered how truly rich I was when I traveled to third world countries. During a year spent in Mexico in my early twenties, I felt for the first time what it means to be a "minority." I have a picture of me, the only blond, sitting in a sea of dark-haired people in a concert I attended in Mexico City. It made me somehow feel like I was "out of place." I didn't quite "fit in" with those around me. Then it began to dawn on me how various types of "minorities" might feel when they realize that they are different in some way than most of the people around them. Lacking a sense of belonging can make people feel like they need to build alliances by forming groups (churches, clubs, gangs, etc.) with those who are similar to them. Thus, many people attend churches where their language is spoken, live in communities where folks share familiar customs and culture, and support businesses where the owners look and act like them. After all, being an outsider is uncomfortable.

The picture these texts give us is one of the Lord gathering the outcasts together, welcoming all those who have been on the sidelines of life so that they all feel included, like they belong, like there's a place for them. They may have been ostracized for some reason in the past, but now they are accepted with open arms, given a seat at the table, and made part of the family—God's family.

Not only that but He gently binds up the wounds made by their previous rejection and heals the broken hearts caused by past cruelty, prejudice, and cold indifference. He did this as Jerusalem was being rebuilt in Old Testament times. He did it when He came to live, interact, and die as the Savior of all humankind as described in the New Testament. Think of how He treated the lepers, the woman at the well, the children, the woman caught in adultery, the Samaritans, the demoniacs, and many others. And He does it again in our day, as He continues to accept all those who come to Him, choosing Him as their personal Savior. Best of all, we have heaven to look forward to, where there will be no outcasts—just children of God, who are saved by grace, healed of their broken heartedness, and overjoyed by the endless and magnanimous blessings of fellowship and belonging they will experience throughout eternity!

April 21

Greedy

"So are the ways of everyone who is greedy for gain; it takes away the life of its owners" (Proverbs 1:19).

The book of Proverbs is so chock full of useful and pithy advice that I hate to start with a negative verse, but this one hit me right off the bat. It seems to me that a life well lived is all about finding balance. Often this means that priorities need to be set, and then a person can make informed decisions about what things they will trade in exchange for what other things at each stage of life in order to reach their goals.

Unfortunately, some people are only interested in reaching career or financial goals at the expense of everything else. They don't value other things, such as their family, their health, or their spiritual condition. All is sacrificed to the god of greed. We all know people like this, and perhaps, heaven forbid, we have even been such people. This points out the need to stay in close contact with the Lord throughout our lives in order to keep our priorities straight!

Today, when I hear the word greed, two people in particular come to mind. One was a young man who determined, above all else, to become a millionaire by the time he was thirty years old. Initially, he worked at several occupations until he found out that the real money-makers were dealing in drugs. He dedicated all of his time, effort, and talent to this endeavor—and he made lots of money. But along the way he lost his family, his reputation, his freedom (for a stint in jail), and even his health. He was so busy wheeling and dealing twenty-four seven that he didn't take time to sleep regular hours or eat properly, and by his forties, he started having heart issues. When he finally took time to go to the doctor, he was given only about six months to live. He had become rich but worked so hard he never had time to enjoy his profit. Now it was too late, and he discovered that he was truly poor in many other aspects of life.

The second man I think of was already older when I met him. I'll call him Mr. B. He was a friend of my father's, who would stop by to visit from time to time when he wasn't too busy with his real estate holdings. My father would talk to him about the Lord, but Mr. B never really had time to spend on devotional activities. He was always busy selling this property or buying that piece of land. Then, of course, he had to hire and fire the people who were managing these real estate holdings, make sure to find the right tenants, and meet regularly with his accountant to help him pay taxes on all that he owned. Eventually, he found himself embroiled in several lawsuits related to his holdings and was forced to secure the services of an attorney. With all this going on in his life, he had never found time to marry or have a family. He had so many irons in the fire, so to speak, that the stress started taking its toll on his health. He thought he owned properties, but in reality, the properties owned him. As he aged, he wasn't able to keep up with all the issues he was juggling. He eventually lost almost everything, dying a poor man in every sense of the word.

In this context, I can't help but think of other people I have known, who, while appearing to live an otherwise normal existence, and sometimes even claiming to be Christians, are still greedy in the little things of everyday life. By this I mean they are always overreaching and selfishly grasping for more, regardless of how it might harm or deprive those around them. You know, those folks who always have to be the first in line, always have to get the biggest piece of pie, constantly compete for the best seat, the highest position, the most money. They insist on winning every argument, always having the last word about any topic, and don't care whose feet they step on to get ahead. They are penny-pinching tightwads, not willing to share any of the blessings that have been showered upon them, and least of all, their money. Their greed destroys them as vessels for God's goodness to flow through to a hurting and needy world. And, more times than not, ultimately destroys their very souls. On this subject, we hear the words of Jesus in Matthew 16:26 echoing down through the ages, when He asks, "For what profit is it to a man if he gains the whole world, and loses his own soul? Or what will a man give in exchange for his soul?"

April 22

Do Good!

"Do not withhold good from those to whom it is due, when it is in the power of your hand to do so" (Proverbs 3:27).

Upon reading this text, I immediately thought of the famous quote by John Wesley, who said, "Do all the good you can, by all the means you can, in all the ways you can, in all the places you can, at all the times you can, to all the people you can, as long as ever you can."

What a comprehensive declaration of what a Christian's life should look like! The first time I heard this quote was from the lips of my father, who was an avid reader and often shared with us the thoughts of the great men he was reading about. Through the years, I may have heard it again a time or two from a teacher or preacher along the way. But the time it really settled into my soul was when I was chairing an education department at a Christian college here in the United States and was searching for a devotional thought to share with the faculty members with whom I worked. I had started in my new position just a few months earlier and was feeling quite optimistic and enthusiastic about all that we could accomplish together over the next few years with a mantra such as this!

To my surprise, when I eagerly presented John Wesley's famous quote as a motto for us to adopt and asked for the thoughts of my colleagues, one of the older, well-respected professors abruptly stated, "It sounds exhausting to me!" With that, the whole office climate changed, and the air went out of my optimistic bubble! I realized then and there that I, the new kid on the block, was in for an uphill battle in trying to instill enthusiasm in folks who were tired, burnt out, demoralized by years of toil and struggle and not about to take advice from some young, naïve whipper-snapper, who thought she had all the answers.

Despite the cool reception Wesley's assertion received that day, I still continue to regard it as a pretty good summary of how a dedicated Christian should live. Of course there will be times when we get tired of doing what's right, but the Lord has promised to walk beside us, giving us the strength we need for each day and for every task He asks us to accomplish in His name and for His sake. In Isaiah 40:31, we're assured, "But those who wait on the LORD shall renew *their* strength; they shall mount up with wings like eagles, they shall run and not be weary, they shall walk and not faint."

In fact, the Bible is replete with verses that advocate good works. The first one that comes to mind is Hebrews 10:24, which says, "And let us consider one another in order to stir up love and good works." Then there's 2 Thess. 2:16, 17: "Now may our Lord Jesus Christ Himself, and our God and Father, who has loved us and given *us* everlasting consolation and good hope by grace, comfort your hearts and establish you in every

good word and work." After He has established us in good works, He then wants us to maintain them, as this next verse found in Titus 3:8 makes clear: "This is a faithful saying, and these things I want you to affirm constantly, that those who have believed in God should be careful to maintain good works. These things are good and profitable to men." Finally, we are encouraged that our labors will not be in vain in Galatians 6:9, 10, which reaffirms a Christian's duty to do good whenever possible, as it states, "And let us not grow weary while doing good, for in due season we shall reap if we do not lose heart. Therefore, as we have opportunity, let us do good to all...."

What more clear admonition do we need? All that remains is to ask God for wisdom to know what good He would have us do in the world and to claim His promise for the strength to do it well!

April 23

Foolishness

"The way of a fool is right in his own eyes, but he who heeds counsel is wise" (Proverbs 12:15).

There it is—short and sweet. The admonition to seek counsel from others. For our own sake, really. To help us learn what we can from other people and make our decisions and actions wise ones. I got to thinking about all the areas of life

where it's helpful to get advice from others and came up with this initial list of ten. They range from simple to complex, but the order doesn't make any difference since I merely alphabetized them as a way of organizing my comments.

1. Addictions – My husband has been involved in substance abuse counseling for a number of years now, and he is always amused when people who are obviously hooked on alcohol or drugs claim that they don't have a problem. They are living in denial, which often blocks them from realizing their true condition. Only by seeking advice from an objective person, hopefully one who is specially-trained in this area, can they finally begin to understand how the given substance is destroying their lives and take steps to turn their lives around.

2. Appearance – Even in this seemingly simple area of life, the advice of others can often be quite helpful. However briefly, we should all take an objective look at ourselves in the mirror before going out the door. But there are times when we're not near a mirror and can be benefitted by the honest answer of a close friend to questions like: Is my slip showing? Do I have something stuck in my teeth? Is my tag sticking out?

3. Communication – Getting feedback on both our written and oral communication is very important, not only in our native language but especially in any foreign language in which we are trying to express ourselves. As missionaries, the members of our family often had to speak or write in our second language, which was like walking through a mine field of linguistic errors. We needed almost constant assistance from native speakers of Spanish in order to get our messages across without embarrassing ourselves or offending someone else. When we got too proud, thinking we didn't need the help of a native speaker, is when we made the most mistakes.

4. Cooking – I have learned that cooking is an art—one at which I'm not very talented. Since my husband and I like to open our home up to guests, however, it's something I continually strive to perfect. In this area, I can take all the advice I can get!

5. Crafting – Through the years I have had friends who are great with their hands. They sew, knit, crochet, draw, arrange flowers, along with many other creative activities. If I want to learn any of these things well, my best course is to ask one of these experts and then to follow their advice carefully.

6. Editing – No matter how much an author writes, it seems there's always something that can be improved with the help of an editor. We get so involved with the content of what we're writing that we sometimes make mechanical errors. We overlook a word that is misspelled here or a punctuation mark there. Or, we may need suggestions on how to make our ideas more clear or our writing more interesting. Only an injudicious person would try to write a book or article without having their work reviewed by an editor.

7. Marriage – Whew! This is a big one. How many miserable marriages might have been avoided if people would have sought wise counsel before tying the knot? Or even after marriage, what positive changes could have taken place if they had decided to go to a marriage counselor to help them work out their problems and preserve their family life?

8. Music – What wise musician doesn't seek expert advice from a professional in his or her field in order to make his or her performance better?

9. Raising children – What a challenging responsibility this is! Here we need to avail ourselves of all the wise counsel we can get—books, articles, counselors, teachers, pastors, relatives, more experienced parents, and, of course, the Bible.

10. Traveling – One of my pet peeves is to ride in a car with someone who refuses to ask for directions. Especially when the driver thinks he knows where he's going, but he doesn't have a clue. These same people often don't wish to consult a map or even use their GPS. In trying to seem wise on their own, they actually become foolish.

I'm sure you can think of other examples from daily life where it is important to ask for counsel. But, most important of all, of course, is to ask the Lord for counsel on how to live our lives here on earth so that they will be filled, not with foolishness, but with wisdom.

April 24

Friends

"The righteous should choose his friends carefully, for the way of the wicked leads them astray" (Proverbs 12:26).

This injunction to choose our friends carefully could not be stated more clearly. Anyone who has taught school at any level has seen many examples of otherwise "good" kids being led to misbehave or develop a negative attitude because of their friends. Unfortunately, the types of bad behavior seem to worsen with age. Although this phenomenon can actually happen at any age, it is especially prevalent when young people hit puberty and become teenagers. At this awkward stage of development there is a marked need to fit in with peers and to gain a sense of belonging by the acceptance of others who are about their age. As a result, many young people are first influenced to drink, use drugs, or become promiscuous due to their association with other youth who see these activities as not only acceptable but desirable in order to be accepted in the "in crowd." Some of these young people act out in order to gain attention while others tend to engage in generally unacceptable activities in order to manifest their rebellion against parents, teachers, authority figures, or even just the status quo.

One real danger here is that once an individual has started down the wrong road, it can be very difficult to completely change course later in life, especially once various addictions have them trapped in the sticky tendrils of dependency.

The prison where my husband works is filled with people who committed serious crimes either while they were under the influence of some addictive substance or simply because a "buddy" suggested the criminal activity, and in their moral immaturity or poor judgment, they joined in, doing things they would never have dreamed of doing when they were surrounded by better associates. Often the ringleaders paint an illegal act as exciting or "fun," focusing on what they can get away with as opposed to what is right or what the ultimate consequences might be. Of course, Satan exults when he can destroy the life of an individual, frustrate their potential, and negate not only the good this person might have accomplished in their life but also turn them into a recruiter for evil themselves, pulling others down into the depths of sin with them.

So, what's the answer? Do we become "helicopter parents," constantly hovering over our children, controlling their every move? We know of a pastor who has decided to cancel all youth activities in his church so that the young people will not be able to meet together and be a bad influence on each other. If we take this approach, how will our children survive when they have to face the difficulties of life without us? How will they learn to make correct choices on their own when we have orchestrated and controlled every aspect of their lives until they turned 18? Unfortunately, we know children who have grown up in these circumstances and who have bolted from their families and the church at their first chance of freedom.

Granted, it's very difficult to be parents these days and to wisely decide when to shelter our children and when to allow them to spread their wings, begin making their own choices, and deal with the resulting consequences. I don't believe that thwarting their natural desire to socialize with others their own age is the answer. Nor do I believe in letting teenagers go wherever they want with whomever they want without age-appropriate supervision. What I have seen work is to provide lots of engaging and interesting activities with their peers, together with adequate amounts of adult involvement and guidance. We also need to live lives that are good examples for them and pray for them without ceasing!

Even as adults, the question of who we adopt as our close friends can affect our lives for good or for evil. Should we eliminate social interaction with worldlings altogether in order to not become tainted by the ungodly all around us? How, then, could we fulfill our mission as Christians to preach the gospel in all the world, to break down the walls of division between us, and go out and seek the lost as Jesus did? Like most things in life, it's a fine balance. The way I see it, we need to be "social to save," yet we should reserve our closest friendships for those who believe as we do and will encourage us toward an ever-closer relationship with the Lord.

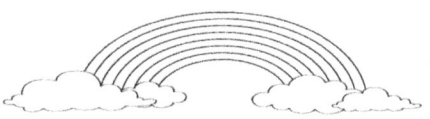

Discipline

"He who spares his rod hates his son, but he who loves him disciplines him promptly" (Proverbs 13:24).

Okay, now we've waded into deep water! This controversial text has been hotly debated on both sides for decades, with whole books being written to support one point of view or the other. I must admit that after becoming a mother and serving many years as an educator, I come down on the side of the need for fair and consistent discipline in the development of a happy, healthy, and well-rounded child, who will be a blessing in both the church and the world.

Obviously, as a mandated reporter for suspected child abuse, I have seen misguided parents who have taken the whole "rod" idea to an inappropriate and even tragic level. This verse is not talking about that kind of discipline. It is addressed to God-fearing parents, who love both the Lord and their children. It admonishes us of the importance of disciplining our children promptly before disrespect, rebellion, and bad habits get a foothold in their young lives. This advice is strongly supported by another important verse on discipline, found in Ecclesiastes 8:11, which states, "Because the sentence against an evil work is not executed speedily, therefore the heart of the sons of men is fully set in them to do evil."

I believe the words "promptly" and "speedily" in this context can be taken to mean not only early in life, as illustrated by the popular saying, "As the twig is bent, so grows the tree," but also the necessity of nipping an inappropriate attitude or action forming in a child's life in the bud. Over and over again, I have seen parents who simply ignore bad behavior, hoping it will just disappear by itself over time, to the detriment of both the child's character and the society in which he or she will become a citizen. Other parents are overly lenient, citing the excuse that, "They're too young to know what they're doing," or "They really don't know any better." If true, that is precisely the responsibility of the parents: to teach their children what is right and what is wrong. If we have brought children into this world, we should consider it our duty to teach, lovingly guide and mentor them, as well as to provide a good example for them to follow.

Unfortunately, schools today are teeming with children who have not been taught the difference between right and wrong before beginning their formal education. Thus, it is left to teachers, principals, and school counselors to try to accomplish this task after many bad habits have already become entrenched. In addition to academic subject matter, these children need to be taught how to take turns, how to wait in line, the importance of keeping their hands to themselves, the need to respect adults, words to avoid when talking with classmates, how to share, how to listen to others, ways to manage anger, the value of perseverance, how to work as a member of a team, and a host of other psycho-social skills that they have not learned at home. If students have not learned essential social skills and adopted important personal values by the time they have entered junior high or middle school, it is often too late to salvage them, barring a miracle at some time later in life, after they have squandered their youth, ruined their health, or damaged their families, failing to become the blessing to the world that God meant them to be.

One day, when I was calling a mother about the absence of her seventh-grade truant son, she responded, "What do you expect me to do about it? I can't control him!" Unfortunately, too many parents today are in this same boat. The child has been allowed to do as he or she pleased for so long, that now the parents have lost all their influence. They have to depend upon the schools to try and keep their wayward children in line. And when the schools are no longer able to manage the rebellious behavior, the penal system has to take over, all at a huge cost to our society.

Obviously, I am not naïve enough to suggest that providing fair, consistent, and loving discipline to children is an easy task. But I believe that if we ask for the Lord's wisdom and grace daily, doing the best we can with each child who has been entrusted to us, we can claim the beautiful promise on this subject in Proverbs 22:6: "Train up a child in the way he should go, and when he is old he will not depart from it."

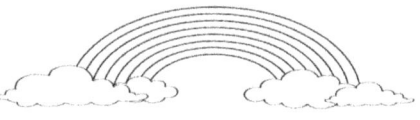

April 26

Keeping Watch

"The eyes of the LORD are in every place, keeping watch on the evil and the good" (Proverbs 15:3).

I really didn't think much about this verse until I heard Steve Green and a children's singing group doing it on one of his great CDs for kids. It's basically a collection of children's memory verses set to music. We bought it for our young daughter, and it was so delightful that we played it over and over again. Subsequently, all of us learned this special set of verses by heart in short order.

The part of the song we tried to emphasize, of course, was the fact that Jesus was watching over us all the time to protect us and guide us, even when we were not aware of His vigilance.

Recently, however, a friend brought up some horrible atrocity taking place in another part of the world and commented, "I don't see why God doesn't just wipe those evil people off the face of the earth immediately!" It set me to thinking. His query brought to mind two great existential questions that surface in our consciousness whenever we talk about the evil we see in the world all around us.

1) Why is there so much evil and suffering in the world? and
2) Why does an all-powerful God allow it to continue for so long?

You'll remember that these issues came up in a couple of earlier devotional thoughts, back when we were discussing the experience of Job. The short answers are:

1) We live in the midst of a great cosmic conflict between good and evil, where Christ and Satan are locked in a fierce battle to win over the hearts of all the created beings in the universe. Unfortunately, along the way there is some temporary collateral damage to the inhabitants of the earth. And, by the way, to Jesus Himself.
2) God continues to be patient with wayward human beings, not wishing that any should perish, but that all should come to repentance and gain eternal life (see 2 Peter 3:9)! He's providing as much time as possible for everyone to finally decide whether or not to claim His precious gift of redemption. However, He is keeping track of everything that evil people are doing so that fair judgment and justice can be served when this great spiritual war is finally over, and Jesus comes to this earth again to take us to a place not defaced by the awful stains of sin. On occasion, He does punish someone immediately, but usually He allows each of us another chance to follow Him. Meanwhile, it's our job to just keep trusting that God knows best.

The basic answers are easy to set forth in words, but they are much more difficult to wrap our heads around and make peace with in our own personal lives or the lives of those who are dear to us. Once we do, however, we can find our needed measure of peace, knowing that the Lord is keeping track of the evil deeds, as well as the good, and eventually there will be a day of final reckoning, where each person, good or bad, will be held accountable "according to their works" (Rev. 20:12). Our all-powerful God, after all, is also omniscient and omnipresent, so we can be assured that nothing that happens to us in this life escapes His loving and watchful record-keeping gaze.

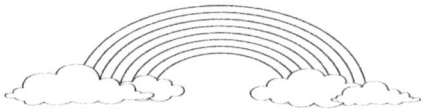

What's Better?

*"Better is a little with the fear of the LORD, than great treasure with trouble.
Better is a dinner of herbs where love is, than a fatted calf with hatred"
(Proverbs 15:16, 17).*

Solomon uses many different comparisons in his pithy proverbs. I find these two particularly impactful because they address two core values that should be present in the life of a true follower of the Lord.

First, in verse 16, he addresses the topic of riches. In the busyness of over working, over committing, and over achieving, it is easy to get our priorities mixed up and begin thinking like the world around us—that life is all about climbing the career ladder, making money, and buying the things everyone else has whether we need them or not. It's not that these things are sins in and of themselves, but if they distract us from developing our spiritual nature and cause us to lose our close relationship with God, we have paid too high a price for our worldly success. You will recall that we have discussed this topic in previous devotionals, and the same key text we quoted there is also applicable here: "For what profit is it to a man if he gains the whole world, and lose his own soul?" (Matt. 16:26)

Then, in verse 17, Solomon turns his attention to our relationships with others. He gives us a course correction, if we are focused more on what we're serving than with whom we're sharing a meal. Have you ever been to a Christmas celebration where hours and hours of time and boatloads of money were spent on brightly decorating the house, buying an overabundance of gifts, and preparing a variety of festive foods, only to see the inhabitants of the home fighting with each other throughout the whole holiday season? What's wrong with this picture? It's that the family has missed the whole point of Christmas, which is about Jesus coming to this earth to give us the real gifts we need to share with those around us—namely, love, joy, and peace.

Once I knew a couple who traveled quite a bit. Usually, they stayed in medium-priced hotels whether their trips were made for business or pleasure. On one occasion, however, they knew they were going to be near a world-class luxury hotel, at which they had always dreamed of staying because they had heard so much about it. Since they didn't know if they would ever be in that particular area again, they decided to splurge and booked a weekend at the magnificent property.

It offered amenities that even exceeded their expectations! The hotel itself was surrounded by a well-landscaped golf course and set at the top of a hill with a spectacular view of the nearby ocean. The rooms were large and well-appointed with spa-type tubs. Several sparkling swimming pools adorned the hotel grounds, and guests could choose to dine at five or six different specialty restaurants with exotic menus. The hotel lobby was beautiful and spacious, with walkways leading to many unique boutiques to explore. If all of that weren't enough, guests could choose from a number of exciting activities, including horseback riding along the beach, jet-skiing, and evening cruises. A more perfect location for lovers to spend an unforgettable weekend couldn't be imagined!

Unfortunately, the couple got into a spat over some little insignificant thing on their way to the dream destination, and despite their beautiful surroundings and the unusually large outlay of money for the excursion, they spent a horrible weekend fighting and barely speaking to each other! What a terrible waste of time and money! They would have had a much happier weekend, even in a modest hotel, had they invested more time in enriching their relationship! The moral of the story is, people who are in truly loving relationships enjoy a banquet regardless of when, where, or what meal they are joyously sharing together!

April 28

Discretion

"The discretion of a man makes him slow to anger, and his glory is to overlook a transgression" (Proverbs 19:11).

There are many texts in Proverbs about the subject of anger. Some say that a man who cannot control his temper "stirs up strife" and "abounds in transgression" (Prov. 29:22). Others say not to go with an angry man, lest you become like him (see Prov. 22:24, 25), or that a *"man of great wrath will suffer punishment"* (Prov. 19:19). Probably the most well-known text in Proverbs about anger is found in chapter 16, verse 32, which says, *"He who is slow to anger is better than the mighty, and he who rules his spirit than he who takes a city."* One of my favorites, however, is Proverbs 14:29: *"He who is slow to wrath has great understanding, but he who is impulsive exalts folly."* It seems to hit the nail right on the head!

So, why did I choose the text at the top of the page for reflection today? Because of the word "discretion." In looking up its meaning on the internet, I found several insightful definitions: the outward manifestation of wisdom; good judgement; taking everything into account before speaking or acting; and even the words "tactful" and "trustworthy." One explanation of the meaning described discretion as consideration of the social context in a given circumstance so as not to offend others. This elaboration of the term gave me a lot of food for thought.

How easy it is, as humans, to blurt out something in our anger without taking into consideration how our words will affect those around us. Not only the person to whom the words are addressed but any innocent bystanders (such as children) who may be close enough to suffer collateral damage. Once spoken, thoughtless, hurtful words cannot easily be taken back. Even if the perpetrator of the injury later apologizes, it may take a long time for the injured party to heal and often leaves an ugly scar on their heart. Angry actions are similar. Once you have murdered someone in a rage, even if you wanted to, you cannot bring that person back to life or make up for the suffering and painful feelings of loss you have inflicted on the lives of their family and friends. So many inmates in our prisons find themselves there as a result of a raging and uncontrolled temper. Thus, they have ruined their own lives as well as the lives of their victims.

Nowadays, anger management classes abound in an effort to help people, both in and outside of the penal system, to learn to control their tempers. But how much better it would be if we never developed the evil habit of losing our tempers in the first place. A person who is always angry moves through life like the proverbial bull in a China closet, leaving devastating destruction in their path wherever they go. May the Lord help us to practice discretion rather than destruction in our daily lives!

Before leaving today's text, I would also like to comment on the last half of it. The part about it being our "glory to overlook a transgression." This implies we should be the kind of person who maintains a broad and magnanimous outlook on life, focusing more on the positive words and actions of those around them rather than the negative—giving other people the benefit of the doubt and not always searching to find fault, blame, and questionable motives in the people with whom we interact. In the event that a once angry person does reach the point where he or she chooses to apologize for thoughtless words or foolish actions, the only way we will be able to begin to live with them harmoniously in the future is if we ask God to give us this "largeness of heart" so that true forgiveness and healing can restore peace to our lives.

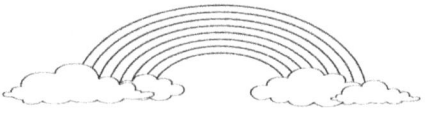

April 29

A Good Reputation

"A good name is to be chosen rather than great riches, loving favor rather than silver and gold. The rich and the poor have this in common, the LORD is the maker of them all" (Proverbs 22:1, 2).

At first glance, I thought the two texts above, although written one right after the other, were totally unrelated. However, after more careful consideration, it seems to me that they are related in this way. In the beginning, before we were ever labeled rich or poor, the Lord made each one of us. We came fresh from His hand to reflect a unique image of God, and we were on a level-playing field as far as our reputation was concerned. According to the first verse, however, we are the ones who "choose" to develop a good name, which subsequently can bring us "loving favor."

Some will argue that being born into a wealthy family, in a certain country, or of a particular race or gender already gives one an advantage regarding their place in society and what others think of them. However, we are not looking at external indicators of identity, but internal traits of character by which people are known within their given community. Regardless of race, age, socio-economic status, or gender, our personal reputation develops as we interact with those around us over a period of time.

Have you ever known a rich person, who by all accounts should have had a perfectly lovely disposition, but turned your stomach when you occasioned to see their arrogance, ill-temper, or sense of entitlement, as if the world owed them a living? Although they may look beautiful on the outside, once you understand the smallness of their character, your view of them changes, and the series of negative impressions they leave on you and others eventually forms a poor reputation. Of course, the opposite is also true. A person who initially seems quite common, or even unattractive, can change your opinion of them quite quickly when you see them exhibiting some of the beautiful fruits of the

Spirit, such as love, joy, peace, etc. Their consistently helpful words and actions will soon render them a good reputation among their friends, family, and co-workers.

Two points I glean from these verses are, first, that we should place a higher value on developing a good name than perhaps we have in the past. This might mean putting more time and effort into being a good person than in pursuing some of our more worldly goals, such as making a lot of money. Second, the fact that we can and should "choose" to have a good name, which means that how our reputation develops within our spheres of influence is really up to us. Every day we are called to make choices about how we will act, what we will say, and how we will say it. We are carving out our own destiny as we choose how to build a good, reputable character. As humans, we will make some mistakes along the way, but if we depend upon the Lord to help us, He will assist us not only in creating a good reputation but also in building a good character, which will serve us well, both here and in eternity.

One last note on this topic. Due to the fact that our reputations are so valuable, it follows that it is a serious offense when we do something that smears or sullies someone else's good name. Whether done through gossip, in written form, or electronically, it is wrong. We do not like people doing this to us, and we should determine, as true Christians, not to do anything to ruin the reputation of others.

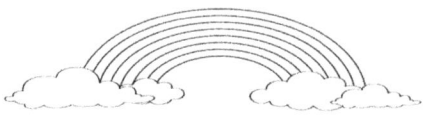

April 30

Overworked

"Do not overwork to be rich; because of your own understanding, cease! Will you set your eyes on that which is not? For riches certainly make themselves wings; they fly away like an eagle toward heaven" (Proverbs 23:4, 5).

In previous devotional thoughts, we have already discussed the folly of being so laser-focused on making money that we fail to dedicate sufficient time to other important aspects of our life, which suffer as a result. Sometimes things suffer to the point of being too late to undo the damage our lack of balance has caused. Our health is broken, our families are in tatters, and our relationship with God is all but non-existent.

Obviously, the Lord wants us to work. He assigned the work of tending to their garden home to Adam and Eve. He told the Israelites that they should work six days a week and worship Him on the seventh. He sent his apostles out to evangelize all nations of the earth. And Jesus Himself worked side by side in a carpenter's shop with His earthly father until He started His public ministry at age thirty. He has given us work as a blessing, a place to use our talents and abilities to do something worthwhile in the world. Even good things, however, have their limits, and work is one of them. In fact, the Lord thought it was such a good idea not to overwork that He created the Sabbath to help us remember to stop our regular weekly pursuits for a time of rest, recreation, and reflection on His goodness and grace for at least one day out of every seven.

These verses really hit home with me since I have been an avowed workaholic for most of my adult life. I was often consumed by my work. It gave me identity, purpose, and fulfillment—not to mention money. I threw myself into it with enthusiasm and zeal, always setting goals for improvement and reaching for the next level of success. After teaching or working as a school administrator all day, I would either teach adult education classes or take advanced study classes myself at night until I obtained my doctoral degree. It was all very challenging and rewarding, but I'm sure that if I hadn't known about the Sabbath, or taken seriously the admonition to rest on it each week, I would have burned out at an early age.

I had a friend who was also working full time while trying to finish a graduate degree. She was so obsessed with reaching her goal that she never took time to back away from it long enough to give her body and mind a rest from the constant pressure she felt. The last I knew of her, she had suffered a nervous breakdown and, to the best of my knowledge, never did achieve her academic goal. Unfortunately, the quality of the rest of her life was also negatively affected.

So here, it's as if the Lord is telling us, "Cease from the rat race! Take time to enjoy your family and friends. Take time to practice your hobbies, reflect, and travel. Take time to restore your soul by communing with Me and all of nature, which I have created for your pleasure. Take time to 'smell the roses' at regular intervals in your life. Adopt a lifestyle that will bring balance back into your life so that you can enjoy it to the fullest, just as I intended you to do!" I believe it's a timely message for our day and age.

A Wise Child

"Listen to your father who begot you, and do not despise your mother when she is old…. The father of the righteous will greatly rejoice, and he who begets a wise child *will delight in him. Let your father and your mother be glad, and let her who bore you rejoice" (Proverbs 23:22, 24, 25).*

We have already discussed the need for fair and consistent discipline in a child's life, but these verses are actually addressed to the children. What should their attitude be toward their parents? Well, we know from the fifth commandment (see Exod. 20:12) that children must honor their parents. And in the New Testament, children are admonished by the apostle Paul to "obey your parents in the Lord, for this is right" (Eph. 6:1). These verses seem to be aimed primarily at underaged children, who are still living under the care and protection of their parents.

The verses we are contemplating in Proverbs today, however, seem more like advice for mature children. How should our aging parents be treated once we have reached adulthood? The Asian custom of venerating one's elders is an idea that seems to have died, if it ever did exist, in modern American society. Often today, the older a person gets, the less they are valued and respected. And unfortunately, the more they are ignored or discarded.

As children of God, together with our elder brothers and sisters in the Lord (our parents), these verses in Proverbs counsel us to continue to listen to our parents and care for them as they age. (I especially like the part that says, "Do not despise your mother when she is old.") As challenging as this can sometimes be, these verses ask us to go beyond usually-expected norms, and by our righteousness and wisdom, make our fathers rejoice greatly, our mothers be glad they bore us, and both of them delight in us! For me, this paints a picture of parents who are both proud and happy that they brought children into the world. All of their hard work, sacrifice, instruction, time, effort, and prayers have paid off, and they can spend the remainder of their lives in joy and satisfaction, knowing that their labors as parents have not been in vain.

This, of course, is the ideal scenario that many of us in this sinful world will never be able to fully attain due to a host of mitigating circumstances, but that does not preclude us from reaching for the closest proximation possible. I believe the point here is to continue to respect our parents and maintain a close relationship with them in order to bring happiness into their lives, just as we would want our own children to do for us.

Turning to our own children, how can we make them wise in this regard? How can we weave these values into their lives? Respect for both the father and the mother as well as their elders, in general, is something that should be taught to children in the home at an early age and then expected and monitored throughout the various stages of development. As a teacher, I have observed this phenomenon over and over again. Those parents who insist on respect get it, while those who don't rarely receive it, and the disrespect grows along with the child. As Christians, may the Lord help us to fulfill our roles faithfully, both as children and as parents.

May 2

Boasting

"Do not boast about tomorrow, for you do not know what a day may bring forth. Let another man praise you, and not your own mouth; a stranger, and not your own lips" (Proverbs 27:1, 2).

Have you ever been in the insufferable presence of someone who continually boasts? Sometimes it's about who they are or how good they are at something. Often, it's about what they have done in the past, and at times, what they are planning on doing in the future—which as this passage points out, nobody on earth has control over. Conversations with these people can quickly turn into a one-sided monologue, which leaves everyone else looking for the nearest exit in the room.

The better part of wisdom suggests that you do your best in life, but allow others to praise you, always keeping in mind that the main person we are trying to please is the Lord, who, after all, is the Creator of all of our talents as well as the Source of our energy, strength, and ability to use our gifts from Him in a way that will bless humanity.

Does this mean that we can never talk about our accomplishments or describe our abilities to anyone? Obviously, there are several instances in life where this is necessary. One is during a job interview, and another related circumstance is when we are creating a resume for a future employer to study in order to determine whether we are the right person for the job in question. Writing an autobiography or discussing your past with a possible future mate who is trying to learn all they can about you might be other occasions to deviate from the general rule. However, even in these cases, a touch of humility will go a long way to making our assertions about ourselves more palatable.

Another question that may arise from verse 1 is, does this mean we shouldn't make plans for the future? Since we don't know what's going to happen in the future, does it make sense to set life goals, such as what degree I plan to get in college, what profession I want to pursue, where I will go on vacation next year, or how I will plan for retirement? Goals, however large or small, provide the fuel that motivates our daily activities in life. They become a framework that helps to give our lives direction and purpose. There are two caveats here. One is that we need to be as certain as possible that our goals are aligned with what we perceive as God's will for us, and the second one is that we should be willing to change or lay aside our plans when it becomes obvious that God has chosen a different path for us.

At first we were slightly amused, but upon further examination, we were impressed by the way that Puerto Ricans deal with this issue. Whenever they are talking about something in the future they always add the phrase, "*Si Dios quiere,*" which basically means, "If the Lord wills it." As Christians, I think this would be a mindset that we could all benefit from adopting when we are talking about or planning for the future. It reminds me of the old adage, which goes roughly like this, "Live like the world could end tomorrow, but plan as if you are going to live another hundred years."

Whenever we are tempted to "get too big for our britches," it behooves us to consider the condescension of Jesus in leaving His throne of glory to come to this world to suffer so that He could save us. That thought alone should help us "nip our bragging in the bud," bathing all of our words and actions in a healthy dose of humility.

May 3

In Authority

"When the righteous are in authority, the people rejoice; but when a wicked man rules, the people groan" (Proverbs 29:2).

Such a pithy statement about the influence a leader has over those he leads! A righteous king, leader, or boss can bless his subordinates in so many ways, while those same kinds of "superiors" who are wicked can cause people untold frustration and suffering. This holds true wherever leaders exert their power, whether at home, at work, or, dare we mention it, as the ruler of a country.

This verse reminds me of some of the bosses I have had in the past. Some were quite arbitrary and unfair, holding tightly the reins of power, while others served more as mentors or helpful friends, even outside the four walls of our mutual workspace. As a past professor, my first inclination here would be to launch into a discussion about the various leadership styles, listing the advantages and disadvantages of each one. However, in order not to go off on a tangent in this short devotional thought, suffice it to say that a worker generally learns quite quickly which bosses are "good ones" and which are "bad ones," based on his or her goals and interpersonal relationship skills. Is the leader more centered on what will only get him or her ahead or on serving other people in some way so that their lives will be improved?

At several points in my life, such as when I was between jobs or during my summer breaks from teaching, I signed up to work for an organization called Kelly Girl (now I believe the name has been changed to Kelly Services), where I agreed to be a temporary secretary for a variety of different companies while their regular employees were sick, on vacation, on maternity leave, or just because they needed extra clerical help during busy seasons for their business. It was interesting because I worked for a different company almost every week. I got a front row seat in observing the management styles of many different bosses. I worked in hospitals, government offices, real estate, engineering firms, the hospitality industry, schools, and universities, to name a few of my temporary assignments. Needless to say, I usually knew by the end of the first day which

places fostered a positive work environment and which places were toxic. Later, when a given company would have an opening for a full-time position, if I was in the market for one, I could easily decide based on the person who would be my supervisor, whether I wanted to work for one company or another. (Of course, the employers felt the same way, often testing a temp worker for a month or so before deciding whether to offer her a permanent job.)

Besides stating a simple fact regarding the far-reaching impact of those in authority, I think this verse offers us, as God's representatives in the world, an opportunity to examine, reflect upon, and perhaps even change how we exert our power, and thus our influence, over those whom we supervise. The best place to start, of course, is at home. Then practicing our "God-likeness" at work, at school, at church, or wherever else we have been placed in a position of authority. May the Lord help us to become leaders who, like Him, are both competent and gracious, bringing blessings to those who associate with us through our example, our words, and our actions.

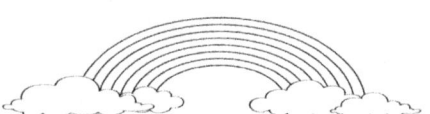

An Angry Man

"Do you see a man hasty in his words? There is more hope for a fool than for him.... An angry man stirs up strife, and a furious man abounds in transgression" (Proverbs 29:20, 22).

The book of Proverbs has a number of enlightening verses about anger. In April, we discussed anger as it relates to discretion. The two verses we are focusing on today tie together hasty words and transgressions as negative by-products of the emotion of anger. Let's take a moment to ponder each one.

First, I want to discuss hasty words spoken by someone who is angry. The Bible tells us that this is worse than foolish. Just think of all the relationships that have been destroyed by these kinds of words. Often impulsive statements escape from our lips that we wish we could take back once our anger subsides. But the damage has been done. Even if we later apologize, the scars remain. And if we continue a pattern of saying similar things, the wound is reopened, trust is lost, and the future of the relationship is in peril. How essential it is, then, that we ask the Lord to control our words—always. But especially when we lose our tempers.

Now, let's turn our attention to verse 22, which tells us that not only does an angry man stir up strife but he will also abound in transgression. I translate this to mean that he will sin with his actions as well as his words when he is under the influence of his anger. The word "furious" conjures up a person (man or woman) who has totally lost control of themselves. As a result they are much more likely to commit "crimes of passion," as they are often called. As we've discussed before, the prisons are filled with people who had at some point become so filled with wrath that they killed another human being or committed some other terrible crime that they never would have dreamed of doing if they had not allowed their temper to get the best of them. How do we avoid becoming one of these perpetrators ourselves?

I believe we need to be taught from our earliest years that it is not okay to have a temper tantrum whenever we don't get our way. As parents, we need to both teach and model the importance of controlling our emotions, and even when we do pass through experiences that warrant anger, we need to look for healthy ways to deal with it. Like anything else, practice makes perfect. We need to develop positive habits in this regard, taking a deep breath and taking a moment to think about optimal ways to deal with the anger we feel, rather than striking out in a manner that hurts others, and that we, ourselves, will probably deeply regret once we are in our right mind again.

Fortunately, as Christians, we are assured of heavenly help in this area of our lives. Galatians 5:22 and 23 inform us that patience (longsuffering, in some versions) and self-control are both "fruits of the Spirit." Thus, when we ask the Lord to come into our lives, and He inhabits us with His Holy Spirit, we can also ask Him to take the old "angry man" out of our characters and gift us with all of His beautiful characteristics of love, joy, peace, longsuffering, kindness, goodness, faithfulness, gentleness, and self-control. Praise the Lord!

The Law of Kindness

"She opens her mouth with wisdom, and on her tongue is *the law of kindness" (Proverbs 31:26).*

Having just reflected on the various fruits of the Spirit yesterday, I can't help but mention when considering today's verse that kindness is also one of the virtues on that list. In this last chapter of Proverbs, the one that describes the much-lauded "Proverbs 31 woman," this is the verse that caught my attention.

What might the "law of kindness" include? I can think of a lot of things it wouldn't include: shouting, cursing, name-calling, sarcasm, shaming, and making fun of someone else are the first inappropriate behaviors that come to mind. Along these lines, I remember teaching one year in an elementary classroom with fairly thin walls, and I could hear the teacher next door yelling at, criticizing, and demeaning his students in an angry voice on and off throughout the day. I guess he thought the only way to control his class was by intimidating them with loud, angry words and mean comments. Needless to say, I determined that none of my children would ever be assigned to his class, and I also steered other parents away from placing their children within his care. Fortunately, it wasn't long before word got around, and he was removed from his post at that school.

On the other hand, I have known many very kind and patient teachers, who have made a world of difference in the lives of their students through their words of gentle encouragement. Some of these teachers have made such an impact on their students that many years later, they are still remembered, even by name, as people who helped them bloom and get started on a positive and productive path through life! Indeed, for some young people today, who come from horrible family circumstances, the school is the only place they ever hear positive and encouraging words. Make no mistake, kind and thoughtful words are powerful!

So, if I were to write a "law of kindness," I would address not only the actual content of the words but also the tone and the manner in which they are delivered. The content would be wise, true, and well-considered to help and not hurt the receiver of the message. The tone would be inviting and encouraging and at an appropriate volume. And the manner of delivery would include pleasant facial gestures and non-threatening body language as well as a judicious time and place to deliver a message to the hearer.

A topic directly related to this one is that of gossiping or using our tongue to spread ugly rumors that could hurt, or even ruin, another person's reputation. Avoiding this harmful practice would also need to be included in my "law of kindness." Of course, it goes without saying that labeling people, or bullying them, has no place in the life of a dedicated follower of God. I believe one way to judge whether our words are appropriate is to ask ourselves if they would be acceptable in heaven. If not, it's time for us to learn to speak more kindly now.

Seasons

"To everything there is a season, a time for every purpose under heaven: a time to be born, and a time to die; a time to plant, and a time to pluck what is planted" (Ecclesiastes 3:1, 2).

Whenever I hear these verses, a popular folk song of my youth called "Turn! Turn! Turn! (To Everything There Is a Season)" by The Byrds springs to mind. If you're about my age, you can probably hear the melody wafting through your memory, too. The words are so impactful and specific that I can't help but reiterate the key verbs in the next few verses of this lyrical biblical poem: to kill, to heal, to break down, to build up, to weep, to laugh, to mourn, to dance, to cast away stones, to gather stones, to embrace, to refrain from embracing, to gain, to lose, to keep, to throw away, to tear, to sew, to keep silence, to speak, to love, to hate, and lastly, in verse 8, two weighty nouns appear: "A time of war, and a time of peace" (see Eccles. 3:3–8). Upon meditation, these words provide us with a lot of food for thought.

I love these verses because they remind us that life is full of stages. There will be many ups and downs in our experience. There will be times of strong and changing emotions. Things that are important to us at one stage of life will be replaced by other things at a different age, time, and place along our journey. This helps to give us a healthy perspective, knowing that "this too shall pass" when moving through difficult times and warning us not to get too giddy, thinking we know all the answers when things are going well for us. After all, a full life on this earth will include most of these phases sooner or later.

This can be encouraging for us, personally, when we are experiencing grief, difficulties at work or home, illness, or financial setbacks. We can take hope in the knowledge that the dark valley we are currently walking through will not last forever. Parents and teachers can also take comfort in the fact that the current phase of silliness, rebellion, or teenage immaturity in the lives of the young people with whom they interact will not last forever.

As an educator, I believe that all of us, but especially the youth, would be benefitted by the study of human growth and development. It would help us realize that the particular phase we are going through at any given time is usually normal, and that it generally is something that we can expect to grow out of with time and wise choices. This would not only alleviate anxiety but also prepare people for the inevitable changes that will take place over the course of their lifetime. I am also a strong believer in the idea that the church can provide assistance in this regard by making resources on where they can find help when going through difficult stages of life available to its members and its community. Larger, more affluent churches can offer classes on things like grief recovery, divorce recovery, anger management, conflict resolution, and twelve-step programs as well as programs on healthy lifestyle changes.

I would like to offer one cautionary note while we're discussing the different phases through which humans pass. It's wise not to judge someone in a different place than us since we have not walked in their moccasins, so to speak. How many of us have been humbled by things like telling other people how to raise their children, only to find out how very challenging it is after having our own! We should not think that everyone should feel exactly as we do in a given situation. Although there are many similarities across human populations, and we all do pass through the basic stages of human development—childhood, adolescence, adulthood, some type of family life, and old age—we all come from such different family backgrounds, cultures, experiences, educational levels, and socioeconomic circumstances. We must learn to respect what others are feeling and provide them, just as our gracious God does with us, the space and time they need to work through their own individual seasons of life.

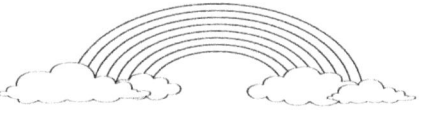

May 7

Walk Prudently

"Walk prudently when you go to the house of God; and draw near to hear rather than to give the sacrifice of fools, for they do not know that they do evil. Do not be rash with your mouth, and let not your heart utter anything hastily before God. For God is in heaven, and you on earth; therefore let your words be few" (Ecclesiastes 5:1, 2).

When I first remember hearing this passage as a college student, I wrestled with its meaning. Now, however, with a few more years of experience under my belt, it speaks to me of the need to maintain humility and reverence in our relationship with God, especially when we come to His house of worship. I don't think it means to be so solemn and serious that we can't enjoy the service but just that we should come as listeners and learners.

Just try to take it in. The Omniscient God, who created and sustains the whole universe, condescends to interact with us personally! And not just one day a week, when we attend a church service, but every day, whenever we call upon Him, as if it weren't enough that He already created us and then died for us here on earth in order to provide us with eternal salvation! Not to mention that it is only by His ongoing mercy and grace that we continue to breathe and that our hearts keep beating for the duration of our lifetimes. How can we keep from worshipping such a powerful and magnanimous God as that! Another related question is how can we keep from rendering reverence to such a wonderful Being?

The author of Ecclesiastes puts us in our place when he states that, "God *is* in heaven, and you on earth; therefore let your words be few." Too often we think we know all the answers, but only because we do not know how much we do not know. In the light of the all-knowing mind of God, whatever knowledge we have is like a small rain puddle compared to the boundless ocean of God's intelligence. No matter how much training, education, or experience we have in any area, we still have so much more to learn. Thankfully, God is going to be our Educator throughout eternity, yet even then, we will just have scratched the surface of His never-ending knowledge. As an educator who believes in the value of lifelong learning, I look forward to a chance to continue to be a student through the endless ages, with Jesus as my wise and fascinating Teacher! I will explore, learn new things, and satisfy my curiosity to my heart's content!

Now back to the part of verse 2, which admonishes us not to be "rash with your mouth," and not to "utter anything hastily before God," these are my conclusions. First, we should not make any pledges or vows that we do not intend to keep in God's presence because He takes our words seriously. Second, there is no place for boasting before God. Boasting only shows our ignorance about who God really is and who we really are, making us look foolish. Third, we should not cause those who come to church to truly worship God to miss out on the blessings He has for them by our secular and inappropriate speech. Nothing should be said in church to distract the worshippers from the message the Holy Spirit wants to share with them on that sacred occasion. As a longtime church member, this is an area in which I think we all need to improve. I'm convinced that walking prudently in God's house in these simple ways will enhance the worship experience for us all.

May 8

Grasping for the Wind

"As he came from his mother's womb, naked shall he return, to go as he came; and he shall take nothing from his labor which he may carry away in his hand" (Ecclesiastes 5:15).

In the first four chapters of Ecclesiastes, the author uses the phrase "grasping for the wind" eight times. Then, here in chapter 5, he explains in a little more detail what he means. We all arrived in this world with nothing, and we shall depart with nothing, at least as far as material possessions are concerned. Earlier, in

Ecclesiastes 3:20, he has tried to make this same point by succinctly stating, "All go to one place: all are from the dust, and all return to dust."

In modern terms, we might ask the question, "Why are we killing ourselves in the incessant rat race to get ahead, make more money, and buy bigger and better possessions when neither our monetary status nor any of the things we "own" will mean anything to us when we die? Add to that the thought that for most of us, our lifespan will end somewhere between seventy to ninety years on this earth. So how should we spend our "one life to live" on this planet during the years between our birth and our death?

This is a theme we have touched upon in previous devotional thoughts, and, as we can see, it's the question Ecclesiastes seeks to answer. What it does not recommend is wasting our precious allotment of time in grasping for things that are not of eternal consequence. The word "grasping" implies someone reaching out to get ahold of something with a degree of urgency or even desperation. While the term "the wind" speaks to us of something transient, changeable, and without substance. In my mind's eye, I can see a mountain climber reaching up to grab a rope to pull himself to the top, only to find it isn't attached to anything and falling to his death while still clutching the useless rope in his hand!

A little later in this book, Solomon provides a few suggestions about some positive ways we should be spending our time. Meanwhile, these verses cause me to reflect upon how I am allocating my time, effort, strength, health, and money, and subsequently, to reorder my priorities. I think they are a call to focus more on that which is permanent, rather than temporary, and an invitation to concentrate more on people than things as well as on my relationship with my eternal, heavenly Father.

Obviously, we all need to work to fulfill our basic needs: food, housing, clothing, some type of transportation, and training or education that will help us be able to provide for our families. I also believe that God expects us to utilize the various talents He has given us (including our funds) to be a blessing to our communities, churches, and the world around us, as we seek to support projects that will advance the work of God here on earth.

So, we circle around again to the idea of maintaining balance in our lives. How do we do this? I believe that it's by making wise decisions based on keeping our priorities straight, always aware that what we have here is temporary, while our real treasures are being stored up for us in heaven.

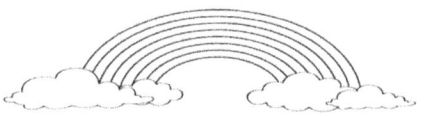

Your Might

"Whatever your hand finds to do, do it with your might; for there is no work or device or knowledge or wisdom in the grave where you are going" (Ecclesiastes 9:10).

In this verse Solomon tells us what we should do with our brief span of years on this earth. Continuing with his theme on the shortness of life, he strikes a more positive tone by admonishing us that whatever we choose to do, we should commit to doing it well. So it's okay to be dedicated to our work, just so we don't become workaholics to the point that our health, families, and religious experience suffer as a result of our labors.

In looking up the word "might," I find these synonyms: strength, power, force, and capacity. Secondary definitions include the nouns valor, potency, powerfulness, and influence. To elaborate on the meaning here, I think it would be fair to add words such as conscientiousness, intention, focus, effort, commitment, dedication, and purpose. In other words, as Christians, I believe we represent our God by the quality of work we produce. Whether we choose the work or it is assigned to us by someone close: parents, teachers, bosses, managers, pastors, military personnel, the government, or even masters (as in the cases of Joseph and Daniel), it is our duty to do it as well as we can. Our work makes a statement about who we are, our values and characters, as well as our beliefs.

I would also assert that these same high standards of work should be evident in our household chores, menial tasks, and any artistic endeavors we undertake, not just in our professional lives out in the work-a-day world. I have had the pleasure of knowing many people who, in addition to doing excellent work at their bread-and-butter day jobs, also employ some of their time in becoming amazing musicians, artists, writers, or craftsman of various kinds. Indeed, because we are made in the image of the God of creation, the number of things we can create for our own happiness and for the benefit of others seems to be limited only by our imaginations!

As a parent, I can't help but think that our creative, heavenly Father must be pleased when His children use their God-given talents to make lovely or useful things to better the world around them. Just as I feel proud and happy when I see our daughter living up to her potential in all the ways in which she has been blessed and gifted by God!

Thus, precisely because our time is short, what we do while we're here matters. And how we do it matters even more! In whatever arena we find ourselves, our work testifies to the kind of God we serve. He faithful, responsible, thorough, effective, efficient, patient, kind, helpful, fair, collaborative, a lover of the beautiful, and so much more. For some of our co-workers, this may be the first, or even the only, view that they will get about what God is like. So, as we said yesterday, a balanced person will not spend an inordinate amount of time working to make a living at the expense of all the other important aspects of life, but whatever our hands finds to do, we must do it with all of our might.

May 10

Casting Bread

"Cast your bread upon the waters, for you will find it after many days"
(Ecclesiastes 11:1).

This verse always sparks my imagination since it is so general in scope. First, we are not told what "waters" to cast our bread upon. We assume it means when we are interacting with other people—co-workers, family members, friends, those in need. But maybe it includes institutions or perhaps even enemies? The advice is pretty open-ended.

Then, we are admonished to cast our "bread." We might take this in a more literal sense, as in sharing food with those who have very little. But it could also be interpreted to mean a random act of kindness, a donation to a worthy cause, or the sharing of a spiritual blessing, as in the giving of a Bible study (spiritual bread) to a truth-seeker.

The last part of the text, the part that carries the promise, is also non-specific. We "will find it." In other words, some future benefit or blessing will come back to us as a result of our time, money, effort, or other generous action. Here, the thought of a boomerang comes to mind. You throw it up into the sky, and eventually, it turns around and comes back to you!

Finally, the last phrase, "after many days," holds us in suspense. It tells us when this good deed will return back to us...but not precisely. Many days could be in several months, after the passage of a number of years, or possibly in our old age. It could also mean sometime in the life to come. I know many spiritual "seed sowers" who never saw the results of their words and actions during their lifetime, but who will be very happily surprised when they arrive in heaven and finally hear the rest of the story about the influence of their godly and generous lives. In any event, whether the serendipitous return of our boomerang happens sooner or later, it is an event which will bring joy to our hearts. In the meantime, we have the assurance that our labor is not in vain in the Lord (see 1 Cor. 15:58.)

To summarize, a modern translation of this verse might read something like, "Our good actions now will result in rebounding good re-actions to us later." Of course, what we are going to get out of it should not be the motivating force for our helpful behavior toward others, rather it is like frosting on the cake of the satisfaction we receive by doing God's work in the world. It allows Christians to live in a kind of exhilarating expectation, looking forward to all of the good and surprising secrets the Lord has to share with us in the future!

Allow me to share a beautiful example of exactly what this verse describes. Sometime after my brother had started practicing medicine, a young immigrant couple was brought to him to see if he could help them. The woman was pregnant, and the husband had lost his job. They had no health insurance, no money, and no immediate family living in this country. The wife knew no English, but the husband's broken conversation skills informed my brother that this was a high-risk pregnancy, and the woman had already had one miscarriage. They didn't know where else to turn. To make a long story short, my brother cared for them until she came to full term, and then safely delivered the baby. He also helped them find a place to stay until they could get on their feet again financially.

Many years later, after retirement, when my brother's cancer-stricken wife needed more care than he alone could provide, he started looking for someone who could help him, not only with caretaking but also with all the numerous chores of keeping a household going single-handedly. Suddenly, and we believe providentially, that same immigrant couple, who had remained friends of our extended family through the years, stepped forward to meet the challenge. He had helped them in their time of need, and now they were willing to help him in his. What an unexpected blessing! It was the perfect fulfillment of casting his bread upon the waters and receiving it back "after many days!"

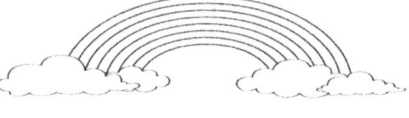

May 11

The Conclusion

"Let us hear the conclusion of the whole matter: fear God and keep His commandments, for this is man's all. For God will bring every work into judgment, including every secret thing, whether good or evil"
(Ecclesiastes 12:13, 14).

After giving much counsel, the "preacher" of Ecclesiastes—presumed by scholars to be King Solomon—ends the book with the pithy conclusion cited above. He sums up all of his wisdom and advice by asserting that humanity's primary duty is to show reverence to God by keeping His commandments, along with a reminder that they are, after all, the standard by which all of our actions will eventually be judged.

It's interesting that Solomon makes a point of saying that "every work," whether "good or evil," including all those things that humans think are being done in secret and that we think we can cover up and get away with, will be brought to light on the day of judgment. They will all be judged by the same all-encompassing standard of the law of God!

This brings two very important topics to the forefront of our thoughts. First, how important is the much-ignored law of God that He proclaimed to Moses with His own voice on the mountaintop and traced in tablets of stone with His own finger! Anyone who reads the Bible with any frequency must readily admit that there are many references, in both the Old and New Testament, where

God makes it abundantly clear that He wants His people to obey the Ten Commandments. Unfortunately, we disregard these simple commands only at our own peril. Nowadays, many people don't realize that they are the foundation of the moral fiber of our society. However, since being bound by moral restraints is not popular in our day, people choose not to emphasize what God has asked us to do. We don't want to have our behavior curbed by the law, which God has actually given to guide and protect us from the encroachment of evil into our lives. And we certainly don't want to think about anyone judging us—even God Himself!

As a result, we are now watching society crumble before our eyes. Lying has become a way of life for some. Adultery is almost accepted as commonplace among worldlings. Who respects their parents anymore? Stealing is okay if you can do it without getting caught, and who can carve out a whole day, out of only seven in our busy week, to celebrate the Sabbath that the Lord asks us to dedicate to Him? It seems our world has been turned completely upside down from the principles that God asks us to live by. Bad has come to mean good, and in many places, good is now termed bad.

As we take a step back to try to get some perspective on why this is so, we remember that we are in a great controversy between good and evil and that Satan has been hard at work in our world, trying to make as many people as possible turn away from God. Satan would have us ignore the principles outlined in the Ten Commandments and ultimately to be lost. Heaven forbid that those of us who call ourselves followers of God, although in the minority, would allow Satan to separate us from God in this way! These verses remind us that it is our duty to obey the commandments the Lord has laid out for us. This is our path to safety.

Which now brings up the second thought. As human beings, with a carnal nature that we inherited from our ancestors, our flesh often wars with us, making us weak to do God's will. The good news, though, is that a Savior has come to show us how to resist temptations to do wrong by using God's Word. He also gave us a perfect example of how to live in this world, even while we are preparing to live in the world to come. He gives us strength to obey through the presence of the Holy Spirit in our lives. But best of all, He died to save us so that when we do make a mistake and transgress His law, we can come to Him to ask forgiveness, knowing that He will shower us with His mercy and grace, giving us the courage to go forward with an even greater desire to do His will in the future. Praise God that He is helping us to better obey His law day by day, molding us into the wonderful people with whom He will rejoice to spend eternity!

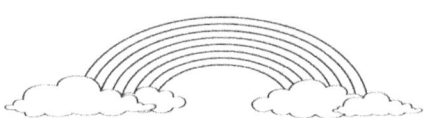

His Banner

"He brought me to the banqueting house, and His banner over me was love"
(Song of Solomon 2:4).

While this book of the Bible has many beautiful word pictures about romantic love, depicting the relationship of Solomon and a beautiful, young Shulamite woman, and comparing it with the overwhelming love and devotion the Lord has for His bride, the church, today's verse is my favorite. Food and shelter are basic human needs, both of which are provided by the king to his beloved in this passage. Just so, the Lord provides for our basic needs when we trust in Him. Not in a cold or careless manner, but with great intention and even celebration, He rejoices in a close relationship with us! That the magnificent Creator of the universe cares that much about me is mind-boggling and wonderful at the same time!

We are all familiar with what a banquet is: a special dinner, a feast, or a formal or ceremonial meal. In this case we are talking about a type of ceremonial meal that might indicate the promise of a sealing of a relationship or a solemn covenant between two people in love, who have chosen each other above any of their other relationships. The fact that it takes place in a whole "banqueting house" denotes a large space, which hints of a party-type environment where the couple can celebrate their joy in having found each other with many other people who have gathered to support them and wish them well.

The word "banner" has several meanings, but when used as a noun could mean a flag, placard, poster, sign, hanging, standard, or streamer. These synonyms can carry slightly different connotations, yet all indicate that some kind of announcement, usually celebratory in nature, is being publicly communicated. When I read today's verse, in my mind's eye, I can imagine a proud groom enthusiastically waving a large, colorful streamer in the air above his bride, declaring his love to her for all to see and hear! A modern-day equivalent might be a huge "Just Married" banner plastered across the back of an unusually-decorated and noisy car, as a newly-wed couple drives off to their honeymoon, joyfully announcing their new status to the whole world!

This short verse has been memorialized in a catchy little song that I first remember singing in a kindergarten class. It begins, "He brought me to His banqueting table; His banner over me is love," and ends after several more stanzas, again with the words, "His banner...over me...is love!" Like many songs for young people, this one had hand movements that went with it, which served to help us remember and internalize the message it carried. Occasionally, I recall, we would even make little flags and wave them over our heads while we sang. Once implanted there, it can be a melody that is hard to get out of your head, but it made me feel loved and special as a child. And in recently rereading these words during my devotional time, I find that they also make me feel loved and special as an adult! How encouraging and uplifting it is to know that the Lord rejoices over His special relationship with me! "His banner...over me...is love!"

May 13

A Hymn of Praise

"'Behold, God is my salvation, I will trust and not be afraid; for YAH, the LORD, is my strength and song; He also has become my salvation.' Therefore with joy you will draw water from the wells of salvation. And in that day you will say: 'Praise the LORD, call upon His name; declare His deeds among the peoples, make mention that His name is exalted. Sing to the LORD, for He has done excellent things; this is known in all the earth. Cry out and shout, O inhabitant of Zion, for great is the Holy One of Israel in our midst!'" (Isaiah 12:2–6).

Many people believe that only the Psalms contain actual hymns of praise, but here Isaiah proves that idea wrong. This beautiful song, found in Isaiah 12, was so impactful and full of praise that I couldn't help but include all of it in today's passage for reflection.

I love the fact it points out that the Lord is our strength and song as well as our salvation. To me, this means He will supply the strength we need to meet the many challenges we face in this life, and He will enable us to do it with a measure of joy, helping us to remember that He is going to walk with us all along the way. After all, here we are told that He is "in our midst."

Often, I find myself humming a little song as I go about my daily duties, even during more difficult times. Sometimes my husband will hear me and say, "What are you doing? Why are you making that noise?" Usually I am doing it unconsciously, marking the rhythm in the background, while consciously focusing on something else. But his question makes me catch myself, and I'll stop and try to identify the little ditty going on in my head. More often than not, it is a hymn I have been practicing on the piano lately. When I am able to tell him what song I am humming, it also makes me ask myself

why I am doing it. The only answer I can find is that the Lord has put a song in my heart, and I feel thankful to Him.

Isaiah 12:3 paints a cheerful word picture in my mind when I read it. Recently, I had the privilege of attending the fiftieth anniversary convention of a self-supporting ministry called Maranatha, which has helped build churches and schools for needy communities all over the world for the last half century. There they announced that in recent years they have also started drilling wells in places that are largely destitute of clean water. The women, whose job it is to bring the water, often have to walk large distances on a daily basis just to obtain enough of this precious substance to survive. Maranatha showed us video footage of some of the villages in Africa where these wells have been installed, and the marvelous difference it has made in the lives of the villagers. Right before the first water is drawn from a well, people from the surrounding area gather around to witness "the miracle." As the water gushes forth, the people break out in wide smiles, and an impromptu celebration of song and dance ensues. Life-bringing water is now readily available to them, saving the women much time and effort, and supplying the means to improve their hygiene and health as well as their economic situation since they are now enabled to cultivate and irrigate crops. Their lives have been changed forever!

Similarly, when we drink from the Lord's "wells of salvation," our lives will never be the same again. Our whole perspective changes as we drink deeply from His Word, and things that used to seem impossible are now more than possible because of His provision! No wonder Isaiah goes on to exclaim that we should give praise, sing, and shout about the "excellent things" the Lord has done for us, declaring His deeds among the people so that all will know the greatness of "the Holy One of Israel," who is in our midst!

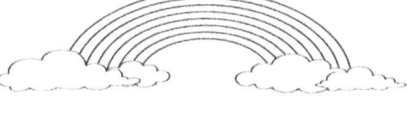

May 14

Punishment

"I will punish the world for its evil, and the wicked for their iniquity; I will halt the arrogance of the proud, and will lay low the haughtiness of the terrible" (Isaiah 13:11).

So often I hear people say that God couldn't be good because He allows so much evil to go unpunished. If He is all-knowing and all-powerful, why do we see so many terrible things happening around us every day? And will criminals ever be brought to justice? Will wicked people ever be made to answer for their crimes?

These are questions we have dealt with earlier in the year but from other perspectives. We have talked about the role of free will that God has given each of us, and God's patience in waiting for us to make the right decision about following Him or not. We have discussed discipline, and it's place in the life of a Christian. And we have confronted the fact that a day of judgment is coming for all of us—for some of us sooner, and for some of us later, but ultimately, because God is just, it will come. We simply don't know when. And that is one of the unanswered questions of life that, as we examined when studying Job, only our omniscient and omnipotent God can answer.

Meanwhile, our job is to trust His Word. And here His Word is very clear. He will "punish the world for *its* evil, and the wicked for their iniquity." You will remember that in Ecclesiastes we are also admonished that even every "secret thing, whether good or evil" will be judged by the Lord (see Eccles. 12:14). For people who love justice and fairness, it is a comfort to know that God will set everything right by the end of time. Of course, in the meanwhile, as representatives of God's character on earth, we must do all we can to foster justice in our families, in society, and to all who are within the reach of our influence.

But what about those people who commit heinous crimes and seem to get away with it? What about the child molesters, the serial killers, and the cruel and power-hungry Hitlers of the world, who sometimes seem to fall through the cracks in our justice systems? This verse also assures us that the Lord "will halt the arrogance of the proud, and will lay low the haughtiness of the terrible." Earlier in this chapter, sinners are told to "Wail, for the day of the LORD is at hand! It will come as destruction from the Almighty. Therefore all hands will be limp, every man's heart will melt, and they will be afraid" (Isa. 13:6–8). The punishment that is coming will not just be a slap on the wrist. Sinners who do not repent before the end of their lives will be facing the living God who will exercise "vengeance" upon them for all of the evil done in their lifetimes as well as the evil they encouraged others to do for them (see Rom. 12:19, KJV). If you've ever felt the force of a hurricane, an avalanche, or a tsunami, you will realize how weak and helpless humanity is in the face of natural disasters. Multiply that power a hundred times to get just a glimpse of how much less they will be able to resist the unleashed wrath of God upon the wicked!

Unlike Jonathan Edwards, a fiery preacher of times gone by, most Christians today do not spend a lot of time thinking or talking about the punishment of the wicked because for God's loving character, it is called a "strange act" (see Isa. 28:21, 22, KJV). In fact, some people argue that because God is so good, kind, and loving, He will NOT actually punish people for their sins. They seem to imagine God as a kind of lenient Santa Claus, who isn't really worried about the sins of the people to which He brings undeserved gifts, or a benign grandfather figure, who simply winks and looks the other way when they get into mischief.

It's obvious to me that these people have not spent much time reading the Bible because in both the Old and New Testaments, we find many references to the judgment of God as well as to the final destruction of the wicked. While it is true that He has labored incessantly throughout the centuries for the salvation of as many people as possible and even paid for their forgiveness with His own life, eventually, for the good of the entire universe, divine patience will come to an end. The Scriptures make clear that those who choose to hang on to their sins until the end (either of their lives or of the world) will be destroyed along with them. Yes, we can rest assured that the wicked will be punished.

But, thankfully, the story doesn't end there. Then, we are told, the righteous, who have also been judged, will receive their recompense. Because they have repented of their wrong-doing and chosen to accept the wonderful robes of salvation granted to them by Jesus, the Lord knows they are safe to save. They will not contaminate the atmosphere of heaven with evil. Their gracious reward is the recreation of a perfect and sinless new earth in which all of God's faithful people will safely and joyfully dwell with Him throughout eternity!

Declaration of Triumph

"And it will be said in that day: 'Behold, this is our God; we have waited for Him, and He will save us. This is the LORD; we have waited for Him; we will be glad and rejoice in His salvation'" (Isaiah 25:9).

*I*n most of the book of Isaiah, the prophet has been focusing on contemporary problems of his day. In chapters 24 and 25, however, he seems transported to a time at the end of earth's history. In chapter 24 he warns of the impending judgment on the earth, while in chapter 25, He praises God for the future deliverance of His people. It is there that this beautiful passage, which some have called "the shout of triumph," leaps off the page and into our hearts. It awakens a desire to be among those people at the end of time who will be ready to claim Him as "our God" and "be glad and rejoice in His salvation."

In the verses previous to this glorious declaration, Isaiah has delineated numerous reasons why God's people should praise Him. He has been a strength to the poor and to the needy in their distress. He has been a refuge from the storm and a shade from the heat. Even more wonderful, He will swallow up death forever and wipe away tears from all faces as well as taking the rebuke away from His people.

As I contemplate the various segments of this verse, I am first struck by the amazing promise found here that death itself will be destroyed forever. If you have lost a loved one during your lifetime, then you will understand the devastating sense of loss their death brings. In fact, even as Christians, we can be overwhelmed by grief. At such times, it is reassuring to know that, having lived on earth among us for more than thirty years, the Lord understands our pain when death occurs, and He comforts us with the promise that we will never have to experience death again. In fact, after death is finally destroyed, He Himself will wipe away our tears! And, of course, from other passages in Scripture we have the promise of the resurrection, which consoles us with the fact that we will be reunited with our loved ones who were also faithful. We will live together with them in eternal bliss! No wonder God's people are filled with gladness and rejoicing when He comes to save them!

Through the ages, many of the saints have been rebuked, rebuffed, and rejected by non-believers. Now the taunts, the false accusations, and all the shame and blame that they have had to endure will be swiped away in an instant, as the Lord comes to claim those who have followed His precepts, and the wicked suddenly and finally realize how terribly wrong they have been in following Satan's path for their lives instead of God's.

The SDA Bible Commentary also highlights the patience of God's people, as they have waited for many years and through many trials and tribulations, for the coming of their Savior. They have had to endure the rise of false doctrines, false christs, and even the final great deception of Satan, yet they remained faithful to Jesus. All of this has made their yearning to be rescued by Him from this dark world even stronger and their joy and rejoicing at His appearing even greater! God grant that we be among those proclaiming victory at His second coming!

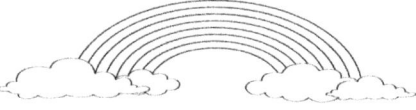

May 16

Perfect Peace

"You will keep him in perfect peace, whose mind is stayed on You, because he trusts in You" (Isaiah 26:3).

With so few things in this sinful world that can qualify as "perfect," this verse, although a beautiful promise, presents us with some challenges. How is this kind of peace defined? Have I ever achieved it? If so, how can I maintain it?

For some deeper insight into this topic I, once again, consulted *The SDA Bible Commentary*, which suggests that "perfect submission to the will of God [like Jesus had], brings the blessing of perfect serenity" (*The SDA Bible Commentary*, vol. 4, p. 203). It also asserts that though "Perfect peace will be the inheritance of the saints in the kingdom of God..., it may (also) be the happy experience of God's children here" (*Ibid.*). Well, in practical terms, what would that look like? This same source fleshes out how this kind of calm serenity would be reflected in everyday life with "a cheerful countenance, an unruffled temper, and a vigorous, glowing experience that stimulates all with whom we come in contact" (*Ibid.*). More than that, "The mature Christian is at peace with God, with himself, and with the world about him" (*Ibid.*).

Let's unpack that last thought, starting with being at peace with God. To me, this means not only being in submission to His will but actually doing it. We need to live in a state of ongoing forgiveness, thereby maintaining a clear conscience before our Creator. I believe this surrender of our will to the Lord will also result in feeling at peace with ourselves. Many problems that we struggled with before will be resolved while others will no longer seem so important once we begin to see them from God's perspective.

Now to deal with that part about being at peace with the world around us. Although there have been periods in my life where I have felt this kind of peace, I must admit that it seems very difficult to maintain one's serenity while living in this sinful world. Just when I think that I may have a handle on it, some trial or tribulation, some irritating person, or untenable situation always arises to cause me consternation and rob me of my peace.

Of course, as we know from reading the experiences of Paul, Daniel, and other examples from the Bible, that true peace of heavenly origin, the kind that is gifted to us by the Holy Spirit, will not depend on our surrounding circumstances. It will be a deep inner tranquility that this world cannot understand nor be able to give or take away from us. In fact, in John 16:33, as Jesus is speaking with His followers, He says, "These things I have spoken to you, that in Me you may have peace. In the world you will have tribulations; but be of good cheer, I have overcome the world."

So, how do we not only attain this heavenly brand of peace but also maintain it despite the vicissitudes of life? Philippians 4:6, 7 gives us the secret: "Be anxious for nothing, but in everything by prayer and supplication, with thanksgiving, let your requests be made known to God; and the peace of God, which surpasses all understanding, will guard your hearts and minds through Christ Jesus." We can glean further assurance by this promise the Lord made in John 14:27, right after telling His disciples about the Holy Spirit who would come to help them after He had gone back to heaven. He said, "Peace I leave with you, My peace I give to you; not as the world gives do I give to you. Let not your heart be troubled, neither let it be afraid."

Thus, the Scriptures teach that we can obtain this heavenly gift of the Holy Spirit, even now, despite being surrounded by the world's conflict, confusion, and chaos, by keeping our minds stayed on the Lord, surrendering to His will, and continually claiming His promises for peace.

Lord, please help us to learn to abide in Your perfect peace.

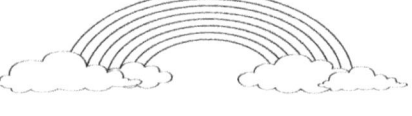

May 17

Talking Clay

"Woe to those who seek deep to hide their counsel far from the LORD, and their works are in the dark; they say, 'Who sees us?' and 'Who knows us?' Surely you have things turned around! Shall the potter be esteemed as the clay; for shall the thing made say of him who made it, 'He did not make me'? Or shall the thing formed say of him who formed it, 'He has no understanding'?" (Isaiah 29:15, 16).

As a child, growing up in the suburbs of Los Angeles, I had little exposure to actual clay. The Merriam-Webster Dictionary defines clay as "an earthy material that is plastic when moist, but hard when fired and is used in making pottery." My parents, who worked hard to make ends meet for their family of five, didn't have much money to spend on toys, landscaping decorations, or artistic extras. Of course, I was introduced to the modern colorful, plastic-like substance that we molded into shapes in elementary school. But the real, earthy type of clay lay outside my realm of existence until I got older and started to travel to other states, including Arizona and New Mexico. There I found a host of items, both practical and artistic, that had been made by various Native American tribes. Museums and historical sites are filled with a variety of clay pots, which were used for cooking, carrying water, storing food, and many other purposes. These are in addition to vases, cups, and numerous artistic figurines, some of which were probably eventually worshiped as gods by some indigenous people groups. What they fashioned out of material that looked only like mud to me was amazing, speaking volumes about their creativity and resourcefulness.

We know from many references in the Scriptures, as well as from archeological digs in the Holy Land, that the people in biblical times molded and utilized clay in much the same way as the Native Americans. In the days before plastic, glass, and metal cooking pots and pans, pottery was an everyday commodity. It could easily be made, sold, traded, and colorfully decorated. Everyone was familiar with it, which made it a good object to use when teaching spiritual lessons to the people. This was the same method Jesus later used in His parables—using something they knew a lot about in order to help the common people understand spiritual truths that were new to them.

I believe the first time I saw a real potter making something out of clay on a potter's wheel was in church some twenty years ago, when a progressive pastor arranged for this to happen on the platform while she was preaching as an object lesson for this passage. She wanted to create a picture in our minds of how the Lord works with us, forming us into something beautiful and useful if we allow Him to guide our lives. She was successful in planting her lessons on this topic in our imaginations, as I can still remember a number of her main points to this day. One was how something that seems as useless as mud can become an object of value, so we should never give up the hope, either for ourselves, or others, that God can turn our lives around.

Another point was the marvelous and creative skill of the Potter. And, of course, the necessary properties of the clay that rendered it completely surrendered to the all-knowing Master's hands. We also learned that after being formed, the pottery needed to be fired in order to make it strong and durable. Even when not perfect, the finished product could be a work of art, and when several of the same kind of pieces were carefully examined, each was a little different in some way. Each piece was therefore unique. Insightful lessons all.

In this passage, the prophet is talking about how foolish it would be for the created inanimate object to think it knows more than the Creator who brought it into being. How would an unformed lump of clay ever have the nerve to question the design and purposes of the omniscient Master Potter? These are good questions to reflect upon whenever we get too big for our britches and think that God doesn't know everything about us: what we do in the light, what we do in the dark, who we are, what we're made of, where we come from, and where we're going.

When you think about it, this is actually good news. Instead of rebelling and talking back to God, or worrying that He doesn't know what's best for us, we can just rest like a lump of clay and trust in His loving and skillful hands to turn our characters into a treasure more beautiful than we ever could have imagined!

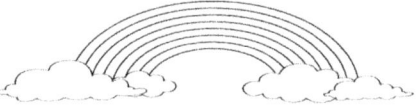

May 18

The Voice

"Your ears shall hear a word behind you, saying, 'This is the way, walk in it,' whenever you turn to the right hand or whenever you turn to the left" *(Isaiah 30:21).*

Have you ever had the experience of being very busy and focused on some work you were involved in, when, unexpectedly, you felt that God was tapping you on the shoulder and calling you in an altogether different direction? My husband and I did, and whenever I read today's text, memories of that experience flood my mind. It also makes me think of that verse in John 10:27 where Jesus says, "My sheep hear My voice, and I know them, and they follow Me." The voice we heard in the spring of 1996 was not audible, yet its gentle urgings came to both of us on the same day and was confirmed by a chain of circumstances that occurred over the ensuing year.

While at church one Sabbath, my husband and I were sitting in different places so that he could videotape our daughter's part in the program, but we both felt moved by the sermon we had heard that morning about Christian service. We discussed our strange new feelings about the topic over lunch. We both had good, well-paying jobs at the time, a nice new home, and a beautiful Christian school in the community where our daughter was doing well. We had a pleasant group of friends, as did our daughter, and our relatives lived fairly close by. Why would we want to leave and serve in a foreign field when we were so comfortable where we were? But maybe it was because things were so good for us that we felt guilty just sitting on the sidelines, soaking in all of our blessings and not being out there sharing our education and talents in some place in the world that might need us more. Perhaps God had a bigger plan for us? There were many reasons why serving as missionaries just didn't seem practical right now, so we decided to simply pray about it and see what would happen.

Amazingly, just a week or two later, we were chatting with some friends at church when they made a surprise announcement.

They told us that they had just accepted a call to serve at Antillian Adventist University in Puerto Rico, and they were preparing to leave by early summer! We were shocked by their news, but even more incredulous when, out of the blue, they said that the university needed more staff members, and since we already spoke Spanish and had graduate degrees, they asked if we would also apply to serve there. In fact, the husband told us that he was friends with the academic dean and would personally recommend us. He even suggested that we provide him with our resumes before he left so that he could hand deliver them! Wow! That certainly gave us something to reflect upon. My husband and I had both been interested in mission work in the past—but for some reason, he thought he might like to serve in Russia, while I was picturing an assignment in Mexico or some other Central American country. Neither of us had ever dreamed of going to Puerto Rico. We were strangely stirred by the suggestion. Could this be God's plan? Had the Lord been preparing us for this invitation by the impactful sermon we had recently heard? We didn't yet know, but we did know that applying to go as regular missionaries was a long and arduous process, so we decided to keep praying, submit our resumes, and watch to see which doors the Lord would open or close.

It was truly awe-inspiring to see the way the Lord removed all the barriers to accepting this call over the following months. We participated in several phone interviews, were required to receive medical clearance, passed the scrutiny of the mission finance committee, and were asked to submit twelve positive recommendations each! At any of these points we could have been rejected, but surprisingly, the process kept moving smoothly forward, until one day, in the spring of 1997, the official letter confirming our call arrived in our mailbox. By this time, after observing God's providential leading in our life over the year since we first heard His still, small voice in church that Sabbath morning, we were convinced that "this was the way" in which He was guiding us, and we determined to "walk in it." Although there were still many unknowns about what mission life would be like in our new and different culture, we decided to trust the One who had led us this far, leaving all the details of the future in His capable hands. Looking back, we're glad we did, for we spent four very pleasant and productive years in the mission field.

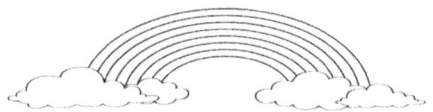

Beside All Waters

"The work of righteousness will be peace, and the effect of righteousness, quietness and assurance forever. Blessed are you who sow beside all waters..." (Isaiah 32:17, 20).

I have linked these two verses together because I think the first one defines what it is we should be sowing while the second verse indicates to whom. Also, the first verse declares what the effect of our work of righteousness will be while the second promises a blessing to those who do this work broadly—basically wherever they go.

Our best example of someone who did this, of course, is Jesus. Just think about the wide spectrum of people He influenced for good over the course of His brief thirty-three year lifespan here on earth. First, He influenced the lives of the members of His family as well as His friends and neighbors in the humble town of Nazareth. Once He began His ministry in earnest, He spoke to the common people wherever He found them, sometimes in small groups and sometimes to multitudes. He preached in synagogues, small towns, and the countryside. He welcomed children to His side and healed the sick. He ministered to both men and women, Jews and Gentiles, rich and poor, powerful and weak, foreigners and outcasts. Wherever He went, He did the "work of righteousness," bringing light, hope, joy, and faith to all those He encountered.

Notice His methodologies for spreading righteousness far and wide: He spoke, He touched, He preached, He taught, and He healed. He shared a meal with some people and cast demons out of others, depending on what the folks He was interacting with needed. His whole ministry was focused on meeting people's needs while at the same time filling the spiritual void in their hearts and lives.

One of the best ways He employed to put human beings on the path of righteousness was to set an example for them—and not only them but also His followers throughout the centuries, including us! Through His example He taught us all that we should be baptized. He also taught us how to meet temptation with Scripture and how to pray. You'll remember Him talking about our duty as citizens to "render therefore unto Caesar the things which are Caesar's; and unto God the things that are God's" (Matt. 22:21, KJV). He attended worship services regularly and participated in them. He demonstrated how to properly keep the Sabbath and the importance of interacting with everyone equally, with fairness and respect. As an educator, I appreciate the example He set of how to teach spiritual truth through both real-world illustrations (such as the wheat and the tares) and stories and parables (like the famous one about the prodigal son). Most importantly, His example taught us how to love others, how to be patient and kind, how to forgive, how to trust in God, and how to "sow beside all waters."

As we study His life, we realize that He showed us in many different ways how to live our own lives as children of God as well as how to carry on "the work of righteousness" He began. This will bring peace, quietness of soul, and "assurance forever" to those with whom we share His gracious goodness and who ultimately choose to accept His marvelous salvation.

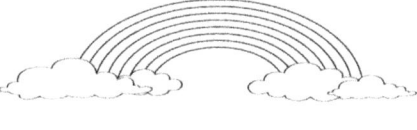

May 20

Everlasting Joy

"And the ransomed of the LORD shall return, and come to Zion with singing, with everlasting joy on their heads. They shall obtain joy and gladness, and sorrow and sighing shall flee away" (Isaiah 35:10).

After wading through several chapters about judgment on the nations who worship false gods and disobey the Lord's precepts, Isaiah turns chapter 35 into a fiesta when he prophesies regarding the future glory of Zion. This last verse in the chapter, however, really puts the frosting on the cake! It describes the amazing and eternal joy that the ransomed will experience in their new heavenly home.

Have you ever been so overcome with gladness that you couldn't help just breaking out in songs of praise? If so, you've experienced a small foretaste of what your future life will be like in heaven. I have been really happy and felt like celebrating at various points in my life—but the times I've felt the closest to heaven are when I have taken part in singing "The Messiah" in a mass choir with full orchestra accompaniment—including the timpani and the trumpets!

On the other hand, have you ever been so overwhelmed with sorrow that you just couldn't stop sighing? For at least six months after going through a terrible divorce, I would find myself inadvertently letting out a long, breathy sigh whenever I reflected on all of the dire ramifications of what I was going through. I suppose it was simply an involuntary response of my body in order to help me deal with the sorrow and stress I was feeling since I only rarely found myself sighing either before or after that dreadful experience. It would make an interesting research topic.

In any event, apparently, I'm not alone in this response, which seems to be somewhat common to those of us living in this world of sin and sadness. What a blessed promise it is to know that all of our heavy sighing, along with the sorrow and distress that cause it, will "flee away" in the earth made new. In fact, they shall be replaced by singing, joy, and gladness. And not just the fleeting joy we know here from time to time but everlasting joy!

This sets me thinking about what a glorious God we serve. First, He created humankind and gave us a beautiful garden home, filled with light, joy, and wonder. Despite the fall, He still provided us with a world that sustained human life and retained enough of its original beauty to speak to us about His love and powerful majesty. When the time was right, He came to earth to show us how to live, as we discussed yesterday, and then, in His crowning act of grace and mercy toward us, He died to erase our sins. Now, He's preparing a wonderful new home for us and has given us many inspiring promises in His Word to encourage us along our way. So, after allowing today's verses to sink into our souls, we should also consider some of the related reassuring promises, such as this one, found in John 14:2, 3: "In My Father's house are many mansions; if *it were* not *so*, I would have told you. I go to prepare a place for you. And if I go and prepare a place for you, I will come again and receive you to Myself; that where I am, *there* you may be also." Hallelujah!

May 21

Renewed Strength

"He gives power to the weak, and to those who have no might He increases strength. Even the youths shall faint and be weary, and the young men shall utterly fall, but those who wait on the LORD shall renew their strength; they shall mount up with wings like eagles, they shall run and not be weary, they shall walk and not faint" (Isaiah 40:29–31).

I just couldn't pass up commenting on this well-known passage because the older I get, the more I appreciate it. In my youth I thought it bore a great promise for more strength after a person had overworked or overexerted themselves in some way. While I'm sure that's still true, since hitting my sixties, with the various and sundry health challenges that almost unavoidably come as a person ages, I have taken these texts much more seriously and claimed the strength they promise much more frequently! And not just for me but also for friends, relatives, and church members who I know are currently needing the Lord's strength from day-to-day.

I see the Lord's strength as being multifaceted. While I believe these texts are speaking about physical strength, they also offer us spiritual and emotional fortitude. Anyone with heart problems knows that there are just some days when you feel weak as a kitten. Experiencing shortness of breath is another thing that can cause real fatigue. Of course, there are a host of other physical conditions where we feel the need to be infused with the strength of the Lord—everything from cancer to influenza.

But today I want to think a little more about the intangible kinds of strength the Lord will give us when we wait upon Him as this text suggests. Have you ever been emotionally weakened by heartbreak, fear, or betrayal of your trust? Here I believe the Lord promises to heal our emotional wounds when we come before Him so that we can find the strength to love again, to trust others again, or to overcome our fears in order to live a more abundant life and accomplish what we know the Lord is asking us to do. To me, spiritual strength includes things such as giving us the power to successfully face temptations, implanting in us the desire to study His word and pray, and gaining the ability to understand spiritual truths with the aid of the Holy Spirit. Possessing the courage of our convictions to stand up for what's right while others simply ignore the promptings of conscience or unabashedly witnessing and sharing the gospel with others as the Lord gives us opportunity are other situations where we need spiritual strength. Perhaps you can think of others.

One person who always springs to my mind when reflecting on what it means to be spiritually strong is an elderly resident named Beverly in a nursing home we used to visit on weekends. (You'll remember I've mentioned her before.) Although she was physically weak, in fact, she was bedbound most of the time, but she was still vibrant spiritually. We often observed her reading her Bible or smiling and talking cheerfully with those around her, and whenever we would sing a hymn in her room, she would join in since she knew all the words by heart. Instead of complaining, she would talk about something she was reading or ask us about how we were doing. It seemed we had met a living saint. When she passed away, it was as if a bright light had been extinguished, yet the memory of her spiritual fortitude lingers on for those of us who were privileged to know her. Lord, give us the spiritual strength of a Sister Beverly!

May 22

Fear Not

"Fear not, for I am with you; be not dismayed, for I am your God. I will strengthen you, yes, I will help you. I will uphold you with My righteous right hand"' (Isaiah 41:10).

Of the many places in the Bible where the Lord tells us not to fear, I believe this one is my favorite because of the beautiful promise with which it comes. I have both claimed this promise and been consoled by it on numerous occasions over the course of my lifetime.

It has encouraged me when passing through relationship difficulties and worrying about what my future held in store. It has been a staff of support on which I have leaned before a surgery or medical procedure. It has given me the courage to witness to others and to prepare for various public-speaking presentations not only in my work-a-day world but also when fulfilling church duties.

Looking back, I can recall several times where I clung tightly to this promise when accepting a new work assignment which I viewed as challenging, knowing I could only be successful with the Lord's daily assistance and blessing. The first time was when I had been working as an administrative secretary in a large Southern California hospital for a couple of satisfying years, when, out of nowhere, I got a phone call from a nearby university. They wanted to interview me for an assistant director position in their recruiting department! How in the world did that happen? It turns out that a gal who worked across the hall from me in the administrative wing, and who I knew only casually, had recommended me to her father, the director of recruitment. He must have put a lot of stock in his daughter's judgment because he was even willing to come to the hospital where I worked, about twenty-five miles from his office, and interview me on my lunch hour so that I wouldn't have to take time off of work to see him. I knew nothing about recruitment at that time, but in view of his enthusiasm, I decided to do the interview anyway, mostly out of curiosity of what such a position might entail.

So, we agreed to meet the next day at noon in the hospital's chapel. The picture of the job he painted sounded really exciting to me! Basically, I would travel around Southern California and Arizona to represent the university, answer questions from potential students and their parents, and meet with past students to encourage them to re-enroll for the following year. I would schedule assemblies of junior and senior high school classes, set up a booth with promotional literature at college day events, and meet with students at community colleges on assigned transfer days. At times when travel was not required, I would meet with potential students who came to my office, provide tours of the campus, and sit on the admissions committee. There would also be some phone work, a bit of administrative assistant-type correspondence to be done, and the creation and dissemination of a speakers' bureau brochure, which would get members of the faculty out in the community to represent the institution. He explained that I would have a lot of autonomy, a flexible schedule, an office assistant to cover the bases when I was out of the office, and my own personal travel expense account. For longer excursions, I could also request to use a company car, so as to reduce the wear and tear on my own vehicle.

The more he shared about the position, the more excited I became, but it was coupled with a fear that maybe I would be biting off more than I could chew! I was in my twenties at the time and had never held a job that required a lot of public speaking before. The scope of the work took my breath away! I loved traveling, and talking with all kinds of people, and would be honored to represent the university that I myself had had the privilege to attend. However, I knew it would be so challenging that I would need to depend on God every day to give me the wisdom and the ability to tackle this huge assignment and that the public nature of the position would stretch me in many ways. So, I told the director that I would need to think and pray about it. What happened next bowled me over!

Before the hour-long interview ended, he actually offered me the position and said that he would call me in a couple of days to see what I had decided! I was in a daze for the next forty-eight hours, praying and trying to weigh the advantages against the disadvantages. Both joy and fear fought to control my emotions. Finally, and with the assurance of this promise that the Lord would be with me, strengthen me, help me, and uphold me, I had the confidence that whatever He had called me to do, He would enable me to do. As a result, by the time the director called me back, I had made up my mind to accept the position. I felt like I was jumping off the high diving board into a pool that I didn't know much about, but being the risk-taker I am, and feeling the Lord's hand guiding me, I took the plunge! Looking back, I'm so glad I did! It was one of the best jobs I ever had!

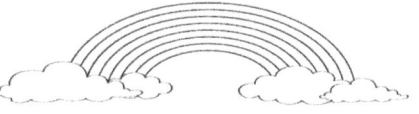

May 23

Return to Me

"I have blotted out, like a thick cloud, your transgressions, and like a cloud, your sins. Return to Me, for I have redeemed you" (Isaiah 44:22).

As humans, we tend to experience spiritual mountaintops, perhaps after a spiritual retreat or a special week of prayer, as well as spiritual valleys. The valleys can be caused by any number of things. The loss of a loved one, which leaves us in shock. How could God allow this to happen? A sudden betrayal, or a difficult divorce, leaving us drained physically, emotionally, and spiritually. An illness that just hangs on or the fear-producing diagnosis of one. Unanticipated financial losses or just the daily grind to try to keep our head above water and put food on the table. In fact, anything that causes us pain, confusion, grief, fear, or doubt can begin to erode our trust in God. Sometimes, in our anger and despair over what has happened in our life, we even turn our backs on God and walk away from Him deliberately. While at other times, our close relationship with Him simply dries up because we have not maintained our daily devotional program, allowing the many pressures or even some of the more distracting pleasures of this world to consume our time and attention. As a result, we find ourselves in a spiritual valley, or worse, having severed our relationship with God completely!

At this juncture, Satan has an advantage over us because, in our weakened spiritual condition, he knows we are likely to believe one or both of his most successful lies. One is that, surely God doesn't love us anymore now that we've drifted away from Him. And the second is that after all the bad things we've done, how can we ever come "home" again? We've gotten so far off the path that we might as well just give up on trying to return to our Heavenly Father. We convince ourselves that neither God nor His followers will ever be able to forgive us. In fact, in our shame, sometimes we can't even forgive ourselves.

But praise God, the Scriptures, like today's verse, don't lie. They give all who want to change directions and come back to God the promise that He does still love them. In fact, He died to redeem them and is beckoning them to return! And not only will He forgive their sins but He will totally blot them out! Whenever I read this verse, I can't help but think what it is like to be looking out the window of an airplane and see a town below one minute, and the next minute, due to thick cloud cover, not being able to see anything under the clouds at all!

Fortunately, all who have fallen from grace at some time in their life can take hope from this verse. A little farther along in Isaiah says that, "All we like sheep have gone astray; we have turned, every one, to his own way…" (Isa. 53:6), which means that we are not the only ones who have veered off the path. All of us, at one time or another, have made mistakes. All of us need forgiveness and grace. Jesus talked many times about His willingness to forgive us and receive us back into a close relationship with Him, but to my mind, never illustrated it so beautifully as in the parable of the prodigal son (see Luke 15:11–24). If you haven't read the story recently, today would be a good time to read it again. Linger especially over the part that describes how the father welcomed the errant son home with open arms and great joy and gladness! How can we resist returning to a loving God like that?

May 24

Gray Hairs

"Even to your old age, I am He, and even to gray hairs I will carry you! I have made, and I will bear; even I will carry, and will deliver you" (Isaiah 46:4).

In previous devotionals we have talked about related topics, such as old age, retirement, and the need for renewed strength. But this verse is special in that it assures us that even when we become so

aged that we can no longer carry our own weight or have become so disabled that we have lost our mobility or even our capacity to think clearly and make rational decisions, the Lord will actually carry us! We can still trust our waning lives into His faithful and loving arms. He reminds us here that, after all, He is the One who made us; therefore, He is the One who knows our weaknesses and limitations better than anyone else. He also promises in this text that He will deliver us!

As I have watched people age and seen some who, due to a forgetful memory, diminished brain function, or the onset of some type of dementia, are now making unwise decisions or acting out toward others in ways they never would have done before, I have often commented to my husband that I'm glad the Lord doesn't just judge us on the words and actions of the last few years of our lives when we may have "lost a few of our marbles," as my father used to say.

When I read this verse today, I can envision the Savior, despite all of our problems and lost capacities, grabbing us up in His warm embrace, and comforting us by saying, "Don't worry! I remember who you were at your best as well as at your worst, and there's nothing you can do to make me not love you. I've got your back. Just trust me for a little while longer—until all your trials and tribulations will come to an end in a glorious future with me!"

It reminds me of when I was small, and my bigger than life six-foot, four-inch father would say in his loud, booming voice when we came to a busy and dangerous street corner, "Wait!" Then he would scoop me up and carry me, sometimes on his strong shoulders, to the other side where I could safely run and play again! It also reminds me of the times when my little sister was a baby, and she wouldn't stop crying and refused to go to sleep for anyone else in the family. My father would cradle her in his caring arms and pat her gently and rhythmically until she finally drifted off into the deep and peaceful slumber of a trusting child.

I'm so comforted knowing that that is what the Lord has promised to do for us gray-headed ones as well! It doesn't matter how we look, how old and decrepit we've become, or what disabilities we've acquired. We may have lost our teeth, our hearing, our eyesight, or our mobility. Our memories might be fading, and some of our words and actions may seem irrational to others. Our hair might be gray or we may have lost it altogether! None of this matters to the Lord or changes the depth of His love for us. All that matters to Him is us knowing and embracing that each of us are His child, and He is our loving and protective heavenly Father. As we age and feel ourselves getting weaker, let's learn to simply rest our weary souls in His faithful and all-powerful embrace!

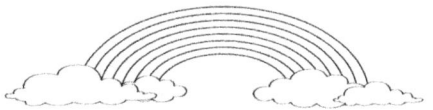

Beautiful Feet

"How beautiful upon the mountains are the feet of him who brings good news, who proclaims peace, who brings glad tidings of good things, who proclaims salvation, who says to Zion, 'Your God reigns!'" (Isaiah 52:7).

According to *The SDA Bible Commentary*, this was an expression of the joy and excitement of the watchers on the walls of Zion when they looked out and saw a messenger coming toward the city who they knew was bearing glad tidings! To the Jews of Isaiah's time, who were suffering under the yoke of an alien nation, there was "no more joyous message than that of deliverance and peace" (*The SDA Bible Commentary*, vol. 4, p. 287). Although this passage had a literal interpretation, it could also be applied to the proclamation of the good news of the gospel, which would be revealed with the coming of the promised Messiah, who would free them from sin and evil. In fact, many Bible scholars see the last verses of Isaiah 52 as a prelude to the description of the Messiah as set forth in chapter 53.

Later, in the context of the New Testament, Paul refers back to this text, using it to describe the messengers who "preach the gospel of peace, who bring glad tidings of good things!" (Rom. 10:15). In his ongoing effort to recruit more volunteers to work in the promulgation of the gospel of Christ, Paul also says this: "How then shall they call on Him in whom they have not believed? And how shall they believe in Him of whom they have not heard? And how shall they hear without a preacher? And how shall they preach unless they are sent?" (Rom. 10:14, 15). Here was an invitation to the early followers of Jesus to do all they could

to spread the good news of the gospel to the then-known world.

Interestingly, this invitation to share the message of salvation with others echoes down to us who are followers of Jesus today. It is still motivating pastors, teachers, doctors, and missionaries of all kinds to go wherever the Lord sends them. They are working to proclaim the glad tidings of peace, love, joy, and hope to those who continue to sit in darkness, unaware of the blessings of becoming a believer in the God who created them, who opened the door of salvation to them, and who, as this verse points out, still reigns!

After my family accepted a call to go to the mission field, we attended a mission institute program to help us prepare for the many cultural, linguistic, and environmental changes we would experience in our new place of labor. Most of all, our family, as well as about ten or twelve others who would be going to various parts of the world, sought to prepare ourselves spiritually. We worshipped together each morning and evening as well as shared our testimonies about how we had felt God calling us to serve Him in this way. I remember that today's text was one we studied about and prayed over frequently during that time.

Since then, I'm happy to report, I have actually been privileged to see and experience some of the glorious results of the "beautiful feet" of those pioneers who went before us into different parts of the world, changing the lives of all those who were ready to accept the good news of the gospel. I've seen the many converts crowding humble church buildings, the establishment of schools, universities, and hospitals, and evangelism adopting numerous new ways through technology and the media to reach people in the far-reaching corners of the world!

Of course, the Lord also calls people to work for Him in their own countries of origin. Wherever we are called to serve, it's good to know that the Lord sees our feet as "beautiful" whenever we are sharing with others His wonderful glad tidings!

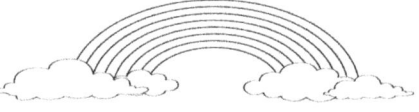

May 26

Seek the Lord

"Seek the LORD while He may be found, call upon Him while He is near. Let the wicked forsake his way, and the unrighteous man his thoughts; let him return to the LORD, and He will have mercy on him; and to our God, for He will abundantly pardon" (Isaiah 55:6, 7).

In early 2020, a very prominent sports figure, together with his young daughter and seven other healthy, vibrant people, died suddenly in a terrible helicopter crash. The nation was in shock! The day had started out like so many others. None of these people realized that it would be the last day of their lives. They were so full of life with many plans for the years ahead. But, unfortunately, terrible and sudden accidents of all kinds are a common occurrence while we are living here on this sinful planet. Not only accidents by various modes of transportation but ones that happen at home, our place of work, or through natural disasters, which claim many lives every year. This doesn't even include dangerous illnesses or the ever-increasing loss of life as a result of terrible crimes, such as mass shootings!

Sadly, these fatal occurrences can invade our lives at any age, killing us quickly and unexpectedly.

As the old saying goes, "None of us has a lease on life." It is a precious gift, which can be swept away from us at any time. Thus, it follows that we should take advantage of every day we have to live the best life possible and enjoy the blessings of an abundant life, filled with thanksgiving, joy, and laughter. And we should work to be the best parent, child, sibling, or worker we can, while we still have the chance! Our time on earth is short, even if we live to one hundred, which few of us will.

The interesting thing to consider here is that we can only live our best lives if we have a close relationship with the Lord. These verses suggest how we can do that. We need to "call upon Him while He is near." In the process, we need to forsake our wicked ways (as well as our unrighteous thoughts), return to Him, as we discussed a couple of days ago, and ask for His mercy and forgiveness. What will His response be? We are promised that He will "abundantly pardon!" So, what are we waiting for?

Once our sins and mistakes are forgiven and our consciences are clear, we are ready to begin living the kind of abundant life that the Lord created us to enjoy. As newly-cleaned and empty vessels, we will now have room for the in-filling of the Holy Spirit, which will give us all the beautiful fruits of the Spirit we need to live a worthwhile life. As a result, we will be able to bless all those around us with the most precious attributes of love, joy,

peace, longsuffering, kindness, goodness, faithfulness, gentleness, and self-control, as delineated in Galatians 5:22, 23.

Would those you spend the most time with—your family, friends, and co-workers—testify that these fruits of the Spirit are exhibited in your current interactions with them? If not, take heart! We can start today! If we will seek the Lord while we still have time left as well as while we still have the mental capacity (for some of us who are older) to do so, He will wipe our slate clean, giving us another chance, every moment of our lives, to become more like Him. This passage reminds us that we need to seek Him now! We need to call on Him to restore us to a right relationship with Him now! Tomorrow may be too late!

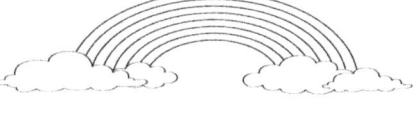

May 27

The Robe of Righteousness

"I will greatly rejoice in the LORD. My soul shall be joyful in my God; for He has clothed me with the garments of salvation, He has covered me with the robe of righteousness, as a bridegroom decks himself with ornaments, and as a bride adorns herself with her jewels. For as the earth brings forth its bud, as the garden causes the things that are sown in it to spring forth, so the LORD GOD will cause righteousness and praise to spring forth before all the nations" (Isaiah 61:10, 11).

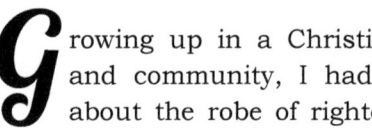rowing up in a Christian household and community, I had heard much about the robe of righteousness that

the Lord will provide to those who love Him. I just never knew exactly where the phrase came from. After checking with my Bible's concordance, it seems that this passage is the most complete depiction of not only this heavenly garment but also its purpose.

Notice that verse 10 tells us plainly that the Lord himself clothes us in "the garments of salvation." The purpose of the beautiful robe of righteousness is to cover us, making us fit to be His much-loved bride. Who doesn't like to get new clothes, especially before a celebratory event or a banquet of some kind? Here, however, we don't have to worry about going shopping or finding just the right size. The Lord will provide exactly what we need, and more than that, it will fit us perfectly! We won't need to try to conceal our blemishes caused by sin, or our bulges, born of our selfish rebellion, because once we have betrothed ourselves to our loving Groom, He will make sure that we are covered completely by His own perfect righteousness. We will be able to enter the wedding feast in great confidence, with no insecurities or complaints—just thanksgiving and praise upon our lips!

Something as simple as a woman putting on foundation, or what some call liquid makeup, when it matches our skin tone and is applied skillfully can serve as an illustration of how our unique imperfections can be covered over entirely when we submit to the One who has not only created us but died to save us individually.

Another humble example comes to mind when I think about my bathtub. Recently, it suffered an unsightly chip. After worrying about it for a while, I finally decided to do something to improve its looks and to try to keep it from getting any worse! So, I went down to the local hardware store and found a spray can of white flat enamel made to be used either inside or out, so it could withstand the water to which it would be frequently exposed. To my joy, just a few coats covered the chip completely. When it dried, that area blended right in with the white enamel in the rest of the tub. Why hadn't I done something to fix this problem sooner?

Sometimes we do something similar with a little sin that pops up here or there in our lives. It is causing a black mark on our character, but since it's small, we figure we don't have to deal with it right away. We're too busy with other things. At times, we just don't feel like doing anything about it. We've become spiritually lazy. Worse yet, we may have actually gotten used to its presence in our lives. In fact, if we just "close the shower door," so to speak, we hope that nobody else will even notice it.

When this is our experience, we should beware, knowing that not taking care of the little problem as soon as possible will only result in bigger and more consequential problems later on. We need to remember that 1) Jesus is the solution to our sin problem, 2) He is available to take care of it immediately, and 3) when we simply ask, He will forgive us, covering our sins perfectly!

What's more, accepting His offer to wear His complete sparkling white robe of righteousness is our passport to the heavenly experience recorded in verse 11, where we'll stand amazed as we watch the Lord "cause righteousness and praise to spring forth before all the nations." We will not be alone. Many others from around the world who have chosen to accept His garments of salvation will enter into the great wedding feast, each one rejoicing in the generous and appropriate clothing He has provided just for them!

Broken Cisterns

"For My people have committed two evils: they have forsaken Me, the fountain of living waters, and hewn themselves cisterns—broken cisterns that can hold no water" (Jeremiah 2:13).

In this chapter the Lord has communicated to Jeremiah His disappointment in the children of Israel, who seem to have forgotten all that He has done for them. He also voices His disapproval of their idolatrous worship practices. He recounts His mercy in bringing them out of bondage in Egypt, His faithfulness in providing for all their needs in the wilderness, and His blessings in leading them into the "bountiful country" of Canaan (Jer. 2:7). Then He decries the fact that instead of remembering His gracious acts on their behalf, they have forsaken His ways and turned to the worship of idols—objects made by their own hands out of wood and stone! What an insult to the Almighty, who wanted them to proclaim His glory throughout the land they had so marvelously inherited. Instead, they had defiled the land and made their heritage an abomination.

To make matters worse, not only had the common people fallen into idolatry but their leaders had also gone astray! The priests, who were supposed to teach the law, no longer had a close relationship with God; the rulers were setting a horrible example by their own transgressions in this regard; and even the prophets of the day were prophesying by the popular heathen god named Baal! No wonder the Lord had to call a new young prophet, one who was true to Him, to wake the people up to their horrible spiritual condition, to entreat them to return to the one and only true God, and to warn them of the consequences if they continued in their course of idol worship. It was a difficult and daunting task for Jeremiah, but he delivered the messages God gave him for the Israelites faithfully throughout his lifetime.

Today's verse is simply a brief summary of the Lord's complaints against His people, and to make the matter clear, the Lord uses a metaphor, stating that they had left the "fountain of living waters" (Himself) to build cisterns for themselves which were broken, rendering them impossible to satisfy their (spiritual) thirst. In a land where water was so precious, this was an illustration that couldn't fail to be understood by Jeremiah's listeners. The word "cistern" is not one that most of us use in our daily speech these days, but it means much the same as it did back then. It is generally some kind of underground tank that is used for storing water. Obviously, if the tank is cracked or damaged in some way, it won't hold the life-giving liquid it was meant to store, bringing serious consequences to those who depend on it.

It set me to thinking about the "cisterns" so many of us have made for ourselves today. We so easily turn our backs on the One who has given us life and breath and continues to sustain us daily, in exchange for fleeting interests, pleasures, riches, or popularity, only to find that in our time of need, those things can't provide the kind of long-lasting satisfaction that we crave. Too late we discover that our supposedly trustworthy "cistern" has cracks in it. This reminds me of another analogy with a similar moral, where a man climbs to the top of the ladder of success, only to find that it was leaning against the wrong building! May the Lord help us to keep our priorities straight by keeping our focus on worshiping only Him.

May 29

True Glory

"Thus says the LORD: 'Let not the wise man *glory in his wisdom, let not the mighty* man *glory in his might, nor let the rich* man *glory in his riches; but let him who glories glory in this, that he understands and knows Me, that I* am *the LORD, exercising lovingkindness, judgment, and righteousness in the earth. For in these I delight,' says the LORD" (Jeremiah 9:23, 24).*

These verses make me think of the anecdote where a little boy is showing his muscles to his neighborhood friend, boasting about how strong he is, when his well-built father shows up to whisk him off his feet and carry him home to supper. Everything is relative. The little boy thought he was strong until his much stronger parent showed up. In comparison, he was very weak. Of course, we can't even begin to explain the difference between our strength and the Lord's—whether we're talking about mental prowess, moral or physical strength, or material riches. There really is no comparison!

I fear that some people may take this passage to mean we should not set temporal goals or strive to reach our highest potential in whatever area of life we pursue. As if it is wrong to celebrate our achievements or feel a healthy pride and sense of satisfaction when we have put forth effort and persevered until we have accomplished a worthy objective. I think we need to remember the verses scattered throughout the Bible that tell us to strive for excellence in all we do. Ecclesiastes 9:10, for example, says that whatever our hand finds to do, we should "do *it* with your might," while 1 Corinthians 10:31 says that whatever we do, we should "do all to the glory of God."

Unfortunately, I have known both parents and teachers who never expressed encouragement or celebrated when the children under their care did a good job on something, whether it came to academics or any other area of life where they excelled. I even knew a family that decided not to celebrate their daughter's eighth grade graduation because they thought it would make her too proud! What a shame! Children need words of encouragement to guide them along the right path as well as to feel motivated to continue to put the time and effort into something that requires discipline and determination to do well. Whether in music, sports, projects, assignments, or tests, there are many little victories in a child's life that, though seemingly small to an adult, are very meaningful to them. These little accomplishments are benchmarks that demonstrate their progress, build confidence, and develop character, preparing them to eventually take on more challenging responsibilities so they can become successful in adult life. This is borne out by a gem of a quote by Ellen White that I came across recently. It counsels,

> Whenever the mother can speak a word of commendation for the good conduct of her children, she should do so. She should encourage them by words of approval and looks of love. This will be as sunshine to the heart of a child and lead to the cultivation of self-respect and… character. (*Testimonies for the Church*, vol. 3, p. 532)

On this same page, it goes on to advocate the importance of cultivating sympathy, affection, and caring about the everyday childish interests of children. Thus, mothers will be able to "bind their children to their hearts."

Obviously, we don't want to focus so much on self-esteem that we neglect our duty to correct children when they are moving in a wrong direction or treat them as if they can do no wrong. It is our responsibility to guide them, not to spoil them with a lot of undue fanfare or unmerited compliments. But harsh, critical words, or simply ignoring what they are doing well, will discourage them to the point that they will lose their interest and pleasure in doing good things and begin looking for affirmation in all the wrong places. Balance is key here.

After all, even as adults, we do better when we receive positive feedback as opposed to criticism or no feedback at all. I believe what the Lord is telling us in these verses is not to become proud or arrogant about our strengths, thinking that we are better than others (who may be much better at other things than we are). We shouldn't get so caught up in our preferred areas of endeavor that we forget all about the God who actually gave us the ability to acquire our gifts and talents and who maintains our very lives day by day. To me, in this last verse it seems the Lord is concluding His admonition by saying that we shouldn't get so caught up with earthly things that we don't take the time necessary to get to know Him well. We should be very familiar with His strongest attributes so that as we grow spiritually, we can become ever more like Him. Because, ultimately, that will be our most important accomplishment!

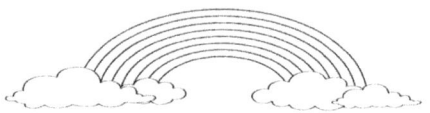

The Footmen

"If you have run with the footmen, and they have wearied you, then how can you contend with horses? And if in the land of peace, in which you trusted, they wearied you, then how will you do in the floodplain of the Jordan?"
(Jeremiah 12:5).

I know that at first glance this may seem a strange verse for a devotional thought, but on closer examination, it really does apply to our experiences today. Have you ever been so upset with someone or some situation that you almost "lost your Christian experience" over it? If so, take note of what *The SDA Bible Commentary* has to teach us about this passage of Scripture. It brings out four important points, all stated in the form of questions.

Just to provide a little context at the outset, in ancient Israel, there were several kinds of fighters when a battle was being fought. There were the ordinary soldiers that fought on foot, and then there were the more intimidating calvary who fought on powerful horses. Thus, the commentary explains that the word "footmen," as used here, is a figure of speech representing the "ordinary vicissitudes of life," whereas the word "horses" (or horsemen), represents life's more difficult experiences. Now, we get to the four questions posed by the Bible commentators:

1) If we neglect the minor tasks of life, how can we undertake the greater responsibilities that may come to us?
2) If we succumb to the smaller temptations of everyday life, how can we overcome in the greater crises of life?
3) If we cannot endure the lesser troubles of life, how can we withstand the terrible tribulations that may yet come upon us?

4) If we fail to meet the situations of the present day with faith and trust, how will we be able to stand the almost unendurable hardships and almost overmastering delusions that will come upon us during the "time of trouble?" (*The SDA Bible Commentary*, vol. 4, p. 408)

As you can see, we have plenty of food for thought here. As I turn these questions over in my mind, they challenge me. First, I think of the importance of all the small tasks and duties in preparing me for whatever the Lord calls me to do in the future. Second, I consider the importance of resisting the lesser temptations, so I develop the habit of choosing what's best before the bigger ones come. Next, I should not make every mole hill into a mountain. It would serve me well to complain less about small irritations and concentrate more on the important issues of life. I was recently in a Bible study class where we were discussing being prepared for all the dire things that could happen to us in the last days, but in the meantime, we're not even prepared to quit gossiping today about this person or that who, in our hyper-sensitive state, we feel has slighted us in some way. If we can't even act like Christians now, when we are enjoying relative peace and creature comforts of all kinds, how will we ever be ready for whatever spiritual tests may come to us at the end of time?

Finally, I'm impressed with the need to strengthen my faith and trust in God for both now and whatever the future may bring. In our human nature, we are always tempted to try to solve all our problems ourselves, often forgetting that the Lord is standing by ready to help us when we ask Him. One of the great advantages of making it a habit to trust Him and immediately ask for His help is that it soon becomes very clear to us that

He is working behind the scenes for our good. We recognize the answered prayers, the rearranged circumstances on our behalf, and we have a fresh and glowing testimony of what the Lord has done for us, not only to strengthen our own faith but to share with others so that their faith can be bolstered as well. So, I'm inspired today to start keeping up with at least the footmen!

May 31

Our Future

"For I know the thoughts that I think toward you, says the LORD, thoughts of peace and not of evil, to give you a future and a hope. Then you will call upon Me and go and pray to Me, and I will listen to you. And you will seek Me and find Me, when you search for Me with all your heart" (Jeremiah 29:11–13).

We can't leave the book of Jeremiah without pausing to enjoy the wonderful comfort found in this famous passage. In times of discouragement and feelings of hopelessness, what Christian hasn't grabbed on to the beautiful promises of verse 11 like a life jacket? I know I have. How reassuring to know in our times of need that the Lord is aware of our dilemmas and is actually thinking about us! And what is He thinking? Not about our weaknesses and mistakes, but about how He can bring peace into our lives to replace whatever evil we are experiencing. Then, He goes the second and third mile to promise us hope in our despair

and a future even though we couldn't see any way to move forward before or muster the courage to even try.

I don't know about you, but I've been there. Walking in the fog of depression, seeing all my plans and dreams for the future crushed. Not able to see any light at the end of a long, lonely, and dark tunnel. During these times of difficulty and doubt, I, not unlike Elijah, just wanted to lie down and die. What kind of worthwhile future could the Lord possibly fashion out of the messed up pieces of my life? At such times, this verse, even when claimed in weak faith, can begin to provide a glimmer of hope, like putting a comforting cream over an open wound and bandaging it up so that it can heal.

Reading on, we see that verse 12 gives us some guidance on what to do to increase the possibility that our future will be brighter. The Lord entreats us to call upon Him, promising that He will listen to us. Just the knowledge that the all-loving, all-knowing, and all-powerful Creator of the universe is willing to take time to listen to us begins to calm our troubled souls.

Then, the frosting on the cake (you may have noticed I like that expression) is that in verse 13, He gives us another almost unbelievable promise when He says that we will actually find Him, the Solver of all of life's problems, when we search for Him with all of our heart. This means when we lay it all on the line, throwing ourselves upon His mercy, surrendering what's left of our life to Him, then we will come to really know Him. This experience will bolster our faith and help us understand that He actually can create a new and meaningful future for us. Even if this experience only happens when we are close to death, like the thief on the cross, we can take hope in knowing that He has already planned an incredibly wonderful new life for us in eternity. Either way, here or in heaven, we win when we hang on to our Savior regarding our future. He's always planning for us in love.

My own experience has been that when I've been at the end of my rope and earnestly asked for His intervention in my life, He graciously provided the motivation for me to continue climbing. He has also given me some wonderful mountaintop vistas in my new future that I never could have imagined! He gave me a Christian family, purposeful and rewarding work, great friends, and some very interesting places to labor in His cause. Often, when we think we've come to a dead-end in life, the Lord opens marvelous new paths for us!

Recently, I heard someone talk about a gift they received that had a concise and insightful saying engraved on it. I think it provides the perfect poetic conclusion for our discussion today. It read: "Just when the caterpillar thought the world was over, it became a butterfly!"

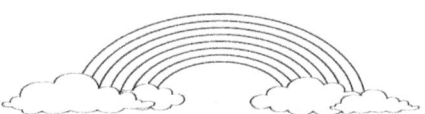

June 1

His Treasuries

"He has made the earth by His power; He has established the world by His wisdom, and stretched out the heaven by His understanding. When He utters His voice—there is a multitude of waters in the heavens: 'He causes the vapors to ascend from the ends of the earth; He makes lightnings for the rain; He brings the wind out of His treasuries'" (Jeremiah 51:15, 16).

As I write this, the mountains behind our house are all shrouded in mists, and a damp fog hides the snow that is falling at the higher elevations today. I like these verses because they give us a small glimpse of the continuous workings of God in the natural world all around us. Some people believe that after God created the world, He got busy with other things in the universe and basically left us to fend for ourselves. But anyone who spends much time in nature can trace His hand in the beauty of the flowers, the glory of a sunset, the inspiration of a mountain, the wonder of the fall colors, or the power of a thunderstorm—not to mention the built-in instincts of all the different species of animals who know how to care for themselves and their offspring, and the absolute miracle of a new baby being born into the world! For those willing to open their eyes to the marvelous creations and interventions of our Maker all around us, we can't help but feel awe, gratitude, and the heartfelt response of praise!

And these are just the things we can see here and now in a sin-damaged environment and with our limited senses. What other wonders will the Lord bring out of "His treasuries" when our minds and senses are expanded and He unfolds the mysteries of the universe to us throughout the ages of eternity? What beauties will we behold, what melodies and harmonies will we revel in, what heightened feelings of joy and thanksgiving will we experience? I can only refer to one of my favorite texts again, which says, "Eye has not seen, nor ear heard, nor have entered into the heart of man the things which God has prepared for those who love Him" (1 Cor. 2:9). What unimaginable enjoyment we have to look forward to in the life to come!

Not only should these verses remind us of the majesty of our God but they should also trigger a desire to break forth in praise to Him. Recently, while practicing piano, I came across this well-known hymn, which Christians have used for centuries to try to express their gratitude for all of God's handiwork, their love in response to His mighty acts, and their praise to the One who is the Source, the Maker, and the Sustainer of all creation! It's hymn 2 in *The Seventh-day Adventist Hymnal*, and it's entitled "All Creatures of Our God and King." Relish it with me today!

All creatures of our God and King, lift up your voice with us and sing: Alleluia! Alleluia! O burning sun with golden beam and silver moon with softer gleam: Oh, praise Him! Oh, praise Him! Alleluia, alleluia, alleluia!
O rushing wind and breezes soft, O clouds that ride the winds aloft: Oh,

praise Him! Alleluia! O rising morn, in praise rejoice, O lights of evening, find a voice. Oh, praise Him! Oh, praise Him! Alleluia, alleluia, alleluia!

O flowing waters, pure and clear, make music for your Lord to hear. Oh, praise Him! Alleluia! O fire so masterful and bright, providing us with warmth and light, oh, praise Him! Oh, praise Him! Alleluia, alleluia, alleluia!

Let all things their Creator bless, and worship Him in humbleness, oh, praise Him! Alleluia! Oh, praise the Father, praise the Son, and praise the Spirit, three in One! Oh, praise Him! Oh, praise Him! Alleluia, alleluia, alleluia!

What better way to welcome the beginning of a new month than to immerse ourselves in robust praise to our Creator God!

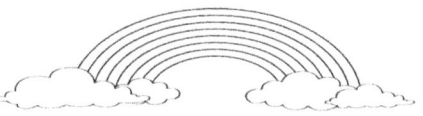

June 2

His Faithfulness

"Through the LORD's mercies we are not consumed, because His compassions fail not. They are new every morning; great is Your faithfulness" (Lamentations 3:22, 23).

As I am writing this, we are in the throes of the coronavirus pandemic, and life as we knew it has been turned upside down. We have been asked to employ "social distancing" in order to slow the spread of this feared and fast-growing illness throughout not only the USA but the world. So, for the time being, those of us who are a bit older as well as those with pre-existing and chronic health issues are being asked to isolate themselves at home. All unnecessary travel is discouraged, and many small businesses, restaurants, theatres, libraries, churches, and even schools have been shut down—in an all-out effort to save people from catching, and worse yet dying from, the dreaded disease. It is a trying time—a time to turn to the Lord and to seek and appreciate evidences of His faithfulness despite whatever difficulties we are experiencing. Focusing on His faithfulness will encourage us and give us courage to press on.

As it turns out, just yesterday—ready or not—my husband and I had an unanticipated opportunity to practice this spiritual discipline! While experiencing all of the turmoil of the coronavirus, we also had many other unexpected occurrences. First, we had a huge snow storm. My husband, who had a doctor's appointment in the morning, had to call to say he would be late because he would have to clear the driveway of snow before backing the car out of the garage. Due to the storm, which also came with strong winds, we had a power outage. When my husband did start out for his appointment, he had a car accident just a few blocks from home, sliding off the pavement due to icy roads. After he got the car out of the ditch, with the help of a good Samaritan, he was drenched from the snow, and although the damaged car could be driven, he had to come home to change clothes.

He was further delayed by needing to file a claim with our insurance company for the repair of his vehicle. By now we realized that instead of just taking off a few hours in the morning, he would have to call his boss to let him know he would be missing the whole day of work in order to deal with the aftermath of the accident.

Finally, upon arriving at the doctor's office, waiting for the power to come back on, and for a number of other patients who were now in line to see the doctor before him, he learned that several of the employees were out that day, so he would have to wait until they returned to work in order to finish his physical exam. When he got home, he wanted to eat his lunch, but he had forgotten it in the car, which he had left with a mechanic close to the doctor's office in town, since by then all of the power steering fluid had leaked out, and he really couldn't drive it any farther.

Fortunately, the mechanic was kind enough to bring him home. Once he ate something, we busied ourselves with trying to figure out how we were going to pay for what looked to be some expensive repairs. Several hours later, the mechanic called to tell us the car was no longer leaking fluids, so we could pick it up and take it to the body shop for the other repairs it needed. With reticence, I got up from my sick bed to go out into the snowy winter weather with my husband in my car, so we could pick up his poor banged-up vehicle. He drove it carefully to the auto body shop recommended by the insurance company, leaving it there so that they could fix it in an undetermined number of days once the required parts arrived. My husband would need to use my car to get back and forth to work until then, making it necessary for me to cancel a long-awaited doctor's appointment.

Subsequently, we decided, since we were already out of the house, to go pick up a few items we needed at the store, but my husband had left the shopping list in the pocket of the wet pants he had changed out of when he first came home after the accident. It didn't matter much because most of the store shelves were empty of the things we wanted to buy, due to the panic over the coronavirus quarantine recommendations.

As the day finally grinded to an end, we looked at each other and said, "What a day! Nothing went as we had planned!" Yet, despite our frustrations, we had to admit that the Lord had been faithful through it all. He was merciful in saving my husband from injury or death in the accident. He showed compassion through the kindness of the neighbor who came to help pull the car out of the snow and the mechanic who offered him a ride home. We also caught a glimpse of the Lord's faithfulness in that we had just received an unexpected tax refund that would help us pay the deductible to repair the car, with the insurance company picking up the tab for the rest! I'm glad we have experienced God's faithfulness, both now and in the past, regardless of whatever trials and tribulations we're facing, because it assures us that He will continue to care for us with every new day that dawns. It is, in fact, our way of tracing His rainbows amidst the clouds.

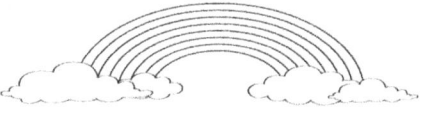

June 3

Self-Examination

"Let us search out and examine our ways, and turn back to the LORD; let us lift our hearts and hands to God in heaven" (Lamentations 3:40, 41).

Usually we are so busy examining everybody else or just so busy, period, that we don't dedicate much time to reflect upon the areas where we ourselves need improvement. I have discovered that one of the benefits of retirement is that I have more time for such reflection. As I look back at my words, actions, and motives from day to day, I must admit that I find myself going to the Lord to ask for forgiveness, for wisdom, and for guidance to do better in the future more often than I did when I was younger. Rather than seeing this continuous course correction as a negative, I believe it is a necessary part of the process of sanctification. We know we are already justified because of what Jesus has done for us, but sanctification—becoming more like the Lord—"is the work of a lifetime" (*Christ's Object Lessons*, p. 65).

In the book of Lamentations, Jeremiah is still trying, even after the destruction of Jerusalem and the captivity of many of its occupants by the Babylonians, to point the Israelites back to the God of heaven who loves them. He wanted to encourage them to worship God with both their hearts and hands, or in other words, with both their thoughts and their actions. I believe his suggestions, however, are also applicable to anyone wanting to grow spiritually today.

As with any evaluation, we need to start with some standards or criteria against which to measure our progress. Of course, the logical place to start would be with the Bible. Then, we might want to seek guidance from our faith community. Upon further consideration, we might also want to hone in on the Ten Commandments, which provide us with a concise checklist of behaviors that are right and wrong. This can be quite tricky, however, because sometimes, like the Pharisees of old, we think we understand what the criteria are for becoming holy only to miss the essence of it by a long shot. Sometimes, I fear that, like them, we are tempted to put more credence into the rituals of worship and the traditions of our religious affiliation than into the importance of getting to know the Lord for ourselves. I think we can avoid this when we focus more on Jesus—His life, His words, His actions—all the while asking the Holy Spirit to teach us how to become more like Him.

I believe that all of the sources of inspiration listed above have their place, but Jeremiah seems to be asking us to dig deeper. Besides just looking at the standards, he's asking us to take inventory on where we stand personally, particularly in the areas in which we feel the Holy Spirit working on our hearts at a given place in our spiritual journey. This will entail asking ourselves some hard questions about the appropriateness of our words and actions. Otherwise, we will never get to the important steps of conviction and repentance. Conviction will help us choose to change as we come to know our deficiencies while repentance will help us turn away from sin or error in order to come closer to the Lord. It is at that point, after experiencing His forgiveness, His victory, and His guidance on how to grow spiritually that we will feel like doing what Jeremiah expresses in the second verse above; we should lift our hearts and hands to the Lord to praise Him for His goodness in continually helping us grow to become more like Him!

June 4

The Lowest Pit

"I called on Your name, O LORD, from the lowest pit. You have heard my voice: 'Do not hide Your ear from my sighing, from my cry for help.' You drew near on the day I called on You, and said, 'Do not fear!'" (Lamentations 3:55–57).

Have you ever been in an actual pit? Jeremiah was. The princes of King Zedekiah didn't like the messages of warning and prophecies of destruction that he was given by God to share with his brethren in an effort to save them from the results of their apostasy. As a result, they threw him into a pit in the middle of a dungeon in Jerusalem. They would have left him there to die if God had not answered his petition for help and raised up an advocate for him, an Ethiopian by the name of Ebed-Melech, who worked in the king's house. How interesting that it was a foreigner, not one of his own countrymen, who took pity on Jeremiah and asked the king to remove him from the pit. Sometimes the Lord uses unanticipated ways and unexpected people to answer our prayers.

In any event, the pits that we generally find ourselves in today tend to be emotional pits of despair or spiritual pits of sin and degradation. Although not actual, physical pits, they produce in us a type of desperation and hopelessness akin to what Jeremiah suffered. When we arrive at the lowest points of our lives, what many recovering addicts call rock bottom, that is when we suddenly realize that without divine intervention we will not survive. If, at that point, we surrender our will to God and cry out for His deliverance, like Jeremiah did, we will see the amazing hand of God working on our behalf to free us from the pit in which we find ourselves.

While it is nice to experience spiritual highs and days in our Christian walk that take us on straight and sunny paths, it seems that we often grow more rapidly when we slip, stumble, and struggle along the way, recognizing our need and receiving the Lord's help on a regular basis, thus building our faith and strengthening our personal relationship with Him. One benefit of experiencing God as He answers our cries for help is that it gives us a testimony of His grace and goodness to share with others. This can inspire other people to turn to Him and to foster hope that they will also be able to climb out of whatever dire situation in which they are presently wallowing.

I like that this passage ends with the expression "Do not fear!" It shows that while the Lord is working in the background with the circumstances of our lives, He also cares about our feelings and tells us not to fear in order to bring us peace and comfort. After all, He is our loving heavenly Father, and He wants to ease our anxiety by trusting that He will take care of everything, much the same as a kind earthly father would want to do for his child. This discussion brings to mind the wonderful promise where the Lord tells us, "Fear thou not; for I am with thee: be not dismayed; for I am thy God: I will strengthen thee; yea, I will help thee; yea, I will uphold thee with the right hand of my righteousness" (Isa. 41:10, KJV). How wonderful to know that, just when we think our lives are over, and we see no way to move forward or escape from the lowest pit we've ever been in, we can cry out to God, and know that He will not only hear us, but uphold us with His righteousness. We just need to trust Him!

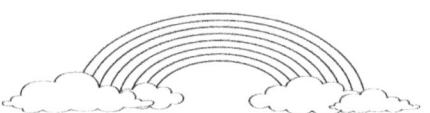

Unsuspected Idols

"They will throw their silver into the streets, and their gold will be like refuse; their silver and their gold will not be able to deliver them in the day of the wrath of the LORD; they will not satisfy their souls, nor fill their stomachs, because it became their stumbling block of iniquity" (Ezekiel 7:19).

Ezekiel is another prophet who was tasked with warning and admonishing God's people. He was called to this work during the dark seventy-year period of time when they were in captivity in Babylon. He himself was carried away to Babylon before the final assault on Jerusalem. When the judgement on Israel was near, God gave Ezekiel the above message regarding those who had valued their riches and the idols made from them more than the living God. In fact, the riches themselves had become idols, and as such, they became barriers between them and the Lord. Their money became an actual "stumbling block" to their spiritual health.

Volume four of *The SDA Bible Commentary* suggests that both their money and their idols were things they would have to cast away in order to survive the coming destruction of Jerusalem as well as the long trek they would be taking between there and the destination of their captivity in Babylon (see p. 600). The material things they had trusted in would not be of any help to them under such dire circumstances but rather a hindrance.

Could it be that we are also trusting too much in the material things of life? Trusting more in them than in the God who created us? Loving them, like Lot's wife, who turned back to see her beloved possessions one more time instead of obeying God's merciful mandate to flee in order to save her life from the destruction that fell on Sodom and Gomorrah? Of course we care about the material things that make our lives so pleasant and comfortable—our house, our car, our furniture, our clothes, and our money—but we mustn't make them our idols because, in the end, they will never be able to save us. They will not serve us at the end of time during the final time of trouble that we know is coming upon the world. They won't help us even before then, when we go through a war or some type of natural disaster. Floods, fires, earthquakes, hurricanes, tornadoes, and volcanic eruptions can all sweep away our treasured possessions in an instant.

Because of where I live, the most impacting recent natural disaster for me was the rapid and overpowering firestorm that swept over a town, ironically called Paradise, in 2018. In a matter of hours, approximately 90 percent of the town was leveled. Houses, businesses, hospitals, schools, churches, and offices were all swallowed up in the flames before most people had time to grab anything, barely escaping with their lives. And many did not escape. Most of those who did had to move to other communities because when they finally were allowed to come back home, they found nothing but charred and smokey ruins in their neighborhoods. Most of the banks, stores, gas stations, and other businesses that help sustain life had also been destroyed, along with the whole infra-structure of the town.

First responders marveled at how rapid and devastating the Camp Fire, as they called it, had been. For months afterward we heard the stories of people who had experienced the greatest losses of their lifetime yet were thankful to God just to be alive, realizing that their lives and those of their loved ones were their most valuable possessions. What a strong and solemn reminder to all of us of where we need to place our priorities—not on the temporary things of earth, which we so readily turn into idols, but on the eternal things of God, such as a firm faith in Him and a loving relationship with those He has been gracious enough to place all around us.

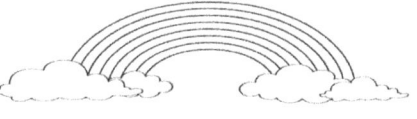

June 6

A Heart of Flesh

"Then I will give them one heart, and I will put a new spirit within them, and take the stony heart out of their flesh, and give them a heart of flesh, that they may walk in My statutes and keep My judgments and do them; and they shall be My people, and I will be their God" (Ezekiel 11:19, 20).

In the midst of stern messages about the future of the errant people of God if they continued to ignore His statutes and judgments, in today's verses, Ezekiel received a word of encouragement about the Lord's vision for them if they chose to return to Him with all their hearts. His desire for them was that they would come back to Jerusalem after their seventy-year captivity in Babylon with humble and teachable hearts so that, with the divine help of the Holy Spirit, they could finally fulfill His purpose for them to share their knowledge of Him with the then-known world.

Unfortunately, ancient Israel did not rise to the level of His aspirations for them.

Today, the Christian church faces a similar challenge. He now asks His modern-day followers to accomplish the sacred task of evangelizing our world. The problem is, we often fall short of His expectations as well. Our only hope of doing better is to ask the Lord, individually, to take away our selfish, cold, and stony heart and, through His Spirit, gift us with a soft, warm, and vibrant heart of flesh. Otherwise, our spiritual lethargy, our carnal nature, our blindness to sin, and our self-centered pride will prevent us from accomplishing God's will in our generation.

How does the transformation from hard hearted to gentle and kind take place? It is the miracle of conversion. The first line tells us that it is the "new spirit" the Lord gives us that turns human beings around. When I think of a person with a hard heart, I see someone who is stubborn, willful, not easily entreated, even cruel. This person could be harsh, critical, unsympathetic, and unmindful of the suffering of others. I remember that the Lord told the Pharisees that the only reason Moses permitted the Israelites to divorce was because of the hardness of their hearts (see Matt. 19:8). On the other hand, a person with a "heart of flesh" demonstrates all the beautiful fruits of the Spirit, including love, joy, peace, longsuffering, goodness, kindness, and gentleness. Like Jesus, he or she would care about others, listen to them, and do everything possible to help them as well as secure their eternal salvation.

Notice what else the Lord wants to give His people according to these texts: one heart, which signifies unity and obedience to His statutes and judgments—not just knowing them but walking in them. He hopes for us to actually incorporate them into our daily lives. Those who allow the Lord to change their hearts in these ways become true and faithful witnesses.

Ultimately, the complete fulfillment of this promise will take place when we come into the New Jerusalem after Jesus' second coming, but our time on earth is our opportunity to begin living now like citizens of heaven. As we do, we become ever more useful tools in sharing God's love and grace with others. We bring Him glory, and we obtain the blessed assurance that we truly are His people and that He truly is our God.

June 7

My Sabbaths

"I am the LORD your God: Walk in My statutes, keep My judgments, and do them; hallow My Sabbaths, and they will be a sign between Me and you, that you may know that I am the LORD your God" (Ezekiel 20:19, 20).

It strikes me that this is one of the clearest "proof texts" regarding God's desire that we hallow His Sabbaths found in the latter part of the Old Testament. It is tucked away in the book of Ezekiel, in a chapter largely devoted to the discussion of the various rebellions of Israel. The Lord Himself is speaking here, reminding His people of how important keeping the Sabbath is to maintaining a strong relationship with Him. In fact, in verse 12, we find almost the same admonition as in verse 20, except He includes the phrase, "that they might know that I *am* the LORD who sanctifies them." In verse 16 of this same chapter, the Lord clearly identifies the reason for their backsliding saying, "Because they despised My judgments and did not walk in My statutes, but profaned My Sabbaths; for their heart went after their idols."

Sadly, I have heard the stories of too many Christians who, because of their busy lives, worldly distractions, or discouragement, begin to quit making it a habit to go to church every week. Their attendance becomes sporadic. They say it's no big deal. They've just found other "good ways" to celebrate the Sabbath. Then they stop spending daily devotional time with the Lord, and their prayer life suffers. They slowly start to distance themselves from other Christians, as they find they have fewer and fewer things in common, and they soon adopt the practices of people all around them who do not keep the Sabbath. Other activities and interests fill the time that used to be used for worship, and like the Israelites of old, they become people who profane the Sabbath. Often, it is a gradual process. The first few times a person breaks the Sabbath, they usually feel some degree of guilt, but with time, they sear their consciences, and before long, they are breaking it almost without giving it another thought. They have slid into a form of modern idolatry, valuing something or someone more than God.

Thinking back, we are reminded of God's injunctions to the Israelites in Moses' day to attend a "Holy Convocation" on the Sabbath. Now, nearing the end of the Old Testament, we see the Lord using a prophet to emphasize, once again, His desire for His people to hallow His Sabbaths. That is not to say that there are other beneficial and acceptable things to do on Sabbath besides going to church: spending a weekend in the great outdoors, visiting the sick or lonely on Sabbath, or just taking some time off by yourself meditating on spiritual themes. But I don't believe that these activities should become the rule, usurping your usual time to worship and fellowship with other believers on a regular basis. Without much trouble, all those other good activities can be scheduled around the roughly three or four hours a week that most Christians gather together to worship the Lord in His house, especially when we know that it pleases Him. Listen to what He says about the Sabbath in Isaiah 58:13, 14:

> If you turn away your foot from the Sabbath, *from* doing your pleasure on My holy day, and call the Sabbath a delight, the holy *day* of the LORD, honorable, and shall honor Him, not doing your own ways, nor finding your own pleasure, nor speaking *your own* words, then you shall delight yourself in the LORD.... The mouth of the LORD has spoken.

If there remains any doubt about how we should hallow His Sabbaths, all we have to do is trace the steps of Jesus in the Gospels where He set an example by His own presence and participation in places of worship on Sabbath throughout His lifetime.

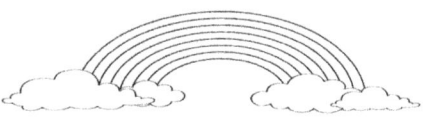

June 8

Death of the Wicked

"Say to them: 'As I live,' says the Lord GOD, 'I have no pleasure in the death of the wicked, but that the wicked turn from his way and live. Turn, turn from your evil ways! For why should you die, O house of Israel?'" (Ezekiel 33:11).

In this chapter, the Lord is talking to Ezekiel and charging him to be the "watchman" for God's people (see verse 7). This assignment requires that Ezekiel receive the warnings God gives him and pass them on faithfully to the Israelites. The Lord is so serious about this that He says if Ezekiel doesn't "blow the trumpet" of warning, and people are lost as a result, He will require their blood at his hand, meaning that it would be Ezekiel's fault (see Ezek. 33:6). If, however, Ezekiel spoke out and warned the people to the best of his ability, but they still chose to disregard the Lord's admonitions, then "their blood would be on their own heads," and Ezekiel would be considered innocent (see Ezek. 33:4, 5).

I feel there's a lesson here for us. I think we need to pause occasionally and reflect upon whether we have been faithful watchmen. How many lives could be saved by our faithful witness in our time and place, and, regretfully, how many folks may be lost for the lack of it? I admit that it can be difficult to share God's unpopular warnings regarding what will happen in the future if people don't turn from their wicked practices to God for cleansing. And we don't want to scare anyone away from the Lord by preaching doom and gloom all the time, but by seeking to speak only smooth things to placate people and not ruffle anyone's feathers, I think we have sometimes missed the mark by seeking to please humankind rather than God. These texts affirm to us that, if we are truly God's servants, there are times when we should bravely call sin by its right name and warn folks of the dangers to come if they choose not to turn from sin to righteousness. Otherwise, we have failed to be good watchmen, and some of the responsibility for their destruction will be on us. What a fearful thought that is!

So, how can we do this important yet sensitive work? As usual, we will need to pray for the wisdom of the Holy Spirit, to know not only when and where to "speak a word in season" (Isa. 50:4) but also how to do it in the least offensive way possible. Of course, some people will not accept a rebuke of their behavior no matter how carefully it is delivered. Another thing to consider is that since none of us is exempt from sin and all of us continually need God's grace, these delicate messages must be delivered with humility.

One example I can think of on how to do this in an effective manner is the time in the Old Testament where Nathan is sent to confront David with his sin and does it by telling him a story. Another beautiful occasion is in the New Testament where Jesus, after forgiving her, gently tells the woman caught in adultery to "go and sin no more" (John 8:11). These two incidents, along with many others found in the Scriptures, corroborate the assertion in today's text that the Lord finds no pleasure in the death of the wicked. In fact, this is one of the places where we can actually hear the voice of our compassionate, heavenly Father tenderly imploring us to make the right choice and choose Him, not only so that we can avoid destruction but so that we can live a life worth living! Let's listen to His earnest and loving entreaty today!

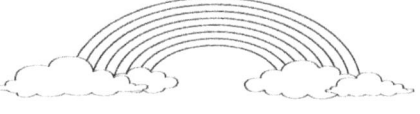

June 9

As Native-Born

"'Thus you shall divide this land among yourselves according to the tribes of Israel. It shall be that you will divide it by lot as an inheritance for yourselves, and for the strangers who dwell among you and who bear children among you. They shall be to you as native-born among the children of Israel; they shall have an inheritance with you among the tribes of Israel. And it shall be that in whatever tribe the stranger dwells, there you shall give him his inheritance,' says the Lord GOD" (Ezekiel 47:21–23).

As the children of Israel are returning to Canaan after their seventy years of captivity in Babylon and resettling in the land that the Lord had given them for an inheritance, we find these very specific instructions from the Lord on how to treat the strangers, or foreigners, in their midst. As I have mentioned before, I taught English to foreigners of all ages over a span of several decades and thus have a special place in my heart for them. Whenever I come across verses that admonish God's people to treat them with kindness and equality, it warms my heart because I recognize that the Lord is mindful of their plight. Living in a foreign country, especially when one doesn't know the language, can be especially trying. (I know this from my many interactions with new arrivals as well as my own years of living in another country.) This experience is made even more difficult if the strangers have suffered extreme poverty or any number of other traumatic incidents (war, natural disasters, etc.) before arriving in the new culture.

How kind and merciful the Lord is in mentioning them here, specifically, to make sure they aren't treated as second or third class citizens in the newly-reorganized Israeli society. I believe that this passage, along with other similar ones reminding the Israelites that they themselves were once "strangers in the land" (Exod. 22:21), provides instructions to God's people today as well—not only in how we treat those coming from other countries but also their children. In fact, I wonder if perhaps this isn't where our government got its philosophy of considering any child born within our shores as an American citizen.

I want to talk a bit about what being treated as a "native-born" citizen would mean. It would mean being granted equal rights as all of the other inhabitants of our great land: the right to vote, the right to gather together, the right to speak out about injustices, the right to worship as one pleases, the right to receive a good education, the right to travel freely from one place to another, and the right to self-determine our career, our lifestyle, and a million little choices we make daily on behalf of ourselves and our families.

It reminds me of what the future society of heaven will probably be like—incredibly diverse, with people from every tongue, tribe, and nation yet with incredible freedom for each of us to pursue all of our interests and fulfill all of our God-given potential! There will be no in-fighting to impede our progress, no labeling of classes or casts to produce pride or prejudice among us, for we will all be treated wonderfully equally by the One who made us and then saved us! Despite our unworthiness, He will joyfully welcome us as if we were native-born citizens to heaven!

June 10

The Cream of the Crop

"Then the king interviewed them, and among them all none was found like Daniel, Hananiah, Mishael, and Azariah; therefore they served before the king. And in all matters of wisdom and understanding about which the king examined them, he found them ten times better that all the magicians and astrologers who were in all his realm" (Daniel 1:19, 20).

Here in the first chapter of Daniel is a short narrative of how he and his three friends, more commonly known today as Shadrack, Meshack, and Abednego, were taken into captivity by the Babylonians. They were among those Israelites who were captured alive by King Nebuchadnezzar's army. Upon their arrival, the king ordered that several well-educated, good-looking, and intelligent young men be selected to be trained in the language and literature of the Chaldeans so that they could be pressed into service in his government.

Daniel and his friends were good candidates for this three-year training program and were thrown into the mix along with many others to prepare for an interview with the king. It soon became apparent that the food and drink that was to be provided to this select group included delicacies and wine that the children of Israel did not consider healthy or kosher. Daniel very courageously spoke to the person in charge of the program to ask for an exception in the dietary plans for himself and his friends. Could they possibly be offered just vegetables and water instead? The manager was doubtful about the benefits of this plan, so Daniel suggested that they undergo a trial of the new diet for just ten days, after which they could be tested. Bible students rejoice in the outcome. At the end of the trial period, the young Hebrews appeared better, more fit, and wiser than all the others in the training group, thus they were allowed to continue with the healthy diet they had requested. When the king interviewed them, it's interesting that he found them ten times better than the others!

What impresses me here is Daniel's courage. There were several factors that would have made it seem almost impossible for him to make such a request. First, he was a mere captive with no human rights as we think of them today. Then, he was young, which might have made him feel inadequate to speak up for what he believed. He was now a foreigner living in a foreign land with a culture and dietary habits very different from his own. He was definitely in the minority here, and he might have been considered impertinent by the Babylonians, who had been kind enough to offer he and his friends food from the king's own table while they were in training. To reject their generous offer, asking for a totally different food plan from the others, might have caused the man in charge of his group to label the young Hebrews as ungrateful and simply kick all four of them out of the program. Amazingly enough, however, their handler decided to give Daniel's strange request a try. Miraculously, God intervened, blessing their faithfulness, courage, and obedience with strength and intelligence to the point that these young men were soon considered to be the top of their class and the cream of the crop! Whenever I read this story, I remember a song that we used to sing as kids in the junior room at church, and I am challenged to live my own life with more courage to stand up for what I believe is right. The chorus goes like this: "Dare to be a Daniel, dare to stand alone! Dare to have a purpose firm! Dare to make it known!" (*Singing Youth*, p. 179).

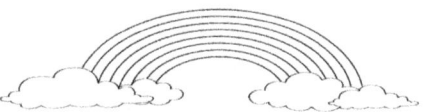

Holy Determination

"Shadrach, Meshach, and Abed-Nego answered and said to the king, 'O Nebuchadnezzar, we have no need to answer you in this matter. If that is the case, our God whom we serve is able to deliver us from the burning fiery furnace, and He will deliver us from your hand, O king. But if not, let it be known to you, O king, that we do not serve your gods, nor will we worship the gold image which you have set up'" (Daniel 3:16–18).

There you have it—a magnificent display of holy determination! It was not timidly whispered privately in the courts of the king, but boldly proclaimed in front of the multitudes who were gathered on the plain of Dura that day to worship the golden image that the king had proudly set before all of his subjects! Talk about peer pressure. After all, everybody else was obediently going along with the king's plan. But even if the social pressure was not enough, the king had prepared a "burning fiery furnace" in which to publicly destroy anyone who dared not to worship him.

When the king discovered that these incentives were not enough, he tried several other approaches—ones that Satan also uses with us when he is trying to bend us to his will. First, he tried to pretend to be gracious by giving them a second chance to bow down, making himself look like a fair and reasonable ruler and the three Hebrews appear to be unreasonable and obstinate. When that didn't work, he threatened to up the ante by making the furnace seven times hotter so their punishment would be even more terrifying. He evoked the response in today's text from the three young men when, in an effort to show how powerful and strong he was, he boastfully asked the question, "And who *is* the god who will deliver you from my hands?" (verse 15).

Have you ever noticed that when someone is trying to force you to do something you have chosen not to do, they often attempt to "browbeat" you by flaunting their position of power and authority in order to scare you into believing that you have no other options but to succumb to their wishes? Not only did these youth reject the lie being perpetrated by the king that their fate was ultimately in his hands, despite the fact that to all human appearances it was, but they saw the king's pride as a blatant affront to the true and almighty God of heaven whom they served.

A number of things, in addition to their stunning faith and courage, strike me as amazing in the answer they gave to the king. They made it clear that they would not bow down to the statue under any circumstances. They had been trained from their youth by their Hebrew families to obey the Ten Commandments, including the second one, which forbade bowing down to idols. Also, they did not try to force God's hand in this crisis by saying they would only obey Him if He rescued them. Instead they focused on making the right choice and leaving the consequences in God's hands. It is a mature faith that believes that while our God can do anything, whatever His will is for our lives will always ultimately be for the best. Our job is simply to obey and trust God, regardless of the results seen here on this earth. After all, if we believe in the Lord, our stories will not end here but will continue to be written throughout the ceaseless ages. Lastly, I'm impressed by their ability to continue to interact with the king in a respectful manner. They did not argue with the king or attack him personally. There was no cursing, name-calling, or yelling, just a calm and steady resolve to do the right thing. May the Lord grant us this kind of holy determination as we seek to serve Him today!

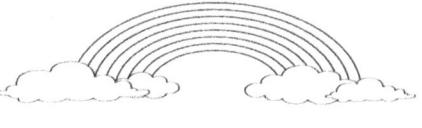

June 12

Pride before a Fall

"The king spoke, saying, 'Is not this great Babylon, that I have built for a royal dwelling by my mighty power and for the honor of my majesty?' While the word was still *in the king's mouth, a voice fell from heaven: 'King Nebuchadnezzar, to you it is spoken: the kingdom has departed from you! ... Now I, Nebuchadnezzar, praise and extol and honor the King of heaven, all of whose works* are *truth, and His ways justice. And those who walk in pride He is able to put down" (Daniel 4:30, 31, 37).*

Closer to the beginning of chapter 4, Daniel had just warned the king of what would happen to him if he didn't repent from his iniquities, including boasting about his own majesty and power, and begin to show mercy to the poor. He told the king clearly that the kingdom would be taken from him, and he would become like a beast of the field, eating grass and being wet with the morning dew for seven years, until he would acknowledge "that the Most High rules in the kingdom of men, [and] gives it to whomever He will" (verse 17) and was ready to proclaim that heaven rules.

Only twelve months later, however, we find him walking around his royal palace bragging again about how rich and powerful he was. Why did he so blatantly ignore Daniel's admonition? Had he already forgotten it, or did he just not believe that Daniel knew what he was talking about? This was unlikely, since this same Daniel had been the only person capable of interpreting his dream about the statue that represented the kingdoms of the world throughout history. Perhaps he simply didn't believe that the God of heaven was powerful enough to bring him down. This would be hard to believe, given that he had witnessed how the Hebrews' God had so wonderfully rescued his followers from the burning fiery furnace.

After the miraculous ways the God of heaven had shown His unquestionable wisdom and power, to the point that

Nebuchadnezzar, himself, had been compelled to utter praises and even make a decree that his subjects should say nothing amiss about the true God of heaven, one would think that he would take Daniel's prophecy very seriously. When looking at the biblical record, we see that the Lord had actually been very patient and merciful to the king, giving him multiple opportunities through his interactions with God's followers there in Babylon to come to know and serve the Most High. But it seemed that Nebuchadnezzar's awe of God melted away quickly after each incident, and he was always just on the verge of becoming a committed believer yet never submitting his life to the One who could change him. Thus, with the passage of time and the apparent resurgence of his selfishness and pride, we see him walking in rebellion to the wise and gracious counsel of Daniel.

As a result, at the end of twelve months, all of the terrible things Daniel had predicted came true. The kingdom was taken from him, and for seven long years, the king acted and was treated like a beast. Only then, after he came to his senses again, was he a changed man, no longer proud but now humble. He was finally ready to surrender to the sovereignty of the true and just King of all kings! Unfortunately, as humans, we all too often follow the same path as Nebuchadnezzar, moving away from God over time, despite His goodness, instead of moving toward Him. May the Lord dissolve our arrogance and pride so we can serve Him as we should and praise Him as the King of the whole universe deserves!

June 13

A Pagan's Faith

"So the king gave the command, and they brought Daniel and cast him into the den of lions. But the king spoke, saying to Daniel, 'Your God, whom you serve continually, He will deliver you'" (Daniel 6:16).

After Nebuchadnezzar passed from the scene, his son, Belshazzar, became the king. Unfortunately, he also exhibited pride and self-aggrandizement, appearing not to have remembered the lessons his father had learned the hard way. One night, when he was hosting a huge and raucous party, worshipping false gods, and desecrating the vessels from the Lord's house by arrogantly drinking wine from them, a mysterious hand appeared and started writing something on the walls of the palace. When all the king's wise men were unable to decipher the strange writing, Daniel was summoned, once again, to interpret what it all meant. Before explaining what the troublesome writing said, Daniel took time to review the past history of the king's late father, and the lesson he had learned that it is "the Most High God [who] rules in the kingdom of men, and appoints over it whomever He chooses" (Dan. 5:21). He also bravely admonished Belshazzar that the true God held the king's breath in His hand and owned all his ways (see Dan. 5:23). Only then did Daniel interpret the inscription, which announced that the kingdom would be taken from the proud and irreverent king, and given to the Medes and the Persians. In fact, that very night Belshazzar was slain, and Darius, a Mede, began to rule in Babylon.

Immediately, King Darius set up three governors to help him rule his vast new kingdom, and Daniel was selected to serve as one of them. The Bible tells us that "Daniel distinguished himself above the governors...because an excellent spirit *was* in him; and the king gave thought to setting him over the whole realm" (Dan. 6:3). When the other governors and state officials saw how much the king favored Daniel, jealousy overcame them, and they began to plot for his downfall. As you'll probably remember this well-known story, the only thing they found to fault Daniel on was his consistent and committed prayer life. Three times a day he stopped to pray to the God of heaven. So, playing on the king's vanity, they drafted a decree specifying that no one in the kingdom should be allowed to ask petitions from "any god or man for thirty days," except the king himself, and that the punishment for anyone who disobeyed would be casting them into the den of lions (Dan. 6:7).

Thinking only of his own power and glory, the king quickly signed the document, feeling quite proud of himself, until he realized that the motivation of his officials was to seek to destroy the faithful Daniel. Although lamenting what he had done, there was no changing the decree because it was the law of the Medes and Persians that statutes could not be changed once established by the king. There seemed no way to avoid the consequences of the decree, so before Daniel was thrown to the lions, the king spoke to him. In the time Daniel had worked for the king, Darius had come to respect him as well as the God of heaven whom he served. It is at this point in the story that today's incredible verse, showing the non-Jewish king's faith in Daniel's God, appears. He unequivocally states, "Your God, whom you serve continually, He will deliver you."

After a long and sleepless night, the king hastened to the den first thing in the morning to affirm the belief he had expressed the night before. Sure enough, Daniel was unharmed! The king was "exceedingly glad," proclaiming that Daniel had not been injured "because he believed in his God" (Dan. 6:23). Even before this miraculous event, how powerful Daniel's witness must have been, as he worked in the government day by day, to have fostered even a pagan king's belief in his God...the true God of heaven. May our work be as flawless, our spirit be as excellent, our devotion to the Lord as inspiring as Daniel's, so that, because of our daily influence, even the "worldlings" around us will be led to believe in our God.

Like the Stars

"Those who are wise shall shine like the brightness of the firmament, and those who turn many to righteousness like the stars forever and ever"
(Daniel 12:3).

Nowadays, when someone speaks about a "star," they are usually referring to a famous and popular TV, movie, or music industry personality. These people are usually very talented, quite attractive, and have the ability to generate a wide fan base. Here, however, in the last chapter of the book of Daniel, he records a prophecy the Lord has given him about the time of the end. After describing some last day events, the chapter begins to declare that in the resurrection, some people will be raised to "everlasting life" but "some to shame *and* everlasting contempt" (Dan. 12:2).

Then, in order to comfort and encourage His faithful people, the Lord provides a beautiful promise in the next verse about what kind of rewards they will enjoy as they enter into life everlasting. He makes it clear that the people He considers "stars" are those who have turned "many to righteousness" (Dan. 12:3). Their stardom will not be a temporary flash in the pan like so many earthly artists. Instead, they will garner love and appreciation "forever and ever" for the wise work they have done on earth to help others be saved. This love will come from both the heavenly hosts and especially from those who otherwise would not be enjoying the wonders of heaven if another human being had not reached out as a co-worker with God to bring them into a saving relationship with the Lord before it was too late. What an encouragement this verse should

be to all those who have labored in the Lord's vineyard, whether as pastors, evangelists, teachers, or missionaries, either at home or abroad, that their labor has not been "in vain in the Lord" (1 Cor. 15:58).

In fact, this encouragement is for anyone who has shared the gospel in any capacity throughout their lifetime, including those who share their testimony in their secular work setting and parents in their often overlooked and underestimated work of raising their children "in the nurture and admonition of the Lord" (Eph. 6:4, KJV). What a gracious, magnanimous God we serve in that He gives all of us many opportunities to experience the joy of working together with Him now (which, by the way, gives our lives meaning and purpose on this earth) so that He can make all of us into "stars" throughout eternity!

I'm not a consistent stargazer, but last night around 2:00 a.m., I happened to be up and looked through my window. In a clear, almost moonless sky, I was amazed by the brightness of the many stars that twinkled there, their light accentuated even more by the dark blue canopy of space surrounding them. Of course, the first lesson that came to mind is the one we often hear that "the darker the night, the brighter the stars," but it came home to me in a new way last night, living as we do now in a world so dark with sin and gloom. Surely, this is a time when the Lord needs us to shine as brightly as we can in order to give hope and inspiration to those who are desperately seeking for a glimmer of light. I noticed something else as I stood there in my nightgown, transfixed by the beauty I had so unexpectedly discovered in the middle of the night. While some stars formed constellations, there were many others that stood out on their own, doing their faithful part to light up their designated place in the sky. It reminded me how we all work differently, some in groups, some independently, but all fulfilling the purpose for which we were created, illuminating the corner of the world where the Lord has so carefully placed us. May we shine ever more brightly for Him!

June 15

Betrothed

"I will betroth you to Me forever; yes, I will betroth you to Me in righteousness and justice, in lovingkindness and mercy; I will betroth you to Me in faithfulness, and you shall know the LORD" (Hosea 2:19, 20).

As the book of Hosea begins, we find a common pattern: God's people are unfaithful, God calls a prophet to disseminate His messages and warn them about the consequences of their wrong choices, and then the Lord pledges His love and forgiveness to them if they will only return to Him. One of the Lord's most tender and intimate pledges in Scripture is the beautiful promise we come across here in the second chapter of Hosea.

The word "betrothed" is an older word, generally used only in the context of that special time of a couple's preparation for an upcoming wedding. Today we would use the term "engaged." In any event, it implies a very close and committed relationship between two individuals who love each other deeply and have promised to be faithful to one another for the rest of their lives. Thus, when the Lord uses this imagery, He is trying to communicate how much He loves His people and just how close He longs for their relationship with Him to be. With powerful and emotional language, He is wooing the children of Israel to come back to their covenant relationship with Him. Down through the centuries since, this language still woos His people today to accept His proposal to marry their lives to His in sweet communion.

Although these verses apply to everyone willing to accept them, anyone who has been divorced can attest to the very special impact of these assurances of love by One who has promised to never abandon us or betray our trust. Others may have experienced deep pain in a failed human relationship (not only from an unfaithful spouse but possibly from an abusive parent, a cruel co-worker, or someone we previously considered a friend, who we discovered to be a traitor), which makes the Lord's promise to stay close to us forever even more meaningful. Other words from this passage also catch our attention. Justice, lovingkindness, and mercy all have an attractive and healing ring to them, but the sweetest word of all is faithfulness. The confessed love of Someone who we know will always be dependable and dedicated to our best interests for the rest of our lives can give us, if we are willing to accept it, the kind of comfort and assurance we need to pick up the pieces of our lives and continue to move forward. As long as we keep our hand in His

for the rest of our earthly journey, we will never travel alone.

The last phrase of this passage is also significant and not to be passed by too lightly. It simply says, "And you shall know the LORD." So we are promised here that when we enter into this close covenant relationship with the Lord, by surrendering our lives to His love and leading, pledging ourselves to love and remain faithful to Him as well, by God's grace, He will make Himself known to us in a way we have never experienced before. We will gain new insights into His character of love and faithfulness, coming to know Him as our personal Savior. What a wonderful trade—our ruin and brokenness in exchange for His strength and salvation! Let's make the deal of a lifetime by accepting His gracious proposal today!

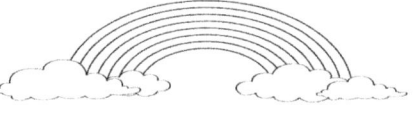

June 16

Righteous Rain

"Sow for yourselves righteousness; reap in mercy; break up your fallow ground, for it is time to seek the LORD, till He comes and rains righteousness on you" (Hosea 10:12).

Perhaps this verse caught my attention because my husband and I are preparing to start a garden in our backyard. I've been surprised by the amount of work and advanced planning this requires. First, you have to pick and mark off the garden plot. Then, in the country where we now live, a fence has to be built around it in order to

keep the small animals and deer from eating all you're trying to grow. After that, the hard ground has to be broken up and enriched with some kind of fertilizer. Subsequently, you must choose and plant your seeds just the right distance from each other so they will have room to grow. While you are patiently waiting for the harvest, you must dutifully keep the weeds out of your garden, make sure it's getting an adequate amount of sunshine, and provide enough water to irrigate whatever you have planted. Having grown up in the suburbs of large cities, I have little knowledge of how to successfully follow these steps, but just enough experience to know that I don't naturally have a green thumb. Thankfully, my husband, who grew up on a ranch, is going to take the lead on this project, so hopefully we will have some nice fresh vegetables to add to our diet by the end of the summer. At least that's our goal.

This text applies the agricultural process to how we grow spiritually. Essentially, it includes four of the steps mentioned above, albeit in a little different order, but the key elements are still there. Breaking up the hard and fallow ground of our hearts is probably the most difficult task we have to do. In fact, without the aid of the Holy Spirit, this action would be impossible. Living in this sinful world, our hearts have become encrusted with sin, selfishness, pride, and rebellion. They have been made hard by worldliness, evil influences, the long exercise of bad habits, and cultivated and inherited tendencies that we may not have even been fully aware of, all pulling us away from God. How important then is our daily devotional time, where we can ask the Holy Spirit to come in and take control of our thoughts, words, and actions so that the seeds of righteousness from the Scriptures can actually take root in our souls.

I envision the mercy alluded to in this text as both the fertilizer of God's grace, which awakens us to our spiritual need, and the continuing active agent that stimulates our growth in Him. As we pray and read the Bible, allowing Him to plant His precious seeds in our lives, He gently waters our souls with the rains of righteousness. This not only gives us more knowledge about Him but also helps us to become more like Him in our behavior from day to day. The harvest, of course, will be the fruits of the Spirit we have talked about so often, as listed in Galatians 5:22, 23: love, joy, peace, patience, kindness, goodness, faithfulness, gentleness, and self-control. When we try on our own to produce this rich harvest, we will see only barren patches in the hard ground of our hearts, but when we surrender ourselves to the Master Gardener, the expert in this field, in due time we will reap the bountiful harvest of righteousness that He has created in us.

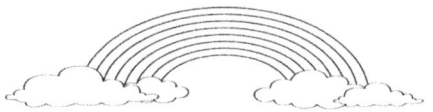

Prudent

"Who is wise? Let him understand these things. Who is prudent? Let him know them. For the ways of the LORD are right; the righteous walk in them, but transgressors stumble in them" (Hosea 14:9).

The dictionary definition of the word "prudent" includes ideas like being shrewd in the management of practical affairs, discreet, judicious, exercising common sense, advisable, expedient, and of course, the more common word, wise. After discussing the judgments of Israel for their sins in chapter 13, Hosea talks about Israel's restoration in the last chapter of his book. He assures the people that the Lord will "heal their backsliding" and "love them freely" if they will only give up their idols and return to Him (see Hosea 14:4). It sounds so easy, yet giving up long-cherished idols was difficult for them just as it is for us today.

To be sure, our idols may look different than the ones worshiped by the ancient Israelites, but they are hard to surrender just the same. Our money, our car, our clothes, our house, our food, our addictions, our work, our unhealthy relationships—any of these things can become our modern idols if they prevent us from experiencing a close relationship with God. This is one of the reasons why taking daily devotional time, where we reflect on and surrender anything that is negatively affecting our spiritual walk with the Lord, is so important for anyone serious about growing as a Christian.

Today's verse is also interesting to me because it says that "the ways of the LORD" are where "the righteous walk" while those very same ways are where "transgressors stumble." The same stimulus creates very different reactions, depending on which way a person is walking. It's like some people love avocados, and other people hate them. Some folks love snowy weather while others avoid it at all costs. There are, of course, a variety of reasons for these opposite reactions, including how we were raised, our culture, our personal tastes, and our past experiences. But in this case, I think it all depends on the general direction of our lives. If we have used our will to choose to follow in the Lord's ways, doing so can be very satisfying to our souls and even joyful. Whereas someone who has not fully chosen to serve the Lord, yet tries to walk on the Christian highway, will find lots of bumps along the road. The journey will feel unpleasant and uncomfortable to the point that many will simply fall off the path and end up at a very different destination.

This discussion reminds me of the story of the rich young ruler. At first, he thought he wanted to become a Christian, but once he understood that he would have to surrender his idol of riches, he decided that following Jesus was going to cost more than he was willing to pay. Meanwhile, the true disciples of Christ gladly gave up everything just to have the privilege of serving the Lord, spending time with Him, and absorbing the spiritual truths He came to share with them. What made the difference? The Bible tells us that spiritual things are spiritually discerned. This is an important key. In order to appreciate the true value of spiritual riches over earthly ones, we have to be open to spiritual growth, which only happens effectively when we accept the gift of the Holy Spirit that the Lord is longing to give us. When this blessed experience occurs, our tastes will change. Spiritual things will become attractive to us, while worldly things will lose their unhealthy appeal. It is at this point that we become truly "prudent" because we have chosen, day by day, to walk willingly in the "ways of the LORD" that will lead us to eternal life.

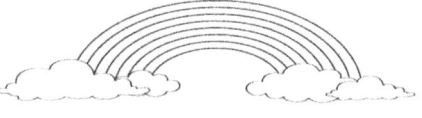

June 18

The Outpouring

"And it shall come to pass afterward that I will pour out My Spirit on all flesh; your sons and your daughters shall prophesy, your old men shall dream dreams, your young men shall see visions, and also on My menservants and on My maidservants I will pour out My Spirit in those days" (Joel 2:28, 29).

We have talked many times in this book about the critical role of the Holy Spirit in the life of the followers of God. These texts speak of receiving the Holy Spirit, not just at the time of justification, when we first accept the Lord's sacrifice as an atonement for our sins, nor even during sanctification, as we grow to become more like Him throughout the course of our lives. These verses describe an outpouring of the Spirit in such a measure that we won't have room to contain it, and it will spill out in ways that we have not experienced before.

The SDA Bible Commentary explains that if the Israelites returned wholeheartedly to the Lord in Joel's time, they would have received this spiritual blessing. Having rejected their covenant with the Lord, these promises were transferred to spiritual Israel instead. "Peter identified the events on the day of Pentecost as a partial fulfillment of Joel's prophecy (see Acts 2:16–21)" (*The SDA Bible Commentary*, vol. 4, p. 946). Although the Holy Spirit had drawn the disciples to the Lord and was actively working in and through them, they were filled with the Spirit in a new and heretofore unseen way on this special occasion, resulting in their ability to speak in tongues, prophesy, heal people, and preach the gospel with convicting power. It also filled them with amazing and relentless motivation to share what they knew about the Lord throughout the then-known world in obedience to the great commission Jesus had given them before He returned to heaven.

This being the case, why did Peter refer to Pentecost as only a "partial fulfillment" of this promise? Most Bible scholars agree that this first outpouring was what believers call the "early rain," but there will also be a "latter rain" close to the end of time. In fact, Peter translates the word "afterward," found at the beginning of this verse, as "in the last days." In her masterful book, *The Great Controversy*, Ellen White corroborates the view that the people of God will receive another great outpouring of the Spirit when she states that this prophecy of Joel will "reach its full accomplishment in the manifestation of divine grace which will attend the closing work of the gospel" (p. ix). In an agrarian society, of course, the early rain helped the seeds planted to germinate, while the latter rain will prepare the crops to be harvested. These showers from heaven are both essential. In the spiritual realm, the disciples were the first to preach the gospel, and those of us who are living in the last days will be the last to do so before Jesus returns to take us home. What a blessing to know that we won't be left alone to finish the great gospel commission on our own. We are here promised that supernatural strength to help us finish our mission will be provided.

June 19

The Valley of Decision

"Multitudes, multitudes in the valley of decision! For the day of the LORD is near in the valley of decision. The sun and moon will grow dark, and the stars will diminish their brightness. The LORD also will roar from Zion, and utter His voice from Jerusalem; the heavens and earth will shake; but the LORD will be a shelter for His people, and the strength of the children of Israel" (Joel 3:14–16).

Here again, due to the failure of the children of Israel to follow the Lord's leading, this passage has subsequently been applied to spiritual Israel—including those of our generation. The "valley of decision" in the first phrase has "frequently been used to describe earth's multitudes, the destinies of whose souls hang in the balance" (*The SDA Bible Commentary*, vol. 4, p. 950).

The term "day of the LORD" in the second phrase is generally used in Bible prophecies to depict a time of judgment and punishment that occurs toward the end of time, shortly after the close of probation, once all of the people of earth will have finally decided once and for all whom they will serve—either Christ or Satan. Indeed, the subtitle of this section in my Bible reads "God Judges the

Nations." By that time there will be no turning back from whatever decision we have made. Our eternal fate will be sealed.

While this passage goes on to describe a number of fearful events, which will take place when our patient Savior finally calls a halt to the world's sin and suffering and comes as the righteous Judge to execute judgment on the impenitent, notice what happens during this time to the people of God. While the wicked are now fearful and hopeless as a result of their own selfish, evil choices made over the course of their lifetimes, verse 16 tells us that this same all-powerful Judge will simultaneously be a shelter and source of strength for those who have chosen to be faithful to Him. What a difference in ultimate destinies our choices will make!

So, the burning question now is why are so many people halting in the valley of decision, gambling away their chance of salvation when the Day of the Lord is so near? Even if the Lord does not return in the next hundred years, which is doubtful given all the signs of the end we are observing today, our own lifetimes limit the number of days in which we have to make the all-important decision to serve the Lord. None of us have a lease on life, and with the uncertainties of sickness, crime, accidents, and natural disasters in this sinful world, our lives could easily be swept away at any moment, and for us, our probationary time would come to an abrupt end.

Interestingly, the pivotal choice to become a Christian will then make a difference regarding all of the other, smaller decisions we make throughout the rest of our lives. It will change who we decide to marry, what kind of career we choose, how we spend our free time, where we live, how we treat other people, and even the things we add or subtract from our diet! In the life of a true believer, all our other choices will automatically fall into alignment with that most important one, which, by the way, makes life's decisions easier to make. "What would the Lord do in this situation?" This will become our mantra.

As people who have already decided to follow the Lord, when we find that our choices become harder to make, we need to take inventory of our spiritual condition to see if maybe we have backslidden from a close walk with the Lord. If so, we need to get out of that dangerous valley of decision by recommitting ourselves to Him as soon as possible. Abiding under the shelter of His love is the only safe place for us to be!

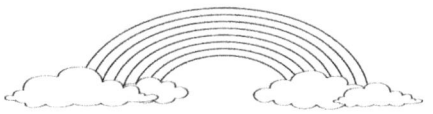

A Mighty Stream

"Seek good and not evil, that you may live; so the LORD God of hosts will be with you.... But let justice run down like water, and righteousness like a mighty stream" (Amos 5:14, 24).

These two verses, both from chapter 5 of the little book of Amos, seemed to me to go together. The first one is admonishing us to look for whatever is good in this world. The text right before it admits that the children of Israel, much like us, were living in an evil time. They could either just go with the flow and wallow in the sin and degradation all around them, or they could focus on and even seek to increase the good in the world. It seems we have a very similar choice to make in our day. The second verse poetically describes what standing for justice in an unjust world might look like—something like a cool drink of water to the thirsty on a hot day. Then, just imagine a mighty stream of righteousness pouring forth from God's people bringing hope, encouragement, and blessings to those groping in the spiritually dry desert all around them!

As I mentioned at the beginning of this month, while I am writing this devotional, the whole world is struggling with the unprecedented coronavirus pandemic. It is a pandemic the likes of which has not been seen for a hundred years, and it threatens our way of life as we have previously known it. Our routines have been interrupted, and many of our well-laid plans have flown out the window, at least for the foreseeable future. Vacations, weddings, graduations, community celebrations, sports events, concerts, church services, and even birthday parties have had to be cancelled or at least postponed indefinitely.

In an attempt to mitigate Covid's spread, businesses have come to a standstill; stores, malls, restaurants, theaters, and sports events venues have all been closed. Even schools and colleges have shuttered their doors for the last part of this past school year, and most instruction has been converted by hard-working teachers into "distance learning" modalities in order to meet the new norm of social distancing, requested by our government leaders and public health professionals in order to squelch the contagion and try to lower the alarming and ever-growing death rate of this relentless disease. It is estimated that approximately one out of five Americans has lost their job as a result of all the mandated shut-downs, adding financial stress to the fear of infection, the grief of loss, the loneliness caused by social isolation, and the gnawing anxiety about what the future may hold. No wonder depression, suicide rates, and panic attacks are all on the rise. Many people are desperate right now as they seek to balance keeping food on the table with the need to keep their families safe.

What a call to action by God's people during this difficult time! I have been heartened by the streams of righteousness seen in the sacrificial actions of healthcare workers, toiling to the point of exhaustion to care for the multitudes of sick people crowding their hospitals, in the host of willing volunteers making millions of masks and protective wear as soon as they understood the need, and the hundreds of ordinary people who have stepped up to assist in much-needed food bank operations across the country to keep families fed until they can get on their feet again! Not to mention the great number of resourceful people, including younger folks, who have found ways to raise money for specific needs, sent out encouragement through electronic media, and found creative ways to thank those essential workers who are still on the front lines trying to keep the basic elements of society functioning. I laud the many pastors who are continuing their ministry through phone calls, emails, and online church services, as well as those reaching out through various media ministries to people all around the globe who need the blessed hope of the gospel now more than ever! And, in this time of crisis, they may be more open to hearing it than ever before!

Therefore, may this evil time in history be recorded as a period when God's people chose to seek for the good—when they pleased the Lord by becoming modern heroes, who grasped this opportunity to meet the needs of those around them, thus pouring out a mighty stream of righteousness.

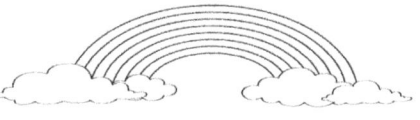

June 21

An Unlikely Prophet

"Then Amos answered, and said to Amaziah: 'I was no prophet, nor was I a son of a prophet, but I was a sheepbreeder and a tender of sycamore fruit.... And the LORD said to me, "Go, prophesy to My people Israel." Now therefore, hear the word of the LORD...'" (Amos 7:14–16).

These words occur in an interesting interchange between Amaziah, the priest of Bethel at the time and who should have been supporting a prophet with important messages for Israel, and Amos, who had unexpectedly been called upon by God to warn His errant people. Even Amos himself was surprised that the Lord had chosen him as His mouthpiece, as indicated by the tiny thumbnail sketch he presents about his life here. After all, he was not a priest, and nobody in his family line had been a prophet. He had no formal education or pedigree. He was simply a poor, humble, sheep herder, who tended the animals and the sycamore trees out in the countryside. Who would have ever dreamed that such an unlikely person as he would become a prophet? But the Lord saw in Amos an honest, hardworking servant of the Lord and knew He could depend on Amos to deliver the straight warnings and messages that His people needed at that time.

Meanwhile, Amaziah and the other religious leaders had falsely been prophesying only the more popular "peace and safety" kind of messages, basically lulling the king and the people into a spiritual sleep that deceived them into thinking their many iniquities and unfaithfulness to God would not have any consequences. Perhaps out of jealousy that God had chosen another spokesperson or maybe to retain his power and popularity among the people, Amaziah had started complaining to King Jeroboam of Israel that because of his dire prophecies, Amos had been conspiring against the king, and the scheming priest dramatically declared that, "The land is not able to bear all his words" (Amos 7:10). His hope, of course, was that the king would banish the unworthy newcomer, silence the doom and gloom prophecies (no matter that they were true), and allow Israel to resume its comfortable spiritual lethargy.

Three thoughts come to my mind when reading this passage. First, how similar this pattern to what was seen in Jesus' day, when, while the priests and religious leaders were busy fussing over their rituals, traditions, and their own power, the Lord had to look elsewhere to find a servant who would preach the straight and convicting messages of God. Thus, John the Baptist, a rough and unlettered person preaching fearlessly out in the wilderness, became the one the Lord called to prepare the way of the Lord. He was another unlikely but faithful prophet, who stepped up when called to become God's man of the hour.

Second, how difficult it is to be a prophet. Many people do not want to hear their timely but unpopular messages, claiming that they are just pessimistic or depressing wet blankets. Prophets have often been ridiculed, mistreated, had their motives questioned, their characters maligned, or even lost their lives by the very people they were trying to save! The same is true for modern messengers of God. How important it is that, as followers of the Lord, we try to make the way easier for our truth-preaching pastors and evangelists by believing, praying for, and supporting those brave souls who have taken up the challenge to become spokespeople for God despite difficult circumstances.

Finally, I am impressed with the Lord's grace, patience, and mercy toward humankind in that He continues to send us messages of warning and instruction today, sometimes through unlikely people. He does this even when His words are often rejected or ignored in order to save as many of us as He possibly can. What a gracious and long-suffering God we serve!

Deceitful Pride

"The pride of your heart has deceived you, you who dwell in the clefts of the rock, whose habitation is high; you who say in your heart, 'Who will bring me down to the ground?' Though you ascend as high as the eagle, and though you set your nest among the stars, from there I will bring you down,' says the LORD" (Obadiah 1:3, 4).

I don't completely understand why human beings would even imagine to see themselves as equal to the task of warring with the God of the universe. I suspect, however, that Satan, the father of lies, promotes this idea, just as he did among the angels of heaven. Somehow he has sold the idea to too many of us that we are strong, independent, and intelligent enough to control our own lives and don't need God or anyone else to tell us what to do or how to do it. We are either ignorant of or choose not to acknowledge the scope of the great controversy between good and evil, between God and Satan, that is now taking place in the universe. Unfortunately, just as we overestimate our strength, we also underestimate Satan's stealth and power to lead us astray. No matter how good and capable we think we are, without the power of God on our side, our sin-soaked souls are sure to lose the battle with the devil over our salvation. Not to mention numerous smaller daily struggles with temptation, addiction, doing our duty faithfully, and a million other stumbling blocks common to humankind.

Pride, however, may be one of the worst sins of all because it deceives us into thinking that we are pretty good, especially when we compare ourselves to other people who we think are worse than we are in one way or another. It blinds us to our need for improvement, our need to change things that are not leading us closer to God, and even our need for a Savior! We fall into the trap of denial, and where a sin or shortcoming is not recognized or admitted, it can't be addressed successfully. Meanwhile, like the Pharisees of Jesus' day, especially if we have been practicing religion for any length of time, we are tempted to think that we're doing okay when we may be way off base when it comes to actually doing the Lord's will in our life.

Have you ever dealt with someone who is 100 percent sure he or she is right, when in reality, that person is 100 percent wrong? What about someone who doesn't want to listen to anyone else's opinion and simply can't be reasoned with? Sometimes, because of pride, this person will even continue to defend his or her position after being proved wrong or blame his or her mistakes on other people or the circumstances. Surely, this person couldn't be at fault! People who display this kind of stubborn pride are not only insufferable but also unteachable and, therefore, not sensitive to the Holy Spirit's guidance in their lives. I can think of several examples of this type of behavior, but the most common one for me is riding in a car with a driver who is absolutely positive that he is going in the right direction even when he's going in the opposite direction of the desired destination! He doesn't care to check a map or listen to anyone else's opinion about the right way to go. Instead, his deceitful pride tells him that he's right until finally he discovers his error by becoming hopelessly lost. Unfortunately, that is too often what happens in our spiritual journey, which is why we need to ask the Lord to help us sweep the pride from our lives so that we will be humble and teachable enough to listen to and follow His advice.

Instead of opposing, challenging, or hiding from the Lord, we need to choose to join His ranks in the cosmic battle between good and evil. Once we have surrendered our lives to Him, He will give us new perspectives, the ability to see ourselves as He sees us, to clearly understand His directions, and to arrive safely at our ultimate destination of heaven. There our humble and joyful cry will be, "Thank you, Lord, for safely and patiently guiding me all along life's journey!"

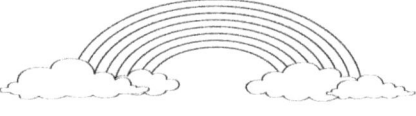

June 23

The Belly of Sheol

"Then Jonah prayed to the LORD his God from the fish's belly. And he said: 'I cried out to the LORD because of my affliction, and He answered me. Out of the belly of Sheol I cried, and You heard my voice'" (Jonah 2:1, 2).

Recently I heard the testimony of a young man who, through a series of poor choices and the unrestrained use of drugs and alcohol, finally found himself at his proverbial rock bottom. Fortunately, through the love and support of his friends and family, he admitted he needed help and enrolled in a life-changing rehabilitation program. His life changed dramatically, and today he is on a different path, heading toward a happy and successful future.

In today's verses, Jonah, a prophet who rebelled against what the Lord had asked him to do and ran in the opposite direction, found himself at rock bottom in the belly of a whale at the bottom of the ocean, with no future but death staring him in the face. The Hebrew word, Sheol, means Hades (the place where dead people go) or hell in our modern terminology. Like many of us who find ourselves in impossible situations, he finally remembered the Lord and cried out to Him to remove him from his dire circumstances and save his life. Since he knew how undeserving he was, he sounds almost surprised when he declares, "...*and* You heard my voice." Sometimes, when we are at the end of our rope, we are also amazed that God still listens to us when we cry out to Him for help, even though it may be because of our own rebellion and bad choices that we have ended up in a seemingly hopeless situation.

So, this time, as I'm reading through the little book of Jonah, I am focusing more on what it tells us about God's character than about Jonah's. In the first chapter, we see that the Lord calls imperfect people to work for Him, even though He knows all our faults, and even when we feel stubborn or rebellious. He doesn't give up on us but arranges circumstances in our lives that will make us think and remind us of our need of Him. His patience and long-suffering in dealing with us is certainly highlighted in His persistence to reach Jonah and turn him around.

We find today's verse in the second chapter of Jonah, where he cried out for help, and the Lord demonstrated His mercy, His forgiveness, and His desire for His children to be reconciled to Him. He also showed His sovereignty, as the mighty fish He had prepared to swallow Jonah now obeyed his Creator's command and spit him out on the beach. Most of the second chapter consists of Jonah's prayer of confession and contrition, along with an expression of thanksgiving and his renewed commitment to do what the Lord asked of him.

In the third chapter, we catch a glimpse of the God of second chances. Once again, he asks Jonah to go preach to the great city of Nineveh. Since the message of warning, that the entire city would be destroyed in a matter of forty days if the people did not repent, was not the easiest message to give, obviously the Lord had to strengthen Jonah for the task.

Amazingly, at least to Jonah, the whole city repented and believed in the God of heaven! The king of Nineveh proclaimed a fast and cried out for mercy, encouraging all his subjects to turn from their evil ways. When they actually did, we find that the Lord listened to their earnest petitions and saved the city with all its inhabitants! Here again, we see manifested the mercy and grace of our God.

Finally, in the fourth chapter, the Lord shows that He is easy to be entreated by His children when He responds to the arguments and anger of Jonah, who, while thinking only of himself, laments the saving of the city of Nineveh because he thought it made him look like a false prophet. You would think he would be rejoicing at how effective his preaching had been and the fantastic results of his efforts! In the interchange recorded here, the Lord condescends to discuss the situation with Jonah, reasoning that it was only right and fair for Him to show kindness to the 120,000 people in the city who had repented and turned their hearts toward God.

The characteristics of God, as displayed throughout the book of Jonah, not only show us what a kind and loving God we serve but also give us the assurance that He will be more than fair and just in all of His dealings with us as well! He will always hear our cry for mercy, too. Even when we find ourselves in our own "belly of Sheol."

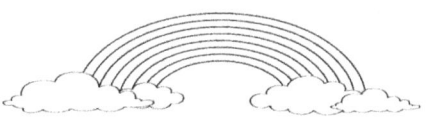

Messianic Prophecy

"But you, Bethlehem Ephrathah, though *you are little among the thousands of Judah,* yet *out of you shall come forth to Me the One to be Ruler in Israel, whose goings forth* are *from of old, from everlasting"* (Micah 5:2).

There were several interesting verses in Micah 4, like the ones that describe Zion's future triumph, when the Lord comes back to reign in it, including the reassuring phrase, "Neither shall they learn war anymore" (Mic. 4:3) that I considered writing about. However, this verse in chapter 5 caught my attention for a number of reasons.

First, it is one of the important prophecies about the coming of the Messiah that helps to tie the Old and New Testaments together. It demonstrates that God's ancient people, at least those who were studying the Scriptures, were cognizant of the fact that a Messiah would be coming in the future to save them. Then, centuries later, in the first book of the New Testament, Matthew quotes this prophecy, along with many others about Christ, to verify to anyone reading his writings that Jesus was, indeed, the fulfillment of the prophecies recorded by the holy men of the Old Testament.

The specificity of this particular prophecy, naming the exact city in which the Messiah would be born, also impressed me. But, most of all, I was struck with the fact that the Lord chose to give such an important prophecy to such a minor prophet as Micah, in such an obscure passage in one of the smaller books of the Old Testament. Although Micah was a contemporary of the much more well-known prophet, Isaiah, the Lord chose to reveal this important tidbit of the actual location of His birthplace to His lesser-known servant. It's interesting to me that God often seems to use some of His most humble servants to deliver some of His most important messages! Once again, I find it interesting that God gives us hope that however insignificant we sometimes feel, God does not overlook us. He has a special place for each one of His faithful followers in His universal plan.

On another note, this is one of those verses that demonstrates to us again the depth of the Savior's condescension. The actual village where the Christ child would be born was generally unimportant, at least prior to the birth of Jesus. (Not to mention the even more humble stable where His amazing birth took place!) To my way of thinking, it would have been enough for the Lord of glory just to visit this earth, let alone really get down to the nitty-gritty of getting His hands dirty by living as one of us for thirty-three years! He could have been born to a prominent rich family in a fancy home with servants. He could have waited to come to earth after society had developed many of the creature comforts we have the benefit of enjoying today, such as electricity, running water, bathroom facilities, cars, microwaves, and refrigerators. Why would He choose to make His appearance in obscure Bethlehem instead of in the famous and powerful Jerusalem, the city of kings? After all, He was the King of the universe, so coming as merely an earthly king to this dark, dangerous, and sin-filled world would have been more than enough suffering and condescension to bear! But He allowed Himself to sink to the lowest state of humanity! Why?

I believe it was because the Lord wanted all His children, including the most poor, the most oppressed, the most unfortunate, and the most disenfranchised among us to feel that He can relate to the unpleasant and uncomfortable circumstances of our lives. He understands those who have suffered because He has suffered. Those who have been tempted because He was tempted. Those who are marginalized because He was marginalized. Made fun of because He was made fun of. Tired and dirty because He walked the dusty roads of Palestine as He traveled around in His mission to seek and to save anyone and everyone who would accept Him.

I'm sure that in the several centuries between when Micah recorded this prophecy and when it was fulfilled, there were many who doubted his accuracy. Surely he was confused or hadn't quite understood God's words to him. Why would the great Ruler of Israel, the long-awaited Messiah, be born in such a place as Bethlehem? But Micah faithfully foretold what the Lord had revealed to him, and at the birth of Jesus, his writings were proven to be true. So, why would the Hope of Israel be born in Bethlehem? Because it was part of the Lord's self-sacrificing plan of salvation, and when the prophecy came to pass, it would build trust in His word, and we would understand that, whatever our status in life, He can relate to us. We can trust Him to be our loving Savior!

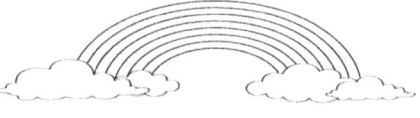

June 25

In a Nutshell

"He has shown you, O man, what is good; and what does the LORD require of you but to do justly, to love mercy, and to walk humbly with your God?"
(Micah 6:8).

In walking through the Scriptures this year, we are finding several places where a Bible writer summarizes in just a few words exactly what it is that the Lord wants from His people in order to maintain a close relationship with Him This is one of them.

Some people in Micah's day were still following a number of the Jewish customs and traditions around worshiping the true God of heaven, although they were carrying them out in a rote manner, more out of habit than with any real devotion. Thus, the rites and rituals of their traditional worship services were dry and had become almost meaning-less. To make matters worse, many of them, through the practice of mixed marriages and long exposure to the pagan religions all around them, had even begun to wor-ship heathen idols. Almost as if they were trying to fill in the gap left by their shallow relationship with the Lord, and in direct dis-obedience to the Ten Commandments, they began making images of wood and stone to worship.

It's interesting to what lengths humans will go to satisfy their soul's innate spiritual hunger instead of just following the Lord's instructions and experiencing the peace and joy that comes when we are living in close communion with Him. Throughout history, people have been known to burn candles, say long, repetitive prayers, make sacrifices to various human-made images, do painful penance or buy indulgences to try to buy heaven for themselves or their loved ones, or go on expensive religious pilgrimages. Some have even sacrificed their own children in an ill-informed effort to reach out to "a higher power," have their sins forgiven, or find some kind of spiritual satisfaction. The problem is that they're looking in all the wrong places!

In Micah's day, even though the Lord had graciously tried time and again through both priests and prophets to teach the children of Israel how to live and how to worship Him in order to find spiritual fulfillment, idolatry

was running rampant. For this reason, God had called upon Micah to deliver the short and direct message found in today's verse. It cut through all the peripheral trappings of religion and got right to the point of what the Lord required of His children. He expected them to live just lives. Justice is a legal term, used in reference to a set of laws or regu-lations. The Lord wanted them to live by the laws He had set up to be a blessing to humanity. Thus, everyone would worship only the Creator God, and people would treat each other equally and fairly. He wanted them to love mercy, showing it to others as He had shown it to them, and He wanted them to walk humbly with their God, with a heart sensitive to His promptings and open to His guidance. Notice that the phrase says to walk "with your God," that is to say, with Him beside you in close company. He knew if they did this, they would find no need to go after any strange imitation of a god or engage in the false worship of human-made objects.

So, what about us today? I believe the same message applies. As we have discussed before, although our idols many look differ-ent now, many of us are embroiled in modern idolatry. As we contemplate this summary of what the Lord requires of us, may He revive us until we can worship Him as He desires—not only with our words and worship prac-tices but more importantly in our heart of hearts and in our daily interactions with others.

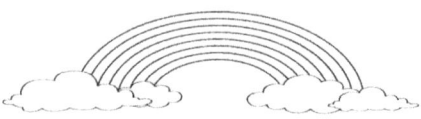

The Depths of the Sea

"Who is a God like You, pardoning iniquity and passing over the transgression of the remnant of His heritage? He does not retain His anger forever, because He delights in mercy. He will again have compassion on us, and will subdue our iniquities. You will cast all our sins into the depths of the sea" (Micah 7:18, 19).

The last chapter of Micah is divided into three parts. In the first section, Micah records the lamentations of the Lord as He sorrows over Israel's many sins. The second part contains Israel's confession while the third section declares that God will forgive Israel "because He delights *in* mercy." What a great way to end the book of Micah. Finally, the people of God show some remorse for their iniquity, and the Lord, who was seeking reconciliation with those He loved all along, declares through His prophet that He will cast all their sins into the depths of the sea. He will have compassion on them, pardon them, and remember their sins no more. What a patient and gracious God, and we can take comfort in the fact that He is the very same God we serve today!

As Christians, we are tempted to lose our balance when we grapple with the subject of forgiveness. Sometimes we diminish the gravity of sin, thinking that it really doesn't matter that much to God. After all, He loves us so much, surely, He won't care if we engage in this little sin or that questionable activity. He will probably just wink and look the other way when we do something wrong, like an over-indulgent parent. (This is what we call "cheap grace," by the way.) Other times we obsess over the sins and mistakes we have committed in the past, unable to believe that God could ever forgive us. How could we

even think of finding His good favor, let alone finally ending up in heaven? These people try to win God over by doing whatever their cruel guilt dictates. They overcompensate by participating in all kinds of unnecessary activities in the hope that they will be able to convince God to save them. Not only do they carry the heavy burden of their past sins but they continue to beat themselves up over present mistakes they are making while on their Christian journey. This ends up being a sad and frustrating existence! If we could only believe God's promises, including those found here in Micah, how much more pleasant our experience would be.

God is serious about the consequences of disobeying Him, so we should not take sin lightly, just shrugging off our errors and mistakes. After all, the Bible tells us clearly that there will be a Day of Judgment where we will have to answer for our actions. But, praise the Lord, this is what the gospel is all about! Jesus already paid the price for our sins so that we wouldn't have to lose our salvation because of them. When we accept His sacrifice for us, repenting and confessing our sins, whether past or present, He has promised us, just as He did the children of Israel, to throw them "into the depths of the sea." This means He will forget all about them, and amazingly, treat us as if we had never sinned! According to 1 John 1:9, "If we confess our sins, He is faithful and just to forgive us *our* sins and to cleanse us from all unrighteousness." Hallelujah! Not only does He forgive us but He gives us power to overcome the sins "that so easily beset us" (Heb. 12:1, KJV). He subdues our iniquity by cleansing and changing us so that we can be more successful in our Christian walk, growing more like our righteous God day by day.

June 27

Dust Clouds

"The LORD is slow to anger, and great in power, and will not at all acquit the wicked. The LORD has His way in the whirlwind and in the storm, and the clouds are the dust of His feet" (Nahum 1:3).

About 100 years after Jonah had preached repentance to Nineveh, causing a great revival in this heathen city, the minor prophet we know as Nahum was called to prophesy against that same city. They had gotten careless and returned to many of their previous bad habits. Their violence and cruelty made all those living in Judah fearful of this powerful capital city of Assyria. Thus, the prophecies regarding its destruction were a source of comfort to the people of Judah. Interestingly, the Hebrew name *Nahum* actually meant comfort or consolation.

In the book named after him, Nahum delineates the downfall and destruction of Nineveh in three short chapters. This proclamation of God's patience yet intolerance of sin as well as His power over all the elements of earth is found in the first chapter. The poetic language used in describing the Sovereign God of heaven and earth caught my attention. (I have been spending more time lately studying the clouds and trying to imagine them as the "dust of His feet.") But Nahum doesn't stop announcing the Creator God's power with just this one verse. He goes on to say that the Lord controls the sea and all the rivers. In picturesque language, he affirms God's power over everything from the fragile flowers to the mighty mountains—which quake before Him. He depicts the hills as melting in God's presence when He finally arises to execute justice.

Notice that the strength that causes fear in God's enemies is the same strength in which His people find a refuge and protection. In verse 6 we find the awesome questions, "Who can stand before His indignation?" and "Who can endure the fierceness of His anger?" While verse 7 states that "The LORD *is* good, a stronghold in the day of trouble; and He knows those who trust in Him." There are only two sides in the cosmic battle between good and evil. I certainly want to be found on the Lord's side when the Day of Judgment comes!

In the meantime, I rejoice in the fact that the Almighty, who made and sustains everything in creation, is my Friend. It is for our enjoyment that He paints such beautiful sunrises and sunsets day after day. He created so many kinds of colorful and fragrant flowers. The wide variety of graceful trees amaze me, and our nearby snow-capped mountains are a constant source of inspiration to me, speaking of His majesty and grandeur! Interesting and companionable animals of every species imaginable bring us delight, and if that

weren't enough, the sea is teeming with an unbelievable number of fish and other exotic creatures! Snorkeling in both Hawaii and the Caribbean, my family and I developed a whole new appreciation for the huge variety of tropical fish that live just under the waves of the ocean! It's like discovering another world! Best of all, the Lord created us as social beings so that we could enjoy interacting with each other. While similar in some ways, each person is unique. We are blessed by our families and friends—each one a living testimony of the magnificent power of God! We keep breathing, and our hearts keep beating because of His faithfulness. He created us in His image out of love, and He sustains us daily out of grace! We can trust such a God!

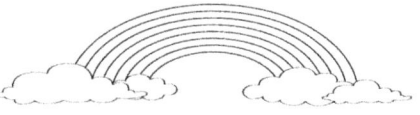

June 28

Keep Silence

"But the LORD is in His holy temple. Let all the earth keep silence before Him" (Habakkuk 2:20).

Habakkuk was another prophet whom the Lord sent to Judah to call them to repentance. It also fell to his lot to warn them about impending judgment if they did not turn away from their entrenched idolatry. A little earlier in this same chapter, he talks about the vision the Lord has given him, and although all that is in it may not happen immediately, it will come to pass.

He encourages the just that they shall live by faith in what the Lord has predicted will happen if they are just patient and wait for it. After that, he launches into the woes that will befall the wicked. The unfaithful people of Judah are again reminded of the futility of worshiping carved and molded idols, regardless of how beautifully they were made of wood or stone. Even if they were overlaid with gold and silver, they had "no breath at all" (Hab. 2:19), and the people could receive no benefit whatsoever from their false deities.

Then, in the last verse of this chapter, the prophet points them instead to the Omnipotent God of the universe, He who is the original Living Being and who has the power to hear their prayers, shower them with blessings, and execute judgment upon the impenitent. In the Jewish religious services, it was customary for the high priest to enter into the Holy Place in their temple to officiate on behalf of the people and ask forgiveness for their sins. During this sacred time, the worshipers were to keep silence until the high priest finished his intercessory work on their behalf. Because of this, the imagery that Habakkuk brought before them in this verse was something they could readily understand. It couldn't help but impress them with two powerful lessons. First, the God of heaven, in His holy temple, was the ultimate Deity they should be worshiping, and second, it was this awesome, true God who they should be standing silently in reverence to, since all they had and were and hoped to be was dependent upon His powerful hand and gracious watchcare.

Unfortunately, it seems that in many of our churches today we have forgotten, like the Judeans of old, the fear of the Lord. In this phrase, to fear God means to respect and reverence Him. It encourages us to walk with humility in His presence and honor Him as the Creator and Sustainer of all, including our very lives.

Yes, Jesus wants us to relate to Him as our best Friend, even our Elder Brother, and God refers to Himself as our loving Heavenly Father, but despite the close relationships that have been granted to us with the Father and the Son, we must never forget their exalted positions in the vast universe, and that it is only because of their great mercy and condescension that we have been provided a seat at the table. A great price has been paid so that we could become part of the heavenly family.

Recently, after observing the reverence displayed upon entering the sanctuary by several new members at church, who used to be Catholic, it became evident to me that I still have some growing to do in this area. They came in very quietly then knelt humbly to pray before the service began. Once seated, they sat quietly and expectantly, awaiting the message they knew the Lord had for them. I noticed that they didn't carry on common, secular conversations with their friends until leaving the church. This reminded me of the kind of reverence Moses demonstrated when he took off his shoes in God's presence because he was on "holy ground" (Exod. 3:5). May I practice more intentionally the kind of "holy ground" reverence that our magnificent God deserves and keep silence before Him in order to more clearly hear His voice.

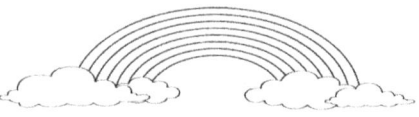

A Hymn of Faith

"Though the fig tree may not blossom, nor fruit be on the vines; though the labor of the olive may fail, and the fields yield no food; though the flock may be cut off from the fold, and there be no herd in the stalls—yet I will rejoice in the LORD, I will joy in the God of my salvation"
(Habakkuk 3:17, 18).

I noticed that in my Bible, which is a New King James Version, this section of Scripture starts with the subtitle, "A Hymn of Faith." After a fairly long diatribe about the coming judgment and destruction of God's errant and rebellious people found in the first two chapters of his book, Habakkuk begins chapter 3 with a long and earnest prayer. He here implores the Lord to remember mercy in the midst of wrath. Although the prophet knows that the Judeans deserve punishment for their sins, he also understands the immeasurable power of the Mighty Creator of heaven and earth, and he is hoping for the best—that at least some of his brethren may have heeded his warnings and will be spared from the wrath of God!

Then, almost at the end of his writings, he declares in this song exactly where he himself stands in relationship to God, despite any calamities that may fall on either him or his people. As described by the introduction to the book of Habakkuk in my Bible, he intentionally "chooses to cling firmly to God regardless of what happens to his nation." Further, "Habbakuk concludes by praising God's wisdom even though he does not fully understand God's ways" (NKJV Broadman & Holman Reference Ed., p. 823).

You will recall that this was the kind of faith that Job expressed when passing through his difficult trials and tribulations.

It's the type of trust in God that keeps a person from being driven to despair, even when they can no longer see a way forward. It goes beyond what is seen to depend on that which is unseen. This is the absolute definition of walking by faith, not by sight (see 2 Cor. 5:7). It is the kind of faith we need to get us through our current darkest days as well as any we might have to face in the future!

But please notice that Habakkuk is not only tolerating and struggling through the loss of material blessings, but he is actually expressing joy in this hymn of faith! He declares, "Yet I will rejoice in the Lord, I will joy in the God of my salvation!" Talk about making a conscious choice to focus on the positive! It reminds me of a funeral I attended recently. The family members decided, as some Christian families do nowadays, to make it a celebration of the deceased's life. There was a short eulogy and then the customary sharing of memories by those who had been close to the person who had passed away. But what really impressed me was that more than half the ceremony was comprised of singing—and not just ordinary songs but robust congregational singing of praises and hallelujahs! Obviously, these people had a hope that extended far beyond the grave, and by giving voice to their strong faith in the Lord's promise of the resurrection, they bore an inspiring testimony to all in attendance of the difference trusting in God can make in our lives. Not only does it buoy us up and carry us through the vicissitudes of life but it also provides us with an eager anticipation of all of the joys and blessings God has in store for us in the future. How we need this kind of faith today!

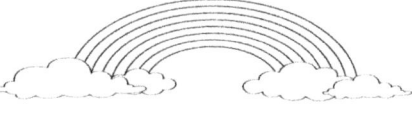

June 30

Like Deer's Feet

"The LORD God is my strength; He will make my feet like deer's feet, and He will make me walk on my high hills" (Habakkuk 3:19).

I am currently using the New King James Version, but the old King James Version of this passage reads like this: "He will make my feet like hinds' feet...." Growing up, as I did, in the suburbs of Los Angeles, I had very little knowledge about deer and even less about what a "hind" was. Subsequently, I learned that a hind was a female deer. Two occurrences in my life caused me to give this verse a second look. First, I had a Christian friend who had purchased and read the book *Hind's Feet on High Places* by Hannah Hurnard. She found the book very inspirational, so she shared several thoughts from it with me. After that, this little verse took on more meaning.

Second, in our golden years, my husband and I have moved to a small rural town in northern California, which has about the same number of deer occupants as humans. They are everywhere! And they make it clear that this was their habitat first. They are just kind enough to allow us to share it with them!

At any time of the day we can look out our windows and see the deer strolling peacefully across our front or backyard. They are so used to humans that they just keep grazing when we drive up and down our driveway and barely even look up when we walk out to get the mail or to work in the garden. My husband has even taken to carrying on a conversation with them while he's out raking leaves! I have started thinking of them as our pets, rather than the wild animals that they are. There are several characteristics that we have come to admire in them, but the one that delights us the most is the graceful way in which they can simply sail over the top of a fence or a hedge when they feel danger (like the neighbor's dog) might be approaching. The beauty and elegance of their quick movements always amaze us.

After doing some research online, I found that the main traits of deer are that they are agile, swift, and sure-footed. They can run securely and with abandonment, placing their back feet exactly where their front feet had just landed. We have observed that, when running away swiftly, they seem to be gently bouncing across the ground, barely touching its surface!

The interpretation of this text in *The SDA Bible Commentary* tells us that "Among the rough crags and the treacherous trails of the mountains the feet of the hind were swift and sure" (*The SDA Bible Commentary*, vol. 4, p. 1058). When explaining the meaning of the "high places," it says, "God's people will triumph over all opposition, and will dwell securely upon the heights of salvation" (*Ibid.*). This part of the verse suggests that God's people will be given the ability to overcome obstacles that come across their path with ease and success, as a result of His strength.

What a beautiful picture this paints for those of us who are following the Lord. May our spiritual strength increase as He makes our feet like those of the deer all around us. May we be agile and graceful as we meet life's challenges, swift to do His will, and secure in the salvation He has already obtained for us!

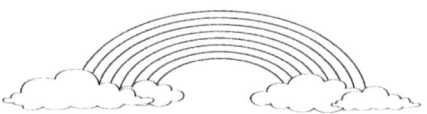

Settled in Complacency

"And it shall come to pass at that time that I will search Jerusalem with lamps, and punish the men who are settled in complacency, who say in their heart, 'The LORD will not do good, nor will He do evil'" (Zephaniah 1:12).

Thankfully, even in this day and age, there are still some people who will intervene when a crime is being committed or go out of their way to help somebody who has an accident or needs to be rescued from a dangerous situation. This text, however, reminds us of those individuals we have all heard about who simply stand by and watch while someone else is in dire need of assistance. Unfortunately, human nature being what it is, there were also these second kind of people in the audience when Jesus told his famous story of the Good Samaritan. He told this parable not only for the people of His time but for all those who would read and re-tell it down through the ages. It makes clear that Jesus expects His followers to step up and do something positive to make the world they live in a better place. Just standing by and allowing evil to prosper and proliferate right in front of us, without doing anything to stem the tide, is not acceptable in the lives of God's children.

Although Zephaniah spent most of his ministry warning the people of Judah that the day of the Lord, Judgment Day, was coming, few of them engaged in a thorough repentance for their sinful practices. In fact, we are told that they were "settled in complacency"—entrenched, if you will, in a dangerous mindset that would prevent them from feeling their need of the Lord in their lives. The blindfold of complacency makes people egoistic, self-satisfied, and self-important. Thus, they resist the possibility that there may be some things in their lives that they need to change. After all, they reason, "I'm pretty good." They casually shrug off the need for any real spiritual reform. They do not take any positive action to be a blessing to others. In this way, they become numb to the wickedness around them. Complicit with the forces of evil, they sink into the state of serving as accomplices on the dark side in the great cosmic battle between right and wrong.

Granted, no one can do everything to stop evil in its tracks, but everyone can do something, in accordance with their time, money, position, talents, and ability to influence others. Today's verse reminds me of the ones in Revelation 3:15, 16, where the Lord says that He wishes His people were either cold or hot—not lukewarm, which would make Him want to spew them out of His mouth! We can readily relate to this illustration, since most of us would welcome a cold, refreshing drink in the heat of summer or a hot, comforting beverage on a cold winter's day. Lukewarm liquids, on the other hand, are usually considered to be insipid, not quite hitting the spot to satisfy our thirst. So, what is the solution for our tepidness? What will heal our absence of enthusiasm or conviction? How do we move from being half-hearted servants to fully-engaged followers, ready to use our hearts and hands to gloriously represent God's will in the world? A deep and heartfelt repentance and reformation is what Zephaniah recommended in his day, and a more perfect message could not be applied as a solution for our spiritual lethargy today. Let us earnestly seek the Lord while He may still be found!

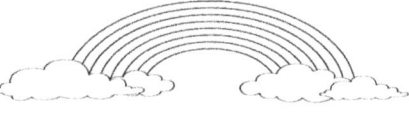

July 2

A Singing Lord

"The LORD your God in your midst, the Mighty One, will save; He will rejoice over you with gladness, He will quiet you with His love, He will rejoice over you with singing" (Zephaniah 3:17).

The year I lived as a volunteer missionary at Montemorelos University, back in my early twenties, I discovered a very pleasant custom that is still part of Mexican culture today. On special days of your life, such as your birthday or Mother's Day, a group of well-wishers who care for you gather early in the morning outside your dwelling, often outside your bedroom window, and sing you a serenade. That way, your special day can be celebrated from the moment you wake up—indeed, that is how you wake up! I can still hear the music of the song, *"Las Mananitas,"* wafting through the morning air from a group of happy voices, frequently accompanied by a strummed guitar, followed by giggling and shouted out wishes for a "Happy Birthday!" as the crowd moves away and people resume their usual everyday activities, leaving you to revel in their surprise gift!

Of course, we've all read books or seen movies where some "Don Juan" warbles out a romantic song to his beloved outside her balcony window. It's as if he simply can't contain his love and must burst out in an offering of song to express his feelings to the one who has captured his heart! Another instance where we often hear song as an expression of love and affection is when a new mother cuddles and croons to her precious baby, "quieting him with her love" and "rejoicing over him with singing." How effectively Zephaniah uses these terms to illustrate God's tenderness and devotion to His people!

I remember being in awe the first time I encountered this verse. Just think of it! The Lord God of Heaven, the Mighty One, as this verse calls Him, rejoices over ME with singing! What does His voice of eternal love sound like, and what words does He choose to express His gladness over ME? Beyond that, if He sings over just one of His children being saved, think how full of inexpressibly beautiful music heaven will be when He is able to spend unlimited time with all of the people who have chosen to accept His invitation to live with Him there forever! I can't help but imagine that, in their joy and gladness, the angels will also want to join in a great chorus of welcome and celebration with more amazing music than we have ever heard before! It will be a glorious concert that I won't want to miss for anything in this world!

In the meantime, the wonderful knowledge that the Lord is in our midst now, that He is mighty to save us today, and that He wants to quiet and calm us, each personally, with His love, is almost more than I can take in. Consider that He rejoices over us with gladness and singing in the present! It's such a happy, reassuring thought that it makes me want to burst out in a song myself—one of unbridled thanksgiving and praise! When was the last time somebody sang you a love song? If you have asked to become one of His children, the Lord is singing in gladness over you even now! Won't you join me in a responsive hymn of praise today?

July 3

Be Strong

"Yet now be strong, Zerubbabel,' says the LORD; 'and be strong, Joshua, son of Jehozadak, the high priest; and be strong, all you people of the land,' says the LORD, 'and work; for I am with you,' says the LORD of hosts"
(Haggai 2:4).

We have talked about strength before in this devotional book: citing the difference between Samson's physical vs. his moral strength (or lack thereof), discussing the spiritual strength that the Lord consistently renewed in a faithful nursing home resident, and claiming the promise of enough strength for the day to accomplish our duties during each (seemingly short) twenty-four hour period.

This text, however, focuses on the Lord giving His people, leaders, priests, and parishioners alike the strength to work in His cause and accomplish His purpose. With the Babylonian captivity behind them, the Jewish people, in their concentration on building their own dwelling places in Judah, had left the rebuilding of the Lord's house undone. For sixteen years, they had largely ignored the need to rebuild the temple in Jerusalem. Thus, the Lord raised up the prophet Haggai to remind the people of their sacred duty. Essentially, he appealed to their consciences by asking them if they thought it was fair that they had all built nice homes for themselves while the house of the Lord still lay in ruins. Then, inspired by the Spirit of God, Haggai stirred up Zerubbabel, the governor of Judah, as well as Joshua (the son of Jehozadak), the high priest, and encouraged them. Even though the project would take a great deal of effort and hard work, especially if the new temple was to look anywhere near as magnificent as the temple which had been destroyed by the Babylonians, the Lord himself had promised to work with them. He would make them strong enough to successfully complete the challenging project so that the work of God could, once again, move forward in the land.

Have you ever faced a huge, complicated, or difficult task that you felt inadequate to complete? Have you been overwhelmed by the magnitude of the project before you, almost paralyzed to begin with the first step, knowing how much determination, blood, sweat, and tears it will require? Bringing this down to practical terms in my own life, I think of my doctoral dissertation, a long and detailed report for a school's accreditation committee or the preparation of a book for publication. In all of these cases, I have to say that it was the strength and consistent support of the Lord that helped me to accomplish each one of these arduous yet worthwhile goals. Of

course, there are many other difficult projects, both short- and long-term, where we need to depend on His presence and strength in order to be successful. Think about it. Raising a God-fearing child, keeping a marriage together through life's ups and downs, moving from one community to another, or committing to care for an elderly loved one are a few common examples. There is also the bigger picture of how to best use our time and talents to do our part in completing the work of God. How will we help to evangelize the whole world? Obviously, we can't bear the weight of this entire assignment on our shoulders alone. Notice that in Haggai's day, all the people were to work together to accomplish the important task the Lord was asking them to complete.

So, for us, I believe the lesson is that we should work together, identifying the part that the Lord would have us play in moving His cause forward. We should depend on His wisdom and strength to do it well while at the same time respecting and supporting the efforts of our co-laborers. Someday, looking back, we will be amazed at the incredible things we have been able to check off of our to-do lists and the marvelous miracles He has wrought through us! In the meantime, this is our charge: "Be strong, all you people...and work; for I *am* with you!"

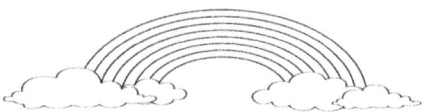

The Apple of His Eye

"For thus says the LORD of hosts: 'He sent Me after glory, to the nations which plunder you; for he who touches you touches the apple of His eye'" (Zechariah 2:8).

The phrase "the apple of His eye" means someone who is cherished above others. It has ancient English origins and is found in several places in the original King James Version of the Bible (using "toucheth" instead of the more modern usage of "touches") where it is utilized to express God's supreme regard for His people. The literal "apple" of the eye seems to refer to the part in its center that allows for the entrance of light.

Volume four of the *SDA Bible Commentary* highlights several important points relative to this verse. The eye "is extremely sensitive to harm" and is "of inestimable value to its owner" (p. 1091). Then there's a thought that really brings home to us how much the Lord personally cares about and identifies with us: "Every blow that strikes His saints, strikes their Lord" (*Ibid.*). Isaiah 63:9 conveys the same comforting thought, just using different language. It says, "In all their affliction He was afflicted." Of course, Isaiah had said something similar back in the well-known and often-quoted chapter 53 of his book, in verses 4 and 5, where he painted a picture of our Savior identifying with us to the point of suffering in our place so that we might be saved. He says, "Surely He has borne our griefs and carried our sorrows; yet we esteemed Him stricken, smitten by God, and afflicted. But He was wounded for our transgressions, *He was* bruised for our iniquities; the chastisement for our peace *was* upon Him, and by His stripes we are healed."

How rare to find a friend who is a true soulmate to the core—someone who will stand with us through not only the good times but also through the bad. Then just imagine a friend who loves you so much that he would also be willing to suffer your punishment and pain so that you wouldn't have to.

The closest human manifestation of this kind of love that I have seen is found in the sacrificial love of a mother for her child. My own mother, for instance, not only suffered the pain of childbirth, bearing the scars of the ordeal on her body the rest of her life, but worked her fingers to the bone in a glass factory during the day to provide for her three children, often staying up long into the night to accomplish her motherly household duties after we had gone to bed. She sacrificed her food so that we might eat; she went without nice clothes so that we could buy what we needed for school; and she had to forego many personal pleasantries and luxuries for years so that our lives might be made easier and more pleasant. In addition, she would have been more than willing to take our sicknesses or injuries upon herself so that we would not have to suffer through them. She always made sure we knew how proud she was of us, and we heard nothing but encouraging words from her when we were growing up. In fact, if a neighbor or teacher ever said anything negative about us, she would always take our side and do everything she could to help and defend us.

(It's a good thing, I guess, that our father was a disciplinarian, or we would all probably have been spoiled rotten!) In any case, we always knew that she loved us fiercely, to the point that whatever concerned us concerned her also. Like God, without taking away our freedom of choice, she identified with us fully and cared for us with every fiber of her being!

That, I believe, is the type of dependable and never-ending love and support that God is wanting His children to know that He has for them! Thus, we can be assured that whatever concerns us is of concern to Him, too. In today's verse, He has pledged to defend and fight for the welfare of those He dearly loves—those who are so precious to Him that He calls them "the apple of His eye!"

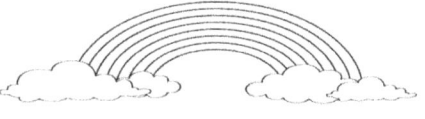

July 5

Plucked from the Fire

"Then he showed me Joshua the high priest standing before the Angel of the LORD, and Satan standing at his right hand to oppose him. And the LORD said to Satan, 'The LORD rebuke you, Satan! The LORD who has chosen Jerusalem rebuke you! Is this not a brand plucked from the fire?'" (Zechariah 3:1, 2).

Joshua was obviously a popular name among the Jewish people, and in the time when Zechariah was a prophet in Judah, a man named Joshua was serving as the high priest. One day when he was doing his priestly duties, he was given a vision of a conversation about him which was taking place between the Lord and Satan, as described in today's passage. Notice that the verse says that although Joshua had not been aware of it, Satan had been right there beside him trying to oppose him. It's as if the curtains had been drawn back, and he had been given a glimpse of the great controversy between good and evil, not only on a grand

scale but specifically as it was taking place in his own life!

How many pastors have become disheartened and discouraged by the opposition and setbacks they have suffered, not realizing that it is supernatural evil powers against whom they are fighting when trying to accomplish God's work in the world. "For we do not wrestle against flesh and blood, but against principalities, against powers, against the rulers of the darkness of this age, against spiritual *hosts* of wickedness in the heavenly *places*" (Eph. 6:12). How much they need our prayers and support instead of our condemnation and criticism! And, although our influence might not be as broad as a pastor's, Satan attempts to trip up any of us who are trying to serve the Lord. 1 Peter 5:8 tells us, "Be sober, be vigilant; because your adversary the devil walks about like a roaring lion, seeking whom he may devour."

Before we throw our hands up in despair, however, we notice that the Lord was also standing beside Joshua to defend and strengthen him. This must have been a great relief and encouragement to him! As a man of God, surely, he had read in the Pentateuch of the omnipotence of the Creator and was familiar with the beautiful promises found in the Psalms. For instance, Psalm 46:1 may have come to his mind. "God *is* our refuge and strength, a very present help in trouble." Knowing that the Lord is more powerful than our adversary and that He is on our side in whatever spiritual battle we're facing can infuse Christians today with the same fortitude and motivation to continue to fight for the right as it gave Joshua.

Finally, we notice a little further down in the same chapter that one of Satan's prime attacks against Joshua was the accusation that he wasn't worthy to serve God because he was clothed in filthy garments, which represented his sins and mistakes. How could a person so imperfect lead other people in worshipping God? It's a tactic Satan still uses today. Since none of us is perfect, and all of us have sinned, what is the solution? The Lord explains that Joshua was a "brand plucked from the fire." A brand was a partially-burned stick used to stir the fire, and the terrible trial of the captivity of the Israelites in Babylon, which decimated and all but destroyed them, represented a fire. The Lord, however, had not only preserved Joshua's life but had also chosen him for this important role of spiritual leadership in which he was actively engaged.

The best part, though, is that the Lord already had a solution for Joshua's unworthiness, just as He does for ours! He took away the filthy garments of iniquity, replacing them with a clean turban and rich robes, representing his forgiving and cleansing righteousness! In His gracious generosity, He has not only plucked each of us out of a sinful and destructive environment but has qualified us and made us worthy, through His merits, to serve as His representatives and spokespeople. What a privilege is ours! How thankful we should be that God doesn't only pick perfect people to do His work. If He did, we would all be disqualified. All He's looking for are people willing to be covered in His perfect garments of righteousness!

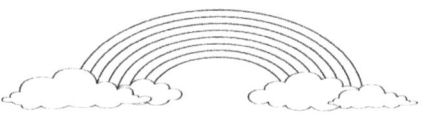

By My Spirit

"This is the word of the LORD to Zerubbabel: 'Not by might nor by power, but by My Spirit,' says the LORD of hosts" (Zechariah 4:6).

Zerubbabel was the governor of Jerusalem and had been named as the head over the first group of captives who had returned from Babylon. It is thought that Joshua, the high priest we discussed yesterday, along with other Levite priests, including the two prophets Haggai and Zechariah, had returned to the ancient Jewish city as part of this group. Things started out well. Zerubbabel had even brought back some of the temple vessels and other sacred objects that had been carried away to Babylon during the captivity to put into the new temple in Jerusalem once it was rebuilt. He reinstated the sacrificial services, the maintenance of the priests according to the instructions of Moses, and the celebration of the Passover. He even went so far as to oversee the completion of the foundations for the reconstruction of the temple.

With the passage of time, however, the urgency to rebuild God's house fell by the wayside. Busy with so many other reconstruction projects and getting the city of Jerusalem up and running again (as discussed in a previous devotional), the governor as well as the inhabitants lost sight of the necessity to put time and effort into rebuilding the temple. Only after strong exhortations from both the prophets Haggai and Zechariah did Zerubbabel reinitiate this God-ordained project. When he seemed doubtful or discouraged about the success of the major reconstruction effort, the Lord encouraged him with today's verse, reminding the governor that it wasn't just with human strength and power that they would accomplish God's bidding but that the mighty Spirit of God would assist them in the accomplishment of this grand and sacred undertaking!

I see several parallels here between us and the people of Zerubbabel's day. Like them, we often get so busy and become so distracted by our personal goals and activities that we forget about God's priorities. Often, we mean well and start out in the right direction, only to find ourselves getting off track due to lack of energy, vision, or motivation. We know we should complete the task the Lord has assigned us, but it just seems too difficult. Like Zerubbabel, we may need a little encouragement that when the Lord asks us to do something for Him, He will give us the strength and ability to do it. As a modern-day prophet has put it, "All His biddings are enablings" (*Christ's Object Lessons*, p. 333).

Here I would like to highlight two important facts about the role of the Holy Spirit in empowering us to do God's will. The first one has to do with the fact that many Christians today believe that the Holy Spirit didn't really become active here on earth until after the Day of Pentecost in New Testament times. On the contrary, if we study the Bible carefully, we will see that the Spirit of God has always played an important part in the affairs of humanity, starting way back at Creation, when we are told that the "Spirit of

God was hovering over the face of the waters" (Gen. 1:2). Today's text is just one example of many that refers to the Spirit's interactions with God's people throughout the Old Testament.

Secondly, to the detriment of our own spiritual growth, I feel we too often undermine the power of this third member of the Godhead and are unaware of our deep need for the Holy Spirit to permeate our lives in order to live the exhilarating and fruitful life the Lord longs to grant to His people. When we don't recognize our need, we don't ask for this mighty gift, which would enliven our testimony and allow us to accomplish great things for God. In the book *Acts of the Apostles*, we find the idea that upon receiving the Holy Spirit, all other blessings will follow in its train (see p. 50). This being the case, like Zerubbabel, we need to quit reciting the problems in trying to build up God's church (literally or figuratively) and despairing over our lack of human resources to get the job done. Instead, we need to cast our vision higher, realizing that God has all the resources of the universe at His command, and it is the Holy Spirit that will make those resources available to us, if we will only ask Him. Praise God for His wonderful promise to us found in Philippians 4:13, "I can do all things through Christ [manifested through His Spirit] who strengthens me!"

July 7

Don't Plan Evil

"Thus says the LORD of hosts: 'Execute true justice, show mercy and compassion everyone to his brother. Do not oppress the widow or the fatherless, the alien or the poor. Let none of you plan evil in his heart against his brother'" (Zechariah 7:9, 10).

Today's verses are an example of another one of those passages where we find a short and sweet summation of what the Lord wants His people to do. Unfortunately, as I am writing this devotional, our country is being plagued by an inordinate and alarming number of crimes—among them mass shootings, human trafficking, and hate crimes of every kind and description. Instead of executing justice, mercy and compassion, as we are admonished in this text, more and more people seem bent on executing (extinguishing life from) those who are different than them—in race, religion, national origin, language usage, or even social class or political persuasion. While we have become somewhat numbed to worldly people perpetrating these kinds of behaviors, it is truly unfortunate that we see some of these same attitudes against our brothers and sisters creeping into the ranks of folks who call themselves Christians. It appears that we are so busy fighting each other that we don't have time to even think about the needs of the widow, the fatherless, the foreigner, or the poor. From God's perspective, we are all His children, and thus siblings of one another in His all-encompassing view, like it or not.

I am intrigued by the last phrase in this Scripture reading. The one that says, "Let none of you plan evil in his heart against his brother." In other words, even just thinking about evil schemes to hurt, get even with, or oppress other people is unacceptable in God's sight. I can see three reasons for this. First, it is an unproductive waste of time. In fact, it is worse than a waste of time because the Lord tells us that if, for example, we even think about killing our neighbor in our hearts, it is counted to us as murder. Also, if we make evil plans, we are much more prone to actually carrying them out. And last, if we are conjuring up evil plans in our minds, we won't have time to make constructive plans for doing good.

It's interesting that even in our secular judicial systems, premeditated crimes are considered more heinous and usually carry a greater penalty than those that happen suddenly or without any malice or forethought. Likewise, planning to do evil carries a greater sentence than if we accidently trespass one of the Lord's precepts. The solution? Don't plan evil. Instead, we should make definite plans to do good. It would be time well spent to let our imaginations think about all the things we could do to help others, especially the widows, orphans, foreigners, and poor among us, and then devise effective ways for putting those good thoughts into positive actions! I like the way Romans 12:21 puts it: "Do not be overcome [even in our own minds] by evil, but overcome evil with good."

So, next time those dark thoughts about another person, laced with anger, jealousy, resentment, or hatred begin to creep into our minds, we need to immediately ask the Lord to take them away and fill the void with His thoughts—with His compassion, mercy, and grace. Then we will be able to treat others with the same unmerited favor that the Lord has granted us.

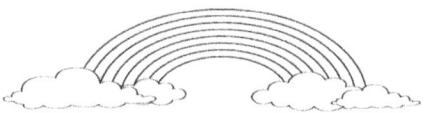

Crown Jewels

"The LORD their God will save them in that day, as the flock of His people. For they shall be like *the jewels of a crown, lifted like a banner over His land—" (Zechariah 9:16).*

This is one of two places in the minor prophets where the Lord refers to His people as His "jewels." The other one is in Malachi 3:17, which reads, "'They shall be Mine,' says the LORD of hosts, 'On the day that I make them my jewels. And I will spare them as a man spares his own son who serves him.'" Imagine how valuable we must be to the Lord that He describes those of us who will be saved as His precious jewels, like glittering gems in His royal crown of majesty!

Growing up in a family of modest means, jewelry did not fit into our meager budget. My parents tried to stretch their income to cover simply the bare necessities of life, like food and school clothes. Thus, jewels, or any kind of jewelry, was a luxury we could not afford. Perhaps that's why I still feel that wearing jewelry is an expensive habit that not only encourages vanity but is also a frivolous use of my still somewhat limited income. Occasionally, however, when I am window shopping at a mall, I will take a moment to study the beautiful colors and the brilliant shine of the pieces a jeweler is featuring in a display case. It serves to remind me of the many jewels that John, the revelator, describes as adorning the structures (i.e. foundations and gates) that we will find in the New Jerusalem. There, in a land without greed, pride, and selfishness, precious gems will be found freely everywhere as a natural part of the beauty of our new home.

Similarly, the beauty of the character of the saints, glistening in robes of righteousness given us by Jesus, will shine like jewels throughout eternity!

Whenever I hear either of these lovely verses, I am immediately taken back to my Primary Sabbath School class, where we sang a song called "When He Cometh." Perhaps you have heard it. The words were written by William O. Cushing more than 150 years ago, and it was set to a tune called "Jewels" by his contemporary, George F. Root. Because it was written so long ago, and is generally considered a children's hymn, it is not found in some of the more modern hymnals. But the words of the song are still engraved in my mind:

> When He cometh, when He cometh to make up His jewels, all His jewels, precious jewels, His loved and His own. Like the stars of the morning, His bright crown adorning, they shall shine in their beauty, bright gems for His crown.
> He will gather, He will gather the gems for His kingdom, all the pure ones, all the bright ones, His loved and His own. Like the stars of the morning, His bright crown adorning, they shall shine in their beauty, bright gems for His crown.
> (*The Church Hymnal*, hymn 418)

Amazingly, even now, as an adult, this simple little song, more than half a century after I first learned it, still conjures up warm feelings of how precious I am in the Lord's sight. It gives me a secure sense of belonging to Him. It also makes me think about how much He wants me to be present with Him forever in heaven. All I can say is hallelujah!

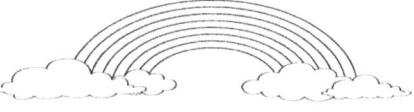

July 9

A Priest's Job Description

"My covenant was with him [Levi], one of life and peace, and I gave them to him that he might fear Me; so he feared Me and was reverent before My name. The law of truth was in his mouth, and injustice was not found on his lips. He walked with Me in peace and equity, and turned many away from iniquity. For the lips of a priest should keep knowledge, and people should seek the law from his mouth; for he is the messenger of the LORD of hosts"
(Malachi 2:5–7).

As we move into the book of Malachi, the last one in the Old Testament, it's interesting to note that this book contains the last writings by a prophet that God's people will receive for the next 400 years until John the Baptist announces the coming of the Messiah. I must say that I am impressed with how practical it is, addressing everything from divorce to tithing. Today, the emphasis is on the duties of the priests, the spiritual leaders and teachers from the tribe of Levi, who had been chosen to conduct the traditional worship services and provide moral guidance and truth to the children of Israel throughout their generations.

Sadly, we find that the priests in Malachi's time were not living up to their holy calling. Chapter 2 begins with the Lord denouncing them for their irreverence and disobedience, for they should have served as faithful guardians of the truths of God as outlined in the previous books of the law and the prophets. Instead of fulfilling their divinely-appointed mission of leading the people through precept and example, their selfishness, wickedness, and hypocrisy had led many astray, to the point that those to whom they should have been ministering now found them to be "contemptible and base" (verse 9). They had corrupted the covenant that the Lord had made with Levi, bringing dishonor and disgrace to the worship of Jehovah. As a result, neither the people nor the Lord found their hypocritical temple services to be a blessing.

To remedy this spiritual declension, the Lord sends Malachi to address it, first by admonishing the priests about their lack of reverence and obedience and then by graciously inviting them to renew their sacred Levitical covenant. This would reverse the curse brought on by their apostasy and restore spiritual life and peace to both the priests and the people. Notice, however, that the Lord didn't stop there. He went on to describe specific expectations He had for the priests, who would stand before the people as His representatives and messengers. In the thumbnail job description delineated in this passage, I find nine qualities the Lord is asking His spiritual leaders to display: reverence, truthfulness, justice, peacefulness, fairness (equity), turning others from iniquity (a positive influence on others), knowledgeable (able to preserve and share spiritual wisdom), lawful (in example as well as in word), and a faithful messenger of the Lord (effectively teaching and preaching God's communications to His people).

Before we become too judgmental about the condition of the priesthood in Malachi's day or even too focused on the qualifications of our modern-day preachers and pastors, let's remember that as New Testament Christians, the apostle Peter exhorts us about the concept of the "priesthood of all believers." What? Does that mean that God expects all of His followers today to leave their own spiritual apostasy behind, renew their own personal covenant with the Lord, and start exhibiting the same qualities He prescribed for the ancient priests? Listen to this text, found in 1 Peter 2:9: "But you *are* a chosen generation, a royal priesthood, a holy nation, His own special people, that you may proclaim the praises of Him who called you out of darkness into His marvelous light." So, I believe the answer is "Yes!"

Has He called us individually from the darkness and curse of sin into His glorious righteousness and light? Yes! Is He willing to forgive us and renew His covenant with us personally? Yes! As part of His royal priesthood, does He make clear His expectations about how we should honor and bring glory to Him in both precept and example? Yes! Under the new covenant, each of us has a part to play in ministering to the spiritual needs of those around us. Then what are we waiting for? The time to start fulfilling our duties as part of His royal priesthood is now!

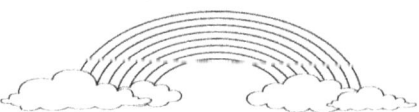

Dealing Treacherously

*"Yet you say, 'For what reason?' [Why won't God accept our offerings?]
Because the LORD has been witness between you and the wife of your
youth, with whom you have dealt treacherously; yet she is your companion
and your wife by covenant. But did He not make them one, having a
remnant of the Spirit? And why one? He seeks godly offspring. Therefore,
take heed to your spirit, and let none deal treacherously with the wife of his
youth. 'For the LORD God of Israel says that He hates divorce, for it covers
one's garment with violence,' says the LORD of hosts. 'Therefore, take heed
to your spirit, that you do not deal treacherously'" (Malachi 2:14–16).*

This is a long passage, but I wanted to cover the whole admonition about the subject of divorce. Why did these verses arrest my attention? For one thing, I have personally felt the pain of divorce, and for another, one of our relatives has recently gone through and, indeed, is still suffering from the trauma caused by this dark and tragic experience. There are, of course, many kinds of divorce. A few are amicable, where people just agree to disagree, and everyone goes their separate ways. But most are bitter, with emotional and often long-lasting struggles over property, on-going financial commitments, custody of children, etc. Sometimes people simultaneously lose their reputations, their jobs, and/or their homes, not to mention their security and self-respect. I have seen time and again, especially in women, the need to rediscover their personal identity now that they are no longer "so-and-so's wife." Unfortunately, in the aftermath of the upheaval, some people also lose their church membership and even their ultimate salvation.

I remember meeting a lovely Catholic lady in our sister city in Mexico, who made all the housing arrangements for a fellow teacher and I when we traveled there one summer to offer a children's art class for purposes of cultural exchange. Over the couple of weeks of our stay, as she got to know us better, she confided in us that her husband was currently living in a nearby town with another woman—and it wasn't the first time. He had trampled on her self-worth and dignity since everyone in her small town knew the situation. When we asked if she had thought about divorcing him, she quickly answered that such an action on her part was out of the question. A divorced woman could not take communion in her church, and someone who didn't take communion could not be saved, according to her priest. Thus, regardless of her pain and humiliation, she was trapped in a sham of a marriage for the rest of her days.

Why do I bring up this case? Because I don't believe it was God's intent that we should use these verses to rub people's noses in their difficult circumstances and to teach that they are excluded from heaven. While the church should support marriages as a sacred covenant and should not condone divorce as a first-choice escape from a difficult one, Jesus said that it was because of the hardness of the Israelites' hearts that Moses had allowed it (see Matt. 19:8). Surely, in these last days, when the love of many waxes cold (see Matt. 24:12, KJV), people's hearts are at least as hard as they were when Moses walked the earth. In cases of infidelity, abuse, abandonment, etc., few of us would argue that a couple should be forced to stay together, especially where children are also being negatively affected. (Paul's discussion in First Corinthians 7 provides more insight on this topic.)

My conclusion is that, as church members, we should not be quoting these texts to condemn people, who are already passing through a difficult time in life, but to encourage them that God is wanting what is best for them. In fact, here He shows His care for the mistreated and oppressed, defending them. These verses give me hope because in them we see the great compassion of a God who doesn't want us to suffer the pain that divorce almost inevitably brings, not only to the husband and wife but also to the children, the extended family, and close friends. After all, He made our hearts, and He knows our need for love, intimacy, and a sense of belonging. That's why He hates divorce. He doesn't hate the person going through it, however, because it is still His will that all of us will be saved.

Notice, though, that He gives the perpetrators of divorce some strong warnings. Through Malachi, He tells them that He no longer wants their supposed worship and their tainted offerings, while they are dealing "treacherously" with the spouses of their youth. He warns them that He has been a witness of their cruel behavior and that they should take heed of the spirit they are manifesting. If they want to be right with the Lord again, they need to repent of their sin and treat their life's companion in a fair and loving manner. So, now is the time, more than ever, to help, support, and pray for each other, leaving all judgment up to the Lord, the only righteous Judge of us all.

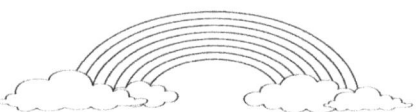

July 11

Overflowing Blessings

"'Bring all the tithes into the storehouse, that there may be food in My house, and try Me now in this,' says the LORD of hosts, 'If I will not open for you the windows of heaven and pour out for you such *blessing that* there will *not be* room *enough* to receive it'" (Malachi 3:10).

Although I have read, heard, and even memorized this verse, it always grips me anew when I come across it because the Lord is actually inviting us personally to test Him in this regard. He's challenging us to engage in a direct interaction with Him, a compact, if you will, and then to stand back with anticipation and see how He will bless us. It's an open opportunity to watch God's intervention in our own lives! How exciting is that? Some people today say they have never seen God interacting directly in their lives, and therefore, they have nothing recent to share with others regarding His goodness and faithfulness to them. I would encourage those people to claim this promise, start paying a regular and honest tithe, and then stand back and watch for the abundant blessings that the Lord will pour out upon them!

In my experience, not all His blessings will be monetary, but some of them will. I'd like to share a couple of them with you. One time, about a year and a half ago, we were planning a family reunion during the Christmas holidays. After paying our bills (including our tithe) in November, it became evident to us that we were not going to have enough money to make the long-anticipated trip in December. We prayed about it and then went on with life. Approximately a week later, out of the blue, we received a mortgage insurance refund check in the amount of

$700—roughly the amount of money it would take for us to make our trip! It was unbelievable! All we could say, over and over as we were making preparations for our journey, was "Praise the Lord!"

Another more recent miracle event occurred, this time concerning a specific kind of offering. Malachi 3:8 mentions not only tithes but offerings. It says that we have also robbed God if we do not bring our offerings to Him. So, a couple of weeks ago I was reading a flyer that came in the mail about a way to evangelize a community by sending out truth-filled literature in specified zip codes. The mission project caught my interest, and I told the Lord, "If a get any extra money in the next month or so, I am going to dedicate it to this purpose." Last week, I was going through my mail when I saw an unusual envelope from a pharmacy. I thought they were probably trying to entice me to buy something from them, but when I opened the envelope, a check fell out. *It's probably one of those fake checks that advertisers send out,* I said to myself. Then I read the brief letter that accompanied the check. They said that in going over their records, they discovered that they had overcharged me for some of the prescriptions I had filled at their store—over four years ago! My mouth fell open in unbelief! Four years ago? And they were just now sending me a refund! Then I remembered the promise I had made to the Lord. Amazingly, they had sent me a check for more than $70, and with thanksgiving and praise, I immediately donated the money, designating it as offering for our local mission project.

What a joy it is to be co-workers together with God, who has more resources at His command than we can even imagine! What a shame that so many people don't experience this joy because they never trust and obey the Lord enough to see the wonders He performs. In fact, a number of years ago, when my husband was pastoring a local church, the conference office for that region shared a report with their workers saying that research had found that only about 30 percent of church members pay a full tithe and even less pay regular offerings! Meanwhile, the Lord continues to faithfully shower down upon them daily blessings, such as health, ample food, a warm home, good friends, a close-knit family, and countless other material and even spiritual blessings! But how much they miss by not taking the Lord at His word through faith! How much richer could their relationship with God be, and how much more of His good work could be accomplished in the church and the world, if everyone committed to doing just his or her little part in returning their tithes and offerings, as the Lord has requested. While this injunction was given to the people in Malachi's day, the Lord expects nothing less from His thankful and faithful children today.

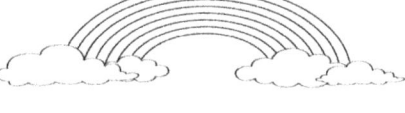

July 12

A Book of Remembrance

"Then those who feared the LORD spoke to one another, and the LORD listened and heard them; so a book of remembrance was written before Him for those who fear the LORD and who meditate on His name. 'They shall be Mine,' says the LORD of hosts, 'on the day that I make them My jewels. And I will spare them as a man spares his own son who serves him'" (Malachi 3:16, 17).

Just a few days ago, we discussed the verse in Zechariah 9:16 where the Lord referred to His people as His crown jewels. Here, in Malachi 3:17, as we mentioned back then, the Lord elaborates on this beautiful concept, stating that we will be His on the day that He makes up His jewels. He also expresses His love to us by saying that He will treat us "as a man spares his own son...." How secure in His tender regard for us these statements should make us feel!

Today, though, I want to focus on the precious promise made to us in verse 16. First, it makes us aware of the fact that when His people speak together about Him, He actually listens to them and hears what they say! Not only that but that a record, a "book of remembrance," is written about those who fear (revere) Him and meditate upon Him. What an amazing thought this is to me! Sure, I've always heard that each of our actions, good or bad, are recorded in heaven in preparation for Judgment Day. But this is more than a bunch of clerical-type angels just writing everything down mechanically. According to this verse, the Lord Himself is listening to us when we talk together about Him, specifically! It gives us the idea that this action is something He's actually anticipating with a special kind of enjoyment, and He wants to remember it in eternity!

This reminds me of the baby books that my mother used to keep for each of her children, recording when each one said their first word, took their first step, got their first tooth, and of course they were replete with pictures! Why did my mother record all of these things in a special book? Because she loved her children so much that she treasured each milestone in their growth and development and wanted to remember each of these details about each beloved child forever! What a sense of warmth and belonging it gave me, knowing that my mother took the time and effort to dedicate a book of memories just for me personally! This is the kind of love and watch care I imagine our heavenly Father having for us when I read this verse about Him keeping a "book of remembrance" for His own precious children.

When I was in my twenties, I had a Christian friend who loved to talk about the Lord. We would share with each other all the good things He had done for us—our answered prayers, His marvelous grace in saving us, and the blessings He showered upon us from day to day. Once, during one of these conversations, we had our Bibles open and came upon this verse in Malachi. Suddenly, we were filled with wonder, realizing that the Lord was listening to us at that very moment and preparing a book of remembrance of some kind for us to enjoy together with Him when we reached heaven— what a great time we will have! It will be kind of like when my mom shared the memories recorded in my baby book with me after I had become an adult. Whenever we dug it out of some bookcase or storage chest, we would always have such fun talking about all of my "accomplishments" and giggling at my baby pictures!

Similarly, today's promise assures me that we have many good times to look forward to when we finally get a chance to sit down to reminisce with our loving Father in heaven. Let's bring joy to His heart now by talking together about Him more often in our everyday lives!

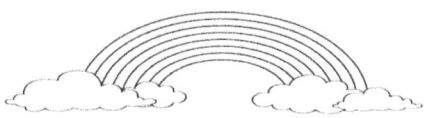

Turning Hearts

"Behold, I will send you Elijah the prophet before the coming of the great and dreadful day of the LORD, and he will turn the hearts of the fathers to the children, and the hearts of the children to their fathers, lest I come and strike the earth with a curse" (Malachi 4:5, 6).

In these final verses of the Old Testament, the Lord has given another practical message to Malachi to share with His people. I can't help but notice that many of these last prophetic messages that the Jewish people will hear for the next 400 years are actually centered around relationships. The injunction to tithe is a demonstration of one's faithfulness and dedication to God; the admonition against divorce emphasizes the expectation that a Godly man will be committed to his spouse; and here, a close relationship between parents and children is advocated.

In reading over comments in the *SDA Bible Commentary*, I gleaned two more insights. One is that "the Elijah message," as this passage is often referred to, is pointing forward to a time when another strong and fiery prophet will appear with God's present truth for the time right before Jesus comes to this earth to accomplish the salvation of the human race. Looking forward to New Testament times, we, of course, have the benefit of knowing that the man of God who would help prepare the people for the Messiah's arrival was John the Baptist. This was a promise that the Lord would not abandon His people nor take the prophetic gift away from them. After several hundred years, John would come with a strong message about the need to repent and re-commit to the Lord, similar to the communications God had given to Elijah to help reform His ancient people. The second insight was that this mention of the need for parents and children to mend and strengthen their relationships was actually a reference to the fifth commandment, representative of all the commandments that the Lord was asking them to return to and obey in order to become His true representatives on earth until the first coming of Jesus.

Many in our day have taught that "the Elijah message" is what we, living near the end of earth's history, also need; but this time, we need it in order to be prepared for the second coming of Jesus. We also need to repent and reform our lives. We need to press together, making sure not to leave our children behind, as we seek to keep all of God's commandments and become His final ambassadors in a dark and chaotic world. In a society where children are often disrespectful and disobedient to their parents and where, too often, parents are abusive or neglectful of their children, what a beautiful and winning witness a Christian home, filled with love and peace, could be! It would be a true example of the loving relationships the Lord wants us to enjoy as well as the righteous characters He wants to form in all those who keep His commandments and teach their children to do so. This has been the Lord's intent even since Moses' time: "And these words which I command you today shall be in your heart. You shall teach them diligently to your children, and shall talk of them when you sit in your house, when you walk by the way, when you lie down, and when you rise up" (Deut. 6:6, 7). May the Lord, once again, turn our hearts to Him and to each other, and may He grant us the kind of families that will honor Him as together we await His coming to take us to our eternal home!

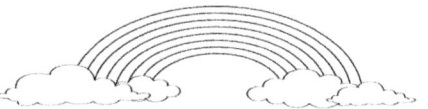

NEW TESTAMENT

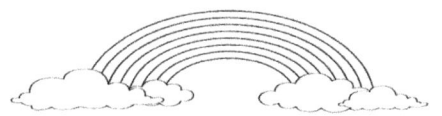

Prophetic Generations

"So all the generations from Abraham to David are fourteen generations, from David until the captivity in Babylon are fourteen generations, and from the captivity in Babylon until the Christ are fourteen generations" (Matthew 1:17).

As we begin our journey through the New Testament, this may seem an unusual text to highlight. It caught my attention for two reasons. It forms a kind of bridge spanning the 400 years between Old Testament times and New Testament times. It also demonstrates that in God's timing, nothing is an accident. I'm impressed by the fact that each of these significant periods of time in the history of God's people were fourteen generations—not more, not less, indicating that the plan of salvation, which would be accomplished by the long-awaited Jewish Messiah, was not just carelessly thrown together. It was meticulously orchestrated by a God of order and precision—One who knew the future and had sent messages through His prophets beforehand about the coming of Israel's Savior.

Matthew's intent in this Gospel was to write from a Jewish perspective to a Jewish audience, in order to establish the legitimacy of Jesus as the Christ. As such, he took every available opportunity to refer back to the Old Testament prophecies, especially those that were specifically about Jesus. In addition, since genealogies were important to the culture in establishing one's heritage, Matthew dedicates more than half of the first chapter of his book to the genealogy of Jesus, going all the way back to Abraham—the person considered to be the father of the Jewish nation. Matthew points out to those who might have been unaware that Jesus was a Son of David, one of Israel's most-lauded kings, as well as a Son of the revered Abraham. To the Jewish mind, what could be a better pedigree than that? It is Matthew's hope that this information, together with all of the prophecies which had been so obviously fulfilled in the life of Jesus, will make a compelling argument that will win many people over to an acceptance of Jesus, not only as the true Messiah but also as their personal Redeemer.

So, when "the fullness of the time had come" (Gal. 4:4), meaning the Lord saw that it was the right time for an important event to take place, in this case, after three periods of fourteen generations each, the momentous and history-changing arrival of the Lord of life, in the form of a baby, burst upon the human scene! Ready or not, humanity's destiny, determined by each person's choice to either accept or reject this heaven-sent Messiah, would be altered forever!

Immediately after establishing Jesus as a Jew by reviewing His genealogy (Israelites would never have accepted a non-Jew as the Messiah), Matthew launches into the amazing biography of Jesus, starting with His miraculous birth. Even a casual reader will notice how frequently he peppers his narrative with references from the Old Testament. He, having been a tax collector, had a writing style that was brief, professional, and to the point, always tailored to be effective in reaching his target audience of compatriots.

And his writing was not without fruit for the kingdom. Even today, many of us modern "children of Israel" are blessed and brought to a fuller faith in Christ by the quoting of the Messiah-confirming prophecies that Matthew so conscientiously employs in his Gospel.

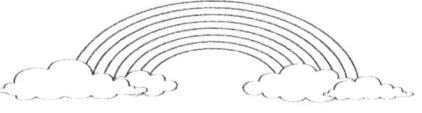

July 15

Divine Affirmation

"When He had been baptized, Jesus came up immediately from the water; and behold, the heavens were opened to Him, and He saw the Spirit of God descending like a dove and alighting upon Him. And suddenly a voice came from heaven, saying, 'This is My beloved Son, in whom I am well pleased'" (Matthew 3:16, 17).

Another firm plank in the upbuilding of our faith that, indeed, Jesus was the long-awaited Messiah occurred with the event of His baptism, just as He was about to formally begin His public ministry. John the Baptist reacted with surprise when Jesus asked to be baptized. He had just recognized and declared Him to be "the Lamb of God, which taketh away the sin of the world" (John 1:29, KJV) to the multitudes who had come to hear him preach in the wilderness. He knew that Jesus was the Savior of the world, and that he, although God's messenger, was merely another sinner. Jesus should have been the one to do the baptizing that day, but Jesus, wanting to set an example for His followers throughout the ages, convinced John that this was the right thing to do. Then, just as He came up from the waters of the Jordan, God showed His approval of Jesus by opening up the heavens, sending His Holy Spirit to alight upon Him and even speaking those words that have resounded throughout history, "This is My beloved Son, in whom I am well pleased." What a beautiful confirmation of the Lord's identity for both Himself and the people of His time as well as for us! His heavenly Father left no doubt in anyone's mind that Jesus was the promised Messiah in the flesh! The subsequent miracles He would perform throughout His life gave further evidence of His divinity, and His mighty resurrection sealed the faith of His followers in Him as their Lord and Savior just as it seals ours today.

At the time of His baptism, Jesus was thirty years old, and this event served to ordain or commission Him to accomplish the great mission for which He had come into the world: "to seek and to save" those who were lost (see Luke 19:10). Up to this time, He had lived a quiet and humble life of service and faithfulness in His hometown of Nazareth. Now, He was to embark on His miraculous public ministry on behalf of humankind—teaching, preaching, and healing people wherever He went. He wanted to make it known that He was dedicated 100 percent to doing God's will, while also dedicated 100 percent to saving those who would accept Him as their Redeemer. Thus, He used not only the title of "Son of God" but also called Himself the "Son of Man," in order to more closely identify with those He came to save.

Some people don't believe in baptism, labeling it as an ancient and unnecessary practice. But the New Testament mentions it often as a meaningful representation that a new convert has died to their old life of sin and become a new creature in Jesus. In addition, it provides an opportunity to declare that they are now 100 percent committed to doing God's will and to fulfilling His purpose for their lives. It gives a powerful testimony to all who know them that they are now on God's side in the cosmic battle between good

and evil. If Jesus thought baptism was an essential way to witness about His relationship with God, who are we to diminish its importance? In fact, many people have felt the first tug on their hearts by the Holy Spirit while witnessing the baptism of a friend or relative.

In the first book of the New Testament, Matthew thought that the subject of baptism was important enough to use as a bookend at both the beginning and end of his writing. Today's passage, found in chapter 3, highlighted the baptism of Jesus, while Matthew 28:19, in the last chapter, gives us the great commission of Jesus to His followers to "Go... and make disciples of all the nations, baptizing them in the name of the Father and of the Son and of the Holy Spirit." In this directive we see that the Lord not only expects us to be baptized but admonishes us to bring others to the experience of baptism as well, all as a public statement that we have passed from death unto life and can truly be identified as His committed followers.

July 16

Heavenly Sustenance

"But He answered and said, 'It is written, "Man shall not live by bread alone, but by every word that proceeds from the mouth of God" ' " (Matthew 4:4).

These, of course, are the famous words of Jesus when Satan first tried to tempt Him in the wilderness soon after His baptism. Satan had been standing by, looking for any way possible to make Jesus unsuccessful in His mission to save the world. He had heard God's words from heaven, declaring Jesus as His Son, and the same old jealousy and hatred that he had felt for Jesus in heaven flooded His soul once again. Now that Jesus was alone in the wilderness and weakened by forty days of fasting, he sought to destroy Jesus and His faith in God's Word. With practiced skill, he crafted three special temptations for Jesus, just as he had worked stealthily to deceive Eve in the Garden of Eden at the beginning of time.

The first temptation, to which Jesus gave the answer above, was with regard to the physical needs and material desires of humankind. Jesus was genuinely hungry, but He saw through Satan's plans. By saying, "If you are the Son of God," Satan was seeking to create doubt in the proclamation God had made so recently by the Jordan River (see Matt. 4:3). He was challenging Jesus to prove His relationship with God by performing a miracle to meet His own needs. On the point of appetite and a desire for material things, which God had not authorized, the whole world had been plunged into sin by our first parents, and Jesus had come to rectify that error. So how did He do it? And how did He successfully overcome the subsequent temptation to be presumptuous about God's protection and care by throwing Himself down from the temple, as Satan suggested? And lastly, what about the temptation to give in to the carnal desire for worldly pomp, pride, and power, which Satan offered Him if He would only bow down and worship the cunning and evil tempter? As always,

Satan mixed some truth with his insidious suggestions, even quoting Scripture, which he twisted to accomplish his wicked designs. This is a tactic he still uses on his unwary victims today.

Thank God, Jesus had studied the Old Testament writings from the time of His childhood and had memorized many of them. His heavenly Father, through the Holy Spirit, had given Him a clear understanding of the truths of God's Word, and His faith in the Scriptures was unwavering. This was the key to His success in standing up to the wiles of the devil and overcoming each temptation thrown at Him. And it will be the key to our victory as well.

The Bible assures us that Jesus not only overcame these three very difficult temptations in the wilderness but all those which He experienced throughout His lifetime. Since He did, He understands the trials and temptations that assail us, His followers, and has made provision for us to overcome evil as well. Listen to this beautiful passage found in Hebrews 4:15, 16: "For we do not have a High Priest who cannot sympathize with our weaknesses, but was in all *points* tempted as *we are, yet* without sin. Let us therefore come boldly to the throne of grace, that we may obtain mercy and find grace to help in time of need." What a gracious invitation our Lord offers us! He will give us the spiritual sustenance we need to withstand all of life's temptations, if we will, like Him, maintain our faith in God's mighty Word and anchor our trust in Him.

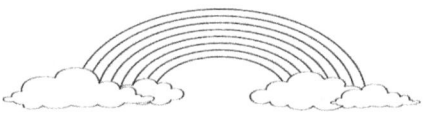

The Call

"And Jesus, walking by the Sea of Galilee, saw two brothers, Simon called Peter, and Andrew his brother, casting a net into the sea; for they were fishermen. Then He said to them, 'Follow Me, and I will make you fishers of men'" (Matthew 4:18, 19).

Almost twenty years ago, I received a call that changed my life. The school year at the university where I was teaching was only a few months from coming to an end when I saw a job advertisement from the State Department of Education for a position as an educational specialist in my exact area of expertise. I would be able to make a real impact in the state where I was living, helping to guide teachers, administrators, and district office employees, as they began to implement a recent law that had been passed regarding how to serve language minority students. The pay was excellent, and the benefits package was generous. There was only one catch—I would have to commute for an hour and a half to work each morning and have an hour and a half return trip at the end of each long day. But the position was so attractive to me that I applied anyway. Several weeks later, I was surprised and happy to be invited for an interview. Shortly thereafter, when the call came offering me the job, it took my breath away! Could I really leave the world of education that I knew so well behind to enter a new and unchartered territory as an employee of the state? Was I willing to take on a three-hour daily commute, through winter weather approximately seven or eight months of the year? I decided to take a leap of faith, and although not knowing what the future would hold, I chose to accept the challenging position I was offered, which changed the trajectory of my life.

In today's passage, Peter and Andrew received a call that changed their lives completely. All their lives they had been fishermen. It was what they knew. It was what they were good at. Their culture, their diet, their friends, their income—all revolved around fishing. Although this new Teacher was compelling, and His messages attractive in a way they hadn't experienced before, could they really just get up and leave everything behind—their nets, their tools of the trade, their boats? Could they risk everything to follow Him into an unknown future and take up His challenge to become "fishers of men," whatever that meant? It would be a giant leap of faith. And yet, something about His call to them inspired them to risk it all and go off with Jesus into a grand new adventure—and it started them on a whole new trajectory as well.

So, what did the call of Jesus entail? Well, first there was the training stage. They listened to His teachings, observed the miracles He performed, and followed Him wherever He led, closely watching His interactions with people all along the way. When He felt they were ready, they entered the practice stage. He sent them out two-by-two to teach and preach and witness for Him. Some days they were more successful than others, but He kept working with them, molding them little-by-little into His image. After His death and resurrection, He poured the Holy Spirit into them, giving them the finishing touch that made them into powerful and effective ambassadors, who were able to convert thousands to Christianity in a day!

Answering the call of God to serve Him in reaching others for His kingdom is the most important decision we can make. He calls all of us, equips us for the work He wants us to do, and then assigns us a special place that no one else can fill. Here, our appearance, our ethnicity, our gender, our age, and our limitations are all immaterial, except as we choose to use them to bring others to the Lord. If we dedicate our whole lives to Him, He will take whatever we bring to the table and both bless and multiply it to the glory of God!

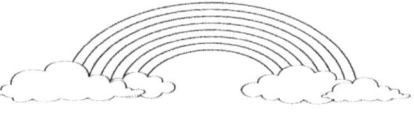

July 18

Be Reconciled

"Therefore if you bring your gift to the altar, and there remember that your brother has something against you, leave your gift there before the altar, and go your way. First be reconciled to your brother, and then come and offer your gift" (Matthew 5:23, 24).

Just after the beatitudes, and shortly before His admonitions in this same chapter to go the second mile and love your enemies, is tucked this less well-known teaching of Jesus. I believe it's not preached frequently because something about it goes against our grain. It makes us a little uncomfortable because we would much rather just gloss over altercations and offenses or pretend they didn't happen or that they don't really matter. They may not matter to us, but to the person offended, they can even be a cause for leaving the church.

In fact, when studies are done regarding why previous members have left the church, a large percentage of them will tell you that it is because of what some other member said or did to them. When these offenses were not addressed, the injured party couldn't get past the hurt, became bitter, and declared, "If this is how church members act, I don't want to be one of them!"

The tricky thing is that although some offenses are obvious, others may have occurred without us even knowing they happened. We had no clue that our simple words would have such a deleterious impact. Let me give you an example. A long time ago, at a family reunion of some sort, while discussing our children, I made a comment about one of the nieces being "so little." It was not spoken directly to her nor did I say it in a derogatory manner. Years later, however, I found out that she had overheard the conversation, taken it as a negative judgment on her value, and held a grudge against me all through her teen years. Who knew?

In mulling over this situation, I came up with an action plan to reduce the problems discussed here. First, I must pray that the Holy Spirit will give me wisdom to know what to say and when to say it—or whether I should speak at all in some cases. Then I must ask the Lord for a sensitive heart to discern if someone has been offended by me. If so, I need to apologize by saying something like, "Please forgive me if I offended you" or "I'm sorry if I upset you." In some instances, it might even be appropriate to ask, "What can I do to make it right?" Now we are really talking about going the second mile, but it makes our apology more credible if we go so far as to try to make amends. "Be reconciled" is how the Bible puts it. The definition of reconciled is to make peace with or restore friendly relations between people.

So far, we've only talked about if your brother has something against you. What if you have something against him? In the spirit of reconciliation, I believe this should also be addressed, if at all possible. Of course, it would require great tact and courage to approach some people, and bringing up the issue may cause more discord and strife than unity, depending upon how we say it as well as how they take it. Once again, we will need to ask the Lord for wisdom. Sometimes the offender may have moved away or died, or we have lost contact with them throughout the years. Then,

instead of opening a can of worms digging up old slights and mistakes, I think we need to go to Jesus, tell Him of our pain, and ask Him to heal us and give us the grace to have a forgiving spirit toward the person who wronged us.

All this begs the question: is it alright to have disagreements with those around us? Of course it is. We each have different backgrounds, opinions, personalities, and perceptions, as part of being the unique individuals God made us to be. Even Paul and Barnabas disagreed at one point about how best to carry out their ministries, so differences will arise between even devout and dedicated Christians. The important thing here is to respect people's right to their opinions, listen carefully in order to consider their point of view, and then, carefully explain why you hold the position that you do. Ultimately, it may be necessary to "agree to disagree," but we need to do so as amicably as possible.

What today's passage tells me is how important relationships are to the Lord. He's basically telling us that if we do not maintain good relationships with each other, we will not be able to maintain a good relationship with Him. He does not accept hypocritical worship or offerings. What He requires is that we learn to love one another as He has loved us.

Lord, please help us to live up to the high standard of relationships that you have modeled for all those who claim to be your followers!

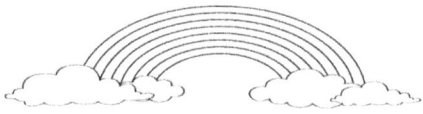

Don't Worry

"Therefore do not worry, saying, 'What shall we eat?' or 'What shall we drink?' or 'What shall we wear?' For after all these things the Gentiles seek. For your heavenly Father knows that you need all these things. But seek first the kingdom of God and His righteousness, and all these things shall be added to you" (Matthew 6:31–33).

A few years back, a catchy little tune which became popular included in its lyrics the words: "Don't worry! Be happy!" It seemed like a mindless little ditty, yet, in some respects, it gave us good council. Proverbs 17:22 tells us that "A merry heart does good, like medicine." And here, the Lord Himself is telling us not to worry. Why? Because He already knows our needs, and He promises that if we just trust Him, He will provide for them. Does this mean we don't have to put forth any effort to pay the bills or keep food on the table? Of course not. As we've discussed before, a number of Bible verses talk about the value of work and how our motto should be, "Whatsoever thy hand findeth to do, do it with thy might" (Eccles. 9:10, KJV). And we should do our work "as to the Lord, and not to men" (Eph. 6:7). What it does mean is that, as Christians, we should not be walking around with a huge burden of worry on our backs, robbing us of our joy, and overclouding our faith and courage. After we have done what is within our power, we need to trust the Lord to do His part.

Allow me to share how the Lord has done this on several occasions in my life. When I was a child, there were a few times when my father would either not be able to find a job, or retain one, because he refused to work on the Sabbath. With three young children

to feed, our family of five sometimes barely scraped by financially. But Daddy always paid tithe regardless of how little his income. (Later, when he had a steady job where he made good money, he often paid a double tithe to show his thankfulness!) Fortunately, during the leaner times, the Lord moved upon the hearts of either our relatives or some of our church members to keep us afloat. When we didn't have enough money for rent, my maternal grandmother, who lived alone by then, took us in. People who knew our cupboards were almost bare brought us bags of food on a couple of occasions. But I think the area where I appreciated help the most was with regard to clothing.

I have always been tall, and in junior high school, right at the age were adolescents are most self-conscious about their looks, I was just about as tall as I am now. This made me stick out like a sore thumb, and it wasn't as if I could just hide behind the other girls my age since I towered over them. About this time, my aunts and cousins, seeing that I was big enough to fit into their old clothes, began to give me their hand-me-downs. We're not just talking about any cast-offs. These women were professional, with good taste, and enough money to buy quality clothing. Wow! What a blessing it was, throughout my teen years, to be the happy recipient of the clothes they didn't want any more! There are other instances where the Lord moved on the hearts of others to help us during my youth—but these are several that stand out in my mind.

As an adult, once I started working and making good money, I tried to pay those acts of kindness forward and help others who I saw in need. I do remember one time, however, after my husband and I were married, when our food supply had run low due to several job changes. An acquaintance from church, who became aware of our situation, kindly brought us enough food to tide us over until the next paycheck. What an unexpected and welcome gesture that was! The Lord knew our need and worked through the kindness of one of His thoughtful followers to faithfully provide for us!

Since then, there have been times when the Lord has simply amazed us with showers of blessings. In one way or the other, the Lord has always seen us through. From personal experience, we have tested His promises and found them to be trustworthy. If we take God at His word and strive to seek Him first, just as He clothes the lilies and feeds the birds, He will provide for our needs in the future just as He has in the past. No need to worry!

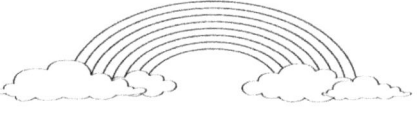

July 20

Distance Healing

"When Jesus heard it, He marveled, and said to those who followed, 'Assuredly, I say to you, I have not found such great faith, not even in Israel! And I say to you that many will come from east and west, and sit down with Abraham, Isaac, and Jacob in the kingdom of heaven.' …Then Jesus said to the centurion, 'Go your way; and as you have believed, so let it be done for you.' And his servant was healed that same hour" (Matthew 8:10, 11, 13).

A number of years back, a simple, unassuming movie called The Gods Must be Crazy came out. It was a strange title, but it made me curious about its content, so I went to see it. I was surprised by the moral lessons it demonstrated. The main character was a small African man, living in an impoverished country, who went to all lengths to try to return something which he thought had accidently been dropped onto Earth by the gods that he believed lived in the heavens. He manifested a firm faith in his purpose and a tenacity to do what he believed was the right thing, regardless of any inconvenience, time, or effort it might cost him. If only we would be so determined to do the right thing!

In today's passage, Jesus was trying to tell the self-righteous religious leaders of Israel that, even though they falsely thought that they had a free ticket to get into heaven simply because they were children of Abraham, there were many non-Jews that would be there because of their strong faith in Him. It was shocking to hear Jesus say that He had not found such faith in all of Israel as displayed by this Roman military man, famously known as "The Centurion" in this chapter. The Jews couldn't really wrap their heads around how an uncircumcised sinner, a foreign soldier, one of the hated occupiers of their land, could ever enter the kingdom of heaven.

Jesus is not looking at all the religious facts we know, what our heritage in the church may be, our wealth, or what country we are from. What matters is the depth of our faith in Him and our willingness to act on it, regardless of where He finds us! Since He is aware of everyone's background, whether rich or poor, educated or uneducated, black or white, from the Eastern Hemisphere or the Western one, He knows and values each person who valiantly and honestly strives to live up to whatever light they have. Sometimes, even unknowingly, they are carrying out His will, just by their determination to do what they believe to be right, regardless of the cost. How amazed some of these people will be when one day they wake up in heaven!

At times, as with the centurion, people don't need to wait for eternity to begin to see the outworking of their strong faith. They begin to see more immediate results here and now. In this case, Jesus simply said, "...as you have believed, so let it be done for you!" And the Bible records that the servant "was healed that same hour!" This happened at a distance, without Jesus ever seeing the servant in person. This story encourages us to pray in faith. It doesn't matter whether the people we are praying for are near or on the other side of the world. If we truly believe in Jesus, He can heal them, inspire them, comfort them, and bless them according to our faith!

Lord, we believe—help Thou our unbelief!

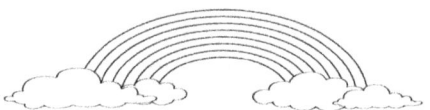

Words!

"A good man out of the good treasure of his heart brings forth good things, and an evil man out of the evil treasure brings forth evil things. But I say to you that for every idle word men may speak, they will give account of it in the day of judgment. For by your words you will be justified, and by your words you will be condemned" (Matthew 12:35–37).

What a powerful warning the Lord has given us here regarding the use of our words! This passage is printed in red in my Bible, meaning that it is a quotation directly from the Lord's mouth. In the verses just previous to this, He was saying that a good tree produces good fruit, and a bad tree produces bad fruit as an object lesson about the fact that a converted person will do good things while one who is still tied to his carnal nature will be doing bad things. Then He makes a point to speak more specifically about the power of our words. We have talked before about not taking the name of the Lord in vain, but this injunction goes far beyond that, saying that we will be judged even by the idle words that we speak. Hmm....I think this might include any silly or shady jokes, name-calling or labeling others in a derogatory way, vociferating upon any topics that are not edifying to the hearers, and most certainly, gossip, or negative words that would injure a person or their reputation. Just think how our speech would change if we could imagine that the Lord was right beside us, listening to all that we said!

According to this passage, in the end we will either be justified by our words or condemned by them. This should surely give us pause to stop and think before we speak. Recently, I saw someone demonstrate how important this is in a children's story at church. The presenter had purchased a new tube of toothpaste. She gave it to one of the children and asked her to squeeze the tube to see how much paste she could get out of it, while the other children counted to ten. Then she said, "Now, we're going to count to ten again, and this time, let's see how much paste you can put back into the tube."

"Oh, no!" The child exclaimed, realizing that she had been given an impossible task! Then the speaker made her point. The toothpaste is like our words—it's much easier for them to come out of our mouths than it is to try to put them back in after we have said something dirty, mean, or hurtful. This is why we need to ask the Lord to help us control our words, monitoring them to make sure that they are kind, helpful, accurate, and encouraging to those around us. Even the adults in the church that day got the memorable lesson!

Too often we take the gift of speech for granted. Only someone who has lost their voice due to illness, an accident, or even just a temporary hoarseness can appreciate how valuable the ability to speak really is and how frequently we take it for granted. I had a relative on my husband's side of the family who had to use her voice almost constantly in her work as an educator. There came a time, however, when she had to have an operation on her throat, and in order for it to heal properly, the doctor told her that she should not speak for three months! What a torture that was! Fortunately, she eventually got better and was able to resume her duties at work.

Not too long ago, I had a similar experience. Due to a respiratory problem, I almost lost my voice. Then, when I tried to talk, I would get short of breath just trying to finish a sentence. It took so much effort to try to carry on a hoarse conversation that I made the attempt less often, and when I did speak, it was in short sentences. How frustrating for a person who likes to talk as much as I do! But it did teach me a couple of things. First,

I did not need to comment about everything, and second, when I did speak, I needed to choose my few words carefully, so they could be as efficient as possible. At this writing, my voice is still not back to 100 percent, but at least I can carry on normal conversations without triggering a coughing episode or a mini asthma attack. Thus, I end today's thought with a prayer:

Lord, help me to appreciate the gift of speech, thanking You for it more often. And then, I pray that You will give me the wisdom and grace to use my words in a way that will bring blessings to others as well as glory to Your name. Amen.

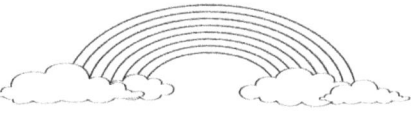

July 22

Mass Healings

"Then great multitudes came to Him, having with them the lame, blind, mute, maimed, and many others; and they laid them down at Jesus' feet, and He healed them. So the multitude marveled when they saw the mute speaking, the maimed made whole, the lame walking, and the blind seeing; and they glorified the God of Israel" (Matthew 15:30, 31).

In our day and age, we regularly hear of mass hysteria, mass mailings, mass shootings, etc., but in Jesus' day, people began to hear about mass healings. And so they came, from near and far, to see this Man who was performing miracles and restoring the health of all who came to Him with a physical need. At the same time, as they listened to His heaven-inspired words,

they also came to realize that He was even more concerned about their spiritual health. Thus, while the physical healings were taking place externally, many people found that the spiritual healing they needed was taking place internally. What a blessing it was to be in His presence, to see the marvelous miracles He was doing, and the Bible says that "they glorified the God of Israel." Of course, this was the objective of Jesus all along—to bring people into a saving relationship with God and to give Him the glory for His wonderful works among His earthly children!

Just think of the amazing testimonies the people who were healed were able to take back to their friends and families, sharing with them how the gracious itinerant Preacher had brought hope and healing to their bodies, minds, and souls! Even those who had long been demon-possessed were suddenly set free and made into new creatures! How could they keep from telling others about their glorious encounter with Jesus that had changed their lives forever!

We may not have experienced a physical healing from Jesus, but those of us who have been saved by Him can certainly bear witness to the fact that He has freed us from the bondage that Satan held us in, and in so doing, He brought spiritual healing into our lives. If we haven't yet experienced this freedom, we need to ask the Lord for it now. If we have experienced His grace making us into new creatures—more like Him day by day—then we, like the people on the hillsides around the Sea of Galilee, should be so filled with gratitude that we can't wait to share the good news with our friends and families! Our personal experience with the Lord will make our testimony real and powerful. Folks can argue with our doctrines, but they can't deny our transforming personal experiences, our own spiritual healing, granted to us by our loving Savior!

Listen to these two quotes on this subject by Ellen White: "No sooner does one come to Christ than there is born in his heart a desire to make known to others what a precious friend he has found in Jesus; the saving and sanctifying truth cannot be shut up in his heart" (Steps to Christ, p. 78). "As witnesses for Christ, we are to tell what we know, what we ourselves have seen and heard and felt.... We can bear witness to what we have known of the grace of Christ. This is the witness for which our Lord calls, and for want of which the world is perishing" (The Desire of Ages, p. 340). This last line is so powerful to me. It tells us that the Lord is calling for exactly that personal testimony which only we can give, and if we don't, people will be lost who could have been saved!

May the Lord give us the courage, grace, and wisdom to "speak a word in season" (Isa. 50:4) to those He puts within our sphere of influence day-by-day, helping to bring a spiritual healing into their lives as well. It's the least we can do after all He's done for us!

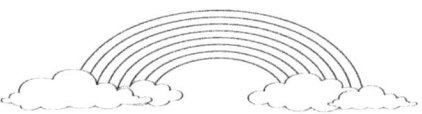

Dead Last!

"And everyone who has left houses or brothers or sisters or father or mother or wife or children or lands, for My name's sake, shall receive a hundredfold, and inherit eternal life. But many who are first will be last, and the last first" (Matthew 19:29, 30).

In our world, everything seems to be upside down from how things work in the kingdom of God. In this chapter, Jesus has just talked to a rich young ruler, who by all external appearances looked like a perfect candidate for heaven, yet he was told that if he wanted to gain eternal life he must, "...go, sell what you have and give to the poor, and you will have treasure in heaven; and come, follow Me" (Matt. 19:21). Not only did this shock the young man but it also shocked the disciples! They reasoned that if people like him couldn't make it to heaven, what hope would anyone else have? So, Jesus explained to them that it was very hard for rich people to follow Him because their treasure consisted of earthly things rather than the things of God. In fact, He stated, "With men this is impossible, but with God all things are possible" (verse 26). Only through God's grace can any of us be saved, but for those who value their money, status, and material wealth and make these things their priority in life, rather than to help others and serve God, it would be extremely difficult for them to come to Him. They are used to being at the top of the heap, the first in obtaining material possessions, the first to receive recognition, the first to display their pride. How could they trade these idols in for a life of sacrifice and service?

Those of us who want to be followers of Jesus today have to ask ourselves the same question. If we always have to be first, looking to be served instead of to serve others, focusing our attention on our wealth of material acquisitions or other earthly distractions, when it comes to our spiritual preparedness to win the ultimate race in life, we will come in dead last!

Jesus, however, did not leave His disciples, then or now, without hope. He honestly told them that in the Christian life there would be sacrifices and losses along life's path, since we live in a world dominated by sin and have to navigate a social order designed by Satan. We may have to give up certain relationships, houses or lands, or personal wealth in the effort to assist those who are less fortunate financially or in order to follow in the footsteps of Jesus more closely. But He promised that for anything lost for His name's sake, we would "receive a hundredfold, and inherit eternal life" (verse 29). Wow! A hundredfold!

The Lord assures us that when we get to heaven, the culture there will be turned right-side-up again, according to God's value system, rendering those who were first here as last and those who were last here as first! We won't have to step on other people in order to get ahead. There will be no ambition or selfish pride exhibited there. We will all be richer than we could have ever imagined—not for a month, a year, or even a lifetime, but for eternity!

How important then that we not turn away from the claims of the gospel, as the rich young ruler did, but that we gladly dedicate all that we have and are to God's service here and now, knowing that by doing so, we are merely banking our treasure in heaven, where soon the Lord will richly reward all of us equally beyond all we can ask or think!

July 24

Caesar's

"'Show me the tax money.' So they brought Him a denarius. And He said to them, 'Whose image and inscription is this?' They said to Him, 'Caesar's.' And He said to them, 'Render therefore to Caesar the things that are Caesar's, and to God the things that are God's'" (Matthew 22:19–21).

As I write this, our country is in the midst of a contentious presidential election cycle. It is interesting to observe how different Christians react to this event. They divide themselves into roughly three groups. Those that believe that anything having to do with politics is bad—having to do with earthly matters instead of heavenly—and so they avoid it completely. Then there are those who decide to follow the path of least resistance and just support the status quo—regardless of how corrupt the government becomes. They may vote, but don't really take time to study the issues at stake for themselves. Meanwhile, the third group sees in an election the possibility to improve the world in which they and their posterity are living between now and eternity. As citizens of a democratic country, in which people actually have a voice in who is elected to office, as well as in which laws are adopted by society, they view voting not only as a sacred right but also as a duty-bound responsibility.

I tend to stand with the third group, and let me tell you why. First and foremost, because I believe that while we're waiting to go to heaven, we should be good citizens in whatever society we find ourselves, casting our influence on the side of right, truth, and justice whenever we can. There may come a day when our voices will be silenced, but while we can still make a difference, we should. Not only to improve our lives but also those of our children and grand-children (if time lasts that long). Secondly, while most believers will find themselves in non-political careers of various kinds, I believe the Lord does call some of His children into this line of service. Consider Daniel, Joseph, Esther, David, and Solomon. Additionally, by squandering our privilege to vote, we waste a freedom that people all over the world have been willing to die for! How can we under-value this right, which is deemed so precious by those who don't enjoy it? It's akin to throwing good food away while we know that people all over the world are starving to death. What a travesty!

Today's verse indicates to me that Jesus was telling His listeners that while they are living on this earth, they will have certain requirements to fulfill as good citizens of the society in which they live. He could have discouraged them from getting involved at all with the Roman government that occupied their land by saying, "Don't pay taxes to Rome—their government is too corrupt!" Or, "Don't pay taxes because all of your money should go to building up the church." Or perhaps, "Don't bother paying taxes because what you have to contribute is too small to make a difference." But He didn't. He simply said, "Render therefore to Caesar the things that are Caesar's, and to God the things that are God's." It's as if He is saying, "Do your honest part to improve the lives of others by participating in whatever helpful ways you can under the government system in which you live, while simultaneously serving Me and waiting for My return." One way to do this, of course, is by paying the taxes that support our governmental infrastructure, providing things such as highways, clean water, schools, and social services across our nation. But there are other ways we can make our communities better, using our time, talents, and innovative ideas to spread the light of the gospel wherever the Lord leads us, even in our political and government-related endeavors.

I would like to end this reflection with a quote that my father repeated often to us when we were children: "All that is necessary for the triumph of evil is for good men to do nothing." As long as the Lord grants us continued freedom and the ability to strive for the best in our country, states, and communities, I am determined to help block the ever-growing tide of evil by overcoming it with good whenever I can—including when I have the opportunity to vote!

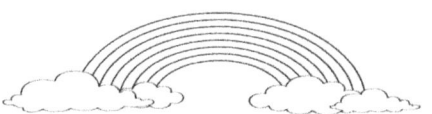

Gnats and Camels

"Woe to you, scribes and Pharisees, hypocrites! For you pay tithe of mint and anise and cummin, and have neglected the weightier matters of the law: justice and mercy and faith. These you ought to have done, without leaving the others undone. Blind guides, who strain out a gnat and swallow a camel!" (Matthew 23:23, 24).

Jesus spends most of this chapter admonishing the scribes and Pharisees, who were supposed to be the spiritual leaders of the Israelites but had strayed away from a living relationship with God. Oh, they still carefully regarded their traditions and were very conscientious to perform all the rites, rituals, and forms of religion that had been passed down to them from their forefathers. But somewhere along the line, with the emphasis on maintaining their religious practices, they had lost the true essence and meaning of what those activities actually stood for. Love for God had been swallowed up in numerous petty rules and regulations through which they sought to become more religious. As they focused more and more on certain works they needed to accomplish in order to find favor with God, they actually lost sight of Him. As part of this re-ordering of priorities by the Pharisees, the important principle of love to others, which would have permeated their lives with justice and mercy, became buried under their insistence on obeying human-made rules. They had great pride in the belief that they were better (more holy, if you will) than those around them because of their strict adherence to even the most minute and burdensome of these seemingly endless regulations.

To be clear, Jesus was not telling them to quit paying tithe or obeying the law of God in general. Instead He was trying to straighten out their priorities. He was encouraging them to work on developing a living faith in God, which would lift their lives to a truly higher plain. They needed to spend more time and effort on becoming just and merciful to those around them than on keeping track of who was and wasn't keeping the most tiny and tedious of their religious rules, which were turning the people away from God instead of attracting them to Him.

It makes me wonder how God sees our priorities. Are we "straining out gnats" and "swallowing camels?" Are we more concerned with what a person wears than the fact that they came to church? Do we judge the vegans at potluck as more holy than the vegetarians? And the arguments over the fitness of people who drink coffee as compared to those who don't seem endless. I once knew of a lovely Christian woman who was told she could no longer play the organ for church because she wore a wedding ring, which had been given to her by her non-church-going spouse. Unfortunately, whole churches have been split up over the color of the new church carpet or whether the acoustics of the building are adequate for the new church organ.

Nowadays, of course, people choose which church to attend based on the worship styles they find there, including the kind of praise music sung during the service. I realize that people are allowed their personal preferences, but to insist everyone else agree with our requirements of what a Christian looks like or that they follow our personal religious rules or be labeled not as "good" as us, gives us a profile very much like the Pharisees of Jesus' day. Could it be that if He walked among us today, He might give us some of the same admonitions? Perhaps we also need to start focusing less on the little external things in favor of concentrating on the more important internal qualities that comprise the life of the true follower of God.

Lord, give us a living faith in You! One that will not only straighten out all our priorities but will also make us the just and merciful reflectors of your character that are so badly needed by our sin-infected world today!

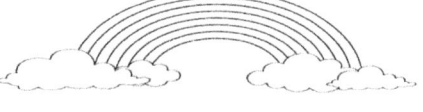

July 26

Well Done!

"His lord said to him, 'Well done, good and faithful servant; you have been faithful over a few things, I will make you ruler over many things. Enter into the joy of your lord'" (Matthew 25:23).

I know there are Christian people who think that giving others a compliment or commending them for something they have done well will ruin their characters and cause them to become proud. That may be the case with constant and unmerited praise, but in this parable being told by Jesus in Matthew 25, both men who used their talents wisely were not only praised but also offered an invitation to "Enter into the joy of your lord." Later in this same chapter, Jesus translates the parable into real life by describing what will happen when He comes again, promising that the faithful will hear these words: "Come, you blessed of My Father, inherit the kingdom prepared for you from the foundation of the world" (verse 34).

Several places in the Old Testament, God commends His people when they are doing what is right. Think of Moses, Job, and Abraham. In the New Testament, the followers of Jesus are also blessed with encouraging words, not only in the Gospels but also in the writings of Paul and other biblical writers. In fact, even Jesus received words of approval and encouragement from His heavenly Father at the beginning of his ministry, right after He was baptized when He heard the proclamation: "This is My beloved Son, in whom I am well pleased" (Matt. 3:17). And this was not the only time. God also audibly pronounced these same words of affirmation toward the end of Jesus' ministry on the mount of transfiguration (see Matt. 17:5).

When I was a child, I was fortunate enough to have parents who motivated me to reach my highest potential through words of affirmation and encouragement. As a result, I always tried to do my best to please them and live up to the high expectations and vision they had for my life. Their compliments on my achievements, on everything from learning to tie my shoes to earning my doctoral degree, motivated me and gave me the confidence to tackle all the challenges that life threw in my direction. I am so thankful for their many positive expressions of love and pride in who I was as well as their approval of my accomplishments, whether large or small.

As an educator, I have often seen the effects of words of commendation on students' behavior, motivation, and academic success. When placed in a positive classroom with a teacher who affirms them, pupils blossom. Not only do they feel a sense of satisfaction that they have done something well (whether it's a physical accomplishment, an artistic expression, or a well-written essay) but they begin to gain the courage to try the bigger and more difficult tasks assigned to them. Thus, they are often more motivated to move successfully from one level of schooling to another. These feelings of competence and success can then be transferred over to other areas of life, ultimately helping them become responsible adults as well as good and productive citizens.

As God so graciously affirms us with His words of acceptance, His encouragement when He sees us doing our best, and His promises of future rewards when we reach His kingdom, let's try to emulate Him in our positive expressions to those around us. It costs so little to tell someone with whom we come in contact—whether our own family members, young scholars, our neighbors, or our friends—that they have done something well. But the effects of our compliments and affirmations can yield such incalculable results. Why don't we determine today to do it more often?

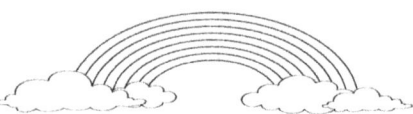

The Least

"And the King will answer and say to them, 'Assuredly, I say to you, inasmuch as you did it to one of the least of these My brethren, you did it to Me.' … Then He will answer them, saying, 'Assuredly, I say to you, inasmuch as you did not do it to one of the least of these, you did not do it to Me.' And these will go away into everlasting punishment, but the righteous into eternal life" (Matthew 25:40, 45, 46).

I chose to use this trio of verses together because one is just the reverse of the other, for emphasis, while the last verse points out the consequences for our behavior in this regard. In my Bible, this section of Matthew 25 bears this subtitle: "The Son of Man Will Judge the Nations." The ensuing verses, including these above, clearly describe on what basis they will be judged.

Many people feel that if they haven't done anything wrong, they are cleared from culpability, but verse 45 points out that Jesus expects us to move beyond the low standard of not doing anything wrong into His example of doing things that are right. This includes doing things that are just and good for those around us, especially those who are in need, not only spiritually but also physically. Here we see the Lord getting really practical. He helps us understand that simple human need in everyday situations is our call to action if we truly claim to be His followers. Passive Christianity ignores the need while active Christianity seeks to meet it. This being the case, we should realize that sometimes our sins of omission can be judged as greater than ones we actually overtly commit.

Recently, I have been thinking about who "the least of these" includes. If our entrance into eternal life is based largely on how we treat these people, it is obviously important to identify who they are. Well, Jesus starts the list off with those who are hungry and thirsty. Then He mentions strangers who have no place to go. After that, He describes people who don't have the clothing they need. He continues with those who are sick, finishing His examples of people in need with those who are in prison. Amplifying His intent here, I believe that between the lines we could add the homeless, orphans, widows, wounded veterans, foreigners, refugees, the poor, those with disabilities, and those who have been discriminated against in a myriad of ways.

What a wide range of ministries this calls us to, challenging us to be the hands and feet of Jesus in a million different ways! What excuse do any of us have not to get involved in being a blessing to the people all around us? The possibilities are endless: programs that provide food and clothing (often called community services today); homeless shelters (and shelters for those who have been evacuated from their homes due to natural disasters); various kinds of children's ministries, including vacation Bible schools, summer camps, and Pathfinder Clubs; donations to orphanages, international relief agencies, and well-digging projects; sunshine bands who are committed to visiting the sick and the elderly; prison ministries; letter-writing ministries to the lonely; English and cultural orientation classes for immigrants to our country; becoming a hospital volunteer; foster care services...the list goes on and on. The question is where will you and I plug in to use our God-given gifts and talents to serve "the least of these"?

The most beautiful part of this passage is that Jesus identifies so strongly with the needs of His human children that He calls them "My brethren," stating that when we have served them, He counts it the same as if we were serving Him. What a profound proclamation this is! It means that when we are meeting the needs of those all around us, we are truly doing the work of God in the world.

July 28

Our Commission

"Go therefore and make disciples of all the nations, baptizing them in the name of the Father and of the Son and of the Holy Spirit, teaching them to observe all things that I have commanded you; and lo, I am with you always, even to the end of the age" (Matthew 28:19, 20).

Thus ends the first Gospel in the New Testament—with the all-inclusive commission given by Jesus to His followers. In fact, the inclusivity of this passage is stunning in two ways.

First, although Jesus was talking to His disciples in the first century, those who had been privileged to walk and work alongside Him during His earthly ministry, it is an almost universally agreed upon belief that He was addressing all of His believers while time should last. None of us should feel excluded from His call upon us to fulfill what is often called "the great commission" of sharing the gospel with others. Jesus is here inviting all

of us who believe in Him to help spread the good news of His salvation—whether we are Jews or Gentiles, men or women, youth or people in our golden years! This means we don't need to wait until someone comes to ordain us to this task officially, for Jesus has already commissioned all of us to engage in the work of soul winning! Not only that but He has also promised to be present with us in all of our missionary endeavors until the end of time.

Second, it's impressive that Jesus is all-inclusive in telling us to whom we should witness and teach to observe all that He had commanded—eventually baptizing them in the name of the Father, the Son, and the Holy Spirit. He makes it clear that we should make disciples of people from "all the nations." This includes those of all language groups, cultures, and belief systems. Back then, without our highly-developed transportation and communication systems, it was a daunting task, even though the then-known world was significantly smaller than we know it to be today, yet those were His marching orders. The disciples must have been somewhat incredulous that they were up to the challenge, until a short time later, at Pentecost, when they experienced the mighty power of the Holy Spirit. In an instant, the Spirit equipped them for the task by not only making them bold to share the gospel but by giving them the gift of tongues, which allowed them to immediately preach and teach in the languages of all those who had come from far and near to the great city of Jerusalem for worship, business, or pleasure. They found that they could speak plainly to the Greeks, the Samaritans, the Syrians, the Egyptians, the Romans, and anyone else they encountered. Thousands were converted in just one day!

Looking back at how the Lord helped His followers then to fulfill His amazing commission should give us faith that today, under the strength of His blessing and the power of that same Holy Spirit, we will also be able to accomplish the task He has set before us. Even though the population of people across the world is burgeoning, He has gifted us with modern technologies today that help us reach them in many different ways that were not possible before. While we're still busy using a number of older standard methods of ministry, we now have so many more tools at our disposal. Without ever having to send out a missionary, get passports, arrange for transportation and housing, and a million other little preparations required by this ministry model, we can now reach people in their own homes, on their own schedule, and in their own language, through gospel television and radio programs, over the internet, or through pre-recorded truth-filled messages on tapes, DVDs, CDs, or small hand-held transistor-like devices.

Praise the Lord that He has provided us today with so many efficient and effective ways to spread the gospel. When I was in high school, I saw the great commission as something overwhelming and impossible to accomplish before the Lord returned. Now, however, I can see how we've been enabled to preach to "all the nations." It seems that all we lack at this point is the outpouring of the Holy Spirit in the latter rain to give us the dedication and the zeal we need to finally fulfill the commission with which we've been entrusted.

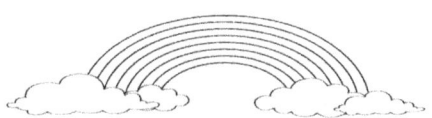

His Purpose

"But He said to them, 'Let us go into the next towns, that I may preach there also, because for this purpose I have come forth'" (Mark 1:38).

The book of Mark starts in chapter 1 with the beginning of Jesus' ministry in Galilee. It briefly describes the preparatory preaching of John, the baptism of Jesus, His temptations in the wilderness, and the calling of four fishermen to become His disciples. By the end of this busy chapter, we find Jesus preaching and healing throughout the region of Galilee, both inside the synagogue and outside of it.

One morning, after a long solitary prayer session with His heavenly Father, His disciples found Him and informed Him that many people were looking for Him to come and continue ministering to them. But the devotional time He had spent that morning with God had further clarified His mission, and He realized that, in order to fulfill His purpose, He must expand the borders of His outreach to include not only the people of Galilee but also those throughout all the surrounding regions. Eventually, with the help of His followers, all the people of the world would need to be reached with the glorious gospel He came to disseminate. Thus, the Savior, with a freshly-renewed focus on His purpose, urged His disciples to move forward with Him into the next towns and the ones beyond that, so that as many people as possible could be reached in the limited time He had on earth. He explained to them that this was the very purpose of His life. It was why He had come.

In this experience of Jesus, I believe there is a valuable lesson for us. Knowing one's purpose in life is essential in order to be effective in our various endeavors. When we lose track of God's purpose for us, it is easy to get caught up in the chaos and confusion of the world around us, and life can become void of its meaning and value. On the other hand, by spending more intentional devotional time with the Lord, the more clear our purpose will become. His Spirit will guide us back into a realization of our reason for living. No matter who we are, when we become believers in Jesus, God has a mission for us to fulfill, just as He had one for Jesus. Of course, the mission of Jesus was immensely greater in scope and responsibility than we can even imagine. But if we surrender our lives to God, He will make us co-workers with Him in His divine work of saving souls for eternity. If we give our time and talents to be employed in this great effort, spending the time necessary with Him to become clear-eyed about our own purpose, He will help us shoulder important responsibilities in His cause that will also be of eternal consequence.

So, what is your purpose in life? What is mine? Are we, like Jesus, continually seeking to commune with God so that we can fulfill the mission He has assigned just for us, individually? Just think about what a sacred trust it is to be a co-worker with God! How crucial, then, is the time we spend with Him in order to receive our "marching orders" day by day! Our devotional life must be consistent, not just intermittent. It must be robust in content and sufficient enough in duration to help us become acquainted with that still, small voice—the one that will lead us to follow in the purposeful footsteps of Jesus.

July 30

Called to Repentance

"When Jesus heard it, He said to them, 'Those who are well have no need of a physician, but those who are sick. I did not come to call the righteous, but sinners, to repentance'" (Mark 2:17).

What exactly was it that Jesus heard that evoked this type of response from Him? Jesus had just called Matthew, a despised tax collector, to follow Him. Shortly thereafter, Matthew invited Jesus and His disciples to dine at his house, along with a number of his tax collector friends, and other common people who the Pharisees considered to be "sinners." Hoping to dissuade Jesus' followers from believing in a person who did not pay attention to all of their strict religious rules (like not eating with sinners) and the social mores of Jewish society, the scribes and Pharisees asked some of those who were with Jesus, "How is it that He eats and drinks with tax collectors and sinners?" (Mark 2:16). Hearing their murmuring in the background, the Lord took this opportunity to once again announce His life's mission—to save as many people as possible.

I like what the SDA Bible Commentary says about this conversation:

If these men were such sinners as the Pharisees claimed, they must be in greater need than other men. Were they not then the very ones for whom Christ should put forth His best efforts? He had come to save men (Matt. 1:21), but if He were able only to save those who were already righteous, He could not be truly a Saviour. The test of His mission as the Saviour of men turned on the point of what He could do for sinners. (*SDA Bible Commentary*, vol. 5, p. 583)

Keep in mind here that the labels of "righteous" and "sinners" were based on the faulty judgment of those who asked the question. Of course, Jesus knew that they were all sinners, and the scribes and Pharisees, who thought they were righteous, were sometimes the biggest sinners of all because of their arrogance and pride, as well as their harsh judgment and condemnation of anyone who didn't play by their own misguided rules. Instead of drawing people toward God, many were actually driven away from God because of the Pharisee's hypocrisy, their unreasonable regulations, and their haughty attitudes. In meditating on this verse, I can't help but ask, could it be possible that some of us who consider ourselves spiritual leaders today might be guilty of doing the same thing? Driving people around us away from God instead of drawing them to Him?

But notice that there is another term to focus on in Jesus' statement. What is He calling those who He came to save to do? He's calling them to repentance. Someone has said that Jesus saves us where we are, but He doesn't leave us where we are. If we are truly converted to Him, we will begin to change, and one of the first steps in following Him as our Savior is repentance for our sinful behavior and attitudes. Of course to get to this step, we must first admit that we're sinners in need of His saving grace. This is why Jesus had said that the prostitutes and

tax collectors would have an easier time getting into heaven than the Pharisees. Though He wants to redeem all of us, He can't save a self-proclaimed righteous person who doesn't realize his or her true condition and thus does not ask for the forgiveness that is believed to be unnecessary. No, the person who thinks he or she is well does not go to a physician—while those who are sick gladly seek the expertise, the care, and the healing they know they need from their doctor.

May the Lord help us to quit looking down on other people, especially those who are so eager to avail themselves of the healing grace of Jesus as soon as they hear about it. And may He help some of us who have been in the church a long time to repent and finally realize our own deep, spiritual need of a Savior.

July 31

We're Family!

"And He looked around in a circle at those who sat about Him, and said, 'Here are My mother and My brothers! For whoever does the will of God is My brother and My sister and mother'" (Mark 3:34, 35).

The reading of this text always brings warm remembrances of a small group of friends from church that my husband and I were privileged to belong to, who met together to read and discuss a number of Christian books and then pray together. At times, when we had a willing pianist, we would

even sing a few songs. We did this on Friday nights for about two years. After a few months, we decided that before starting our meeting, we would share a simple meal together where we could chat and catch up on what had been happening in each other's lives over the past week. What wonderful fellowship we enjoyed!

When we decided to work at a university in Massachusetts, we knew practically no one, and our families of origin all lived on the West Coast—on the other side of the country! Sometimes, we felt quite lonely. But this small group of like-minded believers was an unexpected gift from God to us! It didn't take long after joining it before we all began to feel like family! In fact, we grew even closer to them than to many of our biological family members who did not share our faith, especially to our kind host and hostess, who after a long and demanding work week, cheerfully shared their home with us Friday after Friday. Although we eventually moved back to the West Coast, we still cherish our friendship with these folks, calling and even visiting each other from time to time, despite the long distance between us. We anticipate with joy seeing them more frequently when we all get to heaven!

In today's passage, Jesus was ministering to the multitudes with His disciples sitting around Him, when some Jewish scribes, who were serving as spies for the enemies of Jesus, started accusing Him of being demon-possessed. How else could they explain the miracles that He was performing and the healings that followed wherever He went? They made such an issue of this that finally, Jesus' own mother and brothers, who were sometimes a little embarrassed by the unconventional (at least to the Pharisees) behaviors that He displayed, came to try to persuade Him to "cease and desist." After all, He was going against the norms of Jewish culture and even disputing with the religious leaders of the nation. It was obvious that even Jesus' closest family members did not understand His mission or the methods He was employing to accomplish His great work of redemption. But Jesus used this situation as a teachable moment, emphasizing that those who chose to believe in Him could grow closer to Him and to other believers with shared values than to their very own blood relatives. What's more, they would be counted as part of His heavenly family!

Have you ever been disowned, rejected, or misunderstood by members of your family? Especially over your religious beliefs? If so, do not despair. Jesus understands your situation because He has experienced it Himself. If you let Him, He will comfort you, give you the strength you need to push through it, and best of all, adopt you into the warm and welcoming arms of the eternal family of God.

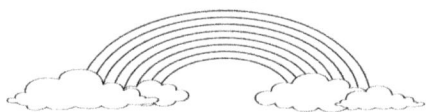

The Seed

"And He said, 'The kingdom of God is as if a man should scatter seed on the ground, and should sleep by night and rise by day, and the seed should sprout and grow, he himself does not know how. For the earth yields crops by itself: first the blade, then the head, after that the full grain in the head'"
(Mark 4:26–28).

Ever since we moved to our current residence, which sits on about a half-acre of land, we've entertained the idea of having a garden. Finally, this past summer, my husband turned this dream into a reality. And now, much to our delight, we are beginning to reap the rewards from his labors. Every time we find a ripe, red tomato, a beautiful yellow squash, a shoot of green onion, or a round fat melon, we marvel at the miracles taking place in that little plot of ground!

As I meditated on this "Parable of the Growing Seed," as my Bible calls it, I thought about all the lessons we have harvested from our garden this year, in addition to the fresh food. First, of course, the most obvious one concerning how the kingdom of God works. When engaged in evangelistic activities, it is humanity's job to scatter the seed, spreading the gospel far and near, and God's job to produce the fruit, working silently and often imperceptibly through the Holy Spirit, until the day when a glorious harvest appears.

A related lesson is what a joy it is to be a co-worker with God. My husband and I were reflecting on what a privilege God has bestowed upon us to labor together with Him for a worthy cause. Both in a literal garden, where we reap what we sow, as well as in the Lord's vineyard, where the spiritual blessings abound. Not only do our efforts help others but we also experience the positive side effects of a sense of fulfillment, a life of purpose, and the excitement of anticipation to see what miracle the Lord will accomplish next! My husband simply tilled the garden plot, planted a few seeds, and then weeded and watered for several months. Like the text says, he slept and went on with the rest of his life, not knowing how the seeds were sprouting and growing until they sprang forth from the ground. Then we just watched to see which plants would produce which fruit. We did our part, and now God is doing His part, making Himself responsible for the outcome of our combined efforts. We can't understand how the seed produces the fruit; we simply trust that the Master Gardener will work miraculously behind the scenes to produce a rich harvest.

This experience has also reinforced the idea that, when working together with the Lord, small and seemingly insignificant actions on our part can result in huge and important results under the mighty hand of God. Lastly, we stand in awe of the fact that each seed has its own particular potential. Although they all receive basically the same required elements of soil, sunshine, and water, each seed grows into the specific plant it is assigned by God to be—producing fruit accordingly. What a lesson for parents, teachers, and pastors. Those with whom we work all have their own God-given individual potential to become what they were meant to be in God's garden. It's our job to plant seeds and nurture them. It's God's job to continue the miracle of growth in each one until the day of harvest.

August 2

A Great Calm

"Then He arose and rebuked the wind, and said to the sea, 'Peace, be still!' And the wind ceased and there was a great calm" (Mark 4:39).

It had been an extremely busy day ministering to the multitudes. Jesus was tired. As the disciples started out in their boat across the water, he fell asleep in the stern. The Bible says that a great windstorm arose, and the waves were beating into the boat, filling it with water to the point that it was in danger of sinking. It was then that the disciples, who had been struggling against the storm on their own, thought of Jesus and called out for Him to help. Immediately, He awoke and came to their aid in a way that only the Creator of heaven and earth could! He simply commanded that the wind and waves settle down...and they did! Even though the disciples had already seen Jesus perform many miracles, this one amazed these rough fishermen—as well as the people in the little boats all around theirs—in a new and profound way. Surely, only the God of the universe could do such a thing, and they could not help but exclaiming in wonder, "Even the wind and the sea obey Him!" (Mark 4:41).

Have you ever experienced "a great calm"? As a retired teacher, this phrase brings me back to the feeling I got at the end of the school day, right after the busy and noisy time of dismissal. At 3:10 in the afternoon, there would be a tremendous bustling about as students put everything they had been working on away, stuffed their homework into their bulging backpacks, grabbed their lunch pails and jackets, and headed for the door, where they were expected to line up in at least a somewhat orderly fashion. When the final bell rang at 3:15, they would rush out to catch the bus, meet their parents, or socialize with their friends at after-school activities. In contrast to the frenetic activity that characterized the last five minutes of the day, the calm that fell over the now empty classroom by 3:20 was palpable. That sudden feeling of great calm is hard to explain to someone who hasn't experienced it firsthand. I would usually just sit down at my desk for a few minutes, take a deep breath, and enjoy the sound of silence, while reflecting upon all that had taken place over the last eight hours. Then I would begin my afternoon tasks of cleaning up the classroom and preparing for the next day's instructional program.

Similarly, over the course of my life, there have also been blessed and soothing times of great spiritual calm that the Lord has provided after I have experienced storms of sadness, anger, confusion, or other types of distress. Sometimes, like the disciples, I have just tried to handle the emergency on my own before suddenly realizing that the Lord would help me if I would just cry out to Him in my time of need. I think the question is, why do we wait so long? Perhaps we think we are stronger than we are to fight life's battles alone, or we don't have enough faith to believe that God is either willing or able to help us. Maybe we doubt His power to change situations that we see as impossible to solve. Apparently, this was the disciples' problem because as soon as the storm was under control, Jesus asked them why they had so little faith. So, I take away three lessons from this verse. First, that I need to seek God early, instead of as a last resort, to help me with my problems. Second, I need to ask Him for more faith to believe that with God all things are possible. Third, I need to revel in the periods of great calm that He brings into my life and thank Him for His amazing power and grace.

August 3

Come and Rest

"And He said to them, 'Come aside by yourselves to a deserted place and rest a while.' For there were many coming and going, and they did not even have time to eat" (Mark 6:31).

Have you ever been too busy to eat? So often as an elementary school teacher, my "lunch hour," which was only about forty minutes in actuality, was taken up by activities such as cleaning up the classroom from the morning, laying out materials for the afternoon, responding to messages from parents or school staff members, making copies, and the list goes on. I was lucky to squeeze in a brief restroom break before the bell rang signaling an end to my always too short lunch period. On a good day, I might get half a sandwich and part of a drink down before running back to my classroom. Working as a college professor was not much different, for there were always students needing advisement, papers to edit, classes to prepare for, and even meetings to attend during my scheduled lunch time.

These days it seems that almost everyone has been caught up in the proverbial "rat race." Between their responsibilities at work, at home, at church, and keeping up with all their children's (or grandchildren's) activities, it seems life has become an endless struggle to keep up with it all. In such a demanding environment, some of our own legitimate needs can sometimes be overrun or neglected to the eventual detriment of our physical health and emotional and spiritual well-being. So, how can we avoid exhaustion and burnout?

In today's text, the disciples had just returned from the brief missionary trips that Jesus had sent them out on a little earlier in this same chapter. They came back brimming over with stories about their adventures in ministry to share with Him. They were tired but happy since they had been able to preach, cast out demons, and heal many people with the power granted them by God. They found Jesus, as usual, surrounded by a multitude of needy people, all jostling about to try to get even a few small moments of His healing time and attention. Recognizing the need to spend what we would call today some "quality time"

with His disciples, allowing them to debrief, rest, and re-charge, and perhaps feeling His own bodily need for a break from the crowds, Jesus requested that they "Come ...apart ... and rest awhile" (Mark 6:31, KJV).

These words should instruct and encourage all of us who are workaholics and remind us that we actually need and should intentionally plan for periods of rest from our hectic everyday lives. This is why Jesus, who created us, also created a weekly Sabbath so that we would not run ourselves into the ground with stress and the cares of this life. On this day every weekend we are invited to come to Him and rest—to spend quality time with Him as well as with those we love. It gives us a chance to reflect, to refresh, and to recalibrate. In the Jewish culture, the Lord also gave the Israelites several important annual holidays to celebrate, knowing that this would help them maintain balance between their work lives and their social and spiritual development. Thus, I believe that by following this same pattern, taking time to celebrate holidays, planning periodic times of "R and R," such as family vacations and keeping the weekly Sabbath, we will also be able to find that blessed rest for which our weary souls long.

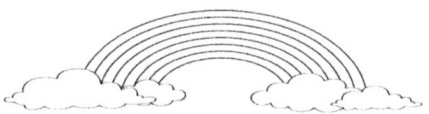

Abundance

"'When I broke the five loaves for the five thousand, how many baskets full of fragments did you take up?' They said to Him, 'Twelve.' 'Also, when I broke the seven for the four thousand, how many large baskets full of fragments did you take up?' And they said, 'Seven'" (Mark 8:19, 20).

Can you remember a time when you felt you just didn't have enough to get by? Enough food, enough money, enough energy, or enough love? Throughout our lives we have all suffered from some type of scarcity. Growing up poor, I can recall many times when our family didn't have enough money to pay the bills or to keep a roof over our heads, so we had to intermittently live with relatives. There were also some times when we had a shortage of food, but the Lord always saw us through somehow. We learned that He had resources of which we were unaware. At times like this, my father, a veritable beacon of faith, would make the most of whatever situation we were in and tell us to trust the Lord, who would provide for all our needs if we trusted in Him. He taught us to walk by faith, not by sight.

In today's passage, the Lord was asking His followers where their faith was. Even though they had seen Jesus perform many miracles, including feeding thousands of people on several occasions from practically nothing, they were still focusing on what they were lacking instead of on their Master's incredible power to meet whatever situation arose. These verses encourage me, as they remind me that Jesus can not only satisfy our needs but provide for us more than we can even ask or think with "fragments" left over (see Eph. 3:20)! After all, the Bible tells us that He owns the cattle on a thousand hills as well as everything else in this world (see Ps. 50:10). His resources are unlimited! When we trust Him, He gives to us generously, abundantly, sometimes in very unexpected ways, until our blessings overflow to the point where we won't be able to receive them! We will often even have enough to share with others.

This brings to mind a certain experience our family had during an economic recession, where both my husband and I had been temporarily out of work, and our cupboards were pretty bare. We were wondering what we were going to do for Thanksgiving that year. One afternoon about a week before the holiday, we heard a knock on our door. When we opened it, we discovered a friend with his arms full of groceries! Knowing our need, he had put our names in to receive a food basket from our local church. The "basket" turned out to be three or four large boxes overflowing with food, along with several bags of fresh produce! My husband had to help him carry it all into the house! That year I can remember feeling especially thankful on Thanksgiving, as we celebrated a wonderful feast where we were able to host both friends and family! What a lesson we got in the marvelous provision and awe-inspiring abundance of the blessings of our heavenly Father!

Ashamed

"For whoever is ashamed of Me and My words in this adulterous and sinful generation, of him the Son of Man also will be ashamed when He comes in the glory of His Father with the holy angels" (Mark 8:38).

I don't know about you, but this text brings conviction to my heart. They say that confession is good for the soul, so here goes. For many years I worked in the public school system, first as a teacher and later as an administrator. Not wanting to step on people's toes, and trying to be politically correct, I rarely spoke of my religion. Of course, because of my lifestyle, my colleagues knew something was different about me. Some things stuck out in the course of rubbing shoulders with them every day. For instance, it didn't take long for them to learn that I was not only a teetotaler but a vegetarian and a non-coffee drinker. If these things didn't make me weird enough, I also did not participate in activities—business or social—on Friday nights and Saturdays. I dressed modestly, didn't swear when something went wrong, and avoided rough and questionable conversations.

Obviously, there were times that these out-of-the-ordinary practices of mine drew questions about why I was so different. In these instances, I was able to share something about my faith, but looking back, I realize that I didn't talk enough about Jesus and the gospel written in His Word. In our modern society, it is usually considered inappropriate to discuss controversial topics like politics and religion at one's place of work, but I wonder if I could have done more to represent God's goodness and invite those I came in contact with to develop a saving relationship with the Lord. Even when working in denominational schools and colleges, I believe I might have been able to do more in this regard. Now, I can only pray that the Lord will forgive my timidity in this area, give me the courage to share Him more boldly, and bless any of the seeds of the gospel that I may have planted along the way.

Even as a retired person, I know I have not outgrown the tendency to feel uncomfortable when my husband gives an audible prayer in a restaurant before eating our meal. What is it about our humanity that sometimes makes us feel ashamed of confessing Jesus in public? I don't know all the answers, but I do know it's something we need to overcome, if, as this verse reminds us, we don't want Jesus to be ashamed to claim us as His friends when He comes again to whisk us away to heaven. We also don't want Him to be ashamed of us on the judgment day, or even now, while we are still going about our day-to-day activities here on earth.

My husband and I have one daughter, who, although not perfect yet, is the pride and joy of our lives. Instead of feeling ashamed of her, we feel just the opposite. We can't stop talking about her to others and regularly brag about her many accomplishments. We have always been happy to introduce her to the people we meet wherever we go. Now, as an adult who uses her gifts and talents to bless others and serve God, she is a wonderful representative of our family as well as our Christian values. Wouldn't it be nice if the Lord could feel this way about us? Let's determine to represent Him well so that He will never have to feel ashamed of us.

By His grace and saving power, may we, His earthly children, fill His heart with nothing but pride and joy!

August 6

Believe

"Jesus said to him, 'If you can believe, all things are possible to him who believes.' Immediately the father of the child cried out and said with tears, 'Lord, I believe; help my unbelief!'" (Mark 9:23, 24).

The cry of the father in this story should frequently be our cry as well. "Lord, I believe; help my unbelief!" Even as long-time Christians, there are so many areas of life where we constantly need to have our faith strengthened. Let me enumerate a few.

Looking back on the trajectory of our lives, we sometimes come upon words we have said or things we have done that seem so terrible we still can't forgive ourselves. As we hash over these sins and mistakes, it is sometimes hard to believe that the Lord has truly forgiven us. In order to have peace, our faith in His forgiveness needs to increase. Think about the sins of David or Saul, who later became Paul. If the Lord was able to forgive them, we should believe with all our hearts that He can completely forgive us as well. A related spiritual battle is the struggle some of us have in believing that He truly accepts us. I think this is why He calls us His children. It paints a picture of us finding a place of belonging, which is close to His heart. Not only that but we can also be assured that He loves us with an incomprehensible love as we think of His investment of time, energy, and effort on our behalf. First, He created us, then He died to redeem us, and now we're told He is preparing a place for us to come and live with Him in heaven forever!

I believe we also need to ask for more faith to trust His guidance in our lives. If we ask Him, He will help us see that His will for our life is best and that He is seeking to guide us along paths that lead to life. Those of us who are a little older have the privilege to look back and see how God has led us in the past, which, if we reflect upon it, will help give us confidence that He will continue to lead and bless us in the days ahead if we will determine to keep trusting Him.

What about our belief in His ability and power to change people—as well as to heal people spiritually, mentally, and physically, if it is according to His will? How many folks have we known who have been totally converted after coming to know the Lord? How many have been healed of some malady or escaped the cruel grasp of a substance abuse addiction? Perhaps you yourself have been strengthened to overcome some nagging temptation through His saving power.

Finally, we need to ask the Lord for more faith to simply believe His Word—all of it. The warnings, the admonitions, and, on the bright side, His precious promises! Just leaning more on His promises and then watching His miraculous interventions in our lives would give a huge boost to our faith! It would also give us a joyful assurance of His salvation—for both time and eternity! Do we really believe that Jesus is coming back soon to take us with Him to live in a glorious place called heaven? If we did, what changes might we make in our everyday lives?

Lord, we believe, at least faintly in all of these things, but today we are begging that You will help our unbelief. Please give us the strong and unshakable faith in You that we all, as Your earthly children, so desperately need! Thank you, heavenly Father! Amen.

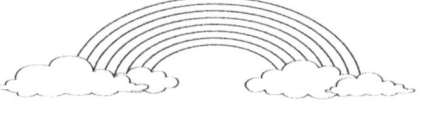

August 7

A Little Child

"But when Jesus saw it, He was greatly displeased and said to them, 'Let the little children come to Me, and do not forbid them; for of such is the kingdom of God. Assuredly, I say to you, whoever does not receive the kingdom of God as a little child will by no means enter it.' And He took them up in His arms, laid His hands on them, and blessed them" (Mark 10:14–16).

What was Jesus doing when this event occurred? He was healing and teaching the people when, as usual, a crowd gathered around Him. His demeanor was so kind, and His words so gracious that even the children were drawn to Him, and the mothers were eager to have Jesus touch and bless their little ones. The disciples, however, guided by the traditional Jewish culture of their time, thought that women and children were beneath the attention of the Master Teacher and that allowing them to approach Him would be a waste of His precious and limited time.

On the contrary, as soon as the Savior became aware of what was happening, we're told that He was not only displeased by what His followers did but that He gently admonished them. As if to emphasize His point, He demonstrated His love and care for the children by immediately dropping whatever else He was doing and calling them to Himself—not to stand at a distance to receive cold and formal words from the King of the Universe. No, He modeled how these precious little ones should be treated by allowing them to come right up onto His lap, by taking them into His loving arms, and by blessing them with His touch! In my mind, it conjures up the kind of picture you'd see at Christmas time, where a Santa Claus figure is surrounded by happy children, some climbing into His welcoming lap, one with the kind man's arm around his shoulder, and others standing around him smiling or eagerly waiting in line to see him with sparkling eyes and joyous anticipation!

As a mother, it gives me great peace and joy to know that Jesus loves our child even more than we do and that it is His greatest desire to bless her! I'm sure that the mothers in this biblical vignette felt the same way. Just imagine how much the crowds who were listening to Jesus teach that day, not to mention His own disciples, were amazed at how important these marginalized mothers and children were to Jesus! Then, while He still had all of their attention, He further elevated the low status of children by saying that whoever would "not receive the kingdom of God as a little child will by no means enter it." This amazing declaration turned their thinking upside down. After all, their society was rampant with people jostling to compete for the highest place, to secure more worldly riches, status, and power.

Even His own disciples were always wrangling over who would take the highest place in Jesus' expected soon-to-come kingdom. The Lord saw this as a teachable moment—an opportunity to drive home the lesson that "there are no 'me-first-ers' going to heaven," as a preacher I know recently coined the phrase. Instead of folks who are motivated by always wanting to be first, to be most honored, to be at the top of the heap, only absorbed by their own selfish desires, without regard to the needs and wants of those around them, the Lord wants to fill heaven with only those who possess the qualities of a small child, as of yet untainted by the world's greed and avarice. He is looking for people to be part of His kingdom who possess such characteristics as innocence, trust, meekness, kindness, gentleness, truthfulness, and unselfishness. Just think what it would mean to live in a kingdom like that! Enjoying perfect peace and harmony, it will be a safe and glorious place where love and rejoicing abound! Of course, that's exactly the kind of place the Lord is preparing for us. The question is, are we preparing for it? Would we be safe to save? Or would we drag into that holy society all the trappings of sin that beset us now? It would be unthinkable! Thankfully, the Master Teacher is also the Master Redeemer, and if we ask Him, He would love to start conforming us to His divine image this very day!

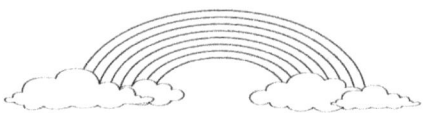

August 8

Signs of His Coming

"Then they will see the Son of Man coming in the clouds with great power and glory. And then He will send His angels, and gather together His elect from the four winds, from the farthest part of earth to the farthest part of heaven" (Mark 13:26, 27).

This is one of those occasions in His ministry when Jesus made a clear and specific promise regarding His second coming, including the assurance that He would then claim His followers to be with Him. Jesus had just been talking with the disciples about "The Signs of the Times, and the End of the Age," as my NKJV titles part of this chapter. Here Jesus pulls back the curtain of time to reveal events that will take place in the future, giving them a brief summary of what will happen before the end of the world.

As we move through the chapter, we see He warned them to beware of deceivers and "false Christs" who would arise (verse 6). He told them that there would be "wars and rumors of wars" (verse 7) and that there would be persecutions of those who preached the gospel to people in all the nations of the world (see verses 10, 11). He described a great tribulation like one not seen since the earth was created, but He also said that God would shorten it "for the elect's sake" (verse 20). Then, right before His glorious second coming, there would be unusual signs in the sun, moon, and stars, and "the powers in the heavens will be shaken" (verse 25). Jesus did not give any specific times or dates for these prophetic events, but regarding His second coming, He simply told them, "When you see these things happening, know that it is near—at the doors!" (verse 29). Then, He emphasized the fact that since no one but

God alone knows the exact day and hour of His coming, it was incumbent upon them, as it is upon those of us who are His modern-day disciples, to "Watch!" (verse 35). We must live in a continual state of readiness, "lest, coming suddenly, he find [His followers] sleeping" (verse 36).

This was one of the last intimate conversations Jesus had with His disciples before He was rudely arrested and snatched away from them to be taken to His death. Since He knew how little time He still had with them, He wanted to prepare them for some of the things to come. He did not do this to frighten them but to warn them of the need to be ready. Most of all, He wanted them to know what signs to look for to encourage them that His return would be soon. He wanted to assure them that His followers would not be left behind to languish in this dark world of sin and sorrow forever. Instead, they could live in the bright hope of His imminent return to rescue them. Then He would take them up to live with Him in a perfect dwelling place that He is preparing for all those who love His appearing (see 2 Tim. 4:8).

The purpose of His promise to come again was meant to give those who He loved not only hope but also courage, strength, determination, and perseverance while living in this weary world. And it should do the same for us! The year in which I am writing this devotional has been filled with sickness, sorrow, fear, financial difficulties, racial tensions, and a plethora of political problems. As we look at all the chaos, hatred, and despair surrounding us, it is sometimes too easy to forget about the "blessed hope" that the Lord has gifted to His followers (Titus 2:13). In the era in which we are living, I believe it is high time to lift our sights above our troubles and seek to focus once again on this marvelous promise of His soon coming. It is designed to give us just the strength, hope, and joy we need to successfully face each new day until He comes!

August 9

Women Disciples

"There were also women looking on from afar, among whom were Mary Magdalene, Mary the mother of James the Less and of Joses, and Salome, who also followed Him and ministered to Him when He was in Galilee, and many other women who came up with Him to Jerusalem" (Mark 15:40, 41).

I've read through the book of Mark many times, yet this passage never really attracted my attention until this most recent reading, where I'm seeking to discover new insights and reflect on them together with you. The apostle Mark has just described the death of Jesus in this chapter, when he takes a moment to list some of the people who are still standing around watching the gruesome scene of the crucifixion. Almost as an afterthought, he tucks in these two verses about some of the women disciples of Jesus. In meditating upon this Scripture, three thoughts came to mind.

First, that even though, as women, they had to stand afar off to observe what was happening, yet they were there. Why did they stay after almost everyone else had left? Surely they took no pleasure in the ghastly event that had taken place that afternoon.

Didn't they, like the male disciples who had fled, have other places to be and other things to do? After all, it was a Friday afternoon, the preparation day for the celebration Sabbath of the busy Passover week. The very reason they had traveled all the way from Galilee to Jerusalem was to participate in this important annual Jewish holiday, yet these women stood there until the bitter end, where they had to be feeling a mixture of misery, horror—and love! Yes, I believe love is what kept them there.

Have you ever sat at the bedside of a loved one until they breathed their last breath, or even, on a much less serious scale, sat as a mother through a terrible piano concert or a lengthy sports competition where your child was not doing well, and both you and he were suffering the whole time? But, as mothers, we are willing to sacrifice almost anything to show our deep love and support for our children. As these female followers of Jesus stood there, I'm sure they were determined to show Jesus their deep love and support, even if only silently. This evidence of affection, support, and devotion in His time of greatest suffering must have been like the "balm of Gilead" to his tortured soul (see Jer. 8:22). At times, when we're walking through dark valleys, just having someone with us who loves us makes all the difference. Their presence is a precious gift.

The second observation I made from this passage is the role that the women disciples of Jesus played in Jesus' small entourage of followers. It says that they "ministered to Him when He was in Galilee." In my imagination, I am trying to picture what that entailed. Perhaps cooking, cleaning eating utensils, carrying water, washing clothes? I don't know. But it's interesting to note that while His male followers were puzzling over His parables, trying to learn evangelistic methods, and fighting over who would be first in His kingdom, His female followers were finding very practical ways to serve Him in the here and now of His everyday life. In fact, even now, at His death, they were determined to

lovingly prepare His body for burial. I'm sure He must have appreciated their small gestures of love and loyalty. Similarly, I'm sure He still appreciates all of the little menial and unseen practical offerings of love that women still contribute in support of their family, friends, and the church today.

Third, it struck me that, although the text mentioned only a few names, it stated that, "many other women…came up with Him to Jerusalem." Usually in the Gospels, we hear mostly just the names of Jesus' male followers with detailed renditions of their exploits, so it is both surprising and refreshing to know that Jesus also had many female followers. Of course, we have to remember the low status of women in that society and the resulting limited roles they could play at that time. Yet here, Mark is inspired to mention them, giving us a slight insight into the close and important relationship they had with their Savior. As modern followers of Jesus, I think we can gain encouragement by this glimpse of women as part of Jesus' inner circle of friends, supporters, and believers.

Thank you, Lord, for the value you give to the many women who occupy a variety of special places in your kingdom!

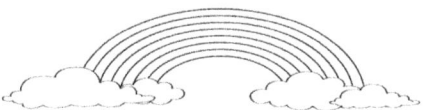

August 10

In Favor

"And Jesus increased in wisdom and stature, and in favor with God and men" (Luke 2:52).

Luke begins his gospel by writing about the birth, childhood, and youth of Jesus as well as the birth of John the Baptist, who will prepare the people to accept Jesus as the Messiah. By the end of the second chapter, Luke has already covered: the circumcision of Jesus (on the eighth day, according to Jewish custom); His dedication at the temple, including blessings by two prophets: a man (Simeon) and a woman (Anna); and His trip to Jerusalem, when He was twelve years old, to celebrate the Feast of the Passover with His parents.

As a parent, as well as an educator, I searched for all the information I could find about the life of Jesus as a young person so that I could teach the children in my sphere of influence about His early life in order to hold Him up as an example of what their young lives should be like. To my disappointment, however, I found very little. The two verses I did find are both here in Luke 2. The first one is found in verse 40, after His family had gone back home to Nazareth after His dedication. So, one can assume it described Jesus as a toddler and young child. It says, "And the Child grew and became strong in spirit, filled with wisdom; and the grace of God was upon Him." The other, verse 52, is today's text. It is proceeded by the return of Jesus and His parents from the Feast of the Passover, which means it took place after He was twelve years old. Although this meant that Jesus was now considered "a man" by Jewish custom,

the verse right before this one provides us with a little more information. It says, "Then He went down with them and came to Nazareth, and was subject to them..." (Luke 2:51). This leads us to believe that He was obedient and respectful of their wishes—something that can be a struggle for many teenagers and young adults. I am thankful that Jesus set this example for them. It is short, sweet, and easy to understand.

Now, though, I want to spend a little more time unpacking what is covered in Luke 2:52. Although it is just one sentence, it addresses all four aspects of a balanced Christian life. When it says that "Jesus increased in wisdom and stature," it is telling us that He grew both intellectually and physically. Then, the phrase "in favor with God and men," informs us that He continued to develop in appropriate developmental ways spiritually (in His relationship with God) and socially (in His relationship with others). Thus, this pithy little statement actually provides us with the complete picture of what a child's life should look like. As parents and teachers, then, it is incumbent upon us to try to provide the necessary instruction and activities that can help them develop in all four of these areas of life, just as Jesus did.

My husband, who sometimes does lifestyle counseling, often teaches this concept to his adult clients. He draws a circle on the board and then divides it into four quadrants. After labeling the four parts of the circle: "Mental," "Social," "Spiritual," and "Physical," he explains that to have a healthy and well-balanced life, people need to continue to grow in a somewhat symmetrical pattern in all four of these aspects of their lives. Then he asks each person to take inventory of their strengths and weaknesses. If they are lacking in any of these areas, the group brainstorms different actions or activities that will help them become well-rounded and optimally-functioning members of society. He contends that if we had taught this construct to our youth, there would be fewer people today who are living unbalanced and unhealthy lives.

May the Lord help us to always keep this model before us as we work with our young people so that they, like Jesus, will be able to develop healthy lifestyles and well-balanced characters that will truly reflect the image of God.

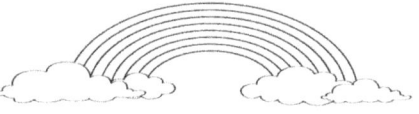

August 11

His Customs

"So He came to Nazareth, where He had been brought up. And as His custom was, He went into the synagogue on the Sabbath day, and stood up to read"
(Luke 4:16).

As Christians, it is one of our stated goals to become more like Jesus. Thus, whenever we catch an overt glimpse of His behavior in the Gospels, we are motivated, as much as possible, to emulate Him. In this one verse, we find that it was Jesus' custom to attend worship services, to attend them on the Sabbath day, and to take an active part in the service when He attended,. Three religious activities that it would be well for His followers to practice as we attempt to follow in His footsteps.

In a previous devotional, we discussed the Christian's duty to attend regular worship services, whenever possible, and the blessings that habit provides. We have also previously discussed how important Sabbath rest is and that the Lord provided the weekly Sabbath for our benefit. But in this passage, we glean a little more insight into who Jesus was and what He valued when we read about His participation in the worship service He was attending.

According to the SDA Bible Commentary, this was the first time the Lord had returned to the synagogue in His hometown, where He had attended regularly as a youth, since beginning His public ministry (see SDA Bible Commentary, vol. 5, pp. 726, 727). It seems that the person who was asked to "read" in a Jewish service not only chose the text but also gave comments in the form of a sermon to elaborate upon its meaning. On this occasion, Jesus chose to share the Messianic prophecy found in Isaiah 61:1, 2. In doing so, He announced to the hometown crowd that He was the long-awaited Messiah. He also rectified their belief that the Messiah would come as a strong conqueror to deliver them from the oppression of the Romans and make the Israelite nation the ruler of the world. Instead, the verses He read described someone who was more concerned about preaching good tidings to the poor, healing the broken-hearted, proclaiming liberty to captives, and restoring sight to the blind. Unfortunately, instead of receiving His correction of their misperceptions about "the Anointed One," they became angry. But that's the story for another day.

Our focus in this text is to study His conduct according to what was customary to Him. We can only become more like our Savior as we understand more fully His daily habits and customs. As He pulls the curtain back on what His ministry is really about, we see that He is concerned for the poor as well as people who were generally marginalized and looked down upon in His day. He spent a lot of His time healing and comforting those who were disappointed and broken-hearted, not to mention all of the physical healings He did for the lame, the deaf, the blind, and countless others. He also came to free the captives of sin.

The Commentary points out that although He did all of these things literally, He also meant them even more in a spiritual sense (see SDA Bible Commentary, vol. 5, p. 728). Thus, it was His purpose to preach good tidings (the gospel) to those who were poor in spirit and hungering for righteousness. He came to heal through forgiveness those who were contrite and repentant over sin. He wanted to restore blessed sight to those who were spiritually blind to the goodness and grace of God and free captives who were bound to their sins by the cruel machinations of Satan. In all these ways, He sought to bring redemption to those who would be saved through the divine plan of salvation. Looking back at His self-sacrificing and people-loving ministry, I believe we have a more than sufficient model to show us what "customs" we should adopt in order to become co-workers with Him in saving the lost all around us.

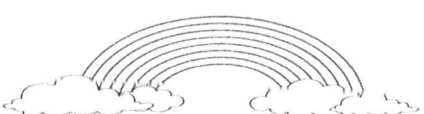

August 12

Covetousness

"And He said to them, 'Take heed and beware of covetousness, for one's life does not consist in the abundance of the things he possesses'" (Luke 12:15).

One day, while Jesus was teaching about the kingdom of God to a crowd that had formed around Him, a person spoke up and entreated Jesus to settle a dispute he was having with his brother over their inheritance. As He often did, Jesus used this occasion as another teachable moment, when He uttered the sentence above. Then He went on to tell a parable about a person who my Bible labels "A Rich Fool" in the subheading for this chapter. According to the story Jesus told the impromptu audience, there was a very rich man who had garnered such an abundant harvest that he didn't have room to store it all. He decided to solve this dilemma by tearing down his old barns and building even bigger ones, which would have plenty of room to store all of his crops and his many material possessions. Then he planned to just sit back, enjoy his wealth, and take it easy for many years to come. At that point Jesus concluded the short parable with a surprise ending. That very night, the rich man would die, and God would ask him, "...then whose will those things be which you have provided?" (verse 20). The moral of the story is quickly summed up in these words: "So is he who lays up treasure for himself, and is not rich toward God" (verse 21).

After this, Jesus took some time to elaborate on this concept with His disciples. He told them not to worry, obsess, or be anxious about what to eat, drink, or wear because God knew what they needed. "Life is more than food, and the body is more than clothing," He said in Luke 12:23. Then He went on to assure them that they were of more value than the ravens or the lilies that God continually provides for and that their job was to "seek the kingdom of God, and all these things shall be added to you" (verse 31). He ended this discourse with more detailed information in verses 33 and 34 of this chapter: "Sell what you have and give alms; provide yourselves money bags which do not grow old, a treasure in the heavens that does not fail, where no thief approaches nor moth destroys. For where your treasure is, there your heart will be also."

It's a message that is still relevant to us today. It is not that we should go without our basic needs being met, but once the Lord has provided these things, our attitude should be one of wanting to build up the kingdom of God by sharing our blessings with not only His church but also to satisfy the needs of those around us. We need to develop an attitude of sharing and generosity that will reap a rich harvest in heaven—not of greed to get more and more material possessions and hoarding whatever we already have. We should ask ourselves, "How can I use my money and worldly goods to bring glory to God?"

So often we get caught up in the sin of covetousness. Is it actually a sin? Yes, you will remember that the tenth commandment addresses the evil of wanting things that other people have. The SDA Bible Commentary defines this malady as "an undue affection for the material things of life, especially those belonging to someone else" (vol. 5, p. 796). It goes on to say, "The man addressing Christ did not need more riches; what he needed was to have covetousness erased from his heart, after which riches would be of little concern to him" (Ibid.). Farther down on the same page it states, "Materialism is at the root of many of the world's major problems today. Dissatisfaction with what we have creates the desire to secure more by forcing others to give up all or part of what they have rather than by toiling honestly ourselves." It asserts that, "Covetousness is the cause of many of the world's insoluble problems." This is probably because it blinds the self-absorbed soul from seeing what is beneficial or best for other people in the frenzied quest to obtain more and more for one's self. A strong case of it can eventually lead to the commission of crimes such as theft and even murder. May the Lord deliver us from the temptation to covet. Instead of the modern mentality of "He or she who dies with the most "toys" wins," our motto should be "He or she who gives the most to others wins—eternal life!"

August 13

Angelic Joy

"Likewise, I say to you, there is joy in the presence of the angels of God over one sinner who repents" (Luke 15:10).

The Lord was in the middle of His "lost items" trilogy. He had just given the parable about the lost sheep, where He proclaimed a similar celebration, found in verse 7. It says, "I say to you that likewise there will be more joy in heaven over one sinner who repents than over ninety-nine just persons who need no repentance." And now, in the parable of the lost coin, as He expresses the rejoicing of the woman who had found it, He likens the celebration she has with her friends and neighbors as similar to the joy that will be felt in heaven over a lost sinner who repents and comes to God.

Back in July, when looking at Zephaniah 3:17, we discussed the glorious thought that the Lord Himself will rejoice over us with singing! But in this verse, we learn that even the angels are participants in the joy which is felt in heaven when a sinner responds to the call to follow the Lord—and is found! Can you just imagine all of heaven erupting into a joyous song of celebration and praise to God every time someone is saved? The idea of heavenly celebration is further cemented in our minds by the parable that follows—regarding the lost son. When the son comes home, the father throws a huge party! The

Bible says, "And they began to be merry" (verse 24). Besides a feast, we're told that there was music and dancing! The father could not contain his joy when his wayward son finally decided to come home to him!

Think of the implications of this in your life and mine. It's hard to wrap my mind around, but it fills me with a humble sense of joy and thanksgiving that not only the Lord but also all the occupants of heaven care that much about me! It makes me want to break into song myself! It certainly motivates me to try not to do anything that would bring them disappointment or ever turn their happiness into sorrow. But there's a third emotion I'm feeling—it's a desire to try to help other people decide to come home to Jesus so that the heavenly party can continue!

What about you? I wonder what you must be thinking about the angelic joy that filled all of heaven when you gave your life to the Lord? Or if you haven't actually given your life completely to Him yet, what a wonderful party will ensue at the moment you do! For many of us, we first made our decision to follow Jesus and be baptized when we were children. For others, we waited to take that all-important step until we felt we understood it better, when we were in high school or college. Then, there are those who didn't come into a personal faith relationship with God until later in their adult life. And some of you may even be accepting Jesus for the first time today! Whenever it happens, whether early or late in life, our decision triggers "joy in the presence of the angels."

Having served as a primary teacher, I can understand what the text means when it says, in verse 7, that there is more joy in heaven over one sinner than over ninety-nine "just persons." Does Heaven not care about all the good people who are already in a saving relationship with the Lord? Of course it does! But in a classroom of second graders, for example, the teacher has to take more time and give more attention to the student who hasn't yet learned to read. Then, when one day he suddenly cracks the code and begins reading, everybody celebrates—him, the teacher, and the parents! Does the teacher love her other students less? No, but she is very happy and proud of the student who struggled to become a reader because now he can join in the joys and benefits of all the other readers in her classroom. In fact, it brings a cause for the whole class to celebrate the new elevated status of that one student! Everyone can join together in celebrating his victory! It should be the same with us.

If we have already been participating in all of the blessings of walking with the Lord, how appropriate it is for us to celebrate, together with all the angels of heaven, when a brother or sister who was previously lost on the path to perdition becomes found and begins walking together with us on the road to heaven! Whenever we are privileged to see this miracle happen, let's take time to praise God right along with all the heavenly host!

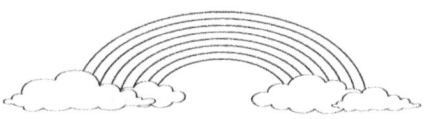

327

A Great Way Off

"And he arose and came to his father. But when he was still a great way off, his father saw him and had compassion, and ran and fell on his neck and kissed him" (Luke 15:20).

In continuation of yesterday's theme—the idea of great celebration taking place when one sinner repents—today's verse highlights not only the father's joy but his overt actions in welcoming his once-lost son home. By this time in the famous parable, the prodigal knows how unworthy he is to receive anything from the father whose love he has spurned, whose money he has wasted, and whose values he has consistently violated. On the other hand, he knows the character of his father; he is a man who lives out the principles of forgiveness, generosity, love, and grace. In his recent awareness of his great need and his decision to come back home, he is now in a position to appreciate those qualities in his father, and his only hope is to appeal to his father's goodness. Realizing the depth of his sin, he has no aspirations of returning to the coveted status of sonship. Will the righteous father be willing to accept the wayward youth's humble request just to be some kind of a servant in the household? Or will he be turned away?

Praise God, we know the answer to the supplicant's plea because we, too, have had to lean on the largesse of our heavenly Father after our forays into sin. Not only have we received unmerited grace but, like the father in the parable, the Lord insists on restoring us to sonship! What's more, we learn that He has been eagerly awaiting us despite all our wanderings, and we see Him excitingly running out to meet us where we are! We know we don't deserve such a royal reception, but His goodness encircles us like a warm embrace, and we are, amazingly enough, invited to attend a wonderful party being held specifically for us—to welcome us home! The experience is beyond belief! Not only for the repentant son but also for us, who have been equally overwhelmed by God's graciousness and goodness, despite our faults and failings!

At the Christian college, from which several members of our family have graduated, there is a wonderful permanent representation of the reuniting of the father with his prodigal son depicted in a large statue gracing the entrance of the institution. In this beautiful work of art, the father is running, coattails flying, arms outstretched, and with an expression of joy and anticipation etched upon his smiling face. It is a powerful reminder to all who visit the university—students, faculty, and guests—that God is always happy, not only to welcome us back into His loving arms but also to run out toward us, even if we are still a long way off. He doesn't demand that we grovel and groan or even go more than half way back to Him. As soon as we realize our need and turn in our hearts toward Him, He makes up the difference to close the gap between Him and the object of His incomprehensible love!

Are you a long way away from God today? If so, ponder with me His eagerness of heart for us to return to Him, no matter how far off course we have wandered. Whether it's for the first time or the 500th time, whenever we decide to turn around from our sinful path and start moving in His direction, we can be assured that the Savior always stands ready to give us a warm welcome and to redeem and restore us to our unmerited status as His sons and daughters! Wow! What a wonderful God we serve!

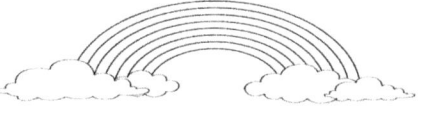

August 15

Our Faithfulness

"He who is faithful in what is least is faithful also in much, and he who is unjust in what is least is unjust also in much" (Luke 16:10).

I know that back in May, we considered the verse in Ecclesiastes 9:10, which admonished us "Whatever your hand finds to do, do it with your might," where we discussed the importance of always doing our best work. But I see today's verse as more of a progressive experience related to the fact that if you do the little things assigned to you well, when larger responsibilities come along, you will be prepared to also do them well. Thus, your faithfulness in little things actually builds your skill level, your self-confidence, and more importantly, your character. More than that, when others, such as parents, teachers, and bosses, see your faithfulness, not only in work but in many other aspects of life, they will begin to trust you to move on to the next level.

This is a verse I quoted often to my daughter as well as my students through the years, regardless of their age. That's because I see this concept as pivotal to all growth in life. For example, in order to learn to multiply and divide, a pupil first needs to learn multiplication tables well. Once a child has basic facts memorized, he or she is ready to go on to more difficult mathematical algorithms. The same goes with reading. A child must first learn the letter sounds before beginning to read words and sentences with any degree of fluency. And on it goes...in the sports world, an athlete first learns basic drills well before going on to play in a competitive game. They practice, spending time and effort to hone their skills, until they become experts. When I first started taking piano lessons, I remember having to start by learning the names of all the notes and practicing scales. Today, although far from being a professional, I play hymns. And I keep practicing them, knowing that by continuing to play the best I can, little by little I will become more proficient.

Consider the prerequisite skills for everyday things, such as learning to cook, driving a car, or learning a second language. I'm sure you can think of many other examples where, by doing your best faithfully day after day, especially in the small things, you create building blocks that can form a strong foundation on which to build in the future. I believe that this is true not only in our work life but also in our spiritual development.

Looking back on my life, I can trace how God was preparing me, even in menial positions, to grow into the person I needed to be for the weightier responsibilities He guided me into farther down the road. It started with the first secretarial job I got right after graduating from college with my first degree—an associate degree in secretarial administration. In my training I had learned how to type rapidly, take shorthand (remember, this was in the old days!), and how to use a stenography machine as well as all the other types of office equipment utilized at that time. At first, since I was so young, the company hired me only as a receptionist and the person who sorted and delivered the mail. Just being happy to have my first real (outside of college) office job, I determined to do my best. Although my title did not include the word "secretary," and my skills were being under-utilized, over the next six months or so, the management observed that I was a competent worker and a faithful employee. I was someone they could depend on to do a good job and an employee they could trust to maintain a professional attendance record and use her work time productively.

It wasn't long before they gave me both a promotion and a raise. By the time our family moved from that area three years later, I had been named the highest paid executive secretary in the company. The Lord used that experience to help me acquire other administrative secretary positions in the future while I finished earning my bachelor's degree in education. I see now that it also helped prepare me for the various leadership roles in which I would serve in both the public and private sectors of education in the years to come. One step, well taken, leads to a greater step. When my daughter was a little girl, she would get nervous about moving from one grade to another. "Mommy, I don't think I'm ready for third grade," she would confide in me. Later, she'd cry, "Mom, I don't think I'm ready for high school." It was the same with college and even grad school. Each time she expressed this "readiness" doubt, I would assure her that, indeed, she was ready. How did I know? Because when she had done well at one level, I knew she would do well at the next. Today's verse holds true. If we are faithful in the little things, God will entrust us with more challenging things. We can be confident that He will help us do them well because we will have established a firm foundation on which to build a beautiful edifice— skill upon skill, experience upon experience, and character trait upon character trait.

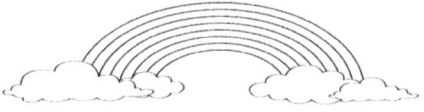

Infinite Possibilities

"But He said, 'The things which are impossible with men are possible with God'" (Luke 18:27).

The moral, rich young ruler, exactly the upstanding kind of person that the disciples thought would be a perfect candidate for heaven, had just turned away from Jesus when He told him to sell his possessions and give to the poor. Although the young man said he had kept the commandments all his life, Jesus saw that there was still something missing. He needed to transfer his "head knowledge" into "heart knowledge" to become part of the kingdom of God. Unfortunately, many modern Christians sitting in church pews today look and act as if they are really good moral people, at least to all outward appearances. But when God searches the heart, He too often sees a believer who is devoid of the essential qualities of compassion, kindness, love, and a motivation to engage in unselfish activities for the benefit of others.

The disciples were amazed when Jesus told them, "How hard it is for those who have riches to enter the kingdom of God" (verse 24). Incredulous they asked, "Who then can be saved?" (verse 26). If a rich, life-long commandment-keeper like the respectable young man wouldn't qualify to become an eventual inhabitant of heaven, how could anyone at all be saved?

It was then that Jesus uttered the statement above, revealing how any of us are saved—only by God's grace and miraculous work on our behalf. How wonderful it is to know that when things are impossible for us, God still has infinite possibilities! When we earnestly desire to follow Him, He exchanges our stony heart for a loving heart of flesh—one imbued with the gifts of the Spirit, which make us willing to give, serve, and sacrifice for those around us. That miraculous change in us helps us reflect the image of God and is what makes us ready to live in the kingdom of heaven.

As I pondered all the things that are impossible for us but more than possible for God, I realized that we are surrounded with evidence of this fact all around us every day. We're so preoccupied with all the earthly cares, problems, and responsibilities of this life, with our noses to the grindstone, that we often fail to look up long enough to recognize the miracles the Lord is performing right before our eyes: the incredible gift of a baby, for instance; the golden glory of a sunrise; the blazing colors of a sunset; or a rainbow set in the sky after a rain shower. The amazing fact that the birds have built-in migration patterns, bees know where to go for nectar, and salmon return to the streams of their birth to spawn. Not to mention the God-given instincts of all the other animals so that each species knows how to survive in their own environment. The awesome power of the wind and waves also speak to us of God's indescribable sovereignty. He placed the stars in the heavens, He owns "the cattle on a thousand hills" (Ps. 50:10), and perhaps best of all, He, the Creator of all things, is able to bring healing to broken hearts, bodies, and relationships. He is a specialist in turning sinners into saints.

So, the next time we get bogged down thinking about all the impossibilities in our lives, we need to remind ourselves that our God is the Lord of infinite possibilities—most of which we haven't even imagined. If we will bring our problems before Him, we will be amazed at how He works things out for our good. But best of all, if we are willing, we will be blessed to experience the most incomprehensible miracle of all—conversion of our own lives to the salvation of our souls! Praise the Lord that He is a God of infinite possibilities!

August 17

Servant Leadership

"And He said to them, 'The kings of the Gentiles exercise lordship over them, and those who exercise authority over them are called "benefactors." But not so among you; on the contrary, he who is greatest among you, let him be as the younger, and he who governs as he who serves. For who is greater, he who sits at the table, or he who serves? Is it not he who sits at the table? Yet I am among you as the One who serves'" (Luke 22:25–27).

While Jesus has just instituted the Lord's Supper, demonstrating once more the depth of His condescension to save humankind, His clueless disciples are arguing about which of them will be the greatest in the kingdom of heaven. The Lord had tried to tell them about His suffering and death, but it was as if His words fell on deaf ears. Before their small meal, which would commemorate His sacrifice until He came back to Earth again, He had even washed their feet, modeling the kind of humility He was looking for from anyone who claimed to be one of His followers, let alone a leader, in the new kind of kingdom He had come to establish.

It makes me wonder what kind of disappointment we cause the Lord today, in our own lives, when we blindly busy ourselves with our own worldly and competitive agenda, not paying attention to His still, small voice urging us in the direction of humbly serving others while we are claiming to serve Him. If we are truly His followers, people should be able to see it in our daily words and actions.

But Jesus is not talking to just anyone in this vignette. He's leaving instructions for those who will become leaders in His cause. Those charged with representing His character to the world after He is gone. It's a tremendous challenge to which He calls them. And at that moment, they seemed woefully unprepared for the task of evangelizing the then-known world. So, what would make the difference? Only the acceptance of the gift of the Holy Spirit, which the Lord promised to send them soon, could make their proud minds humble, their selfish actions benevolent, their harsh speech eloquent and powerful for good, and their hard, uncaring hearts loving and kind. Only the Holy Spirit would be able to equip and inspire His disciples to follow the examples He had set for them so that they could become the servant leaders He needed them to be.

I believe the same applies to us. We have been immersed in our society's dog-eat-dog work culture for so long, running the rat race along with everyone else, that we often seem either unaware or, at the very least, insensitive to the ways and wishes of our Savior. Many of us are just trying to get ahead, clawing our way to what we perceive as "the top," using any methods that we think will help us get ahead. I have worked for many bosses—both within and outside of the church—and of all of them, I can only count a couple who could actually be defined as servant leaders. I remember them clearly because they made such a stand-out impression on me as well as the other workers who were privileged to interact with them.

So, to recap, how do we change? As with the disciples in the first century, our only hope is to ask for and receive the Holy Spirit. When He fills us, we will be imbued with His lovely traits (see Gal. 5:22, 23). He will accomplish the miracle of a Christ-like life. It is He who will empower us to become the servant leaders Jesus asks us to become in every sphere of influence in which we are called to serve.

August 18

He is Risen!

"'He is not here, but is risen! Remember how He spoke to you when He was still in Galilee, saying, "The Son of Man must be delivered into the hands of sinful men, and be crucified, and the third day rise again."' And they remembered His words" (Luke 24:6–8).

As I am writing this page, the whole world continues to suffer through one of the worst pandemics in history. Just yesterday, more than 3,000 people died from the Covid-19 virus in the United States alone! And although an effective vaccine is on the way, we are still projected to lose thousands of folks per day over the next several months until a majority of our citizens are able to get vaccinated. Meanwhile, another staggering statistic confronts us. Since this strange respiratory illness was first identified in our country less than one year ago, more than 305,000 Americans, of all ages and backgrounds, have died from it! And that's not all!

At this point, all the nations of the world have been impacted by this unanticipated malady, and our lives altered in innumerable ways! In an effort to stop the spread of the virus, even something as huge and multi-national as the Olympic Games has been cancelled until we can get this horrible disease under control. In addition to all the problems and inconveniences I've described previously, perhaps one of the worst is that even family gatherings have had to be non-existent or very limited, with every responsible person employing the necessary mitigation strategies of masking, distancing, and constantly washing everything in sight in order to protect ourselves, our loved ones, and the people in our communities. Even so, our losses keep adding up, and many of our friends and neighbors are mourning the death of a loved one.

At a time like this, what could be better news than the blessed hope our Savior has given us that there will be a resurrection! He not only promised this to His followers but He demonstrated it in His own life! Praise God that if we have lost someone we loved or even if our own lives come to an end sooner than expected, we can be assured that we will live again! Jesus, the Creator and Redeemer, also declares Himself as "the resurrection and the life" (John 11:25)! If we believe in Him, we shall be resurrected, just as He was resurrected!

It's important that we don't fall into the same trap as the disciples, who just didn't seem to get it, even though Jesus had tried to prepare them for His death and resurrection by telling them beforehand what was going to transpire! They're suffering was made worse by the fact that they didn't remember His words about the future. I fear the same can happen with us today. If we don't pay attention to His words, we can also be caught completely off guard, forgetting His words about the resurrection and the glorious life that is to follow, thereby increasing our sorrow and suffering at the time of a death. The Bible tells us, in fact, that we are not to sorrow as those who have no hope (see 1 Thess. 4:13–18). What a powerful passage! Thus, I chose today's texts, not because we aren't living through difficult times but precisely because we are! I believe if we can remember His words and the trying circumstances of His death as well as how He, by trusting in God, was able to come forth from the grave victorious, it will give us the comfort and encouragement we need as we walk through our current dark valley of the shadow of death.

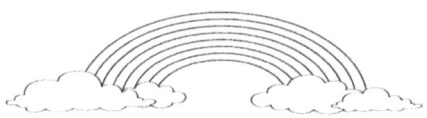

Spiritual Comprehension

"Then He said to them, 'These are the words which I spoke to you while I was still with you, that all things must be fulfilled which were written in the Law of Moses and the Prophets and the Psalms concerning Me.' And He opened their understanding, that they might comprehend the Scriptures"
(Luke 24:44, 45).

This last chapter in Luke covers a lot of ground. It starts by discussing the resurrection, moves to the experience of the two disciples on the road to Emmaus, includes a vignette of Jesus appearing to His followers and opening the Scriptures, so they could better comprehend His mission and better explain it to those they would witness to after His departure, and finally, ends with the ascension. Jesus' ardent desire that His disciples truly understand how the various writings and prophecies of what we call today the Old Testament becomes very clear in this chapter.

First, the angels at the tomb reminded the women who came to properly embalm Him that He had told all the disciples about His impending death and resurrection before any of these things actually happened. Then, Jesus joins the pair of unknowing disciples on their way to Emmaus and expounds to them "all the Scriptures...concerning Himself" (verse 27). Later, when He appears before all the disciples, He utters the words found in verse 44 above. It is evident that prior to His ascension He wants them to clearly understand that His death and His resurrection were all part of the gracious plan of salvation for the inhabitants of the world.

Further, since they will be the witnesses charged with evangelizing the then-known world, verse 45 tells us that He actually "opened their understanding, that they might comprehend the Scriptures," and remember all the things He had taught them over the previous three and a half years. We don't know whether this was an early gift of the Holy Spirit, which they would receive more of at Pentecost, or just the result of His earnest, careful, and patient instruction, made more impressionable by the incredible impact of the events of the Passion Week. What we do know, however, is that they finally got it—comprehension dawned upon them. They had the kind of "ah-ha moment" that teachers throughout the ages have coveted for their students!

Whatever it was that fostered this deep level of comprehension in Christ's original disciples, it's obviously something we need more of today. I don't know about you, but sometimes, when reading the Bible, especially during some of the more obscure passages of the Old Testament, I am slow to understand. I seem to have eyes that cannot see and ears that do not hear. It goes right over my head, and I don't seem to be able to capture the meaning of the verses in front of me. At times like this, I realize that I need the Lord to come and open my understanding so that, like His early disciples, I will finally comprehend what it is that He wants me to know so that I, too, can become an effective witness for Him. Lest I think that I can gain this kind of comprehension on my own, I recall 1 Cor. 2:14, which tells us that spiritual things are spiritually discerned.

Thus, my daily prayer is: Today, and whenever I open your Word, Lord, help me to remember to ask for the spiritual comprehension that only You can supply.

August 20

The Light

"All things were made through Him, and without Him nothing was made that was made. In Him was life, and the life was the light of men" (John 1:3, 4).

Can you remember the last time your electricity went out during the night? We live in a more rural area without city lights or street lights, so when the electricity goes out here, it's pitch black! We have to store a flashlight in each room in order to see how to move from one to the other. What's more, we lose all means of communication with the outside world. Our internet and TV can't work; we can't charge our cell phones; and, because we are an all-electric household, we can't even cook or turn on the heat! The microwave won't work, the food in the refrigerator and freezer is subject to spoiling (if it's a long outage), and worst of all, our electric water pump for our well stops working, so we don't have indoor running water for drinking, showers, toilets, or even washing our hands! It's a dire, and unlivable situation! How thankful we are when our power comes back on! We swear we will never take our access to all the comforts of life through the blessing of electrical power for granted again!

The first verses in the Gospel of John remind us that "the Word" (another term for Jesus) was with God from the beginning. In fact, we're told here that "All things were made through Him, and without Him nothing was made that was made." It's pretty emphatic! So we go back to read about Creation in Genesis. In the first few verses of the first chapter we find: "In the beginning God created the heavens and the earth. The earth was without form, and void; and darkness was on the face of the deep. And the Spirit of God was hovering over the face of the waters. Then God said, 'Let there be light'; and there was light" (Gen. 1:1–3). Thus, all three members of the Godhead were involved in this truly miraculous event of bringing light into the world. Remember, the creation of the sun, moon, and stars didn't occur until the fourth day! Yet, light appeared on the very first day—just because of the presence of Divinity! No other sources of light were necessary. It's interesting to note that, when we go to the last chapter of Revelation, we find a similar statement. It says, "There shall be no night there; They need no lamp nor light of the sun, for the Lord God gives them light" (Rev. 22:5). The conclusion? Where God is, light exists.

I would argue that something similar happens when we meet and accept Jesus into our lives. Prior to that event, we may not be able to see our way, stumbling along in darkness, fear, and confusion. Having worked on college campuses for many years, I have seen a lot of students who were totally lost. Not physically, mind you, but in relation to what major they should choose, what career they should prepare for, or which person they should marry. Some were still struggling over their identity, while others were lost in the darkness of uncertainty about their future due to financial, academic, or even addiction problems. They longed for someone to guide them

who could shed some light on their pathway, helping them to make the right decisions and find the right answers for all their questions. Through the years, I've discovered that adults who do not have a solid relationship with God suffer from some of the same difficulties. We all need to find a way to move forward when passing through the dark experiences of loss, divorce, illness, financial, relational, or job-related challenges. At these junctures, we all long for light.

Thankfully, that's why Jesus came to this earth. He is the Light we need! He who brought light into the world wants to shine that same warming, healing, shadow-dispelling light into all the situations of our life—if we will only invite Him in. Basking in the glow of His presence, we will find encouragement, guidance, grace, peace, hope, and love enough to dispel all of our darkness.

August 21

Saved!

"For God so loved the world that He gave His only begotten Son, that whoever believes in Him should not perish but have everlasting life. For God did not send His Son into the world to condemn the world, but that the world through Him might be saved" (John 3:16, 17).

"Why," you might be asking yourself, "did Dr. Barcelo decide to focus on this—one of the best-known readings in the Bible—for her devotional thought today?" Well, the answer is that I am attempting to focus on verses that I would like to consider more deeply—and this is one of them (actually two). The truth is that I have heard and repeated John 3:16 so many times in my life that, unfortunately, I fear I have taken it for granted. I have just skimmed along the surface of it so frequently that I was no longer giving it the deep reflection it deserves. So, I decided to take some time today to unpack its true and very consequential meaning.

The first idea that begins to sink in when I slow down and really study its components is that God, the Creator of heaven and earth, loves us so much that He took a drastic action to reach out and rescue us from sin. This involved an incomprehensible sacrifice, as He decided to send His very own Son to save us. As I think about how I would feel if someone told me I would have to sacrifice my one and only daughter in order to rescue someone—and especially people of a dubious character—who might not even appreciate it, I begin to realize how costly our redemption was to God the Father. Then, as I consider how much Jesus Himself must love us in order to condescend to leave His throne in glory in exchange for a life of pain, difficulty, and rejection, I stand in awe! Especially considering that He came to this dark and sin-filled world not in our time, with all our modern conveniences (cars, running water, microwaves, and cell phones, to name a few), but during a very dark time in earth's history when people had no indoor plumbing, no electricity, no means of rapid communication, and only very rudimentary methods of transportation. Many people in Palestine at the time were exceedingly poor and had little education (except for the priests and scribes). They knew little about hygiene, about ways to avoid illness, or treat diseases. Subsequently, lifespans were generally short, and the common people had little hope of improving the quality of their impoverished lives. At the same time, the nation of Israel was being occupied by the Romans, who made their lives even more tedious and difficult. If I had been Jesus, I would have chosen to come to a rich and free nation that was clean, with paved roads and provided many places for adequate hand-washing. I would want to be somewhere that was beautiful with lots of amenities to make life in this world at least a little more bearable. Of course, even if He had come under the best of circumstances, this world would have seemed incredibly dark, dangerous, and primitive in every sense of the word for One who had just come from the indescribable light and glory of heaven! But, thank God, our gracious Savior came down to the lowest depths of human existence in order to save those whose lot it was to dwell there. Not only did He humble Himself through the act of incarnation but He bent low to pass through the worst experiences of human existence in order to be able to relate to all of our trials and tribulations— He suffered poverty, exhaustion, filth, pain, rejection, torture, and death—all so that we could be assured that He truly understands us. What He sacrificed for us didn't start at the cross. His whole life was one continual sacrifice for us!

So, why did He do it? This verse answers that question. It says so that "whoever believes in Him should not perish but have everlasting life." Just think of it! "Whoever believes," meaning any one of us who simply believes in Him can be rescued from this life that is dominated by sin and all of its horrible consequences! Not only that...He promises to give us an everlasting perfect life with Him in heaven! What incomprehensible grace and love! Verse 17 finishes off this beautiful passage by telling us that Jesus didn't come down to earth to judge and condemn us but that "the world through Him might be saved." His whole goal in coming to share our experiences as humans was so that He might woo as many of us as possible into returning His love and trusting in Him so that He might be able to save us! It's hard to wrap our minds around, but these texts tell us that it's true. If we believe in Him, we will be saved! As we let it soak in, all that is left to say is, "Praise God from whom all blessings flow!"

August 22

Words of Eternal Life

"From that time many of His disciples went back and walked with Him no more. Then Jesus said to the twelve, 'Do you also want to go away?' But Simon Peter answered Him, 'Lord, to whom shall we go? You have the words of eternal life'" (John 6:66–68).

Recently, we talked about the fact that spiritual things must be spiritually discerned to be rightly understood. That was certainly the case with what Jesus was telling His listening audience on this particular day. He had just told them, "He who eats My flesh and drinks My blood abides in Me, and I in him" (verse 56). He had declared this same idea in several other ways in order to explain the necessity of taking in His words and making them a part of ourselves, just like when we eat bread and it becomes part of us. That's why He described Himself as "the bread of life" (verse 48) and "the living bread" (verse 51). But this concept was so offensive to the Jews that, while shaking their heads, they turned away from Jesus and decided that He wasn't a person they could continue to follow in good conscience. It was a sad day. Fortunately, however, the twelve disciples who were the closest to Him decided to stay. This was not because they understood everything that Jesus had told them but because they had come to believe He truly was the Son of God and that they could find eternal life by believing His words. When Jesus asked if they would leave Him as well, John answered that, as truth-seekers, there was really no one else they could follow. In fact, he goes on to state, "...We have come to believe and know that You are the Christ, the Son of the living God" (verse 69).

Have you ever reached a point in your life where you were hurt, angry, or confused by some bitter experience you had suffered through and didn't understand why God had permitted this to happen to you? I did. It got so bad that I actually stopped going to church for a while. But when I looked for meaning and purpose in a life without God, there was none to be found. Joy, peace, and motivation all fled away. Every day became like the one before it and after it. The wisdom the world had to offer was shallow, and its pleasures were fleeting. Boredom and purposelessness threatened to consume me.

Finally, I decided that even though I did not understand God's ways nor everything He did or said, yet He still had "the words of eternal life." He was still God. In comparison with Him, everything else was empty and insignificant. So, after a little aimless wandering, ultimately, like the twelve disciples, I decided to stay by my faith in Him, even though I might have to wait a while to get all of my questions answered. At least I knew that He had all the answers. In the meantime, He knew my beginning and my end. He gave my days purpose and joy and peace again. It gave my life new meaning to follow, once more, in His footsteps. This is my testimony. I'm sure the disciples, at least the eleven of them who stayed by Jesus until the very end, could share similar stories. Even though there were many times when they didn't really understand what Jesus was doing or saying, they knew they were better off following Him. After all, He was God, and He gave their lives more meaning and purpose than they ever could have imagined for themselves—not only on this earth but in the eternal life He promised them at His second coming! So, when times get tough, and you really can't understand God's words, hang in there! Trust that, as the Son of God, He truly knows what's best. Your life, not to mention your eternity, will turn out far better as a result!

August 23

Doctrine

"Jesus answered them and said, 'My doctrine is not Mine, but His who sent Me. If anyone wills to do His will, he shall know concerning the doctrine, whether it is from God or whether I speak on My own authority'"
(John 7:16, 17).

For some modern-day Christians, "doctrine" has almost become a bad word. I understand that after years of an emphasis on doctrine over relational Christianity, the goal of some of these folks is to emphasize one's relationship with Jesus and their brothers and sisters in the faith, strengthening that aspect of one's Christian walk, while giving very little attention to the constraints of correct doctrine. I would argue that we have a need for balance here. So, I don't think we should throw the proverbial "baby out with the bath water." If we downplay doctrine, I fear we run the risk of disregarding God's stated will and slipping into positions that encourage heresy.

In today's verses, I interpret the Lord's words as upholding the role of doctrine in our Christian experience. Here Jesus plainly says, "If anyone wills to do His will, he shall know concerning the doctrine." In other words, if we truly want to please God and enjoy a close relationship with Him, we will need to put some sincere effort into searching out the truths, the guidelines, and the beliefs that He has left for us to find in His word. After all, wouldn't His true followers seek to learn and practice His instructions in order to follow in His footsteps as closely as possible? As a result, most Christian denominations have given much thought to the doctrinal beliefs of their ecclesiastical body and published materials listing and explaining the doctrines to which they believe their members should adhere.

The publication that I am most familiar with in this regard is entitled Seventh-day Adventists Believe: A Biblical Exposition of 27 Fundamental Doctrines, which was first published in 1988. (Subsequently, the church added a twenty-eighth doctrine in a worldwide General Conference Session.) For those not acquainted with this volume, it is divided into six major categories, under which the related doctrines are listed and expounded upon in more detail, including the biblical references upon which each one was established. Just to provide an overview of the types of doctrines covered in the book and the importance of them in a Christian's life, I will list the six major categories, with a few examples of what's discussed in each one below:

The Doctrine of God (the Trinity, the Holy Spirit)

The Doctrine of Man (Creation, Human Nature)

The Doctrine of Salvation (Life, Death and Resurrection of Jesus, Christian Growth)

The Doctrine of the Church (Baptism, The Lord's Supper, Spiritual Gifts)

The Doctrine of the Christian Life (The Sabbath, Stewardship, Behavior)

The Doctrine of Last Things (The Second Coming, the Millennium, Heaven)

As I reviewed these doctrines, I was struck anew with the important role they play in guiding us along in our Christian journey. Instead of passing through life in the dark, guessing about who God is and what He expects of us, our Bible-anchored beliefs shine a bright light on our pathway, all the way from our conversion to our ultimate arrival at our celestial destination. Today, I thank God for the truth-filled doctrines that will help to lead us home!

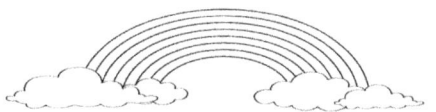

August 24

Abundant Life

"The thief does not come except to steal, and to kill, and to destroy. I have come that they may have life, and that they may have it more abundantly"
(John 10:10).

Chapter 10 of John's Gospel is sprinkled with "I am" statements from Jesus. He says: "I am the door" in verse 9, "I am the good shepherd" in verses 11 and 14, and "I am the Son of God" in verse 36. All of these statements help to establish His authority to make spiritual promises to those who believe in Him, like this wonderful one that declares the reason for His coming to Earth: to give us life—abundant life!

So what does abundant life entail? Synonyms for the word "abundant" include: more than enough, amply sufficient, bountiful, plentiful, and full. Who, then, wouldn't want to live an abundant life? Of course, the definition of a full and satisfying existence might vary, depending upon such factors as cultural background, gender, core values, and even stage of life (age). While browsing through the AARP Bulletin recently, I read that after surveying a number of people who fell into my age bracket (retired), they found that a satisfying life consisted of some degree of economic security and independence, adequate food and housing, readily available healthcare, participation in pleasant (according to their individual interests) activities, strong social bonds with caring individuals (such as family members and close friends), and, not surprisingly to me, affiliation with some type of belief system or faith tradition.

They went on to explain that this last item helped to keep aging individuals more peaceful and hopeful. It tended to give them more stable emotional and mental health as well as a more cheerful outlook on life, in general. When you think about this, it makes sense. After all, Christians who walk all along life's journey with the Lord are blessed every day with His cheering and comforting presence. He gives them forgiveness for their past mistakes and encouragement to continue living the best life they can, regardless of their age or limitations. He gives them love, joy, peace, and hope for a glorious future with Him after all the temporary trappings of this life have fallen away. Christians know that pain, sorrow, crying, illness, and even death itself, will all be destroyed forever, along with sin. They can look forward to the wonderful event of the resurrection, when they will be reunited with their loved ones, and their mortal bodies, ravished by the results of sin, will be changed into marvelous immortal ones forever!

When Jesus talks here about Him coming to give us an abundant life, I see it as playing out in two different dimensions. First, here on earth He gives us an abundant spiritual and faith life that includes all of the blessings outlined above; and second, He will give us a more-than-we-can-imagine abundant life in heaven! Thus, He provides us with the best of both worlds! Why would we even want to resist the abundant life He offers us, especially when we know the horrible alternative? After all, the thief (in this case, the enemy of our souls) seeks only to steal our hope, kill our joy, and destroy our bodies. If we choose to follow him when he lures us with his shallow offers of passing pleasures and fleeting happiness, we will find that, ultimately, he has stolen away our opportunity for a truly meaningful and fulfilling existence in both this life and the next.

Lord, please help us every day to accept your gracious invitation to live our lives abundantly!

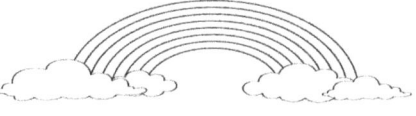

August 25

Other Sheep

"And other sheep I have which are not of this fold; them also I must bring, and they will hear My voice; and there will be one flock and one shepherd"
(John 10:16).

I love the breadth of acceptance of diverse people that Jesus manifests in today's text. Throughout this chapter, He uses analogies on shepherding because shepherds tending their flocks was a common everyday event in the life experience of His hearers, and He knew it would help them to understand what He wanted to teach them. Shepherds of His day lived very close to their sheep. For instance, at night a flock might stay in an enclosure with sheep from other flocks, but in the morning, when their shepherd called them, they recognized his voice, separated from the other sheep, and followed him. Good shepherds had a loving and personal interest in each sheep in their keeping, and the sheep could trust their shepherd to care for them with tenderness and kindness, which is why they were so willing to follow wherever he led them. Thus, Jesus used this pastoral picture as a way to describe the kind of close and loving relationship He wanted to have with His followers.

There were at least two other reasons He chose to use this figure of speech on this occasion. One was that the Pharisees had just expelled the blind man that He had healed from the temple. They were angry with the man because of his powerful testimony regarding what Jesus had done for him, and they didn't know how to explain it. Fearing that more people would believe in Jesus as a result of this miracle, they tried to obscure it by casting the healed man out of the temple. By sharing the illustration of the good shepherd, Jesus wanted to draw a contrast between the tender kindness with which He treated His believers and the harsh and critical manner with which the Pharisees dealt with their followers. Jesus wanted to rectify the impression put forth by these religious leaders that God was harsh and exacting. He wanted people to know that God loved them and wanted to graciously help, guide, comfort, and lead them, much as a good shepherd does with his sheep.

The other reason He used this figure of speech was to introduce to the Pharisees the idea that they were not the only people who could be saved because of the coming of the Messiah. As the children of Abraham, and thus heirs to all the blessings that privileged status entailed, the truth that non-Jewish people could also have a place in God's kingdom was foreign to them. In announcing that He had "other sheep... not of this fold," the Pharisees were flabbergasted. How could that be? But if they had studied the Old Testament prophecies about the Messiah carefully, they would have found that Jesus' mission was to be "a light to the Gentiles," not only the Jews (Isa. 49:6). In actuality, He became the light of the whole world! Anyone who is saved will reach that heavenly state of being because "God so loved *the world* that

He gave" Jesus to come and save anyone who would accept Him as their Savior (John 3:16, emphasis added)!

Having taught international students from many cultural and linguistic backgrounds through the years and sent money to help support mission projects around the world throughout my lifetime, this thought, that anyone who accepts Jesus will be saved, thrills me! Just think how wonderfully diverse heaven will be! I love verses 27 and 28, which explain how this will happen. They say, "My sheep hear My voice, and I know them, and they follow Me. And I give them eternal life...." To me, this means that earnest truth-seekers from around the world, who listen to God's voice speaking to them through the Holy Spirit, will become so attuned to listening and following after their loving Shepherd that when He returns and calls them, whether from their busy lives or their graves, they will recognize His voice and joyfully respond—to receive their eternal reward, safe and sound forever in His heavenly fold!

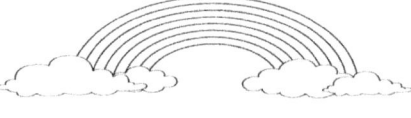

August 26

He Shall Live

"Jesus said to her, 'I am the resurrection and the life. He who believes in Me, though he may die, he shall live'" (John 11:25).

As Bible scholars know, this declaration by Jesus was made to Martha after her brother Lazarus had died.

She was disappointed that the Lord had not come in time to prevent his death, but everything was moving along on God's timetable.

Jesus wanted to use this occasion to test Martha's faith but also to bring glory to God by convincing more people that He, as the Author of Life, also had the power to destroy death. He wanted them, like Martha, to know that He was the actual Son of God, the long-awaited Messiah. In their brief interchange before reaching the tomb of Lazarus, Jesus had announced to Martha, "Your brother will rise again" (verse 23). She expressed that she had faith that her brother would rise in the resurrection "at the last day" (verse 24), not knowing Jesus' plan to raise him immediately. That's when Jesus uttered the famous, "I am the resurrection and the life" statement (verse 25), after which He asked her if she believed it. She responded without hesitation, "Yes, Lord, I believe that You are the Christ, the Son of God, who is to come into the world" (verse 27). His first objective was reached—Martha's faith in Him was firm.

A little later when her sister, Mary, along with many of the Jews who had come to mourn with them, came together in front of the place where Lazarus had been buried, Jesus cried out with a loud voice, "Lazarus come forth!" (John 11:43). And they all witnessed the miracle of the resurrection of Lazarus before their very eyes! Verse 45 informs us that Jesus had reached His second objective. It says, "Then many of the Jews who had come to Mary, and had seen the things Jesus did, believed in Him." God was glorified by what Jesus had done, and His kingdom was increased. Unfortunately, when the people excitedly told the chief priests and Pharisees about the wonder Jesus had performed, they became jealous and angry. Due to all the signs He did, more and more people were following Him, and the Jewish leaders coveted the attention they gave Jesus for themselves. After all, weren't they the religious leaders? Shouldn't the people be coming to them to learn more about God? Their unhappiness grew until they finally decided it was time to plot His death. What they didn't know, of course, is that even Christ's death was part of the whole plan of salvation. It was what would provide a way for even their salvation should they choose to believe in Him as their Savior!

I treasure this verse, not only because it promises us that we, who believe in Him, will be resurrected but also that our faithful loved ones who have passed away and who we miss so much will be reunited with us on resurrection morning! I also thank God that in this same chapter of John 11, the state of the dead is clearly reiterated by Jesus as being like a restful sleep until He comes to raise us to life again. Thus, we find the old expression "rest in peace" to be an appropriate phrase to describe those who die before the second coming of the Lord. In the meantime, John tells us in a smaller book he wrote later that the ticket to eternal life is found in accepting Jesus as our Lord. He sums it up in 1 John 5:11, 12, which says, "...God has given us eternal life, and this life is in His Son. He who has the Son has life; he who does not have the Son of God does not have life." So, this momentous decision for life is ours to make today.

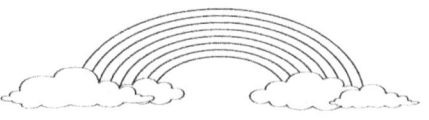

Living Peaceably

"Peace I leave with you, My peace I give to you; not as the world gives do I give to you. Let not your heart be troubled, neither let it be afraid"
(John 14:27).

Previously, we have discussed the Source of perfect peace, whereas today we are grappling with the practical aspects of living peaceably in a conflict-ridden world.

What a valued commodity peace is—especially for those who haven't experienced it for a long time. I can think of several different dimensions of peace. The first is personal, spiritual peace then there is much-to-be-desired familial peace. Next, there is peace within the nation—especially after some long-contested political battle. And finally, there is the allusive goal of eventual worldwide peace.

Since Jesus is talking here with His disciples, it's evident that He is talking about their personal, spiritual peace—peace in one's soul. The kind of peace that is received when we have confessed all of our sins and asked for God's forgiveness. Once we believe He has forgiven us, we no longer need to be plagued with guilt, shame, or bitterness. When we have obeyed the voice of the Holy Spirit and have made ourselves right with God to the best of our ability, He covers us with His blessed robe of righteousness, removes our burdens, frees us from our addictions and besetting sins, and gives us His precious peace as well as a new beginning! Thank God that as Christians, we can avail ourselves of this kind of spiritual peace that goes much deeper than anything this world has to offer.

But what about those other kinds of peace? Sometimes, even in Christian homes, there is a great deal of discord. Occasionally, altercations also spring up between extended family members—sibling to sibling, between generations, or with in-laws or step-relatives. Even in these situations, I can testify that I have seen the Lord bring peace as the result of earnest prayer and the subsequent willingness of the parties in question to find solutions to their problems. On the other hand, because we live in a world of sin, these difficulties may not be ironed out quickly or even during our lifetimes. But as Christians we are given this instruction: "If it is possible, as much as depends on you, live peaceably with all men" (Rom. 12:18). So, we need to ask the Lord to help us in this regard.

At the time of this writing, our country is in the throes of a fierce political struggle that threatens democracy as we know it. This morning when a newscaster asked a private citizen what he thought might happen if we aren't able to heal the deep division in our country, his response was, "I don't know. Maybe there'll be a war!" Unfortunately, people in the USA are more polarized than ever on issues such as race relations, political affiliations, economic necessities, and pandemic solutions. It seems to me that if people of my generation, who have been lucky enough not to know the ravages of war, would speak to some of those who have lived through one, we would be less likely to rush over the edge of the precipice into open conflict. Looking at history, civil wars have often been some of the most devastating. Thus, we need to pray that cooler heads will prevail and that, as Christians, we will work as peacemakers to help heal our nation. In Matthew 5:9, Jesus said, "Blessed *are* the peacemakers, for they shall be called sons of God."

Lastly, there's the problem of "world peace"—that long sought-after objective which always seems to be just out of our reach. In any given time in our history, there has always been war raging somewhere in the world. This, of course, is how Satan wants it since war is so utterly destructive of human life and hope. Although we know from the Bible that on this sin-infested globe, there will always be "wars and rumors of wars." In fact, Matthew 24:6 tells us that they are some of the signs of the times that we will see as we come closer to the end of the world. We know that Bible prophecies regarding the

end of time must be fulfilled. So what is a Christian's stance here? I believe it is still incumbent upon us to pray that war will be avoided for as long as possible and that peace will be maintained as long as possible so that the gospel can still be preached in all the world before probation closes, and it is forever too late for people to be saved. Here, I think our prayer needs to be that God's all-knowing and all-wise will be done, for we know that what worldwide peace we don't experience here will be glorious universe-wide peace throughout eternity in heaven. How we long for that kind of peace! I believe the promise we need to lean on in the meantime is the beautiful one found in Psalm 29:11: "The LORD will give strength to His people; the LORD will bless His people with peace."

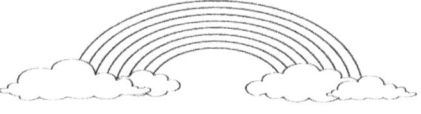

August 28

The Spirit of Truth

"However, when He, the Spirit of truth, has come, He will guide you into all truth; for He will not speak on His own authority, but whatever He hears He will speak; and He will tell you things to come" (John 16:13).

Like all good teachers, Jesus knew that His pupils, in this case His disciples, could only learn what they were ready to learn at the time He was speaking to them. He knew that too much more information than what He was giving them either

wouldn't be understood or would overwhelm them. Thus, in John 16:12, He had just told them, "I still have many things to say to you, but you cannot bear *them* now." This doesn't mean He would just leave them in the dark. On the contrary, after He ascended to heaven, He sent them the Holy Spirit, who would continue to teach them what they needed to learn for the rest of their lives.

Thankfully, as modern-day disciples, He bestows upon us the same gift! Once we accept the Lord and pray for His guidance, He sends the Holy Spirit to us—to guide us, give us wisdom, and to teach us those things we need to know to grow in our spiritual life. He very gently helps us to understand spiritual truth little by little, as we are ready for it. But that's not all. Yes, He helps us learn doctrinal truth, but He also convicts us of personal sin and motivates us to repent. He comforts us when we need consolation—in fact, one of His other names is "the Comforter." As He walks through life with us, He also impresses us to say or do things that will be a blessing to those around us. And, when we listen to His still, small voice with an open heart and mind, He will help us make the most important decisions of our life.

This is a verse I have treasured for a long time, both for myself and for others. As a teacher, preacher, literature evangelist, or someone who gives Bible studies, you know that, although you are being used by God to reach someone for Him, it is the continuing and convicting power of the Holy Spirit that will lead them into all truth. We plant the seeds, which is the great commission that the Lord has given to all of His followers, but the Spirit of God produces the harvest. We realize that we are limited by time, space, or circumstance to teach another person all that they need to know, but thankfully, when we have done the part assigned to us, we can trust God that He will continue to send others to help them along their journey, all under the tutelage of the Holy Spirit. What a blessing it is to realize that the Lord has condescended, despite our weaknesses and limitations, to make us co-workers with Him in the great work of preparing souls for His kingdom!

Whenever I become discouraged with the spiritual progress of someone I have been working with and/or praying for, or even the slowness in my own spiritual growth, I am encouraged by the wonderful promise found in Philippians 1:6, which I believe is a marvelous complement to today's text. In it, Paul is writing to the folks he has worked with and prayed earnestly for in Philippi. They have become Christians. Paul knows they aren't "finished believers" yet, but he knows he cannot be with them continually to help foster their spiritual growth. (It is somewhat like a parent whose grown children live somewhere far away.) So, he commends them to God with these comforting words of faith, which still give all of us cause for courage and hope today. He says: "Being confident of this very thing, that He who has begun a good work in you will complete *it* until the day of Jesus Christ."

Thank you, Holy Spirit, that if we are only willing, You will continue to lead us into all truth throughout our lives!

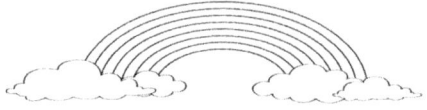

Future Believers

"I do not pray for these alone, but also for those who will believe in Me through their word" (John 17:20).

As we near the end of the Gospel of John, we find a chapter dedicated to talking about the prayers of Jesus. In John 17:1–5, we see Jesus praying for Himself just a little before He is betrayed and arrested in Gethsemane. Subsequently, in verses 6–19, He concentrates on praying for His disciples. Amazingly, in verses 20–26, He prays for someone else who is obviously very important to Him, or He wouldn't have taken time to lift them up in prayer to the Father so close to the time of His death. He takes time to pray "for those who will believe in Me through their word" (verse 20). Whose word? The word of His disciples—both their spoken word, which they preached while they were still alive, and their written word, which has survived the centuries and comes down to us today in the form of the New Testament! Here, Jesus is praying for all FUTURE believers. That means us who are studying this very Gospel of John today! Jesus prayed for us! What a wonderful and encouraging thought this is! Suddenly, my worship time when I am reading my Bible becomes much more personal. It turns into a sacred time of intimate relationship with Jesus who prayed for me so shortly before He sacrificed His life to accomplish my salvation! He looked down through the centuries between then and now, and He prayed for me! I can hardly wrap my mind around it—but I'm so thankful that He chose to demonstrate His care for me in such a direct way.

But now a question arises. What exactly did Jesus pray for? After saying that we will believe in Him through the word of His then current disciples, He begins praying that we will be one. He implores, "That they all may be one, as You, Father, *are* in Me, and I in You; that they also may be one in Us, that the world may believe that You sent Me" (verse 21). He continues, "…that they may be made perfect in one, and that the world may know that You have sent Me, and have loved them as You have loved Me" (John 17:23). Then, He prays that they "may be with Me where I am, that they may behold My glory which You have given Me; for You loved Me before the foundation of the world" (verse 24). He ends this marvelous chapter with these words, "And I have declared to them Your name, and will declare *it*, that the love with which You loved Me may be in them, and I in them" (John 17:26).

When I boil His prayers for me down, I understand He was praying not only that would I learn to believe in Him from the words of Scripture, but that I would experience unity with fellow believers, that someday I would behold His glory and be with Him where He is, and last but not least, that I would experience that kind of exquisite heavenly love that He shares with His Father in heaven. How would this be accomplished? By Him living in us. How can that happen? It occurs automatically when we surrender our lives to Him. The beauty of this transaction is that once He lives in us, our words can help other people to become believers as well! Our testimony, like that of the disciples, can also help others to trust in Jesus. And once they believe in Him, the testimony of their words can reach out to others. It becomes a beautiful, recurring cycle all the way to the end of time.

Thank you, Lord, for thinking of us, and praying for us, melting all the years of distance between us and bringing us close to you!

August 30

Promised Return

"Now when He had spoken these things, while they watched, He was taken up, and a cloud received Him out of their sight. And while they looked steadfastly toward heaven as He went up, behold, two men stood by them in white apparel, who also said, 'Men of Galilee, why do you stand gazing up into heaven? This same Jesus, who was taken up from you into heaven, will so come in like manner as you saw Him go into heaven'" (Acts 1:9–11).

While Jesus had previously mentioned to His disciples that He would be returning to this earth again sometime in the future, this promise, made by angels at the time He was actually ascending into heaven, was perhaps the most meaningful to them. Although they would miss Him terribly, the promise that they would see Him again gave them comfort and hope as well as the motivation to witness to others so that they could also be ready for His promised return.

These words of a promised return jog my memory, and I realize that I have had several personal experiences where I was asked to wait until someone I loved would return to me. The first time I can remember is when I was about four years old. We lived on a military base in Arizona where my dad was stationed

at that time. This particular base had a huge child care building, which at my age seemed sort of like a big gymnasium. It had all kinds of toys lined up along the walls, and children were running around and shouting in glee, as children tend to do when they are playing. The first time, and as I can recall, the only time my younger sister and I were taken there to be cared for was one day when my father and mother had to go to some meeting where children were not allowed. My brother, who was older, was already in school, which is why he didn't share this somewhat scary experience with us.

The constant noise bouncing off the walls and the few adult strangers who we had never met before, but who were assigned to take care of us, left us feeling very uncomfortable in this fearful new environment. This was true even though our parents, while signing us in, assured us that we would be okay and promised that they would return soon to take us home. When they left, we whined for a while, but since we couldn't change the situation we were in, our attention drifted to the toys around the room. Some of the "teachers" tried to get us to play with a few of the other children, but during every pause in activities, I kept my eye on the door from which my parents had left. At our tender age, what we wanted most was just to be with our parents again. What kept us going throughout that seemingly too-long day was that we trusted our parents, so we believed their promise that they would be coming back for us.

I can imagine that the disciples had some similar feelings when their beloved Master departed from them. At that moment, they must have felt some sense of abandonment, being left in this strange, dark world without the One who had become the center of their lives. In mercy, heavenly messengers were sent to bolster the disciples' faith, reminding them that Jesus had told them He would return and that He would come back in the same manner in which He had just left them—in the clouds of heaven. This is what sustained them throughout what sometimes seemed like a too-long wait. Although they kept busy doing the work He had commissioned them to do, it was their greatest desire just to be with Jesus again.

As present-day believers, we should glean the same comfort and hope from Jesus' promise to return soon. Knowing that if He doesn't come during our short lifespan, we will be awakened at the resurrection from what will seem like a very short sleep to see Him coming in the clouds of glory. That means that for older folks like me, His coming will be within the next decade or two, at the latest! May the Lord increase our faith in Him and help us to be prepared spiritually for that glorious day!

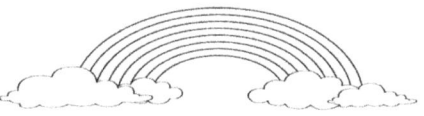

August 31

Such as I Have

"Then Peter said, 'Silver and gold I do not have, but what I do have I give you: In the name of Jesus Christ of Nazareth, rise up and walk.' …So he, leaping up, stood and walked and entered the temple with them—walking, leaping, and praising God" (Acts 3:6, 8).

I don't know if you've ever been confronted by a beggar, but to me, it is always an uncomfortable experience. Growing up in Southern California in the 1950s and 1960s, I had never been approached by a beggar. When I went to serve as a young missionary in Mexico in the 1970s, however, it became a frequent occurrence. As long as I stayed on the college campus where I was working, I was pretty sheltered, but whenever we went to the large city of Monterrey, which was about an hour's drive away, it seemed we encountered beggars on just about every street corner. Locals with whom I was shopping told me to just ignore them for two reasons: one, because they said many of them were just pretending to be needy, and they actually earned more money by begging than by working, and two, due to my unusual appearance (tall, blonde, and blue-eyed), it was obvious that I was an American.

If I showed any signs of generosity, I would immediately become a target for all the beggars in the vicinity. Their advice seemed hard and cold, yet with the little I was earning on a missionary stipend, once I began giving to them, I found I didn't have enough left to buy the items I had come to the city to purchase. On the other hand, when I just ignored them, my conscience bothered me, and I would begin to argue with myself about the best way to deal with this awkward situation. My feelings ranged from compassion to revulsion whenever I was faced with the difficult dilemma. Finally, I decided to ask others to purchase whatever I needed in the city so that I only went there when it was absolutely necessary.

Thus, I can relate to the scene depicted in these texts. I can see and hear the beggar at the temple door, asking all who entered for alms. As Peter and John passed by, I can imagine him reaching out and pleading for whatever change they could muster to help sustain his miserable existence. We know this man had been lame all his life, since the Bible says he had been in this condition "from his mother's womb" (Acts 3:2). Every day someone brought him to this place, where he hoped to find mercy from those who were ostensibly children of God. Perhaps Peter and John had seen him there in front of the temple before, but on this particular day, they were moved by the Holy Spirit to stop and pay attention to his pleading voice and outstretched hands.

As the poor man waited expectantly, he was probably disappointed to hear Peter's words declaring that he did not have any money to give him. But, as he listened, Peter continued, saying that what he did have, he would give him. Then Peter, taking him by the right hand, proceeded to lift him to his feet, as he declared: "In the name of Jesus Christ of Nazareth, rise up and walk!" At that, the man's disappointment must have dissolved into surprise—then hope—and finally, tremendous joy, as he felt the strength come into his ankles and feet for the first time in his life! Not only did he stand up and walk but verse 8 tells us that he entered the temple with Peter and John—walking, leaping, and praising God! The people in the temple that day who knew him, and there were many, were filled with wonder and amazement at the miracle that God had wrought for him through the humble disciples of Jesus. This opened the way for Peter and John to preach to a large crowd about Jesus, resulting in about 5,000 new believers!

Sometimes we think we have little to share with the people in need around us. But if we allow the Holy Spirit to work through us, using whatever gifts God has given us, I believe we will be amazed at the results! Spiritual blessings can sometimes accomplish much more than silver or gold ever could!

Holy Boldness

"Now when they saw the boldness of Peter and John, and perceived that they were uneducated and untrained men, they marveled. And they realized that they had been with Jesus" (Acts 4:13).

When I read this verse, I was immediately struck with its two clear concepts. The first was how unafraid these disciples were to talk about Jesus and to preach in His name wherever they went. Imagine how much courage this took when they knew they were surrounded by the enemies of their Lord. In fact, some of these same rulers, elders, and scribes who were in their audience now had been among those responsible for His death, but the boldness of the disciples did not stop with their preaching. When the jealous and angry rulers and scribes saw the miracle of the healing of the lame man (discussed yesterday) and how many people were becoming believers by listening to what the disciples said about Jesus, they severely threatened Peter and John, forbidding them to teach or preach any more in the name of Jesus.

To this they bravely answered, "Whether it is right in the sight of God to listen to you more than to God, you judge. For we cannot but speak the things which we have seen and heard" (Acts 4:19, 20). These two disciples had a very clear understanding regarding the commission Jesus had given them to fulfill. They knew that their work was to witness for Him by sharing the things they had seen Jesus do and the words they had heard Him say. It was now their job to make believers wherever they went; come what may. Threats of persecution, imprisonment, and even death could not stop them. What

had changed these men from the frightened and cowering people who were hiding out from the authorities in that upper room in Jerusalem just a few short days ago after the crucifixion of Jesus?

Well, that's the second thing that stands out to me in today's verse. The priests and rulers could not help but notice that something unexplainable had happened to these untrained and uneducated common folk who had been following Jesus around for the last three years or so. They had thought that after the death of Jesus, all His followers would be traumatized and intimidated to the point that they would simply slink away, effectively stopping the Christian movement of their day. But now, they found the reverse to be true. His followers had become emboldened; their presence was commanding; their words were powerful, and they were even performing amazing miracles! What was the difference?

After His resurrection, Jesus met with them, explaining again the plan of salvation and pointing out that His substitutionary death to save humankind was part of that plan. He then told them to go and make believers in all parts of the then-known world. He would send the Holy Spirit to empower them to complete this task. Once they were filled with the gift of the Spirit, there was no stopping them! Their holy boldness was evident to all with whom they came in contact, and the only obvious reason was that "they had been with Jesus," and He had forever changed them! This verse encourages us that when we spend time with Jesus, He will change us, too! If we accept His gift of the Holy Spirit into our lives, people will realize that we have been with Jesus as well. He will refine us and polish off our rough edges, making us eager to witness to others of what we have seen and heard of Him in our own Christian experience. Most amazing of all, He will give us the holy boldness we need to finish His work in the world today so that He can come again soon!

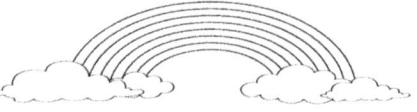

September 2

All Things in Common

"Now the multitude of those who believed were of one heart and one soul; neither did anyone say that any of the things he possessed was his own, but they had all things in common" (Acts 4:32).

Another huge change that the reception of the Holy Spirit had made in the lives of the disciples was their incredible generosity! As more and more people accepted Christ, some had lost work, homes, and even families because of their new beliefs. The Bible tells us that those who had houses or lands sold them so that the proceeds could go to help the new believers who had nothing. They brought not only money but also their possessions to share with those who were less fortunate. A system was worked out where the believers who had more than others came and laid their belongings in front of the apostles, "and they distributed to each as anyone had need" (verse 35). Talk about a true socialistic society!

Unfortunately, history has taught us that most nations who have tried that form of government have failed. In a sinful world, though the idea of everyone sharing everything in common sounds just and fair, after a few years, those who are running such a government usually end up richer as time goes by, and everyone else becomes poorer. Selfishness and an ambition for more and more power tend to gradually take over, and the utopian ideals seem to fade away. Anyone who has tried to live together with others, holding all things in common, whether a roommate, a co-worker, a cult member, or even as the member of a family, can testify how difficult this idealistic notion can be to carry out successfully!

So why did it work for the early church? Today's verse tells us that they "were of one heart and one soul." Once the people were converted to Christianity and imbued with the Holy Spirit, their beliefs, values, and goals became aligned to the point that they willingly shared whatever they possessed with their new brothers and sisters in Christ. What amazing unselfishness! Verse 33 tells us that "with great power the apostles gave witness to the resurrection of the Lord Jesus. And great grace was upon them all." As the focus of the new believers turned from earthly to heavenly treasures, that grace they had received by understanding the redemption given them through the life, death, and resurrection of Jesus unleashed their generosity. They wanted to give all they had to establish and promote the cause of God. This included caring for the poor and needy among them. Imagine what our churches would be like if we continued this generous and grace-filled practice today!

As I think back over my life, I can remember several instances where I can catch just a glimpse of what these early believers might have felt as they first struggled to give up their possessions. One was when my family and I believed that God was calling us to the mission field. We gave up our house, our jobs, our friends, etc. to accept the call. We did, however, keep many of our belongings, which were moved with us to our new place of service. Even so, the sacrifices we had made tugged at our American materialistic hearts. Obviously, the Lord was still working on pruning our naturally selfish characters. Another time, when my mother came to live with us for the last six years of her life, I experienced what it was to live more communally. During that time, we pretty much shared all things in common. The house, our food, utilities, transportation costs, and any other household expenses. It took some adjusting, but because we loved each other, we made it work. Of course, the fact that we each had our own bedroom and our own bathroom helped a lot!

Reflecting on what my selfishness rating would be today, I realize I still have a lot of room for growth in that department. The generosity of the early church stands as a shining example of how Spirit-filled brothers and sisters should share with others in times of need. May the Lord help us to be sensitive to His leading in this area of our Christian experience.

September 3

Divine Vision

"But he, being filled with the Holy Spirit, gazed into heaven and saw the glory of God, and Jesus standing at the right hand of God" (Acts 7:55).

Whenever I read the story of Stephen, the first martyr of the early Christian church, I stand in awe of his calm and Christ-like demeanor. He, along with six other faithful men, had just been chosen as special leaders to see that the needs of the new believers were taken care of. This position was somewhat analogous to what we would call "Deacons" today. So, the apostles laid hands on these seven wise and Spirit-filled men, commissioning them to this practical and much-needed work. The new organizational structure would free the apostles to dedicate more time to prayer and the ministry of the Word. Apparently, their plan was successful because Acts 6:7 tells us, "Then the word of God spread, and the number of the disciples multiplied greatly in Jerusalem, and a great many of the priests were obedient to the faith."

Although it was not one of the primary responsibilities of the newly-assigned deacons to preach, it's obvious from Stephen's story that they still did from time to time. In fact, in Acts 6:8, it says, "And Stephen, full of faith and power, did great wonders and signs among the people." A little later, in verse 10, we're told that when some people arose to argue with what he was saying, "they were not able to resist the wisdom and the Spirit by which he spoke." Unfortunately, then as now, there are always wicked or simply jealous people who will work to oppose or even stop someone who is doing good work in the world. In this case, a group who called themselves the "Freedmen" accused Stephen of blasphemy, stirred up a crowd against him, and dragged him before the Jerusalem Council to be judged. There they found some false witnesses to speak against him, and the high priest asked him if these trumped-up accusations about him were true.

During this charade of a trial, those assembled there knew he was not guilty, for verse 15 declares, "And all who sat in the council, looking steadfastly at him, saw his face as the face of an angel." Nevertheless, they continued with the proceedings. Why

do people choose to believe lies instead of the truth? This is a topic for a different day, but it's amazing to me that in spite of all the wonders he had performed and the supernatural shining of his face, they continued to try to find fault with him, just as they had done with Jesus. Their hatred blinded them to the obvious evidence God supplied that they were trying to silence the very ones He had sent to minister to them.

When Stephen was allowed to speak, he gave a marvelous, wide-sweeping address about God's dealing with His people throughout earth's history. First, He talked about God's covenant with Abraham, the father of their race. Then he recounted the history of the Jewish patriarchs in Egypt and how God had delivered them from slavery through Moses. He talked about the wilderness tabernacle and Solomon's temple, where God had sought to meet with His people. As he reminded them of all the times the Israelites had rebelled against the Lord, ignoring and persecuting God's prophets, rejecting the Holy Spirit, and falling into idolatry, the members of the council began to get uncomfortable. The message struck too close to home, as Stephen declared that modern Israel was following in the rebellious footsteps of their fathers.

When he declared that they had betrayed and murdered the "Just One" (Acts 7:52) whom God had sent from heaven to redeem them—the long-awaited Messiah—they were overcome with anger and rushed to silence him. They threw him out of the city and stoned him. After proclaiming the truth the Holy Spirit had given him to preach to the religious leaders of the Jewish nation, Stephen was at peace, although he knew his death was imminent. In fact, while he was dying, he prayed that the Lord would receive his spirit, and, like Jesus did, he prayed for the forgiveness of those who were taking his life. Even in death, Stephen was a powerful witness for the Lord. His martyrdom was not in vain, as it bore precious fruit for the gospel. As the cruel Saul stood by watching, the noble and peaceful manner in which Stephen died left a lasting impression that would eventually help to convert him into one of the most ardent disciples of Jesus.

As Stephen breathed his last, the Lord gave his faithful servant the beautiful divine vision depicted in today's verse. Instead of focusing on the angry faces and foul shouts of his murderers, His mind was transported to the glorious sights and sounds of heaven! When our work is done, and we walk through the valley of the shadow of our own death, may the Lord grant us the same noble and peaceful end of our days.

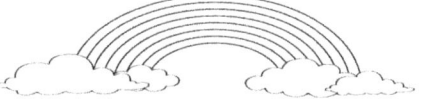

September 4

Poisoned and Bound

"Repent therefore of this your wickedness, and pray God if perhaps the thought of your heart may be forgiven you. For I see that you are poisoned by bitterness and bound by iniquity" (Acts 8:22, 23).

When reading the eighth chapter of Acts, I came upon this scathing rebuke by the apostle Peter. The person he addressed it to was a man named Simon, who had been a fairly well-known and respected sorcerer in the area of Samaria. His story is interesting. When Philip preached about Jesus in his city, many men and women believed the gospel message and asked to be baptized. Not wanting to be left out, and amazed by the miracles and signs that Philip performed, he asked to be baptized as well. A little later, Peter and John came to town. Although the new believers had been baptized with water, they began to lay hands on them so that they would also be baptized by the Holy Spirit. Simon was very impressed when he saw the power of the apostles in this regard and wanted badly to get in on the action. He offered them money to buy this power. Peter, who was incensed by Simon's ambition for power and mercenary spirit issued this strong response: "Your money perish with you, because you thought that the gift of God could be purchased with money! You have neither part nor portion in this matter, for your heart is not right in the sight of God" (Acts 8:20). Then he uttered the words found above. Evidently, the Holy Spirit had given Peter insight into the motivations of this man, who had long been accustomed to people following him because of his sorceries. Apparently, he thought that giving people the Holy Spirit by laying his hands on them could become just another attraction in his bag of tricks.

Simon's response to Peter's words caught my attention. He said, "Pray to the Lord for me, that none of the things which you have spoken may come upon me" (verse 24). It seemed like a sincere request, but we are left wondering. The next verse goes on to the ensuing activities of the apostles, and the end of Simon's story is uncertain. It's like one of those children's books where the readers have to use their imaginations to make up their own ending. Did Simon repent and become a true follower of Jesus? Or did he return to covet his power over the people and continue his life as a sorcerer to his own perdition?

We don't know what decision Simon made, but we can decide how our lives will turn out. Living in this world of sin, we have all, at one time or another, been "poisoned by bitterness and bound by iniquity." Our sins may be different than Simon's, but we have also been tainted by worldly ambitions, tempted to grasp for more fame, money, or power, or bound by old bad habits or addictions of one kind or another that prevent us from living our best life. Like Simon, we have also been introduced to the gospel of Jesus and have the opportunity to choose which way we will go. Will we continue in our previous wicked and self-seeking ways, catering to our own gratification, hiding behind a facade of Christianity simply to fulfill our own selfish motivations, or will we sincerely repent and ask the Lord to forgive us and make us into His true and faithful followers for the rest of our days? We get to write the rest of the story of our life, and the decision we make will determine our own destiny and can help shape the destiny of those who live within our shadow.

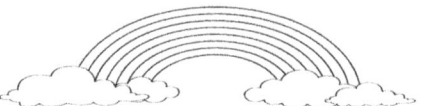

An About Face

"Then he fell to the ground, and heard a voice saying to him, 'Saul, Saul, why are you persecuting Me?' And he said, 'Who are You, Lord?' Then the Lord said, 'I am Jesus, whom you are persecuting. It is hard for you to kick against the goads.' So he, trembling and astonished, said, 'Lord, what do You want me to do?' Then the Lord said to him, 'Arise, and go into the city, and you will be told what you must do'" (Acts 9:4–6).

So, there we have it, in a nutshell, the pivotal event that forever changed the life of Saul, the Jewish zealot, into Paul, the great apostle who evangelized for Christ in most of the then-known world and authored a large part of the New Testament of the Bible. As a result, we still read his writings today to find spiritual strength, guidance, admonition, bright hope for the future, and saving faith in the love and grace of God. As current believers in Jesus, how thankful we should be for the conversion of this man we now call Paul and the inspired messages he left as his legacy.

I'd like to take a few minutes to analyze these three verses a little more closely, beginning with the question that many people ask right at the outset—what does the word "goads" mean? Since I first heard this conversion story as a child, I've wondered why Jesus told Saul, "It *is* hard for you to kick against the goads." Well, my dictionary says a "goad" is "a pointed rod used to urge on an animal." In other words, it is something that can prod or prompt to some kind of action. It makes me wonder if Jesus wasn't referring to Saul's conscience being prod or pricked by the Holy Spirit to quit persecuting the Christians, ever since the martyrdom of Steven, and possibly even before that event, as he saw the godly demeanor

and peaceful countenances of those he was persecuting, supposedly in the name of religion. Although outwardly he continued to project himself as a Pharisee of Pharisees, perhaps inwardly he was beginning to wrestle with some new and disturbing thoughts. Was he really doing the will of God in persecuting the Christians?

On the road to Damascus that day, Jesus gave a clear and piercing answer to that question. He said that by persecuting the Christians, Saul was actually persecuting Him—the Son of God, the Lord of Lords, the long-awaited Messiah!

The primary spiritual lessons I learned from this reading are, first, that Jesus identified Himself so closely with His followers that whatever afflicted them afflicted Him! The sorrow of the disciples was His sorrow, and their pain was His pain. I understood this concept so much better after becoming a parent. Whatever hurt my child hurt me. When we begin to realize that whenever we suffer, Jesus suffers with us, we enter a whole new realm of closeness with Him.

The next lesson is that not all of Paul's education and religious training nor his intellect or the power, which had been granted to him by the priests and rulers of Jerusalem, could assure that he was, indeed, doing the will of God in his life. What made the difference was that He actually saw Jesus for himself and accepted Him as the Savior of his life. Only then did he receive his marching orders from the Lord and was assured that he was now truly doing the will of God.

Finally, after reading a few more verses down in this chapter, I saw how the Lord connected Saul to His church in Damascus. Ananias, a faithful believer, was sent by God to heal Saul from his blindness, to lay his hands on him so he could be filled with the Holy Spirit, and to baptize him. Then Saul spent several days with the believers in Damascus for fellowship and orientation to his new way of life. This reinforces the idea that, as Christians, we need each other. No person, even a great person, is an island. We are all an essential part of the body of Christ, as members of His church, and should band together to strengthen and encourage each other as we seek to fulfill the ministry God calls us to in this difficult world.

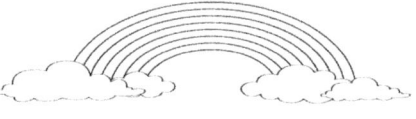

September 6

An Epiphany

"Then he said to them, 'You know how unlawful it is for a Jewish man to keep company with or go to one of another nation. But God has shown me that I should not call any man common or unclean'" (Acts 10:28).

The apostle Peter had just had a strange dream about a sheet coming down from heaven loaded with animals—including some which were considered unclean by the Jewish people. In fact, he had the same dream three times. In it, a voice told him to kill and eat the animals. As Peter was pondering what this unusual vision meant, three foreign men from Caesarea came looking for him at the house where he was staying. The Bible says that the Holy Spirit told him to go with these men, saying, "I have sent them" (Acts 10:20). When he talked with them, they shared a compelling story.

They had been sent to find Peter by a man named Cornelius. He was a centurion who feared God and had developed a good reputation among the Jewish people with whom he worked. Peter was even more surprised when they divulged that an angel had instructed Cornelius to invite Peter to his home to preach. It was then that the meaning of his strange dreams came to him. Obediently, he followed the men back to the home of Cornelius, where he found a house full of people waiting to listen to him talk about Jesus. It was then that he revealed to this group of Gentiles, in the words found in today's text, what God had taught him through his recent dreams.

The apostle was pleasantly surprised to find so many Gentiles gathered together who were so eager to hear the gospel of Jesus Christ. In Acts 10:34, 35, we find him reiterating this idea of God's acceptance of all people: "Then Peter opened *his* mouth and said: 'In truth I perceive that God shows no partiality. But in every nation whoever fears Him and works righteousness is accepted by Him.'"

Before he had finished his sermon that day, Peter saw the Holy Spirit be poured out upon the people who heard his words. Some Jewish folks who had come with Peter were amazed, but he asked, "Can anyone forbid water, that these should not be baptized who have received the Holy Spirit just as we *have*?" (Acts 10:47). It was an exciting day of ministry!

Unfortunately, upon his arrival in Jerusalem a few days later, the people in the church were not so happy about what they had heard about Peter rubbing shoulders with the Gentiles and even baptizing them! Patiently, Peter explained the whole story to them, starting with the dream the Lord had given him in order to break through his prejudice about who could be followers of Jesus. We pick up his defense in Acts 11:15–17, where he says,

And as I began to speak, the Holy Spirit fell upon them, as upon us at the beginning. Then I remembered the word of the Lord, how He said, 'John indeed baptized with water, but you shall be baptized with the Holy Spirit.' If therefore God gave them the same gift as *He gave* us when we believed on the Lord Jesus Christ, who was I that I could withstand God?

Suddenly, they were enlightened with the same epiphany that God had given Peter just a short time before. After a brief silence signaling a period of reflection, "...they glorified God, saying, 'Then God has also granted to the Gentiles repentance to life'" (Acts 11:18). Without this critical awakening, the disciples wouldn't have welcomed the new believers that were being converted from all parts of the world into the early Christian church, and the goals of Jesus' great commission could not have been accomplished. It is a good lesson for us. In order for God's work to prosper, we need to ask the Lord to break down all our walls of prejudice and separation to accept new believers just as Jesus has accepted us with open arms!

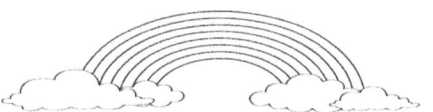

Holy Joy

"But they shook off the dust from their feet against them, and came to Iconium. And the disciples were filled with joy and with the Holy Spirit" (Acts 13:51, 52).

Acts 13 describes the evangelistic activities of Paul and Barnabas in the region of the city of Antioch. The Bible tells us that this was the area where Christ's followers were first called Christians (see Acts 11:26). As was their custom, these two disciples went into the synagogue on the Sabbath day to worship. They sat down and listened to the reading of the day, after which the rulers of the synagogue asked them if they had any words of exhortation to share with the people (see Acts 13:15). This was their chance to talk about Jesus, and they didn't have to be asked twice!

Paul launched into an historical outline of the way that God had worked with the Israelites through the years, proclaiming boldly that Jesus was the long-awaited Savior of Israel. He explained how the life, death, and resurrection of Jesus was a fulfillment of prophecy and that He had been sent from God to forgive His people of their sins. Their powerful preaching left an impact on the people that day, and on the following Sabbath, practically the whole city came out to hear what Paul and Barnabas had to say. The large crowd made the rulers of the synagogue envious, so they began to contradict and oppose the words that Paul was speaking. When their arguments became blasphemous, the two evangelists addressed them directly, saying, "It was necessary that the word of God should be spoken to you first; but since you reject it, and judge yourselves unworthy of everlasting life, behold, we turn to the Gentiles" (Acts 13:46).

When the Gentiles heard this, they were happy, and many of them received the messages that the two men preached gladly. In this way, the gospel of Jesus was spread throughout that region. In the meantime, however, the disgruntled Jews stirred up trouble for them with the leading and prominent people of the city in order to persecute Paul and Barnabas, eventually expelling them from that general area. But the seeds of the gospel had been planted there, and their preaching was bearing fruit in all who would listen. Thus, they followed the instructions the Lord had left with them, that whenever they were turned away, they should shake the dust off their feet and move on (see Matt. 10:14). They should have no regrets, no grudges, no discouragement or resentment. They were just to continue on their way to the next place of labor that the Lord led them to—happy to be able to spread the gospel to a whole array of others who might be willing to accept it!

A couple of summers when I was in college, I worked as a literature evangelist (also known as a colporteur). A group of us would go to an assigned territory each day. We pedaled religious books from door to door, and especially in the heat of summer, it could be a difficult job. It had its rewards when someone started a stimulating conversation regarding their spiritual journey or thanked us for coming or for praying for them. But it was hard to keep from being discouraged when someone slammed the door in our face, swore, or spoke harshly to us. It was also hard to keep working cheerfully after a long day of work with no sales because no sales meant no money earned for our college tuition.

So how were the apostles in the early church able to keep their courage up as well as maintaining their evangelistic zeal? Today's text tells us that they were filled with joy—holy joy—because they were filled with the Holy Spirit. They knew they were doing the important work that the Lord had assigned to them. Thus, although they were aware that not everyone would accept the gospel, they understood that it was their job to plant seeds wherever they went, leaving the harvest to God. They trusted that their labors would not be in vain, and they knew that the Lord would continue to sustain

them, strengthen them, and bless them as they sought to do His will. This is why, despite rejection, opposition, persecution, mistreatment, threats of violence, and trials of every kind, they were still able to shake off the difficulties of the past and press forward to continue their work—not moaning and complaining, but with joy, with singing, and with praise to God on their lips! What a lesson to us today to do less complaining and more praising, to maintain our courage as we strive to do God's work along the way, knowing that He will make Himself responsible for the results. Our job is not to worry and fret, but to ask God for that same gift of the Holy Spirit that the disciples enjoyed so that our countenances will also be radiant with joy—holy joy!

September 8

Unusual Prisoner

"And now I urge you to take heart, for there will be no loss of life among you, but only of the ship. For there stood by me this night an angel of the God to whom I belong and whom I serve, saying, 'Do not be afraid, Paul; you must be brought before Caesar; and indeed God has granted you all those who sail with you'" (Acts 27:22–24).

I love reading about the escapades of the apostle Paul. Being a risk-taker and someone who loves to travel and explore, I am challenged and inspired by his many missionary trips as well as his intrepid boldness in preaching the gospel and his unwavering sense of purpose, regardless of the circumstances in which he finds himself.

In this story, the Jews who didn't believe Jesus was the Messiah stirred up opposition against Paul. They sought to stop his powerful preaching by accusing him falsely and asking the governor to imprison him. After being imprisoned for several years in order to placate the Jewish leaders, a new governor named Festus came to the region. A while later, when King Agrippa came to visit, Festus sought council from him on what to do about Paul's case. One day they decided to give Paul an audience and listened while Paul not only eloquently defended himself but also appealed to the haughty rulers to accept Christ for themselves! A little later, while talking about what to do with Paul, they agreed that he had done nothing wrong. King Agrippa stated that if Paul had not appealed his case to Caesar, he might have been set free.

But, his imprisonment notwithstanding, God had a plan for Paul's life. He would continue to be a prophet, a preacher of the gospel, and an evangelist wherever he went. Even to the seat of the greatest power in the then-known world—to the Caesar in Rome! On the way there, however, he would witness to the other prisoners, to the people on the islands where they stopped along their voyage to Rome, and even to the sailors on the ship on which he was traveling. Did the fact that he was a prisoner even put a dent in Paul's courage or weaken his confidence that he was God's messenger to those around him? Not in the least!

At the outset, he prophesied that beginning their journey as late as they did was dangerous. When they disregarded his words and suffered through a terrible storm, he was the person who stepped up and encouraged them, saying that God had promised him that none of their lives would be lost! He was going to trial in front of Caesar, yet he was the one telling the captain, the sailors, and the other prisoners not to be afraid! When they saw him give thanks to God and eat, they were also encouraged to eat something, despite their dire circumstances, because Paul told them again that their lives would be spared, even though the ship would not. When the shipwreck occurred, the captain followed Paul's lead, and every man on the ship survived.

They discovered they were on an island called Malta. Here, too, Paul's ministry continued. First, when bitten by a poisonous snake while gathering fire wood, he simply shook the deadly animal off, and though the islanders expected him to die immediately, he suffered no ill effects. Then, when the father of Publius, the leading citizen of the island, got very sick, Paul prayed and laid hands on him, healing him. When the islanders saw Paul's power to heal, many others who were sick came to him and were also healed. What an unusual prisoner Paul was! In fact, the islanders thought that maybe he was a god—healing, preaching, and helping others, all along his journey. He cheerfully assured them that his power came from the one God of heaven.

When he finally arrived at his destination, the place where he would eventually lay down his life for the gospel, he met and talked with the Jews, preached to the Gentiles, and wrote letters of encouragement and admonition to the believers he had evangelized in various cities and towns throughout his life of ministry and service. Many of these letters became part of the New Testament and are still offering words of guidance and comfort for those of us who believe in Jesus today! Think of it! Centuries later, Paul's ministry is still blessing others and bearing fruit to the glory of God! Despite his circumstances, whether free or in chains, Paul kept living a fulfilling and adventurous life in the center of God's will! May the Lord help us to do the same.

Without Excuse

"For since the creation of the world His invisible attributes are clearly seen, being understood by the things that are made, even His eternal power and Godhead, so that they are without excuse, because, although they knew God, they did not glorify Him as God, nor were thankful, but became futile in their thoughts, and their foolish hearts were darkened. Professing to be wise, they became fools" (Romans 1:20–22).

know I've mentioned this before, but I just can't understand how anyone who has observed a glorious sunset, contemplated the vastness of the teaming seas, the grandeur of the majestic mountains, or even welcomed a newborn baby into this world could deny or doubt the existence of God. On the micro level, we study the intricacies of one human cell, and on the macro level, we gaze in awe at the mysteries of the universe on a clear, star-studded night.

Who else could have created such wonders as surround us on a daily basis than a very powerful and highly intelligent Designer? Who could have taught the geese their migration patterns, the salmon how to return to the rivers where they were spawned, or the squirrels to store up provisions for the winter? Consider the intricacies of a single snowflake, the glory of the bursting colors in a spring flower garden, or the miracle of germination from a small, hard apple seed, from which comes a lovely and fruitful apple tree! We could go on and on describing the undeniably amazing creations that only a Master Planner could have provided for our sustenance and enjoyment. His wondrous works also tell us of His love for us in that He didn't just accomplish the minimum for our survival but He also added flourishes that He knew would bring us pleasure and help us understand His care for us. Just a few examples would include that He produced an innumerable variety of plants and animals, supplied fragrances to the flowers and budding trees, and provided humans with built-in senses so that we could see, hear, taste, smell, and touch the marvelous objects of His creation.

All of these things should turn our hearts toward our Creator, but unfortunately, many of us have become so busy with the cares and occupations of our hectic lives that we don't take time to even notice the miracles of creation all around us, let alone stop to think about and thank the Supreme Maker of all things. The *SDA Bible Commentary* tells us that people do not have any excuse for not believing in God:

> The invisible things of God may be clearly perceived by the mind with the help of the created works of nature. Even though blighted by sin, the "things that are made" testify that One of infinite power created this earth. All around us we see abundant evidence of His goodness and love. Thus it is possible for even the heathen to recognize and acknowledge the power of the Creator. (*SDA Bible Commentary,* vol. 6, p. 478)

A few paragraphs later on the same page, it goes on to say, "The revelation of God through conscience and nature is sufficient to enlighten men as to the divine requirements. In the face of this revelation, they are without excuse for the non-performance of duty, that is, for their idolatry and for hindering the truth." A few quotes from page 479 in the *Bible Commentary* are also helpful in understanding today's passage:

> The unwillingness to honor God as the divine Creator was the real source of the darkened minds and abominable practices of the Gentiles.... Unwillingness to give thanks to God for His love and goodness toward men is one of the causes of corruption and idolatry. Ingratitude hardens the heart and leads men to forget the Being to whom they are unwilling

to express thankfulness. (*SDA Bible Commentary,* vol. 6, p. 479)

A few paragraphs down, it explains how humans who think they are wise actually become foolish once they reject God in their lives. "Men had sunk so deep in ignorance and sin that their minds had become dark and senseless, and they no longer perceived or understood the truth. To produce such darkness has ever been Satan's purpose..." (*Ibid.*).

Finally, we're told, "Salvation depends upon the right exercise and development of this power [the power of choice] in choosing to have faith in God and to obey His will" (*Ibid.*). What an admonition! If we choose to ignore or reject all the evidence that God has provided to us of His existence, we will stand without excuse on the coming day of judgment.

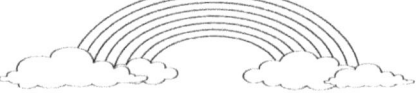

September 10

Common Ground

"For all have sinned and fall short of the glory of God, being justified freely by His grace through the redemption that is in Christ Jesus" (Romans 3:23, 24).

Recently, I was talking with a relative about how much easier it is to start up a conversation with a person with whom you have something in common. My husband is a good example of this. Coming from a Spanish-speaking country, every time he sees someone who looks like they might speak his native tongue, he greets them and

asks if they speak Spanish. If so, he launches into a friendly conversation about where they or their ancestors are from in Mexico, where he's from, if they know anyone in common, etc. The banter takes off from there. I can be shopping, and by the time I reunite with him ten or fifteen minutes later, I find him laughing and talking with a new friend as if they've known each other for years. In that amount of time, he's already learned all about their family, what they do for a living, their belief system, and on occasion, he has even shared some Spanish religious literature with them!

I have also felt the pull of having something in common with people I had not previously met. In my twenties, I agreed to go as a volunteer missionary to a college in northern Mexico and work there for one academic year. The first few weeks were difficult as I struggled with culture shock and homesickness. Only the ground and the sky seemed the same as what I was used to—everything in-between was different! The language, the customs, the people, the foods, the sights, the smells...you name it! It was like living on a different planet. As a result, whenever I saw an American who was speaking English, my immediate impulse was to rush up and hug them! Whatever other differences we had, they all melted away. Suddenly, I shared common ground with these previous strangers, making our conversations helpful and our brief encounters comfortable. I believe that's what our relationships and conversations with fellow Christians should look like, given we have all moved from the common ground of sin into the kingdom of the saved.

Today's passage reminds us of how much common ground we actually have with the people all around us—whether we know them or not. After all, we have all sinned and fallen short, in one way or another, from the glory of God—from representing Him correctly. These verses make it clear that we all start from a level playing field when it comes to salvation. Whether we are rich or poor, male or female, young or old, we all begin our walk with God as sinners. Thankfully, these texts also point out that we are all eligible to become justified and receive God's grace in order to experience "the redemption that is in Christ Jesus." What's more, we are told that He gives us His grace freely! We don't need to be wealthy or privileged in some special way to receive the blessing of His salvation. We don't even need to travel to some religious shrine or stand in long lines for an audience with Him.

So, how do we go from being sin-filled people to sinless people? How does this miracle of transformation take place? The Lord gives us the answer to this question in 1 John 1:9, where it says: "If we confess our sins, He is faithful and just to forgive us *our* sins and to cleanse us from all unrighteousness." What a wonderful promise! From God's perspective, no matter where we come from or whatever limitations we have, we are worthy to be saved! In fact, Jesus wanted us to be saved so much that He sacrificed His life in order to accomplish it! We only need to come to Him and ask that He forgive and justify us, covering our lives with His marvelous mercy and undeserved grace! But it doesn't stop there. As we continue to walk with Him, we need to continue to ask for His saving grace on a daily basis, until we walk with Him right into heaven, where we will enjoy common ground with all those who have been saved throughout eternity!

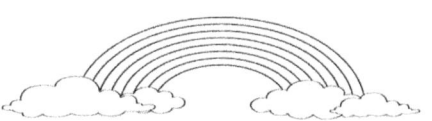

Newness of Life

"Therefore we were buried with Him through baptism into death, that just as Christ was raised from the dead by the glory of the Father, even so we also should walk in newness of life. For if we have been united together in the likeness of His death, certainly we also shall be in the likeness of His resurrection, knowing this, that our old man was crucified with Him, that the body of sin might be done away with, that we should no longer be slaves of sin. For he who has died has been freed from sin" (Romans 6:4–7).

Our passage for today is longer than usual because Paul does such a good job here at explaining how a sinner is transformed into the likeness of Christ. The subtitle for this chapter in my Bible is "Dead to Sin, Alive to God." There are three ideas in these texts that I'd like to unpack a bit. The first is the experience of baptism. Have you ever heard a person who had been recently baptized say, "I didn't feel any different after baptism as before," while others immediately begin living a life obviously touched by God? What makes the difference?

We know that the holy rite of baptism by itself does not hold any magical powers; it simply serves as a public symbol of a change that has taken place in the heart and mind of an individual. And what is that change? It's a decision and a determination to henceforth die to self and live for God. When we repent of our past sins and ask for the Holy Spirit to come in and take control of our lives, it is then that we begin walking in the newness of life described here. Some people are changed almost instantaneously while others simply begin a slow but consistently-advancing march toward godliness. In either case, if we believe by faith that our sinful, "old man" has died and been buried, it will be much easier to think of post-baptismal life as a new one,

lived through the power of the Holy Spirit as we continue to surrender to Jesus.

Unfortunately, some people don't understand that where there is little surrender, there is little power. It's as if they want the dead man who has been buried to keep raising his ugly head from the grave and controlling them even after they have started a new life. This will, of course, ultimately take them on a downward path toward perdition rather than the resurrected life journey that the Lord wants to give them.

This brings me to the topic of the resurrection of Jesus, which, although alluded to in a figurative sense here, can't help but remind us that as followers of Jesus, the day will come when all of us will be literally resurrected from the dead just as He was! This resurrection won't be to simply a new life here on earth but a glorious eternal life with Him in heaven! And it will be more than worth any dying to self that we have done here. The Lord has promised us this in 2 Corinthians 4:17, which assures us that "...our light affliction, which is but for a moment, is working for us a far more exceeding *and* eternal weight of glory."

Lastly, these texts give us the assurance that through God's power we will be able to overcome all of the sins that enslave us—from cruel addictions to long-held cultivated and inherited tendencies to evil. In our Bible reading for today, we are told in verse 6 that "our old man was crucified with *Him*, that the body of sin might be done away with, that we should no longer be slaves of sin." Then verse 7 presses the point home, saying, "For he who has died [to self] has been freed from sin" (brackets added). There are a couple of other verses in this same chapter that give us some additional guidance on how to start walking in newness of life. Romans 6:16 asks, "Do you not know that to whom you present yourselves slaves to obey, you are that one's slaves whom you obey, whether of sin *leading* to death, or of obedience *leading* to righteousness?" Then verse 13 sums it up: "And do not present your members *as* instruments of unrighteousness to sin, but present yourselves to God as being alive from the dead, and your members *as* instruments of righteousness to God."

September 12

It's All Good

"And we know that all things work together for good to those who love God, to those who are the called according to His *purpose" (Romans 8:28).*

Today we arrive at a very well-known and much-quoted verse by Christians. In fact, it has become a kind of mantra for some. I was one of those people…until life got a little rocky, and I went through some very difficult situations that I didn't understand When I asked God for answers for why certain things had happened—what was their purpose—I have to admit that I felt somewhat mad at Him when I didn't seem to get ready reasons for them. One of the advantages of age, however, is that looking back, it's possible to see how events that I once considered unacceptable have, at times, brought positive results of which I never could've dreamed. I have witnessed this phenomenon not only in my life but also in the lives of those around me.

Some examples I can cite include the painful change of schools in junior high that resulted in the forming of lifelong bonds with wonderful Christian friends; the relative who went to prison (where we thought his life would end), but he finally found the Lord and turned his life around; the divorce that brought conversion and compassion into a spiritually-dry life; unplanned or undesirable activities of every kind that eventually turned into life-changing events; the list goes on. Sometimes, as we reflect, we remember choices that we thought were mistakes but the Lord turned into ultimate blessings!

Does this mean that we will always get the answers we seek regarding why bad things happen to good people (including us)? Of course not! So, how do we come to believe this text that boldly proclaims that everything will ultimately work together for good in a Christian's life, apart from our own limited experiences? For one thing, I've found it helpful not to underestimate the power of reviewing our own past experiences to see how the Lord has intervened in our lives. Remembering these outcomes will give us the courage to keep trusting the Lord in the future, even when we pass through dark seasons. Importantly, our past experiences can also serve as an encouragement to others, which is why it's so important to share our testimonies of evidences of the Lord's hand working things out for our good with our fellow Christians.

It seems to me, though, that there are at least two other essential truths that will help us believe this promise. One is the firm belief that God is truly sovereign on this earth as well as in the entire universe which He created and sustains. And second, we need an unshakable trust in His character of fairness and infinite love. I believe that although we may not see everything work together for good here on this sinful planet during our lifetimes, at the end of earth's story, it will all make sense in the light of God's wisdom and grace.

Thus, as Christians, we will be able to declare, "It's all good." We will not say this in a Polyanna-ish way that makes light of what has happened or ignores the difficult passages in our lives; we will say it as a proclamation of confidence in God's goodness and gracious watchcare over His beloved children.

September 13

Living Sacrifices

"I beseech you therefore, brethren, by the mercies of God, that you present your bodies a living sacrifice, holy, acceptable to God, which is your reasonable service. And do not be conformed to this world, but be transformed by the renewing of your mind, that you may prove what is that good and acceptable and perfect will of God" (Romans 12:1, 2).

Generally, when reading this verse in the past, I have thought about presenting our bodies to God in the sense of giving up carnal sins, unhealthy practices, addictions, etc., in order to have a healthy existence in which to serve God better. And I still believe that is true.

Looking back at the Old Testament, however, I have come to realize that the Bible describes a variety of different kinds of offerings or sacrifices that humans can make, which still involve our bodies in some way. Monetary offerings, of course, are the ones mentioned most often, together with the offerings of bulls, sheep, goats, doves, etc., as part of the ceremonial laws followed in the ritual worship services of the Israelites. But according to Old Testament writers, testimonies of God's goodness, praises to His glory, and songs of thanksgiving are also considered as acceptable "sacrifices" or offerings to bring when we come together to worship the Lord. I'm convinced that these last three activities are ones we need to include more frequently in our modern worship services.

In the next section of this same chapter, Paul goes on to describe how Christians can serve God through their spiritual gifts as a way of becoming living sacrifices. While there are many kinds of spiritual gifts, some mentioned here are prophecy, ministry, teaching, exhortation, giving with liberality, leading diligently, and those who show mercy with cheerfulness.

In addition to specifically-mentioned gifts, Paul reminds us that simply behaving like a Christian can make us into living sacrifices. Since he outlines this better than I could, let's read what he says in verses 9-21:

Let love *be* without hypocrisy. Abhor what is evil. Cling to what is good. *Be* kindly affectionate to one another with brotherly love, in honor giving preference to one another; not lagging in diligence, fervent in spirit, serving the Lord; rejoicing in hope, patient in tribulation, continuing steadfastly in prayer; distributing to the needs of the saints, given to hospitality. Bless those who persecute you; bless and do not curse. Rejoice with those who rejoice, and weep with those who weep. Be of the same mind toward one another. Do not set your mind on high things, but associate with the humble. Do not be wise in your own opinion. Repay no one evil for evil. Have regard for good things in the sight of all men. If it is possible, as much as depends on you, live peaceably with all men. Beloved, do not avenge yourselves, but *rather* give place to wrath; for it is written, "Vengeance *is* Mine, I will repay," says the Lord. Therefore "If your enemy is hungry, feed him; if he is thirsty, give him a drink; for in so doing you will heap coals of fire on his head." Do not be overcome by evil, but overcome evil with good.

By giving many specific examples of the behavior the Lord expects from His saints, Paul leaves little doubt about how to live our lives as living sacrifices. All that's left is for us to ask the Lord for the grace and power to live up to His high and holy expectations.

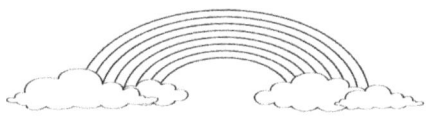

A Stumbling Block

"So then, each of us shall give account of himself to God. Therefore let us not judge one another anymore, but rather resolve this, not to put a stumbling block or a cause to fall in our brother's way" (Romans 14:12, 13).

The phrase "stumbling block" in this passage was interesting to me, so I looked up its origin on *Wikipedia*. This is what I found. "The origin of the metaphor is the prohibition of putting a stumbling block before the blind (Leviticus 19:14)." It also quotes *The International Standard Bible Encyclopedia* as saying, "The concept of a stumbling block was especially appropriate to a rocky land like Palestine, where stones and pebbles are plentiful on all the unpaved roads." The citations also include additional definitions, such as "snare for an enemy," "cause of moral stumbling," or "anything that leads to sin" (Wikipedia: The Free Encyclopedia, *https://www.wikipedia.org*, [accessed March 2022]).

In English, the connotation of this verb means to trip somebody up or to cause someone to sin. I found that this term appears twenty-nine times in the New Testament, and 1 Peter 2:8 uses two synonymous phrases: "a stone of stumbling" and "a rock of offense." I discovered that this term has been very commonly used by Jews, Protestants, and Catholics alike, and in modern times, it has even creeped into usage by the secular world.

So, now let's get practical. How does this text apply to the life of a Christian today? I have read that a Christian can become a stumbling block when he or she commits an evil act or does something that appears to be evil, knowing that it will lead others into sin or what they believe to be sin, like when

Paul said that he would not eat meat in front of fellow believers if it would cause others to stumble (see 1 Cor. 8:13). Digging deeper here, we come to understand that we can become a stumbling block by a behavior or even an attitude about something that leads another into sin or destructive behaviors or actions. Paul tells us that "when you thus sin against the brethren, and wound their weak conscience, you sin against Christ," and he further warns us that because of our decisions, some of our brethren could even perish (1 Cor. 8:11, 12) How important, then, that we pay attention to how our actions are influencing those around us. As parents, teachers, and church leaders, we have been trained to think about how our behaviors are affecting those under our charge, but here, we are reminded that each one of us, regardless of our position in life, is in some sense our brother's keeper and should try to leave footprints that others would be safe to follow.

As we learned in our mission training before going abroad, this can be tricky business if you have to live and work in different cultures. Just to provide one of many possible examples: in one part of the world, good Christians are required to wear wedding rings in order to signal their dedication to family life, while in another part, a church member can be denied any church office for wearing such a thing since it is considered jewelry. As most of us can attest, even in the same country, many issues arise that can cause contention, especially between one generation and the next. Things such as appropriate clothing, worship music preferences, movie-going, meat-eating, wine-bibbing, Sabbath-keeping practices...the list goes on and on. How can we deal with so many inconsistencies in the church and still strive not to be a stumbling block to others, or even, perhaps, allow their behavior to become a stumbling block to our own Christian walk?

Well, the Lord has tried to make it easier for us by admonishing us at the outset that we should not judge each other because "each of us shall give account of himself to God." To me, this means that my primary duty is to make sure that I am living according to His directives to the best of my ability, keeping my eyes on Jesus as opposed to those around me. I should know what I believe and why I believe it, while at the same time being sensitive to the context and culture in which I am living in order not to be a "rock of offense" to the people within the circle of my influence. This is no easy task since I will need to live with enough flexibility to be a blessing to people who are different, while at the same time being careful not to be hypocritical by living one way in one context and another way in a different context. I believe that these are some of the things we need to bring to the Lord to be worked out in our private devotional time with Him, asking for His wisdom to guide our actions in each situation so that we will not be a stumbling block to our sojourners along the way. May the Lord guide our steps.

September 15

Just Imagine

"But as it is written: 'Eye has not seen, nor ear heard, nor have entered into the heart of man the things which God has prepared for those who love Him'"
(1 Corinthians 2:9).

When I was a little girl, I can remember when the Disneyland Theme Park opened up in Anaheim, California. Soon, the kids in school who were privileged enough to have been some of the first ones whose parents had taken them there began to talk about its glories! We heard it was a magical place with rides, restaurants, parades, a castle, and famous Disney characters wandering around and taking pictures with the lucky children who attended this marvelous wonderland! Then, some of my relatives, including my own cousins, went! They could talk about nothing else for days. They brought back souvenirs, sang popular Disney songs, and exclaimed over the thrill it was to go on their favorite rides. It was better than they had even imagined it would be, and they couldn't wait to go back! Needless to say, their testimonials and excitement over the attractions they had experienced there thoroughly stirred up the active imaginations of those poor urchins who had yet to experience "The Happiest Place on Earth," as it was called. I was one of them. Since my parents could not afford to take the three of us children, we had to content ourselves with just dreaming about it. We could only imagine how great it would be to go there one day!

Then it happened! I had a cousin who was an only child, whose parents wanted to take her there, and they invited my little sister and I to go along to enjoy the place together with her! How joyfully we accepted their kind invitation! It was totally unanticipated, and nothing we had earned. How could we be so fortunate? As these thoughts danced around in our heads, we gladly started preparing for the big day. We could hardly wait for it! Finally, after what seemed like a very long time, the marvelous day arrived! And we were not disappointed! It was more spectacular than we had even dared to imagine!

I think of heaven in that same way. Prophets have told us about it; we have listened to testimonials of those who have gone before us; and we have been caught up in the excitement of our fellow believers. But how could we ever go to such a spectacular place? We can't afford it or earn it nor do we deserve it. It is so fabulous that our senses—our eyes and ears—can't even take it in. Nor has it "entered into the heart of man," meaning we can't even imagine in our mortal state how incredible and glorious the things—the attractions—will be in that heavenly "magic kingdom" that the Lord is preparing for those who love Him! Shockingly, not because of any merit on our part, but out of His own gracious generosity, we hear His unbelievable invitation come to us through the Scriptures, and we begin to prepare to go with Him. Although the wait seems long, the Bible assures us that our ultimate indescribably wonderful destination will be more than worth it. Heaven will not only be a place beyond our wildest imaginations but it will also be the dazzling kingdom where all of our dreams really do come true!

The *SDA Bible Commentary* brings out, however, that this declaration is also true on a here-and-now practical level. It promises us that some of the things the Lord has prepared for those who love Him are wonderful blessings that the Lord will fill our lives with even while we are still on this earth. The gospel gifts us with an ever-increasing knowledge of God and victory over the sin that has bound us in the past. It brings all that God provides for the welfare and happiness of His earthly children, including forgiveness, assurance of salvation, "justification and sanctification, the joy and peace that the grace of God imparts to the believer, and his ultimate deliverance from this evil world" (*SDA Bible Commentary*, vol. 6, p. 671). Indeed, the joy and peace the Lord gives to believers who put their trust in Him day-by-day is something that is unimaginable to non-believers who are wandering through this life in darkness and lost in a sense of hopelessness. This verse tells us that no matter how much time we might spend trying to imagine the glories of heaven, our estimations will never even be close to the real thing. But praise God that He begins to give us a foretaste of the many benefits of His future, glorious kingdom even now!

Such Were Some of You

"Do you not know that the unrighteous will not inherit the kingdom of God? Do not be deceived. Neither fornicators, nor idolaters, nor adulterers, nor homosexuals, nor sodomites, nor thieves, nor covetous, nor drunkards, nor revilers, nor extortioners will inherit the kingdom of God. And such were some of you. But you were washed, but you were sanctified, but you were justified in the name of the Lord Jesus and by the Spirit of our God" (1 Corinthians 6:9–11).

I'd like to reflect upon this passage from three points of view. First, from the apostle Paul's. Here, Paul is making the point, in no uncertain terms, that active sinners will not go to heaven. He wants to make it very clear to the new believers that they should not be continuing to practice the behaviors he has listed here once they have made a decision to follow Jesus. Becoming a Christian should create a marked change in how those who bear the name of Christ live. Paul wants them to understand that salvation is not cheap grace. It requires giving up those things that are not pleasing to God, and instead, through His power, beginning to walk in "newness of life" (see Rom. 6:4).

Then, from the standpoint of a new believer, I think these words would give them great encouragement and hope, while at the same time reminding them about activities that were no longer acceptable for people who claimed to be citizens of the kingdom of God. Just think of the joy of the new believer upon realizing that no matter how black the sins were or whatever lifestyle was practiced before conversion, by the acceptance of Jesus as his or her Savior, he or she was now a new person in Christ. In verse 11, Paul assures them of this, saying "But you were washed, but you were sanctified, but

you were justified in the name of the Lord Jesus and by the Spirit of our God." What a wonderful affirmation to them of God's transforming power!

The third perspective I'd like to share regarding today's passage brings us to modern-day Christians. Not to those who are called "new believers," but to those of us who could be identified as "old believers," if you will. Sometimes, it seems that we take on an air of pride and become judgmental about who the Lord will allow to become one of His followers. I have heard some of this tribe declare, for example, that a person who once practiced a homosexual lifestyle could never be saved. Obviously, that's not what Paul is telling us. In fact he says, "Such were some of you." It is because of this critical phrase that my husband, as a prison chaplain, can continue working for the salvation of thieves and extortioners as well as other inmates who have committed every crime imaginable.

Paul addresses sinners of every kind, who have now repented and been washed by the transforming grace of the Lord, as people called to be saints, and members of the marvelous kingdom of God! There is hope of salvation for everyone because Jesus says "whosoever will" may come (see Rev. 22:17, KJV). Thus, I have concluded that we should withhold our judgment of those we consider as unredeemable and wait to witness the miracles that God will perform in lives submitted to Him. In the meantime, I think we would do well to ask ourselves if there are any behaviors here that we have not completely eradicated from our own lives, such as coveting (wanting things that belong to others) or reviling (harshly criticizing others in anger). We need to ask the Lord to give us the victory over these things so that all of us who name the powerful name of Jesus will be able to stand together, faultless and sanctified, on the sea of glass one day soon!

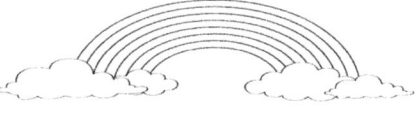

September 17

For Our Admonition

"Now all these things happened to them as examples, and they were written for our admonition, upon whom the ends of the ages have come. Therefore let him who thinks he stands take heed lest he fall. No temptation has overtaken you except such as is common to man; but God is faithful, who will not allow you to be tempted beyond what you are able, but with the temptation will also make the way of escape, that you may be able to bear it" (1 Corinthians 10:11–13).

As a child, my father required all of his children to memorize verse 13 of the above passage so that we could lean upon it whenever we were tempted to engage in spiritually detrimental behaviors throughout our lives. Looking at it today, I still see it as a precious promise, but I appreciate it as one made even stronger because of the context in which it is found.

In this chapter, the apostle Paul is preaching to new Jewish believers in the city of Corinth, a place known for a number of wicked practices, including idolatry and immorality of every kind. He knew these Christians would face many temptations. So, before uttering the promise that God would help them to overcome whatever they would have to face in the future, he reminded them of the past. That is, what had happened to the Israelites when, turning their backs upon God's provision and protection and ignoring the marvelous miracles He had done on their behalf, they continued lusting after things that were attractive to their carnal natures. As a result, most of them died before they ever saw the beautiful land of Canaan.

So, why was Paul referring to this unsuccessful history of their forefathers anyway? And why had Moses written it all down? How could a story of failure encourage them to live a more holy life? Because, as Paul explained, it was all recorded for their admonition—to provide examples of what they shouldn't do. If they would learn from the mistakes their ancestors had made in the past, their gracious Lord hoped they would not repeat them.

In addition, Paul gave them another helpful piece of instruction on how to avoid temptations. When they were doing well, it was important for them not to become too proud of themselves, to the point they forgot to depend upon the Lord. Many stories in the Old Testament have taught us that just when a person starts thinking that he or she is a pretty good individual, the next thing that happens is he or she has fallen into temptation, and the resulting sins have disrupted his or her walk with God. Some, of course, have even been eternally lost. No wonder the Lord is doing everything He can to save those who confess Him as their Savior.

Paul also encourages the new proselytes by telling them not to be dismayed when confronted by temptation because it is a normal part of the Christian's battle against evil. Therefore, they should know that these struggles are common to all those who are daily striving to serve the Lord to the best of their ability. They can take heart in the assurance of this beautiful promise Paul shares with them. When they ask for the Lord's help in these times of need, He will make a "way of escape." In other words, He will give them the victory!

As we read these words today, as people even closer to being those "upon whom the ends of the ages have come," we are privileged to benefit from the same admonitions that Paul shared with the ancient believers in Christ. After all, as we realize that the Lord has preserved the Scriptures until these last days precisely to assist us in our Christian walk, we can be blessed just as Paul's audience was in the early days of the Christian movement.

Thank you, Lord, for providing all this valuable information "for our admonition." May we heed it, both for our salvation and for Your glory!

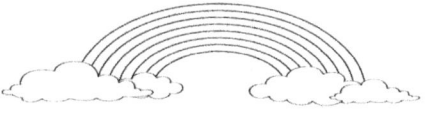

September 18

Unity in Diversity

"There are diversities of gifts, but the same Spirit. There are differences of ministries, but the same Lord. And there are diversities of activities, but it is the same God who works all in all" (1 Corinthians 12:4–6).

I love this chapter because it introduces the metaphor of how the Christian church can be compared to the body of Christ. Although we are all different in so many ways—how we look, think, talk, and live—Paul here declares that we can still achieve unity as members of God's church. How can this be when we come from different cultures, races, family histories, language groups, genders, social and educational levels, generations, and diverse life experiences? It seems impossible! But as the angel told Mary when she received the news that she would become the mother of Jesus, "For with God nothing will be impossible" (Luke 1:37).

Of course, nobody said it would be easy! But I believe today's verses can certainly help us get started in moving out of our comfort zones and expanding our thinking in ways we never would have done on our own before becoming Christians. After all, it is obvious from nature that the Lord loves diversity, or He would never have made so many amazing varieties of flowers, trees, animals, fish and birds! Let's just start by looking at flowers, for instance. Not only do they display various shapes and sizes but they also come in a riot of bright colors, have different fragrances, and bloom according to their own internal schedules. By this and a thousand other examples in God's creation, we have evidence that there is nothing small, limited, or boring about God's character, creativity, or thinking! His mercy is wide; His power reaches beyond the heavens; and His love is deep! Why wouldn't He want His diverse children to reach out and witness in creative ways to the other diverse people that He wants to save throughout the world?

So, verse 4 tells us that the Spirit of God has given diverse gifts to the individuals in His church. Later in this chapter, Paul goes on to list what some of those spiritual gifts are: preaching, teaching, prophesying, healing, helps, performing miracles of various kinds, administration, etc. Then he discusses

how each one is needed. It's important that each person exercises his or her gifts to the best of his or her ability—each individual must do his or her part. Paul then makes the comparison, beautifully explaining that just as each part, even the small or hidden parts of the body, must work efficiently in order for the body to be healthy, so each church member must use his or her gifts as well as they can in order for the church to function smoothly and effectively.

Verse 5 goes on to say that although we are going about ministry in a variety of ways, we are still serving the same Lord. This means that just inviting people to church or holding evangelistic meetings like we've done so often in the past is not the only kind of ministry that will bring people to the Lord. I think of the story of H.M.S. Richards Sr., who decided back in the mid-1900s to begin a radio ministry. When he started, he got a lot of criticism from the brethren for his crazy idea of reaching people over the air waves—especially through an instrument so worldly as the radio! But his ministry was successful and has been responsible for bringing thousands of new believers into the church through all the years since then! Nowadays, we use a plethora of media to evangelize an amazing array of people groups, including individual hand-held radios, television programs on networks which span the globe, computer Bible study and interactive programs, CDs, DVDs, podcasts, sermons posted on YouTube, and all the other forms of social media that have been invented over the last decade or two. We now have ministries designed to reach every kindred, tribe, language, and people group, all with the goal of preparing them for the Lord's second advent, in order to fulfill the great commission He gave us at His first advent.

Finally, verse 6 informs us that the Lord will work through many different kinds of activities to draw people to Himself. Yes, He will continue to bless the more traditional preaching and teaching activities of the church, but we can also reach people through music, health lectures, language instruction, youth socials, visitation programs, community service projects, and the list goes on...as far as our individual God-given creativity can take us!

So, where does the unity part come in? To my way of thinking, two things will help us get there. First, we have to adopt not only tolerance for differences but also try to practice the open-minded, open-hearted, gracious, and charitable traits of our Savior as we work side-by-side. And second, we need to realize that we are all on the same team, striving to reach the same goal of bringing as many people to the Lord as possible, even though we may do it in a different way than our brothers and sisters. Unity in diversity—that is how we will get the job done!

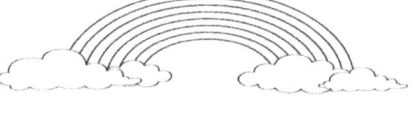

September 19

Clanging Cymbals

"Though I speak with the tongues of men and of angels, but have not love, I have become sounding brass or a clanging cymbal. And though I have the gift of prophecy, and understand all mysteries and all knowledge, and though I have all faith, so that I could remove mountains, but have not love, I am nothing" (1 Corinthians 13:1, 2).

This chapter is one of the most well-known and most often quoted of any found in the Christian Bible. As a child, I understood love because of the care of my parents. As a young person, I have to admit, my view of love became colored by all the stories and expectations surrounding romantic relationships. Later, as a parent, I understood better the sacrificial aspects of love. Now, however, after living a full life and observing human interactions for roughly

seven decades, I have a little different perspective. Obviously, I still believe that God's love for us is beyond our understanding and unchangeable, but I have come to see the warm glow of human love through the revealing prism of how people treat the old, the weak, and the poor as well as their own family members behind closed doors. This, to me, has become the defining factor, the gold standard, if you will, identifying those whose character is saturated with divine love as opposed to those who are only play-acting as Christians.

I'm sure you have known people and maybe even been one yourself at times in your life who can readily pray in public and say all the right words in church or some other religious setting. Perhaps they have studied the Scriptures for years, have an extensive knowledge of biblical history and literature, and are well-respected as spiritual leaders in their community, yet their words and actions seem somehow dry and automatized instead of being infused with light and the power of God's love. Upon observation, it becomes clear over time that their motives are based on self-interest rather than what might be best for those around them. And in an unguarded moment, angry words may slip out, tinged with underlying malice or bitterness.

Thus, we find two basic groups in Christian circles—those who are making beautiful heavenly music in the world simply by their presence and those who are merely making unharmonious noise within their spheres of influence. In trying to tease out in more specific terms just how these two groups might look in their everyday interactions with others, I came up with this list, for starters:

Clanging Cymbals' Typical Activities

- Always wanting to be first or get the biggest or best of anything
- In constant competition with others in order to feel superior
- Showing no patience with anyone not willing to match their pace in life
- Lack of ability to take time to listen to others (including frequently interrupting them)
- Lack of caring for others' physical limitations or health needs
- Lack of showing any interest in the activities or projects of others
- Exhibiting a spirit of criticism or sarcasm
- Using harsh and unkind words (including "put-downs")
- Frequently expressing negativity or rudely arguing with others
- Displaying bouts of uncontrolled anger
- Manifesting a countenance of discontent or an aura of unhappiness

Music Makers' (True Lovers') Typical Activities

- Being patient with those who move at a slower pace
- Being courteous by putting others first
- Taking time to listen to the thoughts and concerns of others
- Taking interest in the hobbies, activities, or projects of others
- Showing sympathy for those with physical limitations
- Being gentle in their interactions with others
- Rendering tender touches to family members
- Giving words of encouragement to others
- Speaking kind and loving words (including terms of endearment)
- Showing unselfishness in meeting the needs of others (with time, money, etc.)
- Manifesting a smiling countenance with a pleasant and peaceful influence

I'm sure you can think of more—both negative and positive—activities that reveal whether we are spreading God's love to those around us or just fooling ourselves when we claim to be Christians. The point is that we need to stop and take inventory of ourselves on occasion, rather than just rushing through life without being mindful of whether we are really representing God or not. May the Lord help us to truly understand and practice His love so that we can become more than just "clanging cymbals" to the world around us.

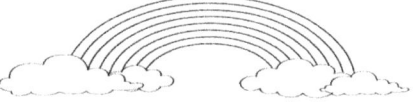

September 20

Incorruptible

"Behold, I tell you a mystery: We shall not all sleep, but we shall all be changed—in a moment, in the twinkling of an eye, at the last trumpet. For the trumpet will sound, and the dead will be raised incorruptible, and we shall be changed. For this corruptible must put on incorruption, and this mortal must put on immortality" (1 Corinthians 15:51–53).

This passage, which is often read at Christian funerals, is one I love to dwell upon. Can't you just imagine the sound of trumpets piercing through the air, the shouts of victory by those who "are alive *and* remain" (1 Thess. 4:17), and the expressions of wonder and praise spilling forth from those who are coming up from the grave with new and glorious bodies?! What a sight to behold! Better yet, what an experience to live!

Since the word "incorruptible" is not one I use frequently, I looked it up on Google to get a better grasp of its meaning. The first meaning I found dealt more with the physical aspects of things—in this case, that would be our physical bodies. The definitions here included "not susceptible to corruption, death, or decay, everlasting, not marred or impaired, imperishable, indestructible, and perpetual." When reading these words, I couldn't help but think of some of the comic book heroes with conjured up superpowers that are so popular in today's media culture. At that time, our God will infuse us—you and me—with the true superpower of being indestructible! Not only that but our bodies will become eternal—"this mortal *must* put on immortality!"

In addition, our new bodies will not carry any of the impairments or limitations that plagued us during our lives here on earth. Just think of it! This means that none of us will ever have to deal with cataracts or wear glasses again! We will be able to throw away forever our hearing aids, our crutches, our wheelchairs, and any other assistive devices we have had to depend on during our sojourn on earth. My mother, who contracted polio as a child, will never limp again. People with deformities of every kind as well as those who bear deep emotional and mental scars will suddenly be able to leave all of their sin-caused ailments and maladies behind forever, as they ascend into heaven, clothed now in a new and perfect body, gifted them by their loving Savior.

But Google didn't stop with the first definition. It continued on with one related to the inside qualities of a person. Listen to this host of synonyms for the word "incorruptible:"

> Above suspicion, scrupulous, trustworthy, incapable of being bribed or morally corrupted, just, loyal, moral, unchangeably honest, ethical, virtuous, irreproachable, honorable, righteous, blameless, guiltless, principled, and finally, a person of integrity with high moral values that cannot be altered when tested.

Wow! What a list! What will it be like walking around in heaven with people who possess these incredible character traits? As Christians, we have worked on them on earth, trying to become more like our Lord day-by-day. But now, He will erase all of our deficiencies, clothing us with His spotless and pure robe of righteousness. Then we will be sealed forever as true children of God. Will these robes be something we can see externally, like the garments of light worn by Adam and Eve before the fall or will they be simply an internal outshining of light, like the face of Moses after he descended from Mt. Sinai? We don't know. But we do know "that we shall be like Him, for we shall see Him as He is" (1 John 3:2).

And so, my desire is to be made incorruptible—inside and out—at the Lord's second coming. And we know that it is sooner now than "when we *first* believed" (Rom. 13:11). Thus, I join with the apostle John in his heartfelt prayer recorded in Revelation 22:20: "Even so, come, Lord Jesus!"

Not in Vain

"But thanks be to God, who gives us the victory through our Lord Jesus Christ. Therefore, my beloved brethren, be steadfast, immovable, always abounding in the work of the Lord, knowing that your labor is not in vain in the Lord" (1 Corinthians 15:57, 58).

Recently, I heard a sermon on this topic, which included a story about a missionary who went to serve in a remote part of Africa. He and his young wife worked very hard trying to win over the people of a certain village to Christianity. Despite their arduous and sacrificial efforts, the village largely rejected them, making them live outside their boundaries. But once a week, the chief did allow a young boy to visit the couple in order to sell them eggs. The wife decided that if this was the only person she could talk to about Jesus, she would make the best of it. So every week during his "sales visit," she would tell the youngster as much as she could about Jesus, teaching him songs and how to pray along the way.

Then disaster struck. The couple, who by that time had a child of their own, both came down with malaria. When his wife died, the young missionary gave his daughter to another missionary family to raise and left Africa for the United States in bitterness and despair, never wanting to hear anything about Christianity again. It so happened, however, that the missionary family who had adopted his daughter for him also ended up in the United States after a number of years. Growing up in a Christian home, the daughter, now a young woman, read an article one day about a village in Africa that had been almost entirely converted to Christianity and even started a Christian school—which she discovered had been named after her birth mother!

It turned out that the young egg salesman her mother had so faithfully taught about Jesus had not only become a Christian himself but had persuaded the majority of the members of his tribe to become Christians as well! Eagerly, the daughter searched for her birth father to share the wonderful news of the results of his family's labors during their difficult and painful time in the mission field! But the father, now old and sick, did not wish for his daughter to contact him. When the persistent young lady refused to give up, the father finally agreed to a short visit. It was then, in joy, that she shared the article about the amazing results of a young missionary family's work—their very own family's work, as it turned out, in that far-flung corner of the world! And because of the Christian school founded by their first strong, young convert, people in that area were still coming to Christ! By the time she told him that the school had even been named after her mother, in love and appreciation for the first missionaries who had served in their region, tears were streaming down the old man's face. "And so, father," she exclaimed, "I just had to find you while you were still alive to let you know that the arduous labors of you and mother were not in vain! People are still coming to the Lord because of your sacrifices!"

Having served in the mission field with my own family, this story strikes a chord in my heart. It is comforting to know that our labors are not in vain in the Lord, and that by His grace and providences, they will bear eternal fruit. What a comfort! And also a blessed encouragement—to continue to remain steadfast, "always abounding in the work of the Lord." Sometimes we, who don't see the end from the beginning, are tempted to get discouraged when our efforts do not seem to be appreciated or when we don't see some kind of immediate results. But when we are serving the Lord, based upon the principles of His eternal word, He gives us this promise: "My word...shall not return to Me void, but it shall accomplish what I please, and it shall prosper *in the thing* for which I sent it" (Isa. 55:11). Coming back to today's verses, verse 57 assures us that we can thank God in advance because He always "gives us the victory through our Lord Jesus Christ." Even though, at times, it looks like we're losing, if we're trusting in Him and His word as we go about our daily tasks—whether at home, the workplace, at church, at school, or abroad—we can be assured that we are on the winning team! Take heart! Our labors are not in vain!

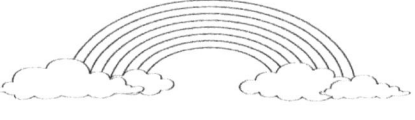

September 22

Sharing Comfort

"Blessed be the God and Father of our Lord Jesus Christ, the Father of mercies and God of all comfort, who comforts us in all our tribulation, that we may be able to comfort those who are in any trouble, with the comfort with which we ourselves are comforted by God" (2 Corinthians 1:3, 4).

A few days ago, I watched a religious program on television where a young woman shared the testimony of her difficult and painful journey after losing her first baby at childbirth. She shared that she had been able to hold the child, whom they had already named, for several hours before having to say goodbye for good and leaving it in the hospital. Her grief was so overwhelming that she couldn't see a path forward and was convinced that she would never know joy again. Subsequently, about six months later, she discovered that she was pregnant again, and although she was terrified every day that she would lose this baby as well, she and her husband earnestly prayed that the Lord would give them the courage and strength to move through the second pregnancy safely, one day at a time.

Finally, after the successful birth of this child, she said she began to feel joy again. Now she has a total of three healthy children. She has never forgotten her first baby and believes her whole family will be able to meet and live with him forever in heaven. Although it was still hard for her to talk about, she had decided to share her experience in the hope that it might give someone going through a similar dark valley the courage and stamina to hold on to their faith in God. She wanted others in despair to know that they could regain their happiness and sense of purpose in life, too, because our merciful God not only suffers with us but comforts and heals us, binding up all our wounds!

To me, this woman's testimony is a perfect example of the meaning of today's passage. Have you suffered some terrible tragedy in your life? Have you leaned hard on God through the experience and discovered He has graciously assisted you to the other side of your grief and pain? Not only, that but many of us have unexpectedly discovered that we can now be even better witnesses of His grace and glory, especially to those who are struggling with adverse circumstances similar to what we've gone through, whether it's the death of a loved one, divorce, loss of a job, a diagnosis of cancer or some other debilitating disease, or perhaps financial ruin—the list goes on. But, if in looking back, you recognize the comfort, help, and providence of God in bringing you through it, share your experience with others. This is not to brag or suggest you know all the answers, but to simply and humbly tell them how the Lord has helped you. Who knows? Only a few words from you could be just the encouragement they need to get over the hump, pointing them to the Lord and giving them the strength and hope they need to move forward toward a brighter day.

I have lived on both sides of this equation—sometimes being the one who received the help and encouragement and sometimes being the one who provided the help and encouragement, so I can attest to the fact that it's a blessing to participate in this authentic and powerful interaction, regardless of which side you find yourself on. In fact, this may be some of the greatest evangelistic work of our lifetime. May the Lord teach us how to gently comfort those in tribulation, as the "God of all comfort" has graciously comforted us!

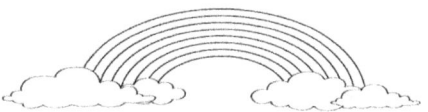

Fragrance

"Now thanks be to God who always leads us in triumph in Christ, and through us diffuses the fragrance of His knowledge in every place. For we are to God the fragrance of Christ among those who are being saved and among those who are perishing" (2 Corinthians 2:14, 15).

Have you ever walked into a room where you were silently greeted by a lovely fragrance? Perhaps it was created by air freshener, a scented candle, someone's perfume, or the subtle whisp of scent from a bouquet of fresh flowers. In any case, unless you are allergic to such things, your senses generally lull you into a calm and pleasant reaction, making you glad you came to visit this place.

Sometimes a sweet-smelling aroma emanates from a person. If the person wears the same fragrance often enough, it can become their signature scent, to the point that others always think of them when they perceive that particular smell. For instance, I can remember a friend of our family who often needed a ride to various activities. Whenever she entered our car, her perfume immediately diffused throughout the car's interior. My daughter always thinks of her second-grade teacher whenever she smells a certain Estée Lauder perfume, and my son-in-law connects me with the scent of a specific brand of hairspray that I frequently use. It's great when the smell people associate us with is a pleasant one. It is not so great, however, if they begin to identify us as individuals with an unpleasant odor—such as bad breath, urine, or body odor.

The interesting thing, though, is that sometimes we aren't even aware of what other people are experiencing in our presence. We may have become so used to a given fragrance—or smell—that we're oblivious to it. The best personal example of this I can recall happened when I was a freshman in college. One day when I was playing some sport in the gym, I sat down to rest a minute next to a young man about my age. Imagine my chagrin when he started up a friendly conversation by asking, "Do you use Noxema?"

"Yes," I answered, surprised that a perfect stranger would know such a thing about how I washed my face in the morning. "Why do you ask?"

"Oh," he replied, "because my sister uses it, and you smell just like her." He said it kindly enough and then innocently bounded off to continue his game, but I immediately changed my morning skin care routine. Without even being aware of it, I had been broadcasting something about my personal life. I decided I definitely didn't want to be known around campus as the girl who diffused the medicinal smell of Noxema wherever she went! Today, my signature scent is a lovely perfume called *L'air du Temps*.

This passage is a strong reminder that, whether we are aware of it or not, we all have an influence on those with whom we interact. Notice that the text enjoins us as Christians to spread the knowledge of God and the "fragrance of Christ" to those among us "who are being saved," as well as to "those who are perishing." This means both fellow-believers and non-believers, folks in the church and out of the church. People hear our words; they watch our gestures; they measure our actions, all to come to a conclusion about what kind of a person we are. Are we authentic or hypocritical? Can they trust us to become a loyal friend, a dependable co-worker, a true follower of Jesus? Do we live up to our professions of faith, serving as a true sweet-smelling savor for God? Or do we leave the foul-smelling stench of selfishness and sinfulness wherever we go?

I'm sure you've heard the saying, "Some people bring happiness when they come; others when they go!" I believe we all need to take stock occasionally, as objectively as possible (perhaps with some input from those around us), on what kind of fragrance we are leaving behind. What example? What influence? What legacy? Is our Christian scent so strong it overpowers people, making them want to flee? Or is it so weak that nobody can sense our message? May the Lord help us to develop our own appropriate signature scent. One that will truly represent our gracious Lord, drawing others closer to Him by the sweet fragrance we diffuse wherever we go.

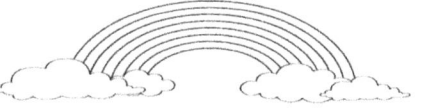

September 24

Liberty

"Now the Lord is the Spirit; and where the Spirit of the Lord is, there is liberty" (2 Corinthians 3:17).

When I was a little girl, my father was in the Air Force, and as I've mentioned before, we lived on a military base. Even though we were fairly isolated from the rest of the world, since the base was situated out in the middle of the Arizona desert, I have some very positive recollections of our life there. Our community had three big swimming pools with diving boards, where we spent many hot summer afternoons cooling off. It also had its own theater, store, and large lawns where the "military brats" (as some people called us) could play with the children of other military families. The base also boasted its own medical clinic, which is where my father worked.

Looking back, one of my best memories of living in such a place was enjoying the marvelous marching bands that would parade around on holidays, loudly filling the air with patriotic Souza marches, much to everyone's enjoyment! In that environment I remember feeling safe and secure as a child, fortunate to be living where the community's camaraderie, solidarity, and patriotism were palpable. At the same time, I was taught to honor those who had sacrificed their lives so that the rest of us could live so freely and happily and got used to seeing slogans posted around the base like, "All gave some, some gave all" and "Freedom isn't free."

It occurs to me now that the same thing is true for those of us who are Christians. Someone else—in this case our Lord and Savior—sacrificed everything in order that we might be privileged to live our lives in freedom and happiness. What has He freed us from? Some examples include sinfulness, addictions, guilt, fear of death and what lies beyond it, hopelessness, and lives without purpose. Not only that but Jesus has given us freedom of choice, which He never violates, so that we can choose each day whether we want to be part of the special community of people who will faithfully and joyfully serve Him or not.

It always impresses me that the Lord created us with free will, even though it meant that we might choose to use this gift to turn away from Him. But this fact reinforces for us the undeniable truth that true love can never be forced. People must always be able to freely choose who they will love. You've probably heard the old adage that goes something like this: "Satan's kingdom is based on the love of power, but God's kingdom is based on the power of love." Thus, wherever we see people being forced against their will into obedience or compliance with religious practices, regulations, or edicts, we are able to discern which spirit is at work

in that situation, and it is not of heavenly origin. For where "the Spirit of the Lord *is*, there *is* liberty."

So, what are the implications for us here? First, I feel a debt of gratitude to Jesus for entrusting me with the ability to freely choose Him as my Redeemer. I also thank Him for freeing me from the slavery of sin and its rueful effects, not only in this life but throughout the eternal life to come. What's more, I realize that I need to be more Christ-like in how I treat those around me. Folks don't have to think, feel, or do everything the way I do. They have the right to exercise their own free voluntary will.

When it comes to being a parent or teacher, it is our job to "train up a child in the way he should go" (Prov. 22:6), while striving to model the graciousness of God in the process. I can instruct them, guide them, and set boundaries for them, and yes, even discipline them—in a way that is appropriate to their error and in accordance with their particular stage of development. However, I must remember to always emphasize that they have a choice to make regarding their own behavior, and each choice will result in either positive or negative consequences not only for them but also for the people around them. Suffice it to say that whole books have been written on this topic. The point is that, regardless of a person's age or station in life, we need to respect their God-given power of choice. Let freedom ring!

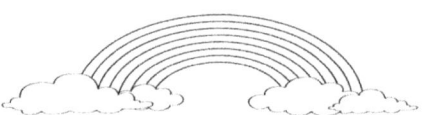

𝓑linded

"But even if our gospel is veiled, it is veiled to those who are perishing, whose minds the god of this age has blinded, who do not believe, lest the light of the gospel of the glory of Christ, who is the image of God, should shine on them" (2 Corinthians 4:3, 4).

How close have you ever come to being literally blinded? Many of us have worn corrective lenses to improve our vision over the years. And I have often wondered what life would have been like if glasses were never invented—perish the thought! Many very intelligent people would never have been able to read, write, invent, or make the myriad other contributions they have for society over the years. Recently, I underwent a cataract surgery that was unsuccessful, leaving my vision impaired rather than improved. It gave me a whole new appreciation for the blessing of clear sight!

Today's passage talks about spiritual blindness. It says people's minds have been blinded by "the god of this age," preventing them from receiving "the light of the gospel" of Christ. Some folks are so busy, weighed down by their responsibilities and the cares of this life, that they don't have time to even think about spiritual realities. They have developed a blind spot when it comes to the role that religion might play in their lives. Others are so focused only on themselves and their personal goals and gains that they have something called tunnel vision. They only see what's straight in front of them, losing sight of the needs of others or the call of God on their lives or even that there is such a thing as eternity to consider. Earthly thoughts and activities have totally obscured their spiritual vision. While this loss of sight

may have occurred almost accidentally on the part of some people, others actually choose not to believe. They willfully let their opportunities to know God slip between their fingers, rejecting the promptings of the Holy Spirit until it is too late. Way back in the 1500s, a man by the name of John Heywood coined this phrase: "There are none so blind as those who will not see." In Matthew 13, Jesus talks with His disciples about people who are willingly blind, saying that they have eyes but do not see (see Matt. 13:15). They have made a fatal choice.

Unfortunately, even as confessed Christians, we sometimes discover, especially if we are trying to grow more like Christ, that we still have a few blind spots. How can we improve our spiritual eyesight? In John 9:25, we find this testimony from the man who was born blind but was healed when He met Jesus. When the pharisees questioned him about the miracle he had experienced, he simply declared: "One thing I know: that though I was blind, now I see."

The good news is that Jesus wants to do the same thing for us. In talking to the last-day church, He describes our current spiritual condition, including blindness, of which we are not even fully aware. His counsel, therefore, is that we buy from Him "eye salve, that you may see" (Rev. 3:17, 18). He asks us to come to Him in order to cure our spiritual blindness. He will help us see not only our true condition but also the efficacy and glory of His salvation for our souls. Our earthly blinders will be removed, and we will begin to see things from God's wide perspective instead of our narrow and selfish point of view. In light of these offered improvements to our visual acuity, let our daily cry be, "Lord, be Thou my vision!"

September 26

The Inward Man

"Therefore we do not lose heart. Even though our outward man is perishing, yet the inward man is being renewed day by day. For our light affliction, which is but for a moment, is working for us a far more exceeding and eternal weight of glory, while we do not look at the things which are seen, but at the things which are not seen. For the things which are seen are temporary, but the things which are not seen are eternal" (2 Corinthians 4:16–18).

We have a lot to unpack with this passage. It builds on our topic of spiritual vision from yesterday but with a little different slant. In these verses, the emphasis is on what's happening in the "inward man" of an individual—the part deep inside us, where only we and God can see what's really happening. This has to do with our character development and things such as motives, goals, aspirations, decisions for right or wrong when we are tempted, and whether or not we are becoming more like Jesus day by day. Although these are things which are generally thought to be invisible, they are of the utmost importance. In verse 18 above, Paul reminds us that "the things which are seen *are* temporary, but the things which are not seen *are* eternal."

In today's modern materialistic society, we tend to put too much emphasis on how people look, the clothes they wear, the houses they live in, or the car they drive. The things we can see and touch are so important to us that it's easy to get distracted from thinking about eternal realities. One day when I was obsessing about some piece of furniture that had gotten scratched in a recent move, my Christian friend came out with a statement that put my priorities straight again, when she said, "Just remember, it's all going to burn." I was a little shocked, but she was right. No matter how hard we work or how many possessions we collect in a lifetime, we can't take material things with us when we die. And in earth's final conflagration, we know they will all be destroyed. Our characters, on the other hand, are destined to go with us into heaven (see *Christ's Object Lessons*, p. 322).

I'd like to take a minute to briefly consider each of the other two verses in today's passage. First, in verse 16 we are encouraged to "not lose heart" about the fact that our outward bodies are perishing. This is comforting to those of us who are senior citizens because the changes we see taking place in our bodies as we age can be quite disconcerting—wrinkled skin, yellow or missing teeth, thinning hair, sagging muscles, to name a few. So, it's nice to know that the Lord still values us just as much as He did when we were young because

His focus is on the people we are becoming on the inside. Then, verse 17 reminds us that whatever we are going through on this earth is only temporary and will seem like a "light affliction" when compared with the "exceeding *and* eternal weight of glory" that we will experience in heaven. So, no matter what we are going through now, be it cancer, poverty, heartache, disabilities, etc., these things will soon all be behind us forever.

Thank you, Lord, for the encouragement we receive upon reading these verses in our golden years, knowing that You are continuing to make us beautiful on the inside, if we will just let You, all the days of our lives.

September 27

The Trade

"For you know the grace of our Lord Jesus Christ, that though He was rich, yet for your sakes He became poor, that you through His poverty might become rich" (2 Corinthians 8:9).

The first time I visited a third-world country, back in the 1970s, I was surprised to learn that most items on display in an impromptu marketplace, usually set up in the town's plaza, did not have a definite price. Instead, the vendors would hold up their wares and call out a suggested price. Then, if something caught a buyer's eye, he would offer a lower price for it, and the haggling would begin. The vendor's goal, of course, was to make as much

profit as possible, while the buyer wanted to get the best bargain possible. Thus, they would loudly negotiate back and forth until a final price could be agreed upon by both parties. As a Westerner, it took me a little while to learn the skill of bargaining, so I didn't get duped into paying too much for things. Eventually I got better at it so as not to get fleeced so often! Since then, I've discovered that in many parts of the world, a great deal of shopping still occurs this way and often includes simply bartering, or trading one item for another, without the need for regular money.

In Bible times, bargaining and trading one thing for another were common practices, so Paul knew those who read his letter in Corinth would readily understand this concept. In this case, however, he wasn't describing a fair trade. In fact, the one thing was not anywhere near equal to the other. Who in the world would give up their riches and become poor so that others, through this person's poverty, could become rich? It was incomprehensible! Which is why Paul used this illustration—so that the believers could catch a glimpse of the unimaginable generosity and grace of Jesus Christ! He, who was the Lord and King of all heaven and earth and who made everything and owned all the riches of the universe, condescended to give it all up in order to come to earth to save poor sinners, who could never pay Him back for His marvelous sacrificial life and death on their behalf! What's more, this trade not only rescued them but also made them heirs of all the riches that He had given up in order to put salvation within their reach! What wonderful, matchless, magnanimous love! So, what was their part of the deal in order to gain all of this wealth? Simply to believe Jesus was who He said He was and to personally accept His sacrifice for them! Without a doubt, this was the greatest bargain in human history!

But, praise God, it didn't stop there! The Lord Jesus wants to make this same gracious trade with us today! Our sinful hearts in exchange for His unspeakable grace and glory! Just think of the ramifications of such an amazing transaction! Forgiveness and cleansing from sin now, His ever-loving presence to comfort and guide us throughout our life's journey, and a whole treasure-trove of riches we can't even imagine in the future when He takes us up to heaven to live with Him forever! How can anyone resist such a deal? Why would anyone want to? If we combined all the wealth of all of the richest people who have ever lived on the face of the earth, it would not even begin to compare with what the Lord is preparing for us in heaven (see John 14:2)! And the constant spiritual blessings that will be poured out upon us will make any other kind of wealth seem insignificant, as we lose ourselves in the chorus of praise and thanksgiving around the throne of God!

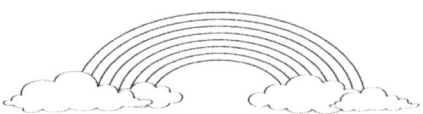

Strength in Weakness

"Concerning this thing I pleaded with the Lord three times that it might depart from me. And He said to me, 'My grace is sufficient for you, for My strength is made perfect in weakness.' Therefore most gladly I will rather boast in my infirmities, that the power of Christ may rest upon me. Therefore I take pleasure in infirmities, in reproaches, in needs, in persecutions, in distresses, for Christ's sake. For when I am weak, then I am strong"
(2 Corinthians 12:8–10).

As Paul nears the end of his second letter to the Corinthians, he reveals something of his personal spiritual struggles in the form of an oxymoron. This contradiction of terms probably left them scratching their heads at first, as it is also likely to do to us. How could the Lord tell Paul that His "strength is made perfect in weakness"? And how could Paul boldly declare, "For when I am weak, then I am strong"? This phrase doesn't make sense to our carnal minds, where being strong is so highly valued, and weakness in almost any form—physically, at work, at play, mentally, emotionally—is almost always disparaged. Only when we employ our spiritual eyesight can we begin to understand.

After prayerful consideration, these are some of the insights I've gained from this difficult yet, at the same time, precious passage:

- Often leaders have struggles of which their constituents are unaware. They could be wrestling with health, spiritual, family, or financial issues, since their feet are made of clay just like the rest of us who live on planet earth. We need to pray that they will find the strength they need to continue to carry on their particular assignments from the Lord.
- Weaknesses can make our witness more authentic, as people see that despite our typical human problems, we don't let them stop us from serving the Lord. Paul set such an inspirational example in this regard. Despite what he describes as a personal "thorn in the flesh" (verse 7), in addition to trials and tribulations of every kind, he kept his eye on the goal of sharing Christ with the world with dedication and determination.
- When we are beset with infirmities or limitations of various kinds, it's so easy for us to excuse ourselves from working for the Lord. After all, we reason, someone who is smarter, healthier, richer, or more talented could surely do a better job. That's a good time to stop and remind ourselves that the Lord has a work for each one of us to do for Him. We will be able to reach someone who nobody else could sometimes precisely because of the difficulty we're dealing with that they can relate to.
- Weaknesses, as Paul points out in this chapter, help keep us humble. They

help us realize that we never could have done the work He asked us to do on our own, and so we learn to lean on His mighty strength. The more we depend on Him, the stronger we become through the power of His Holy Spirit working through us. Thus, like Paul, we can say that "when I am weak, then I am strong" as a co-worker with our all-powerful Lord.

- When we work for the Lord with a loyal and loving heart, trying our best to do His will, He has a glorious way of making up for all our deficiencies.

- Finally, before leaving this chapter, I want to stop and bathe in the statement the Lord makes in verse 9 that His grace is sufficient for you. If we claim it, as Paul did, it can become a wonderful promise we can apply to our own lives whenever we feel we're in over our depth, or when our problems are so dire, it feels impossible to go on. As long as we continue to do our best, always trusting in Him to supply what we're lacking, we can depend on Him to carry us victoriously over the finish line!

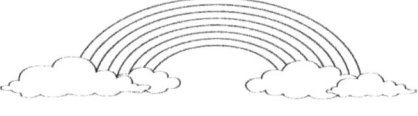

September 29

Sons of God

"For you are all sons of God through faith in Christ Jesus. For as many of you as were baptized into Christ have put on Christ. There is neither Jew nor Greek, there is neither slave nor free, there is neither male nor female; for you are all one in Christ Jesus. And if you are Christ's, then you are Abraham's seed, and heirs according to the promise" (Galatians 3:26–29).

In my Bible, this passage is entitled "Sons and Heirs." I was just going to consider the first verse, but the other verses in this section provided such a thorough elaboration of its meaning that I just had to include them. Paul points out here that anyone who believes in Jesus and is baptized into Him—regardless of nationality, social status, or even gender—has equal standing as a member of God's family. More than that, He not only claims us as a son or daughter but makes us heirs of all of His spiritual and material riches! What a merciful and gracious Savior Jesus is! It makes one wonder why we don't praise Him more!?

Today's verses should give a great deal of comfort to those of us who can't claim to be ethnically nor genetically Jewish, since it assures us that even though we are not born children of Abraham, yet all of the promises made to him and his descendants now belong to us who are believers in Christ. We didn't ask for these blessings. We didn't earn them. And yet, in His great mercy and love, we have been grafted in by our faith in Jesus and stand as much a part of God's family now as anyone who has ever lived.

Before moving on, it's interesting to note here the importance Paul places on the rite of baptism. Living in the midst of variously heathen, idolatrous, and religiously-proud (yet mistaken) people, Paul valued the public commitment each new believer made for Christ at the time of baptism. Each person baptized gave a strong testimony about the power of God to change them from whatever they were before into a child of God. They became an inspiration to neighbors, family, friends, and other observers, giving them the courage to also step forward and confess their belief in the Messiah sent from God to save them. Thus, baptism became an effective evangelistic tool in itself, and the seeds it planted in hearts brought forth a harvest in the burgeoning number of people joining the early church—sometimes as many as thousands in a day!

Have you noticed that baptisms can have a similar effect today? This is why, at the time of a baptism, the officiating pastor often makes a call for others who would like to be baptized to either come forward or to contact him to find out more about what it means to surrender our lives to God and become a part of His family. Watching someone else commit their lives to the Lord, especially if it is a person we know and love, tends to have a softening influence on the heart and makes us more susceptible to the promptings of the Holy Spirit. We are told that toward the end of the world, a latter rain of spiritual power will fill the church to overflowing, and we shall again see thousands of baptisms in a day! What a joy it will be to suddenly see the family of God growing by leaps and bounds—His newly-adopted, beloved sons and daughters becoming part of our very own heavenly family in the process! May it happen in our lifetimes!

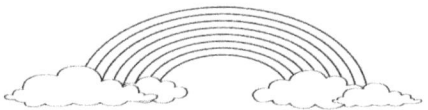

Works of the Flesh

"Now the works of the flesh are evident, which are: adultery, fornication, uncleanness, lewdness, idolatry, sorcery, hatred, contentions, jealousies, outbursts of wrath, selfish ambitions, dissensions, heresies, envy, murders, drunkenness, revelries, and the like; of which I tell you beforehand, just as I also told you in time past, that those who practice such things will not inherit the kingdom of God" (Galatians 5:19–21).

Yesterday, we talked about the fact that all who believe in Jesus will inherit the kingdom of God. Yet in today's verses, Paul takes the time to enumerate some practices that will actually prevent people from inheriting that kingdom. Why does Paul choose to get specific in this way? You will remember that those Paul was writing to were new believers—some fresh out of idolatry, or heathenism—who did not have Christian friends or family to model for them the appropriate way to walk in the Spirit. Often Paul, as well as the other apostles and evangelists, only stayed with these "babes in the faith" a short while after their baptism before moving on to evangelize other areas. Think about the newly-baptized people you have known. They now believe in Jesus, but they naturally have questions about how to live out their new-found status as a son or daughter of God in everyday life. Just as we teach our children about which activities are appropriate or not in their young lives, Paul knew that these folks could benefit by some more detailed instruction as they sought to grow in the Lord.

As it turns out, however, some of us who have walked a little longer in "the Way" still need reminders from time to time about various "works of the flesh" that we should no longer be practicing. Thus, as modern-day believers, we find that we can still benefit from Paul's ancient writings to the Galatians. Let me elaborate. As mature Christians, we would never think to commit adultery or murder. But how many professing Christians do you know (perhaps even yourself) who still struggle with outbursts of wrath, who express hatred of others or who are often involved in dissensions within the church? Although some of us might shun activities like drunkenness and revelries out of hand, we may find ourselves indulging readily in some of the less obvious hidden works of the flesh, such as jealousy, envy, or selfish ambitions. One interesting thing I have found about the Christian walk is that there is always room for growth. Whether we started believing in the Lord yesterday or multiple decades ago, if we are committed to growing closer to Him, He will continue to show us areas in our life where we can improve so that we can build character, bless others, and become ever more like Him.

Besides giving us an opportunity to take inventory of our personal spiritual growth, another benefit I see in a list like today's is that it disabuses people of the idea that unrepentant sinners who are still practicing such things without remorse will be freely welcomed into heaven. The teaching of "once saved, always saved," regardless of the kind of life a person is currently living is equally dismissed here. The doctrine of "cheap grace" is popular in some circles today, but Paul makes clear that once we begin to walk with the Lord, there will be changes in our lives. Sinful practices will start to fall away while new God-inspired interests and activities will take their place.

Lest you think Paul is focusing only on the negatives, tomorrow we'll study the frequently discussed fruits of the Spirit, where he lists some of the positive characteristics seen in those who have truly become the children of God.

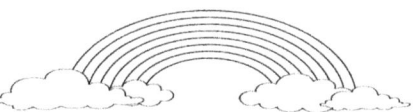

Fruit of the Spirit

"But the fruit of the Spirit is love, joy, peace, longsuffering, kindness, goodness, faithfulness, gentleness, self-control. Against such there is no law" *(Galatians 5:22, 23).*

While yesterday Paul was admonishing new believers against various negative behaviors in which they should not be involved, today's verses, which fall directly behind yesterday's, highlight what qualities should be found in a true Christian's life. Commonly known as the "fruit of the Spirit" passage, here Paul paints a beautiful picture for Christians everywhere to aspire to, for as we surrender ourselves to the Lord, He has promised to gift us the Holy Spirit. As a result, these wonderful Christlike characteristics will begin to make themselves manifest in our lives.

If, however, these traits do not seem to be growing in us, it begs the question "Why?" Perhaps we are not truly surrendered to the Lord. Maybe we haven't asked to be filled with His Spirit. It could be that we are not spending enough time with Him in our prayer sessions or devotional life for His characteristics to rub off on us. Whatever the case, these verses call us to a higher standard of Christian living. After all, if we are preparing to live in heaven someday soon, we need to start living like heavenly citizens now, don't you agree?

Just think about it. Who of us Christians wouldn't want to become more loving, more joyful, or more peaceful? Most of us would buy into the idea of being more joyful, kind, and gentle. Being faithful, patient, and self-controlled might be a little more challenging, but with God's help, we're promised that all things are possible.

When Paul says, "Against such there is no law," I think he means that instead of living underneath the law, looking up at it as our goal in order to meet some minimum standard of behavior, our ceiling as growing Christians goes far beyond the minimum rule of behavior, stretching us ever more heavenward! In this sense, we are actually living above the law. This reminds me of those students I've had through the years who are not satisfied with just a grade but are always wanting to learn more, to get "extra credit," to go the extra mile! May we be as eager to receive the fruits of the Spirit in our Christian walk, not for the sake of "good works" but as a natural outgrowth of our close relationship with the Lord. Our desire to become more like Jesus not only pleases Him but also makes us better ambassadors for Him to those around us.

Recently, I heard a person not of our denomination say about one of our church members, "He is such a good representative of Jesus in our community."

I immediately thought, *What a wonderful thing to have someone say about you!* I found it interesting that the speaker didn't know this member from work, as a neighbor, or in a church setting. He knew him as a music student—something he did as a hobby. Imagine what the world would be like if every Christian left that kind of a footprint in the communities where they live, whether at work, at worship, or even in their recreational activities! So, my prayer today is:

Lord, please give me the fruits of the Spirit, in whatever order or combinations that you see fit, so that I may bring blessings to the world around me, praise to You, and glory to God the Father. Amen.

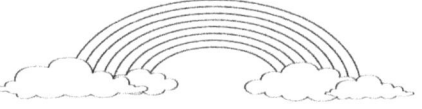

October 2

Burden Bearing

"Bear one another's burdens, and so fulfill the law of Christ" (Galatians 6:2).

What does it mean to bear one another's burdens, and how do we do it? In the verse just prior to this one, Paul has given us a clue as to one way to do it. He says, "Brethren, if a man is overtaken in any trespass, you who *are* spiritual restore such a one in a spirit of gentleness [notice the fruit of the Spirit at work here], considering yourself lest you also be tempted" (Gal. 6:1). So, we know that some people are carrying around a "burden" of sin, and they can be helped by a wise and gentle brother or sister to find forgiveness and restoration.

Wondering what else the word "burdens" might entail, I consulted the *SDA Bible Commentary*, which says:

The golden rule calls upon every follower of Christ to consider other's problems as if they were his own. The application of this principle in personal relations, in the home, the community, the school, and the church...would solve the ills of the world. The grace of Christ alone makes it possible to apply this principle.... (*SDA Bible Commentary*, vol. 6, p. 985)

On the same page, it goes on to state that our Savior was the great "Burden Bearer," and before He ascended to heaven, He left a commandment for His followers to "love one another" (*SDA Bible Commentary*, vol. 6, p. 985). In fact, He declared that love was the principle upon which "all the law and the prophets" (*Ibid.*) were based and that this love included love for humankind as well as love for God. Thus, we fulfill the law of Christ when we take an interest in other people's problems and apply the golden rule (found in Matt. 7:12) as we interact with them.

I noticed that the *Commentary* also mentioned the words "weight" and "heaviness" as synonyms for the word "burdens." The first word paints a picture for me of someone weighted down with the worries and cares of this life while the second one speaks to me of a person whose life is heavy with sorrow.

Now that we have all of this information, what might burden-bearing look like in a Christian's everyday life? Obviously, there are thousands of possibilities in each of our lives, so I tried to narrow it down to what it might look like in my life. I could help a crying child learn how to tie his shoes, teach a first grader how to read, help a child who can't get a drink of water reach the faucet. I can imagine talking to a teenager about his schoolwork and helping a college student choose her major. I can see helping a graduate student who just needs a pep talk to keep working toward her goal. I can be there for an adult student who needs a word of encouragement to keep struggling to learn English as a second or third language, so they can make a place for them and their family in this new environment. I might call a person to express my condolences for their loss or serve on a committee to solve some problem in my church or community. I can let a person with a heavier load go before me in the grocery line, make a meal for someone in need, or lend some money to a brother to get past a rough patch in life. I might write a letter, send a note, or give a quick call to a person who is lonely, or just to express my joy in knowing them. I might even start taking a little more interest in some of my husband's hobbies! And the list goes on... What might your list look like?

October 3

Reaping

"Do not be deceived, God is not mocked; for whatever a man sows, that he will also reap" (Galatians 6:7).

In our journey through the Bible, we have come across several recurring themes. The concept of planting and harvesting is one of them. Because it illustrates the meaning of today's text so well, please indulge me in discussing our garden once again. Anyone who has farmed or even grown a garden knows that the time of harvest is usually a most joyous time. Even my husband's small plot of vegetables and a few fruits fills him with eager anticipation. Will the tomatoes be large and juicy? Will the lettuce make it through the summer? And how many ears of corn will he produce this year? When will the onions be ready to use in our cooking? Will the melons survive the ravishing of the birds? Will the garlic and squash plants yield as much as last year? These questions can only be answered at the end of the growing season, which will bring either pride and satisfaction that all the work and watering have paid off or frustration and disappointment that all the labor and nurturing of certain plants did not render the expected results.

As a laborer for souls, I can say that I have experienced both emotions—joy and sorrow—a sense of satisfaction that my labor was not in vain as well as disappointment when my efforts seemed not to pay off. At those times I have to do three things. First, remind myself that every seed planted has a growing season—and some require more time to germinate than others. The second thing is to ask myself if there is something I could have done to make the sowing more fruitful, and the third and obviously most important thing I need to do is earnestly pray that the Holy Spirit will continue to work in His quiet, patient, and effective way for as long as possible in order to produce an abundant harvest for God's kingdom.

I have learned that in soul-winning, patience is a great virtue. We have people in our extended family for whom we have prayed for years before they finally made their decision to follow the Lord. As I've mentioned previously, we also have a relative who we nearly gave up on when he went to prison, only to be surprised with joy when he found the Lord while he was serving his sentence! I now believe that it's our job to plant seeds, and the Master Gardener's job (with whom we are privileged to work) to gather in His harvest.

In its context, however, this verse speaks to us about more than planting seeds for the purpose of soul winning. It also reminds us, once again, that there is a day of judgment, in which all the evil seeds of sin and rebellion we have planted in our lifetime will also bear fruit. We have discussed this theme before, but it bears repeating in this context. Some people today believe that there is no such thing as a Judgment Day. Others believe that God is too gracious and kind to punish evil words and acts, but the Bible is clear that judgment will come to all those who have not asked the Lord to forgive their sins and cover them in His robe of righteousness. It is because God is so gracious and kind that He will judge the earth and finally eradicate all the filthiness of sin from the universe so we will never have to suffer from any of its horrific results again. Eternal life will then be filled with joy, peace, and love for every forgiven saint!

There is a verse in the Old Testament that complements this one in such simple, straightforward language that Steve Green made it into a children's memory verse song a few years back. It says, "The eyes of the LORD *are* in every place, keeping watch on the evil and the good" (Prov. 15:3). It doesn't matter what dark corner of the world a person tries to hide in when committing their evil deeds, for nothing is hidden from the Lord. We find that Jesus Himself reiterates this thought in the last book of the Bible when He talks about what will happen when He returns to earth. He says, "And behold, I am coming quickly, and My reward *is* with Me, to give to every one according to his work" (Rev. 22:12). So, here we have both a warning and a promise. If we did good work we will be rewarded when Jesus comes, and if we did evil work, we will be paid in kind...according to our work. Our God is both just and fair. What a reminder to always be cognizant of the fact that the Lord is watching all that happens on earth and to ask Him to help us do only those things which are pleasing in His sight.

Hang in There!

"And let us not grow weary while doing good, for in due season we shall reap if we do not lose heart. Therefore, as we have opportunity, let us do good to all, especially to those who are of the household of faith" (Galatians 6:9, 10).

Chapter 6 of Galatians is chock full of great passages for those of us who are walking in the Christian way, but I especially appreciate these last two verses found near the end of Paul's letter to the Galatians. While continuing with the theme of reaping in yesterday's verse, the apostle seems to strike a higher note here in a couple of ways. First, he assures us that we will reap if we hang in there, and second, he encourages us, while doing good in the world wherever we can, we should not forget to be good and kind to our own Christian brothers and sisters. He adds it almost as an afterthought, as if saying, "By the way, be sure to take care of each other."

It set me to thinking about ways in which we could nurture each other in the church. Of course, there are all the traditional ways: sending a cheery card, making a long-overdue phone call, preparing a casserole for someone bereaved or alone, providing transportation to church or a doctor's appointment, sharing produce from your garden, the list goes on. But then I thought about some of the helpful activities that aren't so common yet would be a blessing to other Christians in today's "household of faith."

For instance, recently my son-in-law helped me set up my new computer, saving me a couple hundred dollars and a lot of frustration. What a blessing that was! Nowadays, if we don't have time to write a letter, we can send a quick text, just to let people know that we are thinking of them and praying about their concerns. When I was living alone, I remember just how much I appreciated it when a neighbor would come over to check the oil in my car, put air in my tires, or best of all, offer to wash my car for free! Talk about a kind gesture! Helping a church member move is one of the best ways possible to do good for them. I speak from experience! Just spending time with someone who is lonely and working on projects together with them, whether painting a room or planning a Sabbath School class, can be a real gift. I'm sure you can think of many other creative ways to do good for your fellow Christians, and if we ask the Lord about it, He will give us wisdom to know just what activity is best for each circumstance. It's a great feeling knowing that we can be co-workers with Him, not only in bringing blessings to the world at large but also, and especially, to those who already love and serve Him. Regardless of our faith status, we all appreciate kindness, and all of us can use some form of assistance from time to time.

I like that Paul admits that the road of good works is not always a smooth one when he tells us not to "lose heart." Trying to do nice things for others can sometimes be discouraging. Others may fail to show appreciation for your actions, misread your motives, or criticize the way you did something. In Paul's day, a believer could be persecuted, jailed, or even killed while trying to do God's bidding. Nevertheless, Paul tells us to keep doing good. It should be the practicing Christian's way of life. And if we "hang in there," we're promised we'll reap a harvest of blessings when the Lord returns to take us home.

October 5

Heavenly Places

"But God, who is rich in mercy, because of His great love with which He loved us, even when we were dead in trespasses, made us alive together with Christ (by grace you have been saved), and raised us up together, and made us sit together in the heavenly places in Christ Jesus" (Ephesians 2:4–6).

*I*n this passage, at first glance, Paul seems to be referring to what will happen to believers in the future. After being saved from our sins, we will be made "alive together with Christ." Although our physical bodies will die, our gracious Lord will resurrect us, and we will go to heaven where we will reign together with Him in the glorious place where His throne resides. What a beautiful picture these verses paint of His great love and rich mercy for us upon whom He has poured out His unmerited favor! And how did we obtain this royal treatment? Simply by believing in Him and trusting Him for our salvation. What a deal!

Not only does He save our souls from wallowing in the darkness that sin has brought into our world here and now but He actually promotes us to become joint-heirs with Him in enjoying all of God's goodness for unending ages to come! This will be more wonderful than we can describe or even imagine!

All we can say is, "Praise God from whom all blessings flow!"

Besides the eternal blessings promised in these verses, the *SDA Bible Commentary* helps us contemplate some of the more immediate benefits of choosing to follow Jesus:

Those who see Christ sitting at the right hand of God may dwell in the atmosphere of heaven while here on earth. Believers now belong to the heavenly world, in that Christ's entrance to the heavenly courts was a pledge of the entrance of all who would accept salvation. The spiritual life on earth then becomes a foretaste, an anticipation, of the heavenly life. Christ is with us by the Holy Spirit, and He counts us as already dwelling with Him. (*SDA Bible Commentary*, vol. 6, p. 1007)

What a powerful statement this is! We "may dwell in the atmosphere of heaven" now! Our spiritual life can become "a fore-taste...of the heavenly life." As I let these words sink in, I reflected upon times in my life when I had felt I was already sitting in heavenly places with Christ. At least two specific times come to mind from when I was sitting in church services. The first was an early morning church service, where the morning sunlight was streaming in through the glass windows above where a true man of God was preaching about the all-important theme of righteousness by faith. The Holy Spirit's presence was palpable, and it felt as if the whole congregation had been lifted to the very gates of heaven!

Another time, I was part of a huge university church service, where the congregation was regaled with amazing organ and choir music, and when we were invited to stand and join our 2,000 voices to the anthem of praise, we felt transported to a heavenly place where angels continually sing the praises of God! Now, camp meetings come to mind—what a celebration of God's goodness as, for several days in a row, we focus on spiritual themes, listen to beautiful music, amazing testimonies, and stirring sermons, and eat and talk with family and friends, both old and new! What a foretaste of heaven!

Then there are huge general conference sessions, where believers from around the world gather together to thank God for His goodness during the previous five years and make church plans for the five years to come. This also gives us a chance to meet and greet folks we have served with in different parts of the USA as well as various parts of the world. I think heaven will be a lot like that. But, as I think of it, the most personal "heavenly place" I have found is in my own home in the quiet of the morning when I sit down for my daily devotional time. There, with my Bible, a Bible study guide, a place to write my petitions and praises, a morning devotional book, and my prayer list, I feel the Lord's presence with me. He gives me the courage, hope, and guidance I need, so in that sense heaven has already begun!

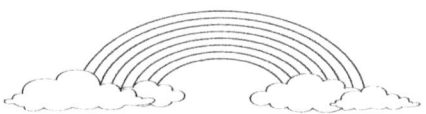

October 6

The Fullness of God

"That He would grant you, according to the riches of His glory, to be strengthened with might through His Spirit in the inner man, that Christ may dwell in your hearts by faith; that you, being rooted and grounded in love, may be able to comprehend with all the saints, what is the width and length and depth and height—to know the love of Christ which passes knowledge; that you may be filled with all the fullness of God" (Ephesians 3:16–19).

These rich verses reveal part of Paul's passionate prayer on behalf of the believers in Ephesus. He tells them that he has just bowed down before the Father of the Lord Jesus Christ to make this earnest petition. His evangelistic heart yearns for them to understand God's immeasurable love for them and to be filled with the very "fullness of God."

What exactly does the term "the fullness of God" entail? This passage itself gives us some clues. It states that the believers would be "strengthened with might through the Holy Spirit," that Christ would dwell in their hearts by faith, and that they would be "rooted and grounded" by their deep knowledge of God's love for them. One can't help but notice that Paul is suggesting here that those who would be filled with God's fullness will be privileged to experience a close and personal relationship with all three members of the Godhead. How does this happen? When invited into our lives, I believe the Holy Spirit will still, even in our day, gift us with spiritual strength; the Lord will still make Himself manifest in our lives through His presence; and we will still be overwhelmed by the knowledge of the Father's great multi-dimensional love.

Once again, the *SDA Bible Commentary* provides some valuable spiritual insights. It states:

> The church, like a vessel, is to be filled to the brim with heavenly grace, so that the individual members composing the body of Christ exhibit or reflect something of the 'fullness of God.' Paul is presenting a most exalted view of the nature of man, and of his possibilities of growth in grace. Man was made in the image of God. He was given capabilities of development and the high privilege of becoming a partaker of the 'divine nature.' (*SDA Bible Commentary*, vol. 6, p. 1018)

This certainly gave me food for thought. What a high calling God has called us to as Christians! This means that our possibilities for becoming more like our Lord are limitless! For me, two ideas highlight the graciousness of God in this regard. No matter where we start on our personal ladder of character improvement, the Lord loves and accepts us and encourages us as we grow. No matter how much we become like Him in our lifetimes, there will still be infinite possibilities for us to continue to grow to be ever more like Him throughout eternity!

Although Paul was initially praying for the new believers of Jesus in his time, his prayer, like all of the Bible, transcends time and space, applying to believers in our age as well. So, I accept Paul's prayer for today's Christians, including me! May we also comprehend and receive God's love in such a way that we experience the "fullness of God" in our own lives and then join in the prayer for those around us—children, siblings, students, friends, colleagues, and neighbors—so that they may be receivers of the same rich blessings!

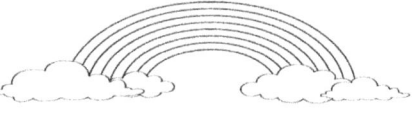

October 7

Winds of Doctrine

"...that we should no longer be children, tossed to and fro and carried about by every wind of doctrine, by the trickery of men, in the cunning craftiness of deceitful plotting, but, speaking the truth in love, may grow up in all things into Him who is the head—Christ" (Ephesians 4:14, 15).

We live in a part of the country that experiences strong winds certain times of the year. Yesterday was one of those times. As I sat looking out my large dining room window, I marveled at the strength of the wind, bending all the branches on even large trees in one direction and causing a roaring sound, something like the sound of waves crashing on an otherwise quiet beach. Meanwhile, the leaves were dancing in every direction. Some clung tightly enough to the branch that bore them to remain on the tree, but many finally gave up the fight against the unrelenting force of the wind and blew away, eventually to become part of the refuse of fall along with many other dead leaves.

Generally, we think of doctrine as a positive thing. These verses remind us, however, that there can be "winds of doctrine" which can have a negative effect on our spiritual lives. As we know from God's word (see 1 Peter 5:8), Satan, our adversary, "walks about like a roaring lion, seeking whom he may devour." He is always in the business of trying to confuse us and convince us to believe things that are not true nor helpful to our efforts to stay close to the Lord. Often, he mixes just enough truth with error that we fall for his schemes. At times, he uses pastors, teachers, and other people we look up to, perhaps unwittingly on their part, in order to influence us to believe falsehood. Then there are those who, as today's passage points out, are downright tricky, cunning, and deceitful, and they twist the gospel into something that brings them personal gain—sometimes monetary, sometimes to increase the numbers of people who will come to hear them speak or join their cult, with the motivation to increase their own power and influence.

Unfortunately, history has taught us that there seem to be many people who are just looking for a strong leader to follow. Regardless of where his teachings may lead. If a person with a degree of charisma proclaims a strong message with great confidence, amazingly, he begins to collect a following. A few examples in the last century include Hitler, Jim Jones, David Koresh, Charles Manson, and a parade of television preachers who have, by their behavior, brought disrepute upon themselves as well as dishonor upon the gospel. We may wonder why people were gullible enough to follow such leaders. Were they very attractive or eloquent or so popular that their followers thought they had to be right? Perhaps the "doctrines" taught by these false shepherds were easy to believe because they were based on religious traditions, comfortable cultural practices, or popular philosophies of the day. Occasionally, folks will join a group that purports to have some secret or special knowledge or "truth" that no one else knows. They enjoy participating in a sort of secret society, which only admits a few "privileged" adherents.

Too often, I fear, we think that we could never be caught up in these strange deceptions. But before we ride too high on our horses of false security, we need to take heed to Paul's words that only by continually growing up into Christ and making Him the head of our belief system will we be safe. The closer we get to the second coming, the stronger the winds of false doctrine will become. Even well-established Bible-based doctrines will be twisted in order to derail long-time Christians. Listen to what Jesus says about this in Matthew 24:24 when talking with His disciples about things that will happen near the end of time. He warns, "For false christs and false prophets will rise and show great signs and wonders to deceive, if possible, even the elect." Thus, Paul admonishes Christians, "Therefore let him who thinks he stands take heed lest he fall" (1 Cor. 10:12).

So, how shall we stand against these strong and ever-increasing winds of perverted doctrine? In Matthew 4:4, while overcoming the deceptions of Satan in the wilderness, Jesus shares with us the best way to stay on track. He says, "Man shall not live by bread alone, but by every word which proceeds from the mouth of God." We need to make the truths found in God's word our anchor. In the verse cited earlier above, Peter tells us to "Be sober, be vigilant." Yet, in our own weak strength, we would never be able to defend ourselves from the supernatural forces swirling around us. That's why I thank God for His promises to help us. One of my favorites that I feel can be applied here is found in Philippians 4:13. It victoriously declares, "I can do all things through Christ who strengthens me."

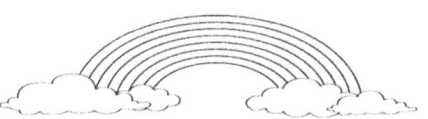

Grace to the Hearers

"Let no corrupt word proceed out of your mouth, but what is good for necessary edification, that it may impart grace to the hearers. And do not grieve the Holy Spirit of God, by whom you were sealed for the day of redemption. Let all bitterness, wrath, anger, clamor, and evil speaking be put away from you, with all malice. And be kind to one another, tenderhearted, forgiving one another, even as God in Christ forgave you" (Ephesians 4:29–32).

*I*n chapter 4 of Ephesians, there are many marvelous verses to ponder, as Paul is discussing what the demeanor of "the new man" will look like (see Eph. 4:24). He had a large number of new converts in Ephesus and wanted to instruct and guide them regarding how to be better reflectors of God's goodness in their interactions with others. The four verses that make up today's passage are rich in helpful content for anyone who desires to be a follower of Jesus. I'd like to consider them one verse at a time.

In verse 29, we are admonished not to allow any "corrupt word" to leave our mouth. In that category I would obviously include swearing of any kind and what we generally call "four-letter words." However, I think harsh criticism, lying, and the telling of any off-color jokes could also be considered corrupt as well as gossiping and name-calling. Basically, anything that we could not imagine coming out of the mouth of our Savior. But the verse doesn't stop there. It also tells us what we should be saying. Anything "good for necessary edification." The word edification means that which builds up, instructs, or encourages. It brings needed help to the endeavor and, loftier still, that which would "impart grace to the hearers." Wow! What a standard to live by! Just imagine what the world would be like if people, or even just those of us who claim to be Christians, began to speak only words that would bring heavenly grace to those within the sound of our voice!

Verse 30 emphasizes just how serious the Godhead takes this injunction when it informs us that we can actually "grieve the Holy Spirit" by using our gift of speech inappropriately. As the One who has been charged with sealing us for the day of redemption, how careful we should be not to offend Him. Here we learn that the words we use could even have an impact on our ultimate salvation.

Although not swearing or calling the listener a derogatory name, have you ever heard someone speak to another with obvious underlying malice, animosity, sarcasm, or disrespect? As we all know, we get messages from others not only by their words but also by their tone, volume, and even their body language! This is why verse 31 outlines a number of negative feelings and attitudes we should "put away" in order to truly impart grace in our communications. Bitterness, wrath, and anger are the first things to eliminate because if they are not found in our heart, neither will they be found in our speech. May the Lord help us to abandon "evil speaking" of any kind—not only in our verbal but also in our non-verbal communications. Could this mean even our writing? What about our text messages and e-mail? Now we have opened a can of worms! But if we want our communications to bring grace to our hearers—in this case, our readers—I'm convinced that we will have to surrender our writing to the Lord's standards as well.

Lastly, verse 31 puts the frosting on the cake. It tells us how to go the second mile in bringing grace into the lives of others. Not only with our kind and encouraging words, but also with our actions. Followers of Jesus must be loving, kind, compassionate, and forgiving. As the Lord has helped us understand what grace is by His loving forgiveness, by forgiving others, we can communicate the blessing of that same saving grace to them.

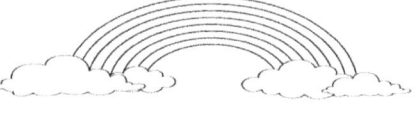

October 9

Bondservants

"...not with eyeservice, as men-pleasers, but as bondservants of Christ, doing the will of God from the heart, with goodwill doing service, as to the Lord, and not to men" (Ephesians 6:6, 7).

In Paul's day, some of the new believers in Christ were bondservants. These were people who were bound to serve others without wages. Some translations use the word slave. However, the word "bondservant," which originated with the Greeks, portrayed a broader sense of the word than our ideas of modern-day slavery. While some servants were considered the property of their masters, at times, a bondservant could be one who worked voluntarily for another for a set period of time, perhaps to pay off a debt. It's interesting to note here that Paul often refers to himself as well as the other apostles as "bondservants of Christ." By the way, Paul also calls all people who have become Christians, whether bond or free, his brethren. What a great example Paul sets for us in treating all believers equally, regardless of their social status or the kind of work they do.

Although we may think that our work circumstances are difficult or our managers have been unfair, just imagine what it would be like to be an unfair or demanding master's bondservant. There was no doubt that this was often an uncomfortable and trying situation. Many people who are unhappy at work tend to do just the minimum to get by. I'm sure this was as true in the first century as in the twenty-first. Today, most unhappy workers are "clock-watchers," who dart out the door the second the clock strikes 5:00 p.m.—whether the task they are working on is finished or not. They do things haphazardly, take every possible break, and harbor a negative attitude toward the boss, the co-workers, and/or the organization for which they work.

But Paul invites the new converts, as well as us today, to adopt a higher level of thinking, living, and working. Instead of focusing on the negative, he urges workers to be positive, to go the second mile in their work, wholeheartedly doing their best, as if their boss was the Lord Jesus Christ instead of just another human being. After all, as Christ's ambassadors to the world, everything we do should represent Him and be done to the best of our ability in order to please Him. This is another one of the Bible's recurring themes. Remember Ecclesiastes 9:10 admonishes, "Whatever your hand finds to do, do *it* with your might...." Biblical examples come to mind. Joseph is my favorite story of a faithful worker in the Bible because despite his sudden lowly status as a slave, the unpleasant duties he was surely assigned, unfair treatment by his master, and the difficult people with whom he most certainly had to interact in the prison, he never lost sight of the fact that he was actually a servant of the most high God. Due to his faithfulness in tasks both large and small, the Bible tells us that God prospered Joseph in all he did. By the end of the story, Joseph was valued and trusted by all and became the most influential leader in Egypt.

Not many of us will end up as powerful and influential as Joseph, but if we use the gifts the Lord has given us faithfully, we can be sure that He will bless us. Our motivation as well as quantity and quality of work can all be improved when we dedicate the labor of our hearts, minds, and hands to the Lord. Regardless of for whom we are working, the Lord will accept and value any sincere effort to work in a way that will bring honor to our real and heavenly boss—the Lord Jesus Christ.

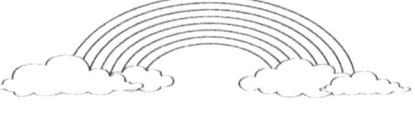

October 10

Knights in Shining Armor

"For we do not wrestle against flesh and blood, but against principalities, against powers, against the rulers of the darkness of this age, against spiritual hosts of wickedness in the heavenly places. Therefore, take up the whole armor of God, that you may be able to withstand in the evil day, and having done all, to stand" (Ephesians 6:12, 13).

Today's passage helps us answer an earlier question this month about how we will be able to stand against the evil swirling all around us in the last days—and it does this by providing details. As an educator, I have always liked object lessons because they increase learning and help students better remember what is being taught. Here, in the second half of Ephesians 6, Paul uses such a method. He illustrates what he is teaching with something they are familiar with from their own life and times. He makes the abstract concrete, bringing the theoretical down to the practical level to make sure his hearers thoroughly understand what he is saying. He knows, after all, that this information will be essential to them being victorious in the great spiritual battle in which they are engaged.

Although some wish to deny it, these texts make it clear that we are all soldiers (brave knights, if you will) fighting in a huge cosmic battle between good and evil, between God and Satan. Not only is it being fought on a universal level but also on a personal level by every person who lives on this earth. Thus, Paul is inspired by God to tell us how we can be successful warriors in this great controversy. It's by taking on the whole strong and shining armor that the Lord—our Commander and King—provides for us!

Paul breaks it down in the subsequent verses in this chapter, and he describes what God's armor consists of, piece by necessary piece: the belt of truth, the breastplate of righteousness, shoes made of the "gospel of peace" (Eph. 6:15), the shield of faith, the helmet of salvation, and the sword of the Spirit (which is the Word of God).

If we will gratefully accept and prayerfully use all of these protective elements of God's armor, He will graciously shield and protect us from the fiery darts of the enemy. They will not be able to destroy us. What's more, we will be able to win in our personal battles against the reign of evil in our own lives, and God will enable us to become courageous knights in shining armor, who will seek to rescue others from the dark and dangerous battleground. In so doing, through our testimony and changed lives, God will also make us effective soldiers in the universal, cosmic war between Christ and Satan. Whenever we are tempted to doubt that we can be overcomers in this fight, we need to listen to Paul's words of encouragement, found in verse 11: "Put on the whole armor of God, that you may be able to stand against the wiles of the devil." And in verse 10: "Finally, my brethren, be strong in the Lord, and in the power of His might." It is only through the magnificent power of His might that we'll become those "knights in shining armor," who will ride victoriously with Him into heaven.

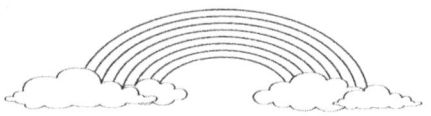

October 11

Completed Work

"Being confident of this very thing, that He who has begun a good work in you will complete it until the day of Jesus Christ" (Philippians 1:6).

Have you ever, in a moment of mis-placed optimism, purchased one of those huge, 1,000-word puzzles, thinking it would be a good winter pastime, only to quit the project half-way through due to boredom, frustration, or distraction?

Fortunately, God does not give up on putting the puzzle pieces of our lives together to form a beautiful picture, even on days when we would give up on ourselves. It doesn't matter if we are sad, mad, sick, weak, frustrated, or just discouraged in our Christian walk. God is standing by to help us make sense of our lives again, if we will only ask for His expert intervention. He was, after all, the Master Designer of the pattern, and His enthusiasm for us to become like Him in character knows no bounds. On dark days, when we want to give up, He can sup-ply the motivation and determination we need to complete the project successfully—through His consistent grace and transform-ing power.

So, in this first chapter of Philippians (one of my favorite books in the Bible), after showing his affection for the new believers by saying that he thanks his God upon every remembrance of them (see Phil. 1:3), Paul seeks to bolster their courage by assuring them that God has promised to complete the work He has started in them through their Lord Jesus Christ. Later, in chapter 2 he explains how this is possible. He says, "for it is God who works in you both to will and to do for *His* good pleasure" (Phil. 2:13). Praise God! This means that when we don't even want to do His will in some aspect of our Christian walk, we can ask Him to help us become "willing to be made willing."

There's no use for us to try to hide our motivations and emotions from the Lord, for He knows us better than we know our-selves. Our only recourse is to simply be honest with Him. When the Holy Spirit con-victs us that we should—or shouldn't—be doing something, our task is to bring it to the Lord, telling Him exactly how we feel and then submitting it to His will. Sometimes He changes our desires immediately, and some-times it takes a struggle, like in the case of Jesus submitting His will to the Father's in Gethsemane. But, early or late, if we remain open to the promptings of the Holy Spirit, stepping out in faith to be obedient to Him, our will becomes changed in miraculous ways. Eventually, we will exclaim like David, "I delight to do Your will, O my God, and Your law *is* within my heart" (Ps. 40:8).

I love Philippians 2:13 because I believe it gives us the key to how Philippians 1:6 will be accomplished. Once we have taken the first step to surrender our will to God's, then He helps us WANT to do what is right. After that, He promises to give us the strength and spiritual power to DO His good pleasure. I believe it is in this way that God is finally able to complete the good work He started in us when He first called us to be His disciples.

Thus, the work of salvation will be completed in us by the Author of salvation. He is a faithful workman. All He needs is for the human material to permit Him to mold it into a beautiful work of art—one that will bring glory to its Maker throughout ceaseless ages!

October 12

Unimaginable Condescension

"Let this mind be in you which was also in Christ Jesus, who, being in the form of God, did not consider it robbery to be equal with God, but made Himself of no reputation, taking the form of a bondservant, and coming in the likeness of men. And being found in appearance as a man, He humbled Himself and became obedient to the point of death, even the death of the cross" (Philippians 2:5–8).

The condescension of Jesus described in this passage is truly incredible! Whenever I read it, I am amazed at all of the steps downward He took in order to save humankind and lift us up out of our hopeless state to prepare us to live with Him one day at the highest level of existence imaginable!

These verses outline at least five ways Jesus humbled Himself in order to become our Savior. First, He, the Creator of heaven and earth, abandoned His almighty position of being equal with God, in order to become one of His created beings. Upon arriving on earth, instead of assuming a role of power and human prestige, He became a very poor and ordinary person. He "made Himself of no reputation." He did not come as a king,

a wealthy man with servants, or even a military general, who might have had fame, authority over other people, or special privileges of some kind to make His tenure here on earth more comfortable.

After all, at the time Jesus lived, such "luxuries" as even the common person enjoys today, like electricity, running water, heaters and air conditioners, microwaves, and refrigeration simply did not exist. Transportation was largely limited to walking or riding a horse or a donkey, if you could afford one. I've often told friends and relatives that if I were Jesus, I would have waited to come down here after we had commodities such as flushing toilets, electric lights, cars, and cell phones! Just thinking of the lack of hygiene, the want of basic conveniences, and the interminable dust and filth on the streets He had to walk makes me shudder.

Not only that but the text also tells us that He came in the form of a man. Thus, He took His second step down by setting aside His immortality in order to become mortal, like those He came to save. He did this in order to experience what humankind living in a sinful world had to experience. He wanted to come close to His children, so He ate and drank what we did; He walked and talked as we did; He got tired and needed sleep like us, and He experienced what it felt like to be tempted to do evil. He tasted the whole range of human emotions, but more than that, He condescended to be born as a helpless baby and to travel through all the stages of human development, just as we do!

Third, He came in the "form of a bond-servant." Not only did He step down from His holy and majestic throne and choose to go lower than any position of power on earth, but when He came, He took the role of a servant. His whole life here was dedicated to serving others. For the first thirty years, He worked for His earthly father in a carpenter shop. Upon beginning His ministry, He spent His time teaching, preaching, and healing those around Him. His life was totally centered on blessing as many people as He could so that they could become part of the kingdom of heaven.

When His time on earth was done, He agreed to die in order to save the human race. He who was the Source of life, who hated sin with all of its ramifications, including the intruder called death, which He never planned that any of His creatures should experience, took a fourth unfathomable step. He chose to sacrificially drink the bitter cup of death Himself so that the humans He loved would be able to live throughout eternity!

Fifth, He chose to die "even the death of the cross." Probably the worst, most torturous death that humankind has ever stooped to invent. It would have been difficult enough for Jesus just to experience a calm death, let alone dying an ignominious death designed for the most evil of criminals.

It's hard for me to wrap my mind around how Jesus was willing to take these five giant steps down from His glory to the level of our degradation. And why? His overpowering love. This is the science of salvation that we will continue to study throughout the ages. But one of my favorite authors, Ellen White, sums it up beautifully like this,

> Christ was treated as we deserve, that we might be treated as He deserves. He was condemned for our sins, in which He had no share, that we might be justified by His righteousness, in which we had no share. He suffered the death which was ours, that we might receive the life which was His. (*The Desire of Ages*, p. 25)

His unimaginable condescension accomplishes our unimaginable glorification! "Wonder, O heavens! and be astonished, O earth!" (*Ibid.*, p. 49).

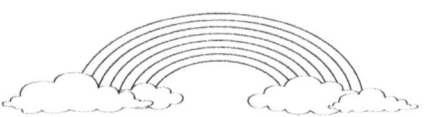

Minor Problems?

"Do all things without complaining and disputing" (Philippians 2:14).

Just after the enlightening verse that tells us it is "God who works in you both to will and to do for *His* good pleasure" (Phil. 2:13), we find Paul giving the early believers this little piece of guidance. Tucked away between two other great verses in this chapter, it is easy to just skip over this seemingly small and simple admonition. When we slow down, however, and take the time to think about it, we realize that complaining and disputing are no minor problems. In fact, they may be even more damaging in our day than they were for the early church.

In our overly contentious society in modern America, people feel it is their right to complain as well as to argue (dispute) with anyone who has a different opinion than they do about almost anything. As Christians, we are not exempt from these feelings. After all, everybody wants to fight for their rights—constitutional, civil, and religious. With the right to free speech in this country, citizens are encouraged to make their voices heard on every topic imaginable and to broadcast their opinions through all the media available to them.

Is this wrong? No, it is a wonderful thing to have the kind of freedoms we enjoy here in the USA. The problem comes when our sense of entitlement pushes us over the red line of civil discourse. Too often we are tempted to misuse our liberty to insult, degrade, curse, or otherwise disrespect those who hold different views than ours. Unfortunately, some people even use our modern means of communication to bolster prejudice, to bully or assassinate character, or to spread hate speech.

So where do we, as Christians, fit into this scenario? Well, it seems to me that we would do well to go back to the verse in Ephesians 4:29 that we studied a few days ago. You'll recall that it admonished us to "Let no corrupt word proceed out of your mouth." (Remember those electronic devices!) It continues, "what is good for necessary edification." And then, most importantly I think, "that it may impart grace to the hearers." So, if you're like me, this certainly gives us some food for thought.

Bringing today's injunction down to a practical level in our everyday interactions, I can't help but ask myself: what would our homes look like if there was no whining and complaining? Where every family member was cheerful, cooperative, helpful, and exhibited a positive attitude? For that matter, what would a church look like where there was no complaining, just everyone doing their best to move the work forward? Or a workplace? I think it would almost feel as if we were in heaven already! Then, when it comes to this idea of disputing, have you ever lived or worked with a person who disagrees with everything you say? It's like constant dripping water, sapping all the life out of you. If you say something is black, they say it is white. If you say a destination is to the north, they say it is to the south. They can argue over the smallest and most insignificant details, wasting precious time and effort, pushing their ideas forward despite all evidence to the contrary.

Again, of course it is part of life to have and discuss various opinions on issues of substance. These kinds of discussions can help us learn and grow as long as they are carried out in a civil and charitable manner. And we do want to stand up for and defend the truth, speaking out on the side of that which is right and good, ideally with judicious tact and sensitivity. We must always remember that as Christians, we have a high standard to meet. After all, we are Christ's representatives in all we do and say. I don't know about you, but I realize that I still have some work to do in this area of my Christian experience. I need to do less complaining and disputing and show more thankfulness and cooperation.

Help me, Lord, to this end.

October 14

Light Bearers

"That you may become blameless and harmless, children of God without fault in the midst of a crooked and perverse generation, among whom you shine as lights in the world" (Philippians 2:15).

More and more, we witness the dichotomy between good and evil, truth and error, light and darkness, as they battle for supremacy in our world. Turning on the evening news we see and hear the litany of almost daily mass shootings, heinous crimes, natural disasters, social and political unrest, and the jostling of nations for more power. One can't help but wonder how much further our current "crooked and perverse generation" can go before filling up its cup of iniquity, just as humanity did before the flood or in the time of Sodom and Gomorrah. As more and more people turn from God, rejecting the wooing of the Holy Spirit until it can no longer be heard, the darkness becomes more pervasive. The darker it gets, the light becomes ever more essential.

Recently, we have experienced several power outages in our area. As night falls and everything becomes pitch black out here in the country, a flashlight suddenly becomes our most valued possession. One is not enough. Each person in the house needs one of their own in order to see where they're going and what they're doing. A good flashlight can keep us from tripping, falling, or running into something that could injure us. Nowadays, thankfully, cell phones can also act as flashlights—that is, until they must be recharged! Unfortunately, the last time our lights went out, I had been on my phone much of the day, so there wasn't much charge left in it, and my trusty flashlight, when I finally located it, was a bit weak, blinking off and on intermittently. It was in need of new batteries! So, it was a long, dark night. Needless to say, I learned my lesson, and now my valuable flashlight has new batteries inside and can be found in the drawer right beside my bed!

The spiritual parallels are obvious. This dark world is a place where many lights have gone out, yet some folks are still looking for a ray of light to help them find their way out of the darkness. People without a light source are in danger of tripping (sinning), falling (being lost), and being injured (buffeted about and controlled by Satan). God has asked His children to be as blameless and harmless as possible so that others will be able to see the light of His presence shining through them. They can only accomplish this task if they are properly charged up about their purpose and have the power of

the Holy Spirit (spiritual batteries) inside of them. All of this will only be successful if the lights can be easily found by those who are searching for them; thus, they must make themselves easily accessible.

We have talked before about the privilege and joy of being co-workers together with God. In today's text, the Lord gives us this invitation to help Him seek and save the lost again. This time, He describes us as light bearers. As earth's history comes to an end, the shadows lengthen, and the darkness closes in. God needs us even more than before to help Him save and gather in those honest-hearted people, who will still respond to His call in the eleventh hour—just before probation closes, and His Spirit is forever withdrawn.

May we not disappoint You, Lord!

October 15

Reaching Forward

"Brethren, I do not count myself to have apprehended; but one thing I do, forgetting those things which are behind, and reaching forward to those things which are ahead, I press toward the goal for the prize of the upward call of God in Christ Jesus" (Philippians 3:13, 14).

When I was in academy, each high school class would pick an inspirational motto to succinctly express their class goals. This motto would then be printed by their class pictures in the

yearbook, displayed on t-shirts and hats, and touted on graduation programs. I can remember at least two of these that I believe were probably inspired by today's passage. One was, "Forward Ever, Backward Never."

Another one was, "Onward and Upward." Perhaps you can remember similar ones from your high school days.

Here, in the two verses above, Paul seems, although not quite as succinctly, to be declaring his motto which includes three main points. First, he is forgetting what is behind. In his case, there was a lot to forget since he was one of the most-feared persecutors of the early Christian church before his conversion. If he had chosen to dwell on his past, it very easily could have discouraged him from his powerful evangelistic work in the present. He might think he was unworthy to preach Christ after what he had done, or he might have become paralyzed by what the fellow believers might have thought about Him. Certainly, Satan must have tempted him from time to time to think that God couldn't really forgive and call him to be a leader in the church, but he pushed all these thoughts aside and chose to forget about the negative things he had done in the past, in order to focus on the work that the Lord had given him to do in the present.

He admits that even now he's not perfect (he's not yet apprehended), but since his conversion to Christ, he knows he is a new creation, with new motives, new purpose, and new zeal to serve God. All of us have done things in the past of which we're not proud. We may have been totally self-absorbed, hurt the people around us, or supported the cause of Satan in some way instead of the cause of God. But, praise God, whether our past has been filled with mistakes large or small, if we truly repent, He will forgive us, cleanse us "from all unrighteousness" (1 John 1:9), and give us a clean slate on which to write the rest of our life. If we don't get bogged down in the past, what a beautiful story of victory He will help us write there.

Next, Paul plainly states that, by faith, he is "reaching forward to those things which are ahead." This implies that, now that He is a Christian, He knows he has great things to look forward to. Even though there will still be bumps along life's road, the Lord has given him tremendous gifts already—grace, forgiveness, purpose, direction, precious promises to lean on, and the presence of the Holy Spirit in his life. He will have the satisfaction of helping to save many souls in his newly-commissioned ministry—and beyond all this, the joys of heaven still await him! We would do well to reach forward, too, since God offers us the same glorious gifts that he supplied to Paul as well as our own custom-designed ministry. Then, trusting in Jesus, we shall also experience the joys of heaven. Talk about something to look forward to!

Finally, Paul points out the need for determination. He reminds Christians that things will not always be easy, and there will be times when we feel like just giving up. Discouragement may try to interrupt our march forward in any number of ways—weariness, pain, sickness, betrayal by others, criticism, etc. So, here, Paul warns us to stay in the game. There is a need for "stick-to-it-ive-ness." The value of the goal "for the prize of the upward call of God in Christ Jesus" is more than worth our effort! Like Paul, we need to decide to press on until the goal is accomplished. Today, I have chosen as my new motto, "Reaching Forward."

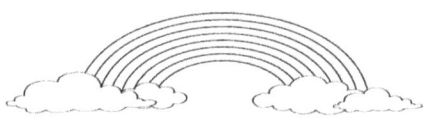

October 16

Citizenship

"For our citizenship is in heaven, from which we also eagerly wait for the Savior, the Lord Jesus Christ" (Philippians 3:20).

Whenever I read this verse, it captures my attention as being something special. There's a great deal of discussion these days about the concept of citizenship, both in the political realm and on social media. Here in the United States, we argue long and loud about who should be able to become a citizen as well as about what an American citizen's rights should be—and what a good citizen's responsibilities should entail. According to the dictionary, a citizen is a person who owes allegiance to a government and is entitled to its protection. While I found this definition a bit limited, it does point out that both the given government and the individual carry some responsibility in this relationship.

If I were writing the definition, I would be tempted to add something about the host of marvelous civil rights—such as voting, free speech, religious freedom, the right to congregate, and to move around the country freely, indeed the ability to get an American passport to move fairly freely around the entire world—that are available to those who can claim citizenship here. Some of us fortunate folks are born into citizenship while many others have had to expend time and money, plus the effort of obtaining and filling out endless paperwork and/or passing through blood, sweat, and tears in traveling from their old country, to finally obtain a place of belonging in their new one. It's interesting that the blessings of our legal citizenship here are so often taken for granted by many of us, yet they are so highly valued by those seeking refuge and opportunity from other parts of the world that they would do almost anything to become an American citizen.

There are so many parallels here between immigrants and our own journey toward becoming citizens of the "heavenly country." For instance, some of us have been born into Christianity while others have gone through great struggles and sacrifices before finding a place in this blessed community of believers. Often, those who have joined the group later tend to value it more than those who have always been Christians and who sometimes take their privileged status for granted. But make no mistake, the wonderful "rights" we receive as Christians—both now and throughout eternity—are worth whatever sacrifices we had to make along the way. As we know, some immigrants to the United States have given up family, friends, jobs, houses, and life in a culture and language that were comfortable for them to gain their goal of American citizenship. Likewise, in the heavenly kingdom, there will be those who gave up everything to become a citizen of that fair land. Another parallel can be found with the simple definition above, which is that we will owe our allegiance to our Savior, since He is the one who made it possible for the country of heaven to open its doors to us, and as citizens of His government, He has pledged to protect us under the shadow of His wings (see Ps. 17:8).

Meanwhile, volume 7 of the *SDA Bible Commentary* emphasizes a few other aspects of citizenship. It broadens the description to include the expectation of faithful loyalty from a citizen to his or her country as well as the fact that a good citizen should conduct himself or herself, wherever he or she goes, in a way that will represent his or her country well. As Christians, we can certainly see how these two elements—faithful loyalty and being a good representative of the heavenly kingdom—would be treasured by the heavenly government we seek to become a part of one day. But then comes the capstone! The *Commentary* explains that in this passage, Paul is emphasizing not what will happen one day but what should be happening now! Even though we are still living on earth, he says, "the Christian's citizenship is already in heaven" (*SDA Bible Commentary*, vol. 7, p. 172). Thus, we should be serving as ambassadors of our heavenly country today! Listen to this beautiful and amazing paragraph:

> The Christian needs a constant awareness of the fact that he is a citizen of heaven. Attachment to one's country leads him to be loyal to it. Wherever he may be living he will conduct himself in a way that will honor the good name of his country. Keeping in mind the kind of life we expect to live in heaven, serves to guide us in our life on earth. The purity, humility, gentleness, and love we anticipate experiencing in the life to come may be demonstrated here below. Our actions should disclose that we are citizens of heaven. Our association with others should make heaven attractive to them. (*SDA Bible Commentary*, vol. 7, p. 172)

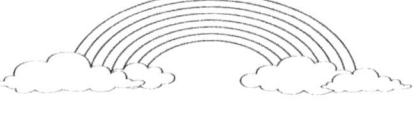

October 17

Meditations

"Finally, brethren, whatever things are true, whatever things are noble, whatever things are just, whatever things are pure, whatever things are lovely, whatever things are of good report, if there is any virtue and if there is anything praiseworthy—meditate on these things" (Philippians 4:8).

I find this verse a good rule of thumb to use whenever I am picking a book to read, a TV show to watch, or a movie in which to invest time. It is also a helpful guide in deciding what music to listen to as well as what conversations to participate in when talking with others. In today's world, with so much aggressive animosity on social media, political division, racial strife, natural disasters in rapid succession, and horrendous crimes filling the evening news, a person has to intentionally search for something positive to dwell on. And meditate? In a whirlwind society with so many deadlines and to-do lists, who has time to actually sit down, catch their breath, and meditate?

But that is the advice given to believers in this text. If we have grown up in Christian homes, most of us have been taught the importance of planning a personal daily devotional time with the Lord. Unfortunately, some of us have not taken this information to heart, and over time, with our busy schedules and the worries, cares, and stress of our everyday existence, having daily devotions is a practice that has frequently gone by the wayside.

It's interesting to note, however, that nowadays some secular meditation gurus have taken up the idea of pausing to focus on positive things as a way to help people relax, achieve better mental health, and find more balance in their lives. They have even turned the concept into a fairly lucrative business.

Meanwhile, as modern-day Christians, we are often losing out on the benefits—physical, emotional, and especially spiritual—that spending time meditating could bring to our lives. In this case, following Paul's injunction, we should be focusing on all the positive things around us. What better material to think about than all the blessings the

Lord has poured into our own lives? What better place to start than during a regularly-scheduled personal devotional time that is rooted deeply in the study of God's Word?

Curious, I looked up all the verses related to the topic of meditation in the small concordance found in the back of my Bible. Here's a taste of what I found to meditate on today:

"I will meditate on Your precepts, and contemplate Your ways. I will delight myself in Your statutes; I will not forget Your word" (Ps. 119:15, 16).

"This Book of the Law shall not depart from your mouth, but you shall meditate in it day and night, that you may observe to do according to all that is written in it. For then you will make your way prosperous, and then you will have good success" (Josh. 1:8).

"But his delight *is* in the law of the LORD, and in His law he meditates day and night" (Ps. 1:2).

"Oh, how I love Your law! It *is* my meditation all the day" (Ps. 119:97).

"Let the words of my mouth and the meditation of my heart be acceptable in Your sight, O LORD, my strength and my Redeemer" (Ps. 19:14).

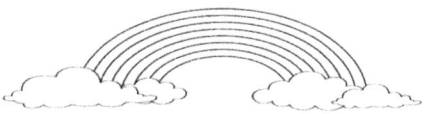

October 18

Promised Provision

"And my God shall supply all your need according to His riches in glory by Christ Jesus" (Philippians 4:19).

Philippians chapter 4 is chock-full of wonderful content. It's most famous verse, and with good reason, is the often-quoted, "I can do all things through Christ who strengthens me" (verse 13). But today's verse is a powerful, overarching promise, and one of my favorite texts in the whole Bible, upon which I have leaned many times through the years. I have claimed it for myself as well as dozens of other people for whom I care. Currently, I am claiming it for a very dear friend, and it gives me great comfort to be able to simply put her in God's capable hands, knowing that He will provide for her needs in better ways than I ever could.

Although in this case Paul was referring to his temporal needs, as he was thanking the Philippian believers for an offering they had sent him in support of his gospel ministry, the *SDA Bible Commentary* makes clear that he was telling them that because of their kind generosity, the Lord would fulfill their temporal as well as their spiritual needs (vol. 7, p. 179). Then it goes on to cite several examples, from both the Old and the New Testaments: Noah saved and provided for during the flood; the Israelites freed and protected during their Exodus journey; Elijah fed by ravens; and the three young Hebrew men preserved in the fiery furnace. Then, there was Mary and Joseph, provided with the wherewithal for their escape to Egypt through the gifts of the three wise men; John the Baptist, sustained out in the wilderness where he was heralding the coming of the Messiah; and the disciples of Jesus, who witnessed firsthand His power to multiply bread in order to feed the hungry.

All these experiences, in addition to the times the Lord has provided for us personally in our own lives, should serve to bolster our faith and help us to trust in the Lord in every time of need. I can think of several such incidents—including securing me a job when I needed it (before I had phone service) by sending somebody to my home from a town about twenty-five miles away to interview and hire me! Spiritually, He has met my need more times than I can count—with camp meetings, small group study sessions, Christian friends, early morning worship services, and the testimonies of others who have come to find Him faithful.

In addition to the examples listed above, there are several other great Bible verses that corroborate the fact that God is committed to caring for His children. Hebrews 1:14 tells us that the very angels of heaven serve as ministering spirits to supply the needs of those who are the heirs of salvation. And Isaiah 33:16 assures us that, even at the end of time, the bread and water of God's people will be sure. Finally, there's that marvelous text in Matthew 6:33, which says, "But seek first the kingdom of God and His righteousness, and all these things shall be added to you."

Knowing that Jesus is supplying our need from "His riches in glory" reminds us that His resources are unlimited. Just knowing that He is the one in charge of taking care of us—He who loved us enough to die for us to grant us eternal salvation—should give us more than enough confidence to claim this truly wonderful promise. After all, as His dear children, He loves to give us good gifts (see Matthew 7:11)! Let's open up our hearts, minds, and souls to be ready to receive them—whether temporal or spiritual—according to what He sees will be for our best good in each situation.

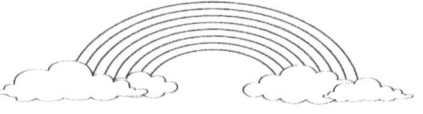

October 19

Spiritual Understanding

"For this reason we also, since the day we heard it, do not cease to pray for you, and to ask that you may be filled with the knowledge of His will in all wisdom and spiritual understanding; that you may walk worthy of the Lord, fully pleasing Him, being fruitful in every good work and increasing in the knowledge of God; strengthened with all might, according to His glorious power, for all patience and longsuffering with joy; giving thanks to the Father who has qualified us to be partakers of the inheritance of the saints in the light" (Colossians 1:9–12).

This is a fairly long quotation, but these verses just seem to beg to be presented together as Paul spells out to the believers in Colosse the many spiritual blessings he is praying for on their behalf. As their spiritual father, he shows his caring and concern for them by first letting them know that he does "not cease to pray" for them. Then he reveals the requests he presents before the Lord so that they may be healthy and productive members of the household of God. The list of petitions he makes on their behalf is impressive:

*That they would be filled with the knowledge of God's will.

*That they would have wisdom and spiritual understanding.

*That they would walk worthy of the Lord.

*That they would fully please the Lord.

*That they would be fruitful in every good work.

*That they would increase in their knowledge of God.

*That they would be strengthened with all His might.

*That they would develop patience and joy in the face of difficulties.

*That they would give thanks to God for qualifying them to be His co-workers.

*That they would be thankful to be "partakers of the inheritance of the saints."

Wow! What a treasure trove of blessings! These are things that any pastor would like to pray for his congregation. More than that, they are things any parent would like to pray for a child, and any grandparent would like to pray for a grandchild. In fact, I believe that just about anyone who is concerned about the spiritual growth and development of others could make good use of this prayer. I must happily confess that I pray it regularly for those who are near and dear to me in my own daily devotions.

As I reflect upon Paul's words, however, it occurs to me that people might think there is some redundancy here. I would argue that there is a shade of difference between "the knowledge of God's will" and the "knowledge of God." The first is to know His instructions for how we should live—such as the Ten Commandments and many other injunctions for God's people scattered throughout the Scriptures—while the second is a knowledge of the characteristics of God's character—who He really is in relation to us.

Another question that may arise is regarding the difference between "spiritual wisdom" and "spiritual understanding." While the word "spiritual" describes both in this passage, "wisdom" refers to the ability to discern right from wrong, to the correct application of knowledge, while "understanding" provides a deeper level of meaning. Not just the cerebral, objective decision-making ability, based on facts, but it includes the concepts of caring and compassion, putting oneself in the shoes of the other. The example that comes to mind is, would you rather have a government-appointed judge or your own mother trying your case? Obviously, one's mother would generally be the best choice because she would better understand your background, culture, personality, current circumstances, etc., and would ideally deliver a fair and judicious verdict, based not just on facts but also on love and grace.

Thankfully, that is how the Lord judges those who become His followers. Thus, Paul here prays that the new believers, like their Lord, will exercise not only wisdom but also "spiritual understanding" in their Christian walk. This means that they would enjoy a deeper relationship with God as well as utilizing both head knowledge and heart knowledge in all their interactions with others. All these centuries later, may Paul's earnest prayer for believers also bless us accordingly.

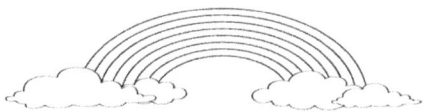

Beware Deceitful Philosophy

"As you therefore have received Christ Jesus the Lord, so walk in Him, rooted and built up in Him and established in the faith, as you have been taught, abounding in it with thanksgiving. Beware lest anyone cheat you through philosophy and empty deceit, according to the tradition of men, according to the basic principles of the world, and not according to Christ" (Colossians 2:6–8).

I'd like to begin today with a quote on this topic from the *SDA Bible Commentary*. Before I do, however, this might be as good a time as any to express my appreciation for this most valuable resource, developed by a team of dedicated biblical scholars, which has enriched and deepened our understanding of God's Word throughout our journey through the Scriptures this year. As a layperson, I have been blessed by the wisdom and expertise shared in its pages, which have helped us avoid the *deceitful philosophy* we're discussing today and focus on *God-centered truth*, purposed to build up and establish our faith. Now for that quote: it states,

> The apostle is not condemning philosophy as such, nor is he denouncing philosophers. What he is warning against is philosophy such as the false teachers at Colossae [aka Colosse] were parading, which was in reality emptiness and vanity, and was promoted by deceit. The context suggests that this philosophy had to do with ceremonial observances, human beliefs, traditions, and materialistic habits and viewpoints, all of which tend away from the gospel of God. (*SDA Bible Commentary*, vol. 7, pp. 201, 202)

A little later this paragraph goes on to say, "The center of this philosophy is the exaltation of man, while God is completely excluded or ignored. The Christian should be forewarned and forearmed against those who teach it. Its end is eternal death" (*Ibid.*).

My daughter loves philosophy so much so that she majored in systematic theology in graduate school. Along the way she was, of course, introduced to many diverse theologies and philosophies. As parents, who had worked diligently to teach her the basic rudiments of the gospel, we were sometimes a bit nervous that she might be swept away by some new or false wind of doctrine. Thankfully, she seems to have come through her seminary program largely unscathed. She does hold a few beliefs different than ours, but she is still a Bible-believing, Christ-serving Christian who shares most of the basic tenants of our faith.

So, what's wrong with philosophy? There's nothing wrong with thinking deeply about the major existential questions of our day and even discussing and debating them. Note from Paul's words that the problem comes in when we base our answers on conjecture, filling in the blanks of our knowledge based on "ceremonial observances, human beliefs, traditions, and materialistic habits and viewpoints." Many humanly-devised philosophies, whether old or new, are not shored up by what God has to say about these ideas in His word. Paul is warning the new believers that if a school of thought does not take into account the wisdom of God, it is deceitful and not to be trusted. In fact, he calls these philosophies empty and vain, saying that ultimately, their end is "eternal death."

It's a pretty strong warning. But Paul has worked so hard to preach the gospel in Colosse and bring these people into a trusting relationship with Christ, he doesn't want anything distracting them from the truth. At the very time the apostle penned these words, there were false teachers in their part of the world spreading deceitful philosophies that he knew, if followed, would bring destruction upon the new believers.

Looking around us today, it seems that Satan hasn't changed his tactics much. The church in our time faces the same danger of getting side-tracked by philosophies tied to the "basic principles of the world," as did the early church. How can we make sure not to be deceived? Paul not only forewarns but also forearms us with the same advice he gave to them. He admonishes Christians to be "rooted and built up" in Christ, "established in the faith" that we've been taught, and "abounding in it with thanksgiving." The message I take away from this is that the more established I am in my faith in Jesus and the teachings of His word, the safer I will become from being deceived by whatever false philosophies are swirling about me, regardless of their source or how appealing they may seem.

Lord, help us to be so firmly established in your truth that we will not be deceived. In our Christian walk, may we stay close to You.

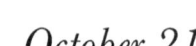

October 21

Off with the Old

"But now you yourselves are to put off all these: anger, wrath, malice, blasphemy, filthy language out of your mouth. Do not lie to one another, since you have put off the old man with his deeds, and have put on the new man who is renewed in knowledge according to the image of Him who created him" (Colossians 3:8–10).

From the time I was a little girl, I have enjoyed trying on different clothes and pretending to be like the people who owned them. I was one of the younger female cousins in a large extended family, and many of my aunts had become professionals who wore fashionable clothing to work. Happily, as the styles changed, or they tired of a particular outfit, many of these nice clothes were handed down to me and my younger sister. Since I had more interest in dressing up, I could pretty much keep whatever suited my fancy. As I donned the blouse, skirt, dress, or suit of a specific relative, I would imagine myself doing her job—thus, I daydreamed of being an executive secretary, an accountant, owning my own business, selling houses, etc. Although the clothing was usually too expensive to wear to my junior high school, I was able to select several well-fitting items for church or special occasions. Just wearing those clothes made me feel like a whole new person!

This is how it should be for the new Christian. In today's passage, Paul is reminding us that once we have put on "the new *man*" of the righteousness of Jesus, the "old man," with his old un-Christlike deeds, should no longer be seen. We should put off the old and put on the new. Then we should begin acting like the person whose clothes we are wearing: our thoughts, our words, our attitudes, and our deeds should all begin to be like the person who has so graciously given us our new garments. The unattractive rags of anger, wrath, malice, blasphemy, filthy language, and lying will no longer fit us. They will seem totally out of place when we are "dressed up" in the beautiful clothing the Lord has handed down to us.

I love these verses because they paint such a vivid picture for me of how a person's life changes when he or she accepts the Lord as his or her Savior. It also bespeaks the fact that our kind Benefactor holds high expectations for His redeemed ones. He wants our characters to represent the beauty of His character. His lovely traits should be seen in us. The sparkle of His joy, grace, and kindness should shine out to all the world through us. Who would ever want to go back to wearing the filthy rags of sin? Let us all determine to say, "Off with the old!"

I'm reminded of the well-known story of our childhood where Cinderella's dirty rags became a glorious gown fit for the palace of a king. But in our case, the robe of Christ's righteousness is our glorious gown, Jesus is our king, and our palace is the kingdom of heaven! Praise God for our own personal "rags to riches" story when we choose to follow Him and please Him in all our words and actions, thus becoming more and more like Him every day!

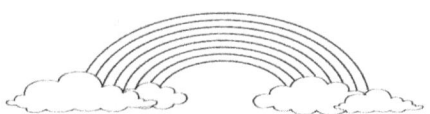

The Bond of Perfection

"Therefore, as the elect of God, holy and beloved, put on tender mercies, kindness, humility, meekness, longsuffering; bearing with one another, and forgiving one another, if anyone has a complaint against another; even as Christ forgave you, so you also must do. But above all these things put on love, which is the bond of perfection" (Colossians 3:12–14).

In today's passage, Paul describes what the characteristics of a "new man" should be (see Col. 3:10). It's quite a list: holy, beloved, merciful, kind, humble, meek, patient, and forgiving. Sounds like a description of the character of Jesus, doesn't it? Of course, that's the point. Christians should represent the Master they are following, but Paul doesn't stop there. He continues, "But above all these things," like modern preachers who say, "If you don't remember anything else I've said today, remember this." More than any of these wonderful traits, Paul wraps up his discussion on Christian character and ties it with a bow when he declares, "Put on love, which is the bond of perfection." Using another metaphor, he makes it clear here that love is like the frosting on the proverbial cake!

Curious about Paul's use of the term "bond of perfection," I looked to see what my trusty *Bible Commentary* had to say. First, speaking of love, it said, "That which should bind together all other qualities is love. No matter how high may be the profession of the nominal Christian, if his soul is not filled with love for God and for his fellow men, he is not a true disciple of Christ" (*SDA Bible Commentary*, vol. 7, p. 212). It then defines the word "bond" as "that which binds together" (*Ibid.*, p. 212). Earlier in Colossians this word is used to refer to the ligaments of the body. "Love binds together into a perfect unity the qualities of the individual Christian and the various members of the...body of Christ" (*SDA Bible Commentary*, vol. 7, p. 212). Thus, the word "bond" in this passage can refer not only to the blending of Christian traits into a beautiful, symmetrical whole in each believer in Christ but also to a unity and peaceful harmony among one another in the community of faith. Finally, I wondered how the word for "perfection" would be explained. The *Commentary* indicated that this word could be described as a kind of "maturity" in the Christian life. "Each in his own sphere is to attain to the highest development" (*Ibid.*, p. 212).

The next logical question, then, seems to be, "Where and how can I obtain this love?" As we have studied before, love is one of the fruits of the Holy Spirit. So, it follows that we need to ask God, the source of all true love, to pour it into our love-thirsty souls through the agency of His sweet Spirit. Once will not be enough. We will need to continue to ask for this precious gift regularly, so we can generously share it with those all around us. I like to look at each Christian characteristic as if it were a flower. Then, when the individual blossoms are all bound together, they become like a beautiful, fragrant bouquet, blessing all who see it and come within the reach of its lovely scent.

How will we know when we have this kind of love? I believe that the actual characteristics named in today's verses will become the best evidence that God's love is resident in our hearts. If we are overflowing with God's love, it won't just hide inside of us but will be poured outward through our loving actions of mercy, kindness, patience, forgiveness, and compassion—outgoing, proactive deeds of love, like those practiced by our Lord when He lived among us. Like the old song says, "They'll know we are Christians by our love!"

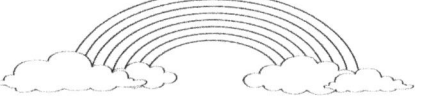

October 23

Singing with Grace

"Let the word of God dwell in you richly in all wisdom, teaching and admonishing one another in psalms and hymns and spiritual songs, singing with grace in your hearts to the Lord" (Colossians 3:16).

We have talked about the place and value of music in the worship of God before thanks to several verses in the Old Testament. But today we have a New Testament injunction regarding the use of music, not only to worship God but also to instruct and admonish one another. The prerequisite here is that one be well-versed in the Word of God. That is what will supply us with the wisdom needed to utilize music in a way which will edify our Christian brothers and sisters.

I like that this verse mentions more than just the use of the Psalms, which come directly from the Bible. It also includes time-honored hymns written by Christians with a close walk with the Lord during their lifetimes. It even suggests the use of more informal "spiritual songs," which may spring from the grateful heart of a believer.

This suggests to me that a variety of musical styles are acceptable both in the worship of God and also as we seek to be a blessing to others. Could this mean that varying worship styles in our churches, especially when the members are from diverse cultures or the service is geared to a generation or two behind us, might be more acceptable to God than we may have previously thought? According to the text, the important thing is that in our worship music we are "singing with grace in our hearts to the Lord."

While meditating on this verse, a traditional hymn came to mind, which I sing from time to time when I sit down to practice the piano. If you've been a Christian for a while, you probably know it, too. Its title is "I Will Sing of My Redeemer." I wanted to share it with you today because I believe it's a great example of a hymn that presents the writer's personal testimony while also instructing others regarding the plan of salvation and amplifying God's saving grace. Thus, the singing of it is right in line with what today's verse is seeking to inspire Christians to do. It's hymn 343 in *The Seventh-day Adventist Hymnal*, if you'd like to sing along.

> I will sing of my Redeemer, and His wondrous love to me; On the cruel cross He suffered from the curse to set me free.

> I will tell the wondrous story, how my lost estate to save, in His boundless love and mercy, He the ransom freely gave.

I will sing of my Redeemer, and His heav'nly love to me; He from death to life hath brought me, Son of God, with Him to be.

Chorus:

Sing, oh, sing of my Redeemer, with His blood He purchased me; On the cross He sealed my pardon, paid the debt, and made me free!

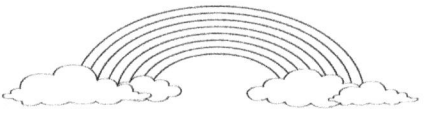

October 24

"As to the Lord"

"And whatever you do, do it heartily, as to the Lord and not to men, knowing that from the Lord you will receive the reward of the inheritance; for you serve the Lord Christ" (Colossians 3:23, 24).

We have come across the phrase "as to the Lord" previously in our study, but we discuss it here specifically in consideration of this passage. In pondering these verses, a number of scenarios come to mind where we might be tempted not to do our best work. The first one has to do with situations where we feel what we are doing is not of much value. As a retired person, I feel myself sinking into this line of thinking when it falls to my lot to do the many repetitive household chores here at home, such as making the bed, doing the dishes, and folding the clean clothes. At these times, it helps to adjust my attitude when I remember that "whatever" I do, it should be done "as to the Lord."

Another pitfall which can trip us up is believing that our work is in vain. When we don't see immediate results when training up a child (see Prov. 22:6), planting a seed, or our labors in various missionary endeavors, it's easy to get discouraged. Why should we put so much time, effort, and resources behind a project that looks, at first glance, as though it's not making a difference? The best answer I can think of is that human experience has taught us that these types of labor take time to produce results. Anyone who has raised a child, planted a garden, or thrown themselves into Christian outreach programs has had to learn to be patient when waiting to see the ultimate outcomes of their efforts. And, at times, the results won't become fully evident until after we have passed from the scene. Once again, we should encourage ourselves with God's promise that if our work is done *in the Lord*, it will *not be in vain* (see 1 Cor. 15:58).

Next, there's the circumstance when your boss doesn't really seem to appreciate you. This can be demoralizing, especially when your financial situation depends upon your job. Perhaps you're doing your work to the best of your ability, but your boss just doesn't seem to recognize how much you are accomplishing or perhaps you have a difference of opinion about what needs to be done and how. Motivations might clash, methods might not align, or there may be a mismatch in the ultimate goals or vision for your particular job description. When the demands are too all-consuming, the employees are not treated with respect, or the pay is too little for the work to be done, it may be time, if possible, to look for another job. In the meantime, focusing on the fact that, as Christians, we are always representing Jesus and that He is our true boss and the One we are always

and ultimately serving, leaning on today's verses can buoy us up. Daniel, of course, is an excellent example of this. No matter which king he was serving, and regardless of the government in charge, he always kept it clear in his mind that the real master he served, over and through it all, was the Lord.

Lastly, co-workers can also make your life on the job miserable in a number of ways. They may make disparaging remarks about you or your work. Perhaps they've set a low-quality work standard and expect you to fall into line. Or there may be little acts of dishonesty that everyone else is participating in, such as stealing things from the company or not putting in an honest day's work, and you are tempted to do the same. If you don't comply you are looked upon as a "goody two shoes" or someone who thinks he or she is better than everyone else. Then, too, as in Daniel's day, you may have co-workers who are jealous of you or envious of your position. They may lie or gossip about you behind your back, sometimes seeking to thwart your work. Once again, today's scriptures provide encouragement for us to continue to work "heartily, as to the Lord and not to men, knowing that from the Lord you will receive the reward of the inheritance; for you serve the Lord Christ." What better motivation could we have for doing our work well, whatever it is, since the Lord, who is our Example and our Master, is at the same time our Judge and the Rewarder of all those who are faithful?!

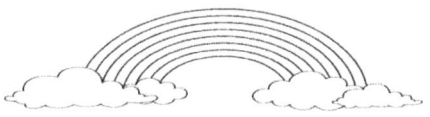

Mind Your Own Business

"...that you also aspire to lead a quiet life, to mind your own business, and to work with your own hands, as we commanded you" (1 Thessalonians 4:11).

Have you ever lived in a community where someone was always sticking their nose into other people's business? Having experienced this in a church setting, I can tell you that it is not only unpleasant but can also create far-reaching social and even legal ramifications. To make matters worse, it's very difficult to change this type of behavior because the perpetrator often feels they are simply doing God's will in telling everyone else what to do and how to do it. Never mind that they may have glaring faults and problems in their own lives. Somehow, they can only concentrate on trying to run somebody else's life! Besides being a busybody, these same folks often tend to spread gossip throughout a community, even to the point of slandering others!

In today's verse Paul is trying to avoid these kinds of problems in the early church by admonishing them to lead quiet, hard-working lives, where they mind their own business. He emphasizes this point again later in his second letter to the Thessalonians, where he says: "For we hear that there are some who walk among you in a disorderly manner, not working at all, but are busybodies" (2 Thess. 3:11). Initially I thought these were the only references that addressed this issue. I discovered, however, that Paul also mentions this topic in a couple of specific places in his writings to Timothy. In the first instance, he is talking about qualifications for deacons and their wives, when he says, "Likewise, *their* wives *must be* reverent, not

slanderers, temperate, faithful in all things" (1 Tim. 3:11). In the second instance, Paul is talking about some of the unacceptable habits of a number of widows in the community of believers. "And besides they learn *to be* idle, wandering about from house to house, and not only idle but also gossips and busybodies, saying things which they ought not" (1 Tim. 5:13).

Obviously, we should take an interest in our fellow believers and provide a helping hand when they are in need, but this can be a delicate work. I have found that two principles can make our attempts at helping our brothers and sisters much more successful. First, we should make sure we're not violating personal, social, or cultural boundaries that might make our actions offensive to them. Then, I believe it's important to ask them what they need. Advice that is not solicited can often be rejected out of hand, and donations in times of disaster can sometimes miss the mark. For example, they could be too much of one thing and not enough of what is really needed in a given situation. For instance, in a recent fire disaster in our state, many people donated food, but nobody thought to donate diapers.

After living in a variety of places, I have discovered a difference in social boundaries, even in diverse sections of the same country. It is a subtle thing, but I learned the hard way that some people are very open to talking about their physical ailments, answering questions about their health, and requesting prayer for specific ailments or anticipated procedures, while in other regions of the United States, people are very "hush-hush" about any health issues they are suffering and may ask only a few people they know well, if any at all, to pray about their situation. They hold their health secrets close to their vest and feel violated if others share their personal information on a wider scale. Nowadays, of course, with the HIPAA law, Americans can even take legal recourse if their health information is shared without their permission.

So, this is an area in which we need to ask the Lord to help us—to control our tongues from gossip, to squelch our tendencies to try to direct the lives of others, and to give us wisdom not to cross people's boundaries so that our involvement in their lives will be perceived by them to be truly helpful as opposed to intrusive.

Lord, help us not to be busybodies!

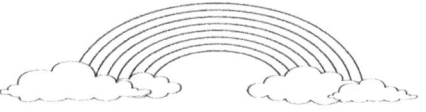

October 26

Caught up in the Clouds

"For the Lord Himself will descend from heaven with a shout, with the voice of an archangel, and with the trumpet of God. And the dead in Christ will rise first. Then we who are alive and remain shall be caught up together with them in the clouds to meet the Lord in the air. And thus we shall always be with the Lord. Therefore comfort one another with these words"
(1 Thessalonians 4:16–18).

What a glorious promise this is! Whenever I read it, I remember the many Christian funerals I have attended where these powerful assurances have brought comfort and hope to the mourners. In fact, verse 13 in this same chapter tells us why we are given this information. It states, "But I do not want you to be ignorant, brethren, concerning those who have fallen asleep, lest you sorrow as others who have no hope." And what a blessed hope this is—knowing that when Jesus comes again, our faithful loved ones will be resurrected, and those of us who are still alive will be caught up "together with them" in the clouds! Just think of the wonder of it all! We will then start our unending heavenly existence, and the Lord promises He will always be with us throughout the rest of eternity!

Unfortunately, I have also attended non-Christian funerals where people did not have this same blessed hope. I can only imagine the depth of their grief believing they will never see their loved one again, nor do they know what will happen to them after they die. It seems their sorrow will never be assuaged, and it is no wonder that there is so much darkness and depression as the friends and family of the deceased person struggle through their devastating loss and pain.

At my own father's funeral, I remember being so buoyed up by the bright and comforting hope brought by the words we are considering today that I felt a new and stronger motivation to share this gift of comfort with others. It has fostered a belief that we should become even more involved than we have ever been in various kinds of evangelistic efforts to try to help mitigate the emotional pain and searing loss they experience after the death of a loved one. What could be a more fulfilling mission than to share Christian comfort and hope with others in one of their greatest times of need?

But there is more to today's passage. Not only does it direct our thoughts toward the joy of our reunions at the resurrection but it also points us forward to the time of our own translation from earth to heaven, if we will remain faithful until the time when Jesus returns to take His children home with Him. Have you ever wished that you could just fly away from this earth and all of its problems? This will be the day when that wish comes true! Just imagine being caught up in the clouds, just as Jesus was when He Himself ascended to heaven after His sojourn here on earth. Sometimes, when I watch puffy white clouds sailing across a blue sky or when I fly through them on an airplane, I muse about what it will be like to live up above them—way above them—as a new, unfettered immortal being! Just think of it... the whole universe will be ours to explore! As a person who loves to travel, these are exciting thoughts indeed!

Thank You, Lord, for both the comfort and the anticipation that we glean from dwelling on your Word.

Pursue What is Good

"See that no one renders evil for evil to anyone, but always pursue what is good both for yourselves and for all" (1 Thessalonians 5:15).

Before ending his first letter to the Thessalonians, Paul admonishes the believers there to "pursue what is good." Then, in the verses that follow this one, he kindly provides guidance by spelling out in more detail what this might look like in the everyday life of a Christian convert:

Verse 16 – Rejoice always,

Verse 17 – pray without ceasing,

Verse 18 – in everything give thanks; for this is the will of God in Christ Jesus for you.

Verse 19 – Do not quench the Spirit.

Verse 20 – Do not despise prophecies.

Verse 21 – Test all things; hold fast what is good.

Verse 22 – Abstain from every form of evil.

As I'm sure you'll agree, this looks like a pretty good list for modern-day Christians to abide by as well. My problem is that it's a little hard to focus on all of them at once. So, as part of my own pursuit of goodness, since there are seven admonitions, and there are seven days in a week, I decided to think about, memorize, and concentrate on practicing one of them each day for the next week—just to absorb them more deeply into my soul.

While some may see this approach as a bit "works" oriented, I believe that when the Bible says we need to pursue something, it implies that we need to put in a bit of effort to follow after it, or in this case, acquire it as an integral part of our character.

Now, I'd like to address the segment of the verse that exhorts us to follow after goodness not just for ourselves but for all. To me, "others" refers to those within our own personal sphere of influence while "all" might refer to everyone on a larger scale, such as everyone in a church, a community, a society, or even a country. In practical terms, this means we will seek that which is good for our children, our friends, our fellow church members, etc., by kindly and generously thinking of what's best for them when we are making our decisions, and, as Christians, we will also be good citizens in view of the greater good of society. To break it down even more, this might include behaviors such as voting for what we believe is best, obeying traffic laws, helping to keep the environment clean, and any number of other civic responsibilities, in keeping with the pursuit of what is good for all. Some Christians I have met feel that since we are planning on leaving this earth soon to go to live in heaven, we need not concern ourselves with making things better here and now. I believe this verse argues against that point of view. Wherever we are, for as long as we're there, we should be making it a better place, seeking the good for all—at work, in our neighborhoods, at church, and in our nation.

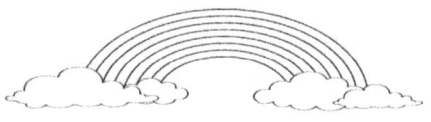

The Love of the Truth

"The coming of the lawless one is according to the working of Satan, with all power, signs, and lying wonders, and with all unrighteous deception among those who perish, because they did not receive the love of the truth, that they might be saved. And for this reason God will send them strong delusion, that they should believe the lie, that they all may be condemned who did not believe the truth but had pleasure in unrighteousness"
(2 Thessalonians 2:9–12).

Have you ever been lied to by someone you trusted? If so, you know the sting of disappointment or perhaps even betrayal when it hits you that neither the information nor the person who told the untruth can be fully trusted in the future. Unfortunately, most of us have experienced this unpleasant occurrence, which seems to take place on both a personal and public scale at an alarming rate these days! We won't even begin to discuss here the current political situation, which has gone completely off the rails when it comes to truth-telling! Long ago, the prophet Isaiah predicted a time like this when he wrote "Justice is turned back, and righteousness stands afar off; for truth is fallen in the street, ad equity cannot enter. So truth fails..." (Isa. 59:14, 15a). Suffice it to say, we all need to beware of who we are listening to and check the facts for ourselves before we decide what to believe.

But we're not alone in our quest for truth. In Jesus' day, Pilot asked his now famous question, "What is truth?" (John 18:38). Throughout time, philosophers, researchers, and scientists of every kind have invested a good deal of time, effort, and money searching for "truth" in their respective areas of interest. Here, however, we are in search of a more existential truth—a spiritual truth.

According to today's passage, knowing what truth is and loving it will make the difference between whether we will be saved or lost.

So, what better place to search for spiritual truth—saving truth—than the Word of God. John 17:17 says, "Sanctify them by Your truth. Your word is truth." The concordance in the back of my Bible supplied me with these additional verses regarding the word "truth." In John 8:31, 32, Jesus Himself said this to the Jews who believed Him, "If you abide in My word, you are My disciples indeed. And you shall know the truth, and the truth shall make you free." In the famous and comforting Psalm 91:4, David assures us that in times of trouble, "His truth *shall be [our]* shield and buckler." The psalmist also talks about truth in Psalm 119:142, where he declares, "Your righteousness *is* an everlasting righteousness, and Your law *is* truth."

Perhaps the most definitive statement about spiritual truth in the Bible is the one made by Jesus found in John 14:6, where He clearly announces to His disciples, "I am the way, the truth, and the life. No one comes to the Father except through Me." One could argue that the disciples had it a lot easier than us in learning to know and love the "Truth" because they got to see, hear, touch, and follow Jesus around for the three and a half years of His earthly ministry. So, where does that leave us? Are we at a disadvantage? Not really, because Jesus thought of us—the Christians who would believe in Him after He had returned to heaven—and He gave us this wonderful promise in John 16:13: "However, when He, the Spirit of truth, has come, He will guide you into all truth; for He will not speak on His own *authority*, but whatever He hears He will speak; and He will tell you things to come." Thus, Jesus has made provision for those of us who ask Him, while abiding in Him and His word (see John 15:7), with the marvelous gift of the Holy Spirit, and He has pledged by that means to guide us into all truth.

In summary, we've learned that God's word and His law contain the saving truth we are seeking and that He, Himself, is the very embodiment of truth. Best of all, we are blessed with the knowledge and assurance that the Holy Spirit, if we allow Him, will not only help us to know the truth that will save us from perdition but to love it. Praise God that His truth will shield us from the lies swirling all around us and from the deceptions that would rob us of salvation!

Lord, please give us your loving Holy Spirit to guide us into all truth!

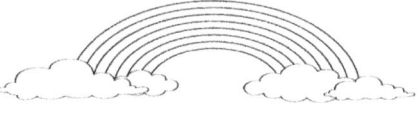

October 29

Everlasting Consolation

"Now may our Lord Jesus Christ Himself, and our God and Father, who has loved us and given us everlasting consolation and good hope by grace, comfort your hearts and establish you in every good word and work"
(2 Thessalonians 2:16, 17).

"**E**verlasting consolation"—the term just rolled off my tongue as I read it. I would venture to say that never have we needed "good hope" and the comfort of God more than when I am writing these words. Between the lingering pandemic, bringing us the fear of falling ill and the sorrow of losing loved ones, as well as crime and mass shootings everywhere from malls to churches, no place seems safe. Add to that the many recent and even-more-alarming-than-usual natural disasters—from devastating fires on the West Coast to crippling winter storms across the Eastern Seaboard—not to mention the current political chaos and unrest in countries around the world, including our own, it's no wonder that people are distraught, depressed, and desperate for consolation! Our souls are longing for liberty from the many sin-induced woes of this world.

Thank the Lord, He understands our need. The Bible is replete with promises that have brought comfort to God's people throughout the long years since His sojourn here on Earth. One good example of this is found in Revelation 21:4, which declares, "And God will wipe away every tear from their eyes; there shall be no more death, nor sorrow, nor crying. There shall be no more pain, for the former things have passed away."

In today's passage Paul is exhorting the believers in Thessalonica that they should continue their good words and work in their region through the strength of the love of God and the grace they had received from the Lord Jesus. As they did so, they were already receiving a down payment, so to speak, of the bright hope and eternal comfort which they would enjoy throughout the ages in their heavenly home. I believe this counsel is also for us.

Recently, I asked a friend what the first thing that came to mind for her was when hearing the term "everlasting consolation."

"No more tears," she said.

"Yes, unless maybe they are tears of joy," I responded. Then I thought of all the painful and difficult things we experience in this life being wiped away when Jesus comes, and it will not be for a moment or even a day but forever and ever. No more sickness, sorrow, pain, death, temptation, trials, lies, betrayals, wars, danger, fears—just everlasting consolation! Praise the Lord! May we, by faith, begin to taste of it now! This week I had the pleasure of hearing (virtually) a congregation singing the hymn "Be Still, My Soul," which is hymn 461 in *The Seventh-day Adventist Hymnal*. I thought the last verse, especially, fit with today's theme:

> Be still, my soul: the hour is hastening on
> When we shall be forever with the Lord,
> When disappointment, grief, and fear are gone,
> Sorrow forgot, love's purest joys restored.
> Be still, my soul: when change and tears are past,
> All safe and blessed we shall meet at last!

A Place in Ministry

"And I thank Christ Jesus our Lord who has enabled me, because He counted me faithful, putting me into the ministry" (1 Timothy 1:12).

In his epistles Paul readily admitted that He had made many mistakes in his life. He had even been an ardent enemy of the truth he was now proclaiming. But after Jesus met him on the road to Damascus, his life totally changed. He was completely converted, and for the rest of his life, he dedicated all his efforts to building up the kingdom of God by serving the Messiah he had once rejected and evangelizing in much of the then-known world. It was as if he was trying to make up for lost time. He preached about Jesus to both Jews and Gentiles, men and women, young and old alike. He started and nurtured fledgling churches. He visited them to encourage the new believers, and he wrote them letters full of instructions on how to live a Christian life.

The two books of Timothy are written to the young pastor of the church in Ephesus. Paul loved Timothy and served as a mentor for him. Here, in chapter 1 of First Timothy, Paul addresses him as "a true son in the faith" (verse 2). As Paul is giving glory to God for His amazing grace in saving sinners, he can't help but stop and share a few words of his own testimony. In fact, this is the chapter where Paul calls himself the "chief" of sinners (verse 15). He knows that if he can be forgiven and entrusted with a place in God's kingdom, anyone can! He described the grace of the Lord as "exceedingly abundant" on his behalf (verse 14), and he felt both humble and grateful for the ministry he was enabled to fulfill in God's cause.

Have you ever felt humbled and thankful for a ministry in which God placed you? I know I have. After working for a number of years in teacher education programs in the public sector, my husband and I received a call to see if we were interested in working as missionaries in a Christian institution of higher education in the Caribbean. Somewhat surprised at this turn of events, we prayed about it and started the long and arduous process of being vetted. We didn't know if the Lord would ultimately open this door for our family, or not. About a year later, however, we found ourselves on a plane to Puerto Rico! We were amazed, humbled, and somewhat in awe of the way that the Lord had changed the direction of our lives and that we had been selected for this sacred commission. Not being sure of all that awaited us, but realizing our lives would never be the same again, we entered this assignment with a mixture of trepidation and thanksgiving! Like Paul, we decided that if God had, by His grace, given us a special place in ministry, we could also count on that same grace to enable us to do it to His glory!

Traditionally, when we talked about a minister, we meant someone, usually a man, who preached and led out in religious services. In the contemporary Christian churches of today, however, we recognize that there are a variety of ways in which people can minister to others, using the diverse gifts God has given them. We get this idea from 1 Corinthians 12:5, which instructs us that "There are differences of ministries, but the same Lord." In fact, this same chapter informs us that we all have a place of ministry in God's service whether in preaching, teaching, healing, administration, translating, or prophesying, and the list goes on. God's work needs ministers of music, those who can run children's ministries, counselors who can minister to families, people who can develop ministries for our youth, young adults, and seniors, and folks who can do member visitation, nurturing those who are spiritually or physically weak. Not to mention Christian writers, missionaries at home and abroad, prayer warriors, and media ministers of all kinds (radio, TV, internet, etc.)

Recently, I attended an ordination service for a young, enthusiastic pastor at a large church whose primary mission was to minister to the poor and needy in an adjacent city. Obviously, there is no lack of positions to be filled in order to serve in ministry. All that's lacking are more converted people like Paul, who will gratefully and faithfully serve in whatever ministry the Lord calls them to, knowing that He will also enable them to do it to God's glory!

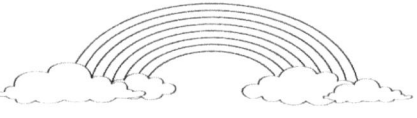

October 31

Spiritual Exercise

"But reject profane and old wives' fables, and exercise yourself toward godliness. For bodily exercise profits a little, but godliness is profitable for all things, having promise of the life that now is and of that which is to come"
(1 Timothy 4:7, 8).

Nowadays the benefits of exercise for physical and even mental health are touted far and wide. Everywhere you look—television, the internet, social media, and popular magazines—all promote the need of the human body to move on a regular basis. In fact, I'm sure you've heard the adage, as I have, of "sitting is the new smoking," in order to motivate people to get up out of their chairs and off their sofas and to develop an active lifestyle. And, of course, scientific evidence abounds regarding the value of regular exercise, not only to lose weight but to build muscle, strengthen bones, improve respiration, boost energy, increase longevity, and decrease feelings of depression.

Here, Paul uses the analogy of physical exercise to compare it with the need for spiritual exercise. Just as our physical bodies require exercise to be healthy, our souls need to engage in spiritual exercise to become strong and healthy. After all, as he points out, physical exercise will only help us in this temporal life, whereas the "exercise" of godliness will benefit us both now and in the life to come. So, while not diminishing the benefits of bodily exercise, this scripture is inviting us to be even more dedicated and devout about becoming more Godlike.

This begs the familiar question we have asked before, "How do I become more like God?" Well, perhaps we could take preliminary stock of ourselves by checking to see if we devote at least as much time each day to godliness as to our physical exercise program. (Although some of us don't spend enough time here either!) After all, it's common knowledge that if we really want to get to know someone and wish to emulate them, we need to spend a lot of time with them, since it is by beholding that we become changed. The Bible expounds on this truth when it says, "But we all...beholding as in a mirror the glory of the Lord, are being transformed into the same image from glory to glory..." (2 Cor. 3:18). God's glory, of course, is His perfect character of love, righteousness, patience, gentleness, kindness, and grace, as described by Paul later in the book of First Timothy. In chapter 6 Paul exhorts Timothy to "pursue" this kind of "Godliness" (verse 11). Thus, becoming more like God should be our most important goal in life.

Just as people can use tools (weights, walking shoes, treadmills, stationary bikes, etc.) to help them exercise, there are tools we can use in order to strengthen our spiritual life. The most common, of course, are reading the Bible, praying, and listening to sermons. But there are many other aides available. Devotional books, like this one, can help busy people "devote" regular time daily to communing with God. Other things I have found to be helpful are listening to sacred music, reading biographies of faith-filled Christians, and making a prayer journal where I can record my answered prayers as well as blessings that I want to thank and praise God for each week. I love to meditate on ways, both big and small, that the Lord is intervening in my life to remind me of His personal care for me. Fellowship with other people who are also making it a priority to grow closer to God is of great help, as well, on our Christian journey. And, last but not least on my list, is becoming involved with either formal or informal outreach programs where I have the opportunity to serve others, share my testimony or my faith, and build spiritual muscle in the process. The best part of all of these spiritual exercises is that they will not only serve me well to meet the challenges of faith I will meet in this short life but also help prepare me for the eternal life to come. Thus, they are more than worth the effort!

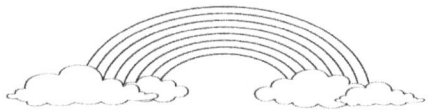

Contentment

"Now godliness with contentment is great gain. For we brought nothing into this world, and it is certain we can carry nothing out" (1 Timothy 6:6, 7).

Yesterday, we talked about godliness. Today, we are talking about contentment, which is actually an element of godliness. When I looked this word up in the dictionary, what a host of lovely synonyms I found: satisfaction, delight, enjoyment, gladness, relish, and ease of mind, to name a few. These nouns evoke a picture for me of someone who is relaxed about their life situation, thankful for what they have, and at peace with God. It's actually a pretty good picture of Jesus, who was never greedy or grasping for power or the material things of this world. He was never envious, jealous, or covetous. He maintained His peace by simply resting in God's will for His life. As we know, He didn't even have a place to lay His head (see Matt. 8:20), but He was not worried because He trusted in God to supply His needs. In fact, in Matthew 6:25–34, He gave His disciples a short treatise on this subject, telling them to stop worrying about what they were going to wear, eat, or drink. Instead, He told them not to even worry about what was going to happen tomorrow but to make the kingdom of God and His righteousness their priority, and He would take care of their future.

In this chapter, Paul is discussing the errors of greed and covetousness. He goes so far as to say in verse 8, "And having food and clothing, with these we shall be content." It's a verse that's hard to come to grips with in twenty-first century America. In our materialistic society, it sometimes seems like we're in a race to see who can collect the most stuff before we die! Even though, in today's short and not-so-sweet passage, we are brought up short by the reminder that, after death, these things will cease to be our belongings. They will mean nothing to us! All that work to acquire them and all the worry to protect and care for them will seem like a waste of time and effort in eternity...unless they were used to help build up the kingdom of God. Does this mean that modern-day Christians should all go around living like vagabonds? Is it a sin to own and enjoy nice things?

This is a concept I have wrestled with, and though I am not a theologian, the following are my conclusions. As humans we all have basic necessities, especially if we have been blessed with a family. We need a home (with some furniture, of course) for shelter and protection; we need good, healthy food and water; we need clothes appropriate to the weather and our daily activities, and most of us need some mode of transportation. (As modern mothers, most of us would also expect, at minimum, to have a stove, refrigerator, washer, dryer, and a microwave!) The possession of these things is not bad. We use them to nurture our families, fellowship with friends and extended family, and extend hospitality to others. I would argue that these activities are all in line with what could be considered as building up the kingdom of God. The problems arise when we

1) love our possessions more than we love God

442

2) use our possessions to "lord it over" other people who have less

3) spend so much money on these things that we have nothing left to invest in the Lord's work

4) invest so much time in working to pay for extravagant and unnecessary "toys" that we neglect our health or rob our families of time we should spend with them

5) allow our things to bog us down, keeping us from being agile in responding to God's call to serve in a new location.

A related problem is feeling covetous of the possessions of other people to the point that we can no longer be satisfied with what we have let alone be thankful to God for our material blessings!

Lord, help us not to make an idol of our possessions, but to seek first Your kingdom and Your righteousness. May we set our priorities straight and be satisfied—content— with what we have. Amen.

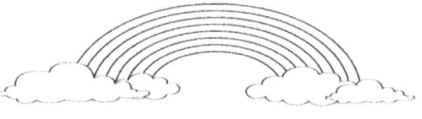

November 2

The Love of Money

"But those who desire to be rich fall into temptation and a snare, and into many foolish and harmful lusts which drown men in destruction and perdition. For the love of money is a root of all kinds of evil, for which some have strayed from the faith in their greediness, and pierced themselves through with many sorrows" (1 Timothy 6:9, 10).

These verses are really just a continuation of the discourse started yesterday because they flesh out in more detail the difficulties that arise when we are not content with what we have. Granted, as humans, we would all like to improve our lot in life in one way or another, but at some point, after meeting our need for the basic necessities we discussed yesterday, it would be well to reflect upon how much more in the way of material possessions, including money itself, we really need. When our cupboards, refrigerators, and freezers contain more food than we could—or should— ever eat, when our closets, drawers, and storage areas are bursting at the seams with clothes we never wear (one of my problems), and when we have three or four modes of transportation sitting in our driveways, perhaps this would be a good time to take stock of why we keep trying to acquire more.

I suppose greediness is one reason. The carnal man is always grasping for more than he already has, indeed, for all he can get for himself. Unfortunately, this can eventually lead to wanting what belongs to other people as well. Here, of course, he is moving into the territory of covetousness, which results in breaking the tenth commandment of God's law. After crossing this line, it's only a short journey to breaking other laws like, "Do not steal" or "Do not lie."

Thus, Paul nips our selfish greed in the bud by clearly stating where it leads. Even desiring to be rich is a snare to our spiritual life because it makes us fall into temptation "and *into* many foolish and harmful lusts which drown men in destruction and perdition." Then he warns that even "the love of money is a root of all *kinds of* evil," which can cause people not only to abandon their faith but to pierce themselves through with many sorrows. Wow! Could Paul have used any stronger language?

So, among the questions that beg for an answer here are: how far are we willing to go in acquiring money and/or material possessions? Are we more interested in making money than in maintaining our integrity, keeping our faith and moral fiber intact, or improving our relationship with God? As Jesus so earnestly asks in Matthew 16:26, a verse we have talked about before, "For what profit is it to a man if he gains the whole world, and loses his own soul? Or what will a man give in exchange for his soul?"

As we know, Judas sold his soul for only thirty pieces of silver. What's our price? Satan is always tempting us on this point, in ways both large and small, because He knows our natural tendency is to be selfish.

He tries to deceive us with the notion that once we obtain the riches that we desire, we will finally be content. He hides the fact that in getting things, our greedy addiction usually only strengthens, leaving us dissatisfied until we obtain ever more than we had before!

Should we conclude, then, that possessing money and material things is always bad? Keep in mind that the verse says "the love of money is the root of all *kinds of* evil." What is most important to us in life? Where do our priorities lie? Do we love God more than our money? If so, we will delight in using it, along with all we possess, to build up God's kingdom here on earth. Later in this chapter, Paul actually addresses those Christians who are already rich, giving them instructions on how they should live. In verses 17–19, he gives this admonition:

> Command those who are rich in this present age not to be haughty, nor to trust in uncertain riches but in the living God, who gives us richly all things to enjoy. *Let them* do good, that they be rich in good works, ready to give, willing to share, storing up for themselves a good foundation for the time to come, that they may lay hold on eternal life.

This shows us that whether we are rich or poor we can be content in the knowledge that God has a place for us in His family if we will not make an idol out of whatever we possess but instead concentrate on being "rich in good works."

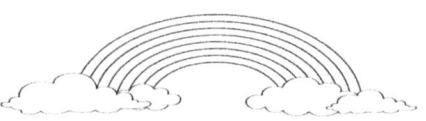

Persuaded

"For this reason I also suffer these things; nevertheless I am not ashamed, for I know whom I have believed and am persuaded that He is able to keep what I have committed to Him until that Day" (2 Timothy 1:12).

Tradition has it that this second letter to Timothy, Paul's spiritual son, was the last epistle he wrote before his death. He was in prison in Rome at the time and surmised his death was imminent. Thus, he wanted to encourage Timothy, as well as others who would read this final letter, to be faithful in maintaining their belief in the truth and steadfast in preaching the gospel, despite trial and persecution.

Paul did not sugarcoat his message. He understood clearly that he was imprisoned because of teaching and preaching the gospel of Jesus Christ. Not because he was a common criminal or a person of questionable character, but because He was not ashamed of Jesus, nor was he ashamed to teach and preach in His name across the Mediterranean world. In fulfilling his calling as an apostle of Christ, he had suffered much—false accusations, beatings, shipwreck, chains, and prison more than once—yet he was not turned aside from his mission. However, he knew that those who followed in his footsteps would also suffer and might be tempted to give up their faith. He wanted to set an example that would give them courage and hope, regardless of any difficulties they might face, and his wise words to them still encourage us today. In 2 Timothy 1:7, he reminds Timothy that "God has not given us a spirit of fear, but of power and of love and of a sound mind." How can he talk about having a sound mind and not being overcome by fear when he is, at that moment, sitting in a dark Roman prison awaiting death? Because, as he admonishes the believers to do, he is focused on the power and love of God. He believes the Lord's promise that he will be resurrected to live in a far better place and entrusts his life into God's hands.

Later, in verse 13, he exhorts Timothy to "Hold fast the pattern of sound words which you have heard from me, in faith and love which are in Christ Jesus." Then, in verse 14, he states that we can remain loyal to the gospel "by the Holy Spirit, which dwells in us." Chapter 2 begins with a tender entreaty: "You therefore, my son, be strong in the grace that is in Christ Jesus" (verse 1), and a few verses down we find this declaration: "You therefore must endure hardship as a good soldier of Jesus Christ" (verse 3). That puts a different spin on things. Paul is preparing those who come after him by letting them know that the Christian life will not be easy and take them down a path strewn with flowers; instead, it will be like serving as soldiers in Christ's army, where believers are engaged in a universal battle between good and evil. A battle to save not only our lives for eternity but to save as many others as possible who will accept the Lord as their Savior. Thank God that Jesus is our great Commander, and we know that He will ultimately be victorious!

In the second part of today's verse, Paul goes on to reveal why his faith and courage remain strong despite his sufferings. He proclaims, "for I know whom I have believed and am persuaded that He is able to keep what I have committed to Him until that Day." He knows the Lord, and whatever comes, he trusts in His sovereign plan. Paul is completely persuaded (convinced) that, as he departs this life, he can commit both his ministry and his new converts into God's hands, and the Lord will take care of it all until the day of His glorious second coming. Then everything will be made right. Our battles will all be behind us, death itself will be abolished, and we shall bask in the blessings of immortality, sharing an eternal life in the light of God's presence, making anything we have suffered in this life seem insignificant in comparison!

This surrender of all that Paul valued set me to thinking. When I come to the end of my life, will I be ready to commit all that is important to me into the Lord's hands? Will I cheerfully and carefully mentor my successors to carry on the work into which I have poured all my time, energy, and strength? I hope, like Paul, I will be thoroughly persuaded to turn all that I leave behind over to Him—my past work, my current unfinished projects, my prized possessions, my friends, my church, and certainly my family, not to mention my earthly body itself—simply trusting in the knowledge that He is able to do what's best with it all until that marvelous day when we meet again!

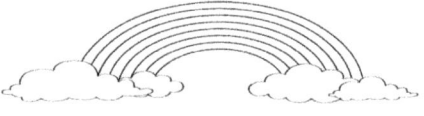

November 4

Avoid Disputes

"But avoid foolish and ignorant disputes, knowing that they generate strife. And a servant of the Lord must not quarrel but be gentle to all, able to teach, patient, in humility correcting those who are in opposition, if God perhaps will grant them repentance, so that they may know the truth" (2 Timothy 2:23–25).

Having lived and worked around educational institutions most of my life, disputing the opinions of others, proving one's own position, and striving to arrive at "ultimate truth" were common activities. Colleges and universities value the study of fine points, they encourage independent thinking, and they even sponsor debate clubs in order to train students on how to express and defend their opinions, and what's more, how to win an argument. I agree there may be some occupations where these skills could really come in handy, such as when a lawyer is defending a client in a court of law.

The problem arises, however, when we incorporate this spirit of "always having to be right" into our daily lives, sometimes to the detriment of our relationships. What's worse, and this is a trap into which I myself have fallen, is that we have tried to bring people to the Lord by arguing with them. Not a very effective strategy! I think that sometimes, in my youthful exuberance to share the gospel, I may have scared more people away from the kingdom of God than into it. One day, in a conversation with another pastor's wife, she reminded me that our focus when trying to save the lost should not be to be right at any cost, but to love at any cost! It was a paradigm shift in my witnessing style.

Does this mean that there is no place for sharing the truth with people? Should we allow them to believe anything they want in order not to ruffle anyone's feathers? Does this relieve us from any responsibility to evangelize the world, which Christians have seen as their calling since Jesus told His disciples to go into all the world and preach the gospel to all nations (see Matt. 28:19, 20)? We might ask, "What place does doctrine hold in our modern, permissive society, where anything goes?" In many of the large and popular churches of today, as long as people say they are Christians, their doctrinal beliefs are immaterial. Does the Lord care what they believe?

I included the third verse in today's passage because it helps us answer these concerns about the role of doctrine in the Christian's life. Yes, doctrines matter, but notice that the emphasis here is on how they are presented. So, this is what I've learned from Paul's guidance to believers on this topic. First, don't go around arguing with people all the time regarding every little point of doctrine. Agree with them where you can in order not to generate strife, which could ultimately lead them to reject the truth simply because they reject your approach. Second, we're admonished to be gentle and patient with everyone (including the young, the old, and even those in our families). And third, teach them in humility. This is where any correction of opposing views can take place. When this last verse says that it is here that God may grant them to know the truth, we are reminded that we need to leave room for the Spirit of God to do His holy and effective work to convince people to believe and accept doctrinal truths. If we follow Paul's advice not to engage in foolish disputes but choose instead to use God's methods, we can be assured the Lord will be able to more successfully use us as the vessels through which people will come to "know the truth."

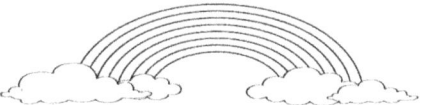

Thoroughly Equipped

"All Scripture is given by inspiration of God, and is profitable for doctrine, for reproof, for correction, for instruction in righteousness, that the man of God may be complete, thoroughly equipped for every good work" (2 Timothy 3:16, 17).

Since my husband and I grew up mainly in sunny Southern California and then worked for a number of years in the Caribbean, we were totally unprepared for the winter weather we encountered upon moving back to the States and being called to serve in the upper Midwest and, for a time, on the East Coast. While the easterners just took it in stride, we were not accustomed to dealing with so much cold and snow—for approximately six months of every year! We immediately realized that the clothes we were used to wearing would not be adequate. We needed to buy some specialized clothing in order to brave the blustery winter weather ahead of us. Thus, we began to equip ourselves with the necessary items—gloves, boots, scarves, earmuffs, and several types of overcoats and jackets to protect us—depending on the weather for a given winter day. Whether it was wet or dry, snowy or windy, or just plain COLD, once we were thoroughly equipped, we were able to successfully go about our business. Admittedly, it took us a little longer to get dressed for the day, but once we stepped out into the frigid air, we were glad we had put forth the extra effort. It made all the difference in our ability to survive and even thrive in such a harsh environment.

The Bible is like this. As people of God, living and working in the harsh environment of sin, the Bible can thoroughly equip us not only to survive as Christians but to thrive! It is our preparation and protection while we seek to do the good works of God. Regularly studying it, of course, takes a certain amount of time and effort, but the results in helping us live purposeful and productive lives will be more than worth it!

Today's passage assures us that all Scripture is inspired by God; therefore, we can trust it to guide us. Paul goes on here to delineate specific ways in which the Bible can assist us in our Christian walk. He says it is useful to us in determining doctrine. Additionally, it provides reproof and correction if we have begun to go off track spiritually as well as giving us "instruction in righteousness" so that we can continue to grow more like Jesus every day!

The New King James version tells us that by incorporating God's Word into our lives in this way, we may "be complete, thoroughly equipped for every good work." The old King James version of the Bible that many of us grew up with, states verse 17 this way: "That the man of God may be perfect, thoroughly furnished unto all good works." Whichever version we read, it is clear that by immersing ourselves in His word, we will become totally prepared—outfitted, if you please—to meet the challenges of life. All of our notions of unworthiness, inability, or inadequacy to do God's work can be thrown to the wind in the light of this declaration. By ourselves, we might freeze up when contemplating accomplishing the tasks that God has assigned us as His witnesses in the world. But armed with the strength of His truth, shrouded in the garments of His grace, protected by His promises, and empowered by His mighty words, we can be confident that He has prepared us for all that lies ahead.

November 6

The Well-Finished Race

"I have fought the good fight, I have finished the race, I have kept the faith. Finally, there is laid up for me the crown of righteousness, which the Lord, the righteous Judge, will give to me on that Day, and not to me only but also to all who have loved His appearing" (2 Timothy 4:7, 8).

I selected today's passage because recently I have been privileged to watch some footage of several events in the Olympic Games. One can't help but be inspired by the total dedication of the Olympic athletes, regardless of the country they represent or the contest in which they compete. Most of them have been practicing their sport for years, trying to hone it to the highest level of perfection in the hope of being named the best in the world, not to mention the medal and honors they will receive if they can place as one of the top three in their event.

I was particularly impressed with a cross-country skier, who obviously gave all she had to her contest. With her last ounce of energy and one huge gasp for air, she fell just across the finish line, sprawled out on the snowy ground for the next five minutes or so, trying to muster the strength to get up and acknowledge her cheering fans. She lay there totally exhausted yet overjoyed at her victory—she had won the race!

I like to envision the apostle Paul like that. Since his conversion, he had given his all to the work that Jesus had assigned him. Despite discouragements, setbacks both within and without of the church, persecutions and privations throughout his ministry, he did not let anything detain him from accomplishing his mission (see 2 Cor. 11:24–28). As we just saw in the reading for November 3, He had been beaten, stoned, shipwrecked, without shelter, and imprisoned—in fact, he was still a prisoner in Rome at the time he was writing this very epistle, yet he was not having a pity party, nor was he discouraged or downhearted. He had dedicated everything to the Lord—his intelligence, education, time, effort, money, influence, talents of public speaking and writing, and now, as if with one last burst of zeal, he was ready to lay down his very life for the cause of God.

Was he exhausted? Probably—yet he was also filled with joy because he knew he had given his all! He also knew that his efforts would not be in vain. There would be precious fruit from his sacrifices, and all the seeds of the gospel he had planted along the way as he was "running his race." Already, he had seen the new believers in Christ form churches in most of the population centers in the middle east where he had lived, taught, and preached. The intrepid evangelist knew he had "run a good race." He also knew that He would win a prize, but unlike an Olympic medal of gold, silver, or bronze, the Lord Himself would bestow a crown of righteousness upon him, honoring him with an award of eternal worth and glory!

So, now it's our turn to run the race. Will we do our best? Will we give it our all? Will we dedicate all we have and are to the cause of God? Will others be saved due to our efforts? Will we please the righteous Judge of heaven and earth? Will we receive the prize of eternal worth that He is preparing for us when we come to the end of our race? These are weighty questions.

Thankfully, Paul gives us hope and encouragement as he pens the last line of verse 8, where he adds, almost as a postscript: "And not to me only but also to all who have loved His appearing." Unlike the Olympics, in this race we are promised that we can all win the prize of the crown of righteousness! The Lord knows that we do not all possess the amazing talents and the prodigious energy of the apostle Paul, but if we put it all on the line, dedicating what we do have to Him, we can also run our race with distinction! How comforting to know that when we are running the race representing Him, He will be there at the finish line, just waiting to celebrate our victory with us!

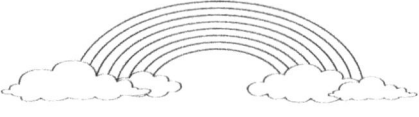

November 7

Good Works

"This is a faithful saying, and these things I want you to affirm constantly, that those who have believed in God should be careful to maintain good works. These things are good and profitable to men" (Titus 3:8).

We have touched on the topic of good works on several occasions this year, but I believe this subject is so important for Christians that it warrants another look. After all, this verse exhorts us to "affirm constantly...to maintain good works." In just a cursory reading of the book of Titus, Paul uses the term "good works" at least six times (and the book only contains three short chapters!). Today's verse seems to be the capstone, but if we look at several of Paul's other references to good works in this short epistle, we catch a better understanding of the kinds of behaviors he is admonishing believers to demonstrate and maintain.

To make his meaning clear to Titus, the young pastor at Crete to whom he was writing, Paul discusses what "good works" might look like for different groups of people in his fledgling church. First, he describes the qualifications of elders:

> [They] must be blameless, as a steward of God, not self-willed, not quick-tempered, not given to wine, not violent, not greedy for money, but hospitable, a lover of what is good, sober-minded, just, holy, self-controlled, holding fast the faithful word as he has been taught, that he may be able, by sound doctrine, both to exhort and convict those who contradict. (Titus 1:7–9)

Many people think that "good works" means witnessing to non-believers, but these texts make it evident that the term includes serving the church as well.

Next, he talks about the older men in the congregation. He states that they should "be sober, reverent, temperate, sound in faith, in love, in patience" (Titus 2:2). Then he describes the role of the older women, saying they should "be reverent in behavior, not slanderers, not given to much wine, teachers of good things" (Titus 2:3). And this is where the young women are mentioned. The older women are to "admonish the young women to love their husbands, to love their children, *to be* discreet, chaste, homemakers, good..." (Titus 2:4, 5). It was interesting to me that being a good homemaker is also considered good works! Finally, he addresses the young men of the church, exhorting them to be "sober-minded, in all things showing yourself *to be* a pattern of good works; in doctrine *showing* integrity, reverence, incorruptibility, sound speech that cannot be condemned, that one who is an opponent may be ashamed, having nothing evil to say of you" (Titus 2:6–8). I like that he tells the young men to be "a pattern of good works," taking a leadership role in spiritual excellence.

Before leaving this discussion regarding what good works should look like in the church, Paul stops to remember even the bondservants (perhaps due to his own chains) who have become Christians, urging them to "be obedient to their own masters, to be well pleasing in all *things*, not answering back, not pilfering, but showing all good fidelity, that they may adorn the doctrine of God our Savior in all things" (Titus 2:9, 10). I love that last statement. Imagine, even the bondservants can "adorn the doctrine of God" by doing the kinds of good works that Paul has described here.

After studying the book of Titus, I fear that sometimes our view of good works has been too limited and narrow, even falling into disrepute in some modern-day churches who have claimed as their mantra, "We are saved by faith, not by works!" While that is true, Paul seems to agree with another apostle, James, who writes, "I will show you my faith by my works" (James 2:18). In fact, Paul provides clarity on this topic in Ephesians 2:10 when he indicates *we are not saved by our good works, but to do good works!* Finally, he emphasizes their importance to the Christian in Titus 2:14, where he says that we are trained by the saving grace of Jesus, "who gave Himself for us, that He might redeem us from every lawless deed and purify for Himself *His* own special people, *zealous for good works*"! (emphasis added).

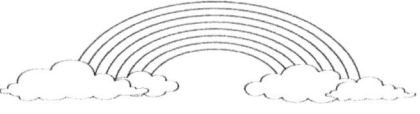

November 8

Thankful Prayers

"I thank my God, making mention of you always in my prayers"
(Philemon 1:4).

Is there someone in your life for whom you are always praying? As a mother, my daughter is someone for whom I am always making mention whenever I talk to the Lord. At the same time I am asking for her protection and that the Lord will give her wisdom, grace, and guidance, I am also profoundly thankful to Him for bringing her into the world and for the amazing gifts He has given her to share in her sphere of influence.

In this case, Paul is writing to his beloved spiritual brother and co-worker in the cause of God. This short book is a warm and heart-felt letter to Philemon, asking him to graciously forgive and take back his runaway slave, Onesimus, who is now a changed man, having become a believer in Christ. He does this with great tact and tenderness, loving all the believers in the early church as though they were family. His evangelist's heart overflows with thanksgiving for each of them, and he is praying for them without ceasing—much like a Christian parent does for his or her children.

In looking up what the *SDA Bible Commentary* says on this verse, here is some of what I found: "Sharing with God the joys and sorrows of life as friend to friend, is prayer at its best" (*SDA Bible Commentary*, vol. 7, p. 379).

"... Paul reminds Philemon of the deep respect and gratitude the apostle feels toward him" (*Ibid.*).

"There is an abundance of encouragement in the certain knowledge that a beloved and respected friend is praying for us, that this friend has full confidence in our integrity and sanctified judgment. Such is the assurance that Paul gives Philemon" (*Ibid.*).

This verse, short and sweet as it is, reminds us of the fact that, as Christians, we should not only love and be thankful for our brothers and sisters in the church but should often be found in prayer for one another. I believe this should be done not only in a formal way at worship services, at prayer meetings, and in church prayer teams but also informally as we lift our hearts to God in prayer throughout the day. In a church that believes in intercessory prayer, it may be difficult to remember all the prayer requests that come to us in a given week, which is why I have found it helpful to maintain a personal prayer list. This is the only way, especially at my age, that I can remember to pray specifically and consistently for all the people who have asked me to pray for them. I also find my list helpful in being able to check off the prayers that have been answered, giving me renewed faith and filling my heart with praise and thanksgiving to God. As I find opportunity to share these answered prayers with others, their faith can also be strengthened.

In recent years, my list has gotten so long that I have divided it up into sections and then assigned a section to each day of the week. First of all, I pray for nuclear family members and folks in our extended families on both sides—mine and my husband's. I then pray for our many friends—from the past as well as the present. Church members and their requests make up another section of the list, which are followed by those who are fighting illness, the bereaved who need comfort and strength to go on,

and people we have worked with in the past, hoping to see them soon in the kingdom of God. My husband and I join in prayer for all our Christian educational institutions, for the pastors of the churches with which we're associated, and church administrators at all levels. We pray for wisdom for our government and its leaders, we remember the millions of refugees around the world, and we pray for those who so selflessly work to alleviate their suffering.

Last, but certainly not least, we pray for the many media ministries that are seeking, through radio, television, and the internet, to reach people around the world for Jesus. All of this, in addition to our perpetual prayers for our loved ones and "emergency prayers" for people in sudden and great need is a huge task—but it is a privilege and a blessing to us! We are honored to be called to such important work, always keeping in mind Paul's instructions to Christians, found back in Philippians 4:6, to mix thanksgiving for what God has already done into all of our petitions: "Be careful for nothing, but in everything by prayer and supplication, with thanksgiving, let your requests be made known to God."

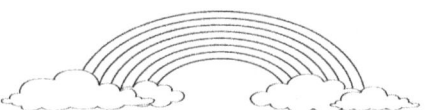

Culture Clashes

"God, who at various times and in various ways spoke in time past to the fathers by the prophets, has in these last days spoken to us by His *Son, whom He has appointed heir of all things, through whom also He made the worlds"* (Hebrews 1:1, 2).

The author of the book of Hebrews is primarily addressing the many Jews who had adopted Christianity and were seriously grappling with which Jewish customs to retain, and which could be laid aside, now that Jesus was the center of their worship and the means of their salvation. For years, they and their ancestors had based their relationship with God on the ancient religious ceremonies first initiated by Abraham, then taught by Moses, and continued by the prophets and holy men of the Old Testament. After all, the beginnings of their way of worship had first been suggested fresh out of Eden by God Himself, when Cain and Able were asked to offer a sacrificial lamb to show that they had faith in the promise that God would send a Savior who would die to redeem them and their parents from their sins. Had God changed His mind? Had the patriarchs and priests been mistaken in teaching and practicing the many temple-related ceremonies that had given structure to their religious life for so long?

Paul and the other apostles worked hard to explain that Jesus was the Messiah to whom all their religious practices pointed. Now that He had come and sacrificed His life to save all who would accept Him, the sacrificial system, along with its elaborate trappings, was no longer necessary. They taught the new believers that they had been living under the old covenant between God and His people, but now that Jesus had come, they would be living under a new covenant—a new agreement, if you will, between them and God. God's own son, the One who had helped create the worlds (as today's passage points out), had become their only-one-time-needed Sacrifice, their all-sufficient Atonement, and their heavenly High Priest.

Once this glorious truth had sunk in, the new believers felt a religious freedom in Christ that they had not experienced before. Yet, old habits die hard, and even though they now understood why the sacrificial system was no longer necessary, they still had a few questions about other parts of their Jewish culture. Should they continue to keep all the feasts? Would they still maintain a kosher diet? Would circumcision be required of Christians? What place would the Ten Commandments and the many ceremonial laws of the Old Testament hold in their lives now? Another major issue, even for the apostles, as we found out in the story about Peter being reticent to go to the house of Cornelius to preach the gospel, was how the Jewish Christians should relate to non-Jewish Christians. Should the "foreigners" adopt Jewish customs, such as circumcision, in order to become acceptable members of the early Christian church? These were all issues that had to be ironed out in the first years of Christianity—and it wasn't a simple matter, since new converts with diverse cultures, lifestyles, and languages were quickly responding to the gospel from all over the ancient world. Only as the leaders allowed themselves to be guided by the Holy Spirit were they able to make wise decisions regarding how to deal with the many complicated issues which arose.

As members of a worldwide church, with people from many cultural and language groups joining our ranks on a daily basis, we should be able to relate. We find so many pressure points among folks who come from very different backgrounds trying to "fit in" to the body of Christ. We argue about worship styles, what people should wear, appropriate church music, gender roles, dietary requirements, Sabbath-keeping practices, which version of the Bible to use, and many other issues. It seems to me that our only safe course of action is, like the early church leaders, to ask the Holy Spirit to guide us in making wise decisions.

As God has communicated with the prophets in Old Testament times, and through the apostles in New Testament times, today's text assures us that now, in these last days, God's Son, none other than Jesus Himself, the One who God has "appointed heir of all things" and through whom the worlds have been made, will speak His will to us also. But we need to be prepared. There may be some areas where we will need to let go of cherished and well-ingrained past practices and open our minds to the new things the Lord is desiring to teach us, in order that we may live together in a way that truly represents His love and His grace.

November 10

Neglect

"Therefore we must give the more earnest heed to the things we have heard, lest we drift away. For if the word spoken through angels proved steadfast, and every transgression and disobedience received a just reward, how shall we escape if we neglect so great a salvation, which at the first began to be spoken by the Lord, and was confirmed to us by those who heard Him"
(Hebrews 2:1–3).

While meditating on this passage, there were three ideas that I wanted to give more consideration to—one from each verse.

In the first verse, we are reminded of how easy it could be to "drift away" from the Lord if we don't give "more earnest heed" to the truth we've been privileged to hear. Have you ever been to the beach and left something, a raft or an innertube perhaps, in the water while you ran to get something up on the seashore? When you turned around to go back to the waves, however, you couldn't help but notice that the items you left, taking your attention from them for only a few minutes, had drifted from where you left them. Sometimes, depending on the strength of the ocean's movements that day, it can be quite a distance away. It seems to me that our religious experience is something like that. If we don't pay attention (give heed), the strong currents of worldliness and sin that are swirling all around us, can, however imperceptibly, make us drift away from the Lord.

Meanwhile, the second verse confirms for us that "every transgression and disobedience" has already in Bible times, or will in the future, receive "a just reward." We have discussed this concept before. While the whole idea of judgment may be bad news to those who aren't practicing Christians, it's good news to those of us who are. Why? First, because 1 John 1:9 says that "If we confess our sins, He is faithful and just to forgive us *our* sins and to cleanse us from all unrighteousness." This is wonderful news! We have no reason to fear the judgment because Jesus has taken away our sins. Second, how reassuring it is to know that justice will one day prevail, and the Lord will finally set everything right that happened during our sojourn in this world. We serve an all-knowing God who is just and fair.

Finally, the third verse confronts us with the momentous question, "How shall we escape if we neglect so great a salvation...." You know, the word "neglect" doesn't seem so bad—just a little lack of attention here and there or simply becoming busy with other things that demand our time and interest for a while. But we've all heard sad stories of parents who have been charged with criminal neglect—withholding necessary attention to the harm, or even death, of their children. Whether we're talking about plants, animals, or children, a little period of neglect can be disastrous—even fatally dangerous. Just so, neglecting our spiritual life by failing to maintain our daily devotional time with the Lord, by not talking to Him or reading His word, can have disastrous consequences, not only in this temporal life but also resulting in our loss of the eternal life to come.

In summary of this trilogy of verses, I believe their purpose is to warn us to value the truth we've heard, paying earnest attention to our spiritual life, lest we drift away from God and fall under judgment, thus losing out on the wonderful gift of salvation the Lord has sacrificed so much to prepare for us.

Lord, help us not to neglect your great salvation!

Like His Brethren

"Therefore, in all things He had to be made like His brethren, that He might be a merciful and faithful High Priest in things pertaining to God, to make propitiation for the sins of the people. For in that He Himself has suffered, being tempted, He is able to aid those who are tempted" (Hebrews 2:17, 18).

As I sit down to write today, I can't quit thinking about an interview I saw on the morning news. The program anchor was talking to a thirty-something American young man about why he had decided to leave the relative peace and freedom of the United States to volunteer to join the Ukrainians in their fight against the invading Russian army. He informed the listening audience that he was just one among many other men from a variety of countries who had seen the news about what was happening in Ukraine and felt that it was their individual duty to do something to help "their brothers." He said he felt it was his calling—what he had been born for. He was an American military veteran who had just the skillset needed now in the heat of the battle. He had seen the suffering of many innocent people on TV and wanted to help them. He also knew that they could use more volunteer soldiers to assist them in their fight for their freedom and identity as a nation. So, leaving his family and country behind and setting aside any thoughts about his own danger, not to mention the hardships of war, he answered the call of his human brethren, fighting side by side with them until they could claim that victory was theirs!

His courage, bravery, and selflessness reminded me of what Jesus did for us. When the call came for help to save humankind from sin and perdition, Jesus volunteered. He left the peace, freedom, and glory of His heavenly existence as well as those who loved and worshiped Him behind, disregarding the suffering and sacrifices He knew He would face in the high-stakes battle between good and evil that was raging here on earth. He couldn't just stand back and watch while human beings were being cruelly attacked by Satan—especially when He knew He had the tools to help us win the fight against our overpowering and merciless adversary.

His choice, however, came at great personal cost. Let's take just a moment to consider His amazing condescension for us once again. It cost Him a lifetime of pain—emotional, physical, and spiritual. It cost Him sacrifices that we can't even comprehend, rejection, misunderstanding, and indignities that no one should have to endure. Eventually, it even cost His life. But, perhaps the most meaningful thing He did so that we would be able to relate to Him and trust Him to bring us to victory was to become one of us! Today's passage tells us that, "...in all things He had to be made like *His* brethren." Just think of it, He got hungry like we do, He got tired like we do, He experienced poverty and pain, AND He was tempted like we are. This, in fact, is why, "He is able to aid those who are tempted." Praise God! Because Jesus came down to us and became like our Big Brother, living and suffering and fighting against temptation just as we do, He understands us! What's more is that His sacrifices, His help, and His victory still apply to us today. They're as efficacious for Christians now as they were in the days of His earthly sojourn, and we know that they even reach back and save those who have trusted in God since the beginning of time.

Happily, thinking and talking about the courage, bravery, and selflessness of Jesus on our behalf inspires those same qualities in us. With His help, we know that the war against sin can be won, that we can get the victory over temptation, and that our exceedingly strong Big Brother, the very Captain of Salvation, is on our side!

November 12

The Throne of Grace

"For we do not have a High Priest who cannot sympathize with our weaknesses, but was in all points tempted as we are, yet without sin. Let us therefore come boldly to the throne of grace, that we may obtain mercy and find grace to help in time of need" (Hebrews 4:15, 16).

This is another one of those great passages in the book of Hebrews that gives us the sweet assurance that Jesus understands and sympathizes with us. It reminds us, once again, that He "was in all *points* tempted as *we are.*" Just let it soak in…He was tempted to disobey His parents; He was tempted to lose His temper; He was tempted to be impatient with others, to break all of the commandments, to get revenge on the people who mistreated Him, to speak unkind words to the people who crowded around Him for healing and hope day after day, to live an intemperate life, to desire riches or earthly power, to give up on saving us, and even to quit trusting in His heavenly Father.

The difference is, although all these temptations and more swirled around Him from the cradle to the grave, as the expression goes, He remained spiritually strong and sinless. Where we, in our human weakness failed, He, in the strength of His relationship with His heavenly Father, succeeded! And He did it for us because He loved us. He stood in the gap between us and God, as our perfect Substitute. It is for this reason that He is worthy to be our heavenly High Priest, mediating for us and representing us in the courts of heaven.

Whenever I read this text, I am reminded of brave Queen Esther, going uninvited before the throne of the powerful King of Medo-Persia, risking her own life to plead for the lives of her people, the Israelites. (See the Old Testament book of Esther for a refresher on the rest of the story.) In our case, however, we need have no fear because the King sitting on the throne of grace has extended a personal invitation to each one of us. Not only that but He has also told us to come boldly—as if that is where we belong! Whatever faults, mistakes, guilt, or shame we are carrying can be cast aside when we enter into His presence. Of course, we still need to ask for forgiveness and help to overcome our sins, but we come to Him knowing that He will accept us and restore us to a close relationship with Him. Why would He do this over and over again? Because He loves us, and having walked in our shoes as an earthly inhabitant, He thoroughly understands us. We don't need an intermediary, for we each have the privilege of coming to Him personally to present our petitions. Any day, anytime, anywhere...the Lord is always available to us. He has already done everything within His power to grant us eternal life, yet He chooses to continue to interact with us throughout our lifetimes. Listening to our concerns, forgiving us, encouraging us, giving us hope, and blessing us with material and spiritual blessings at every turn.

What a gracious Savior! What in this world could ever be important enough to keep us from falling before His throne in praise and thanksgiving every morning, knowing what He has done for us? Especially because He has promised that when we do, we will "obtain mercy and find grace to help in time of need."

November 13

Our Anchor

"This hope we have as an anchor of the soul, both sure and steadfast, and which enters the Presence behind the veil" (Hebrews 6:19).

Once upon a time, I had a father-in-law who was an auto mechanic. As a young man, he had served in the US Navy, and that experience had such an influence on his life that when he decided to start his own business, he called it the "Anchor Garage." It turned out to be a wise decision because soon other Navy veterans, who had also been inalterably shaped by their military service, came in to get their cars repaired in a place where they felt they could relate to the owner of the shop. He was an excellent mechanic with fair prices. Soon, by word of mouth, many other people in the area started bringing their cars to him, and he ended up with a thriving business in that same location for many years.

Personally, I know very little about anchors. I don't know anyone else who served in the Navy, nor have I ever had the pleasure of owning my own boat. But theoretically, at least, I understand the importance in keeping a boat where one wants it to stay. So, when I read today's text, I get an immediate mental picture of my soul staying safe from all the buffeting waves of life. And what does the verse say is this strong anchor that can keep my soul sure and steadfast even among life's strong and unexpected storms? Hope!

Hope in what? In this part of chapter 6, the author of Hebrews is talking about the wonderful hope of salvation found in Christ. He is the *"Presence* behind the veil," who is serving in the heavenly sanctuary as our High Priest, making sure our sins are forgiven and our path to eternal salvation is clear. Finding and maintaining a close relationship with Jesus is what will give us hope for a better future, not only in this short life but also for the eternal life ahead.

Whenever I think of an anchor in a spiritual sense, my mind turns to a traditional old hymn I am just now learning to play on the piano. It is hymn 534 in the *The Seventh-day Adventist Hymnal.* The words were written by Priscilla J. Owens, and the title is "Will Your Anchor Hold?" Consider its wonderful message with me:

Will your anchor hold in the storm of life, when the clouds unfold their wings of strife? When the strong tides lift, and the cables strain, will your anchor drift, or firm remain?

If 'tis safely moored, 'twill the storm withstand, for 'tis well secured by the Savior's hand; and the cables, passed from His heart to thine, can defy the blast, through strength divine.

It will firmly hold in the straits of Fear, when the breakers tell that the reef is near; though the tempest rave and the wild winds blow, not an angry wave shall our bark o'erflow.

It will surely hold in the floods of death, when the waters cold chill our latest breath; on the rising tide it can never fail, while our hopes abide within the veil.

When our eyes behold, in the dawning light, shining gates of pearl, our harbor bright, we shall anchor fast to the heavenly shore, with the storms all past forevermore.

Chorus:

We have an anchor that keeps the soul steadfast and sure while the billows roll; fastened to the Rock which cannot move, grounded firm and deep in the Savior's love.

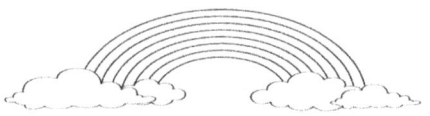

To the Uttermost

"Therefore He is also able to save to the uttermost those who come to God through Him, since He always lives to make intercession for them"
(Hebrews 7:25).

In this section of Hebrews, the author is talking about Jesus as our wonderful High Priest. In Old Testament times, the Israelites worshipped God through the sanctuary services that God had ordained in order to point the people forward to the coming of the Messiah—who would be the ultimate sacrifice for sin. In that system, many priests were needed to officiate and facilitate the worship services. When Jesus came, however, only one Priest—the Lord Himself—was required from then on. It is through Him alone, who "always lives to make intercession" for us, that we are saved "to the uttermost."

The word "uttermost" is not often heard in our usual modern discourse, but it means to the greatest extent possible, to the maximum amount, to the highest degree, to the most extreme level, the furthest imaginable, or as more commonly used today, simply as "to the utmost."

As I meditate on this verse, three ideas come to mind. First is how completely we are saved. It doesn't matter what we have done, how long we have sinned, or how far off track we have wondered, the perfect life of Jesus and His all-encompassing sacrifice are more than enough to cover all our sins. And He doesn't just cover them up. He totally forgives them and then wraps us up in His impeccable robe of righteousness. In this way, He saves us "to the uttermost." What a gracious Savior He is!

Second, this verse tells us who is saved. It says, "those who come to God through Him." Nowadays, people try to find a relationship with God in all kinds of ways—through transcendental meditation, mediums, cults, self-improvement schemes, philosophers, or even through their departed loved ones—just about any way imaginable, except through Jesus Christ. When the apostle Peter was talking to the unbelieving Sanhedrin about Jesus Christ of Nazareth, he boldly declared, "Nor is there salvation in any other, for there is no other name under heaven given among men by which we must be saved" (Acts 4:12). The Bible makes clear throughout the New Testament that accepting Jesus is the way to finding God and to receiving the gracious salvation that only He can offer. The critical factor is our decision to come to Him. We get so distracted by the sights and sounds around us, by our busyness, and by our general lack of interest in spiritual things that we fail to take the all-important step of coming to Jesus. In His great love, the Lord continues to call to us, even up to the last chapter in the Bible. In Revelation 22:17 He still entreats us: "And the Spirit and the bride say, 'Come!' And let him who hears say, 'Come!' And let him who thirsts come. Whoever desires, let him take the water of life freely."

The other thought that impresses me in today's text is the amazing availability of Jesus. Notice the phrase, "He always lives to make intercession for [us]." It's what He lives for! To help us! Whenever we need Him! The heavenly sanctuary in heaven never closes.

Jesus is there to listen to us, forgive us, cleanse us, and save us twenty-four seven! To the uttermost!

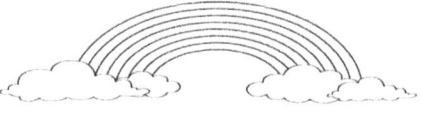

November 15

The New Covenant

"For this is the covenant that I will make with the house of Israel after those days, says the LORD: I will put My laws in their mind and write them on their hearts; and I will be their God, and they shall be My people"
(Hebrews 8:10).

As we discussed yesterday, this part of Hebrews compares the old priesthood with the new priesthood. It also compares the old system of worship with the new and the old earthly sanctuary with the new heavenly one. All of these things that were part of the "old covenant" were changed after the coming of Jesus. Believers in Jesus are now called to be part of a "new covenant." In this covenant, even the characteristics of the believers themselves have changed. Previously, worshippers were focusing on not only the external laws of the Ten Commandments but also on the civil injunctions in the books of Moses as well as the many ceremonial laws of the scribes and pharisees. Clearly, theirs was a very legalistic society.

Fortunately, the new covenant that Jesus offers His people is built on "better promises" (Heb. 8:6). His emphasis is on the inner self. He wants to free us from concentrating on rules and regulations, becoming obsessed with our own progress or comparing ourselves with those around us. Our focus instead should be on Jesus and all that He has done for us. He says that for those who believe in Him, He will actually write His laws in our minds and on our hearts.

So, what does this look like in real life? Does the Lord encourage us to disregard civil or societal rules? No, as long as they don't run counter to His expressed will. We know this from His famous statement about rendering "unto Caesar the things which are Caesar's; and unto God the things that are God's" (Matt. 22:21, KJV). Will we, then, disregard the Ten Commandments which were written by the very finger of God? No. Listen to what David says in Psalm 19:7: "The law of the LORD *is* perfect, converting the soul." Even Paul, who argues so eloquently in chapters 5–8 of his letter to the Romans that we are not saved by the law but by grace, writes,

"Therefore the law *is* holy, and the commandment holy and just and good" (Rom. 7:12). And we find that the Lord Himself commented on this issue when talking to the multitudes who followed Him to hear His words of life. He said, "Do not think that I came to destroy the Law or the Prophets. I did not come to destroy but to fulfill. For assuredly, I say to you, till heaven and earth pass away, one jot or one tittle will by no means pass from the law till all is fulfilled" (Matt. 5:17, 18). Then, in verse 19 He continues: "Whoever therefore breaks one of the least of these commandments, and teaches men so, shall be called least in the kingdom of heaven; but whoever does and teaches *them*, he shall be called great in the kingdom of heaven." Obviously, the Lord doesn't "throw the baby out with the bath water," as the saying goes. In other words, He makes clear that while the ceremonial laws, which He has come to fulfill, are no longer necessary, He re-establishes His eternal law by declaring this about the decalogue: "If you love Me, keep My commandments" (John 14:15). This is how the new covenant is different—because everything we do as Christians should be borne out of our love for God. "I delight to do Your will, O my God, and Your law *is* within my heart" (Ps. 40:8).

In the new covenant we are not just keeping the law to avoid punishment or gain a reward. When we are truly converted, we will want to do the will of God. If we're not yet at that point, how do we arrive there? Fortunately, the Scriptures provide a number of wonderful texts on this topic, but one that we have discussed before and that I lean on in this regard is found in Philippians 2:13. It says, "...for it is God who works in you both to will and to do for *His* good pleasure." We simply and humbly go to the Lord and ask Him to transform us so that we will want to do whatever He asks of us, until our will merges with His will. We need to claim the promise in today's text that He will write His law in our hearts. In my experience, this is not just a one-time request but something we should ask for on a continuing basis in order to fully enjoy living under the gracious provisions of the new covenant.

Hold Fast Your Confession

"Let us hold fast the confession of our hope without wavering, for He who promised is faithful" (Hebrews 10:23).

Over and over the writers of the New Testament urge believers to stay strong in their hope of salvation through Jesus Christ. They realize how faith can wane over time—especially if Christians get preoccupied with worldly things, quit witnessing to others about their blessed hope, and become irregular in gathering together with other believers. In the face of opposition, temptation, and persecution, many Christians will be turned away from their faith in Jesus. Thus, the qualities of perseverance and endurance are encouraged in those who have chosen to follow Christ. In fact, while talking about the signs of the end of the world, Jesus says it succinctly: "But he who endures to the end shall be saved" (Matt. 24:13).

The last few verses of Hebrews 10 reinforce this idea, elaborating a bit more on why our hope and faith should be unwavering:

Therefore do not cast away your confidence, which has great reward. For you have need of endurance, so that after you have done the will of God, you may receive the promise: 'For yet a little while, *and* He who is coming will come and will not tarry. Now the just shall live by faith; but if *anyone* draws back, My soul has no pleasure in him.' But we are not of those who draw back to perdition, but of those who believe to the saving of the soul. (Heb. 10:35–39)

The *SDA Bible Commentary* puts it nicely in volume 7, where it talks about God's faithfulness to us:

God is faithful in keeping His promises—of deliverance from Egypt and entrance into Canaan, and of deliverance from sin and entrance into the blessings of salvation in Christ Jesus. Since God is faithful and does not waver in fulfilling His promises, we should be faithful and not waver in accepting them. (p. 463)

This reminds me of a story found in a book called *501 Illustrations* by Robert Pierson. Here is a paraphrased version of "Illustration 31" on pages 43 and 44 in that volume.

One day when a father and his nine-year-old daughter were swimming in the ocean, they got separated when the tide began to go out. With the tide running so swiftly against him, the father knew he wouldn't be able to reach and save his daughter without getting some help—and quickly! He called out instructions to her: "Float and swim quietly. Don't become excited. I'll be back for you soon with a boat." By the time the father returned with a boat, the child had been swept out to sea by the tide. It took a little while for the men in the boat to find her. When they did, they found her calmly floating and swimming around as her father had instructed her. When they all arrived safely back on the shore, people gathered around to ask the little girl how she had been able to remain so calm and keep afloat so far out at sea all alone.

With the perfect faith of a child she responded, "My daddy told me that he would come back. I knew he would come, so I wasn't afraid. I did what he told me to do, and I was all right until he returned."

Confidence in her father's promise and obedience to his word saved the child's life. Similarly, confidence in our heavenly Father and obedience to His Word until He returns for us will save our lives eternally.

November 17

Vengeance

"Of how much worse punishment, do you suppose, will he be thought worthy who has trampled the Son of God underfoot, counted the blood of the covenant by which he was sanctified a common thing, and insulted the Spirit of grace? For we know Him who said, 'Vengeance is Mine, I will repay,' says the Lord. And again, 'The LORD will judge His people.' It is a fearful thing to fall into the hands of the living God" (Hebrews 10:29–31).

Another word for vengeance is retribution. It is a punishment inflicted in retaliation for an injury or offense—a paying back, if you will, for a wrong or evil deed. It evens the score, bringing justice for crimes, small and large, which have been committed by a malefactor. In this chapter, the author of Hebrews has just reminded his audience of the penalties suffered by the Israelites who rejected or failed to recognize the authority and jurisdiction of the law of Moses in Old Testament times. He argues that those who are living after Jesus came and suffered here on earth to save us will certainly receive a much more severe punishment if they choose to reject His sacrifice

and grace on their behalf. He then reminds them that there will be a day of judgment, and the Omniscient God, who has witnessed everything, will be the ultimate Judge. It is our living, all-wise God who will finally set everything right again in His vast universe!

As we have traveled through the Bible, we have come across this topic of judgment on several occasions. Because, as Christians, we have spent so much time telling people about the Lord's mercy, forgiveness, and grace, some people have doubted there could be such a thing as a Judgment Day. How could such a kind and loving God judge and destroy people? The answer is simple. They have rejected and despised His gracious offer of salvation that came at so great a price to the Godhead, and in the process, they have ruined, for time and for eternity, not only their own lives but many of the lives around them. It is because He is a God of love that He eliminates the terrible pandemic of sin and all of those who have chosen to continue to be infected by it from the universe.

The Bible tells us that because the evil works of sinners have not been punished rapidly, many continue to sin with impunity, thinking that they will never be held accountable for their despicable deeds (see Eccles. 8:11). And through the years, even Christians have asked why the Lord is waiting so long to return to earth and deal with the sin problem. We will see that the apostle Peter addresses this question by explaining that God patiently waits because He wants as many people as possible to choose to be redeemed (see 2 Peter 3:9). Make no mistake, however, in the meantime He is keeping track of all that is taking place. You'll remember that we talked before about Proverbs 15:3, which tells us, "The eyes of the LORD *are* in every place, keeping watch on the evil and the good." And also Ecclesiastes 12:14, which says, "For God will bring every work

into judgment, including every secret thing, whether good or evil." And when He determines the time is right, He promises, "And behold, I am coming quickly, and My reward *is* with Me, to give to every one according to his work" (Rev. 22:12). For those who have turned their backs on God, the Bible tells us, "...in flaming fire taking vengeance on those who do not know God, and on those who do not obey the gospel of our Lord Jesus Christ. These shall be punished with everlasting destruction from the presence of the Lord and from the glory of His power" (2 Thess. 1:8, 9).

Sometimes when we are hurt or offended, we are tempted to take the law into our own hands and seek revenge against those who have injured us or our loved ones, but today's verse reminds us that we should leave punishment for evil up to God. We can be assured that in His divine judgment and unquestionable wisdom, He will fairly mete out the appropriate punishment for each individual who has not accepted protection from perdition by accepting Jesus' gracious robe of righteousness. All who have been mistreated can trust the Lord to make it right for them in the end.

Saving Faith

"But without faith it is impossible to please Him, for he who comes to God must believe that He is, and that He is a rewarder of those who diligently seek Him" (Hebrews 11:6).

No journey through the Bible is complete without a stop at Hebrews 11, that great "Faith Chapter." Here we are reminded of numerous heroes of the faith who can be found throughout Scripture. Starting with Abel and Enoch, we are reminded of those who faithfully believed in God through the ages. Noah and Abraham come next, followed by Isaac, Jacob, Joseph, and Moses. Several women, including Sarah and Rahab, are also included in the narrative. The Lord is holding these folks up as examples for us—not because they were perfect but because they demonstrated their faith in God by moving forward to accomplish His will in their life and times. Just as faithful believers today are called to do.

So, I set out to see what the Bible says about this essential quality. There is, of course, the most well-known definition of faith, which is found in the first three verses of this chapter:

> Now faith is the substance of things hoped for, the evidence of things not seen. For by it the elders obtained a *good* testimony. By faith we understand that the worlds were framed by the word of God, so that the things which are seen were not made of things which are visible. (Heb. 11:1–3)

In 2 Corinthians 4:18, Paul further elaborates on this idea, saying of believers, "while we do not look at the things which are seen, but at the things which are not seen. For the things which are seen *are* temporary, but the things which are not seen *are* eternal." This is what it means when Christians try to explain faith to non-believers by declaring, "For we walk by faith, not by sight" (2 Cor. 5:7).

Let's take a minute to look more closely at the experience of Noah: "By faith Noah, being divinely warned of things not yet seen, moved with godly fear, prepared an ark for the saving of his household, by which he condemned the world and became heir of the righteousness which is according to faith" (Heb 11:7). The people of Noah's day had never seen water fall from the sky before, so of course they thought he was crazy when he announced that there was going to be so much rain that it would cause a worldwide flood. The current "scientific evidence" for such a phenomenon just didn't exist. Why was he wasting his time and energy preparing for something that no one around him believed could ever happen? It's because he was living his life based on his faith in the invisible, non-tangible information God had given him, rather than the temporal and tangible information he was getting from the world around him. He was walking by faith— the kind that brought him both temporal and eternal salvation!

We find that Abraham had a similar saving faith experience. "Abraham believed God, and it was accounted to him for righteousness" (Rom. 4:3). Saving faith is not just some ethereal philosophy or passive feeling. People who have true faith act on it—they live their lives based on believing what God has told them. James argues that people who say they have faith but don't put it to work in their lives don't have the real article. Speaking of Abraham's faith, James said, "Do you see that faith was working together with his works, and by works faith was made perfect?" (James 2:22).

According to Acts 26:18, we are "sanctified by faith" in the Lord. So how do we obtain this saving kind of faith? Ephesians 2:8 teaches us that it is by God's grace that we "have been saved through faith, and that not of yourselves; *it is* the gift of God." So, faith, like every other good gift, comes from our gracious and loving God. He is the One we need to go to when we have doubts, fears, or feel our spiritual weakness. It is His Spirit who will give us the kind of faith that will empower us to become heroes of faith, believing and acting on God's will, in our day!

November 19

A Heavenly Country

"But now they desire a better, that is, a heavenly country. Therefore God is not ashamed to be called their God, for He has prepared a city for them"
(Hebrews 11:16).

In talking about those ancient followers of God who have lived lives of faith, the author of Hebrews says, "These all died in faith, not having received the promises, but having seen them afar off were assured of them, embraced *them* and confessed that they were strangers and pilgrims on the earth" (Heb. 11:13). In fact, it is said of Abraham that he "dwelt in the land of promise [Canaan] as *in* a foreign country, dwelling in tents...for he waited for the city which has foundations, whose builder and maker *is* God" (Heb. 11:9, 10). For the faithful throughout the ages, their birthplace became less important than what would become their ultimate resting place—with God in heaven. So it will be for faithful believers in God until Jesus comes again. Our true homeland will be where God is—in a place He has prepared especially for us. We base this on the Lord's own gracious promise found in John 14:2, 3: "In My Father's house are many mansions; if *it were* not so, I would have told you. I go to prepare a place for you. And if I go and prepare a place for you, I will come again and receive you to Myself; that where I am, *there* you may be also."

In our world today, we have many refugees. They leave their home country due to war, poverty, natural disasters, persecutions, and so forth. They come to a new country with the hope of a better life for themselves and their children. They are looking for a future life that will be better than their past one. How wonderful it is when they find a safe and secure place that they can finally settle down and call home. As Christians, we all look forward to a future life better than the one we have experienced in this world of sin, sickness, and despair. And praise God, the scriptures we have reviewed today assure us that He is preparing not only a country but also a city. There is even a specific place (a mansion) especially designed for us so that we will feel eternally safe and sound and completely at home in our new heavenly country! There we will become grateful and glorified citizens in our new homeland.

In view of all this, it seems to me that our goal should be not to disappoint the One who has done so much to plan and prepare such a wonderful future for us. Especially since we have done nothing to be worthy of such loving generosity, and it is only by His incredible grace that we have any opportunity at all to become recipients of such opulence and splendor. Perhaps we can understand a small measure of what the Lord's disappointment would be like if we don't choose to go home with Him by thinking about how earthly parents would feel if their grown child refused to come home and spend a holiday with the family, after they'd spent weeks planning, cleaning, cooking, buying gifts, and preparing everything especially for the arrival of the son or daughter they love so much!

Unfortunately, many of us are so preoccupied with the things of this world that we spend little to no time thinking about the world to come. This reminds me of the following story:

> An old friend of David Livingstone's youth stood with the thousands who watched the casket bearing the famous explorer's body being drawn to its last resting place in Westminster Abbey. 'He made the wiser choice,' the old man said ruefully as he thought back upon his own life of waste and selfishness. 'I put the emphasis upon the wrong world.' (*501 Illustrations*, p. 114)

Lord, help us not to put our emphasis on the wrong world, but like your faithful servants in the past, help us to place our sights, by faith, on the real yet unseen glories of the world to come. Amen.

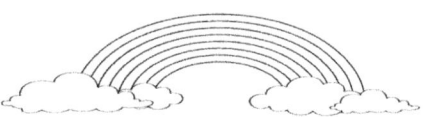

A Cloud of Witnesses

"Therefore we also, since we are surrounded by so great a cloud of witnesses, let us lay aside every weight, and the sin which so easily ensnares us, and let us run with endurance the race that is set before us, looking unto Jesus, the author and finisher of our faith..." (Hebrews 12:1, 2).

We have discussed several of the ideas brought forward in these verses before: running the race of the Christian life, which Paul talks about in 2 Timothy 4:7, 8; the need to lay aside our sins, found in Colossians 3:8–10; and how "He who has begun a good work in [us] will complete *it*" (Phil. 1:6), thus describing Jesus as both "the author and finisher of *our* faith." But today, I want to look a little deeper into this concept of "a cloud of witnesses."

The term in today's title has always brought me a sense of curiosity as well as a bit of amusement. In my mind's eye, I can see a bunch of beings from different places in the universe peering over the edge of the clouds and watching with great interest what is happening here on earth—especially in the lives of those who claim to have faith in God. It's almost as if we were actors in a play with hosts of spectators looking down on us from their heavenly balcony seats. Reflecting upon this idea now, it dawns on me that I probably haven't taken this scenario seriously enough in the past.

First, just to provide some context, if I believe that this earth and everyone on it is involved in a great cosmic battle between good and evil (and I do), then it makes perfect sense that inhabitants (such as those mentioned in Rev. 4:4–6) of heaven as well as others from across the universe would be eager to keep up with how our planet, which was loved so much that God sent His son to rescue it, is doing. Surely, this would also make these beings interested in our individual progress in grappling with right and wrong (see *The Triumph of God's Love*, p. 398). We know this is true for the angels in heaven, since God has utilized them to help us in so many ways since the days of creation. They have delivered glad tidings, such as at the birth of Jesus; given messages of warning, as in the case of Sodom and Gomorrah; fought in defense of humans, as they did for David; released faithful men like Paul, Silas, and Peter from prison; and presented prophecies to God's servants, like Daniel and John the Revelator, throughout history. In addition to all that, as most of us have been taught since we were small children, we each have been assigned our own individual guardian angel! Both Psalms 34:7 and Matthew 18:10 talk about the role of angels in watching over us. But my favorite verse on this topic is found in Hebrews 1:14. Referring to the angels, it says: "Are they not all ministering spirits sent forth to minister for those who will inherit salvation?" Having invested so much in our welfare, how could the angels not be interested in our progress through this world?

Who else might be observing us? I believe there are unfallen beings on other worlds in the universe, based on two sources. The Bible (in texts such as Job 2:1 and Job 38:7), and in the writings of Ellen G. White, not only in the reference given above in *The Triumph of God's Love* but also very specifically on page 543 in her book, *Adventist Home.* Since we were the only planet to engage in the great tragic experiment of sin, naturally others want to see how it plays out. Only in that way will the universe be safe from anyone ever wanting to choose to be contaminated with evil again.

We need to take a moment here to disabuse anyone of the notion that our deceased relatives are watching us from heaven. The Bible tells us that they are asleep and "know not any thing" until they are awakened on resurrection day (Eccles. 9:5, KJV). Ecclesiastes 9:5, 6 is just one of the verses that makes the current state of the dead very clear.

Unfortunately, the errant idea that our loved ones who have died are seeing all that we do, and even sending us messages, although very popular in our modern culture, is not biblical. It is one of Satan's many deceptions.

There is a final group, however, who I would include in those who are watching all that we are doing in life, and that group is composed of our current friends, living family members, and especially our children. We need to remember that our words, decisions, and actions should be modeling an example of how a faithful Christian lives, leaving an indelible impression for good upon all those affected by our influence, encouraging them to also follow the Lord on the well-watched pathway to heaven.

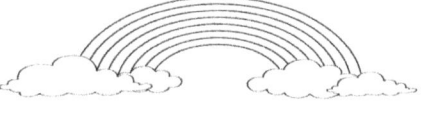

November 21

Benedictions

"Now may the God of peace who brought up our Lord Jesus from the dead, that great Shepherd of the sheep, through the blood of the everlasting covenant, make you complete in every good work to do His will, working in you what is well pleasing in His sight, through Jesus Christ, to whom be glory forever and ever. Amen" (Hebrews 13:20, 21).

As I was finishing the last of the fourteen Pauline Epistles of the New Testament, I wanted to take note of how the revered apostle finished his remarks. What were the last words he spoke to the beloved new believers he had spent the latter part of his life converting and so ardently nurturing? In my Bible, the New King James Version, the last five verses of Hebrews 13 have a subtitle of "Benediction, Final Exhortation, and Farewell." That section begins with verses 20 and 21 (cited above). As you can see, he has attempted to pack one last sermon into one long sentence!

He wants to make sure that the Christians stay focused on the Lord Jesus, and all He has done for them. In verses 22 and 23 Paul takes care of a little housekeeping, and then, in verse 24, he exchanges greetings. Finally, in verse 25, he ends his letter with this famous benediction: "Grace *be* with you all. Amen."

A benediction, of course, is the pronouncement of a blessing, usually given at the end of a worship service. In his case, Paul is very consistent about invoking a blessing on his readers at the end of each of his letters. In fact, when I went back and looked, I was surprised to see that he had used a very similar blessing, always one with the word "grace" in it, to finish up all of his writings from Romans to Hebrews! If you have the curiosity to go back and check, as I did, you will discover that usually the familiar blessing, "Grace be with you all," is found in the last verse. There are a few exceptions, however, especially in some of his earlier books. Romans, for example, places this phrase in Romans 16:24, and then goes on for three more verses, giving the believers a more robust blessing in the form, again, of a sermon in a nutshell. In 1 Corinthians 16, the "grace-filled" blessing is located in the next to the last verse, so he can express his love for his precious readers in verse 24. It says, "My love *be* with you all in Christ Jesus. Amen."

Meanwhile, in Ephesians, he puts a small twist on the phrase by stating, "Grace *be* with all those who love our Lord Jesus Christ in sincerity. Amen" (Eph. 6:24). I think my favorite, though, is the benediction found in 2 Corinthians 13:14, which includes all three persons of the Godhead. It reads: "The grace of the Lord Jesus Christ, and the love of God, and the communion of the Holy Spirit *be* with you all. Amen."

The importance the apostle placed on the Lord's grace is obvious, always using it in his final caring words to the fledgling believers across the various places where he had planted churches. Perhaps because he himself had been a recipient of that grace, and it had turned his life around so significantly! Grace is often defined as "unmerited favor" from God, sometimes as "unmerited help" or "unmerited salvation." Synonyms I found included approval, acceptance, virtue, an act of kindness, mercy, courtesy, or clemency. Whatever description is used, words are not enough to express the feelings of warmth, protection, acceptance, forgiveness, hope, joy, and thanksgiving, not to mention a new sense of purpose, experienced by Christians who have allowed the Lord to touch them with His marvelous, life-changing grace. No wonder Paul always included the grace that comes to us from the Lord Jesus Christ in his numerous benedictions. It was the best blessing He could wish upon them as he finished his inspired writings. Just think what an impact it would make on others today if Christians finished their letters and other communications with the same blessed benediction: "May the grace of our Lord Jesus Christ be with you." Our final parting words could remind us all of what is truly important in life.

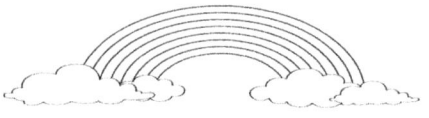

Trials and Tribulations

"My brethren, count it all joy when you fall into various trials, knowing that the testing of your faith produces patience. But let patience have is *perfect work, that you may be perfect and complete, lacking nothing" (James 1:2–4).*

Trials and tribulations...how we hate them! Unfortunately, here on this earth we meet with many of them on an almost daily basis! There are trials of disease, poverty, unreached dreams, and broken relationships, including the loss of loved ones through death. We also experience afflictions such as pain, disappointment, boredom, and difficult home or work situations. In addition, sometimes we even suffer from tribulations like those the early Christians had to deal with, such as opposition and persecution.

What is the normal response people have when confronted with life's unpleasantries? Generally, irritation! Fight or flight! Naturally, we want to extricate ourselves from our difficulties as soon as possible. There are times, however, when we don't have control over the situation, and we just have to bear with it. This is where the need for patience—what the Bible sometimes calls "long-suffering" kicks in. Today's passage actually counsels us to "count it all joy" when we're going through trials, since they can help us develop patience, which will ultimately render our characters "perfect and complete." It's interesting to note here that our natural carnal responses are almost opposite to what our desired spiritual responses should be.

Does this mean we should sadistically seek uncomfortable situations and painful experiences? I think not. Rather that we should approach them with a positive attitude, looking for the good that can come out of what initially seems bad. I am currently reading a book by Pastor John Bradshaw called *The Hope of Glory*, which provides two illustrations of this idea. The first one is about a young military man who was expecting to board a plane that would bring him home to his family, only to discover that his name had inadvertently been left off the list of authorized passengers. He couldn't believe it! In his disappointment, he was angry and upset the whole day—until the news came that the plane on which he would have been a passenger went down in the Atlantic Ocean, and everyone aboard was lost! What had seemed bad to him actually turned out to be good for him. The second illustration discussed the biblical story of Jonah. Being swallowed by a whale seemed at first to be a very bad thing—until he realized that the Lord had used this specially-prepared fish not only to save his life but to deliver him to where he needed to be in order to evangelize Nineveh and accomplish God's mission for his life. God was looking at the bigger picture, and He knew that Jonah's preaching in that place would result in salvation for the whole city!

So, remembering that too-often-doubted promise, "And we know that all things work together for good to those who love God, to those who are the called according to *His* purpose," found in Romans 8:28, how do we develop this kind of knowledge, this assurance, this kind of faith in God that will help keep us calm and unruffled amid life's trials and tribulations? Even if we don't see all the bad things turn into good ones during our lifetimes? Certainly, this is a challenge! And it will take a lot of patience and trust in the Lord's wise providence.

As I ask myself how these qualities of patience and trust can be obtained, I realize that that is the very purpose of trials—they help us practice trusting in the Lord from day to day as well as to wait upon Him to bring good out of our current difficulties. Then, when we see His interventions in our personal lives, our answered prayers, and the blessings He has poured out upon us, our trust in Him grows. Once we are convinced that He really does want what's best for our ultimate good, we can wait until heaven to understand the reasons for the problems which were never resolved while we were still on earth. This kind of experiential relationship with the Lord improves and strengthens our patience. Thus, it improves and strengthens our characters, making us more like our Savior. It is in this way, while always asking for the Lord's guidance and support, that we can actually profit from our trials.

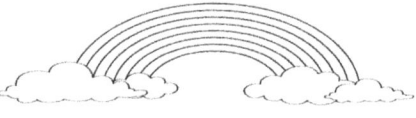

November 23

Good Gifts

"Every good gift and every perfect gift is from above, and comes down from the Father of lights, with whom there is no variation or shadow of turning"
(James 1:17).

Gifts! Just the word elicits pleasant feelings. For me, it conjures up good memories of exciting Christmas celebrations from years gone by. When I was a child, our whole extended family used to gather together at my grandmother's house—aunts, uncles, cousins, children, and grandchildren. We ate, talked, laughed, and of course, opened gifts! I can remember each of my aunts—and there were five of them, bringing in large bags of beautifully-wrapped presents (like female Santa Clauses) when they arrived, and then setting them under the large festive tree in Grandma's den until they filled half of the room! As children, we could hardly wait for the designated time to start opening our presents. Finally, someone would don a Santa's cap and begin calling out names. We squealed with joy whenever it was our turn to go get a gift and then began unwrapping it with great anticipation. I remember receiving dolls, board games to share with my siblings, an occasional toy, and sometimes, a lovely dress. After exclaiming over each item, I would store my stash of presents in a corner of the house until it was time to load up our cars and head for home with a warm glow in our hearts. We could hardly wait for our next family holiday celebration!

Why were they so special? Well, partly because of the delicious food—nobody created homemade apple pie like my Aunt Margie, and my grandma's fruit and Jell-o ring as well as her smooth butter-dribbled mashed potatoes were works of art. Then there was the easy conversation, the laughter, and the warm hugs from relatives who hadn't been seen for a while. My grandma's house was something beautiful to behold, decked out in red, green, and gold, and finished off with a little sprig of mistletoe right in a strategic place above the dining room door, where unsuspecting relatives could suddenly be plied with kisses! Looking back, I realize that all of these things were gifts of love in themselves. But as a little girl, the highlight of such an occasion was experiencing familial love and the sense of belonging to a huge family that cared enough about me to select personal gifts especially designed to meet my wants and needs.

I believe Jesus's gifts are like that. Some are general in nature, experienced by everyone who belongs to His large extended family—the changing of the seasons, the beauty of a sunset, the wonder of the stars, the grandeur of the mountains, the taste sensations of a ripe peach, the fragrance of the flowers, the indescribable poetry of a symphony, the sudden shining of a rainbow appearing behind the clouds—all of those things that we can enjoy with our senses. But that's just the start of His gift-giving! Because He wants to assure us that we belong to the family of God and that He cares for us personally, He designs gifts, especially to meet our individual wants and needs. He gives us each the breath of life, a measure of health, special talents, familial blessings, material blessings, and perhaps most importantly, spiritual blessings. He answers our prayers, gives us wisdom when we request it (as promised in James 1:5 from this same chapter), and guides our footsteps by His Spirit. And He does none of this grudgingly. The Bible tells us He is even more eager than our parents to give us good gifts. In Luke 11:13, He declares: "If you then, being evil, know how to give good gifts to your children, how much more will *your* heavenly Father give the Holy Spirit to those who ask Him!" What a promise!

Like my grandmother, who planned ahead and expended the time, energy, and effort to make sure we would be able to enjoy our family's holiday celebrations, the Lord has planned ahead and expended the time, energy, and effort required to assure that we will be able to enjoy His family's celebrations in heaven. He gave the gift of His own life in order to secure the personal gift of salvation just for you. It is His very best gift. All you have to do is accept it!

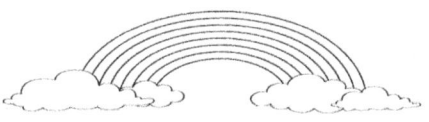

The Implanted Word

"Therefore lay aside all filthiness and overflow of wickedness, and receive with meekness the implanted word, which is able to save your souls. But be doers of the word, and not hearers only, deceiving yourselves" (James 1:21, 22).

I love the book of James because it is simply overflowing with practical, down-to-earth advice to Christians on how to live their daily lives. In this passage, James tells the believers that after they lay aside their carnal lifestyles they must receive "the implanted word." Why? Because it is able to save their souls! Then he drives his point home by explaining that this doesn't mean just listening to the Word—it means actually embedding it into their lives to the point that they are practicing what they've heard. James then goes one step further to say that if they are not "doers of the word," they are deceived if they think they are Christians just by listening to the gospel. To be true followers of Jesus, they needed to make a decision to accept the gospel and then take definite action to live it.

In looking at the definitions of "implanted," I found two clarifying descriptions: "to set firmly or deeply" and "to fix in the mind or spirit." Besides the word "embed," I came across several other helpful synonyms: entrench, fix, ingrain, lodge, and simply "to plant." Nowadays, we might say something like, "They needed the gospel to sink in," or "They needed to absorb the gospel." While considering this good advice from James, I can't help but think it sounds like a message that modern-day Christians could profit from as well. So, how do we ingrain the Word of God into our lives?

Since I was raised a Christian, I had the privilege of hearing, reading, and even studying the Scriptures throughout the years. When I started writing this book, however, personally analyzing selected verses, looking at their context, finding the meaning of key words, studying what others had to say about them, and trying to figure out how they applied to my own life, I was able to digest what the Bible was saying in a new way. This type of study of the Word has been a shot in the arm to my spiritual life. I'm more convinced now than ever that if we want to make the Word an integral part of our lives, we need to spend more time immersed in it, making sense of its meaning regularly for ourselves. Naturally, this doesn't mean that we can't still benefit from hearing others preach the word—but I don't believe it can take the place of our own time in the Bible.

Earlier this year, we talked about the idea of memorizing Scripture. I continue to believe that's another effective way to make God's Word part and parcel of our lives. While on this topic, I want to reiterate how important it is for children to memorize Scripture from an early age. That way the Spirit of the Lord can bring these passages to their mind in times of temptation as well as strengthen and comfort them in times of spiritual need. My husband and I have both found it a blessing to lean on God's promises, learned in childhood, whenever needed throughout our lifetimes. We should always remember that the way even Jesus, our example, overcame Satan's strong temptations in the wilderness was by His dependence upon "... every word that proceeds from the mouth of God" (Matt. 4:4). For these reasons, I believe that Christians must continue the age-old practice of learning not only memory verses but also larger portions of God's word. What better way to implant God's Word into our hearts and minds for our reference and edification on a moment's notice in order to meet life's challenges successfully?

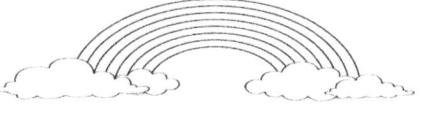

November 25

Pure Religion

"Pure and undefiled religion before God and the Father is this: to visit orphans and widows in their trouble, and to keep oneself unspotted from the world" (James 1:27).

You'll remember back when we were studying the book of Acts that, shortly after Pentecost, when the early church was just getting organized, many dedicated believers were selling their material goods in order to support their mission to evangelize the world, but they were also doing this to support their brethren in need and the widows who had joined their ranks. Upon becoming Christians, some of the believers had lost all they had because of persecution. Women and children, in particular, may have been rejected by family and lost financial support because of their new religion. To meet this crisis, loving and unselfish members of the new sect willingly stepped forward. They found that by pooling their resources, holding everything in common, as described in Acts 4, the church could continue to flourish. Let's review this chapter, focusing on verses 32–35. It reads,

Now the multitude of those who believed were of one heart and one soul; neither did anyone say that any of the things he possessed was his own, but they had all things in common. And with great power the apostles gave witness to the resurrection of the Lord Jesus. And great grace was upon them all. Nor was there anyone among them who lacked; for all who were possessors of lands or houses sold them, and brought the proceeds of the things that were sold, and laid *them* at the apostles' feet; and they distributed to each as anyone had need.

As the church grew, the need for people to serve those who came for help on a daily basis also grew. The apostles saw fit to meet this challenge by assigning seven deacons to carry this important work out in a fair and orderly manner. This new organizational structure helped to quell complaints by the Greek believers that their widows were being neglected, as compared to what the widows of the Hebrews were receiving (see Acts 6:1).

Another instance in which helping widows is mentioned is found in 1 Timothy 5. Here, Paul lays out some interesting guidelines for how widows should be treated. While he admonishes the church to honor and continue to assist them if they are truly in need, he also encourages believing family members to help support them if they are able. "But if any widow has children or grandchildren, let them first learn to show piety at home and to repay their parents; for this is good and acceptable before God" (1 Tim. 5:4).

Unfortunately, in today's society, those who are poor and destitute are often looked down on, which is just the opposite of how Jesus treated anyone who was marginalized. He honored the poor widow who generously put all that she had into the treasury of the temple and memorialized her unselfish act for all time (see Mark 12:41–44). Think of the widow of Nain. While crowds of people were jostling about trying to get Jesus's attention, He stopped to notice a poor mother's grief, and with unspeakable love and mercy, He raised her son from the dead.

As we think about orphans in relation to today's text, it's instructive to consider a number of statements Jesus made about children. Here are a few examples: "Let the little children come to Me, and do not forbid them; for of such is the kingdom of God" (Mark 10:14); "Whoever receives one of these little children in My name receives Me; and whoever receives Me, receives not Me but Him who sent Me" (Mark 9:37); "But whoever causes one of these little ones who believe in Me to stumble, it would be better for him if a millstone were hung around his neck, and he were thrown into the sea" (Mark 9:42); "Take heed that you do not despise one of these little ones, for I say to you that in heaven their angels always see the face of My Father who is in heaven" (Matt. 18:10).

Then, you'll recall that famous dialogue in Matthew 25, where Jesus is talking to the saved, and says, "For I was hungry, and you gave Me food; I was thirsty and you gave Me drink; I was a stranger and you took Me in; I *was* naked and you clothed Me; I was sick and you visited Me..." (verses 35, 36). The amazed saints will ask when this all occurred. "And the King will answer... 'Assuredly, I say to you, inasmuch as you did *it* to one of the least of these My brethren, you did *it* to me'" (verse 40).

A lovely verse in Psalm 146:9 sums it up: "The LORD watches over the strangers; He relieves the fatherless and widow...." And as the true followers of Jesus, guess who's been assigned to help Him do just that? All those who want to practice pure religion.

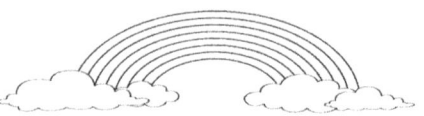

The Poor

"My brethren, do not hold the faith of our Lord Jesus Christ, the Lord of glory, with partiality. For if there should come into your assembly a man with gold rings, in fine apparel, and there should also come in a poor man in filthy clothes, and you pay attention to the one wearing the fine clothes and say to him, 'You sit here in a good place,' and say to the poor man, 'You stand there,' or, 'Sit here at my footstool,' have you not shown partiality among yourselves, and become judges with evil thoughts? Listen, my beloved brethren: Has God not chosen the poor of this world to be rich in faith and heirs of the kingdom which He promised to those who love Him?" (James 2:1–5).

This is a fairly long passage, but it demonstrates clearly the kind of partiality, favoritism, or prejudice that Christians can be prone to—even in their religious gatherings. Sadly, this is an age-old problem, as prevalent in today's churches as it was in the early days of Christianity. It stems from the fact that, as humans, we tend to judge a person's internal worth by external appearance. Not only that but we rather enjoy lording it over people, who we feel we are "better than" in some way. Prejudice both springs from and strokes our pride. Unfortunately, this behavior, sometimes obvious and other times more subtle, is exercised not only on poor people but also on strangers, people of a different race or language, older people, and on occasion, even children. As Christians, it's something we need to guard against.

As I have revealed before, when I was a child, my family was very poor. Not the kind of poverty experienced in third-world countries, but we were poor by American standards. Compared with all my cousins' families, we were the poorest. This was evidenced by their nice houses, matching furniture, latest-style clothing, and the richest even had a swimming pool! Meanwhile, we moved from pillar to post on a regular basis (sixteen places by twelfth grade), had water with cereal when we ran out of milk, and wore hand-me-downs. Stretching the dollar to pay the rent on time and keeping food on the table were the primary concerns of my parents. I share this to say that I can relate to feeling "less than" because of financial limitations. Thankfully, my parents instilled in me a can-do attitude, which inspired me to get a good education, thereby raising my socio-economic status considerably once I became an adult. But the lessons I learned as a poor little girl have stayed with me, causing me not to judge people simply on their external differences.

I find it of interest that when talking with His disciples one day, Jesus stated, "For you have the poor with you always" (Matt. 26:11). I've contemplated why this is so. It's almost as if interacting with people who are different socio-economically than us is a real test of character for everyone—because the poor, unlike their more affluent neighbors, have to develop patience and trust in God for their sustenance, while the rich, in serving the poor, find it a check against their pride and selfishness.

Think back to the story of the rich young ruler found in the 19th chapter of Mathew as an example of this. When Jesus told him that in order to be perfect, he should sell his belongings and give to the poor, it was too much for him. Even though he had obeyed the law all his life and thought of himself as a good person, he failed the selfishness test. Jesus tried to help him by promising that if he was unselfish, he would have treasure in heaven. But the young man chose to keep his "great possessions," along with his social status (see Matt. 19:22). It was an unhappy choice—for him, for those he could have helped, and for Jesus. The Bible tells us that he went away sorrowful. He's not alone. Many people think that making money and hoarding possessions will make them happy, only to find out that they have rejected salvation as a result of their self-centered lifestyle. They have exchanged the cheap trinkets of this world for the exceedingly great treasures of the kingdom of heaven.

It may be difficult for the proud heart to understand that being accepting and generous with the poor around us makes us more like Jesus, and becoming more like Jesus ultimately makes us happier. However, I like the succinct way that King Solomon summarizes the idea when he says: "He who despises his neighbor sins; but he who has mercy on the poor, happy *is* he" (Prov. 14:21).

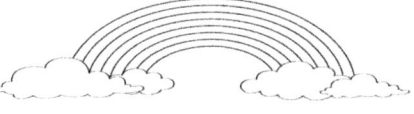

November 27

Dead Faith?

"Thus also faith by itself, if it does not have works, is dead. But someone will say, 'You have faith, and I have works.' Show me your faith without your works, and I will show you my faith by my works" (James 2:17, 18).

Lest you think we were done with the faith versus works issue, in his book, James invites us to delve deeper into the subject. As you know, it is one that has been debated by Christians for years, yet it still continues to be a point of contention in some circles. One camp insists that faith in Jesus is all you need to be saved, while others, like the apostle James, argue that faith without works is dead. It's an assertion he reiterates several times in this chapter. He discusses a number of examples to make his point.

First, he states that if a brother or sister is without food or clothing, and a believer does nothing except throw a few platitudes their direction, his faith profits nothing. Second, he reminds his readers that even the demons believe in God—and tremble because they know they are living outside of His will and doing the works of Satan rather than the works of God. Thus, the mere fact that they believe in God is not going to save them. Third, James likens faith without works to a dead body with no spirit (life or breath) in it: "For as the body without the spirit is dead, so faith without works is dead also" (James 2:26). His fourth example may be the most convincing. He talks about Abraham, spiritual father of the Jewish people, and the fact that his faith in God was accounted to him for righteousness. James asserts, however, that the way Abraham demonstrated this faith, this genuine and saving faith, was by His obedience to God. He left his home in Ur upon the Lord's direction, took Isaac to Mt. Moriah during the fearful test of his faithfulness, and attempted to serve God throughout his life. So, in verse 22 of this chapter, the apostle describes the relationship between faith and works in this manner: "Do you see that faith was working together with his [Abraham's] works, and by works faith was made perfect?"

I believe these illustrations are instructive because they help us understand that saving faith and good works need to go hand in hand in the life of a mature Christian. They are not opposing concepts, but cooperating ones.

When thinking about the topic of faith versus works, my mind goes back to the story that Jesus told about the good Samaritan found in Luke 10:25–37. No one can contend that either the first man who passed by, a priest, or the second one, a Levite, was not a believer in the true God of heaven. However, their faith was useless because they did not act on it to benefit the victim of the crime. Only the Samaritan put his faith into action by caring for the injured man the way a true believer in God should have. At the beginning of this famous parable, a Jewish lawyer had started his dialogue with the Savior by asking, "Teacher, what shall I do to inherit eternal life?" (verse 25). At the end of their conversation, after Jesus had made his point about what saving faith looked like in the actions of the good Samaritan, He answered the question that had been posed by simply saying, "Go and do likewise" (Luke 10:37).

Faith, of course, is essential, but James says it is his works that will show whether his faith is alive or dead. Our works should reveal the same about our lives. Near the beginning of His ministry, when Jesus was preaching to the multitudes in the sermon on the mount, He declared, "Let your light so shine before men, that they may see your good works and glorify your Father in heaven" (Matt. 5:16). May this be the result of our living faith!

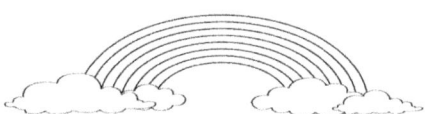

Fire!

"Even so the tongue is a little member and boasts great things. See how great a forest a little fire kindles!" (James 3:5).

Last summer, about a dozen of my husband's relatives came to spend a few days with us. We decided to plan some outings while they were here, including a boat ride on a local lake. Due to drought-like conditions, our area has been plagued by wildfires over the last two summers. We had heard rumors about a small fire, said to have been started by a stray electrical spark, quite a ways south of the lake. But on the day of our excursion, the morning was bright and sunny, and when I called to make sure our rental boat would still be available, they assured me that it would. Upon arrival, we noticed that there was a plume of grey smoke in the distance. The sky above the lake, how-ever, was still blue. So, we clambered into the boat, enthusiastic about our joy ride.

About an hour later, as we got close to the south shore of the fairly-large body of water, we noticed the sky growing dark with huge black clouds of smoke. Obviously, the fire was coming our direction at a pretty fast clip. We had rented the boat for the morning and didn't want to cut our excursion short, so we decided to drive to the other end of the lake to eat our lunch in a still decently smoke-free area. By the time we'd finished eating, the smoke had caught up with us. We started to get alarmed. Soon, the whole lake was enveloped in acrid smoke, affect-ing both our visibility and our breathing, so we headed back to the rental dock as fast as we could. What had started as a small fire in the distance had obviously turned into something much more serious—and much closer to where we were parked than we had anticipated. Fortunately, we were able to drive away from both the ominous fire and the irritating smoke, suffering nothing more than a few ashes caught in our hair. We later learned of all the damage this fire had caused, leaving many houses and trees all around the once-beautiful lakeshore charred and black in its wake. It took several weeks of arduous labor on the part of fire fighters to finally extinguish the flames.

Today's verse reminded me of this expe-rience. Gossip can be especially hard to squelch, once it has started its rounds, and although beginning small, it can eventually do great damage. We have talked about the power of words before and how important it is for us to choose them wisely in order to not create our own damaging firestorm. In a number of subsequent verses of James 3, he takes his admonitions about the tongue a bit further. They advocate for consistency on the part of those claiming to be Christians. Listen to what he says:

> But no man can tame the tongue. *It is* an unruly evil, full of deadly poison. With it we bless our God and Father, and with it we curse men, who have been made in the similitude of God. Out of the same mouth proceed blessing and cursing. My breth-ren, these things ought not to be so. Does a spring send forth fresh *water* and bitter from the same opening? (James 3:8–11)

Have you ever looked up to a Christian leader—perhaps a preacher, a teacher, or even a parent, only to be crestfallen when you hear them saying something that is inappropriate in an unguarded moment? It could be a swear word, an off-color joke, or maybe a volley of harsh and angry words spoken to someone in their own family or church family. Especially for non-believers, people new to their faith, and young people, the shock and disappointment of an incident like this can leave them feeling like most Christians are nothing more than hypocrites! Unfortunately, we have all said things without thinking from time to time. Sometimes when irritated, sometimes in anger, but as mature Christians, we should make it a habit to remember that both fresh and bitter water do not come from the same spring. This is an area in which we can all work to become more consistent and more Christlike. To do so, we shall have to pray, as David did, "Set a guard over my mouth, LORD; keep watch over the door of my lips" (Ps. 141:3, NIV). Amen.

November 29

Sow Peace

"For where envy and self-seeking exist, confusion and every evil thing are there. But the wisdom that is from above is first pure, then peaceable, gentle, willing to yield, full of mercy and good fruits, without partiality and without hypocrisy. Now the fruit of righteousness is sown in peace by those who make peace" (James 3:16–18).

While I am writing this, the war in Ukraine is raging. Every day now my television screen is filled with the horrific images of war—demolished cities, loud and fiery explosions, mass graves, and people fleeing with one or two bags containing all that is left of their shattered lives. Their dazed faces are an indication of what they have suffered in a sudden conflict in which they had no fault. They were merely innocent citizens, going about their daily lives in the wrong place at the wrong time, as far as a neighboring dictator was concerned. It's amazing as well as frightening to realize how much misery and devastation can be caused by just one selfish person, crazed with a lust for power. Now, many of those Ukrainians who have survived are on their way to an unknown destination. These victims can only hope and pray that, in whichever country accepts them as refugees, they will be provided with their basic necessities—food, water, heat, and shelter from the cold of winter. Perhaps even more importantly, they hope for peace and safety, not only for themselves but especially for their terror-stricken children. Right now, no one knows if they will ever be able to return to their war-torn land, just as no one can predict when the fighting will cease or what the final outcome will be.

Apart from folks in the military, few Americans of my generation have ever had to live through a war. But whenever I have talked with my parents about their experiences during World War II and the Korean Conflict or heard an interview with a holocaust survivor or had the privilege to meet a person who has served in Vietnam, Iraq, or Afghanistan, it has begun to sink in just how fortunate and blessed I really am! The relative peace we enjoy and too often take for granted in the United States should be a cause of great thanksgiving every day of our lives!

So, how do we sow peace? How do we create it and sustain it? Not just in our world or in our nation, where we may not have much control or influence, but in our communities and families—the places where our personal influence counts the most. According to today's passage, we will need to start by putting away envy and self-seeking. Partiality (prejudice) and hypocrisy will also have to be eliminated. Those characteristics will need to be replaced with pure wisdom from above. That heavenly wisdom will help us to become peaceable, gentle, willing to yield, full of mercy, and best of all, fill us with the fruits of righteousness. Only then will we be able to become true peacemakers. Only then will we be able to reflect Jesus— the Prince of Peace.

In the famous discourse of Jesus known as The Beatitudes, we find several related and encouraging promises: "Blessed *are* the meek, for they shall inherit the [new] earth" (Matt. 5:5); "Blessed *are* the merciful, for they shall obtain mercy" (Matt. 5:7). And most to the point, "Blessed *are* the peacemakers, for they shall be called sons of God" (Matt. 5:9). Let's start sowing peace today.

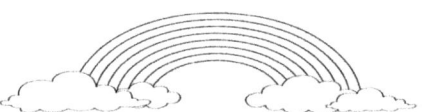

Tomorrow?

"Come now, you who say, 'Today or tomorrow we will go to such and such a city, spend a year there, buy and sell, and make a profit'; whereas you do not know what will happen tomorrow. For what is your life? It is even a vapor that appears for a little time and then vanishes away. Instead you ought to say, 'If the Lord wills, we shall live and do this or that'" (James 4:13–15).

How often we take our life and even our health for granted. Today's passage struck me with new force after learning this week of the death of a friend who was in his fifties. He had valiantly fought cancer for several years. When he was finally declared cancer free, he and his family, filled with eager plans for the future, bought and moved into a new home. Shortly thereafter, the whole family came down with Covid. His wife, son, and daughter all recuperated within a few days, but our friend, with his weakened immune system, had to be hospitalized for several weeks, where he finally succumbed to the deadly virus that has ended so many lives over the past few years. We, along with his other close friends and extended family, were devastated by the news!

Other recent unexpected events have brought home to me how vulnerable and weak we humans really are and how our productivity can be cut short not just by death but by various health concerns, such as a thirty-five-year-old suffering a heart attack that changes his life's trajectory or a person in her prime contracting pneumonia, leaving her with COPD. These kinds of occurrences can change the plans we've made for our lives in an instant, reminding us that we are not in total control of our lives, even though we often think or act as if we were.

The truth is none of us knows how long we have on this earth—especially living in the throes of a world-wide pandemic! This is why Psalm 90:12 tells us to "number our days." My modern interpretation of this is to "be humbly thankful for each new day, and make the most of it." Given that our lives are like "a vapor that appears for a little time and then vanishes away," we should always be cognizant of the fact that it is God who grants us the breath of life, and He who receives it back to Himself to reserve for us until the resurrection morning. During the time in-between, we need to recognize the fact that it is only by God's grace and power that we can accomplish anything. We show we realize this by saying, "If the Lord wills, we shall live and do this or that." I've shared before how amazed I have been to discover that in a number of languages, including the Spanish I encountered in both Mexico and Puerto Rico, this phrase was a regular and often-used figure of speech. Everyday conversations were laced with, "*Si Dios Quiere.*" When I first heard it, I couldn't help being amused that the students in our classes sometimes seemed to have a better understanding of God's supremacy over their lives than some of their American missionary teachers! It was a paradigm shift for me.

All this is not to say that, as Christians, we shouldn't make plans. Every well-ordered life and well-done project is the result of wise planning. It's just that whatever we plan needs to be in keeping with what we believe is God's will, and, if circumstances warrant, we should be willing to change our plans upon the promptings and direction of the Holy Spirit.

There's a curious little verse in Proverbs 16:9 which says, "A man's heart plans his way, but the LORD directs his steps." A similar thought is found in Psalm 37:23: "The steps of a *good* man are ordered by the LORD, and He delights in his way."

Help us, Lord, to acknowledge your power and supremacy over our lives and to follow your will in each step we take, until you lead us into the joys of that healthy and everlasting life you have planned for us in heaven! Amen.

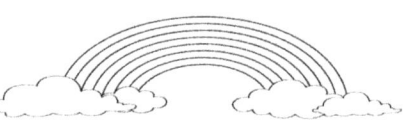

Fervent Prayer

"Confess your trespasses to one another, and pray for one another, that you may be healed. The effective, fervent prayer of a righteous man avails much. Elijah was a man with a nature like ours, and he prayed earnestly that it would not rain; and it did not rain on the land for three years and six months. And he prayed again, and the heaven gave rain, and the earth produced its fruit" (James 5:16–18).

I'm fond of this passage because it is like a mini-sermon in only three verses. Not only does it admonish us to pray earnestly but it provides us with a real-life example of another person who was a follower of God getting his prayers miraculously answered!

I have often thought that the reason Elijah was so successful in experiencing answered prayers was because he was a prophet. And we have many instances in the Bible of prophets receiving incredible results from their petitions to God. I think of Moses, earnestly imploring the Lord for a way of escape for the Israelites when they were fleeing from the Egyptians, and God parting the Red Sea so they could all arrive safely on the other side. Then there was Elisha, requesting that the lost axe of the students in the school of the prophets would be found, and then discovering it floating on the top of the water. Daniel slept safely in the lion's den because he had prayed and put his life in the hands of God. John, the revelator, was praying fervently while he was in exile on the isle of Patmos when the Lord broke into his solitude with amazing visions about the future, but prophets were not the only Bible characters whose prayers were answered in marvelous ways.

I believe we can take heart, reading the biblical record of the many ordinary people, like us, who received extraordinary answers to their earnest prayers. Out of his frequent devotional conversations and deep faith in God, David overcame Goliath; the fleeing Jacob was given a comforting dream about heaven's continuing connection with him; and because of Joseph's relationship with God, he prospered in all he did, finally ending up as the prime minister of Egypt. We have the stories of women of faith as well. The foreigner, Ruth, who because of her love for her mother-in-law and her God, was honored to become part of the genealogy of Christ. Queen Esther fasted and prayed for three days before successfully requesting that the king save the Jewish people from annihilation. Then there was Hannah, whose fervent prayers for a child resulted in the birth of Samuel, who became a strong spiritual leader in Israel.

Of course, the New Testament is amply supplied with amazing answers to the prayers of those who were followers of Jesus. The apostle Paul was given power to cast out demons and boldness to evangelize throughout the then-known world, while Peter was given the gift of healing and was miraculously freed from prison by angels in answer to the prayers of the early church on his behalf. In fact, after the Day of Pentecost, all of the disciples of Christ performed miracles, including the ability to preach in languages they had never spoken before! Even the wonderful gift of the Holy Spirit was given in response to their unified prayers for it.

It's helpful for us to review biblical history on the subject of prayer. Remember, "... all these things happened to them as examples, and they were written for our admonition, upon whom the ends of the ages have come" (1 Cor. 10:11). Jesus invites us to experience our own meaningful answers to prayer. He says, "Until now you have asked nothing [comparatively speaking] in My name. Ask, and you will receive, that your joy may be full" (John 16:24). Of course, we always need to ask in accordance with God's will. James 4:3 makes this clear when it states, "You ask and do not receive, because you ask amiss, that you may spend it on your pleasures." God, in His unlimited wisdom and foresight, always knows what is best. If we trust Him and keep our own record of the prayers He has answered for us in the past, our faith will grow ever stronger and our fervent prayers ever more effective.

December 2

Wanderers

"Brethren, if anyone among you wanders from the truth, and someone turns him back, let him know that he who turns a sinner from the error of his way will save a soul from death and cover a multitude of sins" (James 5:19, 20).

Have you ever known a wanderer from the truth? Have you ever been a wanderer from the truth? The world is so filled with distractions, temptations, and trials, it's no wonder we sometimes fall off the straight and narrow pathway to glory.

Here, in the last two verses of James' book, he gives hope to those who have made mistakes that they can go home again. They should not immediately be rejected and disfellowshipped from the church. In fact, the "dirty laundry" of their sins does not need to be hung out and paraded around for all to see. Instead, in his ever-practical manner, James describes what a grace-filled reaction to a person in error should be. Someone (perhaps that should be you or me?) should attempt to turn the "sinner from the error of his way." If this gentle entreaty on the part of a brother or sister is successful, the result will be at least two great outcomes. First, a soul will be saved from (eternal) death, and second "a multitude of sins" will be covered.

If this kind advice had always been followed, think of the large number of missing members the Christian church would have been able to restore to their ranks throughout the years. This is not to say that people living in open sin or rebellion to the truth should be accepted back into the fold immediately or that their wrong-doing should be ignored by a church body, such as a board that has been charged with the duty of deciding who should be voted in as members and who may not yet be ready. But if a "wanderer" shows remorse and an interest in returning to the Lord and once again becoming part of the body of Christ, it behooves us, who are also dependent upon the grace of the Lord for our own salvation, to assist in this delicate work of restoration. It's worthy of note that experience has taught us when a person is able to maintain some degree of self-respect through this process, by focusing more on the Lord's love and forgiveness and less on his or her past errors and mistakes, the more likely he or she is to re-integrate successfully into God's family.

When we lived in New England, we came across a ministry dedicated completely to this important work of restoration. Given the number of individuals who have left the church, it's amazing that more Christians haven't felt called to do the same. Yes, we want to put forth effort to gain new members, but in doing so, we should not forget those who have fallen away and might be reclaimed for the kingdom of God. After all, wanderers were so important to Jesus that He told the now well-known parable about the Father waiting for the return of the Prodigal Son to illustrate His desire to bring home again those who had lost their way. There are young people wandering who have been drawn away by the attractions of the world, divorced people who lost their connection to God's family when their own family was broken apart, elderly people who have been forgotten by our modern busyness and lack of concern, as well as those who chose to live a life apart from God and now don't know how to find their way back to Him. Many of these, if approached with kindness and courtesy, would be happy to know that they could be "accepted in the Beloved" (Eph. 1:6) once again by both God and their former brethren.

The following lovely quotation informs us of the most effective way to draw both new and old members alike. It says, "If we would humble ourselves before God, and be kind and courteous and tenderhearted and pitiful, there would be one hundred conversions to the truth where now there is only one" (*Testimonies for the Church*, vol. 9, p. 189). Thus, by exhibiting His traits in our interactions with them, many former wanderers, like that Prodigal Son, will gently find their way back to where they belong. Remember Jesus' own words, "And I, if I am lifted up... will draw all *peoples* to Myself" (John 12:32).

Help us, Lord, to engage in our own ministry of restoration, starting with those who are closest to us—our own family and friends.

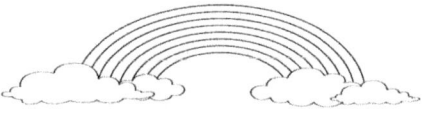

Reserved!

"Blessed be the God and Father of our Lord Jesus Christ, who according to His abundant mercy has begotten us again to a living hope through the resurrection of Jesus Christ from the dead, to an inheritance incorruptible and undefiled and that does not fade away, reserved in heaven for you"
(1 Peter 1:3, 4).

Few things are so frustrating, not to mention embarrassing, as finding an empty seat near the front of a church program or concert, only to discover when you make your way forward that the seat is reserved for someone else! When this happens, you crouch down and make your way sheepishly back to the beginning of the too-long aisle, desperately scanning the audience for an empty and unsaved seat where you could slip in without causing too much commotion. On the flip side, almost nothing is so gratifying as arriving at a venue and finding there is a great seat or table reserved especially for you. Immediately, you feel relieved, and like this is a place where your presence is welcomed. Someone has planned ahead and prepared a specific place with you in mind! That's how I feel when I read today's passage. Think of it. The risen Jesus, in His abundant mercy, has reserved an incorruptible inheritance in heaven just for me!

One summer I was on a fairly long road trip and decided to stop and spend the night in Reno before continuing my trip across the vast desert that lay ahead. Since the city is known for its abundance of hotel rooms, I didn't think to make a reservation ahead of time. What I didn't know was that there was a huge convention in town that week, and most of the rooms had been reserved for its many attendees. The ones that were left were either charging an exorbitant price or were not places where I, as a woman traveling alone, felt safe to spend the night. I spent several hours driving from north to south and east to west looking for an appropriate place to find rest and shelter. When I finally found an available room where I thought I would feel comfortable, I gave in and decided to pay the ridiculous amount they were asking simply because I was too exhausted to continue looking for something more reasonable. I checked in so late I wasn't able to enjoy any of the amenities of the hotel for which I had paid so dearly! This experience reminded me of the value of reservations. Since then, I always plan ahead, making sure to book any needed accommodations before leaving home. I've learned that I can't just assume there will be an appropriate place where I can stay, and I don't want to be left out in the cold.

Similarly, in our spiritual journey, we can't just assume there will be a place for us in heaven if we haven't planned ahead and made a reservation by accepting the Lord's generous offer to save us. He wants to provide a safe haven where we can rest securely throughout eternity. No longer will we have to worry about the darkness and dangers closing in around us as we travel life's road alone, nor fear the ultimate destination of our journey. By confirming that we want Him to be our personal Savior, He will begin to travel with us, helping to smooth out the rough places along the road, guiding us to take all the right turns in life. Then, when we reach our final destination, He will fling the doors of heaven wide open so that we will be able to enjoy all the amenities He has planned specifically for the happiness of His loved ones! Not only will we feel welcome, but the accommodations will be more than comfortable, and perhaps best of all, He has already picked up the tab!

What incredible plans the Lord has in store for us! No wonder Peter starts this passage proclaiming praise to God! We should praise Him, too—every time we think about the marvelous inheritance He's reserved for our future!

December 4

Living Stones

"Coming to Him as to a living stone, rejected indeed by men, but chosen by God and precious, you also, as living stones, are being built up a spiritual house, a holy priesthood, to offer up spiritual sacrifices acceptable to God through Jesus Christ" (1 Peter 2:4, 5).

As I write, our home is undergoing a remodeling project. It has given me a new appreciation for how much work goes into building a structure. In our case, it took a day to do just the demolition required, to clear away the old in order to make room for the new. The two young men (They all seem pretty young to me now!) who came to do the work had to be experts in their field. They had to become familiar with our house—to know where to turn both the electricity and water off and on, etc. They had to bring the right materials, along with the tools of their trade. Now, they are engaging in hard physical labor, combined with perseverance and patience, until the job is completed. Meanwhile, my job is to trust they know what they're doing and (I hope!) rejoice at the finished product of their handiwork!

In Jesus' day, large construction projects began with a very strong corner stone, upon which all the other stones of the building depended. This foundational stone was called the "chief cornerstone." One day, when talking with the priests and pharisees, Jesus showed He knew God had made Him the chief Cornerstone of salvation by quoting Psalm 118:22, 23: "The stone *which* the builders rejected has become the chief cornerstone. This was the LORD's doing; it *is* marvelous in our eyes." Thus, at the same time, He also showed He realized that many of the supposed religious leaders of His day, whose job it was to build up the church, would reject Him. Despite this, He had given His life over to be sacrificed for humankind, knowing that for those who accepted Him, it would mean the difference between eternal death and eternal life. Only in this way would He be successful in "bringing many sons to glory" (Heb. 2:10).

In today's Scripture reading, Peter describes Jesus as "a living stone...chosen by God *and* precious." But he doesn't stop there. As followers of Jesus, Peter states that we are also "living stones... being built up a spiritual house." So, who is it putting this spiritual house together? None other than Jesus, who is not only the chief Cornerstone but also the Master Builder! Now, going back to the work of a builder, we can draw several parallels. First, before Jesus can build anything new, He helps us demolish all the sins and habits of our old carnal life. Being

the expert that He is, He comes very close to us when we pray, so we can get to know each other well. To make us strong spiritually, He uses specially-designed materials: His Word, sermons, spiritual songs, and Christian fellowship with like-minded believers. His primary tool is the gift of the Holy Spirit, who helps us use and apply all we need to become part of His spiritual house. At times, usually because of our selfishness or stubbornness, the labor to make us like Christ can take a while. But thank God, He continues working on us patiently and perseveringly as long as we remain surrendered to Him. In Philippians 1:6, His Word gives us this assurance: "being confident of this very thing, that He who has begun a good work in you will complete *it* until the day of Jesus Christ." Our job is to trust the Master Builder and then rejoice with Him in heaven one day when His wonderful work in us is finished!

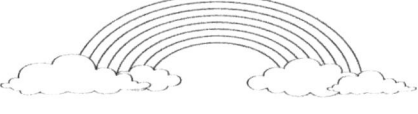

December 5

Called to Blessing

"Finally, all of you be of one mind, having compassion for one another; love as brothers, be tenderhearted, be courteous; not returning evil for evil or reviling for reviling, but on the contrary blessing, knowing that you were called to this, that you may inherit a blessing" (1 Peter 3:8, 9).

In my Bible, this section of 1 Peter 3 bears this subtitle: "Called to Blessing." I like it. Some Christians think that if

they haven't been called into ministry or to become a missionary or do some other great work, their responsibilities stop wherever their job title does. Here, however, Peter speaks to the fact that, as Christians, we all have a calling—a life purpose, if you will. There's a reason for our existence which goes beyond just making a living.

So, how can we fulfill our calling to be a blessing? Peter gives us a list. He exhorts us to:

- *Be of one mind*
- *Have compassion*
- *Love as brothers*
- *Be tenderhearted*
- *Be courteous*
- *Don't return evil for evil (be revengeful)*
- *Don't revile those who revile you*

It's interesting to note that these are things believers can do regardless of their other responsibilities in life. We can do them whether we're male or female, young or old, well-educated or not educated, rich or poor, black or white, English-speaking or not. We can do them, of course with the help of the Holy Spirit, whether we work for the church or in a secular setting. And wherever we are, even in our own homes, we will be witnessing because we will be reflecting the character of Christ.

I believe that it's useful to take an inventory every so often of how we're doing in this regard. Personally, although I can still see room for improvement in all of them, the characteristics I seem to have the most

trouble with are the first one and the last one. After many years of working in academia, I've been trained to question details, argue over philosophies, and debate various opinions. So, "being of one mind" with the people around me, even other believers, can be difficult—and especially challenging in the light of today's theologically and politically-fractured environment. Then, the reviling thing, returning angry words for angry words, is something with which I continue to struggle. So, obviously, these are areas where I still need to grow.

I want to share with you an encounter I had recently with a non-believer. I had to share a piece of painful information with him about a family member. Because it was difficult, I hesitated, not knowing how he would respond. Would he be critical, judgmental, harsh? Finally, since I knew he would be hearing about it sooner or later, I spilled the beans. To my surprise and relief, he reacted with gentle delicacy and great compassion. I was moved. As I got off the phone, I couldn't help thinking how Christ-like he had been. If only those of us who claim to be Christians could be such gracious sounding boards, it's hard to imagine what the impact on our world would be.

All I can say is, *"Lord, help us to live up to our calling so that we can be more like you— spreading blessings all around!"*

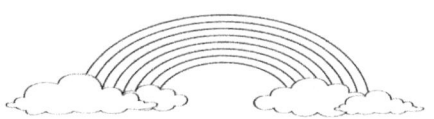

He Cares

"Casting all your care upon Him, for He cares for you" (1 Peter 5:7).

There it is. Short and sweet—a band aid for our broken, bruised, and hurting hearts and a comforting balm for our burden-ridden souls. A sure place of solace in our times of need.

I can still vividly remember the first time I heard the hymn I'm going to share with you today. It was a very dark time in my twenty-something life. I was sitting on a pew in a large church with a couple of thousand parishioners, but I was so lost in my thoughts that I wasn't really aware of them. I felt alone. My head was down, and my heart was broken. Suddenly, I heard a voice that sounded like an angel. It seemed like the song, one I had never heard before, was being sung directly to me. *"Does Jesus care?"* As the lovely strains rang out, I knew that God had sent this comforting message in song just for me that morning. My heart melted, as the "balm of Gilead" poured over my soul (see Jer. 8:22). I don't remember what else happened in the worship service that day, but when I left, I carried a warm sense of healing and new hope, not to mention awe and gratitude that the Lord was so interested in me individually that He sent that lady to sing those words of consolation into my soul just when I needed them most!

On your dark days, maybe this hymn will bring some comfort to you as well. It's hymn 181 in *The Seventh-day Adventist Hymnal* and contains three verses, full of questions we all ask when we're hurting. Then, after each stanza comes the affirming chorus, assuring us of the blessed answer and reinforcing today's precious verse found in 1 Peter 5:7. This is how it goes:

Does Jesus care when my heart is pained too deeply for mirth and song; As the burdens press, and the cares distress, and the way grows weary and long?

Does Jesus care when my way is dark with a nameless dread and fear? As the daylight fades into deep night shades, does He care enough to be near?

Does Jesus care when I've said goodbye to the dearest on earth to me, And my sad heart aches till it nearly breaks—is it aught to Him? Does He see?

Chorus:

O yes, He cares—I know He cares! His heart is touched with my grief; When the days are weary, the long nights dreary, I know my Savior cares. (He cares.)

The Lord is so gracious in the many ways He reaches out to us in our times of need—through His word, through nature, through other people, and through His gentle Spirit gently nudging us in the way that we should go, but one of my favorite ways is through inspirational music. Several decades after the incident I shared above, I was driving down the street, burdened with all my adult worries and responsibilities, when a wonderful song by Amy Grant called "Carry You" floated out of my car radio. It brought me instant relief, reminding me of today's admonition to cast all your care upon Him.

Knowing that He cares and wants to help us with our burdens, whether large or small, always soothes my troubles because I know that if I trust Him, He will make sure everything turns out right in the end. Regardless of what's happening in your life today, may this thought bring you the blessings of comfort, healing, and sweet peace that only the presence of Jesus can supply when we truly understand how much He cares for us.

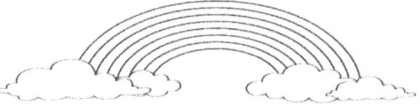

December 7

The Lion Roars

"Be sober, be vigilant; because your adversary the devil walks about like a roaring lion, seeking whom he may devour" (1 Peter 5:8).

This is a verse I quoted often to my daughter during her growing-up years, especially during the intense peer-pressure days of high school. Kids that age have to make so many important decisions that will affect the rest of their lives, and those making poor choices always seem to influence some of the ones who would otherwise make good decisions. College can be just as bad, or even worse, depending on each student's circumstances. Young adults are under a lot of pressure to decide on what their major will be, who they will date or marry, what defines them as individuals, and what kind of a relationship they will have with God. It's always been my position that young people need a lot of intercessory prayer during this critical time of life.

The truth, however, is that Satan, our adversary, is seeking to trip up every one of us. He is a formidable foe, with thousands of years of experience, who knows millions of ways to cause human beings to sin and to tear them away from a saving relationship with the Lord. Whether we are young or old, he is constantly setting traps for us. Whenever we take our eyes off Jesus, we can hear the enemy of our souls roaring like a lion in the background of our daily situations.

The tools that Satan uses are many, starting with our own carnal natures. Sometimes he is very subtle, like a chess player, setting things up slowly for our ultimate demise. Other times, the swiftness of his cruel actions takes us completely by surprise. He uses not only other people, including some we have looked up to, but also stressful situations at work and at home and discouraging circumstances that have left us vulnerable to his evil suggestions. I think this quotation says it well:

It is Satan's constant effort to keep the attention diverted from the Saviour and thus prevent the union and communion of the soul with Christ. The pleasures of the world, life's cares and perplexities and sorrows, the faults of others, or your own faults and imperfections—to any or all of these he [Satan] will seek to divert the mind.... We should not make self the center and indulge anxiety and fear as to whether we shall be saved. All this turns the soul away from the Source of our strength. (*Steps to Christ*, p. 71)

Knowing that this powerful "lion" is out to get us, what can we, as his weak and sin-battered prey, do to protect ourselves from his wiles? We have to do the same thing that Jesus did when He was tempted by Satan to do wrong—depend on God's word. There are two mighty promises that I have found amazingly helpful when doing battle with our powerful predator. I'm sure you can find more, but these are two that I have depended on through the years:

1. "No temptation has overtaken you except such as is common to man; but God *is* faithful, who will not allow you to be tempted beyond what you are able, but with the temptation will also make the way of escape, that you may be able to bear it" (1 Cor. 10:13).
2. "Therefore submit to God. Resist the devil and he will flee from you" (James 4:7).

Whenever I read this verse, I get a mental picture of a large, burly beast suddenly turning tail and running in the other direction when he sees the invincible weapon of the Scriptures in the hands of his intended victim. Make no mistake, we will have multiple encounters with the lion throughout our lifetime. But despite his fearsome roar, we know that we will have victory over him as long as we keep our eyes on Jesus, with our hearts and minds protected by the powerful Word of God.

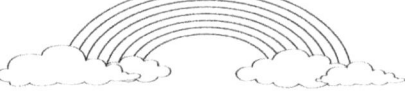

December 8

Precious Promises

"Grace and peace be multiplied to you in the knowledge of God and of Jesus our Lord... by which have been given to us exceedingly great and precious promises, that through these you may be partakers of the divine nature, having escaped the corruption that is in the world through lust"
(2 Peter 1:2, 4).

Yesterday, we talked about the power of God's promises in keeping us from yielding to temptations. Today's passage talks about the worth of God's promises. Here Peter tells us that they are "exceedingly great and precious." Why?

Because, he says, they have been given to us by the Lord so that through them we "may be partakers of the divine nature, having escaped the corruption *that is* in the world...." This being the case, how much we should value them!

When Christians seek to become better reflectors of God's character, what a blessing it is to know that by assimilating the precious promises He has so graciously provided, we can actually partake of His nature. Like Lot in Sodom, we do not have to be tainted by the corruption that surrounds us in the society in which we live. We can choose to lift our hearts and minds to a higher reality when we eat, sleep, and breathe, (and dare I say, commit to memory?) the precious gems found in God's Word.

Let's review a few of the more frequently referenced promises using the familiar King James Version of the Bible, from which many of us learned verses by memory when we were growing up. Here they are organized under some common Christian themes, many as presented in the American Bible Society's *Pocket Scripture Book* pamphlet, originally produced to provide encouragement and inspiration for those serving in the military.

Joy — "They that sow in tears shall reap in joy" (Ps. 126:5).

"Our soul waiteth for the LORD: he is our help and our shield. For our heart shall rejoice in him, because we have trusted in his holy name" (Ps. 33:20, 21).

Peace — "And the peace of God, which passeth all understanding, shall keep your hearts and minds through Christ Jesus" (Phil. 4:7).

"Peace I leave with you, my peace I give unto you: not as the world giveth, give I unto you. Let not your heart be troubled, neither let it be afraid" (John 14:27).

Security — "The LORD is my light and my salvation; whom shall I fear? the LORD is the strength of my life; of whom shall I be afraid?" (Ps. 27:1).

"The name of the LORD is a strong tower: the righteous runneth into it, and is safe" (Prov. 18:10).

Hope — "For thou art my hope, O Lord GOD: thou art my trust from my youth" (Ps. 71:5).

"Be of good courage, and he shall strengthen your heart, all ye that hope in the LORD" (Ps. 31:24).

Strength — "The LORD is my rock, and my fortress, and my deliverer; my God, my strength, in whom I will trust..." (Ps. 18:2).

"My flesh and my heart faileth: but God is the strength of my heart, and my portion for ever" (Ps. 73:26).

Guidance — "In all thy ways acknowledge him, and he shall direct thy paths" (Prov. 3:6).

"Thou shalt guide me with thy counsel, and afterward receive me to glory" (Ps. 73:24).

Forgiveness — "If we confess our sins, he is faithful and just to forgive us our sins, and to cleanse us from all unrighteousness" (1 John 1:9).

"Bless the LORD, O my soul, and forget not all His benefits: who forgiveth all thine iniquities; who healeth all thy diseases" (Ps. 103:2, 3).

<u>Salvation</u> – "For by grace are ye saved, through faith; and that not of yourselves: it is the gift of God; not of works, lest any man should boast" (Eph. 2:8, 9).

"For God so loved the world, that he gave his only begotten Son, that whosoever believeth in him should not perish, but have everlasting life" (John 3:16).

This smorgasbord of scriptures is really just an appetizer, if you will, to the abundant feast of spiritual food the Lord has prepared in His Word for all of His children until He returns to take us home. Bon appétit!

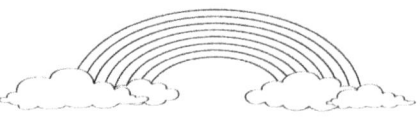

December 9

Fruitful Growth

"But also for this very reason, giving all diligence, add to your faith virtue, to virtue knowledge, to knowledge self-control, to self-control perseverance, to perseverance godliness, to godliness brotherly kindness, and to brotherly kindness love. For if these things are yours and abound, you will be neither barren nor unfruitful in the knowledge of our Lord Jesus Christ" (2 Peter 1:5–8).

Today's passage covers more verses than usual because they seem to go together as a set. In my Bible, the subtitle for this section of the chapter is "Fruitful Growth in the Faith." Over the years, I have also heard it called "Peter's Ladder of Christian Virtues."

Although we have just been reading in Paul's writings that we are saved by grace and not by works (see Eph. 2:8, 9), Peter is telling us here that we should give all "diligence" to making our calling and election sure (see 2 Peter 1:10). In order to gain more insight into how these two ideas harmonize, I turned once again to the *SDA Bible Commentary*.

Regarding verse 5, the fact that God has showered us with so many blessings

> ...is reason enough to stimulate us to greater zeal in pursuit of righteousness. God has done His part; we must now do ours.... We are to add our diligent pursuit of Christian virtues to the gifts God has already bestowed. Working along with God, the Christian is enabled to develop the sanctified life. (*SDA Bible Commentary*, vol. 7, p. 597).

On the word "virtue" in verse 5, "Peter's thought may be paraphrased, 'in connection with your faith, supply moral excellence.'

By heeding such counsel the Christian will build a balanced life" (*Ibid.*).

The word "knowledge," also in verse 5, is believed to refer to one's "practical understanding of God's ways and plans for the individual rather than to a merely intellectual knowledge" (*Ibid.*).

In shedding light on verse 6, the same page of the *Commentary* further defines each of three virtues: first, "temperance" as "self-control;" then, "patience" as "a brave, steadfast perseverance under adversity;" and third, "godliness" as "a reverence for God," which will keep the Christian "humble and gentle."

In verse 7, there are two virtues to flesh out. "Brotherly kindness" is the first, meaning "love of the brethren." We shall love other members of the church with the kind of affection one has for blood relatives. And finally, "love" (also known as charity):

> This is the true Christian affection that seeks only the good of the one loved.... This is the capstone of all the preceding qualities listed by Peter. It is the greatest of all virtues; it is that which must govern all we do. All the virtues meet in this greatest emotion; and all others fail and are less than nothing without it. (1 Cor. 13:1–3) (*Ibid.*)

In explaining verse 8, the *Commentary* presents Peter's bottom line for why the acquisition of these virtues is so important. Those who have developed these characteristics will not be idle, barren members of the church.

> Christian service, rendered through the operation of these basic qualities...will be productive. As money well invested is expected to yield dividends, as a field cultivated is expected to produce good crops, so the Christian life, well furnished with every needed virtue is certain to produce results. (*SDA Bible Commentary*, vol. 7, p. 598)

Thus, we have learned that our salvation occurs in two parts. Justification happens the moment we accept Jesus as our Savior, and it is given to us as a gift through God's gracious generosity, whereas sanctification—becoming more like Jesus—takes place over the rest of our lifetime. If we function "in continual connection with the Saviour," we shall not be unfruitful (*Ibid.*). As we choose to be active participants, the Lord will help us grow into flourishing, fruitful Christians who will successfully bring others into the joy of His kingdom.

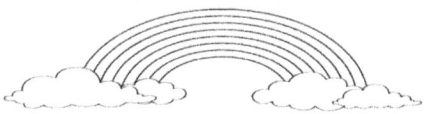

Eyewitnesses

"For we did not follow cunningly devised fables when we made known to you the power and coming of our Lord Jesus Christ, but were eyewitnesses of His majesty" (2 Peter 1:16).

For years I've watched a news program in the evenings called "Eyewitness News." This title is meant to convey confidence in the validity and authority of the news stories presented by the show's producers. They do their best to interview people who were either directly involved in the incident they're reporting on or who were eyewitnesses of what took place. People who can say, "I saw it with my own eyes!" are always more believable than just some uninvolved bystander simply spreading hearsay. This is the point Peter is making here.

> The fact that the apostles had been eyewitnesses of the life, ministry, death, resurrection, and ascension of Christ convinced them that He was indeed the promised Messiah, the Son of God. In turn, this conviction imparted irresistible power to the message they proclaimed. (*SDA Bible Commentary*, vol. 7, p. 600)

When the apostles preached, they weren't just making up fables to entertain their hearers or to gain attention for themselves. They had been privileged to walk with Jesus on a daily basis, to marvel at His miracles and be moved by His teachings. Three of them, including Peter, had actually seen the magnificent glory of their Master on the mount of transfiguration. What's more, they had heard the very voice of God proclaiming, "This is My beloved Son, in whom I am well pleased. Hear Him!" (Matt. 17:5).

It's one thing to hear others discuss religious topics or to read historical facts about the Lord or to study doctrinal points in His word. This is all "head knowledge," and it has its place in the Christian's life. But what we need is to experience a "heart knowledge" about Jesus by accepting Him as the Lord of our individual life. Only then can we qualify as an eyewitness— one with up close and personal information, a first-hand account of the veracity of God's love and grace. Armed with such an authentic and powerful message to share, we, like the first disciples, will be able to turn the world upside down for the Lord. Too often, I fear, we discount the value of our testimonies as an important tool for bringing others to Christ. A Christian's prayerful and thoughtfully presented testimony can be a wonderful source of inspiration, encouragement, and even conviction. Many who have previously felt lost and hopeless have found new courage by listening to the story of someone like them who, through being with Jesus, have discovered new hope, purpose, and joy in their lives.

It was only because of the disciples' real experiences with the Lord that they were able to evangelize with such power, and the same will be true for those who are called to preach the gospel of Christ today. We may not see His glory except with our mind's eye. We may not audibly hear God's voice except through the whisperings of the Holy Spirit. We may not witness the same miracles that

Jesus performed in person, but we will be able to trace His hand of providence at work in our own lives and be blessed to see the wondrous miracle of conversion taking place in the lives of those who have chosen to accept Jesus as their personal Savior.

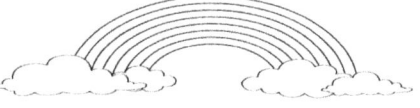

December 11

The Sure Word

"And so we have the prophetic word confirmed, which you do well to heed as a light that shines in a dark place, until the day dawns and the morning star rises in your hearts; knowing this first, that no prophecy of Scripture is of any private interpretation, for prophecy never came by the will of man, but holy men of God spoke as they were moved by the Holy Spirit"
(2 Peter 1:19–21).

The King James Version is the one my generation grew up with, so the way I learned verse 19 was like this: "We have also a more sure word of prophecy; whereunto ye do well that ye take heed, as unto a light that shineth in a dark place, until the day dawn, and the day star arise in your hearts." I like the "sure word of prophecy" translation better than "the prophetic word confirmed," but either way the meaning Peter is conveying is that God's Word, given through the prophets, is trustworthy.

Here he is referring, of course, to the Old Testament, which was the part of the Scriptures available in his day. He, along with the other disciples, had seen how the prophecies there, especially those about the Messiah, had been fulfilled in the life of Jesus. To that, they were now able to add their personal testimonies about the miraculous life of Jesus, together with the evidence they had seen regarding His divine origin. In this way, they were able to "confirm" the prophets' words.

A number of the Lord's disciples were inspired not only to preach about their experiences with Him but also to leave a written record to encourage and guide those who would become followers of Jesus in the future. In time, as we know, these books, messages, and letters would be compiled into the New Testament, giving us the whole Bible as we know it today. Despite the arguments of non-believers and the ardent efforts of Satan to destroy the Bible and its influence over the centuries, its publication has not only survived but thrived! Only God could have assured that His Word, written by prophets and apostles of old, would be protected and preserved throughout the ages in order to be delivered into our hands "upon whom the ends of the ages have come" (1 Cor. 10:11)—and in the modern languages which we speak today!

In this passage Peter wants us to know two things. First, in the writing of the Scriptures, the authors were not just charlatans of some kind, writing their own thoughts and ideas, but "holy men of God" who were moved by the Holy Spirit to share messages that God wanted to communicate to His people. Second, Peter is telling his readers that those who "heed" the sure Word will receive light to dispel the darkness, and as a result, "the Morning Star" (Jesus Himself) will "arise in [their] hearts." It's a gracious and salvific promise.

How wonderful to know that God is still using the messages in His sure Word to bring light, guidance, instruction, and encouragement, not to mention salvation, to His modern-day people. I want to end today with the cry of a sincere believer's heart regarding the Scriptures. It's from a well-known song that Christians have sung for more than a century now to express and acknowledge all that the Bible is to them. I'm sure you've heard it. It's hymn 272 from *The Seventh-day Adventist Hymnal*, and it's entitled "Give Me the Bible."

Give me the Bible, star of gladness gleaming, to cheer the wanderer lone and tempest tossed; no storm can hide that peaceful radiance beaming, since Jesus came to seek and save the lost.

Give me the Bible, when my heart is broken, when sin and grief have filled my soul with fear; give me the precious words by Jesus spoken, hold up faith's lamp to show my Savior near.

Give me the Bible, all my steps enlighten, teach me the danger of these realms below; that lamp of safety, o'er the gloom shall brighten, that light alone the path of peace can show.

Chorus:

Give me the Bible, holy message shining, Thy light shall guide me in the narrow way. Precept and promise, law and love combining, 'till night shall vanish in eternal day!

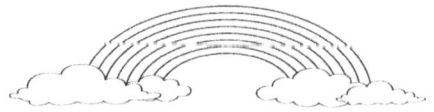

Slackness?

"The Lord is not slack concerning His *promise, as some count slackness, but is longsuffering toward us, not willing that any should perish but that all should come to repentance" (2 Peter 3:9).*

Whew! What a slew of negative definitions I found when I looked up the word "slack." When used as an adjective it can mean: not using due diligence, care, or dispatch, careless, sluggish, not busy or active. Synonyms include: derelict, lax, negligent, remiss. The noun "slackness" is defined as the quality or state of being slack or behaving slackly. On the other hand, when I looked up the word "longsuffering," I found the meaning to be patiently enduring lasting offense or hardship. Synonyms were patient, forbearing, tolerant, and uncomplaining. In modern speech we'd probably say, "It means putting up with something painful or unpleasant for a long time."

Comparing these two terms, I would argue that in His constant interactions with humanity, God has proven over and over that He is the opposite of slack while being the epitome of longsuffering, as shown by His continuous patience in enduring the lasting offense of sin. Why does He continue to put up with it? Today's verse tells us. It's because He is "not willing that any should perish but that all should come to repentance." How long will He wait? We don't know, but we do know that there will come a day when sin and sinners (those who cling to sin) will be erased from the universe and a joyful, sin-free eternity will begin. We also know that we can depend on Him to make

the right decision because it will be according to God's perfect timing.

There is a philosophical school of thought whose adherents believe that there is a God (or some kind of creative being), but He just made the world and then went off to let it fend for itself. As if He got busy somewhere else in the universe, lost interest in us, and simply left us on our own, with an aimless, dark, and unknown destiny. The Bible, however, paints a picture of a loving God, who is not only interested in the world at large but in every aspect of our individual lives. As believers in the true God of the Bible, how encouraged we should be when we do even a brief review of just a few of the gracious and marvelous interactions of God with His people over the course of history as documented in His word.

First, in the Old Testament:

* God created men and women in His own image (Gen. 1:27).

* An active, personal God didn't just speak humans into existence, as He did with other things, but He actually "formed man *of* the dust of the ground, and breathed into his nostrils the breath of life" (Gen. 2:7).

* God made everything that His servant Joseph did prosper (Gen. 39:23).

* The Lord freed the Israelites from Egypt with many miracles and guided them through the

wilderness with a fire by night and a cloud in the daytime (Exod. 13:21).

* He parted the Red Sea, so His people could walk across it on dry ground, escaping from the Egyptians (Exod. 14:21).

* He provided manna for them to eat along their journey—for forty years! (Exod. 16:35)

* He slated their thirst with water from a rock in the desert (Exod. 17:6).

* God gave Elijah a stunning victory over those who worshipped idols on Mt. Carmel (1 Kings 18:27–29).

* He spared the lives of the three Hebrew young men who trusted in Him and walked with them in the fiery furnace (Dan. 3:25).

* He saved the life of His faithful servant Daniel in the lion's den (Dan. 6:22).

Lest we think God only interacted with humankind back in ancient times, here are a few New Testament examples:

*God "so loved the world that He gave His only begotten Son, that whoever believes in Him should not perish but have everlasting life" (John 3:16).

*The mission of Jesus was not just to wait for people to come to Him but to sacrifice His life in order to do all He could to seek and save the lost (Matt. 18:11).

*At the end of His life, as Jesus was ascending to heaven, He promised His disciples that He would come back again someday to take them to heaven, and in the meantime, He would be building mansions for them to live in (John 14:1–3).

*He promised that His presence would be with them always, through the gift of the Holy Spirit, who would empower them to evangelize the world as well as to perform miracles as they ministered to others (Matt. 28:20; Acts 2:4).

*Through this same Holy Spirit, the Lord would also grant spiritual gifts to His people to help build up and bless the church (1 Cor. 12:4–11).

Thank God that He is so patient, loving, and interactive with the beings He created! We can be confident that He has not forgotten us. Thank God for all the wonderful stories in the Scriptures that encourage us and help us understand the nature of our caring, heavenly Father! And thank God that, if we trust Him, He has promised to personally guide and bless our steps as well (see Prov. 3:5, 6)!

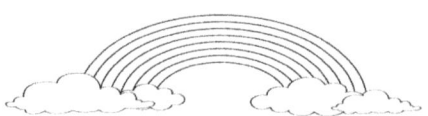

December 13

The Day of the Lord

"But the day of the Lord will come as a thief in the night, in which the heavens will pass away with a great noise, and the elements will melt with fervent heat; both the earth and the works that are in it will be burned up. Therefore, since all these things will be dissolved, what manner of persons ought you to be in holy conduct and godliness...?" (2 Peter 3:10, 11).

In talking about "the day of the Lord," Peter, who is undoubtedly referring to the much-anticipated time when Jesus returns to the earth, also brings us back to a discussion of the judgment—after which the earth and everything in it will be destroyed by fire. When that day comes, the Lord will stand up and declare that enough is enough as far as sin and all of its terrible circumstances is concerned. His long-suffering will have finally reached its limit. His righteous wrath will be expressed by the heavens, as we know them, dissolving with "a great noise" and even the very elements melting "with fervent heat."

When I try to imagine what that will be like, it reminds me of some of the uncontrollable wildfires we've experienced in northern California over the last few summers. Even at a distance, the heat radiating from these massive fires can be felt, as they roar through the forest like a mighty ocean of flames, turning everything in their path to ashes. Some survivors say it's the closest thing to hell they've ever experienced.

Like a wildfire, the day of the Lord will come unexpectedly. In fact, verse 10 says it will surprise us suddenly, like "a thief in the night." Fortunately, it is in our hands whether we survive this last day holocaust of destruction or not. Will we be happy and relieved to see Jesus bursting through the skies to come and rescue us or terrified, cringing with an indescribable dread, and begging the rocks and mountains to fall on us to hide us from His glorious, shining presence? God has done everything He can to provide us with salvation, but it's our choice whether or not to accept it.

In verse 11, Peter challenges his readers with a serious question. In light of the things he has described, he asks, "What manner *of persons* ought you to be?" Then he answers his own question by admonishing them to be persons of "holy conduct and godliness." In the subsequent verse, He tells them that those who have made the choice to be God's people will not only look forward to the day of the Lord but will also want to help hasten it by sharing their testimony and knowledge of God with others. The goal is to rescue as many people as possible from the horrors of sin before the doors of mercy close, and it is forever too late for them to be saved. In the end, only those who insist on clinging to sin will ultimately be destroyed with it.

With a change of tone at the end of this section of the chapter, Peter comforts and encourages believers by turning their sights from the scenes of destruction of this old earth to the unimaginable delights of the promised new earth. He reminds us that as children of the God of the universe, it is our privilege to eagerly look forward to "new heavens and a new earth in which righteousness dwells" (verse 13). As we draw to the close of his second epistle, Peter exhorts believers, whom he refers to as "beloved," to remain steadfast in their relationship with the Lord. In verse 14 he writes, "Therefore, beloved, looking forward to these things, be diligent to be found by Him in peace, without spot and blameless." He warns them not to be "led away with the error of the wicked" (verse 17), and he urges them to continue to "grow in the grace and the knowledge of our Lord and Savior Jesus Christ" (verse 18) in a blessed benediction.

How wonderful it is to know that we do not need to fear the awesome day of the Lord if we have chosen to become one of His own by accepting His gracious salvation!

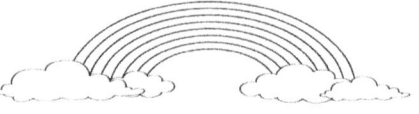

December 14

Fellowship

"But if we walk in the light as He is in the light, we have fellowship with one another, and the blood of Jesus Christ His Son cleanses us from all sin"
(1 John 1:7).

I have mentioned before the warm Christian fellowship we shared when we had the privilege of belonging to a small prayer group while living in Massachusetts. It was even more precious to us because, at that time, all of our blood relatives lived on the other side of the country. If you have ever had the pleasure of belonging to a small, close-knit group of fellow believers, perhaps you can relate.

As I look back over the years, I can truly say I am amazed at how much I have enjoyed interacting with people with very diverse backgrounds. Often having very little in common, except our shared faith, we have experienced great fellowship as we've lived and worked together. I have had a best friend in college from Nigeria, stayed in the homes of "like believers" in the Virgin Islands, and taught with other professors from India, Haiti, and Panama. We have hosted church administrators from Brazil as well as other South American countries for Sabbath lunches and relished family friends from Colombia, Venezuela, Costa Rica, Pakistan, and various islands in the Caribbean. We were so happy when the warm people of Puerto Rico welcomed us with open arms when we served there for four years, and because my husband's family is from Mexico, we can naturally claim many friends of Mexican descent. What a blessing it is to attend worldwide church conventions, where we can reunite with our brothers and sisters from around the world. It is truly a foretaste of heaven!

In these three short epistles, John, who has often been referred to as the disciple whom Jesus loved, emphasizes the fact that if we are enjoying a loving relationship with the Lord, it will also spill over into loving relationships with those around us—and especially those who are also walking in the light. I like the way the *SDA Bible Commentary* interprets this verse:

> As a traveler will follow the light of a guide along a dark and unknown road, so the child of God will follow light from the Lord along the road of life.... If we walk in the light we walk with God, from whom the light shines, and have fellowship not only with Him but also with all others who are following the Lord. Serving the same God, believing the same truths, following the same instructions on the pathway of life, we cannot fail to walk in unity. The slightest sign of ill will between us and our brethren should make us review our own conduct, to be sure that we are not veering away from the lighted path of life. (*SDA Bible Commentary*, vol. 7, p. 631)

As I read this, I found myself nodding in agreement with the beautiful picture these words painted—until I got to that last sentence. It amplified the meaning of the often overlooked "If" at the beginning of today's verse: "If we walk in the light...." This is the prerequisite in order to experience the heavenly fellowship that the Lord wants us to enjoy as His children. So how will we know if we're still walking on the path that leads to heaven? "The slightest sign of ill will between us and our brethren should make us review our own conduct"! This is a wake-up call. Is it remotely possible in today's rough and tumble political world to achieve even a small measure of unity? It's a question that I find challenging.

Since the Lord made each one of us to be unique, I don't believe He wants us all to share the exact same thought patterns, and thus, like robots, agree on everything. Knowing how He loves diversity (just think of the wide variety of plants, animals, etc., He created!), I think there is room in God's world for differing opinions, especially considering our diverse upbringings, cultures, races, genders, and language backgrounds, not to mention our educational and socio-economic levels. Perhaps what will help keep us on the straight and narrow is the way in which we interact when sharing our strongly-held opinions. If we could just imagine that Jesus is in the room and model our conversations after His gracious manner—with no shouting, put-downs, name-calling, etc.—and respecting each person's right to their own opinions, I believe it would go a long way toward creating and maintaining the kind of fellowship that should be shared by Christians, despite the raucous battle of ideas that is raging all around us.

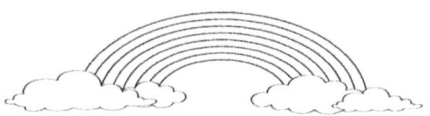

Forgiveness

"If we confess our sins, He is faithful and just to forgive us our sins and to cleanse us from all unrighteousness" (1 John 1:9).

Surely this verse is one of the great pillars of the Christian faith. It has been quoted for centuries to assure sinners that they can be free of all of their sins, mistakes, guilt, and shame if they will only confess them to the Faithful One—Jesus Christ, our Savior. It was for this very reason that the Lord came to our earth. He chose to take the penalty for our sins, so we could escape the darkness that iniquity brought on this world and experience the light and joys of the heavenly home He has gone to prepare for us. What a gracious God we serve!

But that's not all. In this small verse, He declares that He will not only forgive us our sins but will also "cleanse us from all unrighteousness." Here He promises to break the chains of sinful habits, including our vicious and destructive addictions, and even erase the stains on our souls that have been caused by our association with evil. I think the following illustration explains this concept well:

The story is told of a boy who learned God's method of forgiveness in a simple, yet convincing manner. The little fellow could not grasp the meaning of having his sins "blotted out," and insisted that his mother tell him where his sins went when the Lord forgave him.

"Bring me the slate you were writing on this morning," his mother suggested.

When the slate was produced, the mother found it clean and bright with no trace of writing on it.

"Where is the writing that you put on it this morning, Freddie?" she asked.

"Why, nowhere, Mamma; it's just gone."

"And that's what happens to your sins, too. When God forgives them, they are all gone!" Mother explained.

What a blessed assurance! The Lord holds nothing of the past against us. He blots it all out. In Christ's righteousness we stand before our heavenly Father as though we had never sinned. (*501 Illustrations*, p. 138)

Today's verse is one of the key texts my father insisted that all his children memorize at a young age. I must admit it has served me well through the years. No matter my error, this precious promise of the Lord has given me assurance of forgiveness, relief from guilt, and the comforting confidence that the Lord will help me do better in the future. Restarting each day with the proverbial "clean slate" should provide a wonderful motivation for us to be the best people possible in order to bring honor and glory to the generous God who has granted us this marvelous gift of forgiveness.

There's also an additional fringe benefit to basking in God's unmerited favor. When we truly realize the depth of God's grace to us, it's so much easier to forgive others. As we recognize and assimilate the forgiveness of God, it has the lovely tendency to overflow from our lives, moving us to accept and pardon those who have wronged us, resulting in such blessings as peace and reconciliation. So, claim God's promise of forgiveness now and start enjoying the blessings of a "clean slate" today!

December 16

The Test

"Now by this we know that we know Him, if we keep His commandments. He who says, 'I know Him,' and does not keep His commandments, is a liar, and the truth is not in him. But whoever keeps His word, truly the love of God is perfected in Him. By this we know that we are in Him. He who says he abides in Him ought himself also to walk just as He walked" (1 John 2:3–6).

Today's scriptural reading makes very clear what the test is if we want to examine our relationship with the Lord. As a life-long educator, I believe in the need for periodic assessment in order to gauge a student's grasp of the material being taught. Teachers spend a great deal of time developing assessment instruments to evaluate their pupil's knowledge, not only regarding isolated facts (such as the dates when important historical events took place) but also their understanding regarding broad concepts (such as the meaning of democracy). State-required standardized testing also reveals a student's progress over time—usually from one year to the next. It is often used to compare a student's achievement in different subject areas with the achievement of others of the same age and grade. Meanwhile, performance assessments are a very useful tool for measuring growth in the more hands-on subjects in the curriculum—everything from music to auto mechanics to art to modern languages. Can a student actually employ the skills they have been learning in real life—where the rubber meets the road?

Here the apostle John is actually recommending a type of performance assessment for the converts to Christianity—one that continues to be helpful for Christians in our day. Are we merely professing to be followers of Jesus or are we the real thing? Every teacher knows that when your students love you, they happily keep the classroom rules. On the other hand, if the student-teacher relationship is not good, getting that young person to abide by the rules will become an uphill battle. The same is true in our Christian walk. If we truly know Jesus as our Savior, loving and trusting Him, we will be happy to live by His rules—the Ten Commandments. We will also want to emulate Him and do those things that we know will be pleasing in His sight. This doesn't mean that we'll always behave perfectly, just as the happily compliant children won't always do things perfectly, but the pattern of our outward actions will certainly be an indicator of where our hearts lie. I like this statement found in the *SDA Bible Commentary*:

> True religion is the imitation of Christ. Those who follow Christ will deny self, take up the cross, and walk in His footsteps. Following Christ means obedience to all His commandments. No soldier can be said to follow his commander unless he obeys orders. Christ is our model. To copy Jesus, full of love and tenderness and compassion, will require that we draw near to Him daily. O how God has been dishonored by His professed representatives. (*SDA Bible Commentary*, vol. 7, p. 949)

All of us who have claimed to be Christians know that we have, at times, disobeyed His laws and dishonored Him by our un-Christlike behavior. So how do we do better—not to earn the salvation that He has already provided for us but to live a life that will be pleasing to Him and represent Him appropriately? According to this quotation, the answer lies in drawing "near to Him daily." Spending time with Him, so that we can better abide in Him.

Lord, please transform us into your obedient and loving children. Enable us, by your grace, to pass this test of true Christianity with flying colors!

God's Children

"Behold what manner of love the Father has bestowed on us, that we should be called children of God! Therefore the world does not know us, because it did not know Him. Beloved, now we are children of God; and it has not yet been revealed what we shall be, but we know that when He is revealed, we shall be like Him, for we shall see Him as He is" (1 John 3:1, 2).

This reading reminds me of all of the orphan stories I have heard that have a happy ending. It also calls to mind the parable that Jesus Himself told about the prodigal son. But as I mulled it over, a much-less famous story—the one about Mephibosheth—caught my attention.

You may remember that Mephibosheth was Jonathan's lame son. You can read about him in 2 Samuel 9. King Saul, his grandfather, had been the king of Israel before the popular and prosperous reign of King David. As a small child, his nursemaid had accidently dropped him when she was fleeing from the Philistines as their armies defeated the armies of Israel. As a result, Mephibosheth, although surviving, became a cripple for the rest of his life.

One day, as King David was enjoying peace from his enemies and his royal kingdom was flourishing, he stopped to think about his beloved but now deceased friend, Jonathan. As Saul's son, Jonathan was actually the person who should have ascended to the throne. Instead, he graciously supported the prophet Samuel's anointing of David as the next ruler of the nation. Now he, along with most of the royal line of Saul, had been destroyed. In pondering these events, he remembered a covenant he had made with Jonathan to show kindness to the house of Saul, if anyone was left, after he became king. In curiosity, he requested that a former servant of Saul be summoned to the palace, and then asked this question: "Is there still anyone who is left of the house of Saul, that I may show him kindness for Jonathan's sake?" (2 Sam. 9:1). The servant was probably somewhat suspicious of the king's motives, given that Saul had treated David as an enemy during the last part of his life, but David assured him by stating he wanted to show the remnant of Saul's family "the kindness of God" (verse 3). It's plausible to think that the reason Mephibosheth's life had been spared was that he did not fight in Israel's army due to his physical limitations. Whatever the case, David brought him to his court immediately. Undoubtedly, the young man came before the powerful king with fear and trembling. But his prejudice against this political rival and his fears of annihilation melted away as David kindly explained his purpose. Not only did he wish to treat Mephibosheth as a son, as part of his own royal family, by assigning him a place at the table where he would eat "continually" (verse 7) right along with the king's own sons but he also returned to the shocked descendant the land and possessions that had belonged to Saul and all of his family!

511

I see parallels between David's treatment of Mephibosheth and God's treatment of us. We were half hiding from God, skulking around in the shadows of sin, hoping maybe the King, who we feared and doubted, either wouldn't notice or bother us. However, because of His great love and His promise to His beloved Son to save us, He sought us out. He explains that He simply wants to show us His kindness. Although we've done nothing to deserve it, if we will accept it, He will restore our lost dignity. He gives us a place at His royal table, declaring that we are now His sons and daughters! And finally, He will bestow upon us a royal inheritance!

No wonder John bursts out in holy exclamation, "What manner of love the Father has bestowed on us, that we should be called children of God!" *Amen!*

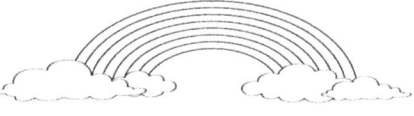

December 18

Victory!

"For whatever is born of God overcomes the world. And this is the victory that has overcome the world—our faith. Who is he who overcomes the world, but he who believes that Jesus is the Son of God?" (1 John 5:4, 5).

Many times in our stroll through the Scriptures this year, we have talked about the great cosmic conflict between good and evil that is raging in the universe, and in which, unwittingly, we have become personally involved. There is no sitting on the fence in this battle. Each of us will decide—in fact, are now deciding every day by our choices—on which side our loyalties lie. Will we dedicate our energies and throw our effort behind good or evil? Will the weight of our influence on those around us promote salvation or perdition? Will we stand on the side of Jesus or Satan?

Sometimes, as we see the rapid rise of iniquity all around us, it's easy to get discouraged and feel that it will be impossible for righteousness to ultimately win the day. We find our world consumed with the seemingly intractable problems of war, poverty, sickness, strife, and suffering of every kind. In addition to all these external struggles, we are forced to recognize that our own carnal nature is also causing internal strife to try to prevent us from living a holy life that will bring honor to our Creator. We become aware, as the old songwriter penned, of "fightings within and fears without" (*The Seventh-day Adventist Hymnal*, hymn 313). So how will we, in our moral weakness, ever be able to overcome the world, the flesh, and the devil? How will we ever achieve victory?

Thank God, today's passage answers that very question. Faith is the victory that overcomes the world! Faith in what? Ourselves? Other weak humans? Some kind of blind scientific optimism? No! The Bible makes clear that it is faith in Jesus, the Son of God, that delivers the victory we seek—in our own hearts, in the world, and in the universe at large! He who first made us and then redeemed us is the Almighty Commander who will ultimately conquer all evil with His unmatched power and overwhelming love, bringing us a glorious victory!

Ever since I decided to write about this text, I have been humming an old beloved hymn written in the late 1800s called, "Faith is the Victory." It is hymn 608 in *The Seventh-day Adventist Hymnal*. Even though a few of the words are rather archaic, the message they carry is still a rallying cry for those of us engaged in Christian warfare today. Be inspired as you sing it along with me!

> Encamped along the hills of light, ye Christian soldiers, rise,
> And press the battle ere the night shall veil the glowing skies.

> Against the foe in vales below let all our strength be hurled;
> Faith is the victory, we know, that overcomes the world.
> On every hand the foe we find drawn up in dread array;
> Let tents of ease be left behind, and onward to the fray;
> Salvation's helmet on each head, with truth all girt about,
> The earth shall tremble 'neath our tread, and echo with our shout.
> To him that overcomes the foe, white raiment shall be giv'n;
> Before the angels he shall know his name confessed in heav'n.
> Then onward from the hills of light, our hearts with love aflame,
> We'll vanquish all the hosts of night, in Jesus' conquering name.

Chorus:

> Faith is the victory! Faith is the victory!
> O, glorious victory, that overcomes the world!

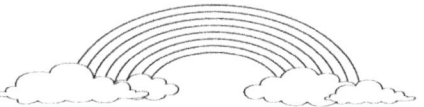

The Doctrine of Christ

"Whoever transgresses and does not abide in the doctrine of Christ does not have God. He who abides in the doctrine of Christ has both the Father and the Son" (2 John 1:9).

*I*n John's shortest epistle, we find him sending a note of encouragement and exhortation to one particular sister in the faith, mentioning that he had gladly observed some of her children "walking in the truth" (verse 4). He then proceeds to remind her, as apostles often did when writing to their converts in the various places where they had started fledgling churches, to continue with the beliefs and practices she had been taught when she first became a Christian. Among these, he enjoined her to continue to walk in Christ's commandments, to love one another in the church, and to beware of false teachers who did "not confess Jesus Christ *as* coming in the flesh" (verse 7). He goes on to emphasize that those deceivers who do "not abide in the doctrine of Christ" are transgressing and do not have God (verse 9). He ends his letter with a strong warning not to fraternize with those false teachers who would lead believers away from their faith in Jesus. It's apparent that in John's day, just as in ours, there are religionists who claim that a person can be saved without believing in Jesus, even though the inspired Scriptures clearly proclaim, "Nor is there salvation in any other, for there is no other name under heaven given among men by which we must be saved" (Acts 4:12). Not to mention, "...that whosoever believeth in him should not perish, but have everlasting life" (John 3:16, KJV) as well as a host of other key texts recorded in the New Testament.

As a citizen of the twenty-first century, I decided to visit the internet to see if it could give me any information on the meaning of "the doctrine of Christ." Happily, it did. I learned that "the doctrine of Christ" is also called "Christology" by modern theologians, and this was the definition I found:

> Christology, Christian reflection, teaching, and doctrine concerning Jesus of Nazareth. Christology is the part of theology that is concerned with the nature and work of Jesus, including such matters as the Incarnation, the Resurrection, and his human and divine natures and their relationship. (Britannica, "Christology," accessed May 31, 2023, https://britannica.com/topic/Christology.)

I would venture to say that the apostles also put a heavy emphasis on additional parts of the life of Jesus as they taught the new believers, especially the crucifixion and its meaning to their salvation as well as His promises to send the Holy Spirit to His followers and to one day come again (the Second Coming) to take them to heaven to live with Him. In any event, I'm sure that coming to know Jesus Himself, as each person's individual Savior, was the center point of all that the apostles taught in the many towns and villages where they evangelized.

I believe the same should be true of our evangelistic efforts today. Yes, there are many things to be taught to new Christians—doctrinal beliefs, historical facts, knowledge about the Bible, lifestyle issues, how to relate to others in a Christ-like manner, etc., but the most important thing, that which cannot be left out, is introducing people to Jesus as their Savior! They must learn of His great love, His forgiveness, His grace, and the loveliness of His character. Once they truly begin to love Him in return, all the other doctrinal pieces will eventually fall into place. Accepting the "doctrine of Christ," they will be enabled to develop a saving relationship "with both the Father and the Son."

The story is told of a man who called his pastor to come visit and encourage him as he lay dying. The sick man asked the minister to read John 14:1–3, which he called "the sweetest texts in the Bible." As the clergyman read the passage, the man who was ill urged him to read faster. When the man of God got to the phrase, "and receive you unto Myself," the sick man exclaimed, "Ah, there it is! That's the portion I love. It's not the mansions I want. It's to see Jesus and to be with Him—that is my blessed hope!" The author of this story concludes, "This is the blessed hope—our greatest anticipation—to be with Jesus throughout eternity. This will be the greatest joy and glory of the redeemed. To see Him, to be with Him—this should be our all-consuming desire!" (*501 Illustrations*, p. 168).

The application of this text for us, then, is to be sure that in all we teach and preach about doctrine, religion, and theology, Jesus—His life and teachings—must always hold the place of preeminence.

December 20

Health

"Beloved, I pray that you may prosper in all things and be in health, just as your soul prospers" (3 John 1:2).

A walk through the Word would be incomplete without making note of the value of a believer's physical health and how it relates to spiritual health. In John's third short epistle, he writes to a beloved local church leader commending him for his faithfulness. He also gives this man, Gaius, encouragement by informing him that the apostle is praying that he will prosper in all the areas of his life, including his health. I know nothing about the age of Gaius, but if he was an older person, as I have now become, I'm sure he was very happy to know that John was praying for his health.

Some folks think that religion is detrimental to good health, but they are wrong. Listen to what Ellen White says about this:

The religion of the Bible is not detrimental to the health of either body or mind. The influence of the Spirit of God is the very best medicine for disease.... The true principles of Christianity open before all a source of inestimable happiness. Religion is a continual wellspring, from which the Christian can drink at will and never exhaust the fountain.... The condition of the mind affects the health of the physical system. If the mind is free and happy, from a consciousness of rightdoing and a sense of satisfaction in causing happiness to others, it creates a cheerfulness that will react upon the whole system, causing a freer circulation of the blood and a toning up of the entire body. The blessing of God is a healing power, and those who are abundant in benefiting others will realize that wondrous blessing in both heart and life. (*Counsels on Health*, p. 28)

Please indulge me to share one more beautiful paragraph from this wonderful book on the connection between religion and health:

Those who walk in the path of wisdom and holiness find that "godliness is profitable unto all things, having promise of the life that now is, and of that which is to come." 1 Timothy 4:8. They are alive to the enjoyment of life's real pleasures, and are not troubled with vain regrets over misspent hours, nor with gloomy forebodings, as the worldling too often is.... Godliness does not conflict with the laws of health, but is in harmony with them. The fear of the Lord is the foundation of all real prosperity. (*Ibid.*, p. 29)

As the above quotes so aptly point out, optimum health is not just the absence of sickness. Whole books, of course, have been written on this topic. Suffice it to say that God is interested in our physical condition and would like us to enjoy the best of health. It has been said, however, that there is a direct correlation between the health of the soul, the health of the mind, and the health of the body. To flesh this concept out a bit, the health of the soul helps us understand our place in the world as sons and daughters of God, created in His image, and what our relationship should be with both God and humankind. Meanwhile, a healthy mind gives us clear perceptions with which to understand God's Word and make wise decisions about how to appropriate its teachings into our daily lives. Finally, a healthy body provides us with the strength and energy needed to carry out God's work in the world—serving others and bringing them into a saving relationship with the Lord.

How important then that we try to maintain our health as much as possible. The *SDA Bible Commentary* makes several points regarding this text. It says, "Because of the close connection between mind and body, when the soul or character prospers, the body is better able to be healthy. Conversely, when the health of the body is neglected and bad physical habits are established, the religious life also suffers" (*SDA Bible Commentary*, vol. 7, p. 695). Then it goes on to emphasize the importance of living a balanced lifestyle. Meaning we need to take time for exercise, social life, and rest as well as work and religious disciplines. It states that "Balance is essential to successful living" (*Ibid.*). Finally, it finishes its discussion of today's verse with this succinct paragraph:

"All who are followers of Christ may well make John's prayer for Gaius their own, for themselves, their households, and their fellow believers" (*Ibid.*).

December 21

Glory to God!

"Now to Him who is able to keep you from stumbling, and to present you faultless before the presence of His glory with exceeding joy, to God our Savior, who alone is wise, be glory and majesty, dominion and power, both now and forever. Amen" (Jude 1:24, 25).

The epistle of Jude, written by the brother of James, is tucked into the New Testament right before Revelation. He starts his letter with a warm greeting before admonishing the beloved believers to "contend earnestly for the faith" (verse 3). Apparently, he was writing in a time when false teachers and apostates were preaching heretical ideas, attempting to dilute the pure faith of the Christians, which they had originally received through the direct teachings of the apostles of the Lord Jesus Christ.

Jude warns his readers that there is a real danger of these false teachers "turning God's grace into unbounded license to do as they pleased" (NKJV Broadman & Holman Reference Ed., p. 1078). These evil men, in their lewd and lustful ways, denied Christ, and they were leading unsuspecting believers into perdition. His description of these

ungodly apostates, found in verses 12 and 13, is very colorful—almost poetic. He says, "*They are* clouds without water, carried about by the winds; late autumn trees without fruit, twice dead, pulled up by the roots; raging waves of the sea, foaming up their own shame; wandering stars for whom is reserved the blackness of darkness forever."

Unfortunately, there are some false teachers now, as then, who tell people that it doesn't matter what they do, as if God doesn't mean what He says in His Word. Others say God is too kind and merciful to hold anyone accountable for their sins. We have discussed this topic before, but if we still have any doubts, Jude dispels them for us in verses 5 through 11 of this chapter, where he talks about the punishment that came to the idolatrous children of Israel and those who rebelled at Korah when they were wandering in the wilderness. He reminds us of the coming judgment to fall on the evil angels, the perdition of disobedient Cain and greedy Balaam, as well as the complete destruction of Sodom and Gomorrah. He even gives us a word picture of the judgment, which will occur at the time of the second coming. "Behold, the Lord comes with ten thousands of His saints, to execute judgment on all, to convict all who are ungodly among them of all their ungodly deeds which they have committed in an ungodly way, and of all the harsh things which ungodly sinners have spoken against Him" (verses 14, 15). The truth is that God is too wise and fair not to judge those who insist on holding on to sin in order to finally purge the universe of its cruel and deadly effects forever. (I liken it to a judge in a court of law who banishes a serial killer from society in order to guarantee its citizens protection as well as lasting freedom from fear and harm.)

The beauty of today's passage, however, for both us and the believers in Jude's day, is that (just to reiterate this important point once more) we don't have to worry about the judgment if we accept the invitation of Jesus to follow Him and receive the salvation that He offers us. As I dissect this reading, reflecting on each section, I gain new spiritual insights. In the first two phrases, we are reminded that it is the Lord that keeps us from stumbling (sinning, or "falling" in the King James Version), and He is the one who will present us, without fault, (clothed in the beautiful righteousness of Jesus) to God. We don't need to be perfect to escape judgment—just hidden in Christ.

Next, I took note of the fact that this occurrence brings great joy to Jesus as well as to God, not to mention how we must feel! At this, Jude breaks into an expression of unbridled praise to God not only for His wisdom, which set up the plan for our salvation, but also for His glory, His majesty, His dominion, and His power! Lastly, Jude declares that these marvelous attributes of God, which deserve our adulation, will continue throughout the ages of eternity—forever! More than that, He already possesses these praiseworthy traits NOW. In the time when Jude wrote his letter, in the time when we read it, from time immemorial in the past, all the way to time everlasting in the future, God is to be praised for His inherent glory as well as for His marvelous love and grace that provided a way of salvation for His people—for you and me! No wonder this last section of Jude's book is subtitled "Glory to God!" *Amen!*

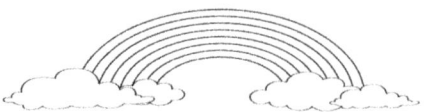

The Loveless Church

"He who has an ear, let him hear what the Spirit says to the churches. To him who overcomes I will give to eat from the tree of life, which is in the midst of the Paradise of God"' (Revelation 2:7).

Having had the privilege of working in several Christian universities, I have heard professors talk about a number of ways in which to study the book of Revelation. For purposes of our devotional readings, this time as we move through the book, I want to spend some time looking at the seven churches, which are described in chapters 1–3. Some see this information as primarily historical, written about specific New Testament churches that existed in chronological order in the past. Others see it as purely prophetic in nature—about, from John's point of view, groups of people who would exist in the future. A third approach is to consider the seven churches symbolically, as descriptions of church members who would exhibit these various characteristics at any time throughout history, including up through the time of the end.

I will be guided by a helpful quotation I found on this in a book by Ellen White called *Acts of the Apostles*:

The Lord Himself revealed to His servant the mysteries contained in this book, and He designs that they shall be open to the study of all. Its truths are addressed to those living in the last days of this earth's history, as well as to those living in the days of John. Some of the scenes depicted in this prophecy are in the past, some are now taking place; some bring to view the close of the great conflict between the powers of darkness and the Prince of heaven, and some reveal the triumphs and joys of the redeemed in the earth made new. (p. 584)

Another clarifying quote is found on the next page in the same volume:

The names of the seven churches are symbolic of the church in different periods of the Christian Era. The number 7 indicates completeness, and is symbolic of the fact that the messages extend to the end of time, while the symbols used reveal the condition of the church at different periods in the history of the world. (*Ibid.*, p. 585)

Thus, with that brief introduction in mind, we will be focusing on the various characteristics of each church named, applying the messages to ourselves, and, since a primary goal of this book is to look for the *Rainbows Amidst the Clouds*, the Scripture reading for each of the next seven days will describe the reward promised to those of each group who overcome their issues in the strength of the Lord. It is our hope, of course, to be among those people!

So, we begin today with Ephesus, the first of the seven churches. Ephesus was a favored and vibrant church, which had originally been started by the apostle Paul.

The first experience of the Ephesus church led to good works. God took delight in the fact that His church reflected the light of heaven by revealing the spirit of Christ in tenderness and compassion. The love that dwelt in the heart of Christ...this was the love that was to be revealed in the lives of His disciples. (*SDA Bible Commentary*, vol. 7, p. 956)

They were commended for their earnest labor, done with fervor, diligence, and zeal. Their "first love" experience with Christ motivated them to do great things for God. Over time, however, they began to lose their ardent affection for the Lord, as selfishness, false theories, and opposition from others, both in and out of the church, crept in to discourage them and distract them from the truth as it is in Jesus. "...as they lost their first love, they increased in a knowledge of scientific theories originated by the father of lies" (*Ibid.*, p. 956). (Sound familiar to our day?) This moral fall from love was affecting their entire religious life, to the point where they could no longer effectively represent their Savior. It was for this reason that

"God in His mercy called for repentance, for a return to their first love and to the works that are always the result of true, Christlike love" (*Ibid.*, p. 957).

It should encourage us today to know that heeding the Lord's call in this regard will not only restore spiritual joy and zeal but will also bring His promised reward to His faithful followers: "To him who overcomes I will give to eat from the tree of life." The beauty of this promise is that believers don't even have to wait until heaven before eating the leaves of the tree of life. "He who receives into his heart the words of Christ knows what it means to eat the leaves of the tree of life. When the believer, in the fellowship of the Spirit, can lay his hand upon truth itself, and appropriate it, he eats the bread that comes down from heaven" (*Ibid.*). This means that our divine education from the loving Master Teacher can begin even now, and then continue throughout eternity in "the Paradise of God."

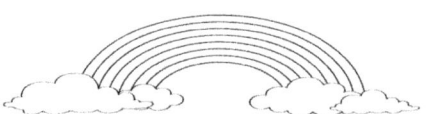

The Persecuted Church

"Be faithful unto death, and I will give you the crown of life. He who has an ear, let him hear what the Spirit says to the churches. He who overcomes shall not be hurt by the second death" (Revelation 2:10b, 11).

Not possessing a wealth of information on the seven churches, I have had to lean more heavily on a number of my husband's resources in order to abstract spiritual lessons here that can be applied to our Christian experience today.

This section of my Bible is subtitled, "The Persecuted Church," which it identifies as the church at Smyrna. The first tidbit of information I found out was that Smyrna was an ancient city on the west coast of Asia Minor. It is now the site of Izmir in Turkey. Just knowing the actual place on the world map where these cities existed makes them more real to me. In any event, this second of the seven churches obviously experienced religious persecution. They were warned ahead of time, however, by Jesus Himself. We know this because in the first chapter of Revelation, while the apostle John was "in the Spirit on the Lord's Day" (Rev. 1:10), he was given this vision regarding the seven churches and then told to write down what he had seen and send it to each church, which was specifically named. When John turned to see the loud voice that was speaking to him, Jesus identified Himself by saying that He was "the Alpha and the Omega, the First and the Last" (Rev. 1:11). A little later He continues, "I *am* He who lives, and was dead, and behold, I am alive forevermore. Amen. And I have the keys of Hades and of Death" (verse 18).

Overcome by the holy Being speaking to him, John tries to describe the Lord's appearance:

Then I turned to see the voice that spoke with me. And having turned I saw seven golden lampstands, and in the midst of the seven lampstands *One* like the Son of Man, clothed with a garment down to the feet and girded about the chest with a golden band. His head and hair *were* white like wool, as white as snow, and His eyes like a flame of fire; His feet *were* like fine brass, as if refined in a furnace, and His voice as the sound of many waters; He had in His right hand seven stars, out of His mouth went a sharp two-edged sword, and His countenance *was* like the sun shining in its strength. (Rev. 1:12–16).

As he tried to take it all in, John didn't understand the meaning of the stars and the golden lampstands, so Jesus explained, "The seven stars are the angels of the seven churches, and the seven lampstands which you saw are the seven churches" (verse 20).

In this scenario, Jesus is represented as walking in the midst of the churches—not sitting far off on a throne somewhere but personally involved with the people He loves. It's also comforting to know that each church has its own special angel assigned to watch over it. I'm sure these two thoughts would be especially helpful to the congregation at Smyrna while they were suffering through their period of tribulation. Other words of encouragement the Lord sends to Smyrna are that He knows their "works, tribulation, and poverty" (Rev. 2:9). He is aware of their situation and understands what they're going through. Finally, the fact that He holds the keys to Hades and Death (see Rev. 2:18), that He Himself has passed through death and is now alive forevermore, means that they do not need to fear. Even if they lose their lives in the struggle with evil, He has the power to bring them back to life—eternal life! They will not "be hurt by the second death," that complete extermination, which is reserved only for the unrighteous.

Thus, His message to Smyrna (as well as to us when we pass through trials) ends with the beautiful promise, "Be faithful until death, and I will give you the crown of life."

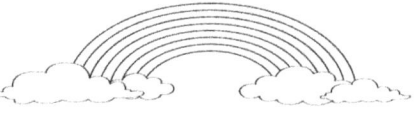

December 24

The Compromising Church

"He who has an ear, let him hear what the Spirit says to the churches. To him who overcomes I will give some of the hidden manna to eat. And I will give him a white stone, and on the stone a new name written which no one knows except him who receives it" (Revelation 2:17).

Pergamos was the third of the seven churches, and the Lord called it the compromising church. Although there were those who, even in the midst of the paganism that surrounded them, had remained faithful, others had compromised their belief in Christ. The common heathen practices of paying homage to idols and immorality began to creep into the church, and some began to adopt the doctrine of the Nicolaitans, who taught that the gospel had made the keeping of the law of God unnecessary. The Lord admonished the believers to repent from these evil practices and beliefs and to hold on to the pure faith that had been delivered to them by the apostles. Those who did and overcame the pressures and temptations of the ungodly culture of their day were promised not one but three interesting rewards, as outlined in today's Scripture reading.

Before discussing these rewards in more detail, however, I couldn't help but notice that the three compromises that the Lord warned the church of Pergamos about are still prevalent in the modern Christian era: giving homage to idols (things we put before the Lord in our lives), various kinds of immorality, and false doctrines which advocate that the salvation provided to us through Jesus voids the law of God. Unfortunately, we, too, not unlike the believers in ancient Pergamos, are facing strong influences that tempt us to compromise our commitment to God. Knowing our struggles and temptations, the Lord encourages us to overcome, just as He has done for His people throughout the centuries. And, happily, the same rewards offered to Pergamos will be enjoyed through ceaseless ages by all who are victorious in Him.

Now let's look at the meanings of the promised manna, the white stone, and the new name. As the manna of the Exodus sustained and strengthened the Israelites during their wanderings in the wilderness, so the Lord strengthens and sustains us spiritually in our walk toward heaven. In John 6:48–51, Jesus describes Himself as the "Bread of Life." Just as the children of Israel needed to gather and eat manna every morning to nourish their physical bodies, we need to partake of the spiritual manna we find in Jesus each day in order to move forward in our spiritual journey. The manna is called "hidden" because its sweetness and power are only savored by those who have "tasted and seen that the Lord is good." Believers in Jesus enjoy blessings not experienced by those who are non-believers.

"There are several viable interpretations of the significance of the white stone. Winning athletes in biblical times were given white stones that served as admission passes [tickets, if you will] to a winners' celebration. The faithful believer's white stone may point to admittance into the ultimate winners' celebration: eternal life in heaven." (*40 Days Through Revelation*, page 38).

I think the meaning of the "new name" is especially nice. Have you ever had a nickname used only by those who know you well? Often this is a name created by friends or colleagues. It usually celebrates something about your personality and generally indicates a close relationship between you and the group of people who use it. In even more intimate relationships, often a pet name emerges. Parents call their children by various terms of endearment (Baby, Sweetie, Pumpkin, etc.), while siblings often develop special names for each other based on shorter, less formal variations of a given name or particular traits of character. My brother, for instance, has always called me by a shorter version of my name since he had trouble pronouncing it as a child, and the label stuck. All these years later, it is still his name for me. Nobody else uses it. But whenever I hear him say it, I'm reminded of our special relationship. People in romantic relationships also share special names for each other, expressing their love and feelings of belonging to one another in a way reserved just for the two of them. I believe God's new name, created for each of us individually, will be something like that. It will undoubtedly say something about our character while at the same time expressing the Lord's love and signifying the special relationship He has with each overcomer. May we be among them!

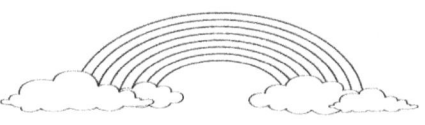

The Corrupt Church

"And he who overcomes, and keeps My works until the end, to him I will give power over the nations—...and I will give him the morning star"
(Revelation 2:26, 28).

The Corrupt Church? You may be thinking that this is a rather strange topic to be discussing on Christmas morning. My husband told me the same thing. I defended myself by explaining to him that we were walking through the Bible chronologically, and this just happened to be the place where we arrived in Revelation here near the end of the year. Then, upon reading the rewards of those in this fourth church called Thyatira, I was happy to see that they were centered on Jesus!

The church at Thyatira was plagued by similar sins as Pergamos, but perhaps to a greater degree because they not only indulged in their ungodly practices but taught them to others. This proliferation of iniquity was not acceptable to the Lord. As a result, this section of chapter 2 is filled with symbols of judgment. He warns them that if they don't repent "all the churches shall know that I am He who searches the minds and hearts. And I will give to each one of you according to your works" (verse 23).

At the same time, He acknowledges those in the church who have continued to do good works for their love, service, faith, and patience. These He encourages to "hold fast what you have till I come" (verse 25). If they do, He promises that He will give them "power over the nations." This applies not only to those in Thyatira who overcome but to all who choose Him as their Savior, following His bidding during their time on earth.

They shall become "kings and priests to...God" (Rev. 1:6), reigning with Him in glory!

But if that's not enough, the overcomers receive something even greater. The "morning star" referred to here is thought to represent Jesus Himself—the constant companionship of "the light of the world" in both their earthly and heavenly sojourns. Listen to the declaration of Jesus in John 8:12: "I am the light of the world. He who follows Me shall not walk in darkness, but have the light of life." Later, Peter remembered this illustration of Jesus and wrote: "We have also a more sure word of prophecy; whereunto ye do well that ye take heed, as unto a light that shineth in a dark place, until the day dawn, and the day star arise in your hearts" (2 Peter 1:19, KJV).

In the classic religious biography of Jesus, *The Desire of Ages*, we find this beautiful description of the relationship between Him and the blessing of light in all its forms.

In the manifestation of God to His people, light had ever been a symbol of His presence. At the creative word in the beginning, light had shone out of darkness. Light had been enshrouded in the pillar of cloud by day and the pillar of fire by night, leading the vast armies of Israel. Light blazed with awful grandeur about the Lord on Mount Sinai. Light rested over the mercy seat in the tabernacle. Light filled the temple of Solomon at its dedication. Light shone on the hills of Bethlehem when the angels brought the message of redemption to the watching shepherds. [We had to get Christmas references in here somewhere today!] God is light; and in the words, "I am the light of the world," Christ declared His oneness with God, and His relation to the whole human family. It was He who at the beginning had caused "the light to shine out of darkness." 2 Corinthians 4:6. He is the light of sun and moon and star. He was the spiritual light that in symbol and type and prophecy had shone upon Israel. But not to the Jewish nation alone was the light given. As the sunbeams penetrate to the remotest corners of the earth, so does the light of the Sun of Righteousness shine upon every soul. (*Desire of Ages*, p. 464)

What a different world we would live in if everyone would accept the light of the presence of Jesus into their lives! He has graciously offered this indescribable gift to human beings from the creation of the world, through the time of the seven churches, and on to the very close of probation. Then, those who are saved will continue to revel in it for eternity! This Christmas, let's determine to receive His most precious gift to us with open arms!

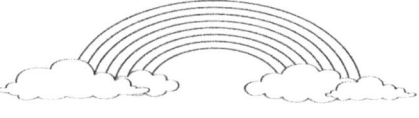

December 26

The Dead Church

"He who overcomes shall be clothed in white garments, and I will not blot out his name from the Book of Life; but I will confess his name before My Father and before His angels" (Revelation 3:5).

The fifth church, the one in Sardis, was labeled the "Dead Church" because the majority of its members' supposed good works were devoid of the love of Jesus. In their pride they had become self-centered and self-absorbed. Their goal was to keep up appearances and work to build and maintain their own reputations. "One may go through the whole round of religious activity, and yet, unless Christ is woven into all that he says and does, he will work for his own glory" (*SDA Bible Commentary*, vol. 7, p. 958). Later, on that same page we read, "They had not held the beginning of their confidence firm unto the end. They had a name to live [up to], but as far as exerting a saving influence is concerned, they were dead. They had a form of godliness without the power" (*Ibid.*).

In the first verse of chapter 3, the Lord speaks to the Christians in Sardis, declaring "I know thy works, that thou hast a name that thou livest, and art dead" (Rev. 3:1, KJV). Their outward show and rote forms of religion were worthless. Some of the believers in Sardis had become converted through the preaching of John the Baptist; others had received the gospel from the apostles, and still others learned from the ministry of Jesus Himself. Over time, however, the pure faith and sound doctrines they had received had been mixed with error. They had not watched diligently and constantly to guard the truth they had received. As a result, their faith had eroded, and their spiritual strength had faded away. Thus, through John, the Lord sent them a warning: "Remember therefore how thou hast received and heard, and hold fast, and repent. If therefore thou shalt not watch, I will come on thee as a thief, and thou shalt not know what hour I will come upon thee" (verse 3, KJV).

There was one ray of hope for Sardis, however, in that there were a few church members who had remained faithful. To these He gave both a commission and a commendation. First, He told them to "Be watchful, and strengthen the things which remain, that are ready to die" (verse 2). Second, He encouraged them who had "not defiled their garments" that "they shall walk with Me in white, for they are worthy" (verse 4).

It is interesting to note that three rewards are promised to those who will overcome during the dark and difficult time of the church of Sardis. As just mentioned, they will be clothed in white garments, generally referring to the white robe of the righteousness of Christ that the saints will be given in heaven. Second, the Lord assures them that He won't erase their names from the Book of Life, the glorious record of all those who have repented of their sins and been redeemed through the gracious sacrifice of Jesus. And third, He

will "confess his name before My Father and before His angels," indicating that He will not be ashamed to admit they are His friends to all the occupants of heaven! In fact, centuries before, the prophet Isaiah had prophesied that when the Messiah saw the results of His arduous work of redemption, He would be satisfied that all He suffered had been worth it (see Isa. 53:11). The redeemed are His precious jewels, His pride and joy, and He is proud to introduce them to the whole universe!

When I was a young person, I had a brother a couple years older than me who was always very popular in school. Not only was he smart academically, but he was also involved in many social and sports activities at which he excelled. His senior year at high school he was even voted student body president. Shortly thereafter, when attending the same school, I found that everybody knew his name. He had left a good impression on the students who had interacted with him and a great reputation with the teachers and staff. As a result, he paved the way for my immediate acceptance, and I received a warm welcome wherever I went on campus. I was able to hold my head high and fit right in simply because I was my brother's little sister! I imagine that our introduction to heaven will be something like that. Simply because Jesus is our elder brother and He claims us as family, we will be welcomed more than warmly and immediately be "accepted in the Beloved" (Eph. 1:6) Not only that but we, together with all of heaven, will burst into a joyous song of celebration and an anthem of praise to Jesus for paving the way for our marvelous salvation!

December 27

The Faithful Church

"He who overcomes, I will make him a pillar in the temple of My God, and he shall go out no more. I will write on him the name of My God and the name of the city of My God, the New Jerusalem, which comes down out of heaven from My God. And I will write on him My new name" (Revelation 3:12).

Finally—a group of believers who were faithful—the church of Philadelphia! Revelation 3:7–13 is filled with commendations for this church, whose name means the church of brotherly love. Obviously, they were representing the Lord well. What a great reputation to have in the world!

I can almost see Jesus smiling as He addresses them. "I know your works. See, I have set before you an open door, and no one can shut it; for you have a little strength, have kept My word, and have not denied My name" (verse 8). Many believe that this open door refers to an open and constant communication between the Lord and those who love Him. Others say this is a door to His continual mercy and grace, which still stands wide open for those who daily ask forgiveness for their sins and mistakes. It may represent both. But whatever the case, this door is described as one that opens into a large area of light, with the glory of the Lord emanating from it.

Jesus continues speaking to His faithful followers, "Because you have kept my command to persevere, I also will keep you from the hour of trial which shall come upon the whole world, to test those who dwell on the earth" (verse 10). Then He declares to them, "Behold, I am coming quickly," with a short, but very meaningful admonition to follow, "Hold fast what you have, that no one may take your crown" (verse 11). In other words,

He was encouraging the faithful to persevere until He returns. To those who do, He promises the rewards listed in today's verse.

In order to understand these rewards better, I unpacked them a little. First the phrase, "I will make him a pillar in the temple of My God." Synonyms for the word pillar include: a rock, a post, column, support, mainstay, tower of strength, or leader. I like to think that the Lord might appoint us as leaders in His heavenly temple. What a sacred responsibility and distinct honor that would be! Then, we find three statements that have to do with names: "I will write on him the name of My God." Next, "And the name of the city of My God." And the last one, "I will write on him My new name." Not being a trained theologian, I can only speculate based on what I have read and heard, but I do know that names were very significant in Bible times. They were often given to assign roles or describe characteristics of a person. Many times, after an encounter with the Lord, people's names were changed to indicate that their lives had been changed. Think about Abram becoming Abraham, Sarai becoming Sarah, and Jacob, after his night of wrestling with the Lord, given the new name of Israel. Even in the New Testament, some of the disciples' names were changed, and Saul was renamed Paul, the great evangelist.

Recently, we discussed the fact that each of us will be given a new and special name by the Lord when we arrive in heaven. Even now, however, once we've adopted the name "Christian," we are indicating that our lives have been changed by our association with Christ. As part of His family, we should be representing Him wherever we go. The fact that He would write the name of the New Jerusalem on us, whether literally or figuratively, speaks to us of God's desire to give us a sense of belonging in His kingdom—like putting an address on us so that wherever we wander in the vast universe, we will always be able to find our way back home. Of all the names of God in the Bible, I don't know which one He will choose as His new name in heaven, but I do know we'll praise Him as the worthy Lamb of God, the King of Kings, and the Lord of Lords! Perhaps He'll use the wonderful name found in Isaiah 63:16: "Our Redeemer from Everlasting!" One thing is sure—the faithful are in for many delightful and meaningful surprises when Jesus comes to take them to their eternal home.

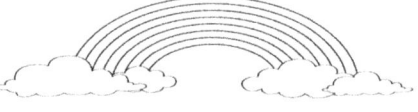

December 28

The Lukewarm Church

"To him who overcomes I will grant to sit with Me on My throne, as I also overcame and sat down with My Father on His throne"
(Revelation 3:21).

The last of the seven churches described in Revelation is the Laodicean—also known as the Lukewarm Church. It got its name from Jesus' statement about it in Revelation 3:15, 16. "I know thy works," He says, "that thou art neither cold nor hot: I would thou wert cold or hot. So then because thou art lukewarm, and neither cold nor hot, I will spue thee out of my mouth" (KJV). The Christian experience of the Laodiceans was insipid, worse than tasteless. Although they had received great light and had many opportunities both to grow spiritually and to share their faith with others, they chose to stagnate. They were not non-believers, nor were they zealous Christians. Although full of self-satisfaction and pride about what they knew regarding spiritual matters, they were devoid of the essential elements of faith, love, and righteousness, which would have made them fruitful in bringing the light of Christ to others.

Unfortunately, to a great degree, the church of today finds itself in a similar back-slidden situation. Listen to what the *Bible Commentary* has to say on this topic:

The message to the Laodicean church is applicable to our condition. How plainly is pictured the position of those who think they have all the truth, who take pride in their knowledge of the Word of God, while its sanctifying power has not been felt in their lives. The fervor of the love of God is wanting in their hearts, but it is this very fervor of love that makes God's people the light of the world.

... Now, more than ever before, are seen pride, worldly ambition, self-exaltation, double-dealing, hypocrisy, and deception. Many are speaking great swelling words of vanity, saying, "I am rich, and increased with goods, and have need of nothing." Yet they are miserable, and poor, and blind, and naked. (*SDA Bible Commentary,* vol. 7, pp. 961, 962)

Despite their apathy and even willful ignorance on the part of some, the Lord still offers hope to those who repent and who ask the Lord to renew and deepen their experience with Him. How can we do this? In verse 20, He paints an inviting picture of Himself as a heavenly vendor of sorts, knocking on our heart's door to sell us the priceless riches we lack. Instead of our wretched and miserable spiritual poverty, He offers us the gold of true faith and love. In place of our own robes of righteousness, which are like filthy rags leaving us naked and ashamed, He gives us the pure, white raiment of His sparkling robe of righteousness. Then, in His kindness and mercy, He cures our blindness with a heavenly "eyesalve" (verse 18, KJV) that allows us to discern spiritual things out of His Word that we never saw or understood before.

And the beauty of it is, He has made ample provision for all who want to obtain these blessings at a price we can each afford! All we have to do is open our individual heart's door to Him. It's a simple act of the will. If we do, He promises to come into our lives and dine with us—filling us with spiritual food that will forever transform our characters—making us like Him. Then, in an unbelievable gesture of grace, when our time on earth is done, He will call us overcomers, granting us to sit with Him on His heavenly throne, just as He came and sat down with His Father after His sojourn on earth.

In the case of every church we have studied, thank God there is hope. If the churches heed the messages and warnings given for them, they will reap rich rewards. At the same time, they will be fulfilling God's purpose for them to diffuse light to the world. Jesus, the true Witness, continues today to make entreaties for a vibrant relationship with Him, not only to groups of believers but also to each of us individually. Every promise, warning, or admonition we read from His Word, every sermon from His messengers of truth, should be cherished as if it were a knock at the door of OUR heart. The more readily we respond, the clearer His voice becomes to us. However, whenever we reject His still, small voice, our heart becomes hardened and less impressionable. The next time Jesus stands knocking at your heart's door, invite Him in immediately, with your whole heart. It's the least you can do, after all He's done for you!

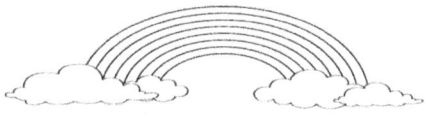

All Things Made New

"Now I saw a new heaven and a new earth, for the first heaven and the first earth had passed away. Also there was no more sea. Then I, John, saw the holy city, New Jerusalem, coming down out of heaven from God, prepared as a bride adorned for her husband. And I heard a loud voice from heaven saying, 'Behold, the tabernacle of God is with men, and He will dwell with them, and they shall be His people. God Himself will be with them and be their God. And God will wipe away every tear from their eyes; there shall be no more death, nor sorrow, nor crying. There shall be no more pain, for the former things have passed away'" (Revelation 21:1–4).

As you will notice, today's scriptural reading is several verses long. As we get into descriptions of the new heavens and the new earth found in the book of Revelation, human words seem insufficient. John, however, does his best to give us glimpses into the glorious visions the Lord has revealed to him. So, I like to use his language as much as time and space permit within the limits of a daily devotional book.

In my seven some decades of life, I have visited and lived in communities where the buildings were old and dilapidated, and I have visited and lived in communities where the buildings were new and beautiful. I prefer the latter. I know there's an argument to be made that old things can provide us with historical facts and interesting stories about the past. Not to mention, handmade antiques of various kinds can be unique and very valuable, but I find that which is new, clean, and beautifully designed to be the objects and structures that appeal to me. In fact, one of the hobbies my husband and I both enjoy is spending a free hour or so visiting lovely models of new homes. We ooh and ahh over thoughtfully-designed floor plans, expensive furnishings, and colorful décor. If the

house has a view, especially of a verdant golf course or snow-capped mountains, we are even more delighted! Then, as we pull away to return to our own humbler abode, we console and encourage each other by reminding ourselves that Jesus is planning something even more wonderful for us in heaven—in fact, the Bible says He's preparing mansions for the redeemed (see John 14:1–3).

In this passage, however, we can't help but notice that some of the things that will be "new" go far beyond just physical structures. Some of the "former things" that are part of our daily lives on this sin-infested earth will not be part of our everyday existence there. In fact, we will never suffer from them again. Just think of it—no more tears, sorrow, crying, or pain! No more death! Emotional, physical, or even spiritual pain will not harass us in the new earth because the Lord will "dwell" among us. His tabernacle will be in our neighborhood, so to speak, so that we, His people, can be near Him, enjoying full access to His healing and loving presence.

Something else will be "new" in that holy land. Unlike now, where we are bombarded daily with news of wars and rumors of wars, the saved, who will be drawn into heaven from every corner of the globe, will all get along peacefully, as they share the same sacred goal of declaring praise to the glorious Savior, who made it possible for them to become citizens of this glorious land! Listen to how this scene is presented:

> After these things I looked, and behold, a great multitude which no one could number, of all nations, tribes, peoples, and tongues, standing before the throne and before the Lamb, clothed with white robes, with palm branches in their hands, and crying out with a loud voice, saying, "Salvation *belongs* to our God who sits on the throne, and to the Lamb!" (Rev. 7:9, 10)

Imagine what it will be like to live in a place where the brotherhood of saints permeates the atmosphere with grace, kindness, and heavenly love! That alone would make the future life worth living!

The last few days we've been discussing the rewards of the faithful in each of the seven churches. The Lord also announces breathtaking blessings on those who are ready to meet Him when He comes. In addition to being raised into an incredible new heaven and a beautiful new earth, as if that weren't more than enough, He also promises: "He who overcomes shall inherit all things, and I will be his God and he shall be My son [or daughter]" (Rev. 21:7). Hallelujah!

December 30

Forever and Ever

"And he showed me a pure river of water of life, clear as crystal, proceeding from the throne of God and of the Lamb. In the middle of its street and on either side of the river, was the tree of life, which bore twelve fruits, each tree yielding its fruit every month. The leaves of the tree were for the healing of the nations. And there shall be no more curse, but the throne of God and of the Lamb shall be in it, and His servants shall serve Him. They shall see His face, and His name shall be on their foreheads. There shall be no night there: They need no lamp nor light of the sun, for the Lord God gives them light. And they shall reign forever and ever" (Revelation 22:1–5).

We have another one of those long scripture readings today. Again, I am at a loss for words to adequately describe the marvels of heaven. Thus, once again I defer to John's descriptions. He begins chapter 22 by painting word pictures for us, first of the crystal river of life, which proceeds from the throne of God and of the Lamb. Then there is a picture of the tree of life, a prolific fruit bearer, whose leaves are for the healing of the nations. These two heavenly icons are replete with symbolism. It is fitting that the river of life begins at the throne of Jesus, the Lamb, who sacrificed His earthly life for our salvation. As our Creator, He is the very source of life. As our Redeemer, He is the giver of immortality. Whenever we feel spiritually weak, He is the One who can refresh us with new spiritual vigor and strength. We are told that once we arrive in heaven, the Lord will gather us on the banks of the river of life to explain the things we didn't understand while on this earth.

Meanwhile, the *Bible Commentary* presents the tree of life in this way:

> The tree of life is a representation of the preserving care of Christ for His children. As Adam and Eve ate of this tree, they acknowledged their dependence upon God. The tree of life possessed the power to perpetuate life, and as long as they ate of it, they could not die.... The fruit of the tree of life in the Garden of Eden possessed supernatural virtue. To eat of it was to live forever. Its fruit was the antidote of death. Its leaves were for the sustaining of life and immortality. (*SDA Bible Commentary*, vol. 7, p. 988)

So, this wonderful tree brought vitality in the past and will again in the future, but here's the really good news for us: as He is the Fountain of life, Jesus was also the unseen Author of the Scriptures (working through His servants) which have come down to us today. Listen to this amazing statement, again from the *Commentary*:

> The Word of God is to us the tree of life. Every portion of the Scripture has its use.

In every part of the Word is some lesson to be learned. Then learn how to study your Bibles. This book is not a heap of odds and ends. It is an educator. Your own thoughts must be called into exercise before you can be really benefited by Bible study. Spiritual sinew and muscle must be brought to bear upon the Word. The Holy Spirit will bring to remembrance the words of Christ. He will enlighten the mind, and guide the research. (*Ibid.*, p. 989)

This bringing of our own thoughts into exercise as we interact with daily small portions of the Bible in order to gain spiritual insights and better understand God's messages to us has been the method and the goal as we've journeyed together through this devotional book this year. Who knew we were already taking spiritual nutrients from the tree of life along the way? I only hope it's been as much of a blessing for you as it has for me.

In today's passage we've concentrated mostly on verses 1 and 2. John, however, does not stop there with his description of the things he saw in his heavenly vision. He goes on to briefly mention God's throne, the servants of God, all with the name of the Lord inscribed on their foreheads, and then the surprising fact that there will be no such thing as night in heaven. What's more, he tells us that we won't need lamplight or even sunlight because the Lord will supply all the light we need. Then, while we're still sitting here trying to take in and imagine for ourselves all that the prophet has told us about heaven, like amazing frosting on an already delicious cake (last time for this idiom, I promise!), John makes one last unbelievable announcement about those who serve God, declaring "And they shall reign forever and ever!" To this I sense an overwhelming wave of joy and gratitude, knowing that once we get to heaven, our happiness is assured throughout eternity. All I can respond over and over is a heartfelt, "Praise God from whom all blessings flow!"

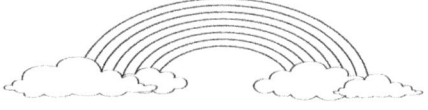

December 31

The Beginning and the End

"And behold, I am coming quickly, and My reward is with Me, to give to every one according to his work. I am the Alpha and the Omega, the Beginning and the End, the First and the Last" (Revelation 22:12, 13).

So, here we are at the end of the year. I'd like to thank you, dear readers, for accompanying me in this walk through the Word. As you know, I started this project in an effort to personally draw deeper meaning from the Scriptures I was reading for my morning devotions. As time went on, however, becoming more aware of those who were taking this journey with me, I began to broaden my scope to include spiritual applications I saw for Christians, in general. Much of the time I was writing this book the Covid pandemic necessitated isolation; thus, it was a real blessing for me to have someone to share my musings with along the way—from Genesis to Revelation. It filled my days with purpose, structure, and inspiration. We have read scriptural passages, reflected on them, studied what some other sources have said about them, sang and prayed together, and even spent time trying to imagine what some of the verses described. All of this under the overarching theme of our continual search for *Rainbows Amidst the Clouds*.

Thankfully, on this joint sojourn, we have had many opportunities to realize beautiful rainbows of hope, demonstrated by God's promises and loving care, woven throughout the Bible—from beginning to end. It is fitting, therefore, to take note of the fact that even in heaven we will find a rainbow. Revelation 4:3 informs us that in the very throne room of heaven there is a "rainbow around the throne, in appearance like an emerald." That dazzling arch will be the ultimate beautiful rainbow to which all the others along our pathway have led us!

Today, as we turn our attention to the very last chapter of the Bible, we close with some of the final words of Jesus. We can't help but notice that here again He is sharing promises with us. First, He will come again—and quickly! Second, He is bringing rewards with Him—according to everyone's work. I believe His statement in verse 13 can also be understood as a kind of promise because He is assuring us that just as He was there at the beginning of earth's history during Creation week, He will also be there when this world comes to an end. His all-powerful presence guards our existence like two sturdy bookends. As His people, we don't need to worry about coming to the end of this world or even the end of our individual lives and falling into oblivion somewhere beyond His knowledge and care. As we've learned from our study together this year, the Lord has lots of wonderful plans for us in our heavenly home. Between now and then, we have His promise that He will be with us always, "even unto the end of the world" (Matt. 28:20, KJV). Thus, we can be assured that He will never leave us nor forsake us (see Heb. 13:5). Thank God that His divine love has us covered from beginning to end!

I'm going to ask you to use your imagination one more time with me as we consider this marvelous quotation of some of what we'll experience in the world to come. It's found in a classic work called *The Great Controversy*:

> There the redeemed shall know, even as also they are known. The loves and sympathies which God Himself has planted in the soul shall there find truest and sweetest exercise. The pure communion with holy beings, the harmonious social life with the blessed angels and with the faithful ones of all ages who have washed their robes and made them white in the blood of the Lamb, the sacred ties that bind together "the whole family in heaven and earth" (Ephesians 3:15)—these help to constitute the happiness of the redeemed. There, immortal minds will contemplate with never-failing delight the wonders of creative power, the mysteries of redeeming love. (*The Great Controversy*, p. 677)

Finally, I leave you with the blessing of this, my favorite paragraph from the same volume:

> The great controversy is ended. Sin and sinners are no more. The entire universe is clean. One pulse of harmony and gladness beats through the vast creation. From Him who created all, flow life and light and gladness, throughout the realms of illimitable space. From the minutest atom to the greatest world, all things, animate and inanimate, in their unshadowed beauty and perfect joy, declare that God is Love. (*Ibid.*, p. 678)

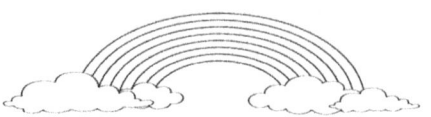

Bibliography

Bradshaw, John. *The Hope of Glory*. Nampa, Idaho: Pacific Press Publishing Association, 2021.

The Church Hymnal. Washington, D.C.: Review and Herald Publishing Association, 1941.

New King James Version. UltraThin Large Print Reference Edition. Nashville, TN: Broadman & Holman Publ., 1996.

Nichol, Francis D., ed. *The Seventh-day Adventist Bible Commentary*. 10 vols. Washington, DC: Review and Herald Publishing Association, 1953–1957.

Pierson, Robert H. *501 Illustrations*. Nashville, TN: Southern Publishing Association, 1965.

Rhodes, Ron. *40 Days Through Revelation*. Eugene, OR: Harvest House Publishers, 2013.

The Seventh-day Adventist Hymnal. Washington, D.C.: Review and Herald Publishing Association, 1985.

Singing Youth. Washington, D.C.: Review and Herald Publishing Association, 1953.

Wikipedia. "*Stumbling Block*." Accessed March, 2022. https://en.wikipedia.org/wiki/Stumbling_block.

Webster's All-in-One Dictionary & Thesaurus (Second Edition). Springfield, MA: Federal Street Press, 2013.

White, Ellen G. *The Acts of the Apostles*. Mountain View, CA: Pacific Press Publishing Association, 1911.

———. *The Adventist Home*. Hagerstown, MD: Review and Herald Publishing Association, 1952.

———. *Christ's Object Lessons*. Washington, D.C.: Review and Herald Publishing Association, 1900.

———. *Counsels on Health*. Mountain View, CA: Pacific Press Publishing Association, 1923.

———. *The Desire of Ages*. Mountain View, CA: Pacific Press Publishing Association, 1898.

———. *Early Writings*. Washington, D.C.: Review and Herald Publishing Association, 1882.

———. *The Great Controversy*. Mountain View, CA: Pacific Press Publishing Association, 1911.

———. *Life Sketches of Ellen G. White*. Mountain View, CA: Pacific Press Publishing Association, 1915.

———. *Steps to Christ*. Mountain View, CA: Pacific Press Publishing Association, 1892.

———. *Testimonies for the Church*, vol. 3. Mountain View, CA: Pacific Press Publishing Association, 1972.

———. *Testimonies for the Church*, vol. 9. Mountain View, CA: Pacific Press Publishing Association, 1909.

———. *The Triumph of God's Love*. Mountain View, CA: Pacific Press Publishing Association, 1950.

TEACH Services, Inc.
P U B L I S H I N G

We invite you to view the complete
selection of titles we publish at:
www.TEACHServices.com

We encourage you to write us
with your thoughts about this,
or any other book we publish at:
info@TEACHServices.com

TEACH Services' titles may be purchased in
bulk quantities for educational, fund-raising,
business, or promotional use.
bulksales@TEACHServices.com

Finally, if you are interested in seeing
your own book in print, please contact us at:
publishing@TEACHServices.com

We are happy to review your manuscript at no charge.

Milton Keynes UK
Ingram Content Group UK Ltd.
UKHW031125221123
433051UK00014B/642